[수능/사관학교/경찰대학] 고난이도 영어 시험을 대비한 유형별 고난도 문제

예리한 분석, 명쾌한 해설의 2025학년도 [사관학교/경찰대학] 기출 문제 풀이

사 주만에 다 끝내는 리얼 문제집

수능/사관학교/경찰대학 1등급 대비
영어 독해 고난도

200제

개정
신판

국순염 편

씨마스

저자 약력

국순엽

- **학력**
  - 서울대학교 영문과(1980~1988)
  - 인천 송도고등학교(1976~1978)

- **경력**
  - 앱솔루트어학원 강사 역임
  - 강동 명문학원 영어 강사 역임
  - 노량진 토플학원 강사 역임
  - KBS 국제방송 영어 앵커 겸 아나운서 역임

- **저서**
  - 고난도 영어 200제
  - 경찰대학 · 사관학교 영어 독해 고난도 240제
  - 경찰대학 · 사관학교 영어 어법 · 어휘 고난도 240제(공저)
  - 가장 사랑하는 친구(역)
  - 호스피스 입문(역)

저자 이메일 sluicegate@naver.com
영어 블로그 https://blog.naver.com/sluicegate 운영

원어민 감수
Alannah Hill
- Dublin Institute of Technology, Ireland
- Editor, JoongAng Daily

머리말

영어독해고난도200제가 출간된 지 벌써 6주년을 맞았다. 그간 본서는 전국 주요 서점의 영어 고난도 판매부문에 상위 랭크되는가 하면 전국 최대 사관 기숙학교의 정식 영어 교재로 선정되는 등 많은 수험생과 선생님들로부터 분에 넘치는 사랑을 받아왔다. 그 사랑과 성원에 힘입어 이렇게 다시 2026학년도 판을 내게 된 데 대해 머리 숙여 감사드리며 본서가 입시 영어 고난도 분야에서 최고의 콘텐츠로 자리매김할 때까지 정진할 것을 약속드린다.

이번 2026학년도 판에서는 두 가지에 역점을 뒀다.

먼저 지속적인 고난도화다. 첫 출간 이후 본서는 끊임없는 고난도화 노력을 통해 난도 강화라는 입시 영어의 큰 맥에 동참해 왔고 그럼으로써 여타 준비서와 차별화를 시도해 왔다. 이번 판에서 필자는 난도와 시의성이 떨어지는 일부 문제들을 교체함으로써 예의 그 고난도화 노력에 한층 박차를 가하고자 했다.

그리고 대수능 대비 강화다. 그간 두 차례 개정을 통해 본서는 대수능 대비 능력을 강화하는 쪽으로 내용의 대폭적인 혁신을 시도한 바 있다. 그런 노력은 이번 판에서도 그대로 이어져 필자는 대수능 출제 포맷을 철저히 분석하는 것은 물론 대수능 관련 지문의 쏘싱을 강화하는 등 본서 집필의 기본 방향을 대수능 대비 강화에 두고 집필했다.

대수능 영어의 고난도화는 이제 거스를 수 없는 추세가 됐다. 빈칸 추론이나 순서, 삽입 지문의 난도는 사관학교나 경찰대 문제와 차별을 논하는 게 무의미할 정도로 어려워졌고 고난도화 추세는 주제나 요지 등 타 유형으로 확대되고 있다. 점증하는 고난도화와 함께 EBS 연계가 낮아지고 정시 모집의 확대로 수능 비중이 높아진 상황에서 이제 기존의 학습 방법만으로는 더 이상 영어 1등급을 기대하기 어렵게 됐다.

이런 상황에서 1등급을 목표로 하는 수험생들의 현명한 선택은 무엇일까? 고난도 문제를 되도록 많이 풀어보고 고난도에 대한 내성을 기르는 것이 가장 확실한 전략이 아닐까? 외람되지만 본서의 한 단계 업그레이드된 콘텐츠는 그런 변화된 요구에 십분 부응할 것으로 기대한다. 본서를 택한 독자 여러분의 탁월한 선택에 경의를 표하며 본서와 함께 모두 소기의 목표를 성취하기를 기원한다.

저자 국순엽 배상

이 책의 구성과 특징

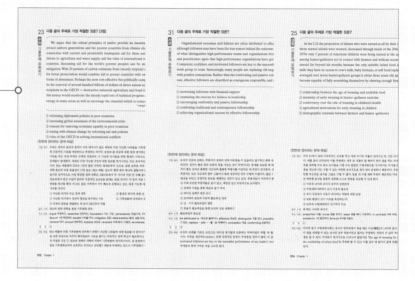

1 일석삼조

수능, 사관학교, 경찰대 영어 독해 수험 준비를 이 한 권으로 끝낼 수 있도록 구성했다. 세 시험은 출제 유형이 대동소이하고 어휘나 독해 난이도에서 큰 차이가 없을 뿐 아니라 출제 경향에서 서로 영향을 주는 측면도 있으므로 이 한 권으로 준비하면서 시너지 효과를 거둘 수 있도록 했다.

2 지문의 포괄성

시대를 초월한 가치를 가지는 고전은 물론 시의성이 최대한 반영된 최신 문장을 골고루 지문에 포함시켰다. 또 글의 성격도 정치, 경제, 사회, 문화, 문학, 과학, 예술, 철학, 시사, 군사 등 출제 가능성이 있는 전 분야를 망라해 이 한 권만 제대로 공부하면 어떤 성격의 지문이 나와도 당황하지 않고 풀 수 있도록 했다.

3 시의성

최근 출제 빈도가 점점 잦아지고 있는 각종 시사 문제나 첨단과학 등에 대한 지문을 다수 포함시켜 시의성 있는 주제에 대한 적응력을 높이고 최신 영어에 대한 대비를 동시에 할 수 있도록 했다.

4 원제와의 유사성

수능, 사관학교, 경찰대에서 한 번이라도 출제된 적이 있는 출제 유형을 모두 포함시켰고 문제의 내용과 형식, 난이도는 물론 지문이나 선택지의 길이까지 기출 문제에 그대로 맞춰 당장 실제 문제로 가져다 써도 손색이 없도록 했다.

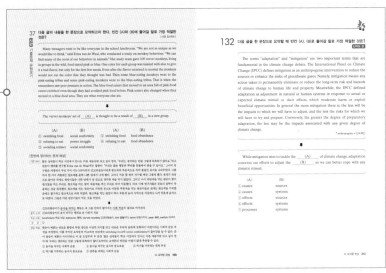

5 난이도 조절

본서의 문제들은 전반적으로 난이도가 높지만 특히 난도가 높은 문제를 각 유형 후반에 배치해 독자의 실력에 맞춰 진도를 나가도록 배려했다. 난이도를 중·상으로 표시해 놓았기 때문에 독자들은 자기 실력에 맞은 부분을 선택해 보다 유연하고 효율적으로 공부할 수 있을 것이다.

6 기출 문제 해설

사관학교와 경찰대학교의 2025학년도 1차 시험 기출 문제를 해설해 부록 형식으로 첨부했다. 정확한 지문 해석은 물론 예리한 문법적 구조 분석과 적확한 정답 해설에도 만전을 기했다.

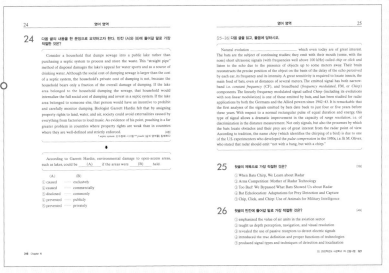

목 차

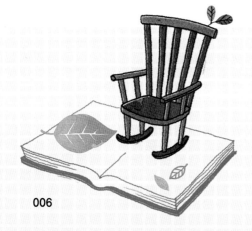

[사관학교/수능/경찰대학 1차 시험 시간표 비교]

구분	시간		
	사관학교	수능	경찰대학
수험생 입실 (입실시간 종료 후에 수험장 입실 및 응시 불가)	08:10~08:30 (20분)	00:00~08:10 (00분)	07:30~08:30 (60분)
수험생 주의사항 안내	08:30~09:00 (30분)	08:10~08:30 (30분)	08:30~09:00 (30분)
답안지 · 문제지 배부	09:00~09:10 (10분)	08:30~08:40 (10분)	09:00~09:10 (10분)
제1교시 - 국어 [공통]	09:10~10:00 (50분)	08:40~10:00 (80분)	09:10~10:10 (60분)
휴식	11:00~11:20 (20분)	10:00~10:20 (20분)	10:10~10:30 (20분)
답안지 · 문제지 배부	11:20~11:30 (10분)	10:20~10:30 (10분)	10:30~10:40 (10분)
제2교시 - 영어/수학[수능]	10:30~11:20 (50분)	10:30~12:10 (100분)	10:40~11:40 (60분)
휴식(사관학교, 경찰대학), 중식(수능)	11:20~11:40 (20분)	12:10~13:00 (50분)	11:40~12:00 (20분)
답안지 · 문제지 배부	11:40~11:50 (10분)	13:00~13:10 (10분)	12:00~12:10 (10분)
제3교시 - 수학/영어[수능]	11:50~13:30 (100분)	13:10~14:20 (70분)	12:10~13:30 (80분)

[사관학교/수능/경찰대학 1차 시험 비교]

과목	학교	사관학교	수능	경찰대학
국어	문항 수	30문항	45문항	45문항
	시험 시간	50분	80분	60분
	문항	공통 [문학, 독서] 30문항 [3점] 20문항, [4점] 10문항	공통 [문학, 독서] 34문항 선택 [화법과 작문] 11문항 　　　[언어와 매체] 11문항 [2점] 35문항, [3점] 10문항	공통 [문학, 독서] [2점] 35문항, [3점] 10문항
영어	문항 수	30문항	45문항	45문항
	시험 시간	50분	70분	60분
	문항	상대 평가 - [영어 I , 영어 II] 듣기 없음 [3점] 20문항, [4점] 10문항	절대 평가 - [영어 I , 영어 II] [듣기] 17문항 [독해] 28문항 [2점] 35문항, [3점] 10문항	상대 평가 - [영어 I , 영어 II] 듣기 없음 [2점] 35문항, [3점] 10문항
수학	문항 수	30문항	30문항	25문항
	시험 시간	100분	100분	80분
	문항	공통 [수학 I , 수학 II] 22문항 선택 [확률과 통계] 8문항 　　　[미적분] 8문항 　　　[기하] 8문항 [2점] 문항, [3점] 문항, [4점] 문항	공통 [수학 I , 수학 II] 22문항 선택 [확률과 통계] 8문항 　　　[미적분] 8문항 　　　[기하] 8문항 [2점] 문항, [3점] 문항, [4점] 문항	공통 [수학 I , 수학 II] 25문항 [2점] 문항, [3점] 문항, [4점] 문항

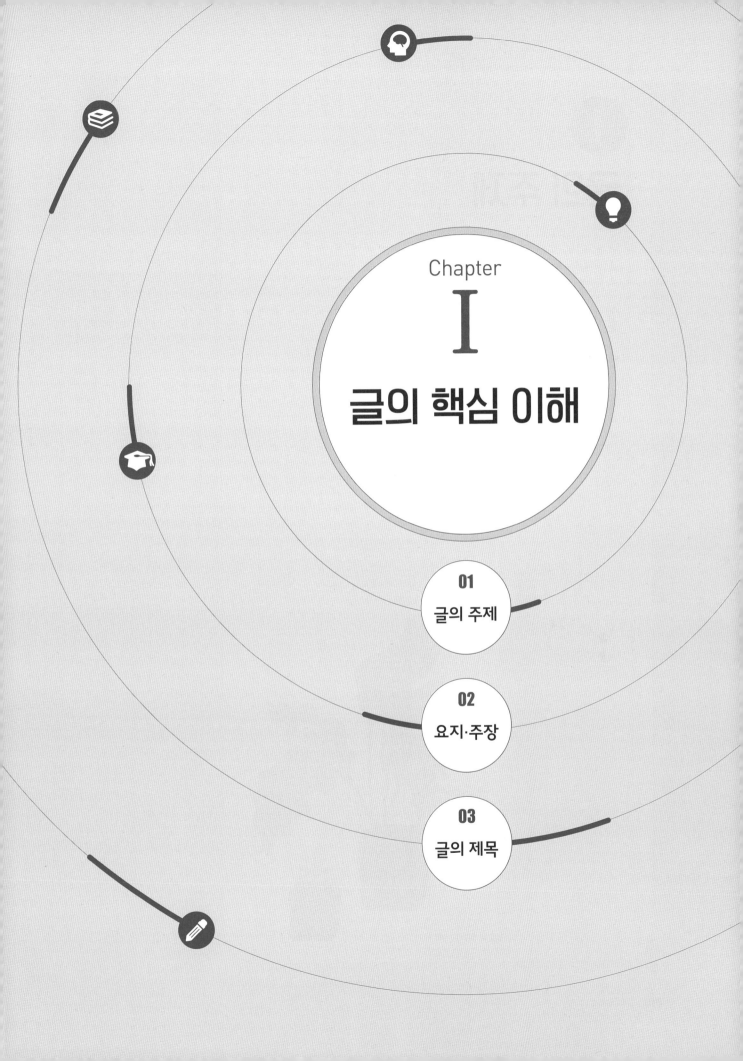

Chapter

I

글의 핵심 이해

1

글의 주제

필자가 글을 통해 전하고자 하는
핵심 내용(controlling idea),
즉 주제를 추론하는 유형이다.

▶ 먼저 주제문을 포착하는 것이 중요하다.

▶ 글의 전개 방식에 따라 주제문은 흔히 글의 초반에 오거나(두괄식), 후반에 오거나(미괄식), 중간에 오거나(중괄식), 처음과 끝의 양쪽에 오거나(양괄식), 문장 곳곳에 섞여 있다(병렬식).

▶ 단락은 흔히 주제문이 포함된 일반진술과 주제문을 뒷받침하기 위한 구체 진술로 양분되고 구체 진술은 예시·연구·실험·조사·보도·인용의 형식을 띠며, 구체 진술이 시작되기 전의 문장이 주제문일 경우가 많다.

▶ 글의 처음 한두 문장과 마지막 한두 문장은 특히 중요하므로 반복해서 읽어 내용을 숙지한다.

▶ 연결사나 상관 표현이 주제문을 암시하는 시그널일 경우가 많으므로 이들을 항상 예의 주시한다.

▶ 글을 읽을 때는 항상 핵심 소재가 무엇이고 그에 대한 필자의 생각은 어떤지를 염두에 두고 읽는다. 핵심 소재를 중심으로 글을 단순화하는 독서 습관이 중요하다.

▶ 정답을 고를 때는 선택지에 글의 핵심 소재가 포함됐는지를 먼저 확인한다. 핵심 단어가 빠진 선택지를 과감히 제외하는 오답 소거 전략을 적극적으로 활용한다.

▶ 주제가 직접적으로 드러나지 않거나 주제문이 아리송한 글에서는 제일 많이 반복되는 단어나 어구를 가려낸 후에 그에 대한 필자의 입장을 파악한다.

▶ 선택지가 주제의 방향과 부합하는지에 따라 선택지를 긍정(+)과 부정(−)으로 나누면 정답 후보를 대폭 압축할 수 있다(±전략).

▶ 선택지 중에서 2~3개는 주제에 대해 필자와 정반대되는 주장을, 나머지 1~2개는 주제와는 무관한 내용을 담고 있는 경우가 많다. 이들은 모두 소거 대상이다.

▶ for example, for instance, Suppose, Let's suppose 같은 예시의 연결어나 예시를 암시하는 표현이 있으면 바로 전 문장이 주제문일 경우가 많다.

▶ Research says, A study suggests, According to an experiment, Reports say 와 같이 연구, 실험, 조사, 보도, 인용이 시작되는 표현이 있으면 바로 앞 문장이 주제문일 가능성이 크다.

▶ but, however, yet, still 같은 역접의 연결사가 들어있는 문장, 이른바 꺾이는 문장은 그 문장이나 다음 문장이 주제문일 가능성이 있다.

▶ 결어나 요약, 인과를 나타내는 연결사 즉 thus, therefore, consequently, accordingly, as a result, in short, in brief 등이 올 때는 그 문장이 주제문일 가능성이 크다.

▶ 무엇을 정의하는(define) 듯한 단정적인 어조의 문장이 주제문일 가능성이 크다.
  e.g. ~ is the key to ~, Definitely(Obviously, Certainly, Absolutely) ~

▶ 의견, 중요성, 필요성, 의무 등을 나타내는 어구를 포함하는 문장이 주제문일 경우가 많다.
  e.g. I think, I believe, In my opinion, It is important, It is necessary, must, need, should, have to 등

▶ 명령문은 필자의 주장이 강하게 들어 있기 때문에 주제문일 경우가 많다.

다음 글의 주제로 가장 적절한 것은? [3점]

We argue that the ethical principles of justice provide an essential foundation for policies to protect unborn generations and the poorest countries from climate change. Related issues arise in connection with current and persistently inadequate aid for these nations, in the face of growing threats to agriculture and water supply, and the rules of international trade that mainly benefit rich countries. Increasing aid for the world's poorest peoples can be an essential part of effective mitigation. With 20 percent of carbon emissions from (mostly tropical) deforestation, carbon credits for forest preservation would combine aid to poorer countries with one of the most cost-effective forms of abatement. Perhaps the most cost-effective but politically complicated policy reform would be the removal of several hundred billions of dollars of direct annual subsidies from the two biggest recipients in the OECD — destructive industrial agriculture and fossil fuels. Even a small amount of this money would accelerate the already rapid rate of technical progress and investment in renewable energy in many areas, as well as encourage the essential switch to conservation agriculture.

* mitigation 완화, abatement 감소, subsidy 보조금

① reforming diplomatic policies in poor countries
② increasing global awareness of the environmental crisis
③ reasons for restoring economic equality in poor countries
④ coping with climate change by reforming aid and policies
⑤ roles of the OECD in solving international conflicts

[한번에 정리하는 문제 해설]

지문 해석 우리는 정의의 윤리적 원칙이 아직 태어나지 않은 세대와 가장 가난한 나라들을 기후변화로부터 보호하기 위한 정책에 대한 근본적인 기초를 제공한다고 주장하는 바이다. 농업과 물 공급에 대한 점점 증가하는 위협과 주로 부유한 국가들에게만 이득을 주는 국제 무역의 규칙에 직면하여, 이 가난한 국가들을 위한 현재의 지속적으로 부족한 원조와 관련하여 연계된 문제들이 발생한다. 세계의 가장 가난한 국민에 대한 원조를 증가시키는 것은 효과적인 (탄소 배출) 완화의 필수적인 부분이나. 탄소 배출량의 20%는 (대개 열대 시역의) 벌채로부터 오므로, 삼림 보존을 위한 탄소 배출권은 너 가난한 국가들에 대한 원조와 비용 효율성이 가장 높은 (탄소 배출) 감소의 형태 중의 하나와 결합시켜 줄 것이다. 아마 비용 효율성이 가장 높지만 정치적으로 가장 복잡한 정책 개혁은, OECD에서 두 가지의 가장 큰 수혜 분야, 즉 파괴적인 산업화 농업과 화석 연료에게서 연간 수천억 달러의 직접적인 보조금을 없애는 일일 것이다. 이 돈의 적은 양이라도 보존 농업으로의 근본적인 변화를 촉진할 뿐만 아니라, 많은 지역에서 이미 빠르게 진행되고 있는 재생 가능한 에너지에 대한 기술적 진보와 투자를 가속할 것이다.

① 가난한 국가의 외교 정책 개혁   ② 환경의 위기에 대한 전 지구적 인식 높이기
③ 가난한 국가에서 경제적 평등을 복구하는 이유   ④ 기후변화에 대처하여 원조 및 정책을 개혁하기
⑤ 국제적 갈등을 해결하는 데 있어 OECD의 역할

글의 소재 원조와 정책 개혁을 통한 기후변화 대처

주요 어휘 argue 주장하다, essential 근본적인, foundation 기초, 기반, persistently 끈질기게, 지속적으로, inadequate 부족한 in the face of ~에 직면하여, benefit 이익을 주다, mitigation 경감, deforestation 벌채, 삼림 파괴, abatement 경감, 감소, reform 개혁 removal 제거, annual 연례적인, subsidy 보조금, recipient 수혜 분야, 수령인, accelerate 가속하다, conservation 보존

정답 ④

정답 해설 탄소 배출에 의한 기후변화에 대처하기 위해서 가난한 나라들에 대한 원조를 더 증가시키고, 선진국의 파괴적인 산업화 농업을 보존 농업으로 바꾸며 화석연료의 사용을 줄이는 대대적인 정책 혁신이 필요하다고 주장하는 글이다. 따라서 주제로 가장 적절한 것은 ④ 원조와 정책의 개혁에 의하여 기후변화에 대처하기이다. 첫 문장에서 정의의 원칙이 미래 세대와 최빈국들을 기후변화로부터 보호하는 것이라고 선언했기 때문에 주제에는 반드시 기후변화가 언급돼야 한다. 이는 ④뿐이다.

31 다음 글의 주제로 가장 적절한 것은?

Organizational successes and failures are often attributed to effective or ineffective leadership, although followers may have been the true reason behind the outcome. When examining the question of what distinguishes high-performance teams and organizations from average ones, most scholars and practitioners agree that high-performance organizations have good leaders and good followers. Competent, confident, and motivated followers are key to the successful performance of any leader's work group or team. Increasingly, many people are replacing old negative conceptions of followers with positive conceptions. Rather than the conforming and passive role in which followers have been cast, effective followers are described as courageous, responsible, and active.

① motivating followers with financial support
② examining the reasons for failures in leadership
③ encouraging conformity and passive followership
④ combining traditional and contemporary followership
⑤ achieving organizational success by effective followership

[한번에 정리하는 문제 해설]

지문 해석 조직의 성공과 실패는, 추종자가 결과의 진짜 이유였을 수 있음에도 불구하고 종종 유능한 혹은 무능한 리더십의 탓으로 돌려진다. 성적이 좋은 팀과 보통의 팀을 가르는 것이 무엇이냐는 문제를 검토할 때 대부분의 학자나 전문직 종사자들은 성적이 좋은 조직은 훌륭한 지도자와 훌륭한 추종자를 가진다는 데 의견이 일치한다. 유능하고 자신감 있고 성취동기가 있는 추종자는 모든 지도자의 업무 그룹이나 팀의 성공적인 임무 수행의 비결이다. 많은 사람들이 추종자에 대한 낡고 부정적인 관념을 버리고 긍정적인 관념을 채택하는 경우가 늘고 있다. 추종자들이 아직까지 빠져왔던 순응적이고 수동적인 역할 대신 이제 유능한 추종자들은 용기 있고, 책임감 있고 능동적으로 묘사된다.
① 경제적 지원을 통한 하급자 동기 부여
② 리더십 실패의 원인 조사
③ 조직에의 순응과 수동적 팔로워십 장려
④ 신·구식 팔로워십의 결합
⑤ 효율적 팔로워십을 통해 조직의 성공 성취하기

글의 소재 팔로워십의 중요성

주요 어휘 be attributed to ~탓으로 돌려지다, effective 유능한, distinguish 구별 짓다, practitioner 전문직 종사자, motivated 성취동기가 있는, replace ~ with ~ ~를 ~로 대체하다, conception 개념, conforming 순응적인

정 답 ⑤

정답 해설 조직의 성패를 가르는 요인으로 리더십 못지않게 요즘에는 부하직원의 역할, 즉 팔로워십이 강조되고 있음을 지적한 글이다. 무엇을 정의하는(define) 듯한 단정적인 문장이 주제문일 경우가 많다. 이 글에서는 'Competent, confident, and motivated followers are key to the successful performance of any leader's work group or team.'이 이에 해당한다. 주제문의 뜻에 가까운 것을 고르면 된다.

In the U.S. the proportion of infants who were nursed at all by their mothers, and the age at which those nursed infants were weaned, decreased through much of the 20th century. For example, by the 1970s only 5 percent of American children were being nursed at the age of six months. In contrast, among hunter-gatherers not in contact with farmers and without access to farmed foods, infants are nursed far beyond six months, because the only suitable infant food available to them is mother's milk: they have no access to cow's milk, baby formula, or soft food replacements. The age of weaning averaged over seven hunter-gatherer groups is about three years old, an age at which children finally become capable of fully nourishing themselves by chewing enough firm food.

① relationship between the age of weaning and available food
② necessity of early weaning in hunter-gatherer societies
③ controversy over the role of weaning in children's health
④ agricultural motivations for early weaning in children
⑤ demographic contrasts between farmers and hunter-gatherers

[한번에 정리하는 문제 해설]

지문 해석 거의 20세기 내내 미국에서는 모유를 먹고 자란 아기의 비율이 낮아지고 또 그런 아기들이 젖을 떼는 나이가 점점 어려졌다. 예를 들어 1970년이 될 무렵에는 생후 육 개월이 될 때까지 엄마 젖을 먹는 유아는 단 5%에 불과했다. 이에 비해 농부를 접촉할 수도 없고 농식품을 구할 수도 없었던 수렵채취인들 사이에서는 아기들이 생후 육 개월이 훨씬 지나도록 엄마 젖을 먹는데 이는 구할 수 있는 마땅한 유아식으로 엄마 젖이 유일하기 때문이다. 우유나 유아용 유동식, 또는 이를 대체할 만한 부드러운 음식을 그들은 구할 수 없다. 일곱 개 수렵 채취 부족의 평균적인 이유 나이는 세 살로 이때 비로소 아기들은 딱딱한 음식을 충분히 섭취해 스스로 영양을 공급할 수 있게 된다.
① 이유의 나이와 유아식 유무의 상관관계
② 수렵채취사회에서 조기 이유의 필요성
③ 유아 건강에서 이유가 차지하는 역할에 대한 논란
④ 농촌 환경이 조기 이유를 촉진하는가?
⑤ 농부와 수렵채취인의 인구학적 비교

글의 소재 젖 떼는 나이와 유아식

주요 어휘 proportion 비율, nurse 젖을 먹이다, wean 젖을 떼다, 이유하다, in contrast 이에 비해, hunter-gatherer 수렵채취인, have access to ~에 접근하다, formula 유아용 유동식

정답 ①

정답 해설 미국과 원시 수렵채취사회는 유아가 엄마에게서 젖을 떼는 이유(離乳)의 나이에 있어 큰 차이를 보이고 있고 그 차이는 엄마 젖을 대체할 수 있는 음식의 유무 때문이라고 필자는 주장한다. 따라서 이 글의 주제는 젖떼기의 나이와 음식의 상관관계로 볼 수 있다. 주제문이 명시적으로 드러나지 않았지만 'The age of weaning for nursed infants chiefly depends on the availability of infant food'로 추론해 볼 수 있고 이를 글의 맨 앞이나 끝에 덧붙여 온전한 paragraph로 재구성할 수 있다.

1. 글의 주제

| 해설 366쪽 |

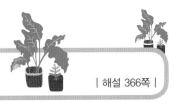

01   다음 글의 주제로 가장 적절한 것은?   난이도 중

It is to be observed that the word value has two different meanings. Sometimes it expresses the utility of some particular object, and sometimes the power of purchasing other goods which the possession of that object conveys. The one may be called 'value in use'; the other, 'value in exchange.' The things which have the greatest value in use have frequently little or no value in exchange; and, on the contrary, those which have the greatest value in exchange have frequently little or no value in use. Nothing is more useful than water: but it will purchase scarcely anything; scarcely anything can be had in exchange for it. A diamond, on the contrary, has scarcely any value in use; but a very great quantity of other goods may frequently be had in exchange for it.

① the value worthy of the intrinsic utility of a commodity
② the value corresponding to the power of purchasing
③ the relationship between commodity usefulness and its value
④ a comparison between value in use and value in exchange
⑤ a proposal to boost the substantial value of a commodity

02

다음 글의 주제로 가장 적절한 것은?

Most of people think of beavers as cute, even appealing, animals, even though the animals belong to the rodent, or rat, family. Many people just don't realize that, like dogs and bats, beavers can become rabid and attack anyone who come near them. In 2013, a fisherman from the eastern European country of Belarus spotted a beaver standing on the side of a country road. When he approached the animal to take a picture, the beaver bit him on the thigh. Tragically, his friends could not stem the flow of blood from the wound, and the man bled to death. Also in Belarus in 2003, a rabid beaver bit two farmers who tried to chase the animal out of a barn. And rabid beavers can turn up closer to home as well. In 2012, an 83-year-old woman was attacked by a rabid beaver while she swam in a Washington lake. The beaver was two feet long and weighed 34 pounds. Two young girls were also attacked while swimming in a lake in Virginia.

* rabid 포악한

① beavers as rabid animals that can attack humans
② the best way to avoid attacks from beavers
③ the reason why beavers have turned into rabid animals
④ the characteristics of the rodent family in general
⑤ people's misunderstanding of beavers as harmless animals

03 다음 글의 주제로 가장 적절한 것을 고르시오. 난이도 중

Certainly, the Kitoi hunter-gatherers of Siberia prized their dogs. Not only did the Kitoi and their dogs share the same diet and parasites, but they shared the same cemetery on the shores of Lake Baikal. Robert Losey, an archaeologist at the University of Alberta, says "The Kitoi had an elaborate mortuary tradition, which they extended to their dogs. They treated them just like a person." Indeed, in some places the gravediggers moved aside human remains to make room for a prized dog. Losey says "One was buried with a necklace of four red deer-teeth pendants, the same type of necklace the Kitoi wore. Another had a spoon tucked beside it and others were found with stone tools." The dogs themselves were carefully positioned. Some were placed in a crouching pose with their heads resting on their paws and others were laid curled on their sides, as if asleep. Two dogs were buried with an adult male human; one curled next to him on his right, the other to his left. "People only do this when they have close emotional bonds with their animals," Losey observes, "and the Kitoi clearly did with their dogs. A dog was a member of the family, and treated as such when it died."

① a Siberian tribe's strategy for survival by taking advantage of dogs
② a close human-dog relationship as shown in burial customs of a Siberian tribe
③ a canine burial custom found uniquely in a Siberian tribe
④ an observation on humans and dogs sharing a dietary tradition
⑤ an analysis of Siberian practices of burying humans and dogs together

다음 글의 주제로 가장 적절한 것은?

According to E-Marketer, during the 1999 holiday season some 34 million individuals made at least one purchase online. Web users are often lulled into believing that browsing online is an anonymous process. In reality, the explosion in electronic commerce has been accompanied by increasingly sophisticated information-gathering techniques. Clearly there is nothing inherently unethical in gathering information on customers when appropriate safeguards are put into place to protect them. Since the dawn of the commerce, bricks-and-mortar store owners have gathered information on their regular customers. However, what has irrevocably altered this information gathering process is the growth of sophisticated technology that enables the collection, dissemination, and combination of detailed information on customers at previously unprecedented levels.

* bricks-and-mortar 실제 매장이 존재하는, 오프라인의

① E-marketing as a likely cause for overspending
② anonymity as the main contributor to online browsing
③ the seriousness of information-gathering in E-marketing
④ technological developments facilitating electronic commerce
⑤ information-gathering as shown in conventional marketing

05

다음 글의 주제로 가장 적절한 것은?

난이도 중

"It lies with the government to satisfy the working classes that there is no justification... er..."(long silence)

On April 22nd 1904, Winston Churchill was addressing the House of Commons. Churchill had been speaking on trade unions in the House for a better part of an hour, when he suddenly lost his train of thought. He stalled for time, but could not finish his speech. He thanked the House for listening to him and sat down and put his head in his hands. He had been in the habit of totally memorizing his speeches. But from this point forward, Churchill decided to forge a system of speech writing that employed copious notes and several revisions. It was this system which helped create the powerful and awe-inspiring oratory which Churchill had envisioned as a 23-year-old in 'The Scaffolding of Rhetoric' and for which Churchill has become famous. So in many ways, it was from this small failure that day in the House of Commons that Churchill's amazing oratory was born. He was making a speech which, though often overlooked, is revered as one of the most important speeches of his life.

① a devastating moment that young Churchill had ever experienced
② a deadly speech that could have cost Churchill his whole career
③ a secret to surviving a moment of big public embarrassment
④ what Churchill drew from a ruined parliamentary speech
⑤ a terrible yet beneficial mistake that turned Churchill into a great orator

다음 글의 주제로 가장 적절한 것은?

Extended solitary confinement has become a standard practice in many American prisons largely because, as prison punishments go, social isolation is not considered especially harsh or painful. That's not the opinion, however, of a small group of psychiatrists, who believe that solitary confinement for extended periods of time is unbearable torture, bound to have devastating and long lasting psychological effects. At a hearing of the California State Assembly Public Safety Committee in 2011, Dr. Terry Kupers, a clinical psychiatrist, pointed out that one-half of all prison suicides are carried out by prisoners in maximum security prisons, who have been confined in isolation for long stretches of time. The suicides, from his perspective, are the result of the "toxic conditions" created when prisoners must remain in cells the size of the closets with no human contact for 23 hours a day. Massachusetts psychiatrist Stuart Grassian, who has studied the psychiatric effects of long-term isolation for a decade, echoes Kupers's assessment of the practice. Grassian insists that long-term isolation is a form of torture that should be eliminated from the list of prison punishments.

① the reason why social isolation can be a viable option
② a proposal to effectively prevent prison suicides
③ the case for the abolition of prison punishments
④ the toxic side effects of long-term solitary confinement
⑤ the effects of social isolation on healing

07
다음 글의 주제로 가장 적절한 것은? 난이도 중

Some people say that education should have no positive purpose, but should merely offer an environment suitable for spontaneous development. I cannot agree with them, who seem to me too individualistic, and unduly indifferent to the importance of knowledge. We live in communities which require cooperation, and it would be utopian to expect all the necessary cooperation to result from spontaneous impulse. The existence of a large population on a limited area is only possible owing to science and technique; education must, therefore, hand on the necessary minimum of these. The educators who allow most freedom are men whose success depends upon a degree of benevolence, self-control, and trained intelligence which can hardly be generated where every impulse is left unchecked; their merits, therefore, are not likely to be perpetuated if their methods are undiluted. Education must be something more positive than a mere opportunity for growth. It must, of course, provide this, but it must also provide a mental and moral equipment which children cannot acquire entirely for themselves.

① the role spontaneous impulse plays in education
② education as a tool to provide an opportunity for success
③ the advantage of an education based on freedom
④ the need for a more positive and purposeful education
⑤ education befitting an era of ever expanding science and technology

다음 글의 주제로 가장 적절한 것은?

The comforting function of religion has increased in more populous and recent societies: it's simply that those societies inflict on us more bad things for which we crave comfort. This comforting role of religion helps explain the frequent observation that misfortune tends to make people more religious, and that poorer social strata, regions, and countries tend to be more religious than richer ones: they need more comforting. Among the world's nations today, the percentage of citizens who say that religion is an important part of their daily lives is 80%-99% for most nations with per-capita gross domestic products (GDP) under $10,000, but only 17%-43% for most nations with per-capita GDP over $30,000. Even within just the U.S., there appear to be more churches and more church attendance in poorer areas than in richer areas, despite the greater resources and leisure time available to build and attend churches in richer areas. Within American society, the highest religious commitment and the most radical Christian branches are found among the most marginalized, underprivileged social groups.

① the instinctive human desire to seek comfort anywhere, anytime
② misfortune and comfort as a significant religious motive
③ the economic affluence that negatively affects religious inclination
④ destitute regions suffering from a lack of religious opportunities
⑤ contrasting religious realities in poorer and richer nations

09 다음 글의 주제로 가장 적절한 것은? 난이도 중

Education as an event situates personal encounter in the very center of the educational experience. As in *The Calling Saint Matthew* by Caravaggio, education begins when people in need meet. A teacher inspires a student to imitation and becomes a life companion. In his masterpiece, Caravaggio depicts the essence of the educational encounter as a surprise, disbelief, and overwhelming joy of being called to follow the teacher. It is an opening toward the unknown, which happens as the disclosure of truth. Situating this encounter in a deliberate horizon of ambiguity, Caravaggio points towards the relevance of the personal touch, which empowers people who are called to transgress their particular limits and follow the call. In the face of this call, what is asked for is an answer, the most personal expression of responsibility. A teacher brings real light into the student's world: The collision of different worlds promises a new way of life. This novelty cannot be imagined and theoretically constructed but must be lived out to its fullest.

① the joy found in entering the realm of education
② educational motives implied in religious paintings
③ the ideal relationship between teacher and student
④ the importance of personal encounter in education
⑤ the significance of religious inspiration in education

10 다음 글의 주제로 가장 적절한 것은?

Infants are born with different levels of emotional reactivity that influence their care-giving environment. People often refer to highly reactive infants as fussy or difficult and infants who are not reactive as easygoing. A fussy baby might elicit more frustration from his or her caregiver than an infant who rarely cries. Additionally, a fussy baby might elicit a different response from his or her caregiver upon crying than an infant who rarely cries. According to the dynamic viewpoint of temperament posited by Thompson, Cassidy, and others, the difference in quantity or quality of caregiver response to the infant's emotional expressivity has the potential to shape the infant's subsequent emotional expressivity. In turn, the way the infant comes to express emotions elicits further emotional socialization from the parent. Thus, a fussy infant might elicit greater expression of personal distress from a parent, which may increase the infants' negative emotionality over time, whereas another parent who responds to the infants' crying with comforting may decrease the infants' negative emotionality.

* posit 가정하다

① different levels of emotional reactivity indigenous to each infant
② how infants with loud cries are served more and better
③ the risks resulting from caregivers expressing personal distress
④ the advantages of caregivers keeping infants at arms' length
⑤ infants and their caregivers emotionally affecting each other

11 다음 글의 주제로 가장 적절한 것은?

Meditation is by no means a cure-all for our era of mean tweets and mindless tribalism. I have been meditating for years, and yet during one of the recent presidential debates I stress-ate a family-size bag of popcorn. I didn't realize what I had done until I looked down to see my feet surrounded by stray kernels. Nevertheless, I really do believe meditation can help you survive this season of discontent and division. When you are blinded by outrage, you're unable to understand the views of people with whom you disagree. A consistent meditation practice can help you know your biases. Does your heart soar every time the Mueller probe inches closer to the White House? Or do you own a mug emblazoned with the words Liberal Tears? When you are more aware of your tribal instincts, you may be more inclined to venture out of your ideological bubble and examine opposing views. Next thing you know, you are refraining from nasty tweets and even having civil conversations with your uncle. Cutting down on wasted emotional churn frees up energy to do things that really make a difference, like volunteering. Multiply this by enough people and it could inject significant light into America's chasm of toxicity.

① a proposal to guide you to mindfulness through meditation
② ways to survive the era of political and ideological polarization
③ the reason why consistency is required for all meditation practice
④ rampant political biases and their harmful effects on society
⑤ meditation as an effective means to overcome ideological biases

② 요지 · 주장

필자가 궁극적으로 전달하고자 하는
글의 요지나 필자가 주장하는 바를 묻는 유형이다.
때로는 필자가 시사하는 바나 특정 사안에 대한
결론을 묻는 형식을 취하기도 한다.

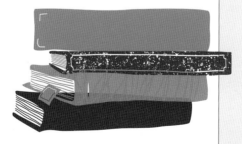

▶ 요지나 주장은 주제를 하나의 문장으로 발전시킨 형태를 띠는 경우가 많다.

▶ 주제는 구 형태로, 요지나 주장은 문장으로 제시되며, 둘은 흔히 문답의 관계를 이룬다.

▶ 따라서 요지나 주장을 파악하기 위해서는 주제문을 파악하는 방법을 따르면 된다.

▶ 주제문이 명시적으로 드러나지 않는 경우 먼저 중심소재를 파악한 다음 이에 대한 필자의 견해를 살핀 뒤에 요지나 주장을 추론한다.

▶ 요지의 방향과 부합하는지에 따라 선택지를 긍정(+)과 부정(-)으로 나누면 정답 후보를 대폭 압축할 수 있다 (±전략).

▶ 선택지 중에서 2~3개는 특정 가치에 대해 필자와 정반대되는 주장을, 나머지 1~2개는 주제와 무관한 내용을 담고 있는 경우가 많다. 이들은 모두 소거 대상이다.

▶ for example, for instance, Suppose, Let's suppose 같은 예시의 연결어나 예시를 암시하는 표현이 있으면 바로 전 문장이 주제문일 경우가 많다.

▶ Research says, A study suggests, According to an experiment, Reports say와 같이 연구, 실험, 조사, 보도, 인용이 시작되는 표현이 있으면 바로 앞 문장이 주제문일 가능성이 크다.

▶ but, however, yet, still 같은 역접의 연결사가 들어있는 문장, 이른바 꺾이는 문장은 그 문장이나 다음 문장이 주제문일 가능성이 있다.

▶ 결어나 요약, 인과를 나타내는 연결사 즉 thus, therefore, consequently, accordingly, as a result, in short, in brief 등이 올 때는 그 문장이 주제문일 가능성이 크다.

▶ 무엇을 정의하는(define) 듯한 단정적인 어조의 문장이 주제문일 가능성이 크다.e.g. ~ is the key to ~, Definitely(Obviously, Certainly, Absolutely) ~

▶ 의견, 중요성, 필요성, 의무 등을 나타내는 어구를 포함하는 문장이 주제문일 경우가 많다. e.g. I think, I believe, In my opinion, It is important, It is necessary, must, need, should, have to 등

▶ 명령문은 필자의 주장이 강하게 들어 있기 때문에 주제문일 경우가 많다.

22 다음 글의 요지로 가장 적절한 것은?

   With the industrial society evolving into an information-based society, the concept of information as a product, a commodity with its own value, has emerged. As a consequence, those people, organizations, and countries that possess the highest-quality information are likely to prosper economically, socially, and politically. Investigations into the economics of information encompass a variety of categories including the costs of information and information services; the effects of information on decision making; the savings from effective information acquisition; the effects of information on productivity; and the effects of specific agencies (such as corporate, technical, or medical libraries) on the productivity of organizations. Obviously many of these areas overlap, but it is clear that information has taken on a life of its own outside the medium in which it is contained. Information has become a recognized entity to be measured, evaluated, and priced.

* entity: 실재(물)

① 정보화된 사회일수록 개인 정보 보호가 필요하다.
② 정보의 효율적 교환은 조직의 생산성을 향상시킨다.
③ 정보 처리의 단순화는 신속한 의사결정에 도움이 된다.
④ 정보 기반 사회에서 정보는 독자적 상품 가치를 지닌다.
⑤ 정보 기반 사회에서는 정보를 전달하는 방식이 중요하다.

[한번에 정리하는 문제 해설]

[지문 해석] 산업사회가 정보에 기반한 사회로 진화해가면서, 하나의 상품, 즉 그 나름의 가치를 가진 하나의 제품으로서의 정보의 개념이 등장했다. 결과적으로 가장 고품질의 정보를 소유한 사람, 조직, 그리고 국가들이 경제적으로, 사회적으로, 그리고 정치적으로 번창할 가능성이 높다. 정보의 경제학에 대한 연구는 정보와 정보 서비스의 비용, 정보가 의사결정에 미치는 영향, 효과적인 정보 취득으로 인한 절약, 정보가 생산성에 미치는 영향, 그리고 (기업, 기술, 혹은 의학 도서관과 같은) 특정 기관이 조직의 생산성에 미치는 영향을 포함하는 다양한 범주를 망라한다. 이러한 많은 분야들이 서로 겹치는 것은 분명하지만, 정보가 그것이 포함되는 매체를 벗어나 그 나름의 생명력을 지니게 된 것은 분명하다. 정보는 측정되고, 평가되고, 값이 매겨지는 인정받는 실재(독립체)가 되었다.

[글의 소재] 정보의 상품 가치

[주요 어휘] evolve 진화하다, 발전하다, information-based 정보에 기반한, commodity 제품, 상품 emerge 부상하다, 떠오르다, prosper 번창하다, investigation 연구, 조사 encompass 망라하다, 아우르다, effective 효과적인, 효율적인, acquisition 취득, 습득, productivity 생산성, corporate 법인의, 기업의, overlap 겹치다, take on 띠다, 지니다, evaluate 평가하다, price 값을 매기다

[정답] ④

[정답 해설] 이 글의 주제문은 첫 문장 'With the industrial society evolving into an information-based society, the concept of information as a product, a commodity with its own value, has emerged.'이며, 이 주제문의 핵심 내용은 마지막 문장 'Information has become a recognized entity to be measured, evaluated, and priced.'에 반복 제시된다. 요컨대 정보 사회의 도래와 함께 독자적 가치를 가진 상품으로서의 정보의 개념이 탄생했다는 것이 중심 내용이므로 글의 요지로 가장 적절한 것은 ④의 '정보 기반 사회에서 정보는 독자적 상품 가치를 지닌다.'이다

05 다음 글의 요지로 가장 적절한 것을 고르시오.

Habits often prove to be quite fragile when changes appear predictably or unpredictably in our lives. How many times have you heard someone complaining or regretting their 'good hobbies' before marriage when they 'had the time'? I have heard it dozens of times and people always try to find excuses for lack of continuity. That's what we do. We find excuses. But if we just spent some time thinking and trying to understand how we function and how habits function, then we might see that habits need training to strengthen them, just like a muscle does, and the more they depend on some external factors or your disposition and mood to be maintained, the more vulnerable they are to interruption. Build your habits strong right from the beginning. If you want to start jogging, do it when it is sunny, do it when it is windy or rainy, do it when you feel happy and do it, by all means, when you feel sad. It is about connecting with a zone of enjoyment per se that goes beyond meeting a bunch of conditions to be carried out.

* vulnerable: 취약한 ** per se: 그 자체로

① 예기치 않은 상황에서는 침착한 태도를 유지하는 것이 중요하다.
② 습관을 꾸준히 유지하려면 훈련을 통해 처음부터 강화해야 한다.
③ 나쁜 습관을 없애는 데는 지속적인 자기 보상이 효과적이다.
④ 자신의 성격에 맞는 취미를 고르면 오랫동안 즐길 수 있다.
⑤ 건강한 생활 습관 형성을 위해서는 휴식과 회복이 필요하다.

[한번에 정리하는 문제 해설]

지문 해석 예상했든 예상하지 못했든 우리 삶에서 변화가 생길 때 습관은 자주 취약한 것으로 드러난다. 누군가가 결혼 전 '시간이 있을 때' 가졌던 훌륭한 취미에 대해 불평하거나 아쉬워하는 것을 당신은 얼마나 여러 번 들었는가? 나는 그것을 수십 번 들었고 사람들은 항상 연속성 부족의 핑계거리를 찾으려 한다. 우리는 그런 식이다. 우리는 핑계거리를 찾는다. 잠시 시간을 내 우리가 어떻게 작동하고 습관이 어떻게 작동하는지를 생각하거나 이해하려고 노력한다면 우리는 근육이 그러하듯 습관을 강화하기 위해서는 훈련이 필요하고, 습관이 유지되기 위해 어떤 외부적 요인이나 우리의 기질, 분위기에 의존하면 할수록 그만큼 중단에 취약하다는 것을 알게 될 것이다. 바로 처음부터 습관을 강하게 만들어라. 조깅을 시작하고 싶다면 맑을 때에도 하고 바람 불거나 비가 올 때도 하고 행복할 때도 하고 슬플 때도 기필코 하라. 중요한 것은 이행돼야 할 다수의 조건을 충족하는 것을 넘어서는 즐거움의 영역 그 자체와 연결되는 것이다.

글의 소재 훈련은 습관을 강화시키는 최상의 방법

주요 어휘 fragile 깨지기 쉬운, 취약한, continuity 지속성, external 외부적인, disposition 기질, 성향, vulnerable 취약한, interruption 중단, by all means 어떤 일이 있어도, 기필코, per se 그 자체로

구조 분석 • It is about connecting with a zone of enjoyment per se that goes beyond meeting a bunch of conditions to be carried out.
→ 'A is (all) about B' 구문이다. 'A는 B에 관한 것이다.'가 원래 뜻이지만 실제로는 'A에서 중요한 것은 B다.'를 의미한다. 강조를 위해 all을 넣기도 한다. ex) Soccer is (all) about scoring goals(축구에서 중요한 것은 골을 넣는 것이다). 문제에서는 상황의 비인칭 it이 쓰였으므로 '중요한 것은 ~ 연결되는 것이다.'로 해석할 수 있다.

정답 ②

정답 해설 습관은 기분이나 외부 요인 등에 매우 취약하기 때문에 이를 강하게 만들려면 근육을 단련시키듯 단련시켜야 한다고 필자는 강조하므로 이 글의 요지로 적절한 것은 ② '습관을 꾸준히 유지하려면 훈련을 통해 처음부터 강화해야 한다.'이다. 필자의 주장은 'Build your habits right from the beginning.'에 함축돼 있는데 명령문 같은 강한 표현은 주제문일 경우가 많다.

34 다음 글의 요지로 가장 적절한 것은?

When infant mortality rates are high, as they are in much of the developing world, parents tend to have high numbers of children to ensure that some will survive to adulthood. There has never been a sustained drop in birth rates that was not first preceded by a sustained drop in infant mortality. One of the most important distinctions in our demographically divided world is the high infant mortality rates in the less-developed countries. Better nutrition, improved health care, simple oral rehydration therapy, and immunization against infectious diseases have brought about dramatic reductions in infant mortality rates, which have been accompanied in most regions by falling birth rates. It has been estimated that saving 5 million children each year from easily preventable communicable diseases would avoid 20 or 30 million extra births.

① Infant mortality rates affect birth rates.
② Infant mortality around the world is declining very rapidly.
③ Disparities of wealth are reflected in infant mortality rates.
④ A primary cause of infant mortality is poor quality of water.
⑤ Good prenatal care has been linked to reduced infant mortality.

[한번에 정리하는 문제 해설]

지문 해석 현재의 개발도상국에서 그런 것처럼 영아 사망률이 높을 때, 부모들은 성인까지 살아남는 아이가 있는 걸 보장하기 위해 많은 아이를 낳는 경향이 있다. 영아 사망률의 지속적인 하락에 의해 선행되지 않은 영아 출생률의 지속적인 하락이 있던 적은 없었다. 인구학적으로 나뉜 이 세상에서 가장 중요한 구별 기준은 개발도상국의 높은 영유아 사망률이다. 더 나은 영양 상태, 의료서비스 개선, 간단한 경구 수분 보충 요법, 그리고 전염성 질환에 대한 예방주사는 영유아 사망률에 급격한 감소를 가져왔고, 이는 대부분의 지역에서 출생률의 감소를 동반하였다. 매년 5백만 명의 아이들을 쉽게 예방할 수 있는 전염성 질병으로부터 보호하는 것은 2천만 명에서 3천만 명의 추가적 출생을 방지할 수 있는 것으로 추산된다.
　① 유아 사망률은 출생률에 영향을 미친다.
　② 전 세계 영유아 사망은 급속히 감소하고 있다.
　③ 영유아 사망률에는 부의 불균형이 반영돼 있다.
　④ 영유아 사망의 일차 원인은 수질 불량이다.
　⑤ 양질의 산전 관리가 영아 사망 감소와 관련 있다.

글의 소재 영유아 사망률과 출생률

주요 어휘 infant 영아, mortality 사망, developing world 개발도상국, ensure 확실하게 하다, 보장하다, sustained 지속적인, precede ~보다 선행하다, distinction 차이, 구별법, demographical 인구의, 인구학의, nutrition 영양, rehydration 재수화, 수분 보충, therapy 요법, immunization 면역, 예방주사, reduction 감소, accompany ~를 동반하다, ~와 함께하다, estimate 추정하다, communicable 전염성의

정　답 ①

정답 해설 이 글은 영유아 사망률이 높은 국가에서 부모는 후손을 확보하기 위해 더 많은 아이를 낳는 경향이 있기 때문에 영유아 사망률과 출생률 사이에는 긴밀한 상관관계가 있음을 개발도상국의 예를 들어 주장하고 있다. 따라서 이 글의 요지로 가장 알맞은 것은 ①의 '영유아 사망률은 출생률에 영향을 미친다.'이다. 이 글의 주제문 'There has never been a sustained drop in birth rates that was not first preceded by a sustained drop in infant mortality.'에 주목하면 어렵지 않게 풀 수 있는 문제이다.

2. 요지 · 주장

| 해설 371쪽 |

12 미국의 유가에 관한 다음 글의 요지로 가장 적절한 것은? 난이도 중

Periodically, the price of gasoline soars and infuriated Americans blame Congress, the White House, and the Organization of the Petroleum Exporting Countries(OPEC). According to an editorial by an American local newspaper, however, if Americans want to know who is really responsible for high gas prices, they should look in the mirror. "The real cause of gas-pump sticker shock," says the editorial, "is American consumers' addiction to the automobile and the life style it allows." The editorialist goes on to point out that far too many Americans act as if they are entitled to own big, gas-guzzling cars and oversized pickup trucks, which together account for a sizable portion of the vehicles sold in this country. The result? America has an insatiable appetite for oil, and OPEC simply takes advantage of our dependence on its product. Rather than demanding lower gas prices, says the editorial, Americans should be driving as little as possible and insisting that their leaders do more to make mass transportation available, reliable, and affordable.

* sticker shock 비싼 가격을 보고 놀람, gas-guzzling 연료를 많이 소비하는

① OPEC는 미국의 과도한 석유 수요에 편승해 막대한 이득을 취한다.
② 고유가는 정부 정책에 일차적 책임이 있다.
③ 고유가 해소를 위해서는 자동차 연비의 획기적 개선이 필요하다.
④ 고유가의 근본 원인은 소비자들의 자동차 중독 때문이다.
⑤ 자동차 사랑과 자동차 문화는 미국 고유의 가치로 인정돼야 한다.

13 다음 글의 요지로 가장 적절한 것은?

Essentially combat is an expression of hostile feelings. But in the large-scale combat that we call war hostile feelings often have become merely hostile intentions. At any rate, there are usually no hostile feelings between individuals. Yet such emotions can never be completely absent from war. Modern wars are seldom fought without hatred between nations; this serves as a more or less substitute for the hatred between individuals. Even when there is no natural hatred and no animosity to start with, the fighting itself will stir up hostile feelings: violence committed on superior orders will stir up the desire for revenge and retaliation against the perpetrator rather than against the powers that ordered the action. It is only human (or animal, if you like), but it is a fact.

① Hostile feelings prevail in combat but not in wars.
② Modern wars are rooted in hatred between nations.
③ Hostile feelings, after all, are essential to all forms of wars.
④ Hatred between nations substitutes that between individuals.
⑤ Hostile feelings also arise in the course of actual fighting.

14 다음 글의 요지로 가장 적절한 것은?

난이도 중

Physicians and other medical professionals have strongly resisted the use of checklists. It is seen as an insult to their professional competence. "Other people might need checklists," they complain, "but not me." Too bad. To err is human: we all are subject to slips and mistakes when under stress, or under time or social pressure, or after being subjected to multiple interruptions, each essential in its own right. It is not a threat to professional competence to be human. Legitimate criticisms of particular checklists are used as an indictment against the concept of checklists. Fortunately, checklists are slowly starting to gain acceptance in medical situations. When senior personnel insist on the use of checklists, it actually enhances their authority and professional status. It took decades for checklists to be accepted in, let's say, commercial aviation: let us hope that doctors and other medical professionals will change more rapidly.

① 의료인에게도 체크리스트가 필요하다.
② 의료인에게 인간적인 실수는 필연적이다.
③ 체크리스트에 대한 비판은 정당화될 수 있다.
④ 의료계에도 체크리스트 사용이 보편화될 것이다.
⑤ 체크리스트는 의료인의 자긍심을 손상할 수 있다.

15 다음 글의 요지로 적절한 것은?

Over the years Steve Jobs would become the grand master of product launches. In the case of the Macintosh, the astonishing Ridley Scott ad was just one of the ingredients. Another part of the recipe was media coverage. Jobs found ways to ignite blasts of publicity that were so powerful the frenzy would feed on itself, like a chain reaction. It was a phenomenon that he would be able to replicate whenever there was a big product launch, from the Macintosh in 1984 to the iPad in 2010. Like a conjurer, he could pull the trick off over and over again, even after journalists had seen it happen a dozen times and knew how it was done. Some of the moves he had learned from Regis McKenna, who was a pro at cultivating and stroking prideful reporters. But Jobs had his own intuitive sense of how to stoke the excitement, manipulate the competitive instincts of journalists, and trade exclusive access for lavish treatment.

① 잡스는 성공적인 제품 출시의 비결을 꿰고 있었다.
② 잡스는 불같은 정열과 저돌적 추진력의 소유자였다.
③ 잡스는 제품 홍보에 언론을 적절히 이용할 줄 알았다.
④ 잡스는 대중의 소비 심리를 정확히 파악하고 이를 영업에 이용할 줄 알았다.
⑤ 잡스는 때론 경쟁자로부터 배우려는 유연한 자세를 취했다.

16 빅토리아 시대 코르셋에 관한 다음 글의 요지로 가장 적절한 것은? 난이도 중

Early Victorian costume not only made women look weak and helpless, but it made them weak and helpless. The main agent of the debility was the corset, which at the time was thought of not as a mere fashion item but as a medical necessity. Ladies' "frames," it was believed, were extremely delicate; their muscles could not hold them up without assistance. Well-brought-up little girls were laced into juvenile versions of the corset as early as three or four. Gradually their stays were lengthened, stiffened and tightened. By the time they reached their adolescence they were wearing cages of heavy canvas reinforced with heavy steel, and their back muscles had often atrophied to the point where they could not sit or stand for long unsupported. The corset also deformed the internal organs and made it impossible to draw a deep breath. As a result, fashionably dressed ladies fainted easily, suffered from digestive complaints, and felt weak and exhausted after any strenuous exertion.

* atrophy 위축되다

① 디자인의 주안점은 섬약한 여성성을 강조하는 것이었다.
② 많은 여성을 허약 체질로 만든 주범이었다.
③ 모든 연령대의 여성이 즐겨 입던 복식이었다.
④ 부작용이 있었으나 여성들이 미용을 위해 즐겨 입었다.
⑤ 허약한 여성의 신체를 받쳐주는 데 큰 도움을 줬다.

motorcycle에 대한 다음 글의 요지로 가장 적절한 것은?

 난이도 중

In a desperate move to reduce the risk of crashes most states offer rider education programs. Some states even provide the incentive of automatic licensure in lieu of a state-administered written knowledge test or road test once riders successfully complete a rider education course. A 1996 review of the effects of motorcycle rider training on crash risk, however, concluded that there is "no compelling evidence that rider training is associated with reductions in collisions."

The New York Department of Motor Vehicles conducted a large-scale analysis of motorcycle rider training between 1981 and 1985. In the study sponsored by National Highway Traffic Safety Administration(NHTSA), motorcycle operator's license applicants were randomly assigned to one of four groups. One group took the state's existing knowledge and driving test and another took a skills test developed by NHTSA. The two remaining groups were assigned to rider training courses, plus the skills test. Riders who took the state's standard knowledge and driving test had fewer motorcycle crashes in the subsequent two years than riders in the three experimental groups. A 2010 review of international research also found no established link between motorcycle rider training and crash risk.

① Rider training programs should be greatly encouraged as an effective way to reduce crashes.

② Rider training programs can effectively replace any formal driver's licence test.

③ There are no clues yet showing rider training programs help diminish the risk of crashes.

④ Stricter policies on issuing driver's licences are needed to reduce crash risk.

⑤ The role of the knowledge and driving test as a crash deterrent should never be underestimated.

18 다음 글에서 필자가 말하고자 하는 바는?

Because biographies of famous scientists tend to edit out their mistakes, we underestimate the degree of risk they were willing to take. And because anything a famous scientist did that wasn't a mistake has probably now become the conventional wisdom, those choices don't seem risky either. Biographies of Newton, for example, understandably focus more on physics than alchemy or theology. The impression we get is that his unerring judgment led him straight to truths no one else had noticed. But how can we explain all the time he spent on alchemy and theology? Apparently, physics seems to us like a promising thing to work on, and alchemy and theology obvious wastes of time. But that's because we know how things turned out. In Newton's day the three problems seemed roughly equally promising. No one knew yet what the payoff would be for inventing what we now call physics; if they had, more people would have been working on it. And alchemy and theology were still then in the category Marc Andreessen would describe as "huge, if true". Newton made three bets. One of them worked. But they were all risky.

① 뉴튼은 물리학 못지않게 연금술이나 신학에 관심이 많았다.
② 과학자들의 업적은 모험의 소산일 때가 많다.
③ 연금술이나 신학은 과학자들에게 매력적인 연구 대상이 아니었다.
④ 과학자들은 연구 과제 선정에 신중을 기해야 한다.
⑤ 모험은 성공적인 과학 연구에 없어서는 안 될 요소다.

다음 글의 요지로 가장 적절한 것은?

난이도 중

That perceptions and judgements produce and shape passions should surprise no one. Perhaps more surprising is the converse causal relationship: the fact that passions also shape perceptions and judgments. Aristotle says, 'The emotions are all those feelings that so change men as to affect their judgments, and that are also attended by pain or pleasure. Perception does not take place in a purely rational, objective, and detached way. Instead. perception is colored by a rich range of passions and their relatives, moods. Passions foreground some factors within a situation, meanwhile backgrounding others. In particular, anger helps victims to recognize, hold onto, and attach importance to the fact that they have been, or are being wronged. Without anger, people tend not to focus sufficiently on injustices, and so tend not to notice them, or not to take them seriously. They sometimes do not consider them wrongs or even harms. In general, passions are salience and value projectors. They overlay situations with highlight and shadow.

* foreground ~를 전면에 두다, salience 돌출 부분

① passions usually drive us to respond too hastily
② passions affect the way we perceive and judge
③ emotions often get in the way of sound reasoning
④ perceptions should account for the birth of passions
⑤ anger helps perceive the wrongs done unjustly to us

다음 글의 요지로 가장 적절한 것은? 난이도 상

I fully admit that the mischief which a person does to himself may seriously affect, both through their sympathies and their interests, those nearly connected with him and, in a minor degree, society at large. When, by conduct of this sort, a person is led to violate a distinct and assignable obligation to any other person or persons, the case is taken out of the self-regarding class, and becomes amenable to moral disapproval in the proper sense of the term. If, for example, a man, through extravagance, becomes unable to pay his debts, or, having undertaken the moral responsibility of a family, becomes from the same cause incapable of supporting or educating them, he is deservedly criticized, and might be justly punished; but it is for the breach of duty to his family or creditors, not for the extravagance. If the resources which ought to have been devoted to them had been diverted from them for the most prudent investment, the moral culpability would have been the same. Whenever there is a definite damage, or a definite risk of damage, either to an individual or to the public, the case is taken out of the province of liberty, and placed in that of morality or law.

① 개인의 자유는 도덕적 책무를 다할 때에만 허용된다.
② 도덕적 책무는 모든 사회 규약의 제일 원칙이다.
③ 도덕적 책무에 과도하게 얽매이면 개인적 자유를 얻기 어렵다.
④ 개인의 비행은 타인과 사회에 부정적 영향을 끼친다.
⑤ 진정한 자유를 위해서 과도한 욕구는 포기돼야 한다.

③
글의 제목

글의 내용과 성격을 반영하여 글 전체를
대표하는 제목(title)을 추론하는 유형이다.

가이드라인

▶ 제목은 많은 경우 주제문을 그대로 인용하거나 주제문의 일부를 구 형태로 변형해 제시한다.

▶ 그러나 주제를 압축하거나 상징적인 또는 비유적인 어구로 제시할 때도 있다.

▶ 때로는 의문문이나 명령문, 감탄문의 다양한 문장 형태를 취하기도 하므로 의미 파악에 주의한다. 만약 수사 의문문으로 제시되는 경우라면 반대로 해석한다.

▶ 속담이 선택지로 제시되는 경우도 있으므로 자주 사용되는 속담이나 격언의 의미를 정확히 파악해 둔다.

▶ 정답을 직접 찾기 어려울 때는 주제나 요지의 대강의 방향을 파악한 후에 이를 근거로 오답을 가려내 정답을 역추적하는 오답 소거 전략이 효과적일 수 있다.

▶ 대강의 주제의 방향과 부합하는지에 따라 선택지를 긍정(+)과 부정(−)으로 나누면 정답 후보를 대폭 압축할 수 있다(±전략).

▶ 선택지 중에서 2~3개는 주제에 대해 필자와 정반대되는 주장을, 나머지 1~2개는 주제와 무관한 내용을 담고 있는 경우가 많다. 이들은 모두 소거 대상이다.

오답의 예

▶ 필자의 주장과 정반대의 가치를 담고 있는 선택지의 경우

▶ 얼핏 보기에 합리적이고 상식에 부합하나 필자의 생각과 다른 내용이 제시된 경우

▶ 주제와 상관없는, 본문 내용의 일부를 그대로 인용해 오판을 유도하는 경우

▶ 필자의 생각과 방향은 비슷하나 지나치게 지엽적인 내용으로 주제에 대한 대표성을 상실한 경우

▶ 역으로 지나치게 포괄적으로 제시돼 주제를 특정하기 어려운 경우

다음 글의 제목으로 가장 적절한 것은?

수능 기출문제 유형보기

A defining element of catastrophes is the magnitude of their harmful consequences. To help societies prevent or reduce damage from catastrophes, a huge amount of effort and technological sophistication are often employed to assess and communicate the size and scope of potential or actual losses. This effort assumes that people can understand the resulting numbers and act on them appropriately. However, recent behavioral research casts doubt on this fundamental assumption. Many people do not understand large numbers. Indeed, large numbers have been found to lack meaning and to be underestimated in decisions unless they convey affect (feeling). This creates a paradox that rational models of decision making fail to represent. On the one hand, we respond strongly to aid a single individual in need. On the other hand, we often fail to prevent mass tragedies or take appropriate measures to reduce potential losses from natural disasters.

* catastrophe 큰 재해

① Insensitivity to Mass Tragedy: We Are Lost in Large Numbers
② Power of Numbers: A Way of Classifying Natural Disasters
③ How to Reach Out a Hand to People in Desperate Need
④ Preventing Potential Losses Through Technology
⑤ Be Careful, Numbers Magnify Feelings!

[한번에 정리하는 문제 해설]

지문 해석 큰 재해를 정의하는 요소 중 하나는 그 해로운 결과의 거대한 규모이다. 사회가 큰 재해로부터 오는 손실을 방지하거나 줄이는 데 도움을 주기 위해서, 잠재적 혹은 실제적 손실의 규모와 범위를 산정하고 전달하기 위한 대단히 큰 노력과 기술적인 정교한 지식이 자주 사용된다. 이 노력은 사람들이 그 결과로 생기는 수를 이해할 수 있고 그에 의거하여 적절하게 행동할 수 있다는 것을 전제한다. 그러나 최근의 행동 연구는 이러한 근본적인 전제에 의혹을 던진다. 큰 수를 이해하지 못하는 사람들이 많다. 사실상 큰 수는 정서적 반응(감정)을 전달하지 않는다면 의미가 없으며 결정을 내릴 때 과소평가된다는 것이 밝혀졌다. 이것은 의사결정의 이성적인 모델이 설명하지 못하는 역설을 만들어 낸다. 한편으로 우리는 곤궁한 상태에 빠진 한 사람을 돕기 위하여 강렬하게 반응한다. 다른 한편으로 우리는 대량의 비극을 방지하거나 자연재해로부터 잠재적인 손실을 줄이기 위한 적절한 조치를 하지 못할 때가 흔히 있다.

① 대규모 비극에 대한 무감각: 우리는 큰 수에 매몰되어 있다
② 수의 힘: 자연재해를 분류하는 방법
③ 필사적인 곤궁한 상태에 있는 사람들에게 손을 내미는 방법
④ 기술을 통해 잠재적 손실을 방지하기
⑤ 주의하라: 수는 감정을 확대한다!

글의 소재 큰 수에 무감각한 대중

주요 어휘 catastrophe 재난, 재해, magnitude 큰 규모, consequence 결과, sophistication 정교한 지식, assess 산정하다, behavioral 행동의, appropriately 적절하게, cast doubt on ~에 의혹을 던지다, fundamental 근본적인, assumption 가정, 전제, affect 정서적 반응, paradox 역설, represent 표현하다, 설명하다

정답 ①

정답 해설 큰 재해가 생기면 그 규모와 피해액을 표현하는 거대한 수에 매몰되어 그 실상을 파악하지 못하는 경향이 있음을 설명하는 글이다. 그래서 한 개인의 재난에는 강하게 반응하면서, 정작 큰 규모의 재난에는 무감각해지는 역설이 생긴다는 것이다. 따라서 제목으로 가장 적절한 것은 ①의 '대규모 비극에 대한 무감각: 우리는 큰 수에 매몰되어 있다'이다. 이 글의 주제문은 'Many people do not understand large numbers.'이다, 이에 가까운 것을 찾으면 된다.

13 다음 글의 제목으로 가장 적절한 것을 고르시오.

To reconstitute democracy in line with our present situation, we need to challenge the frightening, but false, assumption that increased diversity automatically brings increased tension and conflict in society. Indeed, the exact reverse can be true. Conflict in society is not only necessary, it is, within limits, desirable. But if one hundred men all desperately want the same brass ring, they may be forced to fight for it. On the other hand, if each of the hundred has a different objective, it is far more rewarding for them to trade, cooperate, and form symbiotic relationships. Given appropriate social arrangements, diversity can make for a secure and stable civilization. It is the lack of appropriate political institutions today that unnecessarily sharpens conflict between minorities to the knife-edge of violence. The answer to this problem is not to stifle dissent or to charge minorities with selfishness. The answer lies in imaginative new arrangements for accommodating and legitimating diversity— new institutions that are sensitive to the rapidly shifting needs of changing and multiplying minorities.

① Does Diversity Harm Democracy?
② Are Democracy's Weaknesses Inherent?
③ The Rise of Diversity Is a Threat to Democracy
④ The Majority Rule: A Basic Principle of Democracy
⑤ Democracy Is Contagious: Democratization in Progress

[한번에 정리하는 문제 해설]

지문 해석 현재 상황에 맞게 민주주의를 재구성하기 위해서 우리는, 다양성 증가가 자동적으로 사회 내 긴장과 갈등 증가를 부른다는 무서운, 그러나 그릇된 전제를 의심할 필요가 있다. 오히려 사실은 정반대다. 사회 내 갈등은 필요할 뿐만 아니라 어느 정도는 바람직하다. 그러나 만약 백 명의 사람이 모두 필사적으로 같은 성공의 기회를 원한다면 그것을 두고 싸울 수밖에 없을 것이다. 반면에 백 사람 각각이 서로 다른 목표를 가진다면 그들이 거래하고, 협력하고 상생 관계를 맺는 것이 훨씬 더 보람 있을 것이다. 적절한 사회 제도가 주어지면, 다양성은 안전하고 안정된 문명에 기여할 수 있다. 소수민족 간 갈등을 불필요하게 첨예한 폭력으로 몰고 가는 것은 오늘날 적절한 정체제도의 결핍이다. 이 문제에 대한 답은 반대를 억압하거나 이기적이라고 소수민족을 비난하는 것이 아니다. 그 답은 다양성을 수용하고 합법화하는 창의적인 새로운 제도, 즉 변화하고 증가하는 소수민족의 급속히 변하는 필요에 민감한 새로운 제도에 있다.
① 다양성이 민주주의에 해가 되는가? ② 민주주의의 약점은 내재되어 있는가?
③ 다양성의 부상은 민주주의의 위협이다 ④ 대다수 규칙: 민주주의의 기본 원칙
⑤ 민주주의는 전염성이있다: 민주화 진행 중

글의 소재 민주주의 시금석으로서의 다양성

주요 어휘 reconstitute 재구성하다, 복원하다, in line with ~에 맞춰, challenge 이의를 제기하다, 의심하다, assumption 가정, 전제, diversity 다양성, reverse 역, 반대, desperately 필사적으로, brass ring 성공의 기회, symbiotic 공생의, social arrangement 사회적 제도, make for ~에 기여하다, stifle 질식시키다, 억압하다, dissent 반대, charge ~ with ~ ~ 때문에 ~를 비난하다, accommodate 수용하다, legitimate 합법화하다, multiply 빠르게 증가하다

정 답 ①

정답 해설 사회의 다양성을 억압하지 않고 그것을 수용하고 합법화하는 길만이 현재의 소수민족 간의 갈등을 해결하고 사회적 안정을 되찾는 최선의 방책이라는 것이 이 글의 요지이므로 이 글의 제목으로 가장 적절한 것은 ①의 '다양성은 민주주의에 해가 되는가?'이다. 주제문인 '~diversity can make for a secure and stable civilization.'이나 'The answer lies in imaginative new arrangements ~ the rapidly shifting needs of changing and multiplying minorities.'에 주목하면 쉽게 풀 수 있다.

32 다음 글의 제목으로 가장 적절한 것은?

People can actually do two or more things at once, such as walk and talk, or chew gum and read a map; but, like computers, what we can't do is focus on two things at once. Our attention bounces back and forth. This is fine for computers, but it has serious repercussions in humans. Two airliners are cleared to land on the same runway. A patient is given the wrong medicine. A toddler is left unattended in the bathtub. What all these potential tragedies share is that people are trying to do too many things at once and forget to do something they should do. When you try to do two things at once, you either can't or won't do either well. If you think multitasking is an effective way to get more done, you've got it backward. It's an effective way to get less done.

① Fallacy of Multitasking
② The ABCs of Multitasking
③ Multitasking: Why and How
④ Coping Strategies for Multitasking Demands
④ Simple Truth behind Great Results: Multitasking

[한번에 정리하는 문제 해설]

지문 해석 사람들은 걸으면서 대화하기, 껌을 씹으면서 지도를 보는 것 같이 사실 두 개 이상의 일을 동시에 할 수 있다. 그러나 컴퓨터처럼, 우리가 할 수 없는 것은 두 개의 일에 동시에 집중하는 것이다. 우리의 집중은 이리저리 왔다 갔다 한다. 이것은 컴퓨터에게는 괜찮지만 인간들에게는 심각한 파급 효과를 가져온다. 두 개의 비행기가 같은 활주로에 착륙하도록 허락받는다. 환자가 다른 사람의 약을 처방받는다. 아기가 아무도 돌보는 사람 없이 욕조에 방치된다. 이 모든 잠재적인 비극들의 공통점은 사람들이 너무 많은 것들을 동시에 하려 하고 그들이 해야 할 것을 잊어버린다는 것이다. 당신이 두 가지 일을 동시에 하려고 할 때, 당신은 둘 중 어느 것도 잘 할 수 없고 잘하게 되지도 않는다. 만약 당신이 멀티태스킹이 더 많은 일을 하기 위한 효과적인 방법이라고 생각한다면, 정반대로 이해하는 것이다. 효과적인 방법은 (더 하는 것이 아니라) 덜 하는 것이다.

① 멀티태스킹에 대한 잘못된 생각 ② 멀티태스킹의 기초
③ 멀티태스킹 왜, 어떻게 하나 ④ 멀티태스킹 과업 대처 전략
⑤ 위대한 성취의 비결, 멀티태스킹

글의 소재 멀티태스킹에 대한 잘못된 생각

주요 어휘 bounce back and forth 주고받기다, 왔다 갔다 하다, repercussion 반발, 파급 효과, clear 비행기 이착륙을 허가하다, toddler 걸음마 타는 아기, unattended 보살핌을 받지 않는, potential 잠재적인, multitask 두 가지 일을 동시에 하다, effective 효과적인, get it backward 정반대로 이해하다, 완전히 잘 못 이해하다

정 답 ①

정답 해설 이 글은 우리 인간은 두 가지 이상의 일에 동시에 집중할 수 없기 때문에 멀티태스킹에는 심각한 부작용이 따를 수 있음을 경고하고 있다. 따라서 이 글의 제목으로 가장 적절한 것은 ①의 '멀티태스킹에 대한 잘못된 생각'이다. 멀티태스킹에 대한 부정적인 선택지는 ①뿐이라는 사실에 착안하자. 그리고 역접의 연결사 but로 시작하는 두 문장 'but, like computers, what we can't do is focus on two things at once.' 'but it has serious repercussions in humans.'이 주제를 유도함을 놓치지 말자.

3. 글의 제목

| 해설 376쪽 |

21

다음 글의 제목으로 가장 적절한 것은?

난이도 중

A British University has recently released a survey result indicating a possible relationship between love and money. Psychologists at Swansea University in the UK showed 75 men and 76 women pictures of 50 potential love interests and asked if they'd be interested in a long, short or nonexistent relationship with each person. The researchers then showed some of them images of fancy cars, jewelry, big houses or actual cash to see if that affected how they felt about dating. It did. After the viewers had seen those images, they were shown the photos of the opposite sex again. Compared with the group that was not shown any luxury images, these participants had a higher preference for short-term flings—choosing 16% more such partners.

① Only Love for Its Own Sake Lasts Long
② Can Luxury Affect Our Desire for Love?
③ Is a Short-term Relationship Worth It?
④ Avoid Luxury or Your Romance May Fail
⑤ A Serious Relationship Allows for No Luxury

22 다음 글의 제목으로 가장 적절한 것은?

Between January and May 2007, beekeepers lost one-quarter of their colonies, which is a lot of bees. Anyone inclined to ho-hum at this information should think again because honeybees are not important just to gardeners, who need bees to pollinate their flowers; on the contrary, the disappearance of honeybees could have much wider significance. The truth is the disappearance of honeybees, also known as "Colony Collapse Disorder," could cause a food crisis. Honeybees pollinate nuts, avocados, apples, celery, squash, cucumbers, cherries, and blueberries. And that's not even a complete list. Experts estimate that about a third of the human diet is insect-pollinated, and 80 percent of the time, the honeybee is the pollinator of choice. Honeybees are part of the cycle that brings meat to the table. Cattle feed on alfalfa, and alfalfa crops need bees as pollinators. If scientists can't figure out why honeybees are disappearing, meat eaters might be forced to turn vegetarian precisely at the time when even vegetables are in short supply.

* ho-hum 따분해하다

① Ways to Best Prepare against Food Crisis
② The Reason behind Honeybees' Failure to Pollinate
③ Missing Honeybees: A Possible Cause of Food Crisis
④ Honeybees as the Pollinator of Choice
⑤ Honeybees as Part of the Meat-Producing Cycle

23 다음 글의 제목으로 알맞은 것은?

Health and disease may be considered two extremes of a continuum. At one extreme is severe, life-threatening, disabling illness with its corresponding major effect on the physical and emotional well-being of the patient. At the other extreme is ideal good health, which may be defined as a state of complete physical and mental well-being. The healthy person is emotionally and physically capable of leading a full, happy and productive life that is free of anxiety, turmoil and physical disabilities that limit activities. Between these two extremes are many gradations of health and disease, ranging from mild or short-term illness that limit activities to some extent through moderate good health that falls short of the ideal state. The midpoint in this continuum may be considered a "neutral" position in which one is neither ill nor in ideal good health. In this continuum, most of us are somewhere between mid-position and the ideal state.

① The Inter-dependency between Health and Disease
② Health and Disease: A Continuum
③ Two Extremes of Human Life Quality
④ Why Attaining a Neutral Position in Human Health Matters?
⑤ What It Means for a Patient to Achieve Physical and Emotional Well-being

24 다음 글의 제목으로 가장 적절한 것은?

Dutch students have a new option when it comes to university housing. Instead of the typical cramped and dingy shared apartment or dormitories, they can stay free of charge at Humanitas, a long-term care facility for the elderly. If having a ninety-year-old neighbor sounds a bit odd, the price tag makes up for it. While the average amount Dutch students spend on rent each month is about 366 Euros, living at Humanitas only costs thirty hours of volunteer work per month. For the elderly residents, the students are a window to the outside world. Volunteer hours are spent learning how to send emails, use social media and the like. It's a break from the monotony and loneliness that often characterizes elderly life. Now they can replace conversations about aching bones with gossip about interesting college courses and even dating. For students, the financial incentive is obvious. But having a connection to the wisest members of society also provides a unique perspective on the troubles and triumphs of life. Many students develop close, lasting relationship with their older neighbors, beyond the shared smiles of a one-time visit to a church or club activity.

① What's Good for the Goose is Good for the Gander.
② A Friend in Need is a Friend Indeed.
③ A Stitch in Time Saves Nine
④ Do to Others as You Would Have Others Do to You.
⑤ Many Hands Make Light Work

25 다음 글의 제목으로 가장 적절한 것은? 난이도 중

An enduring, sentimental tie between individuals is what defines friendship, analogous to pair bonding in mates. This individual constancy is mirrored by a collective constancy. Individuals in the social species we have considered come and go; they are born and die; and friendships begin and end. But the overall social organization of the species stays the same. Some turnover in social ties within groups may even be necessary for networks to endure. It's like replacing planks in a boat. This is required to keep the boat seaworthy. But the plan of the boat, like the topology of the social network, remains fixed, even if all the individual boards are eventually replaced. That is, the structure of social networks —arising from all the dyadic friendship ties and the genes within us—is a feature of our species itself. Remarkably, humans share this emergent structure with other social mammals, which highlights how fundamental this property is to all humans, regardless of their culture.

* dyadic 2원적인

① Friendship Survives Any Generational Shift
② Societies Lacking in Social Networks Flourish at Times
③ Human Cultural Norms Reflect Waning Social Networks
④ Social Networks: The Unchanging Support for Human Society
⑤ Collective Constancy: The Primary Determinant for Human Evolution

The reaction of art to an impending change is revulsion, rather than eager anticipation. When science first began to change the lives of men, many artists revolted violently before the vision of a future irrevocably committed to science. This is a futile revolt, since science is the only field of human activity in which progress is incontrovertible and inevitable. Artists, politicians, philosophers can look back to this or that period in past history as a peak of human achievement— be it classical Greece or Renaissance Italy, the civic order of the Roman empire, the solidity of Victorian England, or the golden eras of Indian or Chinese history and art. No such nostalgia is possible in science. Its highest point is the present, and every successive year is bound to be an advance beyond the preceding one. A civilization that refuses to accept this constant progress, and to adjust itself to it, does this at its own risk; and that risk is, right now, appalling.

* incontrovertible 이론의 여지가 없는

① Art Challenging Science: A Futile Attempt
② Science Riding on the Crest of an Artistic Wave
③ Science Never Looks Back But Only Advances
④ The Glorious Past Is What Art Eternally Feeds on
⑤ Retrogress at Your Own Risk

27 다음 글의 제목으로 가장 적절한 것은?

난이도 상

An additional category of exaptations for migrants includes energy storage, namely the laying down of subcutaneous fat reserves. Although considered by many authors to be actual adaptations for migration, the capacity to store energy at times when patchy foods are abundant or when the organism is potentially confronted with an imminent need is found in many if not most resident birds as well. For instance, it is a common strategy in sedentary, resident, altricial birds to feed nestlings intensively prior to fledgling so that when they leave the nest, the fledglings have significant fat reserves. It is also well known that young of at least some resident species lay down large amounts of subcutaneous fat prior to dispersal. Females of some resident species lay down fat reserves preparatory to egg-laying, and many also lay down fat reserves preparatory to undergoing molt or other "lean season" demands. Also, members of both wintering and resident tropical species that exploit temporary resource concentrations have been captured with moderate to heavy subcutaneous fat.

* exaptation 굴절 적응(하나의 목적을 위해 진화한 특성이 이후 다른 용도로도 완전히 적응하는 과정),
subcutaneous 피하의, altricial 만성조(晚成鳥)의, molt 털갈이

① Energy Storage Counts for a Number of Resident Birds
② Subcutaneous Fat: A Major Source of Energy Storage
③ Want to Protect Birds? Conserve Their Habitat First!
④ Why We Need to Feed Migratory Birds Properly
⑤ Food Shortage: A Threat to Resident Birds' Survival

28 다음 글의 제목으로 가장 적합한 것은?

I recently published a new picture book entitled Love. A few weeks into the writing of the book, my wife and I received some bad news, and my daughter saw my wife openly cry for the first time. This rocked her little world, and she began sobbing and clinging to my wife's leg, begging to know what was happening. We settled her down and talked to her and eventually got her ready for bed. As my wife read her a story about two turtles who stumble across a hat, I studied my daughter's tear-stained face. I couldn't help thinking that a fraction of her innocence had been lost that day. But maybe these episodes of loss are as vital to the well-adjusted child's development as moments of joy. Maybe instead of anxiously trying to protect our children from every hurt and heartache, our job is to support them through such experiences. To talk to them. To hold.

① Spare the Rod, Spoil the Child
② Broken Young Hearts Hardly Heal
③ Avoid Crying in Front of Children
④ Good Parenting Entails Controlling Your Emotions
⑤ Children Grow as Much amid Pain as amid Joy

29 다음 글의 제목으로 가장 적절한 것은? 난이도 상

Two specific examples illustrate for us the association between rituals or prayers and uncertain outcome. Gamblers in a game of chance often follow their own personal rituals before throwing the dice, but chess-players don't have such rituals before moving a piece. That's because dice games are known to be games of chance, but there is no role of chance in chess: if your move costs you the game, you have no excuses. It was entirely your own fault for not foreseeing your opponent's response. Similarly, farmers wanting to drill a well to find underground water often consult dowsers in western New Mexico, where the area's local geological complexity results in big unpredictable variation in the depth and quantity of underground water, such that not even professional geologists can predict accurately from surface features the location and depth of underground water. In the Texas Panhandle, though, where the water table lies at a uniform depth of 125 feet, farmers merely drill a well to that depth at a site nearest to where the water is needed; no one uses dowsers, although people are familiar with the method. That is, New Mexico farmers and dice players deal with unpredictability by resorting to rituals, while Texas Panhandle farmers and chess-players dispense with rituals.

* dowser 수맥 탐사가

① Ability is All We Can Depend on When Luck Runs Out
② Rituals and Prayers Sometimes Work Wonders
③ Rituals and Prayers: Silent Healers of Broken Hearts
④ Prayers Don't Hurt: The More of Them the Better
⑤ Uncertainty Heightens Likelihood for Rituals and Prayers

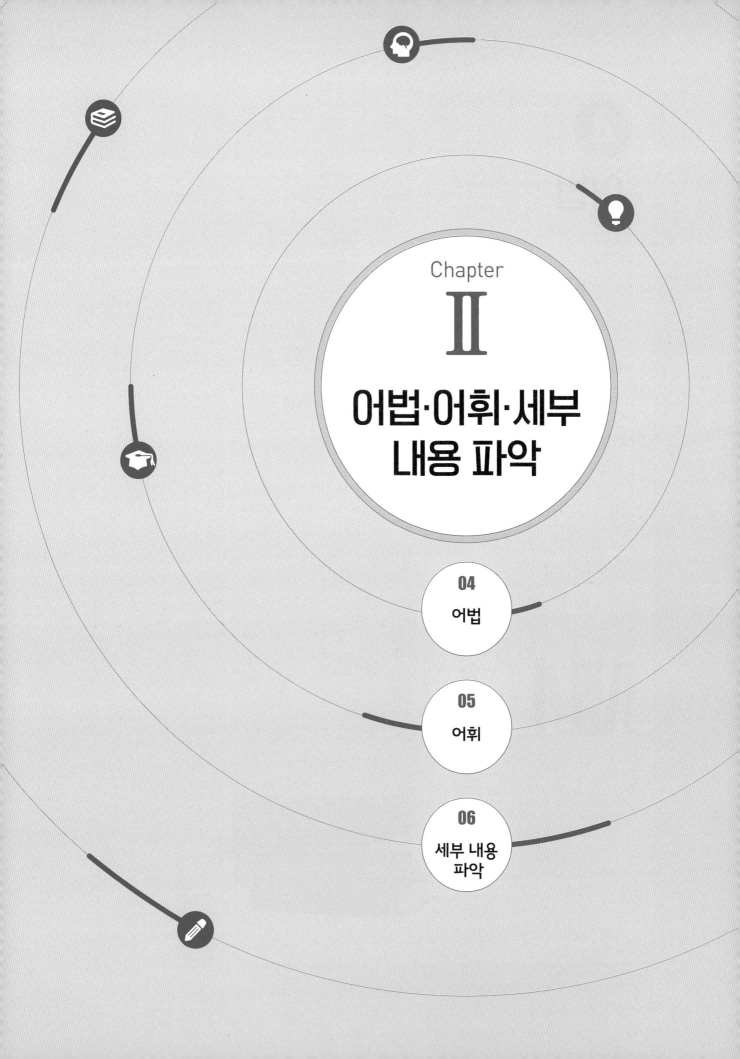

Chapter

II

어법·어휘·세부
내용 파악

④ 어법

제시된 지문에서 표시된 부분이 문법적으로 옳은지를
판단하는 유형이다. 밑줄 친 부분 중 어법에 어긋난
것을 고르는 밑줄형과 네모 안에 제시된 두 표현 중
맞는 것을 선택하는 네모형이 있다.

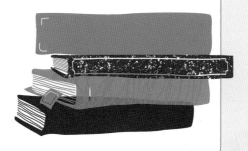

▶ 문장을 대하면 먼저 주어부와 술어부를 나누는, 즉 주술 관계를 파악하는 습관을 들인다.

▶ 모든 영어 문장은 문장 5형식 안에 포함돼 있다는 믿음을 가지고 평소 문장 5형식에 따라 문장을 파악하는 연습을 게을리하지 않는다.

▶ 구와 구, 문장과 문장의 접속 및 수식 관계 파악이 원활해야 하며 이를 위해 접속사의 쓰임과 관계사 용법, 분사구문이나 도치 구문, 생략 구문 등의 파악에 능숙해져야 한다.

▶ 특히, 삽입구나 삽입절이 포함돼 주술 관계 파악이 쉽지 않은 문장이 자주 출제되기 때문에 평소 복잡한 문장의 뼈(문장 성분)와 살(수식구)을 가르는 연습을 꾸준히 해야 한다.

▶ 시험에 자주 출제되는 어법 유형은 20여 가지로 정해져 있기 때문에 빈출 유형을 중심으로 공부하는 습관을 들인다.

빈출 어법 유형

▶ 뒤 문장이 완전한 상태에서 관계대명사, 전치사+관계대명사, 관계부사, 접속사 등의 쓰임을 묻는 유형

▶ 뒤 문장이 불완전한 상태에서 관계대명사, 전치사+관계대명사, 관계부사, 접속사 등의 쓰임을 묻는 유형

▶ 완전한 문장이 나와야 하는 상황에서 술어 자리에 동사가 아닌 준동사가 와서 1문장 1동사 원칙에 위배되는 유형

▶ 등위접속사 다음에 오는 동사의 적절한 형태를 묻는 병렬구조 유형

▶ 완전한 뒤 문장이 오는 동격절의 상황에서 동격의 that 쓰임을 묻는 유형

▶ 준동사가 명사를 후치 수식할 때 현재분사/과거분사 중 어떤 것이 적합한지 묻는 유형

▶ 감정유발 타동사의 능동형(현재분사) · 수동형(과거분사)을 묻는 유형

▶ 주어와 술어가 삽입구나 삽입절에 의해 분리된 상태에서 수 일치를 묻는 유형

▶ 도치 구문에서 동사의 수 일치를 묻는 유형

▶ 수식 관계에서 형용사와 부사 중 적합한 형태를 고르는 유형

▶ be 동사와 do 동사 중 어떤 것이 대동사로서 적절한지 묻는 유형

▶ 5형식 문장에서 형용사와 부사 중 목적보어로 올 수 있는 형태를 묻는 유형

▶ 가목적어 it의 쓰임을 묻는 유형

▶ 목적어가 있는 상태에서 능동태와 수동태의 적절성을 묻는 유형

▶ 수여동사의 능동형과 수동형 중 적합한 형태를 묻는 유형

▶ 'so 형용사/부사 that' 구문에서 so나 that의 쓰임을 묻는 유형

▶ 3인칭 대명사 it나 they의 지칭 대상 파악과 그에 따른 수 일치를 묻는 유형

▶ 가정법 과거와 과거완료의 주절과 조건절의 시제를 묻는 유형

다음 글의 밑줄 친 부분 중, 어법상 틀린 것은?

   Like whole individuals, cells have a life span. During their life cycle (cell cycle), cell size, shape, and metabolic activities can change dramatically. A cell is "born" as a twin when its mother cell divides, ①producing two daughter cells. Each daughter cell is smaller than the mother cell, and except for unusual cases, each grows until it becomes as large as the mother cell ②was. During this time, the cell absorbs water, sugars, amino acids, and other nutrients and assembles them into new, living protoplasm. After the cell has grown to the proper size, its metabolism shifts as it either prepares to divide or matures and ③differentiates into a specialized cell. Both growth and development require a complex and dynamic set of interactions involving all cell parts. ④What cell metabolism and structure should be complex would not be surprising, but actually, they are rather simple and logical. Even the most complex cell has only a small number of parts, each ⑤responsible for a distinct, well-defined aspect of cell life.

* metabolic: 물질대사의 ** protoplasm: 원형질

[한번에 정리하는 문제 해설]

지문 해설 전체 개체가 그러하듯 세포에도 수명이 있다. 그들의 삶의 주기 동안(세포 주기) 세포의 크기와 형태, 물질대사 활동은 크게 변할 수 있다. 세포는 어미 세포가 분열해 두 개의 딸세포를 생산할 때 쌍둥이로 태어난다. 각각의 딸세포는 어미 세포보다 작고, 특별한 경우를 제외하면 어미 세포의 크기가 될 때까지 자란다. 이 기간에 그 세포(딸세포)는 물, 당분, 아미노산과 다른 영양소를 흡수하고 그것들을 결합해 새롭고 살아있는 원형질을 만든다. 그 세포가 적절한 크기로 자라면 물질대사가 바뀌는 데 이는 세포가 분열을 준비하거나 성숙과 함께 전문화된 세포로 차별화되기 때문이다. 성장과 발달에는 세포의 모든 구성인자가 참여하는 복잡하고 역동적인 일련의 상호작용이 따른다. 세포의 물질대사와 구조가 복잡하다는 사실도 그리 놀라운 일은 아니나, 사실상 그것들은 (복잡하기는커녕) 꽤 간단하고 논리적이다. 가장 복잡한 세포조차 단지 몇 개의 구성인자를 가질 뿐이고 각각의 인자는 저마다 독특하고 명확한 세포 생활의 면면을 책임진다.

글의 소재 세포의 성장과 발달

주요 어휘 life span 수명, metabolic 물질대사의, dramatically 극적으로, 크게, absorb 흡수하다, amino acid 아미노산, nutrient 영양소, assemble 결합하다, protoplasm 원형질, differentiate 차별화하다, dynamic 역동적인, interaction 상호작용, distinct 독특한, 다른, well-defined 명확한

정 답 ④

정답 해설 ④ 문장 'What cell metabolism and ~ would not be surprising'에서 주어부를 구성하는 'What ~ complex' 부분은 명사절을 유도해야 한다. 그런데 What에 이어지는 부분이 완전한 문장이기 때문에 관계대명사 What은 올 수 없고, 의문형용사 What도 의미상 적절치 않다. 따라서 What는 접속사 That로 대체돼야 한다.

① 분사구문으로 현재분사 producing의 쓰임은 적절하다.

② was large에서 large가 생략된 형태로 was의 쓰임은 적절하다.

③ 'it either prepares to ~ a specialized cell' 문장은 either A or B 구문으로 이뤄져 있고 A=prepares to divide, B=matures and differentiates into a specialized cell이다. 따라서 differentiates는 당연히 matures와 문법적 형태가 같아야 한다(병렬구조).

⑤ 이 문장은 분사구문 'each being responsible for ~'에서 being이 생략된 형태로 being의 술어(보어)로서의 responsible의 쓰임은 적절하다.

13 다음 글의 밑줄 친 부분 중, 어법상 틀린 것은?

Modern archaeological researchers, some of whom are women, ①have unearthed evidence that suggests the historical soundness of Herodotus' account of the Amazons. These scholars have found numerous graves in southern Ukraine dating from the middle of the first millennium BCE ②containing the skeletal remains of women buried with military paraphernalia such as lances, arrows, and armor. Some of the skeletons indicate that the deceased had been struck on the head or stabbed with a sharp blade, providing support for the view ③which these are the remains of warriors rather than of women who were coincidently buried with weapons. The graves also contain bronze mirrors and gold trim for clothing, as well as jewelry (earrings, necklaces, beads, and arm rings). Perhaps the bodies were buried so that the women would enter the next world with both the weapons they would need as warriors and the ornaments they would desire ④to enhance their appearance. All in all, the archaeological evidence suggests that Herodotus' account of the Amazons was not, as formerly thought, an illustration of his gullibility, but rather historically ⑤sound.

* paraphernalia: (특정 활동에 필요한) 용품 ** trim: 장식
*** gullibility: (남의 말을) 쉽게 믿음

[한번에 정리하는 문제 해설]

지문 해석 │ 몇몇 여성을 포함하는 현대 고고학자들이 아마존족에 대한 Herodotus의 기술이 역사적으로 타당했음을 시사하는 증거를 발굴했다. 이들 학자들은 우크라이나 남부에서 기원전 천년 중반의 무덤을 다수 찾아냈는데 거기엔 여성의 유골들이 창이나 화살, 갑옷 같은 군사용품과 함께 묻혀 있었다. 몇몇 유골들은 사자가 머리에 타격을 입거나 예리한 칼날에 찔렸음을 보여줘 이들이 우연히 무기와 함께 매장된 여성이 아니라 전사의 유해라는 견해를 뒷받침해준다. 무덤에서는 귀걸이나 목걸이, 구슬, 팔찌 같은 보석은 물론 동 거울과 금으로 된 옷 장식도 나왔다. 여성들은 전사로서 필요한 무기와 외모를 돋보이게 하는 데 필요한 장식품을 가지고 저세상에 들어갈 수 있도록 매장된 듯하다. 대체로 보아 이 고고학 증거는 아마존족에 대한 Herodotus의 기술이 이전에 생각됐던 것처럼 그가 남의 말을 너무 쉽게 믿은 예가 아니라 역사적으로 타당했음을 보여준다.

글의 소재 │ 고고학 발굴품에 의해 입증된 Herodotus의 아마존족 관련 기술

주요 어휘 │ archaeological 고고학적, unearth 발굴하다, account 기술, 서술, millennium 천년, lance 긴 창, the deceased 사자(死者), coincidently=coincidentally 우연히, 공교롭게, enhance 높이다

구조 분석 │ • Some of the skeletons indicate that the deceased had been <u>struck</u> on the head or <u>stabbed</u> with a sharp blade, <u>providing</u> support for the view ~
→ stabbed와 struck은 병렬구조로 문법적 형태가 같다(과거분사). providing 이하는 분사구문으로 'and they provide support ~'로 바꿔 쓸 수 있다.

정 답 │ ③

정답 해설 │ ③ 다음에 완전한 문장이 오기 때문에 ③ 자리에는 관계대명사가 올 수 없고 관계부사나 접속사가 와야 하며 여기서는 view를 보충 설명해 줘야 하므로 동격의 접속사 that이 적절하다.
① have는 researchers의 동사로 복수로 수 일치시켰기 때문에 타당하다.
② containing 이하가 graves를 능동으로 수식해 주므로 현재분사 containing의 쓰임은 타당하다.
④ 'to enhance'는 목적의 부사적 용법으로 '~를 높이기 위해'의 뜻으로 쓰였으며 하자가 없다.
⑤ sound는 형용사로 that 절의 주어인 'Herodotus' account of the Amazon'의 보어로 쓰였기 때문에 문제가 없다.

밑줄 친 부분 중, 어법상 틀린 것은?

Mental illness in many ways remains a mystery to us. Some scientists think that it is hereditary. Others think it is caused by a chemical imbalance in the body. Other factors ①considering are a person's environment or perhaps an injury to the brain. Experts have differing opinions as to ②what causes mental illness and different ideas on how to treat it. One method is to place mentally ill people in hospitals and even prisons ③to separate them from society. Another method is to give medications under the supervision of a psychiatrist to modify behavior. Mentally ill persons under medication often ④live in supervised housing. Another method of treatment pioneered by Sigmund Freud is psychoanalysis, ⑤whereby the patient receives many hours of counseling and talk therapy at a psychiatrist's office. The above treatments are often combined.

[한번에 정리하는 문제 해설]

지문 해석 여러 가지 면에서 정신병은 우리에게 미스터리로 남아있다. 어떤 과학자들은 그것이 유전적이라고 생각한다. 다른 이들은 그것이 신체 내 화학물질의 불균형 때문에 발생한다고 생각한다. 고려되는 다른 요인으로는 개인의 환경이나 뇌 손상 등이 있다. 전문가들은 무엇이 정신병을 일으키는지에 대한 의견이 다르고 그것의 치료법에 관한 생각이 다르다. 한 가지 치료 방법은 사회와 격리하기 위해 정신병을 앓는 사람을 병원이나 심지어 감옥에 가두는 것이다. 또 다른 방법은 (환자의) 행동을 바꾸기 위해 정신과 의사의 감독하에 약을 주는 것이다. 투약 중인 정신병 환자들은 종종 감시받는 거주지에서 산다. Sigmund Freud가 창시한 또 다른 치료법은 정신분석인데 이에 따르면 환자는 정신과 진료실에서 많은 시간의 상담과 대화 치료를 받는다. 위의 치료들은 종종 병합되기도 한다.

글의 소재 정신병의 원인과 치료법

주요 어휘 **hereditary** 유전적인, **imbalance** 불균형, **medication** 약물, **supervision** 감독, **psychiatrist** 정신과 의사, **pioneer** 개척하다, 창시하다, **psychoanalysis** 정신분석

정 답 ①

정답 해설 ①의 자리에 오는 동사는 앞의 factors를 꾸며주는 준동사이어야 하고 factors의 술어이므로 반드시 수동의 의미가 있는 과거분사이어야 한다. 따라서 consider의 올바른 형태는 considering이 아니고 considered이다.

② what이 유도하는 의문사절(명사절)이 전치사 as to의 목적어가 되고 있어 문법상 하자가 없다. 의문사절은 전치사의 목적어가 될 수 있다.

③ 'to separate'는 목적의 부사적 용법으로 쓰였으며 '~를 격리하기 위해'를 의미하기 때문에 쓰임이 올바르다.

④ 이 문장의 주어는 persons이기 때문에 이에 맞춰 복수로 수 일치시킨 것(live)은 옳다.

⑤ whereby는 by which와 같고 전치사(by) + 관계대명사(which) 다음에는 완전한 문장이 와야 하는데 'the patient ~ a psychiatrist's office.'는 완전한 3형식 문장이므로 whereby의 쓰임은 문제가 없다.

30 다음 글의 밑줄 친 부분 중, 어법상 틀린 것은? 난이도 중

Effective altruists can accept that one's own children are a special responsibility, ahead of the children of strangers. There are various possible grounds for this. Most parents love their children, and it ①<u>would</u> be unrealistic to require parents to be impartial between their own children and other children. ②<u>Nor</u> would we want to discourage such bias because children thrive in close, loving families, and it is not possible to love people without having greater concern for their well-being than one has for others. In any case, while ③<u>doing</u> the most good is an important part of the life of every effective altruist, effective altruists are real people, not saints, and they don't seek to maximize the good in every single thing they do, 24/7. Typical effective altruists leave themselves time and resources to relax and do what they want. For most of us, being close to our children and other family members is central to ④<u>what</u> we want to spend our time. Nonetheless, effective altruists recognize that there are limitations to how much they should do for their children, ⑤<u>given</u> the greater needs of others.

* altruist 이타주의자

31 다음 글의 밑줄 친 부분 중, 어법상 틀린 것은? 난이도 중

Adults playing with children can find ①themselves in a terrible conflict. The child desperately wants to win because he or she has been taught ②that winning is so important. If the parent plays at full strength in order to teach the child ③how to lose or compete, the child often collapses in tears of frustration. If the parent tries to lose, the child feels patronized or, when he wins, ④engages in a kind of taunting behavior that may be difficult for some parents to tolerate. Fathers sometimes depend on winning at games in order to prove that they can still dominate their children. The film *The Great Santini*, in which a father was driven to intense competition in games with his own son in order to assert his dominant position and maintain his youthfulness, ⑤illustrating the pain of this kind of conflict.

32

다음 글의 밑줄 친 부분 중, 어법상 틀린 것은?   난이도 중

A long time ago, our ancestors discovered that ①ingesting some plants or the body parts of certain animals produced effects that were rather unpleasant or even lethal. Reference to these substances once appeared in a collection of prayers of comfort for the dying and ②referred to a type of spiritual medicine, at the time called a *pharmakon*, which was used principally to ③alleviate suffering near the end of life. Simply put, a pharmakon was a poison. Originally, the term *pharmakos* referred to a human scapegoat, who was sacrificed, sometimes literally by poisoning, as a remedy for the illness of another person, usually someone far more ④important in the local society. Later, around 600 BCE, the term came to refer to substances used to cure the sick. It is of course related to two terms now in use today: *pharmacology*, the scientific investigation into the mechanisms ⑤which drugs affect the body, and *psychopharmacology*, the study of the effects of drugs upon the brain—effects that in turn are defined as "psychoactive."

33

다음 글의 밑줄 친 부분 중, 어법상 틀린 것은? 난이도 중

How are we to learn to be practically wise? There is no recipe, formula, or set of techniques. Skills are learned through experience, and so ①does the commitment to the aims of a practice. That's why we associate wisdom with experience. But not just any experience will ②do. Some experiences nurture and teach practical wisdom; others corrode it. And it is here ③that Aristotle focuses our attention on something critically important: character and practical wisdom must be cultivated by the major institutions in which we practice. Aristotle wrote his book on ethics not simply to underline the importance of practical wisdom to a good life and a good society, but also ④to urge the citizens and statesmen of the Athenian city-state to build institutions that encouraged citizens to learn to be practically wise. Faced with today's "wisdom deficit"—the lack of the wisdom we need to succeed in our daily life and work—he would urge us to examine ⑤whether our institutions are discouraging the wisdom of practitioners and, if so, what can be done to make up the deficit.

34

다음 글의 밑줄 친 부분 중, 어법상 틀린 것은?　　난이도 중

The ears, for the most part, do not require any routine cleaning. Ears are ①like a self-cleaning oven. With the help of gravity and body heat, earwax will gradually find its way out. If wax appears on the outer ear, a cotton swab may be used. If you can't help but ②to go in farther, you are risking wax impaction or injury. If you do get wax ③impacted in your ear, you will be in pain and half deaf. There are over-the-counter preparations that can help relieve wax blockage but warm water in a syringe often works. As a last resort you can see an ear doctor or come to the ER for a good cleaning. It is not uncommon for doctors to see their patients who have violated these rules and ④come to see them to remove the tip of the cotton swab that has fallen off inside the ear. Don't worry, they are prepared. They also remove other things like cockroaches, beads, and pen caps, all of ⑤which they've pulled out of ears.

*impaction 이구경색(귀지 막힘)

35

(A), (B), (C)의 각 네모 안에서 어법에 맞는 표현으로 가장 적절한 것을 고르시오.

난이도 중

In 1898 the British Egyptologists James Quibell and Frederick Green uncovered a sculpted slab of greywacke (a greenish-grey slate-like stone) in the ruins of an early temple at the Upper Egyptian site of Hierakonpolis. Unlike the discovery of Tutankhamun's tomb twenty-four years later, this find would not bring the world's journalists (A) raced / racing to the scene, but its discoverers were almost immediately aware of its importance. Like the Rosetta Stone, this carved slab— the Narmer Palette—would have powerful repercussions for the study of ancient Egypt, (B) spread / spreading far beyond its immediate significance at Hierakonpolis. For the next century or so, it would be variously interpreted by Egyptologists attempting to solve numerous different problems, from the political origins of the Egyptian state to the nature of Egyptian art and writing. No single object can necessarily typify an entire culture, but the Narmer Palette is one of a few surviving artefacts from the Nile Valley that are so iconic and so rich in information (C) that / which they can act as microcosms of certain aspects of ancient Egyptian culture as a whole.

	(A)	(B)	(C)
①	racing	spreading	which
②	racing	spread	that
③	racing	spreading	that
④	raced	spread	which
⑤	raced	spreading	that

36

(A), (B), (C)의 각 네모 안에서 어법에 맞는 표현으로 가장 적절한 것을 고르시오.

While social scientists can surely draw conclusions of academic interest from studies of traditional societies, all the rest of us may also be able to learn things of practical interest. Traditional societies in effect represent thousands of natural experiments in how to construct a human society. They have come up with thousands of solutions to human problems, solutions different from (A) ones / those adopted by our own modern societies. We shall see that some of those solutions—for instance, some of the ways in which traditional societies raise their children, treat their elderly, remain healthy, talk, spend their leisure time, and settle disputes—may strike you, as they do me, as superior to normal practices in the First World. Perhaps we could benefit by selectively adopting some of those traditional practices. Some of us already do so, with (B) demonstrated / demonstrating benefits to our health and happiness. In some respects we moderns are misfits; our bodies and our practices now face conditions different from those under which they evolved, and to (C) what / which they became adapted.

	(A)	(B)	(C)
①	ones	demonstrated	what
②	ones	demonstrated	which
③	ones	demonstrating	what
④	those	demonstrated	which
⑤	those	demonstrating	which

37

(A), (B), (C)의 각 네모 안에서 어법에 맞는 표현으로 가장 적절한 것을 고르시오.

난이도 중

Maybe clever advertisers will figure out a way of getting subliminal ads to work. Even if they do, however, the effects of their ads are unlikely to be as powerful as every day ads (A) presenting / presented at conscious levels. Despite people's blasé attitude toward ads that they see on television, hear on the radio and see in the print media, these ads can shape their behavior in powerful ways. Perhaps the best evidence for this comes from studies that use split cable market tests. Advertisers, working in conjunction with cable television companies and grocery stores, (B) show / to show different versions of commercials to randomly selected groups of cable subscribers. The subscribers agree to use a special identification card when they shop, allowing the grocery stores to keep track of exactly what they buy. The advertisers can thus tell whether people who see a particular commercial are in fact more likely to buy the advertised product. The answer is that they often (C) are / do .

* subliminal 잠재의식의, blasé 심드렁한

	(A)		(B)		(C)
①	presenting	······	show	······	are
②	presenting	······	to show	······	do
③	presented	······	show	······	do
④	presented	······	to show	······	do
⑤	presented	······	show	······	are

다음 글의 밑줄 친 부분 중, 어법상 <u>틀린</u> 것은?   난이도 상

Scientists see extinction as a natural result of the complex interactions between living creatures and their continually changing physical environment. When a species becomes so ill-suited to its environment that ①<u>it</u> cannot compete successfully for food and living space, it is likely to become extinct. The crisis may be brought on by evolutionary changes in the species itself, by changes in the environment, or by the arrival of a new species in the same local area. Large-scale environmental changes can cause "mass extinctions" ②<u>what</u> wipe out enormous numbers of species in a geologically short time. The extinction of a single species is, from scientific standpoint, like a single dot of color in an impressionist painting —significant primarily as a part of a larger pattern. Popular culture, on the other hand, invests the extinction of individual species with deep meaning and its stories about extinctions with a strong ③<u>moralizing</u> tone. Those set in the present portray ④<u>threatened</u> species as sweet, innocent victims of human ignorance and greed. Those set in the past ⑤<u>portray</u> now-extinct species as hapless victims of their own short-comings. Both portrayals are rooted in broader cultural attitudes toward nature.

다음 글의 밑줄 친 부분 중, 어법상 틀린 것은?

Although archaeologists and cognitive scientists have proposed a variety of theories regarding the meaning and purpose of prehistoric art, all agree that the arts are among the evolutionary developments that "embody the very essence of ①what it means to be fully human." Moreover, most theorists distinguish between Paleolithic "art" and the abstract symbols and notations ②where emerged around the same time in the prehistoric record. The fundamentally mimetic character of art—in contrast with the abstract nature of symbolic and notational systems—has been highlighted by the Canadian neuropsychologist Merlin Donald, who offers a ③profoundly illuminating theory regarding its significance. In his *Origins of the Modern Mind*, Donald persuasively argues that mimesis played a crucial role in human cognitive evolution, ④serving as the primary means of representing reality among the immediate ancestors of Homo sapiens, just prior to the emergence of language and symbolic thought. For Donald, the term "mimesis" refers to intentional means of representing reality that ⑤utilize vocal tone, facial expression, bodily movement, manual gestures, and other nonlinguistic means. In his view, it is "fundamentally different" from both mimicry and imitation.

5

어휘

밑줄 친 어휘 중 문맥에 어울리지 않는 것을 고르거나,
네모 안에 제시된 한 쌍의 어휘 중 문맥에 적합한 것을
고르는 유형이다.

▶ 어휘는 영어 공부의 기본이자 입시 준비의 기본이다. 수능, 사관학교, 경찰대 필수 어휘는 반드시 숙지해 놓아야 한다.

▶ 모의고사와 수능 기출 문제에 나오는 단어들은 어휘 준비의 바이블과 같다. 과거 10년간 모의고사와 수능에 출제된 주요 어휘를 중심으로 꼼꼼히 정리하라. 특히, 선택지에 나오는 어휘들은 일종의 표제어로 매우 중요하므로 단 하나도 놓쳐서는 안 된다.

▶ 적절한 어휘 선택을 위해서는 정확한 맥락의 파악이 우선이므로 독해해 가면서 논지의 흐름을 놓치지 말아야 한다.

▶ 빈칸 추론의 경우처럼 올바른 어휘의 단서가 앞뒤 문장에 있을 경우가 많다. 평소에 정답의 단서를 앞뒤 문장에서 찾는 버릇을 들인다.

▶ 빈출 분야의 대표적인 어휘들은 꼭 숙지해야 한다. 가령 진화론과 관련된 대표적 개념 어휘인 adaptation, hereditary, variation, mutation, natural selection 등을 정리해서 암기하는 식이다.

▶ 빈출 어휘에 대한 유의어, 반의어를 평소에 잘 정리해 놓고 숙지한다. 특히 네모형 어휘는 정답이 반의어가 함께 주어지기 때문에 반의어 숙지가 필수다.

▶ 헷갈리기 쉬운 표현들을 평소에 잘 정리해 놓는다.

▶ 어휘 암기에는 무조건적 암기보다는 어원을 따져가며 암기하는 것이 효율적일 수 있다.

혼동하기 쉬운 어휘의 예

▶ adopt/adapt: 입양하다, 채택하다/적응하다
▶ banish/vanish: 추방하다/사라지다
▶ comprehensible/comprehensive: 이해하기 쉬운/포괄적인
▶ complement/compliment: 보충/칭찬
▶ confirm/conform: 확인하다/순응하다
▶ conscious/conscientious/conspicuous: 의식하는/양심적인/눈에 띄는
▶ considerable/considerate: 상당한/사려 깊은
▶ council/counsel: 위원회/조언, 상담
▶ difference/deference: 차이/존경
▶ elect/erect: 선출하다/세우다
▶ imaginable/imaginary/imaginative: 상상할 수 있는/상상의/상상력이 풍부한
▶ inhibit/inhabit: 금지하다/~에 거주하다

▶ literal/literary/literate: 문자대로의/문학의/문해의
▶ medication/meditation/mediation: 의약품/명상/중재
▶ natural/neutral: 자연적인/중립적인
▶ observation/observance: 관찰/준수
▶ rise/arise/rouse/arouse/raise: 일어나다/발생하다/깨우다/각성시키다/높이다
▶ respective/respectable: 각각의/존경하는
▶ royal/loyal 왕립의/충성하는
▶ sensible/sensitive/sensuous: 지각 있는/민감한/감각적인
▶ statue/stature/statute: 조각상/키, 신장/법령
▶ successful/successive: 성공적인/연속적인

다음 글의 밑줄 친 부분 중, 문맥상 낱말의 쓰임이 적절하지 않은 것은?

It has been suggested that "organic" methods, defined as those in which only natural products can be used as inputs, would be less damaging to the biosphere. Large-scale adoption of "organic" farming methods, however, would ①reduce yields and increase production costs for many major crops. Inorganic nitrogen supplies are ②essential for maintaining moderate to high levels of productivity for many of the non-leguminous crop species, because organic supplies of nitrogenous materials often are either limited or more expensive than inorganic nitrogen fertilizers. In addition, there are ③benefits to the extensive use of either manure or legumes as "green manure" crops. In many cases, weed control can be very difficult or require much hand labor if chemicals cannot be used, and ④fewer people are willing to do this work as societies become wealthier. Some methods used in "organic" farming, however, such as the sensible use of crop rotations and specific combinations of cropping and livestock enterprises, can make important ⑤contributions to the sustainability of rural ecosystems.

* nitrogen fertilizer: 질소 비료 ** manure: 거름 *** legume: 콩과(科) 식물

[한번에 정리하는 문제 해설]

지문 해석 자연적인 산물만이 투입 요소로 쓰일 수 있다는 식으로 정의되는 "유기적" 방식이 생물권에 피해를 덜 준다는 주장이 있었다. 하지만, "유기적" 농법의 대규모 채택은 주요 경작물의 소출을 줄이고 생산비를 증가시킬 수 있다. 무기 질소의 공급은 많은 비(非) 콩과 작물의 생산성을 적정 수준 이상으로 유지하는 데 필수적인데 이는 질소성 물질의 유기적 공급이 자주 제한적이거나 무기 질소 비료보다 비싸기 때문이다. 게다가, 거름이나 콩과 식물을 "녹색 거름" 작물로 폭넓게 사용하는 데는 이득(→제한)이 따른다. 많은 경우에 화학 약품을 쓸 수 없다면 잡초를 다루는 일은 매우 어렵거나 많은 수작업을 요하고, 사회가 부유해짐에 따라 이런 일을 기꺼이 하려고 하는 사람들은 점점 줄어든다. 하지만 윤작의 분별 있는 활용이나 수확과 축산업을 종(種)적으로 결합하는 것과 같은 "유기적" 농업에서 사용된 몇몇 방식들은 농촌 생태계의 지속가능성에 중요한 기여를 할 수 있다.

글의 소재 유기농법의 장점과 단점

주요 어휘 organic 유기농의, input 투입, biosphere 생활권, adoption 채택, nitrogen 질소, essential 필수적인, non-leguminous 비(非)콩과의, fertilizer 비료, extensive 광범위한, manure 거름, 퇴비, sensible 분별 있는, 양식을 갖춘, sustainability 지속 가능성, rural 시골의, 농촌의

정 답 ③

정답 해설 ③ 문장의 In addition에 주목하자. 이는 첨가의 연결사로 앞 문장의 내용을 긍정적으로 받아 비슷한 내용을 추가한다. 따라서, 앞 문장에서 언급된 유기농법에 대한 부정적 내용—유기농법이 소출을 줄이고 비용을 증가시키는가 하면 유기적 공급이 제한적이고 비싸다고 하는 등—은 ③ 문장에 그대로 이어져야 한다. 그런데 ③ 문장은 정반대로 (유기농법의 한 수단인) 거름이나 콩과 식물의 사용에 이점(benefits)이 있다고 말하고 있다. 이는 맥락에 어긋난다. 따라서 benefits는 constraint(제한) 등의 부정적인 단어로 대체돼야 한다.

(A), (B), (C)의 각 네모 안에서 문맥에 맞는 낱말로 가장 적절한 것은?

According to descriptive realism, states are, as a matter of fact, motivated exclusively by national self-interest. Their behavior is not influenced by moral considerations. On this view, any appeal to ideology and values in world politics is mere rhetoric, (A) concealing / revealing the pursuit of power, which is at the root of every decision taken in the international arena. Some see this as an (B) avoidable / inevitable consequence of human nature. Since humans are naturally self-seeking, the argument goes, it is to be expected that this will be reflected in their political institutions. For 'structural' realists, by contrast, it is the anarchical nature of the international system—the absence of an 'overarching sovereign' or 'world government'—that explains why states are so preoccupied with their own interests. The absence of a world government makes for an insecure environment which (C) forbids / forces states to seek power in order to ensure their own survival. [4점]

	(A)	(B)	(C)
①	concealing	avoidable	forbids
②	concealing	inevitable	forces
③	concealing	inevitable	forbids
④	revealing	inevitable	forbids
⑤	revealing	avoidable	forces

[한번에 정리하는 문제 해설]

[지문 해석] 서술적 현실주의에 따르면 국가는 사실상 전적으로 국가적 이해에 따라 움직인다. 그들의 행동은 도덕적 배려에 의해 영향 받지 않는다. 이런 관점 아래에서는 세계 정치의 어떤 이념이나 가치에 대한 호소도 권력 추구를 은폐하기 위한 수사에 불과하고, 그것은 국제무대에서 내리는 모든 결정의 뿌리를 이룬다. 어떤 이들은 이것을 인간 본성의 피할 수 없는 결과로 보기도 한다. 인간이 본래 이기적이기 때문에 그것이 그들의 정치 제도에 반영되는 것은 당연하다고 보는 것이 그들의 주장이다. 이와는 대조적으로 구조적 현실주의자들에게 있어서 국가들이 자기 이익에 그토록 사로잡히는 이유를 설명해주는 것은 국제 시스템의 무정부주의적 성격, 즉 지배적인 주권이나 세계 정부의 부재 때문이다. 세계 정부의 부재는 국가들로 하여금 자신의 생존 확보를 위해 권력을 추구할 수밖에 없는 불안한 환경을 조성한다.

[글의 소재] 국가 이기주의는 인간의 이기적 본능 때문인가, 세계 정부의 부재 때문인가?

[주요 어휘] descriptive 서술적, motivate 동기를 부여하다, exclusively 전적으로, rhetoric 수사의, conceal 은폐하다, reveal 드러내다, arena 장(場), 무대, inevitable 피할 수 없는, consequence 결과, self-seeking 이기적인, argument 주장, institution 제도, anarchical 무정부의, overarching 지배적인, sovereign 주권, insecure 불안정한

[구조 분석] • it is the anarchical nature of the international system—the absence of an 'overarching sovereign' or 'world government'—that explains why states are so preoccupied with their own interests.
→ 'it that' 강조 구문으로 'the anarchical nature ~ world government' 부분이 강조되고 있다.

[정답] ②

[정답 해설] 국제 정치에서 이념과 가치에 대한 호소는 수사, 즉 겉치레일 뿐이고 실제로는 권력 추구를 은폐하고 있다는 식으로 흐름이 이어져야 하므로 네모 (A)에 들어갈 적절한 말은 concealing이다. 또, 이어지는 문장에서 '인간은 태생적으로 이기적이고 이 점이 정치 제도에 반영된다.'고 부연 설명한 것으로 보아 '이것을 인간 본성의 불가피한 결과로 보는 것'이 타당하다. 따라서 네모 (B)에 들어갈 말은 inevitable이 적절하다. 앞 문장에서 국가들이 자신의 이해에 사로잡히는 것은 세계 정부의 부재 때문이라고 했으므로 세계 정부의 부재가 국가로 하여금 권력을 추구하지 않을 수 없는 불안한 분위기를 조성한다는 식의 흐름이 이어져야 한다. 따라서 네모 (C)에는 forces가 적절하다. 따라서 정답은 ②이다.

밑줄 친 부분 중, 문맥상 낱말의 쓰임이 적절하지 <u>않은</u> 것을 고르시오.　　　　| 경찰 2022년 |

경찰 기출문제 유형보기

Digital information plays a part in the increasing uncertainty of knowledge. First, the infinitude of information now accessible through the Internet ①<u>dwarfs</u> any attempt to master a subject—it is simply no longer possible to know what is to be known in any area. The response is to focus on ever narrower or more esoteric disciplines or interests, or to admit that all that can be done is to ②<u>sample</u> the field. Second, the stature of knowledge is challenged, because the quality of what can be accessed is often ③<u>unknown</u>. In the printed book, the signs of quality—publisher, author affiliation, and so on—are usually clearly marked. But the quality of information on the Internet is not always so obvious, sometimes deliberately ④<u>unveiled</u>, sometimes simplistic but loud. Even the encyclopedic is not guaranteed: Wikipedia bills itself as 'the free encyclopedia that anyone can edit'. Despite the theory that correct material will usually overcome incorrect, there is nevertheless a caveat that knowledge is always ⑤<u>relative</u>.

[한번에 정리하는 문제 해설]

지문 해석) 디지털 정보는 지식의 불확실성을 높이는 데 한 역할을 한다. 첫째로 이제 인터넷을 통해 접근할 수 있는 정보의 무한성이 한 가지 주제를 통달하려는 모든 시도를 왜소해 보이게 한다—어떤 분야의 사정을 속속들이 안다는 것은 그야말로 더 이상 가능하지 않다. (이에 대한) 대처는 어느 때보다 좁은 비전(祕傳)의 지식이나 관심 분야에 초점을 맞추거나 이제 할 수 있는 것이라곤 어떤 분야든 간 보는 것뿐이라는 점을 인정하는 것이다. 둘째로 접근하려는 것의 질을 종종 알 수가 없어서 지식의 위상이 흔들리고 있다. 인쇄된 책의 경우 품질의 표시가—출판사나 저자의 소속 등—통상 명백히 드러난다. 그러나 인터넷상 정보의 질은 항상 분명하지 않고 종종 의도적으로 드러나거나(→ 은폐되거나) 때로는 단순하지만 요란하다. 백과사전조차 보장할 수 없다. 위키피디아는 누구나 편집할 수 있는 공짜 백과사전이라고 자신을 홍보한다. 정확한 자료가 늘 부정확함을 압도한다는 이론이 있지만 그럼에도 불구하고 지식은 항상 상대적이라는 경고를 잊어서는 안 된다.

글의 소재) 지식의 불확실성 높이는 디지털 정보

주요 어휘) uncertainty 불확실성, infinitude 무한량, dwarf 난쟁이. 왜소하게 만들다, esoteric 비전(祕傳)의, discipline 훈육, 학문 분야, stature 키, 위상, affiliation 소속, 관계, deliberately 고의로, unveil 드러내다, encyclopedia 백과사전, caveat 경고, 공고

정 답) ④

정답 해설) 인쇄된 책의 질을 판단할 수 있는 징후는 출판사나 저자에 관한 정보 등을 통해 명확히 표시되지만, 인터넷을 떠도는 정보의 질은 항상 분명하지는 않다고 했으므로 논지의 일관성이 유지되려면 정보의 질이 고의로 은폐된다는 내용이 이어져야 한다. 따라서 ④의 unveiled는 concealed 등의 단어로 대체돼야 한다.

40 다음 글의 밑줄 친 부분 중, 문맥 상 낱말의 쓰임이 적절하지 <u>않은</u> 것은? 난이도 중

Trust can be fragile in the learning community. It is like any other moral resource in that it can be enhanced or diminished. It is difficult, for example, to respond in a fashion that will make everyone happy, and educators can easily ①misinterpret a colleague's good intentions. Furthermore, leadership often ②entails making choices in response to multiple and sometimes conflicting demands, and teachers may lose trust in the principal when the dominant demand does not ③address their current needs. Without trust, a true sense of community cannot be developed, nor can a collaborative culture exist. Under such conditions, people will cooperate only under a system of formal rules and regulations. In essence, the lack of trust is likely to ④yield a more bureaucratic school where administrators rely on rules and standard procedures for compliance and co-operation. The less trust, the less likely that learning will occur because community building is ⑤feasible in a bureaucratized environment. People in such environments tend to do the minimum necessary to comply with the institutional demands. Schools just do not function well in this kind of climate.

41 다음 글의 밑줄 친 부분 중, 문맥상 낱말의 쓰임이 적절하지 <u>않은</u> 것은? 난이도 중

Think about your reaction if you were sitting in an airliner and the captain said over the intercom, "I hope we'll be landing safely in Cleveland at 7:30 tonight." If you hadn't taken off yet, you'd ①<u>get off</u> the plane. Why? Because the captain's choice of the phrase "I hope" suggested some doubt about a safe arrival. Such ②<u>uncertain</u> language doesn't belong in the airline cockpit or in the sales presentation. If you are in the habit of saying, "I think you'll find our products to be……," you're being too tentative. Prospects prefer a more ③<u>flexible</u> approach, such as "I know you'll agree that……" Tentative language is a normal part of polite conversation and can easily slip into a sales presentation if you're not careful. If your language choices are tentative rather than positive, that tentativeness will be ④<u>associated</u> with you and your product. Use definite positive phrases within your presentation and ⑤<u>save</u> the "maybe's," "might be's," and "I think so's" for polite conversation.

다음 글의 밑줄 친 부분 중, 문맥상 낱말의 쓰임이 적절하지 <u>않은</u> 것은? 난이도 중

If you have already had the experience of coping successfully with some different crisis in the past, that gives you more ①<u>confidence</u> that you can solve the new crisis as well. That contrasts with the sense of helplessness, growing out of previous crises not ②<u>mastered</u>, that, whatever you do, you won't succeed. The importance of previous experience is a main reason why crises tend to be so much more ③<u>traumatic</u> for adolescents and young adults than for older people. While the break-up of a close relationship can be hurtful at any age, the break-up of one's first close relationship is especially ④<u>devastating</u>. At the time of ⑤<u>earlier</u> break-ups, no matter how painful, one recalls having gone through and gotten over similar pain before.

다음 글의 밑줄 친 부분 중, 문맥상 낱말의 쓰임이 적절하지 <u>않은</u> 것은? 난이도 중

The first scientific attempt to explain the origin of the salt in the ocean was made by the Anglo-Irish scientist Robert Boyle in the 1670s. Drawing on his studies of the chemistry of the atmosphere and the phenomena of color, he made measurements which showed that rivers carried ①<u>minute</u> amounts of salt with them as they flowed into the sea. This led to a view of the origin of sea salt which served as the standard explanation for centuries. It is, that minerals are continuously ②<u>discharged</u> from rocks and soil by rainwater, and eventually ③<u>join</u> the runoff which forms local streams, move on to the rivers, and thence into the sea. Each drop of water that enters the sea brings with it some minerals from the land, and these minerals ④<u>vanish</u> when the drop of water eventually evaporates and becomes rain again. In this picture, the river systems of earth form a kind of continuous conveyor belt, ⑤<u>washing</u> materials into the sea and leaving them behind as the water starts its evaporation precipitation cycle again.

* runoff 땅 위를 흐르는 빗물

44 (A), (B), (C)의 각 네모 안에서 문맥에 맞는 낱말로 가장 적절한 것을 고르시오.

난이도 중

It is hard for us to separate information from meaning because we cannot help interpreting messages. We infuse messages with meaning automatically, fooling ourselves to believe that the meaning of a message is carried in the message. But it is not. This is only an (A) allusion / illusion . Meaning is derived from context and prior knowledge. Meaning is the interpretation that a knowledge agent, such as a human, gives to a message, but it is different from the physical order that carries the message, and different from the message itself. Meaning emerges when a message reaches a life-form or a machine with the ability to process information; it is not (B) carried / lost in the blots of ink, sound waves, beams of light, or electric pulses that transmit information. Think of the phrase "September 11." When I say that phrase, most Americans automatically think of the 2001 attack on the Twin Towers. Chileans usually think about the 1973 coup d'état. But when I am saying "September 11" I am just telling my students that I will be back at MIT on that date. Thus, the meaning of the message is something that you construct. It is not part of the (C) context / message , even if it seems to be.

```
         (A)              (B)            (C)
① illusion  ······  lost      ······  context
② illusion  ······  carried   ······  message
③ illusion  ······  lost      ······  message
④ allusion  ······  carried   ······  context
⑤ allusion  ······  lost      ······  message
```

45

(A), (B), (C)의 각 네모 안에서 문맥에 맞는 낱말로 가장 적절한 것을 고르시오.

난이도 중

Why are giant brains so rare in the animal kingdom? The fact is that a jumbo brain is a jumbo (A) [drain / gain] on the body. It's not easy to carry around, especially when encased inside a massive skull. It's even harder to fuel. In Homo sapiens, the brain accounts for about 2-3 percent of total body weight, but it consumes 25 percent of the body's energy when the body is at rest. By comparison, the brains of other apes require only 8 percent of rest-time energy. Archaic humans (B) [benefited / suffered] from their large brains in two ways. Firstly, they spent more time in search of food. Secondly, their muscles atrophied. Like a government diverting money from defence to education, humans diverted energy from biceps to neurons. It's hardly a foregone conclusion that this is a (C) [desirable / undesirable] strategy for survival on the savannah. A chimpanzee can't win an argument with a Homo sapiens, but the ape can rip the man apart like a rag doll.

* foregone 기정(旣定)의

	(A)		(B)		(C)
①	drain	······	suffered	······	desirable
②	drain	······	benefited	······	undesirable
③	drain	······	suffered	······	undesirable
④	gain	······	benefited	······	desirable
⑤	gain	······	suffered	······	undesirable

46

(A), (B), (C)의 각 네모 안에서 문맥에 맞는 낱말로 가장 적절한 것을 고르시오.

난이도 중

There may be large potential gains to be had from international collaboration in a post-transition multipolar world. The presence of such gains, however, does not imply that collaboration will actually be (A) achieved / abandoned. One obstacle is the difficulty of ensuring compliance with any treaty that might be agreed. Two nuclear rivals might each be better off if they both relinquished their atom bombs; yet even if they could reach an in-principle agreement to do so, disarmament could nevertheless prove (B) attainable / elusive because of their mutual fear that the other party might cheat. Allaying this fear would require setting up a verification mechanism. There may have to be inspectors to oversee the destruction of existing stockpiles, and then to monitor nuclear reactors and other facilities, in order to ensure that the weapons program is not reconstituted. One cost is paying for these inspectors. Another cost is the risk that the inspectors will spy and make off with commercial or military secrets. Perhaps most significantly, each party might fear that the other will (C) preserve / renounce a clandestine nuclear capability. Many a potentially beneficial deal never comes off because compliance would be too difficult to verify.

	(A)	(B)	(C)
①	achieved	elusive	preserve
②	achieved	attainable	renounce
③	achieved	elusive	renounce
④	abandoned	attainable	renounce
⑤	abandoned	elusive	preserve

47

(A), (B), (C)의 각 네모 안에서 문맥에 맞는 낱말로 가장 적절한 것을 고르시오.

난이도 상

Of the many questions about memory, one of the most fundamental concerns the types or varieties of memory. In recent years, both psychological and neuro-biological works have suggested that memory is (A) associated / dissociated into processes or systems that are fundamentally different. For example, amnesic patients with brain injury or disease exhibit severe inabilities to recall and recognize recent events and have difficulty learning new facts or other kinds of information. But these patients possess some relatively (B) intact / damaged learning and memory abilities: for example, on tasks such as manual-dexterity learning trials, they perform as well as healthy and uninjured people, even though they may have no conscious memory of having performed the task before. This evidence—that some kinds of learning can proceed normally even when the brain structures that mediate conscious remembering are damaged—(C) supports / contradicts the general proposition that there are distinct, dissociated types of memory.

* amnesic 기억상실의

	(A)	(B)	(C)
①	associated	intact	supports
②	associated	damaged	contradicts
③	associated	intact	contradicts
④	dissociated	damaged	supports
⑤	dissociated	intact	supports

48

(A), (B), (C)의 각 네모 안에서 문맥에 맞는 낱말로 가장 적절한 것을 고르시오.

난이도 상

Archaeologists often talk about studying the past. They don't, really. They study the present—those latter-day bits and pieces of the past that survive, those perduring lines of evidence still accessible to them today that allow them to draw inferences about what happened yesterday. Susan Pearce, one of the major authors addressing issues of archaeological curatorship uses Ferdinand Saussure's (A) similarity / distinction between *langue* and *parole* to illustrate the complexity of interpreting that obscured past. From the wide range of unstructured possibilities are drawn a set of forms that a society's communication systems, material culture, and other cultural forms may take. To be culturally (B) intelligible / intelligent, these forms must be used in appropriate ways informed by culturally constructed rules. These rules of use creating structured, meaningful action are the *langue*. *Parole* represents everyday behaviors—utterance, making a tool, or cooking a meal—drawn from the langue, the physical actions expressing the semiotic structure. Even in ethnographic cases archaeologists don't directly observe the *langue*, but they may be able to draw inferences about it based on observed *parole*, the (C) actual / potential structurally informed behavior of people in their daily lives.

* semiotic 기호의, ethnographic 민족지(誌)적인

	(A)	(B)	(C)
①	similarity	intelligent	actual
②	similarity	intelligible	potential
③	distinction	intelligent	actual
④	distinction	intelligible	actual
⑤	distinction	intelligent	potential

6

세부 내용 파악

선택지의 내용이 지문에 제시된 사실(facts)과
일치하는지 혹은 일치하지 않는지를 묻는 유형으로
빠르고 정확한 독해 능력이 요구된다.

가이드라인

▶ 전기나 설명문 또는 특정 목적의 실용문이 지문으로 제시되므로 비교적 쉬운 내용이다.

▶ 세부 내용을 파악하는 문제는 선택지의 내용이 본문의 내용과 일치하는지 또는 불일치하는지를 묻는 문제다.

▶ 선택지를 먼저 훑어 읽고 지문을 접하면 내용 파악이 한결 수월할 수 있다. 특히 불일치를 묻는 문제의 경우 선택지 중 4개가 옳은 진술이기 때문에 더욱 그러하다.

▶ 선택지의 순서는 지문에서 제시되는 내용의 순서와 일치한다.

▶ 이 점을 활용해, 선택지를 먼저 읽고 이를 지문에서 1:1로 확인하는 방식, 즉 '선택지 ① → 지문 확인, 선택지 ② → 지문 확인' 방식으로 읽어 나가야 정확도를 높이고 시간을 절약할 수 있다.

▶ 선택지와 본문을 매칭하는 데 고유명사나 숫자(연도 포함)를 적극적으로 활용하라. 이 경우 선택지의 고유명사나 숫자는 해당 내용을 본문에서 찾는 데 좌표와 같은 역할을 한다.

▶ 읽어 내려가다가 특정 선택지가 정답이라는 확신이 들면 독해를 멈추고 과감하게 다음 문제로 넘어가라.

▶ 주어진 글의 내용에 의해서만 판단한다. 상식에 입각한 판단이나 주관적 가치에 근거한 판단, 즉 주관 개입은 금물이다.

Jim Marshall에 관한 다음 글의 내용과 일치하지 <u>않는</u> 것은?

The late photographer Jim Marshall is regarded as one of the most celebrated photographers of the 20th century. He holds the distinction of being the first and only photographer to be presented with the Grammy Trustees Award. He started as a professional photographer in 1959. He was given unrivaled access to rock's biggest artists, including the Rolling Stones, Bob Dylan, and Ray Charles. He was the only photographer granted backstage access for the Beatles' final full concert and also shot the Rolling Stones on their historic 1972 tour. He formed special bonds with the artists he worked with and those relationships helped him capture some of his most vivid and iconic imagery. Over a 50-year career, the photographs he took appeared on more than 500 album covers. He was passionate about his work up until the end. "I have no kids," he used to say. "My photographs are my children."

① Grammy Trustees Award가 수여된 최초이자 유일한 사진작가이다.
② 1959년에 직업 사진작가로 일하기 시작했다.
③ Rolling Stones의 역사적인 1972년 투어에서 그들을 촬영했다.
④ 함께 작업한 예술가들과 특별한 유대 관계를 맺지 않았다.
⑤ 500개가 넘는 앨범 커버에 그가 촬영한 사진들이 실렸다.

[한번에 정리하는 문제 해설]

지문 해석) 작고한 사진작가 Jim Marshall은 20세기의 가장 유명한 사진작가 중 한 명으로 여겨진다. 그는 Grammy Trustees Award를 수여한 최초이자 유일한 사진작가라는 명예를 지니고 있다. 그는 1959년에 직업 사진작가로 일하기 시작했다. 그는 Rolling Stones, Bob Dylan, Ray Charles를 포함해서 록 음악의 가장 인기 있는 예술가들에게 그 누구보다 더 많이 접근할 수 있었다. 그는 Beatles의 마지막 콘서트 전체를 무대 뒤에서 접근할 수 있도록 허락을 받은 유일한 사진작가였고, 또한 Rolling Stones의 역사적인 1972년 투어에서 그들을 촬영했다. 그는 함께 작업한 예술가들과 특별한 유대 관계를 맺었고, 그런 관계는 그가 가장 생생하고 상징적인 이미지들을 포착하는 데 도움을 주었다. 50년의 경력에 걸쳐 그가 촬영한 사진들이 500개가 넘는 앨범 커버에 실렸다. 그는 마지막까지 자신의 일에 대해 정열적이었다. 그는 "저에게는 아이가 없습니다. 제 사진이 제 아이일 뿐입니다."라고 말하곤 했다.

글의 소재) 사진작가 Jim Marshall의 삶

주요 어휘) **celebrated** 저명한, **distinction** 구별, 명예, **unrivaled** 필적할 만한 상대가 없는, **access** 접근, **grant** 부여하다, **shoot** (사진·영화를) 촬영하다, **capture** 포착하다, **vivid** 생생한, **iconic** 상징적인, **passionate** 정열적인

정 답) ④

정답 해설) 'He formed special bonds with the artists he worked with and those relationships helped him capture some of his most vivid and iconic imagery(그는 함께 작업한 예술가들과 특별한 유대 관계를 맺었고, 그런 관계는 그가 가장 생생하고 상징적인 이미지들을 포착하는 데 도움을 주었다).'라고 했으므로 ④의 '함께 작업한 예술가들과 특별한 유대 관계를 맺지 않았다.'라는 내용은 사실이 아니다. 따라서 정답은 ④이다.

14 Ruth Gardena Birnie에 관한 다음 글의 내용과 일치하지 <u>않는</u> 것은?

On August 15, 1884, Ruth Gardena Birnie was born to Moses and Louise Harrison in Sumter, South Carolina. Since her parents died while she was very young, Birnie was reared by Martha A. Savage, a teacher. Birnie graduated from Lincoln School, an early African American school in Sumter. Later she taught there for a short period of time. In 1902, when she was eighteen years old, she married Charles Wainwright Birnie, who came to Sumter as its first African American physician. Sixteen years after their marriage, the Birnies gave birth to a daughter, Anna. As Charles W. Birnie's practice grew, he and Martha Savage, Ruth Birnie's foster mother, encouraged Ruth to pursue pharmacy as a profession. She entered Benedict College, then went on to Temple University and received her degree in pharmacy. Upon her return to South Carolina, Birnie became one of the earliest female African American pharmacists in the state.

① 아주 어릴 때 부모를 여의고 Martha A. Savage에 의해 양육되었다.
② 모교인 Lincoln School에서 짧은 기간 동안 가르쳤다.
③ 열여덟 살 때 의사인 Charles Wainwright Birnie와 결혼했다.
④ 남편과 키워준 어머니의 반대를 무릅쓰고 약사가 되려고 했다.
⑤ Temple University에서 약학 학위를 받았다.

[한번에 정리하는 문제 해설]

지문 해석 Ruth Gardena Birnie는 1884년 8월 15일 South Carolina주 Sumter에서 Moses & Louise Harrison의 집안에 태어났다. 그녀가 아주 어렸을 때 부모님이 돌아가셔서 그녀는 교사였던 Martha A. Savage에 의해 양육됐다. Birnie는 Sumter에 있는 초기 흑인 학교인 Lincoln School을 졸업했다. 그녀는 후에 그곳에서 잠시 가르쳤다. 그녀가 열여덟 살이던 1902년 그녀는 이 지역 최초의 흑인 의사로 Sumter에 부임했던 Charles Wainwright Birnie와 결혼했다. 그들이 결혼한 지 16년이 지나 Birnie 부부는 딸 안나를 낳았다. Charles W. Birnie의 병원 사업이 커가자 그와 Ruth Birnie의 양어머니인 Martha Savage는 그녀에게 정식 직업으로 약학을 공부할 것을 권했다. 그녀는 Benedict College에 들어갔고, 후에 Temple University에 진학해 그곳에서 약사 학위를 받았다. South Carolina로 돌아온 후 Birnie는 그 주의 초기 여성 약사 중 한 명이 됐다.

주요 어휘 rear 키우다, 양육하다, African American 아프리카계 미국인의, 흑인의, physician 내과 의사, give birth to ~를 낳다, practice 의사나 변호사의 사업, 업무, foster mother 유모, 양모, encourage 격려하다, 권하다, pharmacy 약학, profession 전문 직업, female 여성(의), pharmacist 약사

구조 분석 • In 1902, <u>when</u> she was eighteen years old, she married Charles Wainwright Birnie, <u>who</u> came to Sumter as its first African American physician.

➜ when은 관계부사, who는 관계대명사로 둘 다 계속적 용법으로 쓰여 바로 앞의 선행사에 대한 추가 정보를 제공한다.

정답 ④

정답 해설 글 후반에 'Charles W. Birnie의 병원 사업이 커가자 그와 Ruth Birnie의 양어머니인 Martha Savage는 그녀에게 정식 직업으로 약학을 공부할 것을 권했다.'고 했으므로 ④ '남편과 키워준 어머니의 반대를 무릅쓰고 약사가 되려고 했다.'는 사실과 다르다.

15 Lewis와 Clark의 탐사에 관한 다음 글의 내용과 일치하는 것은?

| 경찰 2017년 |

In 1803, the US government purchased the entire area of Louisiana from France. The territory stretched from the Mississippi River to the middle of the Rocky Mountains, but no one was really sure where the Mississippi River started or where exactly the Rocky Mountains were located. President Thomas Jefferson commissioned an expedition in this area. It comprised a selected group of US Army volunteers under the command of Captain Meriwether Lewis and Second Lieutenant William Clark. Their perilous journey lasted from May 1804 to September 1806. Their primary objective was to explore and to map the newly acquired territory, and to find a practical route across the western half of the continent. Lewis and Clark departed with forty-three men and supplies for two years. They became acquainted with a sixteen-year-old Native American woman named Sacajawea, which means Bird Woman. With her help, Lewis and Clark obtained horses from the Indians and passed the Indian territory without much trouble.

① 미국은 영국으로부터 Louisiana 지역을 매입했다.
② 탐사는 이미 알려진 Mississippi 강의 시작점에서 출발했다.
③ 탐사대원들은 육군의 추천을 통해 선발됐다.
④ 모든 탐사를 마치기까지 4년 이상의 기간이 걸렸다.
⑤ 탐사 중에 원주민 여성의 도움을 받았다.

[한번에 정리하는 문제 해설]

지문 해석 1803년 미국 정부는 프랑스로부터 루이지애나 전 지역을 사들였다. 그 영토는 미시시피 강에서 로키산맥 중심부에 이르렀지만 미시시피 강이 어디에서 시작하는지, 로키산맥이 정확히 어디 있는지 아는 사람이 아무도 없었다. 토마스 제퍼슨 대통령은 이 지역에 탐험대를 위촉했다. 그것은 Meriwether Lewis 대위와 William Clark 소위 휘하에 선별된 육군 자원병 그룹으로 구성됐다. 그들의 위험한 여행은 1804년 5월에서 1806년 9월까지 계속됐다. 그들의 일차적인 목적은 새로 사들인 영토를 탐사해 지도를 제작하고, 대륙 서반부를 가로지르는 쓸 만한 도로를 찾는 것이었다. Lewis와 Clark은 남자 43명과 2년 치 보급품을 가지고 떠났다. 그들은 Sacajawea – 새(鳥) 여인을 의미 – 라는 이름의 열여섯 먹은 미국 원주민 여성과 친해졌다. 그녀의 도움으로 Lewis와 Clark은 인디언들로부터 말을 얻어 인디언 영토를 큰 어려움 없이 통과할 수 있었다.

글의 소재 미국 건국 초기의 영토 확장 에피소드

주요 어휘 stretch from ~ to ~ ~에서 ~까지 이르다, commission 위촉하다, expedition 탐험대, comprise ~로 구성되다, perilous 위험한, primary 일차적인, objective 목표, map 지도를 제작하다, be acquainted with ~와 친해지다

정 답 ⑤

정답 해설 이 글은 미국 건국 초기 영토를 확장하면서 루이지애나를 프랑스로부터 사들였을 당시의 이야기다. 새 영토 구매와 개발에 관련된 fact를 선택지의 내용과 일일이 대조해 어긋나는 부분을 찾는다. 본문에 부합되는 내용은 ⑤뿐이다.
 ① 프랑스로부터 매입했다.
 ② Mississippi 강의 시작점은 알려지지 않았다.
 ③ 육군 자원병으로 구성됐다.
 ④ 탐사는 1804년 5월에서 1806년 9월까지 계속됐다.

49 다음 글에 나타난 home office의 안전 대비책과 거리가 먼 것은? 난이도 중

One important issue of working in a home office that you should give paramount importance is its safety and security. If you use computers in your business, you need to constantly protect your computer systems from viruses, worms and hack attacks. Given the increasing amount of threat and damage caused by viruses and hackers, you should always make sure that you have the latest firewalls and antivirus software. More importantly, you should give the physical safety of your home office its due consideration. You need to protect your home office from break-in, theft and the chaos that often results. Aside from getting a security system installed, there are a number of measures that you can implement to protect your office. Keep a low profile, making sure that your computer systems and other expensive equipment are hidden from public view. Keep your curtains or blinds closed when you are not in your office, and dim the light—especially at night. It is also very important to get your office and all your equipment insured.

① 컴퓨터 방어벽을 높인다.
② 보안시스템을 설치한다.
③ 컴퓨터는 접근성을 고려해 공개된 장소에 설치한다.
④ 외출 시 커튼이나 블라인드를 친다.
⑤ 사무실과 장비를 보험에 가입한다.

50 다음 글에 나타난 레오나르도 다빈치의 치적과 관계<u>없</u>는 것은?

난이도 중

There have been, of course, many other insatiable polymaths, and the Renaissance produced other Renaissance men. But none painted the Mona Lisa, much less did so at the same time as producing unsurpassed anatomy drawings based on multiple dissections, coming up with schemes to divert rivers, explaining the reflection of light from the earth to the moon, opening the still-beating heart of a butchered pig to show how ventricles work, designing musical instruments, choreographing pageants, using fossils to dispute the biblical account of the Deluge and then drawing a deluge. Da Vinci was a genius, but not simply because he was smart. He was, more important, the epitome of the universal mind, the person most curious about more things than anyone else in history.

* polymath 박식가, ventricle 심실

① 인체해부도를 그린 일
② 강의 수로(水路) 변경을 계획한 일
③ 야외극 안무를 창작한 일
④ 악기를 디자인한 일
⑤ 화석을 이용해 성경의 사실(史實)을 입증한 일

51 다음 글에 나타난 차(tea)의 효능과 관계없는 것은?   난이도 중

Tea, though neglected by some, contains valuable flavonoid, natural substances known to be effective antioxidants. With a cup of a tea a day our protection is improved against free radicals, harmful substances that can cause problems, such as cell deformation and inflammation. These radicals cause cell damage that can lead to cancer and heart diseases. The antioxidant properties in two cups of tea equals four apples or ten glasses of orange juice. Steeping tea bags for some minutes releases the highest amount of antioxidants. It also goes a long way in reducing esophageal cancer by about 20% among males and 40% among females. There is also a likelihood that tea may reduce the size of established tumors in the body. Tea may also decrease blood clotting, another common cause of cardiovascular disease. It's not only the flavonoid contents of tea that may be of immense benefit to us. Tea also contains several of the minerals needed in small amounts for good health such as manganese, potassium and zinc.

* flavonoid 플라보노이드, 토마토 등에서 발견되는 물질로 항암에 효과가 있는 것으로 알려져 있다,
free radical 유리기, esophageal 식도의, potassium 칼륨

① 항산화 작용
② 피의 응고 방지
③ 유리기 분비 촉진
④ 식도암 예방
⑤ 암의 증식 억제

Ulmer에 대한 다음 글의 내용과 일치하는 것은?

난이도 중

Like most kids her age, Ulmer used to hate bees. "I absolutely despised anything that buzzed," she says. But shortly after she was stung, twice, in 2009, the Texas native developed a fascination with them. That's when she learned that honeybees are also going extinct. So Ulmer decided to help—with lemonade. Using her great grandmother's recipe, Ulmer made a blend, sweetened with local honey, to sell at community business fairs, donating 10% of her profits to honeybee-advocate groups. By 2014, her side project was a full-blown business. Now, Me & the Bees Lemonade is stocked at more than 300 Whole Foods stores as well as at Wegmans and other grocers, and Ulmer runs a nonprofit, the Healthy Hive Foundation, to raise awareness about the plight of the honeybee. Next up: finishing her first children's book(it aims to teach kids how to start their own business) and expanding her company. To that end, Ulmer says, "I just hired my dad."

① 벌에 두 번 쏘인 후 벌을 극도로 싫어하게 됐다.
② 토종꿀을 가미한 레몬 음료를 혼자 힘으로 개발했다.
③ 음료 회사 수입의 10%를 꿀벌 후원 단체에 기부한다.
④ 대형 식음료 유통 체인에 자사 제품의 입점을 추진 중이다.
⑤ 최근 아동의 창업을 돕기 위한 책을 발간했다.

53 암에 대한 다음 글의 내용과 일치하지 <u>않는</u> 것은? 난이도 중

The most important discovery in the history of cancer epidemiology is the carcinogenic effect of tobacco. Lung cancer incidence increases rapidly among continuing smokers, but remains roughly constant in ex-smokers. The risk is therefore greatest in those who begin to smoke when young and continue throughout life. Secondhand, or environmental, tobacco smoking is also carcinogenic, but it is hard to quantify the magnitude of the risk. The large increase in male cigarette smoking in most developed countries that occurred during the first half of the twentieth century caused an unprecedented epidemic in the lung cancer rate several decades later. A reduction in tar levels in cigarettes combined with decreases in smoking has subsequently reduced the lung cancer rate in many developed countries. Women in most Western countries began smoking later than men and fewer have stopped, so their lung cancer rates are either still increasing or falling less rapidly.

* carcinogenic 발암성의

① 암의 역학 역사에서 가장 큰 발견은 담배의 암 유발 가능성을 밝힌 일이다.
② 담배를 끊은 사람의 암 발생률은 큰 변화 없이 대체로 일정하다.
③ 간접흡연의 위험 정도를 계량화하기는 쉽지 않다.
④ 20세기 전반의 남성 흡연의 증가는 수십 년 후 폐암 발생률 증가로 나타났다.
⑤ 서구에서 여성의 폐암 발생률은 남성보다 빠르게 줄어들고 있다.

테니스에 관한 다음 글의 내용과 일치하는 것은?

The game of tennis arguably originated with the Egyptians—in friezes on temple walls a ball game is depicted. It came to Europe with the Moors and fascinated the monks who called it la soule. In the 12th and 13th centuries it came out of the monasteries and a glove and handle supplanted the bare hand. Balls became made of leather stuffed with bran instead of wood and in the 16th to 18th centuries it was a game much favored in France where it was called Jeu de Paume, or palm game. Play was started with the cry 'Tenez!' It was a favored game with royal courts and 'real tennis' was played off the walls(there is a 'real tennis' court at Hampton Court Palace). At the first Wimbledon tournament there were 22 players and 200 spectators. The last time men wore long trousers on court was in 1939.

* frieze 프리즈, 띠 모양의 조각, bran 쌀겨

① 테니스가 이집트에서 시작됐다는 설은 근거가 희박하다.
② 테니스가 처음 유럽에 전해졌을 때 수사들은 이를 반기지 않았다.
③ 12~13세기 전까지만 해도 테니스는 맨손으로 쳤다.
④ 궁정의 테니스 경기는 주로 야외에서 열렸다.
⑤ 1939년 이전에는 남자 선수에게 긴 바지가 허용되지 않았다.

아래 글에 나타난 O. Henry의 행적과 관계없는 것은?

난이도 중

Here is where the twists and turns of O. Henry really started. Banking, in particular, was not to be his calling; he was quite careless with his bookkeeping, fired by the bank and charged with embezzlement in 1894. His father-in-law posted bail for him, but he fled the day before the trial in 1896, first to New Orleans, then to Honduras, where there was no extradition treaty. He befriended a notorious train robber there, Al Jennings, who later wrote a book about their friendship. O. Henry sent his wife and daughter back to Texas, after which he holed up in a hotel to write Kings and Cabbages. He learned his wife was dying of tuberculosis and could not join him in Honduras, so he returned to Austin to be with them and turned himself in to the court. His father-in-law again posted his bail so he could remain with his wife until her death in 1897. He was sentenced to 5 years in prison and imprisoned in March 1898 at the Ohio Penitentiary in Columbus, Ohio.

① 장부 정리에 허술했으며 은행에서 해고되고 횡령 혐의로 기소되었다.

② 재판받기 하루 전날 도망해 뉴올리언스와 온두라스를 전전했다.

③ 철도 강도와 친분을 나눴으며 후에 그들의 우정에 관한 책을 쓰기도 했다.

④ 아내가 치명적인 병에 걸린 것을 알고 그녀 곁으로 돌아갔다.

⑤ 장인이 그를 위해 두 번이나 보석을 신청했다.

tuna에 대한 다음 글의 내용과 일치하지 <u>않는</u> 것은?   난이도 중

A tuna is a saltwater fish that belongs to the tribe Thunnini, a sub-grouping of the mackerel family. Thunnini comprises fifteen species across five genera, the sizes of which vary greatly, ranging from the bullet tuna (maximum length: 50 cm, weight: 1.8 kg) up to the Atlantic bluefin tuna (maximum length: 4.6 m, weight: 684 kg). The bluefin averages 2 m, and is believed to live for up to 50 years. Tuna and mackerel sharks are the only species of fish that can maintain a body temperature higher than that of the surrounding water. An active and agile predator, the tuna has a sleek, streamlined body, and is among the fastest-swimming pelagic fish—the yellowfin tuna, for example, is capable of speeds of up to 75 km/h. Found in warm seas, it is extensively fished commercially, and is popular as a game fish. As a result of overfishing, stocks of some tuna species, such as the southern bluefin tuna, are close to extinction.

* genera genus속(屬)의 복수, mackerel shark 악상어, pelagic fish 표층어

① 크기가 다양해 어종에 따라 몸길이가 아홉 배 이상 차이나기도 한다.
② 악상어와 함께 주변 수온보다 낮은 체온을 유지하는 유일한 어종이다.
③ 활동적이고 민첩한 포식자로서 수영 속도가 매우 빠르다.
④ 상업 용도로 많이 잡고 낚기 시합용으로도 인기가 많다.
⑤ 일부 어종은 멸종 위기를 맞고 있다.

57 철새의 이동에 관한 다음 글과 일치하지 <u>않는</u> 것은? 난이도 중

As birds approach the breeding grounds, migration is accelerated but movements are increasingly scattered, possibly indicating a search for a suitable breeding habitat. However, whereas some birds may be searching for new breeding territories, most migrants will return to breeding sites that they have experienced earlier as breeding or juvenile birds, and thereby display site fidelity rather than dispersal. For many migrants, breeding habitat selection often involves return to the territory on which the bird bred the previous year. Return rates vary naturally from species to species and year to year but average around 50 percent for adult small passerines to as high as greater than 90 percent for some long-lived species like gulls. Banding studies demonstrate that adult migrants of many species that have bred successfully in a previous year return to their breeding territories at a rate assumed to be comparable to that of survivorship.

* passerine 연작류, banding study 조류표지법에 의한 연구

① 번식지가 가까울수록 철새의 행동이 산발적인 것은 번식지 탐색과 관계가 있을 수 있다.
② 대부분의 철새들은 이전에 경험했던 번식지로 귀환함으로써 높은 장소 충실도를 보여준다.
③ 많은 철새에게 번식지 선택은 종종 전 해의 번식지로 다시 돌아가는 것을 포함한다.
④ 귀환율은 종에 따라 혹은 해마다 다르나 다 자란 작은 연작류의 경우 거의 90%에 이른다.
⑤ 성인 철새가 전 해에 성공적으로 번식했던 곳으로 귀환하는 비율은 생존율과 비슷하다.

네 명의 학생 사업가에 관한 다음 글의 내용과 일치하지 <u>않는</u> 것은?   난이도 중

On a cool fall evening in 2008, four students set out to revolutionize an industry. Buried in loans, they had lost and broken eyeglasses and were outraged at how much it cost to replace them. One of them had been wearing the same damaged pair for five years. He was using a paper clip to bind the frames together. Even after his prescription changed twice, he refused to pay for pricey new lenses. Luxottica, the 800-pound gorilla of the industry, controlled more than 80 percent of the eyewear market. To make glasses more affordable, the students would need to topple a giant. Having recently watched Zappos transform footwear by selling shoes online, they wondered if they could do the same with eyewear. When they casually mentioned their idea to friends, time and again they were blasted with scorching criticism. No one would ever buy glasses over the internet, their friends insisted. People had to try them on first. Sure, Zappos had pulled the concept off with shoes, but there was a reason it hadn't happened with eyewear. "If this were a good idea," they heard repeatedly, "someone would have done it already."

* the 800-pound gorilla 업계의 시장 지배적 강자

① 비싼 안경 교체 비용 때문에 몹시 화가 나 있었다.
② 도수가 두 번 바뀌었지만, 렌즈 교체를 거부한 학생도 있었다.
③ 안경 가격을 낮추기 위해 거대 안경 회사를 무너뜨려야 했다.
④ 신발을 온라인으로 판매하는 회사의 성공에 자극받았다.
⑤ 온라인 안경 판매 계획에 대해 주변 사람들은 우호적이었다.

다음 글의 내용과 일치하지 <u>않는</u> 것은?

난이도 중

Every year, on the midnight before exams begin, Harvard students take part in what's called the Primal Scream, a venerable tradition that some attribute to our clearly not-so-puritanical forebears. While Founding Father John Adams was making his mark upon history by signing the Declaration of Independence, his son Charles was earning a mark of distinction for being caught streaking with his friends in Harvard Yard. They were thrown out of the school, then later readmitted (clearly if your father is a Founding Father you get at least one get-out-of-jail-free card), and their chilly tradition continues today. More than three hundred years later, the bravest or most intoxicated students gather in front of the Mower Hall, where they proceed to disrobe. Then, the half-frozen, fully naked students begin to jog in a tight pack over the icy ground of old Harvard Yard, huddling together for warmth as hundreds of onlookers come streaming out of their dorms. And for a few brief moments, the anxiety of failing to reach one's potential on exams is replaced by the very real fears of potential frostbite—not to mention potential embarrassment in front of one's peers.

* streaking 벌거벗고 대중 앞을 달리는 행위

① 존 아담스 아들 찰스는 스트리킹에 참여한 적이 있다.

② 찰스는 스트리킹 사건으로 퇴교를 당했으나 복교 조치가 됐다.

③ 스티리킹의 전통은 오늘날도 이어지고 있다.

④ 수줍음을 타는 학생들도 스트리킹에 참여한다.

⑤ 스트리킹 참여 학생들은 잠시나마 시험의 불안에서 벗어날 수 있다.

다음 글의 내용과 일치하지 <u>않는</u> 것은? `난이도 중`

Employees spend between one and three hours a day surfing the web on personal business at work, depending on the study reviewed. Since most studies are based on employee self-reported data, this productivity loss, combined with the concerns employers have for where their employees are surfing the web at work, causes more employers to monitor employee use of the Internet. Employees shop, do banking, visit sports sites, pay bills, chat on Facebook, tweet on Twitter, and more. With most employees, these are occasional activities that they pursue on breaks and lunch. If they do spend a few minutes of work time, they likely make up for it answering email after the kids go to bed. But, a small percentage of employees abuse the privilege. In one company, a disgruntled supervisor was spending 6~7 hours a day doing everything from job searching to looking up recipes and downloading coupons. In another, the change in position of an employee's computer, making the view of its screen impossible by anyone except the employee, made IT suspicious. They found that the employee was downloading and watching adult movies. So, sometimes employers' worst fears are justified.

* disgruntled 앙심을 품은

① 회사원들은 업무와 관련된 인터넷 서핑을 하는 데 평균 1~3시간을 소비한다.
② 업무의 손실과 검색 내용에 대한 우려로 사업주는 사원들의 인터넷 사용을 감시한다.
③ 회사원 대부분은 인터넷 검색을 휴식시간이나 점심시간에 잠깐씩 하는 선에서 끝낸다.
④ 한 회사의 관리자는 하루 6시간 넘게 구직이나 조리법 검색에 빠지기도 했다.
⑤ 한 직원은 자기만 볼 수 있도록 컴퓨터를 옮겨놓고 성인 영화를 시청하기도 했다.

61 Mark Carney에 관한 다음 글의 내용과 일치하지 <u>않는</u> 것은? 난이도 상

Central bankers aren't often young, good-looking and charming, but Mark Carney is all three—not to mention very smart. As the head of the Bank of Canada, Carney, 45, had the good fortune of presiding over a banking system that didn't need a single bailout. Now that the world's richest nations are working to coordinate new financial rules, Carney is clamoring to stay focused on the causes of the crisis—like banks not holding enough capital and Western consumers spending too much—instead of getting distracted by populist zeal. The ex-Goldman Sachs banker, who isn't afraid to crack a joke or roll his eyes, has also been warning Canadians not to take on too much personal debt, since levels in the country have been rising—the sort of straight talk one rarely hears from a person whose job it is to juice the economy.

① 젊고 미남에 매력 있고 아주 영리하기까지 하다.
② 부도 위기를 맞은 은행이 단 하나도 없는 금융 시스템의 수장이 됐다.
③ 민간의 금융 수요에 대해 비교적 호의적이다.
④ 농담이나 감정 표현을 스스럼없이 하는 편이다.
⑤ 국민에게 지나친 개인 빚을 지지 말라고 경고했다.

62 다음 글의 내용과 일치하지 <u>않는</u> 것은?

난이도 상

The early years of X-ray practice in America were described as "a piebald proceeding, a sort of Joseph's coat of many colors, which fitted no one." Indeed, commencing early in 1896, X-ray practice in America remained for more than two decades an unregulated territory, inhabited by a welter of photographers, electrical engineers, physicists, medical novices and other speculative souls. It was only in the 1920's that an organized community of medical specialists, the radiologists, successfully claimed monopoly over the X-ray practice. The slow warming of the American medical community to the new discovery has posed a puzzle to historians. Some explained this as being the results of the difficult theoretical and technical challenges that faced the infant technology. Others concentrated on the social and institutional intricacies involved in the molding of the expertise of the photographer, the electrician, and the doctor into a new profession. Still others pondered over the great epistemological barrier involved in shifting from the tactile and the verbal to the visual.

* piebald 얼룩무늬의, epistemological 인식론적인

① 초기 엑스레이 업계는 여러 부류의 사람들이 거주하는 무규제 공간이었다.
② 1920년대에 이르러서야 방사선계가 엑스레이 독점권을 따냈다.
③ 엑스레이에 대한 의료계의 굼뜬 반응을 역사가들은 비교적 잘 이해하고 있었다.
④ 의료계의 굼뜬 반응의 원인을 신기술의 이론적 기술적 난제 때문으로 보는 견해가 있다.
⑤ 엑스레이 발명으로 인한 인식론적 전환의 어려움이 상당했을 것으로 보는 사람도 있다.

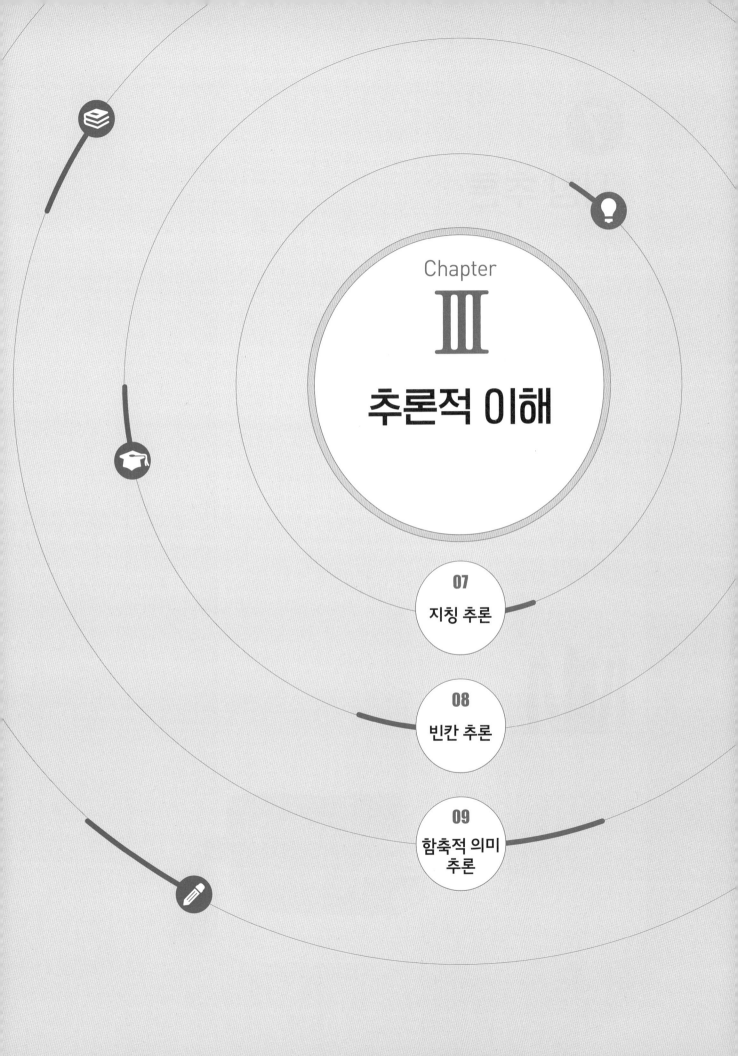

Chapter

III

추론적 이해

7

지칭 추론

글에서 대명사나 명사(구)가 지칭하는 대상이
나머지 넷과 다른 하나를 찾는 유형이다.

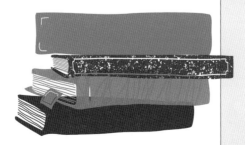

가이드라인

▶ 선택지에 제시되는 대명사는 대부분 글의 중심인물(주인공)이거나 중심소재이기 때문에 글을 읽으면서 이들을 중심으로 선택지의 지칭 대상을 파악해야 한다.

▶ 대명사는 이전에 언급된 명사를 대신하므로 대명사가 나온 문장과 그 앞 문장을 주의 깊게 읽어야 한다.

▶ 글의 흐름이 바뀌어 새로운 정보나 인물이 등장하면 같은 대명사라 하더라도 지칭 대상이 달라질 수 있으므로 장면 전환이 이뤄지는 곳에 등장하는 인물이나 정보에 특히 유의한다.

▶ 비교급 문장에는 정답을 포함한 상반된 두 지칭 대상이 모두 나올 수 있기 때문에 유심히 살펴봐야 한다. 둘 모두가 선택지에 포함돼 있으면 둘 중 하나가 정답이다.

▶ 영어는 같은 말을 반복해서 쓰는 것을 꺼리기 때문에 되풀이되는 말은 흔히 비슷한 뜻의 다른 말로 대체되어 제시된다. 영어의 이러한 대체 표현 관행을 알고 있으면 지칭 대상을 추론하는 데 도움이 된다.

▶ 지칭 대상이 글 안에 있기 때문에 분석·추정하는 능력보다는 지문을 꼼꼼히 읽고 정확하게 이해하는 습관이 필요하다.

밑줄 친 부분이 가리키는 대상이 나머지 넷과 다른 것은?　　　　　　| 수능 2018년 |

Scott Adams, the creator of Dilbert, one of the most successful comic strips of all time, says that two personal letters dramatically changed his life. One night ① he was watching a PBS-TV program about cartooning, when he decided to write to the host of the show, Jack Cassady, to ask for his advice about becoming a cartoonist. Much to ② his surprise, he heard back from Cassady within a few weeks in the form of a handwritten letter. The letter advised Adams not to be discouraged if he received early rejections. Adams got inspired and submitted some cartoons, but ③ he was quickly rejected. Not following Cassady's advice, ④ he became discouraged, put his materials away, and decided to forget cartooning as a career. About fifteen months later, he was surprised to receive yet another letter from Cassady, especially since he hadn't thanked ⑤ him for his original advice. He acted again on Cassady's encouragement, but this time he stuck with it and obviously hit it big.

[한번에 정리하는 문제 해설]

지문 해석 역대 가장 성공적인 연재만화의 하나인 'Dilbert'의 창작자 Scott Adams는 두 통의 개인적인 편지가 극적으로 자신의 인생을 바꾸었다고 말한다. 어느 날 밤, 그는 만화 제작에 대한 PBS-TV의 프로그램을 시청하던 중, 그 쇼의 사회자인 Jack Cassady에게 편지를 써서 만화가가 되는 데 대해 그의 조언을 구하기로 했다. 그가 매우 놀랍게도, 그는 손편지의 형태로 몇 주 안에 Cassady로부터 답장을 받았다. 편지에서 Cassady는 Adams에게 초기에 거절을 당하더라도 낙심하지 말라고 조언했다. Adams는 격려를 받아 몇 편의 만화를 제출했지만, 그는 금방 거절당했다. Cassady의 조언을 따르지 않고 그는 낙심했으며, 자신의 자료들을 치우고 만화 제작을 직업으로 삼는 것을 잊기로 했다. 약 15개월 후, 그는 Cassady로부터 또 한 통의 편지를 받고는 놀랐는데, 특히 그가 첫 번째 조언에 대해 그에게 감사를 표하지도 않았기 때문이었다. 그는 다시 Cassady의 격려에 따라 행동하였고, 이번에는 그것을 끝까지 고수해 명백히 큰 성공을 거뒀다.

글의 소재 만화가 Scott Adams의 성공에 얽힌 일화

주요 어휘 **creator** 창작자, 제작자, **comic strip** (신문·잡지의) 연재만화, **personal** 개인적인, **dramatically** 극적으로, **cartooning** 만화 제작, **rejection** 거절, **submit** 제출하다, **act on** ~에 따라 행동하다, **stick with** ~을 고수하다, **hit it big** 크게 성공하다

정답 ⑤

정답 해설 밑줄 친 ⑤는 Cassady를 가리키지만 나머지는 모두 Scott Adams를 가리킨다. 따라서 정답은 ⑤이다. ⑤가 속한 문장 'About fifteen months later, he was surprised to receive yet another letter from Cassady, especially since he hadn't thanked ⑤him for his original advice.'에서 since ~절의 주어 he는 주절의 주어와 같은 Scott Adams가 확실하다. 하지만 since ~절의 목적어 him은 he(Scott Adams)가 아닌 다른 인물이어야 한다. 왜냐하면 him이 주어 he와 같은 인물이라면 him이 아닌 himself를 써야 하기 때문이다. 그러므로 him은 Scott Adams가 아닌 Cassady를 가리킨다. 한 문장에서 주어와 목적어가 동일 인물이면 목적어는 반드시 일반 대명사가 아닌 재귀대명사를 써야 한다는 점 짚고 넘어가자.

13 밑줄 친 부분이 가리키는 대상이 나머지 넷과 다른 것은?

사관 기출문제 유형보기

Krause describes a memorable encounter with an elder of the Nez Perce tribe named Angus Wilson, who chided ①him one day: "You white people know nothing about music. But I'll teach you something about it if you want." The next morning, Krause found ②himself led to the bank of a stream in northeastern Oregon. He was motioned to sit quietly on the ground there. After a chilly wait, a breeze picked up, and suddenly ③his surroundings were filled with the sound of a pipe organ chord—a remarkable occurrence, since no instrument was in sight. Wilson brought ④him over to the water's edge and pointed to a group of reeds, broken at different lengths by wind and ice. "He took out his knife," Krause later recalled, "and cut one at the base, whittled some holes, brought the instrument to his lips and began to play a melody. When ⑤he stopped, he said, 'This is how we learned our music.'"

* whittle: 깎아서 모양을 만들다

[한번에 정리하는 문제 해설]

지문 해석 Krause는 Angus Wilson이라는 이름의 Nez Perce족 원로 한 명과의 인상적인 만남을 서술한다. 어느 날 Wilson이 그를 꾸짖으며 말했다. "당신네 백인들은 음악에 대해 아는 게 없어요. 하지만 당신이 원하면 내가 그것을 좀 가르쳐 주겠소." 다음 날 아침 Krause는 동북 오리건에 있는 한 개천의 제방 쪽으로 안내됐다. 땅 위에 조용히 앉아 있으라는 몸짓 신호가 그에게 전달됐다. 서늘한 기다림 후에 바람이 거세졌고 갑자기 그의 주변이 파이프 오르간 화음 소리로 가득 찼는데 이는 놀라운 일이었다. 어디에도 악기가 보이지 않았기 때문이다. Wilson은 그를 물가로 데리고 가서 바람과 얼음에 서로 다른 크기로 잘려 나간 한 무리의 갈대를 가리켰다. Krause가 나중에 회상하며 말했다. "그가 칼을 꺼냈어요. 그리고 (갈대) 하나의 밑동을 자르고 몇 개의 구멍을 내더니 그 악기를 입술에 대고 멜로디를 연주하기 시작했어요. 연주를 멈췄을 때 그가 말하더군요. '우리는 이런 식으로 음악을 공부했어요.'라고."

글의 소재 Angus Wilson과의 인상적인 만남

주요 어휘 describe 묘사하다, 기술하다, encounter 우연한 만남, chide 꾸짖다, motion 몸짓으로 신호하다, pick up (바람이) 거세지다, occurrence 사건, reed 갈대, recall 회상하다

구조 분석 Krause found himself led to the bank of a stream in northeastern Oregon.
→ himself가 목적어, led가 목적보어인 5형식 구문이다. Krause 자신이 이끈 것이 아니라 이끌렸기 때문에 수동의 의미가 있는 과거분사 led를 썼다.

정 답 ⑤

정답 해설 ①~④는 글의 필자인 Krause를 가리키지만 ⑤는 Angus Wilson을 가리킨다. 따라서 정답은 ⑤이다.

13 밑줄 친 ①~⑤ 중에서 의미하는 바가 나머지와 다른 것은?

It's really not that hard to build a flying car—the first working model got up in 1947. The real challenge turns out to be building ① <u>a flying car</u> that makes sense. Elon Musk, CEO of both Tesla and Space X, keeps getting asked why he can't mate his two companies and give birth to ② <u>a rocket car</u>. He answered in a series of recent tweets, including: "③ <u>Airborne auto</u> pros: travel in 3D fast. Cons: risk of car falling on head much greater than ④ <u>one moving in two vectors</u>." And Peter Thiel, the famous investor, goes around saying, "We wanted ⑤ <u>real sky cars</u>; instead we got junk."

[한번에 정리하는 문제 해설]

[지문 해석] 하늘을 나는 자동차를 만들기는 그리 어렵지 않아서 작동하는 최초의 모델은 1947년에 나왔다. 정작 어려운 것은 제대로 된 나는 차를 만드는 것이다. Tesla와 Space X 양사의 CEO인 Elon Musk는 왜 두 회사를 합쳐 로켓카를 만들어내지 못하느냐는 질문을 늘 받고 있다. 그는 최근 한 트윗을 통해 "하늘을 나는 차가 3D의 속도로 달리는 것은 찬성하지만 일반 차에 비해 추락 위험이 훨씬 큰 점은 반대한다."고 답했다. 또 유명한 투자가인 Peter Thiel는 "우린 진짜 스카이카를 바랐건만 정작 얻는 건 쓰레기뿐이다"라는 말을 하고 다닌다.

[글의 소재] 하늘을 나는 자동차

[주요 어휘] mate 짝짓다, airborne 공수(空輸)의, pros 찬성, cons 반대, vector 벡터, 방향량, go around saying ~라는 얘기를 하며 다니다

[정 답] ④

[정답 해설] ④는 기존의 자동차를 가리키고 나머지는 하늘을 나는 차를 가리킨다. 3차원(3G)이 아닌 양방향으로만(two vectors) 움직이니까 일반 차임을 알 수 있다. 또 ④가 속한 문장에서 하늘을 나는 차의 추락 위험이 ④보다 훨씬 크다고 했다. ④는 나는 차의 비교 대상이므로 '나는 차' 자신일 수 없다. 비교급 문장에는 정답을 포함한 상반된 두 지칭 대상이 모두 나올 수 있기 때문에 항상 유심히 살펴봐야 한다.

63 밑줄 친 (a)~(e) 중에서 가리키는 대상이 나머지와 <u>다른</u> 하나는? 난이도 중

Throughout her career, Isadora Duncan did not like the commercial aspects of public performance, regarding touring, contracts, and other practicalities as distractions from (a) <u>her</u> real mission: the creation of beauty and the education of the young. (b) <u>A gifted if unconventional pedagogue</u>, she was the founder of three schools dedicated to inculcating her philosophy into groups of young girls (a brief effort to include boys was unsuccessful). The first, in Grunewald, Germany, gave rise to her most celebrated group of pupils, dubbed "the Isadorables," who took her surname and subsequently performed both with (c) <u>Duncan</u> and independently. The second had a short-lived existence prior to World War I at a chateau outside Paris, while the third was part of Duncan's tumultuous experiences in Moscow in the wake of the Russian Revolution. Duncan's teaching and her pupils caused (d) <u>her</u> both pride and anguish. Her sister, Elizabeth Duncan, took over the German school and adapted it to the Teutonic philosophy of (e) <u>her</u> German husband. The Isadorables were subject to ongoing hectoring from Duncan over their willingness to perform commercially, and one, Lisa Duncan, was permanently ostracized for performing in nightclubs.

* hector 괴롭히다

① (a)
② (b)
③ (c)
④ (d)
⑤ (e)

다음 글을 읽고 밑줄 친 the procedure가 가리키는 것은?   난이도 중

Today it is English, rather than any created alternative, that is the world's auxiliary tongue. There are more people who use English as a second language than there are native speakers. Estimates of the numbers vary, but even the most guarded view is that English has 500 million second-language speakers. Far more of the world's citizens are eagerly jumping on board than trying to resist its progress. In some cases the devotion appears religious and can involve what to outsiders looks a lot like self-mortification. According to Mark Abley, some rich Koreans pay for their children to have an operation that lengthens the tongue because it helps them speak English convincingly. The suggestion is that it enables them to produce r and l sounds, although the evidence of the many proficient English-speakers among Korean immigrants in America and Britain makes one wonder whether the procedure is either necessary or useful. Still, it is a powerful example of the lengths people will go to in order to learn English, seduced by the belief that linguistic capital equals economic capital.

① having an operation that lengthens the tongue
② studying English in America or Britain
③ inviting English language tutors to their home
④ enabling them to produce r and l sounds
⑤ paying heavily for private education

65

밑줄 친 (a)~(e)에서 가리키는 대상이 같은 것끼리 올바르게 짝지은 것은? `난이도 중`

In January 1911, Churchill showed his tougher side when he made a controversial visit to a police siege in London, with (a) <u>two robbers</u> holed up in a building. Churchill's degree of participation is still in some dispute: Some accounts have him going to the scene only to see for himself what was going on; others state that he allegedly gave directions to police on how to best storm the building and get (b) <u>the targets</u>. What is known is that the house caught fire during the siege and Churchill prevented the (c) <u>fire fighters</u> from extinguishing the flames, stating that he thought it better to "let the house burn down," rather than risk (d) <u>lives</u> rescuing (e) <u>the occupants</u>. The bodies of the two robbers were found inside the charred ruins.

① {(a), (b), (d)}　　　　　　　{(c), (e)}
② {(a), (b), (e)}　　　　　　　{(c), (d)}
③ {(b), (c), (e)}　　　　　　　{(a), (d)}
④ {(b), (c), (d)}　　　　　　　{(a), (e)}
⑤ {(c), (d), (e)}　　　　　　　{(a), (b)}

밑줄 친 (a)~(e)에서 지칭하는 대상이 나머지 넷과 <u>다른</u> 것은?　　난이도 중

The morning after the Battle of Fredericksburg, the ground before the stone wall at the base of Marye's Heights was covered with (a) <u>wounded and dying Northerners</u>. Hours passed by as soldiers from both sides listened to the cries for water and pleas for help. Finally, Richard Kirkland, a young Confederate sergeant, could bear it no more. He approached his commanding officer, Brigadier General Joseph Kershaw, and said, "General, I can't stand this."

"What's the matter, Sergeant?" asked the general.

"All day I have heard (b) <u>those poor people</u> crying for water, and I can stand it no longer," Kirkland replied. "I come to ask permission to go and give (c) <u>them</u> water."

"Kirkland, don't you know that you would get a bullet through your head the moment you stepped over the wall?" responded the general.

"Yes," said the sergeant. "I know that I may, but if you will let me, I am willing to try it."

The general was moved by Kirkland's request and allowed him to go. However, he refused to allow him to carry a white flag of truce that would have ensured his safety. Despite the danger, Kirkland ventured over the wall, bringing with him as many canteens of water as he could carry. Under Northern fire, he reached the nearest sufferer and gave him water. As soon as (d) <u>they</u> understood his intent, the enemy ceased fire, and for an hour and a half Kirkland tended (e) <u>the wounded</u> unharmed.

① (a)

② (b)

③ (c)

④ (d)

⑤ (e)

67

밑줄 친 (a)~(e)에서 가리키는 대상이 같은 것끼리 올바르게 짝지은 것은?　난이도 중

　　The simplest cases of migration by attraction are those of a people living on poor steppes or plateaus adjoining cultivated land or rich valleys. (a) <u>Agricultural peoples</u> are, as a rule, averse to and ill-prepared for war. The more prosperous their circumstances, the more (b) <u>they</u> are likely to be enervated by their very civilization. They are thus liable at all times to be attacked by (c) <u>neighboring brigands</u>, who in some cases retire to their barren homes with their booty, but in others remain among the conquered people, and, becoming assimilated with (d) <u>them</u>, in due course become more civilized, and in their turn are subject to invasions from (e) <u>their</u> barbarian kinsmen of the borders. Thus is set up an automatic social mechanism which at the same time civilizes the barbarians and invigorate those who have become softened by easy circumstances.

* brigand 산적

① {(a), (b), (c)} 　　　　　　　　　　{(d), (e)}
② {(a), (b), (d)} 　　　　　　　　　　{(c), (e)}
③ {(a), (c), (e)} 　　　　　　　　　　{(b), (d)}
④ {(b), (c), (d)} 　　　　　　　　　　{(a), (e)}
⑤ {(b), (c), (e)} 　　　　　　　　　　{(a), (d)}

8

빈칸 추론

글의 흐름을 파악해 빈칸에 들어갈
최적의 단어, 구, 또는
문장을 추론하는 유형이다.

가이드라인

▶ 빈칸이 있는 문장은 지문에서 정보 가치가 가장 높은 문장, 즉 주제문이거나 주제문과 밀접한 관련이 있는 문장이다.

▶ 빈칸의 단서는 십중팔구 지문 안에 숨어있다. 빈칸 추론은 말처럼 빈칸의 내용을 추론하는 것이 아니라 지문 어디엔가 있을 빈칸의 단서를 찾는 정보 찾기의 콘셉트로 접근해야 한다. 빈칸 추론은 정보 찾기 게임이다.

▶ 빈칸 앞뒤 문장은 빈칸의 단서가 숨어있을 수 있는 매우 중요한 문장이므로 집중적으로 읽어 내용을 완전히 파악하도록 해야 한다. 멀리서 찾지 마라. 문제 해결의 열쇠는 가까운 곳에 있다.

▶ 빈칸 문장 안에 부정적 표현(no, not, difficult, hard, undesirable, unthinkable 등)이 포함돼 있을 때 빈칸에는 정반대 내용이 들어가야 함을 명심하고 함정에 빠지지 말아야 한다.

▶ 빈칸 앞뒤 문장과의 연결 관계도 중요하다. 가령, 빈칸 문장과 앞뒤 문장이 역접의 연결사로 연결돼 있으면 빈칸에 상반된 내용이 와야 하고, 첨가나 강조의 연결사와 연결돼 있으면 이 빈칸에는 기본적으로 비슷한 내용이 와야 한다.

▶ 빈칸에 들어갈 문구는 출제자의 창작이 아닌 원저자가 쓴 텍스트의 일부다. 따라서 늘어지는 만연체보다 짧고 간결한 '영어스러운' 표현일수록 정답일 가능성이 크다.

▶ 시간 부족 등의 이유로 선택지만으로 답을 추론해야 할 때는 주제나 요지의 경우처럼 일단 선택지를 특정 가치를 기준으로 긍정(+)과 부정(-)으로 분류한 다음에 정답 후보를 좁혀나가는 '±전략'이 유효하다.

34 다음 빈칸에 들어갈 말로 가장 적절한 것을 고르시오

Successful integration of an educational technology is marked by that technology being regarded by users as an unobtrusive facilitator of learning, instruction, or performance. When the focus shifts from the technology being used to the educational purpose that technology serves, then that technology is becoming a comfortable and trusted element, and can be regarded as being successfully integrated. Few people give a second thought to the use of a ball-point pen although the mechanisms involved vary—some use a twist mechanism and some use a push button on top, and there are other variations as well. Personal computers have reached a similar level of familiarity for a great many users, but certainly not for all. New and emerging technologies often introduce both fascination and frustration with users. As long as ＿＿＿＿＿＿＿＿＿＿＿＿ in promoting learning, instruction, or performance, then one ought not to conclude that the technology has been successfully integrated— at least for that user. [3점]

* unobtrusive 눈에 띄지 않는

① the user successfully achieves familiarity with the technology
② the user's focus is on the technology itself rather than its use
③ the user continues to employ outdated educational techniques
④ the user involuntarily gets used to the misuse of the technology
⑤ the user's preference for interaction with other users persists

[한번에 정리하는 문제 해설]

지문 해석 교육적 기술의 성공적인 통합의 특징은 그 기술이 사용자들에 의해 학습과 교수, 수행의 눈에 띄지 않는 조력자로 여겨진다는 것이다. 초점이, 사용되는 기술에서 그 기술이 소용되는 교육적 목적으로 이동할 때 그 기술은 편안하고 신뢰받는 요소가 되고 성공적으로 통합된 것으로 간주될 수 있다. (볼펜과) 관련된 작동법이 다양함에도 불구하고 — 어떤 것들은 비트는 작동법을 사용하고 어떤 것은 위에서 내리누르는 작동법 그리고 기타 여러 가지 작동법이 있다. — 볼펜의 사용법을 신경 쓰는 사람은 거의 없다. 개인용 컴퓨터는 많은 사용자들에게 비슷한 정도로 친숙해졌지만 모두에게 그러한 것은 아니다. 새로운 기술들이 종종 사용자들에게 매력과 좌절을 동시에 가져다준다. 사용자의 초점이 용도보다는 기술 자체에 머물러 있는 한 우리는 — 적어도 사용자에게는 — 기술이 성공적으로 통합됐다고 결론 내려서는 안 된다.
① 사용자가 성공적으로 기술에 익숙해지는 한
② 사용자의 초점이 용도보다는 기술 자체에 머물러 있는 한
③ 사용자가 계속 낡은 교수 테크닉을 사용하는 한
④ 사용자가 자기도 모르게 기술 오용에 익숙해지는 한
⑤ 사용자의 다른 사용자와의 교류 선호가 계속되는 한

글의 소재 기술의 교육적 통합

주요 어휘 integration 통합, unobtrusive 눈에 띄지 않는, facilitator 촉진시키는 사람, 조력자, fascination, 매혹 매력, frustration 좌절

정답 ②

정답 해설 이 글은 기술이 어떻게 교육 목적에 부합할 수 있는지, 즉 기술의 교육적 통합을 설명한 글이다. 두 번째 문장에서 초점이 기술에서 그 기술이 봉사하는 교육적 목적, 즉 용도로 이동할 때 그 기술이 신뢰를 얻고 제대로 '통합'됐다고 주장하고 있고, 빈칸 문장에서는 어떤 경우에(빈칸) 기술이 통합됐다고 결론 내려서는 안 된다고 주장하므로 빈칸에는 기술이 용도로 전환이 이뤄지지 않는다는 내용이 들어가야 한다. 따라서 정답은 ② '사용자의 초점이 용도보다는 기술 자체에 머물러 있는 한'이 적절하다.

118 Chapter Ⅲ

27 다음 글을 읽고, 빈칸에 들어갈 말로 가장 적절한 것을 고르시오.

   In its ordinary, normal state, the information-processing system that constitutes consciousness does not focus on any particular range of stimuli. Like a radar dish, attention sweeps back and forth across the stimulus field, noting movements, colors, shapes, objects, sensations, memories, one after the other in no particular order or pattern. This is what happens when we walk down a street, when we lie awake in bed, when we stare out a window—in short, whenever attention is not focused in an orderly sequence. One thought follows another without rhyme or reason, and usually we cannot link one idea to the other in a sensible chain. As soon as a new thought presents itself, it pushes out the one that was there before. Knowing what is in the mind at any given time does not predict what will be there a few seconds later. This _____ of consciousness, although it produces unpredictable information, is the probable state of consciousness. It is probable because that is the state to which consciousness reverts as soon as there are no demands on it. [3점]

① random shift
② strict inflexibility
③ orderly repetition
④ reliable consistency
⑤ constant irreversibility

[한번에 정리하는 문제 해설]

지문 해석 일반적인 정상 상태에서 의식을 구성하는 정보처리시스템은 특정 자극원에 초점을 맞추지 않는다. 레이다 원반처럼 주의력은 특정한 순서나 패턴 없이 차례로 동작이나 색깔, 형태, 물체, 감각, 기억 등에 주목하면서 자극 장을 왔다 갔다 한다. 이것은 우리가 길거리를 걸을 때, 깬 상태로 침대 위에 누워있거나 창밖을 응시할 때, 요컨대 주의력이 질서정연하게 초점이 맞춰지지 않을 때 일어나는 일이다. 아무 이유 없이 한 생각이 다른 생각에 연이어 일어나고, 하나의 생각과 다른 생각을 어떤 합리적인 사슬로도 묶을 수 없다. 새로운 생각이 나타나자마자 그것은 전에 그 자리에 있던 생각을 밀어낸다. 특정 시간에 무슨 생각을 하는지 안다고 해서 몇 초 후에 어떤 생각을 할지 예측할 수 없다. 비록 그것이 예측하지 못한 정보를 만들어내지만 이러한 의식 변화의 임의성은 의식의 개연성 있는 상태다. 개연성이 있다 함은 변화의 임의성이 그에 대한 요구가 사라지자마자 의식이 되돌아가는 상태이기 때문이다.

① 임의의 변화   ② 엄격한 불변성
③ 질서 있는 반복   ④ 신뢰할 만한 일관성
⑤ 끊임없는 비가역성

글의 소재 의식 변화의 임의성

주요 어휘 constitute ~를 구성하다, sensation 감각, sequence 순서, without rhyme or reason 아무 이유 없이, sensible 지각 있는, 합리적인, probable 개연성이 있는, revert 되돌아가다

정 답 ①

정답 해설 빈칸 앞에 지시대명사 This가 쓰였으므로 앞의 내용으로 빈칸의 내용을 추론할 수 있다. 빈칸 앞의 두 문장에서 '새로운 생각이 일어나면 그 자리에 있던 생각을 밀어내고, 특정 시간에 어떤 생각을 하는지 안다고 해서 몇 초 후에 어떤 생각을 할지 예측할 수 없다'라고 했는데, 이런 것은 모두 우리의 의식이 정해진 순서나 패턴 없이 임의로 무작위하게 변하는 것을 의미한다. 그러므로 빈칸에는 ①의 '임의의 변화'가 적절하다. 또 변화라는 가치를 +라 보면 ①을 제외한 나머지 선지는 모두 −이기 때문에 ±전략으로 봐도 정답은 ①이다.

경찰 기출문제 유형보기

For a threat to be effectual, its utterer must have the means to carry it out and want the addressee to act otherwise than would be the case without the prompting of the utterance. Then, once a speaker is seen by the target to be in such a position of power, any utterance forecasting ＿＿＿＿＿＿＿, even if not framed explicitly as involving the utterer's own behavior, can be reasonably understood as a threat. This is how we make sense of remarks that contain no overtly threatening material. For example, when a Mafia boss in a movie says, "Tonight you sleep with the fishes," it is not taken as an invitation to sleep over at the speaker's house in the room with the aquarium, but as a chilling message of imminent doom.

[3점]

① a cordial invitation to an aquarium
② explicit withdrawal of a future action
③ the maintenance of the present status
④ an unspoken agreement of cooperation
⑤ negative consequences to the addressee

[한번에 정리하는 문제 해설]

지문 해석 위협이 효과적이기 위해서는 그것을 말하는 사람이 위협을 실천할 수단이 있어야 하고, 위협이 대상이 위협의 촉발이 없었더라면 사실이었을 것과 다른 행동을 보이기를 원해야 한다(위협으로 상대가 행동의 변화를 보이기를 원해야 한다). 그때 일단 화자가 그런 힘 있는 위치에 있는 것으로 상대에게 보이면 상대에 대한 부정적 결과를 짐작하게 하는 어떤 말도 당연히 위협으로 이해될 수 있다. 비록 그것이 말하는 사람 자신의 행동에 관련된 것으로 명시적으로 표현되지 않는다고 하더라고 말이다. 이런 식으로 우리는 공공연하게 위협적인 요소를 지니지 않은 말들을 이해할 수 있다. 예를 들어 영화에서 마피아 보스가 "너 오늘 밤 물고기와 잠 자"라는 말을 하면 그것은 화자의 집의 수족관 있는 방에서 자자는 초대가 아닌, 다가올 불운에 대한 으스스한 메시지로 받아들여진다.

① 진심어린 수족관으로의 초대
② 미래의 행동을 드러내고 철회함
③ 현재의 상태 유지
④ 협력에 대한 암묵적 합의
⑤ 상대에 대한 부정적 결과

글의 소재 위협이 효과적이기 위한 요건

주요 어휘 effectual 효과적인, utterer 말하는 이, 언표자, addressee 말을 듣는 이, 대화 상대자, prompt 촉발하다, 자극하다, utterance 말, 언설, 언표, consequence 결과, frame 틀에 넣다, 표현하다, make sense of ~를 이해하다, explicitly 명시적으로, overtly 공공연하게, 공개적으로, aquarium 수족관, imminent 임박한

정 답 ⑤

정답 해설 이 문제는 누가 어떤 위협을 느낄 때 그것은 다가올 무엇(빈칸) 때문이냐를 묻는 문제이다. 위협은 당연히 부정적이기 때문에 빈칸에 들어갈 내용은 부정적이어야 하고 이에 해당하는 선택지는 ⑤의 '상대에 대한 부정적 결과'뿐이다. 따라서 정답은 ⑤이다. 마지막 문장에서 마피아 보스가 하는 말이 단순히 수족관이 있는 화자의 집에서 자자는 초대가 아닌, 다가올 불운에 대한 으스스한 메시지, 즉 매우 부정적인 메시지로 받아들여진다고 했으므로 여기서 단서를 얻을 수 있다.

| 해설 398쪽 |

68

다음 글을 읽고 빈칸에 가장 적절한 것은?   난이도 중

The Freudian psychology is the only systematic account of the human mind which, in point of subtlety and complexity, of interest and tragic power, deserves to stand beside the chaotic mass of psychological insights which literature has accumulated through the centuries. To pass from the reading of a great literary work to a treatise of academic psychology is to pass from one order of perception to another, but the human nature of the Freudian psychology is exactly the stuff upon which the poet has always exercised his art. It is therefore not surprising that the psychoanalytical theory has had a great effect upon literature. Yet the relationship is reciprocal, and the effect of Freud upon literature has been no greater than the effect of literature upon Freud. When, on the occasion of the celebration of his seventieth birthday, Freud was greeted as 'the discoverer of the unconscious,' he corrected the speaker and _____ the title. "The poets and philosophers before me discovered the unconscious," he said. "What I discovered was the scientific method by which the unconscious can be studied."

① ostracized
② disclaimed
③ embraced
④ cherished
⑤ disowned

다음 빈칸에 들어갈 말로 가장 적절한 것을 고르시오. 난이도 중

Neuroscientists have found that the wiring of the neo-cortex is amazingly "plastic", meaning it can change and rewire itself depending on the type of inputs flowing into it. For example, newborn ferret brains can be surgically rewired so that the animals' eyes send their signals to the areas of cortex where hearing normally develops. The surprising result is that the ferrets develop functioning visual pathways in the auditory portions of their brains. In other words, they see with brain tissue that normally hears sounds. Similar experiments have been done with other senses and brain regions. For instance, pieces of rat visual cortex can be transplanted around the time of birth to regions where the sense of touch is usually represented. As the rat matures, the transplanted tissue processes touch rather than vision. Cells were not born to _____ in vision or touch or hearing.

① interfere
② specialize
③ abound
④ reside
⑤ indulge

70

다음 빈칸에 들어갈 말로 가장 적절한 것을 고르시오. [난이도 중]

From our most low-level sensory processes to our treatment of other human beings, _____ is one of the basic activities of human brains. Temporal coincidence or spatial proximity can be enough, as many visual illusions show. If we hear a sound about the time we see an object, we assume that the object is making the sound unless we have learned otherwise. We cluster, we classify, and over the course of a lifetime we acquire innumerable category concepts. We use these to speed up our interpretations of the world. If I can judge a novel object to be a member of the category 'cat,' I immediately have access to all sorts of stored information about the new object ('eats meat,' 'may scratch,' 'could not comfortably be swung in my kitchen') without having to work it out anew. This gives me considerable savings in time and energy, and a definite survival edge.

① interpreting surroundings
② discerning objects
③ enumerating details
④ separating specifics
⑤ grouping things

다음 글을 읽고 빈칸에 들어갈 가장 적절한 말은?

난이도 중

Over the years, I've heard lots of complaints from laid off workers who never saw it coming and then are bitter when they are tossed aside because they're apparently no longer getting the job done. They point to a series of glowing annual performance reviews and then suddenly being called into the boss's office to be let go. People aren't usually resentful if they're laid off because the company is suddenly facing a crisis not of their own making (which isn't usually the case). However, what drives people up the wall is when it's clear that the boss has been bothered by some aspect of their performance, but never bothered to mention it to them until the time of their firing. "_____ would have been nice so I could have tried to improve in that area," said one person I know who went through this experience.

① A pink slip
② A kinder guideline
③ A little heads up
④ A contract renewal
⑤ A detailed disclaimer

72

다음 빈칸에 들어갈 말로 가장 적절한 것을 고르시오.

난이도 중

Comparative research between and among species is crucial to understanding the breadth and subtlety of the cognitive mechanisms involved in cooperative behavior. Brian Hare's work, for example, shows that we cannot make generalizations even about primate cooperation because of the lack of _____. Hare compared bonobos and chimpanzees engaged in the same cooperative task. When given a plate of food, a pair of bonobos will react by playing with each other; they tend to share the fruit. A pair of chimpanzees will usually not share, and will avoid contact with each other. In a collaborative task where a team of two had to pull ropes to retrieve a plate of fruit, both the chimpanzee and the bonobo team worked together if the food was cut into small pieces that could be shared. But when the fruit was presented in large pieces, the chimpanzees cooperated less often, and when they did work together, one animal would try to monopolize the reward. This reminds us, again, that behavior will be species-specific.

① a sense of sharing between primate peers
② consistent primate patterns in social living
③ adequate cooperative networks among primates
④ empathic relationship among primates in times of challenges
⑤ communication between primate peers in cooperative settings

73 다음 글을 읽고 빈칸에 들어갈 가장 적절한 말은?

 난이도 중

Designer's move to the business mainstream has sparked a broad debate about who designers are and what they do. Silicon Valley design guru John Maeda distinguishes between three categories: "classical" designers, who create physical objects or products for a specific group of people; "commercial" designers who innovate by seeking deep insights into how customers interact with products and services; and "computational" designers, who use programming skills and data to satisfy millions or even billions of users instantaneously. What's noteworthy is that _____. Classically trained designers are apt to look askance at the artistic abilities of designers from the other groups. Commercial designers question how computational designers can empathize with millions of people they've never met. Computational designers complain that the methods of the other two groups can't be scaled. But many believe that, in the future, the most valuable designers will be those who combine skills and perspectives from all three categories.

① the camps always try to complement each other
② the camps are indifferent to each other
③ the camps are mostly in a cooperative mood
④ the camps don't always get along
⑤ the camps seldom collide head-on.

74 다음 글을 읽고 빈칸에 들어갈 가장 적절한 말은? 난이도 중

One of the strongest pushes from the shape-changing propagandists is the phrase 'body sculpting', heavy exercise of the kind that gives people the characteristic, unnatural body-builder look. If you concentrate on one or a few muscles, and work only on them, you will get a bigger, more defined muscle. That's why skaters develop bigger thighs and weightlifters bigger arms. Going the other way—making an area smaller by losing weight only from one specific area—is virtually undocumented. Remember, doctors disagree on exactly how many body types there are. But look around: there are as many as there are people. Or at least 837. The one thing almost all of the people who say you can change your shape have in common is that _____. Unless they are money-driven, they have no reason to elaborate on something unattainable.

① they are trying to preach to you about something.

② they are trying to sell you something.

③ they are trying to talk you into exercising more.

④ they are trying to warn you about something.

⑤ they are trying to say selective weight loss is a virtual impossibility.

글의 흐름으로 보아 빈칸에 들어갈 가장 적절한 말은? 난이도 중

Amazon has flourished by innovating relentlessly and expanding omnivorously. The retail and tech giant has recently announced that it will be entering the dominion of health care. Word that Amazon was entering health care immediately depressed the value of old-school health-insurance companies. Anyone who has been a customer of either knows why. The health care system in the US is the antithesis of Silicon Valley. Grossly inefficient and user-unfriendly, it may be the least transparent enterprise outside the Kremlin—and just as awash in money. The $3.3 trillion that Americans spent on health care in 2016 was close to Germany's entire GDP that year. It accounted for an astounding 18 % of the US gross domestic product—twice the share other developed countries typically spend on health—and produced a return on investment that would get any CEO fired, as is clearly shown by the fact that _____.

① 2016 saw countless heath care chains close across the US
② life expectancy in the US is actually going down
③ investors in health care stocks have suffered huge losses
④ living standards of Americans have plunged dramatically
⑤ Americans' health index has been improving remarkably

76 다음 빈칸에 들어갈 말로 가장 적절한 것을 고르시오.   난이도 중

All the new media have this in common: they _____. These form the framework of our present human existence. Through space, we perceive all things that are outside ourselves, and through time, both things outside ourselves and those within. The way we see things, other people, and ourselves depends greatly on this link. So do our will, our feelings, and emotions that may be present or absent, stronger or weaker according to the distance and time that separate us from their objects. Overall, the new media shrink the space and time that separate us from people and things. We can place them, hear them, and see them immediately wherever they may be in the world. In a certain fashion, partly virtual, partly real, we can meet them without having to travel any distance with the various constraints that involves, and without having to wait.

① alter profoundly our relationships with space and time
② help us establish basic concepts involving space and time
③ move towards imposing severe constraints on time and space
④ reinforce the roles of space and time in our perceptual learning
⑤ cause our spatial and temporal perceptions to solidify indefinitely

다음 글의 빈칸 (A), (B)에 들어갈 가장 적절한 말로 짝지은 것은?   난이도 중

Some forensic experts argue there might be a relationship between mass shootings and shooters' domestic abuse. Their arguments are underscored by a host of recent massacres, including the one committed by Omar Mateen, who killed 49 people in the Pulse nightclub shooting in Orlando. Mateen is known to have abused his ex-wife. But in scientific terms, the link remains anecdotal. Just because mass shooters are often abusers doesn't mean abusers are more likely to be mass shooters. That's why the red flags appear only ____(A)____: researchers lack sufficient evidence to prove the connection ____(B)____. Susan Sorenson, a professor at the University of Pennsylvania, says, "Right now, we don't have enough data to have a pattern."

	(A)	(B)
①	in hindsight	ahead of time
②	ahead of time	in hindsight
③	in hindsight	afterwards
④	ahead of time	afterwards
⑤	in hindsight	in no time

78

난이도 중

In economics, scarcity is ubiquitous. All of us have a limited amount of money; even the richest people cannot buy everything. But we suggest that while physical scarcity is ubiquitous, the feeling of scarcity is not. Imagine a day at work where your calendar is sprinkled with a few meetings and your to-do list is manageable. You spend the unscheduled time by lingering at lunch or at a meeting or calling a colleague to catch up. Now, imagine another day at work where your calendar is chock-full of meetings. What little free time you have must be sunk into a project that is overdue. In both cases time was physically scarce. You had the same number of hours at work and you had more than enough activities to fill them. Yet in one case you were acutely aware of scarcity, of the finiteness of time; in the other it was a distant reality, if you felt it at all. The feeling of scarcity _____ _____.

① is distinct from its physical reality
② accurately reflects its numerical value
③ leaves one worried about unfulfilled duties
④ causes one to suffer from relative poverty
⑤ is proportional to what it measures physically

다음 빈칸에 들어갈 말로 가장 적절한 것을 고르시오.

Big data creates new opportunities to understand the world around us, but it also creates new scientific challenges. One major challenge is that big data does not fit too well into what we typically think of as the scientific method. Scientists like to confirm specific hypotheses, and to gradually assemble what they have learned into causal stories and eventually mathematical theories. Blunder about in any reasonably interesting big dataset and you will inevitably make discoveries—say, a correlation between rates of high-seas piracy and atmospheric temperature. This kind of exploratory research is sometimes called "hypothesis free," since you never know what you'll find. But big data is much less incisive when it comes to _____. Do pirates bring about global warming? Does hot weather make more people take up high-seas piracy? And if the two are unrelated, then why are they both increasing in recent years? Big data often leaves us guessing.

* incisive 예리한

① identifying possible relationship between piracy and global warming
② distinguishing between hypotheses and proven facts
③ predicting the future based on what's happened in the past
④ detecting possible correlations between two random variables
⑤ explaining these correlations in terms of cause and effect

80

다음 빈칸에 들어갈 말로 가장 적절한 것을 고르시오.

난이도 중

_____ influences our judgement concerning the frequency of related events and, more importantly, their significance. In one study, subjects were given a list of six words and told that these words described a person. They were asked to provide a more detailed description of what this person was like, given the six words they'd already been given. All subjects received the same set of words, but the order of the words was reversed for half the subjects. One group was told that the person was intelligent, industrious, impulsive, critical, stubborn and envious; the remaining subjects were told the person was envious, stubborn, critical, impulsive, industrious and intelligent. Those subjects who had received the list with the more positive adjectives at the beginning of the list offered considerably rosier descriptions. One plausible explanation offered for these results is that whichever words appeared earliest in the list, being so available to the subject, shaped their attitude towards those words that appeared later in the list.

① When certain impressions are created
② How certain habits are formed
③ The ease with which certain ideas come to mind
④ Prejudice against or in favor of others
⑤ The speed at which certain beliefs are shared

다음 빈칸에 들어갈 말로 가장 적절한 것을 고르시오.

Learning consists in adapting our thought schemas to new information from the real world. According to Piaget, this adaptation can occur in either of two ways: assimilation or accommodation. Assimilation consists in interpreting new events in light of pre-existing thought schemas. For example, a baby knows how to grab her favorite rattle with the fingers of one hand, then throw it to hear it make a noise. When she comes across a new object, such as her father's delicate watch, she has no trouble in transferring this motor schema that she already knows to this new object and sending it flying to the ground. Accommodation is the opposite process: altering one's internal cognitive structures to incorporate a new object or phenomenon. Suppose this same baby now encounters a beach ball. At first, she'll try to grab it with one hand, the way she does her rattle. But very quickly, she'll realize that this doesn't work, and eventually she will discover

_____.

① when to give up making further attempts
② how to insist on using one hand
③ how to dodge the ball altogether
④ how to hold the ball with both hands
⑤ how to throw the ball single-handedly

82

다음 빈칸에 들어갈 말로 가장 적절한 것을 고르시오.

난이도 중

Almost every human behavior, from shopping to marriage to expressions of feelings, is learned. In Canada, for example, people tend to view marriage as a choice between two people based on mutual feelings of love. In other nations and in other times, marriages have been arranged through an intricate process of interviews and negotiations between entire families, or in other cases, through a direct system such as a mail-order bride. To someone raised in Winnipeg, Canada, the marriage customs of a family from Nigeria may seem strange or even wrong. Conversely, someone from a traditional Nigerian family might be perplexed with the idea of romantic love as the foundation for the lifelong commitment of marriage. In other words, the way in which people view marriage depends largely on what they have been taught. Being familiar with these written and unwritten rules of culture helps people feel secure and "normal." Most people want to live their daily lives confident that their behaviors will not be challenged or disrupted. Behavior based on learned customs is, therefore, not a bad thing, but it does raise the problem of _____.

① how to deal with cultural integration
② how to seek cultural unity through globalization
③ how to preserve local indigenous culture
④ how to prevent cultural polarization
⑤ how to respond to cultural differences

다음 빈칸에 들어갈 말로 가장 적절한 것을 고르시오.

난이도 중

The aim of this book, *Fifty Key Thinkers on History*, is to provide an introduction to the beliefs and assumptions held by a variety of thinkers on history. It is not a canonical 'top fifty' of all-time greats on the basis of popularity. Many of the thinkers I have chosen would certainly make it onto such a list (for example, Gibbon, Ranke, Thucydides), but the inclusion of others will likely come as a surprise. Nor is it a collection of exemplary thinkers that I expect readers to revere or imitate. My choice of thinkers would make it impossible for anyone to do so. For example, try reconciling the views of Niall Ferguson and Emmanuel Le Roy Ladurie, or even those of G. W. F. Hegel and William H. McNeill. Moreover, in my view one of the hallmarks of a 'key thinker' is someone whose thought has come to be widely regarded in the historical community as a challenge to be reckoned with. Thus, for me, *Fifty Key Thinkers on History* is
_____ .

*canonical 정전의, 표준적인

① as much about provocation as it is about suggestion
② an approach to rediscover hidden history makers
③ an attempt to reconcile conflicting views on history
④ an effort to employ conventional scholastic methods
⑤ a scheme designed to exclude historical extremists

84 다음 빈칸에 들어갈 말로 가장 적절한 것을 고르시오. 난이도 중

Something either exists or it does not exist; there is no halfway point between the two. The lamp sitting on my desk is either really there or it is not. There is no other possibility. We might ask: How about becoming? Isn't the state of becoming between those of being and nonbeing? The answer is no. There is no such thing as just becoming; there are only things that become. The state of becoming is already within the realm of existence. A lamp in the process of being made is not yet a lamp; however, the parts that will go to compose it actually exist, and the lamp's "becoming" depends entirely on their existence. There is then, no becoming in the absolute sense, no transition from nonbeing to being. Elaine, who is becoming everyday a more accomplished musician because of assiduous practice, could not be becoming a musician if she were not already Elaine. There is no becoming with respect to the very existence of a human person. Elaine is "becoming" relatively, not absolutely: She is not becoming Elaine; she is becoming Elaine the more accomplished musician. Again the basic idea behind the principle of excluded middle is that there are no gaps in being. What we call "becoming" is not a passage from nonbeing to being, but a(n) _____ in a thing or in things already in existence.

① alteration
② regression
③ fixation
④ leap
⑤ integration

다음 글의 빈칸에 들어갈 말로 가장 적절한 것을 고르시오.

For decades, we have been measuring intelligence at the individual level, just as we have been measuring creativity, engagement, and grit. But it turns out we were failing to measure something with far greater impact. Researchers from MIT, Union College and Carnegie Mellon have finally found a method for systematically measuring the intelligence of a group as opposed to an individual. Just as we evaluate how successful an individual will be at solving a problem, we are now able to predict how successful a group of people will be at solving a problem or problems. It would be easy to assume that if you put a group of high-IQ people together, naturally they would exhibit a high collective intelligence. But that's not what happens. Indeed, their research found that a team on which each person was merely average in their individual abilities but possessed a collective intelligence would continually exhibit higher success rates than a team of individual geniuses. The researchers concluded that "the general collective intelligence factor that explains the group's performance on a wide variety of tasks" was "a property of the group itself, not just the individuals in it. In other words, _____.

① the whole is greater than the sum of its parts
② the part matters only when it constitutes the whole
③ the part and the whole should be viewed separately
④ individual talents take precedence over collective intelligence
⑤ individuals sometimes outperform the group in problem solving

86 다음 빈칸에 들어갈 말로 가장 적절한 것을 고르시오.   난이도 중

When an object is scaled up in size, its volumes increase at a much faster rate than its areas. For example, if you double the dimensions of every length in your house keeping its shape the same, then its volume increases by a factor of $2^3 = 8$ while its floor area increases by only a factor of $2^2 = 4$. This has huge implications for the design and functionality of much of the world around us, whether it's the buildings we live in or the structure of the animals and plants of the natural world. For instance, most heating, cooling, and lighting is proportional to the corresponding surface areas of the heaters, air conditioners, and windows. Their effectiveness therefore increases much more slowly than the volume of living space needed to be heated, cooled or lit, so these need to be disproportionately increased in size when a building is scaled up. Similarly, for large animals, the need to dissipate heat generated by their metabolism and physical activity can become problematic because the surface area through which it is dissipated is proportionately much smaller relative to their volume than for smaller ones. Elephants, for example, have solved this challenge by evolving disproportionately large ears _____.

① to better listen to what's happening in their vicinity
② to use as fans to keep flies and other harmful insects away
③ to spread out wide in an attempt to scare off potential threats
④ to significantly increase their surface area so as to dissipate heat
⑤ to show off to their peers by looking even bigger than they really are

87

다음 글의 빈칸에 들어갈 말로 가장 적절한 것은?

Edgar Allan Poe must have understood _____. In one of his short stories *The Imp of the Perverse*, Poe's protagonist carries out the perfect murder, inherits the dead man's estate, and lives for years in healthy enjoyment of his ill-gotten gains. Whenever thoughts of the murder appears on the fringes of his consciousness, he murmurs to himself, "I am safe." All is well until the day he remodels his mantra to "I am safe—yes—if I be not fool enough to make open confession." With that thought, he comes undone. He tries to suppress the thought of confessing, but the harder he tries, the more insistent the thought becomes. He panics, he starts running, people start chasing him, he blacks out, and, when he returns to his senses, he is told that he has made a full confession.

① the divided mind
② the placebo effect
③ mantra meditation
④ criminal psychology
⑤ mind-body integration

88

다음 글의 문맥 상 빈칸 (A)와 (B)에 들어갈 적절한 말들로 짝지어진 것은? **난이도 상**

Spending 12 days at the Cannes Film Festival is, for movie lovers, pretty close to paradise, and most years it's extremely easy to _____ (A) _____ the world outside. Not so this year. Even if nearly all critics and journalists dutifully switched off their phones during screenings, most of us couldn't resist powering up immediately afterward to check for news updates. World events don't stop happening as we're sitting in the dark. Plus, security was tighter than ever this year: at press screenings and gala premieres, every saggy backpack and bejeweled handbag was thoroughly inspected by the cheerful staff, women in sleek Mondrian-style dresses that Emma Peel would have loved. Everything in Cannes, including the employees' uniforms, is just a little bit glamorous. That's less a way of _____ (B) _____ an uncertain, scary world than an act of standing as a bulwark against it.

	(A)	(B)
①	keep track of	avoiding
②	lose track of	facing
③	lose track of	seeking
④	lose track of	avoiding
⑤	keep track of	facing

다음 빈칸에 들어갈 말로 가장 적절한 것을 고르시오.

In their now classic article, 'Dilemmas in a general theory of planning', Rittel and Weber draw an important distinction between what they call 'tame' problems and 'wicked' problems. While not necessarily simple, tame problems generally have a relatively straightforward solution that is amenable to expert, technical knowledge. For instance, landing a man on the moon was an extremely complex undertaking, but it was possible to clearly articulate the objective and achieve it through the application of existent scientific knowledge. In problems like this, there are clear cause and effect mechanisms that enhance the likelihood that they can be solved. Wicked problems, by contrast, are intractable, poorly structured and have only temporary or uncertain solutions. For wicked problems, there are no _____. In fact, it is often difficult to define these problems in the first place because they usually involve intertwined normative criteria and empirical conditions or situations.

*amenable ~로 해결할 수 있는, intractable 통제할 수 없는

① unambiguous criteria by which to judge their resolution
② evasive messages to explain their source
③ vague terms to define their characteristics
④ blurred boundaries between proven facts and opinions
⑤ historical background on which to base their definition

90 다음 빈칸에 들어갈 말로 가장 적절한 것을 고르시오. 난이도 중

The Asymmetric Dominance Effect is a cognitive bias in which consumers will tend to have a specific change in preferences between two options when also presented with a third option that is asymmetrically dominated. Simply put, when there is a third strategically important choice, then the consumer is more likely to choose the more expensive of the other two options. An option is asymmetrically dominated when it is inferior in all respects to one option. However, in comparison to the other option, it is inferior in some respects and superior in others. In other words, it is completely dominated by (or inferior to) one option and only partially dominated by the other. When the asymmetrically dominated option is present, a higher percentage of consumers will prefer the dominating option than when the asymmetrically dominated option is absent. The asymmetrically dominated option is, therefore, a decoy _____.

① designed to attract consumers attention to the dominated option
② serving to increase preference for the dominating option
③ serving to distract consumers attention from the superior option
④ helping consumers to access as many options as possible
⑤ designed to implicitly promote the 'buy one get one free' strategy

다음 빈칸에 들어갈 말로 가장 적절한 것을 고르시오.

Evolutionary biologist Jessica Flack and her colleagues manipulated the network structure of a group of eighty-four pigtailed macaques at the Yerkes National Primate Research Center near Lawrenceville, Georgia. They first measured connections based on whom the monkeys groomed or played with. Group leaders were identified by counting the number of times others silently bared their teeth at them during peaceful moments, an act of deference in this species. The scientists then strategically removed the highest-ranked individuals and then compared the resulting social networks to an unperturbed control condition. When the high-ranking individuals were removed, chaos ensued. Conflict and aggression skyrocketed. This analysis sheds light on the impact of leaders on interactions within the group as a whole. First, after the leaders were removed, the group had fewer grooming and play interactions overall. That is, the remaining macaques became less connected to one another. This suggests that stable leadership promotes peaceful interactions not only between leaders and followers, but also between followers and other followers. The existence of popular leaders seems to facilitate social order throughout the group. And given that these interactions create opportunities for beneficial mutual support it is easy to see why natural selection might favor the evolution of an individual interest in, and respect to, _____.

* macaque 아프리카 · 아시아산 원숭이의 하나

① comradeship
② equality
③ upheaval
④ hierarchy
⑤ discipline

92

다음 빈칸에 들어갈 말로 가장 적절한 것을 고르시오.

난이도 상

The way experience and our understanding of experience can influence language has been observed by Galili and Hazan in connection to optical phenomena. They argue that language, historically, was developed under the influence of visual perception and well before our present understanding of vision was reached. As a result, many linguistic constructions do not _____ _____. Phrases in our daily language such as "throw a glance" or "give a look", in the authors' view, are probably related to the ancient, and incorrect, Empedoclean idea that vision involves the emission rather than reception of light by the eyes. In a similar manner, Eshach has shown that the way we talk about shadows in our daily lives may also reveal a strong association between language and ideas regarding shadows; according to him, we talk about shadow as an existing entity, for example, "look at my frightening shadow, my shadow follows me." and so on. Such phrases may lead students, and adults as well, to attribute the properties of material substances to shadows, rather than to understand them as the product merely of the absence of light.

① reflect changing speech patterns of today
② conform to present-day scientific knowledge
③ go against contemporary scientific norms
④ respect time-honored scientific traditions
⑤ serve the role as a communication facilitator

다음 빈칸에 들어갈 말로 가장 적절한 것을 고르시오. 난이도 상

That boundaries are necessary features of post-humanism may seem counterintuitive; after all, blurring and breaking down boundaries is a major feature of much post-human work. Braidotti argues, for example, that the "shared starting point" for post-human theory is a non-dualistic understanding" of the "nature-culture continuum"—that is, we begin post-humanism by blurring the boundaries between these two realms. Post-humanism conspicuously posits a dynamic and indeterminate world: what was distinctly human becomes cyborg; what was distinctly animal becomes invested with consciousness and human-equivalent subjectivity; what were distinctly inanimate machines become animate and, perhaps, sentient. This boundary-blurring extends beyond the humanities (a term itself that recalls a time pre-post-humanism), as in the sciences, too, previously paradigmatic boundary lines _____. The boundaries of thought and consciousness, for example, are more and more being blurred and called into question. Andy Clark describes this new view of cognition in the sciences as that which takes into account "inextricable tangles of feedback, feed-forward, and feed-around loops that promiscuously criss-cross the boundaries of brain, body, and world."

* posit 상정하다

① are showing signs of stability

② are now in a state of transition

③ have had their ambiguity removed

④ have yet to recover their former vitality

⑤ remain the way they were initially drawn

94 다음 빈칸에 들어갈 말로 가장 적절한 것을 고르시오.

Plans to develop infrastructure and mitigate tourism impacts on islands require relevant baseline studies and monitoring of ecological conditions. For example, on Rottnest Island, a major tourism destination in Western Australia, the peak tourism season coincides with peak numbers of migratory shorebirds. In relation to the nexus between tourism and protecting bird habitats, environmentalist A. Morrison-Saunders reported that a proactive monitoring system could identify areas of tourism-conservation conflict, such as fencing off areas where fairy terns are breeding as the birds use different locations from year to year. Saunders also noted that monitoring could have mitigated the magnitude of past tourism-related activity, such as the construction of a road around a salt lake that impacted on the feeding areas for waders and the construction of a power line within the flight path of birds moving between salt lakes which resulted in significant mortality arising from collisions. Saunders went on to report that it took 15 years before the power lines were fitted with warning devices, a situation which could have been avoided if _____ had been in place.

* fairy tern 흰제비갈매기, wader 섭금류

① an epoch-making tourism promotion drive led by local governments
② a gigantic technical upgrade befitting the ultra-modern 21st century
③ an efficient outreach program designed to reduce ecological footprints
④ governments' will to crack down on any attempt to disrupt environment
⑤ a tourism impact monitoring system linked to adaptive management

95 다음 글의 빈칸에 들어갈 말로 가장 적절한 것을 고르시오. 난이도 상

Uncertainty is a basic fact of life and technology is no exception. The first source of technological uncertainty derives from the fortunate fact that there always exists a variety of solutions to perform a particular task. It is always uncertain which might be "best" taking into account technical criteria, economic criteria, and social criteria. Uncertainty prevails at all stages of technological evolution, from initial design choices, through success or failure in the marketplace, to eventual environmental impacts and spin-off effects. The technological and management literature labels such uncertainty a "snake pit" problem. It is like trying to pick a particular snake out of a pit of hundreds that all look alike. Technological uncertainty continues to be a notorious embarrassment in efforts to "forecast" technological change. But there is also nothing to be gained by a strategy of "waiting until the sky clears." It will not clear, uncertainty will persist, and the correct strategy is _____. This may seem an "inefficient" strategy for progress. To the extent that it is, it is one of the many areas in which writers have drawn useful analogies between technology and biology.

① experimentation with technological variety
② commitment to existing scientific principles
③ unwavering trust in technological uniformity
④ vigilance against any rash climatic approach
⑤ restriction on irrelevant academic exchanges

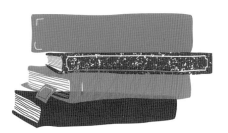

9

함축적 의미 추론

지문 속의 특정 단어나 어구가
실제로 뜻하는 바를 추론하는 유형으로
문맥 파악 능력과 추리력을 필요로 한다.

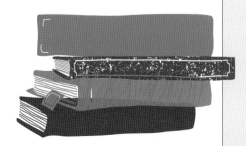

▶ 지칭 추론 유형과 다른 점은 지칭 추론이 지칭 대상이 다른 대명사나 명사를 가려내는 문제인데 비해 의미 추론은 비유적, 함축적 표현에 감추어진 실제 의미를 묻는다는 것이다.

▶ 문제의 밑줄 부분을 전후한 문맥 관계를 정확히 파악해야 한다. 따라서 밑줄 친 부분 앞의 두세 문장을 집중적으로 읽을 필요가 있다. 특히 밑줄 부분이 대명사를 포함하고 있을 때 그러하다.

▶ 밑줄 부분은 글의 주제나 요지와 직결된 경우가 많으므로 주제문을 먼저 파악한 후 밑줄 부분과 대조해서 읽으면 의미 파악이 의외로 쉬울 수 있다.

▶ 빈칸 추론에서 빈칸의 단서가 지문 어딘가에 있는 것처럼 함축적 의미의 단서 역시 지문 어딘가에 숨어있을 가능성이 크다. 단서 찾기, 정보 찾기라는 점에서 함축적 의미 추론은 빈칸 추론과 문제 해결의 접근 방식이 기본적으로 같다.

▶ 밑줄 부분에 선택한 답을 놓고 의미가 통하는지 점검한다.

밑줄 친 hunting the shadow, not the substance가 다음 글에서 의미하는 바로 가장 적절한 것은?

| 수능 2025년 |

The position of the architect rose during the Roman Empire, as architecture symbolically became a particularly important political statement. Cicero classed the architect with the physician and the teacher and Vitruvius spoke of "so great a profession as this." Marcus Vitruvius Pollio, a practicing architect during the rule of Augustus Caesar, recognized that architecture requires both practical and theoretical knowledge, and he listed the disciplines he felt the aspiring architect should master: literature and writing, draftsmanship, mathematics, history, philosophy, music, medicine, law, and astronomy—a curriculum that still has much to recommend it. All of this study was necessary, he argued, because architects who have aimed at acquiring manual skill without scholarship have never been able to reach a position of authority to correspond to their plans, while those who have relied only upon theories and scholarship were obviously "hunting the shadow, not the substance."

① seeking abstract knowledge emphasized by architectural tradition
② discounting the subjects necessary to achieve architectural goals
③ pursuing the ideals of architecture without the practical skills
④ prioritizing architecture's material aspects over its artistic ones
⑤ following historical precedents without regard to current standards

[한번에 정리하는 문제 해설]

지문 해석 건축술이 상징적으로 특히 중요한 정치적 선언이 됨에 따라 로마제국 시기에 건축가의 지위가 높아졌다. Cicero는 건축가를 의사나 교사와 같은 급으로 분류했고 Vitruvius는 "이 같은 위대한 직업"에 대해 말했다. Augustus Caesar 통치 기간 중 개업 건축가였던 Marcus Vitruvius Pollio는 건축에는 실무 지식과 이론 지식이 모두 필요하다는 것을 인정하고 야심 찬 건축가가 마스터해야 할 학문으로 문학, 작문, 제도, 수학, 역사학, 철학, 음악, 의학, 법, 천문학을 꼽았는데 이것은 여전히 많은 추천을 받는 커리큘럼이다. 이 학문은 모두 필요하다고 그는 주장했는데 그 이유는 학문 없이 손 기술 익히기만 목표로 하는 건축가들은 결코 그들의 계획에 부합되는 권위 있는 지위에 도달하지 못하고 반면 이론과 학문에만 의존하는 이들은 분명 "실체가 아니라 그림자를 쫓기" 때문이다.

글의 소재 로마 시대의 높아진 건축가의 지위

주요 어휘 architecture 건축학, 건축술, symbolically 상징적으로, theoretical 이론적인, draftsmanship 제도, astronomy 천문학, argue 주장하다, acquire 획득하다, manual 손의, authority 권위, correspond to ~에 상응하다, ~에 부합하다, substance 실체

구조 분석 he listed the disciplines he felt the aspiring architect should master: literature and writing, draftsmanship, mathematics, history, philosophy, music, medicine, law, and astronomy—a curriculum that still has much to recommend it.

→ the disciplines과 he 사이에 목적격 관계대명사 that(which)가 생략됐고 a curriculum 이하는 'literature and writing ~ and astronomy'와 동격을 이루고 이를 부연 설명한다. it는 architecture를 가리킨다.

정답 ③

정답 해설 밑줄 친 부분을 말한 Marcus Vitruvius Pollio는 건축에는 실무 지식과 이론 지식이 모두 필요하다고 주장했고 밑줄 문장 전반부에서 학문 없이 손기술만 목표로 하는 사람이 높은 지위에 오르지 못한다고 말해 이론 지식의 중요성을 강조했다. 그래서 대조의 연결사 while 뒤에는 실무 지식을 강조하는 내용이 와야 논리적으로 타당하다. 따라서 밑줄친 부분이 의미하는 바는 ③ '실무 기술 없이 건축의 이상을 추구하는 것'이 적절하다.

① 건축계의 전통이 강조하는 추상적 지식을 추구하는 것　② 건축의 목표를 성취하는 데 필요한 과목을 무시하는 것
④ 건축의 물질적 면을 예술적인 면보다 우선하는 것　⑤ 현재의 기준을 무시하고 역사적 선례를 따르는 것

08 밑줄 친 turn them into a big raft to float around on the rivers and lakes가 다음 글에서 의미하는 바로 가장 적절한 것은?

| 사관 2022년 |

One typical exchange begins with Huizi telling Zhuangzi that a king once gave him a gift of a handful of large gourd seeds: "When I planted them they grew into enormous gourds, big enough to hold twenty gallons! I tried to use them as water containers, but they were too heavy to lift; I tried cutting them to make spoons, but they were too shallow to hold any liquid. It's not that I wasn't impressed by their size, but I decided they weren't really useful for anything, so I smashed them." In China at the time, gourds were used for these two purposes, containers or spoons. Hence Huizi's disappointment. Hearing this story, though, Zhuangzi is incredulous. "You are certainly a fool when it comes to thinking big!" he declares. He tells Huizi some stories about people who took apparently useless or trivial items and used them for unexpected purposes, winning great rewards in the process. "Now you've got these gourds," he concludes. "Why didn't it occur to you that you could <u>turn them into a big raft to float around on the rivers and lakes</u>, instead of lamenting how they're too big to use as spoons! It's as though you've got underbrush growing in your mind!"

[4점]

* gourd: 조롱박 ** underbrush: (큰 나무 밑에 나는) 덤불

① conform to established conventions
② show respect for other people's possessions
③ take a look at your current spending habits
④ be flexible when considering the uses of objects
⑤ pay attention to the size of the item you are buying

[한번에 정리하는 문제 해설]

지문 해석 옛날에 왕이 그에게 큰 박 씨 한 줌을 선물로 줬다는, Huizi가 Zhuanzi에게 하는 이야기와 함께 전형적인 말싸움이 시작된다. "내가 그것들을 심자 거대한 박으로 자랐는데 20갤런을 담을 만큼 커졌어. 나는 그것들을 물통으로 쓰려고 했지만, 너무 무거워 들 수가 없었어. 나는 그것들을 잘라 숟가락으로 만들려 했지만, 너무 얇아서 액체를 담을 수 없었어. 그 크기가 인상적이지 않은 것은 아니지만 나는 그것들이 아무짝에도 쓸모가 없다고 결론 내렸고 그래서 그것들을 부숴 버렸어." 당시 중국에서 박은 물통과 숟가락의 두 가지 목적으로 사용되었다. 그래서 Huizi는 실망한 것이다. 하지만 이 이야기를 듣고 Zhuanzi는 의아하게 생각한다. "넓게 생각하는 것에 관한 한 너는 참 바보구나!"라고 그는 선언한다. 그는, 겉보기에는 쓸모없고 하찮은 것처럼 보이는 물건을 가져다 뜻밖의 목적으로 사용하고 그 과정에서 큰 보상을 얻은 사람들에 관한 이야기 몇 개를 Huizi에게 말해준다. "이 박들이 있는데, 너는 왜 그것들을 큰 뗏목으로 만들어 강이나 호수에 띄울 생각을 하지 못했을까! 그것들이 너무 커서 숟가락을 만들 수 없다며 한탄하는 대신에 말이야. 너는 마음속에 덤불을 키우고 있었던 셈이야."라며 그가 끝을 맺는다.

글의 소재 고정 관념에서 벗어나기

주요 어휘 **typical** 전형적인, **enormous** 거대한, **shallow** 얕은, **smash** 부수다, **incredulous** 믿지 않는, 의아해하는, **declare** 선언하다, **lament** 한탄하다, **underbrush** 덤불

구조 분석 ~ instead of lamenting <u>how</u> they're too big to use as spoons ~
➡ how는 의문사가 아닌 접속사로 쓰였고 접속사 that과 쓰임이 같다.

정 답 ④

정답 해설 박으로 큰 뗏목을 만들어 강이나 호수에 띄운다 함은 박의 전통적인 용도인 물통과 숟가락이라는 고정 관념으로부터 벗어나는 것을 의미하기 때문에 ④ '물건의 용도를 생각할 때 융통성 발휘하기'가 정답이다.
① 확립된 전통을 따르기
② 다른 사람의 소지품을 존중하기
③ 당신의 현재 소비 습관을 되돌아보기
⑤ 당신이 사려는 물건의 크기를 신경 쓰기

밑줄 친 it이 의미하는 것으로 가장 적절한 것은?

Closely related to the societal customs of touching are those of spatial relationships. Anthropologists tell us that each of us walks around inside "bubbles of personal space." The size of the bubble represents our personal territory, territorial imperatives, or "personal buffer zones." We neither like nor tolerate <u>it</u> when someone invades our bubbles. We become distinctly uncomfortable. But as we travel to different places around the world, we learn that some cultural bubbles are larger or smaller than others.

① feeling uncomfortable

② walking inside the bubble

③ the size of the bubble

④ someone's invasion of our bubbles

⑤ our personal territory

[한번에 정리하는 문제 해설]

지문 해석 공간적 관계의 관습은 접촉의 사회적 관습과 긴밀히 연관돼 있다. 인류학자들은 우리에게 우리들 각각은 "개인적 공간의 거품" 안을 거닌다고 말한다. 그 거품의 크기는 우리의 개인적 영역, 영역의 규칙, 혹은 "개인적인 완충지대"를 나타낸다. 누가 우리의 거품을 침범할 때 우리는 그 행위를 좋아하지도 용서하지도 않는다. 우리는 분명히 불편해진다. 그러나 세계의 여러 곳을 여행하면서 우리는 어떤 문화적 거품은 다른 것보다 크기도 하고 작기도 하다는 것을 알게 된다.

① 불편한 느낌을 갖는 것

② 거품 안을 거니는 것

③ 거품의 크기

④ 누가 거품을 침범하는 것

⑤ 우리의 사적 영역

글의 소재 공간적 관계의 관습

주요 어휘 societal 사회의, spatial 공간의, anthropologist 인류학자, bubble 거품(거대한 크기의 개별적 거품을 말한다), represent 나타내다, imperative 규칙, buffer zone 완충지대, distinctly 분명히

정 답 ④

정답 해설 'it'는 'when someone invades our bubbles'를 받는다. 따라서 정답은 ④이다. I like it when ~와 같은 문장에서 it는 항상 when 이하의 내용을 가리킨다. 관용적 표현으로 알아두는 것이 좋다. (e.g. 'I like it when you call me an angel.'에서 it은 when you call me an angel이다.)

9. 함축적 의미 추론

| 해설 412쪽 |

96

밑줄 친 부분이 의미하는 바를 가장 적절히 나타낸 것은?

난이도 중

Decisions and decisions. We all make hundreds even thousands of them on a daily basis. And it can all add up and wear a person down. But there is at least one simple way that you can put a stop to it. Barbara Shaw wears virtually the same outfit almost everyday. The public relations executive has a closet full of the same clothes and says that there's zero guesswork when it comes to what to wear to work each day. She says it's a strategy to decrease fatigue from making the same decision over and over again and to free her up to focus on things that matter more. Mark Zuckerberg wears the same thing every day <u>for the same reason.</u> Even President Obama only wears blue or gray suits saying "I don't want to make decisions about what I'm wearing. Because I have too many other decisions to make."

① to save money on clothes

② to enjoy an easy and simple life

③ because he has no time to spare

④ to cut down on decision fatigue

⑤ to follow the latest trend

다음 글에서 화자가 밑줄 친 부분을 언급한 의도로 가장 적절한 것은? 난이도 중

Educators are also grappling with smartphone-related dilemmas. Most schools allow smartphone use between classes and during free periods, but teachers say keeping students off their phones during class has become a tremendous burden. In a move to solve such dilemmas, a high school in California has come up with an idea. Recently, the school teamed up with a local IT company to develop a solution to restrict smartphone access during school hours. The company makes small, lockable phone pouches that students keep with them, but that can't be opened until the end of the day. Alison Silvestri, the high school's principal, says "The changes have already been profound." According to Silvestri, students are more focused and engaged during class, and student journals suggest the high schoolers are feeling less stress. She says fewer fights have broken out this semester—a benefit she attributes to the absence of social media. Silvestri adds "I can't count the number of parents who have asked me, 'How do I buy this for my home?'"

① 학교와 가정을 잇는 핫라인을 설치하려고
② 가정에서 소셜 미디어 접속을 원활히 하려고
③ 가정에서 아이들이 사용할 스마트폰을 구입하려고
④ 스마트폰 잠금장치를 가정에서도 사용하려고
⑤ 자녀의 문제를 실시간으로 학교에 알리려고

98

다음 글에서 밑줄 친 부분이 의미하는 것은? 난이도 중

Inside the Dolby, the site for the Academy Awards, usually during commercial breaks for the live broadcast, industry people and non-industry invitees would pop out of their seats in the auditorium and mill about the different levels of the venue while enjoying free alcohol and refreshments. Though the venue was mostly occupied by white people who would enthusiastically clap and cheer when *Parasite*, one of 2019's most acclaimed films and South Korea's Bong Joon-ho, the mastermind behind it, were called to the stage, views on how the Academy should navigate diversity were varied. "Being inclusive is a very good thing but to use it as a standing point for the work....I don't necessarily agree with that," said Scott Michaels, a consultant who briefly worked with director Quentin Tarantino for *Once Upon a Time in Hollywood*. "I do agree with diversity, of course, but I do think work is stand-alone," Michaels told BuzzFeed News when asked about the overrepresentation of white performers in the acting categories this year. He added, "I'm a big believer in 'the work stands for the work and merit is merit.' I don't think it's right to base merit on demographic."

* mill about ~ 주변을 오가다

① 소수민족 출신의 작품을 무시하는 것
② 수상작 선정에 작품의 질을 중시하는 것
③ 인구 비례로 적당히 상을 나눠주는 것
④ 작품과 제작자의 출신성분을 연계하는 것
⑤ 수상작을 민주적 절차에 따라 결정하는 것

99 다음 글에서 밑줄 친 evidence to the contrary가 의미하는 것은? 난이도 중

T.S. Eliot's famous poem *The Waste Land* stands as a notable instance of a co-authored poem that is consistently attributed to one author alone. There is documentary evidence from Eliot's manuscript that Ezra Pound contributed substantially to the published poem. Pound helped carve out the 434 lines of *The Waste Land* from the 1,000 lines of the first draft, in addition to making major alterations to many other aspects of the poem before it was published. Eliot always acknowledged Pound's significant contribution. As he put it in 1938, Pound "turned a jumble of good and bad passages into a poem." But a large contingent of Eliot scholars have insisted on minimizing Pound's contribution despite this and other evidence to the contrary. The obvious implication of the denial of Pound's contribution to Eliot's writing of *The Waste Land* is that the poem would somehow be perceived as a lesser work than it is now taken to be.

① Eliot's unwavering belief in single authorship
② Eliot's acknowledgement of Pound's contribution
③ Pound's contribution to composing The Waste Land
④ Eliot's refusal to allow Pound to influence his works
⑤ Eliot enthusiasts' being excessively biased towards his works

100 다음 글에서 밑줄 친 a lightning rod가 의미하는 것은?

Education Secretary Betsy DeVos took on one of former President Obama's most controversial regulatory actions: a set of 2011 campus disciplinary procedures for students accused of sexual assault. Arguing that victims of assault were being denied justice, the Obama White House weakened traditional protections for the accused, like presumption of innocence and the right to cross-examine the accuser. DeVos, in a speech at George Mason University, said the system "is shameful, it is wholly un-American, and it is anathema to the system of self-governance to which our Founders pledged their lives over 240 years ago." Not surprisingly, DeVos was immediately attacked. From her poor performance at her nomination hearing to her preference for charter schools over public education and her decision to rescind 72 policy documents on the rights of students with disabilities, Devos has been a lightning rod.

* anathema=파문, 저주, 정면으로 배치되는 것

① a target of criticism
② a focus of attention
③ a source of attraction
④ a bone of contention
⑤ a sight for sore eyes

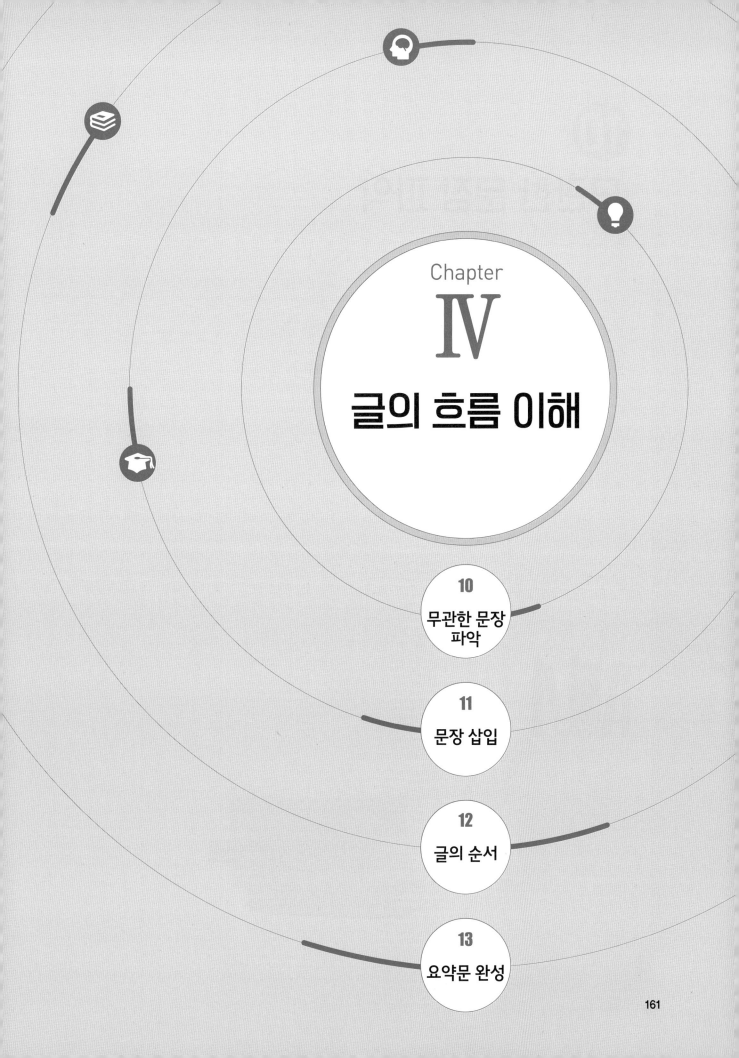

Chapter

IV

글의 흐름 이해

10

무관한 문장 파악

11

문장 삽입

12

글의 순서

13

요약문 완성

10

무관한 문장 파악

하나의 주제를 전개해 나가는 여러 개의 문장 중
글의 흐름과 무관한 문장을 찾아내는 유형이다.

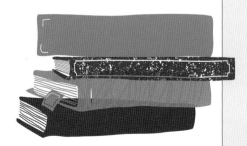

가이드라인

▶ 글을 읽어 내려갈 때 글의 핵심 소재나 주제를 염두에 두어 글의 내용과는 무관한 문장을 찾아내는 근거로 삼는다.

▶ 글의 내용과 무관할 문장일 확률이 높은 선택지의 문장 유형을 숙지한다.

▶ 마지막으로 선택한 문장을 뺀 후 글의 흐름이 자연스러운지 확인한다.

정답일 확률이 높은 선택지의 문장 유형

▶ 겉으로는 같은 소재나 주제를 언급하는 것처럼 보이지만 실제로는 주제나 요지를 뒷받침하지 않거나 정반대의 주장을 하는 문장

▶ 논리적 비약이 있거나 논점을 이탈한 문장

▶ 글의 소재에 대해 불필요할 정도로 지나치게 포괄적이거나 또는 반대로 지나치게 구체적이어서 지엽ㆍ말단에 흐르는 문장

▶ 시제가 일치하지 않는 문장

35 다음 글에서 전체 흐름과 관계없는 문장은?

In the context of SNS, media literacy has been argued to be especially important "in order to make the users aware of their rights when using SNS tools, and also help them acquire or reinforce human rights values and develop the behaviour necessary to respect other people's rights and freedoms". ① With regard to peer-to-peer risks such as bullying, this last element is of particular importance. ② This relates to a basic principle that children are taught in the offline world as well: 'do not do to others what you would not want others to do to you'. ③ Children's SNS activities should be encouraged when we help them accumulate knowledge. ④ This should also be a golden rule with regard to SNS, but for children and young people it is much more difficult to estimate the consequences and potential serious impact of their actions in this environment. ⑤ Hence, raising awareness of children from a very early age about the particular characteristics of SNS and the potential long-term impact of a seemingly trivial act is crucial.

[한번에 정리하는 문제 해설]

지문 해석 SNS 상황에서, 'SNS 도구들을 사용할 때 사용자들이 자신들의 권리를 의식하게 하도록, 그리고 또한 그들이 인권이라는 가치를 배우거나 강화하고 타인의 권리와 자유를 존중하는 데 필요한 태도를 기르도록 돕기 위해' 미디어 정보 해독력이 특히 중요하다고 주장되어왔다. ① 약자 괴롭히기와 같은 사용자 간 위험과 관련하여, 이 마지막 요소는 특별히 중요하다. ② 이것은 아이들에게 오프라인 세계에서도 가르치는 기본 원칙인 '남들이 여러분에게 하지 않았으면 하는 일을 남들에게 하지 말라'와 관계가 있다. ③ 우리가 아이들이 지식을 축적하는 것을 도울 때 아이들의 SNS활동은 권장되어야 한다. ④ 이것은 SNS와 관련해서도 황금률이어야 하지만, 아이들과 젊은이들이 이 환경에서의 자신들의 행동의 결과와 잠재적인 중대한 영향을 추정하는 것은 훨씬 더 어렵다. ⑤ 이런 이유로, SNS의 특수한 특성과 겉보기에는 사소한 행동의 잠재적인 장기적인 영향에 대한 아이들의 의식을 아주 어린 나이부터 높이는 것이 필수적이다.

글의 소재 SNS에서 미디어 정보 해독력이 중요한 이유

주요 어휘 context 맥락, 상황, estimate 추정하다, 판단하다, literacy 문해, 정보 해독, argue 주장하다, acquire 획득하다, 습득하다, reinforce 강화하다, with regard to ~에 관하여, peer-to-peer 개인 간, 사용자 간, relate to ~와 관련되다, encourage 장려하다, 격려하다, accumulate 쌓다, 축적하다, estimate 추정하다, potential 잠재적인, characteristic 특성, seemingly 겉보기에는, 외견상으로, trivial 사소한, crucial 필수적인, 결정적인

정 답 ③

정답 해설 SNS 상황에서 미디어 정보해독력은 특히 그것이 타인의 권리와 자유를 존중하는 자세를 길러 주기 때문에 중요하고 이런 SNS 특성과 자신의 행동이 미치는 영향을 어린이들에게 조기에 숙지시켜야 한다는 것이 이 글의 주된 내용이므로 '지식 축적을 돕기 위해 어린이의 SNS 활동이 장려돼야 한다.'는 내용의 ③은 전체 흐름과 무관하다. 따라서 정답은 ③이다.

다음 글에서 전체 흐름과 관계 <u>없는</u> 문장은?

Subsidies are payments made to businesses or economic sectors with the intention of reducing prices or increasing profitability. ① They are not necessarily used for exports, as farmland is often subsidized with the intention of making food cheaper for domestic consumption, and businesses are often subsidized for the costs of hiring new employees when a government is trying to increase employment levels. ② During the course of economic warfare, one reason subsidies are used is to increase the volume of a specific product, or potentially all products, that the consumers of the targeted nation are purchasing from the businesses of the issuing nation. ③ The other purpose is to make the good produced within one's own nation cheaper to decrease the volume of exports purchased by people domestically. ④ In other words, planned economies are not responsive to market forces, which results in resource inefficiencies and shortages. ⑤ The intended goal of issuing subsidies is to redirect profits and production away from the businesses of the target nation and turn them to benefit one's own businesses.

[4점]

[한번에 정리하는 문제 해설]

지문 해석 보조금은 가격을 낮추거나 수익성을 높일 의도로 기업이나 경제 단체에 제공하는 지불금이다. 그것들은 꼭 수출만을 위해 쓰이지는 않는데, 때로는 국내 소비를 위해 음식 가격을 낮출 목적으로 농지에 보조금을 지급하거나 정부가 고용 수준을 높이고 싶을 때 신규 취업자 고용 비용을 위해 기업에 보조금을 주기도 하기 때문이다. 무역 전쟁 시에 보조금이 사용되는 한 가지 이유는 대상국 소비자들이 발행국 기업으로부터 구매하는 특정 상품, 혹은 잠재적으로 모든 상품의 생산량을 늘리기 위한 것이다. 또 다른 목적은 자국 내에서 생산된 제품을 싸게 만들어 국내 소비용 상품이 수출되는 것을 억제하는 데 있다. (달리 말하면 계획 경제는 시장의 힘에 반응하지 않는데 이는 자원의 비효율성과 부족을 초래한다.) 보조금을 지급하는 목적은 이익과 생산을 대상국 기업으로부터 자국 기업에 이득이 되는 쪽으로 돌리는 것이다.

글의 소재 정부의 보조금 지급 목적

주요 어휘 subsidy 보조금, profitability 수익성, domestic 국내의, consumption 소비, potentially 잠재적으로, issue 발행하다, responsive 반응하는, resource 자원, inefficiency 비효율

구조 분석 • The intended goal of issuing subsidies is to <u>redirect</u> profits and production away from the businesses of the target nation <u>and turn</u> them to benefit one's own businesses.
➜ and 전후 문장이 병렬구조이기 때문에 redirect와 turn 모두 동사 원형이 쓰였다.

정 답 ④

정답 해설 이 글은 정부가 기업이나 경제 단체에 주는 각종 보조금의 지급 목적을 상술하고 있다. 계획 경제의 비효율성을 언급하는 ④는 글의 흐름과 관계가 없다.

32 다음 글에서 전체 흐름과 관계 없는 문장을 고르시오.

Cryptocurrencies have been around since 2009, and in all this time they have never come to play a major role in real-world transactions—El Salvador's much-hyped attempt to make bitcoin its national currency has become a disaster. ① Suppose, for example, that you use a digital payments app like Venmo, which has amply demonstrated its usefulness for real-world transactions. ② So how did cryptocurrencies come to be worth almost $3 trillion at their peak? ③ Why was nothing done to rein in "stablecoins," which were supposedly pegged to the U.S. dollar but were clearly subject to all the risks of unregulated banking, and are now experiencing a cascading series of collapses reminiscent of the wave of bank failures that helped make the Great Depression great? ④ My answer is that while the crypto industry has never managed to come up with products that are of much use in the real economy, it has been spectacularly successful at marketing itself, creating an image of being both cutting edge and respectable. ⑤ It has done so, in particular, by cultivating prominent people and institutions.

[3점]

* cryptocurrency: 암호화폐

[한번에 정리하는 문제 해설]

지문 해석 암호화폐는 2009년 이래로 존재해왔고 그 동안 내내 그것들은 현실 세계의 거래에서 결코 주요한 역할을 맡았던 적이 없다. ─비트코인을 국가 통화로 만들겠다는 엘살바도르의 과도 광고된 시도는 대참사가 되었다. ① 예를 들어 Venmo처럼 현실 세계 거래에서 유용성을 충분히 입증한 디지털 지불 앱을 당신이 사용한다고 가정하자. ② 그런데 어떻게 가상화폐가 한창 때에 거의 3조 달러의 가치를 가지게 되었는가? ③ 미 달러화에 연동되는 것으로 추정되나 무규제 은행 거래의 모든 위험에 노출돼 있고 대공황을 키우는 데 일조한, 은행의 연쇄 파산을 연상케 하는 일련의 붕괴를 경험하고 있는 스테이블 코인을 규제하기 위해 왜 아무것도 하지 않나? ④ 내 대답은 가상화폐 산업이 현실 경제에서 쓰임이 큰 제품을 출시한 적은 없지만 자기 마케팅에 크게 성공해 첨단적이면서도 존경받을 만 하다는 이미지를 창출했다는 것이다. ⑤ 그것은 특히 저명한 인물이나 기관을 육성함으로써 그렇게 했다.

글의 소재 암호화폐가 성공적인 시장성을 갖게 된 이유

주요 어휘 cryptocurrency 암호화폐, transaction 거래, much-hyped 과대 광고된, disaster 재앙, 대참사, amply 널리, 충분히, demonstrate 시연하다, 입증하다, rein in 억제하다, 통제하다, peg 말뚝 박다, 연동시키다, cascade(v) 폭포처럼 떨어지다, collapse 붕괴, reminiscent of ~를 연상시키는, cutting edge 첨단의, prominent 저명한

구조 분석 • it has been spectacularly successful at marketing itself, <u>creating</u> an image of being both cutting edge and respectable.

➡ 순차 진행을 나타내는 분사 구문으로 creating 이하는 'and it created an image of being both cutting edge and respectable.'로 바꿀 수 있다.

정 답 ①

정답 해설 지문은 비록 현실 거래에서 주요한 역할도 해 본적이 없고 이렇다할 금융 상품을 출시하지도 못했지만 암호화폐가 3조 달러라는 높은 가치를 누리고, 규제 대상에서도 빠지는 것은 성공적인 자기 마케팅을 통해 이미지를 개선한 데 그 이유가 있음을 주장하는 글이다. 디지털 화폐 지불 수단을 언급하는 ①은 이러한 흐름과 무관하다. 또, ①의 긍정적인 내용은 첫 문장의 부정적인 내용이나 부정적인 내용을 전제로 하는 ② 문장과의 사이에서 글의 흐름 상 어색하다.

101

다음 글에서 전체 흐름과 관계 <u>없는</u> 문장은? 난이도 중

Much is being done nowadays to produce better newspapers, but much more is yet to be done to produce better newspaper readers. The newspaper is controlled by its readers. ① It is newspaper readers who raise up the newspaper and pull it down. ② It can hardly be any better than the reading public wants it to be or allows it to be. ③ No newspaper can be the pillar of free democracy unless readers have a good understanding of it. ④ Free democracy can only flourish when its constituents are fully committed to realizing a truly egalitarian society. ⑤ Thus, a keen consciousness on the part of the general public as to the role of the newspaper is a prerequisite to the successful maintenance of a democratic society.

다음 글에서 전체 흐름과 관계 없는 문장은? 난이도 중

Bitcoin is a new currency that was created in 2009 by an unknown person using the alias Satoshi Nakamoto. Transactions are made with no middle men. meaning, no banks! There are no transaction fees and no need to give your real name. ① More merchants are beginning to accept them: You can buy webhosting services, pizza or even manicures. ② Bitcoins can be used to buy merchandise anonymously. ③ In addition, international payments are easy and cheap because bitcoins are not tied to any country or subject to regulation. ④ They are stored in a "digital wallet," which exists either in the cloud or on a user's computer. ⑤ Small businesses may like them because there are no credit card fees.

103 다음 글에서 전체 흐름과 관계 없는 문장은?

난이도 중

Most people engaged in the advertising industry agree that in many ways the buying of television advertising time is both more accurate and more complex than the buying of time in print media, because far more is known about the ways viewers watch than is known about reading patterns. ① The exact composition of television audiences, broken down by age, sex, employment, region, family composition, buying habits, and other data, can be continuously analyzed. ② For example, viewers' program switching can be tracked throughout an evening, and the different viewing patterns in houses with multiple sets can likewise be measured. ③ All this makes it possible to pinpoint television viewing of target markets with great accuracy. ④ Thus, viewers often fail to watch programs they have been predicted to watch, and inter-channel competition can make audience levels unpredictable. ⑤ The media buyer will then be able to evaluate precisely which programs and even which breaks in which programs will reach the target market most cost-effectively. There are great differences in price, for example, between peak-time and off-peak spots, and the differences approximately reflect the size and composition of the audiences.

* off-peak 비인기 시간대의

Predators which are deliberately or accidentally introduced outside their normal environments can have enormously detrimental effects. The problem is particularly acute in island settings, where a wide variety of naturally occurring predators and complex food webs are typically absent. ① Island species are thus particularly susceptible to disturbance from the sudden arrival of a new predatory species. ② Desperate efforts for survival by the island species usually ends up generating peaceful coexistence with the invading predators. ③ When alien predators, such as dogs and cats, are introduced into different ecosystems, such as islands, their impact can result in a severe reduction in or even extinction of native species. ④ This is because, in the absence of a co-evolved predation pressure, isolated and endemic island faunas have not evolved evasion and escape mechanisms. ⑤ Island faunas then become easy prey for such introduced predators. This has happened on the Australian continent, where introduced cats and foxes pose a severe threat to existing populations of native marsupials in national parks and nature reserves.

* marsupial 유대동물

105 다음 글에서 전체 흐름과 관계 <u>없는</u> 문장을 고르시오.

난이도 상

Reflective unbelievers find the language of transcendence basically unintelligible, even meaningless, and that is why they say they are skeptics. Or, more pointedly, if they have examined the arguments adduced historically to prove the existence of God, they find them invalid, hence unconvincing. They find the so-called appeals to experience unwarranted: neither mysticism nor the appeal to miracles or revelation establishes the existence of transcendental realities. ① Moreover, they maintain that morality is possible without a belief in God. ② Unbelievers are critics of supernaturalistic claims, which they consider superstition. ③ Indeed, they consider the God hypothesis to be without merit, a fanciful creation of human imagination that does not deserve careful examination by emancipated men and women. ④ This led them to go a long way towards establishing the concept of deity as the most essential element to be considered in all aspects of human life. ⑤ Many classical atheists including Baron d'Holbach, Denis Diderot and Karl Marx, fit into this category, for they were materialists first, and their religious skepticism and unbelief followed from their materialistic metaphysics.

* adduce 제시하다

106

다음 글에서 전체 흐름과 관계 없는 문장은?

난이도 상

Whether deliberately or accidentally, people have been transporting whole range of organisms, breaking natural distribution boundaries and interfering with community structures. The unwanted hitchhikers are usually either well hidden or too small to be noticed—for the entire lifespan or just for its part. ① For most coastal species the open ocean environment is inhospitable, preventing them from spreading into habitats similar to their own but located elsewhere. ② Distances separating such habitats might be too long to overcome either through their active swimming abilities or passive floating in water currents. ③ Mechanisms by which humanity aids introduction of exotic species are called vectors of introduction and these are chiefly associated with shipment activities, marine aquaculture or ornamental species trade. ④ Marine aquaculture is recognized as a viable alternative to wild collection as it can effectively supplement or replace the supply of wild caught specimens. ⑤ Other vectors include the international transport and sale of live marine bait, live seafood, and live organisms for research and education.

* ornamental species 관상용 종

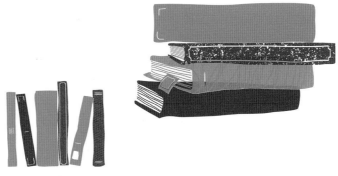

11

문장 삽입

주어진 문장이 지문의 어디에
들어가야 하는지를 묻는 유형으로
논리적 사고와 연결어, 지시어 등의
활용 능력을 측정한다.

가이드라인

- 먼저 지시사나 연결사에 주의하면서 주어진 문장을 천천히 읽는다.
- 지시사(지시대명사, 지시형용사, 인칭대명사)가 있으면 지칭 대상을, 연결사가 있으면 앞 문장과의 관계를 각각 염두에 두면서 지문을 읽어 나간다.
- 주어진 문장에 역접의 연결사(However, But, Still, Yet)가 있는 문장이 들어갈 곳은 다음의 셋 가운데 하나다.
    ⓐ 필자가 주장하는 특정 가치가 전환의 시그널 없이 갑자기 긍정(+)에서 부정(-)으로, 또는 반대로 부정(-)에서 긍정(+)으로 반전되는 곳
    ⓑ 지시사(지시대명사, 지시형용사, 인칭대명사)가 받을 말이 바로 앞 문장에 없는 곳
    ⓒ 연결사의 쓰임이 어색한 곳. 예를 들어 역접의 연결사가 있는 문장이 앞 문장과 논조가 비슷하다든지, 첨가의 연결사가 들어있는 문장이 앞 문장과 반대되는 내용을 가질 경우
- 연결사의 쓰임을 숙지한다.
    ⓐ 역접의 연결사가 있으면 앞 문장과 상반된 내용이 온다.
    ⓑ 예시의 연결사가 있으면 바로 앞에 일반 진술(주제문)이 온다.
    ⓒ 첨가나 강조의 연결사가 오면 기본적으로 앞 문장과 같은 내용(논조)이 온다.
    ⓓ 유사 비교의 연결사(Similarly, Likewise)가 오면 앞뒤 두 문장이 주제는 같고 소재가 다르다.
    ⓔ 대조의 연결사 Rather의 앞 문장은 반드시 부정어를 포함해야 한다.
- 정답 후보 선택지가 결정되면 주어진 문장을 포함하여 글의 흐름이 자연스러운지 다시 읽어 본다.
- 문장 삽입은 글의 흐름이나 연결의 시그널을 이용해 전후 문맥 관계를 따지는 것이기 때문에 기본적으로 글의 순서 파악 유형과 유사하다. 따라서 글의 순서 파악에 적용되는 원칙이 문장 삽입에서도 그대로 적용된다.

글의 흐름으로 보아, 주어진 문장이 들어가기에 가장 적절한 곳을 고르시오. |수능 2020년|

Still, it is arguable that advertisers worry rather too much about this problem, as advertising in other media has always been fragmented.

The fragmentation of television audiences during recent decades, which has happened throughout the globe as new channels have been launched everywhere, has caused advertisers much concern. (①) Advertisers look back nostalgically to the years when a single spot transmission would be seen by the majority of the population at one fell swoop. (②) This made the television advertising of mass consumer products relatively straightforward—not to say easy—whereas today it is necessary for advertisers to build up coverage of their target markets over time, by advertising on a host of channels with separate audiences. (③) Moreover, advertisers gain considerable benefits from the price competition between the numerous broadcasting stations. (④) And television remains much the fastest way to build up public awareness of a new brand or a new campaign. (⑤) Seldom does a new brand or new campaign that solely uses other media, without using television, reach high levels of public awareness very quickly.

[3점]

* fragment 조각내다 ** at one fell swoop 단번에, 일거에

[한번에 정리하는 문제 해설]

지문 해석 최근 몇십 년 동안 텔레비전 시청자의 분열은 도처에서 새로운 채널들이 생겨나면서 전 세계적으로 일어났는데, 이는 광고주들에게 많은 우려를 안겨주었다. (①) 광고주들은 한 군데에서 전송하는 것을 대부분의 사람들이 한 번에 보게 되었던 시절을 향수에 젖어 회상한다. (②) 이것은 대량 소비 제품의 텔레비전 광고를 상대적으로 단순하게—쉬웠다고 말하는 것은 아니지만—만들어 주었는데, 반면에 오늘날에는 광고주들이 별도의 시청자가 있는 다수의 채널에 광고를 함으로써 자신들의 목표 시장의 점유 범위를 시간을 두고 구축하는 것이 필요하다. (③) 그렇다고 하더라도, 다른 미디어를 이용한 광고들은 늘 단편적이었으므로, 광고주들이 이 문제에 대해 오히려 너무 많이 걱정하는 것일 수 있다고 주장할 여지가 있다. 게다가, 광고주들은 수많은 방송국들간의 가격 경쟁으로부터 상당한 이익을 얻는다. (④) 그리고 텔레비전은 새로운 브랜드나 새로운 캠페인에 대한 대중의 인식을 형성하는 단연코 가장 빠른 방법으로 남아있다. (⑤) 텔레비전을 이용하지 않고, 다른 미디어만을 이용하는 새로운 브랜드나 새로운 캠페인이 아주 빠르게 높은 수준의 대중 인지도에 도달하는 경우는 거의 없다.

글의 소재 다채널 시대의 TV 광고

주요 어휘 arguable 주장할 여지가 있는, 논쟁해 볼 만한, fragment 조각내다, 단편화하다, launch 시작하다, 출범하다, nostalgically 향수에 젖어, spot 스폿 광고, transmission 전송, 전달, at one fell swoop 단번에, 일거에, public awareness 대중 인지도, solely 혼자서, 단독으로

정답 ③

정답 해설 ③ 다음 문장은 첨가의 연결사 Moreover와 함께 채널 다양화로 인해 광고주가 얻는 이득을 말하며 채널 다양화에 대해 긍정적 시각을 보여주고 있다. 첨가의 연결사는 앞의 주장을 받아 심화 발전시키는 것이므로 앞 문장에서도 채널 다양화나 광고의 단편화에 대해 긍정적 시각이 제시돼야 한다. 그런데 ③의 앞 문장에는 다양한 채널을 통한 광고가 새로운 생존 전략이 된 오늘날 광고 환경 현실에 대해 언급할 뿐 채널 다양화나 광고 단편화에 대한 긍정적 시각과는 거리가 있다. 한편, 주어진 문장은 다른 미디어에서도 광고 단편화는 보편적 현상이라며 광고 단편화를 두둔하는 어조이므로 Moreover 문장과 자연스럽게 이어진다. 따라서 주어진 문장은 ③의 자리에 들어가는 것이 글의 흐름상 가장 적절하다.

사관 기출문제 유형보기

The efforts and legacy of those humanists, however, have not always been appreciated in their own right by historians of philosophy and science.

The Renaissance was one of the most innovative periods in Western civilization. New waves of expression in fine arts and literature bloomed in Italy and gradually spread all over Europe. (①) A new approach with a strong philological emphasis, called "humanism" by historians, was also introduced to scholarship. (②) The intellectual fecundity of the Renaissance was ensured by the intense activity of the humanists who were engaged in collecting, editing, translating and publishing the ancient literary heritage, mostly in Greek and Latin, which had hitherto been scarcely read or entirely unknown to the medieval world. (③) The humanists were active not only in deciphering and interpreting these "newly recovered" texts but also in producing original writings inspired by the ideas and themes they found in the ancient sources. (④) Through these activities, Renaissance humanist culture brought about a remarkable moment in Western intellectual history. (⑤) In particular, the impact of humanism on the evolution of natural philosophy still awaits thorough research by specialists.

* philological 문헌학의, fecundity 풍요

[한번에 정리하는 문제 해설]

지문 해석) 르네상스는 서구 문명에서 가장 혁신적인 시기 중 하나였다. 미술과 문학에서 새로운 표현의 물결이 이탈리아에서 꽃피웠고 서서히 유럽 전체로 퍼져나갔다. (①) 역사가들이 휴머니즘이라 부른, 문헌학에 강하게 초점 맞춘 새로운 접근법이 학문에도 도입됐다. (②) 르네상스의 지적 풍요로움은 주로 희랍어와 라틴어로 쓰인 고대의 문학 유산을 모으고, 편집하고, 번역하고 출간하는 데 전념한 인문주의자들의 왕성한 활동에 의해 확립됐는데 그것들은 당시까지 거의 읽히지 않았고 중세까지는 전혀 알려지지조차 않았다. (③) 인문주의자들은 이 새로 복원된 텍스트들을 해독하고 해석하는 것은 물론 고문서에서 발견한 사상이나 주제에서 영감을 받아 독창적인 저술을 하는 데도 활동적이었다. (④) 이런 활동을 통해 르네상스 인문주의 문화는 서구 지성사에 획기적 전기를 가져왔다. (⑤) 그러나 이 인문주의자들의 노력과 유산이 철학이나 과학사가들에 의해 항상 정당하게 평가받은 것은 아니다. 특히, 인문주의가 자연철학의 발전에 미친 영향은 아직 전문가들의 철저한 연구를 기다리고 있다.

글의 소재) 르네상스 시기 인문주의 유산에 대한 이해와 몰이해

주요 어휘) legacy 유산, in their own right 정당한 권리로, 정당하게, philological 문헌학의, fecundity 풍요, hitherto 지금까지, 그때까지, medieval 중세의, decipher 해독하다, thorough 철저한

정답) ⑤

정답 해설) 주어진 문장 속에 있는 역접의 연결사 however에 주목하고 어떤 가치가 긍정(+)에서 부정(−)으로, 또는 부정(−)에서 긍정(+)으로 갑작스럽게 변하는 곳이 있는지 찾아보자. ⑤ 앞 문장은 '르네상스 인문주의 문화가 서구 지성사에 획기적 전기를 가져왔다'라는 긍정적인 내용인 반면 다음 문장은 인문주의가 자연철학에 미친 영향이 아직 철저한 연구를 기다린다는 부정적인 내용이 오고 있고 두 문장은 'In particular'에 의해 연결되고 있다. 그런데 강조의 연결사 'In particular'는 기본적으로 같은 내용의 두 문장을 연결하므로 여기서 연결사의 쓰임이 어색함을 알 수 있다. 따라서 주어진 글이 올 곳은 ⑤이다.

25 글의 흐름으로 보아, 주어진 문장이 들어가기에 가장 적절한 곳은?

However, some businesses (for example, small retailers) do not usually find it practical to match each sale to a particular cost of sales figure as the accounting period progresses.

The cost of sales (or cost of goods sold) figure for a period can be identified in different ways. (①) In some businesses, the cost of sales is identified at the time a sale has been made. (②) Sales are closely matched with the cost of those sales and so identifying the cost of sales figure for inclusion in the income statement is not a problem. (③) Many large retailers (for example, supermarkets) have point-of-sale (checkout) devices that not only record each sale but also simultaneously pick up the cost of the goods that are the subject of the particular sale. (④) Other businesses that sell a relatively small number of high-value items also tend to match sales revenue with the cost of the goods sold at the time of the sale. (⑤) They find it easier to identify the cost of sales figure at the end of the accounting period.

[한번에 정리하는 문제 해설]

지문 해석 한 기간의 판매비용(즉 판매된 제품의 비용)은 서로 다른 방식으로 산정될 수 있다. (①) 어떤 업체에서 판매비용은 판매가 이뤄진 시점에 산정된다. (②) 판매는 그 판매에 따른 비용과 밀접하게 연계되기 때문에 손익계산서에 포함하기 위해 판매비용을 산정하는 것은 전혀 문제 되지 않는다. (③) 많은 대규모 소매상(예를 들어 슈퍼마켓)들은 각각의 판매를 기록할 뿐만 아니라 특정 판매의 대상인 상품의 비용을 동시에 계산하는 매장(계산대) 장치를 가지고 있다. (④) 비교적 적은 수량의 고가 상품을 판매하는 다른 업체들 역시 매출 수입을 판매 시점에 팔린 상품의 비용과 연계시키는 경향이 있다. (⑤) 하지만, 몇몇 업체들은─예를 들면 소규모 소매상들─회계 기간이 지날수록 각각의 판매를 판매비용과 연계시키는 것이 대체로 실용적이지 않다고 본다. 그들은 판매비용을 회계 기간 말에 산정하는 것이 더 수월하다고 본다.

글의 소재 판매비용 산정 방식의 상이함

주요 어휘 figure 수치, identify 확인하다, 산정하다, inclusion 포함, retailer 소매상, point-of-sale 매장, checkout 계산대, simultaneously 동시에, relatively 비교적, revenue 수입, accounting 회계

정답 ⑤

정답 해설 들어갈 글은 각각의 판매액과 판매비용을 연계시키는 것이 효과적이지 못하다는 내용이고 그것이 역접의 연결사와 함께 제시된다. 따라서 네모 글은 그와 반대 내용, 즉 판매와 판매비용이 연계되는 내용의 맨 마지막 부분에 와야 한다는 것을 추론할 수 있고 그곳은 바로 ⑤다. 기술적으로, ⑤ 앞까지는 판매와 판매비용이 연계되다가 갑자기 ─ 즉 적절한 전환의 시그널 없이 ─ 비용을 회계 기간 말에 산정한다는, 둘 간의 연계가 깨지는 내용으로 넘어가기 때문에 여기서 글의 논리적 흐름이 단절됨을 알 수 있다. 또 ⑤ 다음 문장의 주어 They는 판매비용을 회계 기간 말에 산정하는 주체이므로, 판매액과 판매비용이 연계되는 바로 앞 문장에는 이를 받을 말이 없음을 알 수 있다.

107 글의 흐름으로 보아 주어진 문장이 들어가기에 가장 적절한 곳은? 난이도 중

Specifically, they found it can help people withstand higher levels of pain and discomfort.

Since the inception of the Ig Nobel Prizes in 1991, prizes have been issued for a number of unusual achievements. (①) For example, a research team from the UK's Keele University was awarded an Ig Nobel for their study on pain and the use of profanity. (②) They discovered that profanity is not only a common response to pain, but also a useful one. (③) In one of their experiments, test subjects were required to hold their hands in icy cold water for as long as they could. (④) Those permitted to swear were able to keep their hands in the water nearly fifty percent longer than those not permitted to swear. (⑤) In a follow-up study, the researchers discovered that infrequent users of profanity benefited the most, whereas those who frequently swore showed little to no difference.

108 글의 흐름으로 보아 주어진 문장이 들어가기에 가장 적절한 곳을 고르시오.

In short, a suitable reward may result in an animal or human displaying certain behaviour more quickly.

American educationalist Edward L. Thorndike embraced the method of testing and separating education completely from philosophy and moving it more into empirical psychology. The use of statistics was central for this, as was the belief that everything in life can be measured. (①) At the time this was expressed as follows: "whatever exists at all, exists in some amount; anything that exists in amount can be measured; measurement in education is in general the same as measurement in the physical sciences." (②) Thorndike introduced careful experimental procedures into research on learning. (③) His most famous contribution is the introduction of the law of effect. (④) According to this law, the effect of a response determines whether the inclination to repeat the same response will grow stronger or weaker. (⑤) Statistics thus became both an academic discipline of education and a part of the broader educational development in how to organize education and schooling.

109 글의 흐름으로 보아 주어진 문장이 들어가기에 가장 적절한 곳은?

난이도 중

As a result, China has had to play a major role in preserving the remaining population of the revered "big bear cat," as the giant panda is called in Chinese.

Counting pandas is notoriously difficult, as they are surprisingly elusive in spite of their size. Methods have changed since the first official census in the 1970's: researchers no longer merely wander the forests searching signs of panda life, but now analyze fecal matter for DNA and study the length of undigested bamboo, which indicates bite size. The current population is fast approaching 2,060 bears, including cubs. (①) The 17 percent increase over 10 years, as reported in the 2014 census, can be attributed to two major factors: a decrease in poaching and an increase in the animal's habitat. (②) Pandas used to inhabit the lush bamboo forests of Southern China, Myanmar, and Vietnam. (③) But now their habitat encompasses only the mountainous regions of western China. (④) The nation has opened 67 panda reserves covering 14,000 square kilometers over the past 30 years, which has helped boost the image of Chinese environmental responsibility. (⑤) Pandas have also been an important symbol of diplomacy between China and the international community.

* fecal 배설물의

글의 흐름으로 보아 주어진 문장이 들어가기에 가장 적절한 곳은?

However, until a century ago, all but 20, if known at all, were curiosities of the chemistry laboratory.

Not only are we consuming materials more rapidly, but we are using an increasing diversity of materials. (①) A great new range of materials has opened up for the use of 20th-century man: refractory metals, light alloys, plastics, and synthetic fibers, for example. (②) Some of these do better, or cheaper, what the older ones did; others have combinations of properties that enable entirely new devices to be made or quite new effects to be achieved. (③) We now employ in industrial processes a majority of the ninety-two elements in the periodic table which are found in nature. (④) Not only are more of nature's elements being put into service, but completely new materials are being synthesized in the laboratory. (⑤) Our claim to a high level of materials civilization rests on this expanded, almost extravagant utilization of a rich diversity of materials.

* refractory 내화성의

111

글의 흐름으로 보아 주어진 문장이 들어가기에 가장 적절한 곳을 고르시오. 난이도 중

It doesn't matter that those fans, for the most part, don't actually understand the Korean lyrics of major hits like "DNA" and "Mic Drop".

In 2017, if you asked most Americans to name just one Korean performing artist, odds are high the answer would have been a resounding "BTS". This seven-member boy band has grown from a local pop sensation to a global phenomenon that's made "K-pop" a household word in households that have probably never even looked at South Korea on a map. (①) How did they do the impossible, and crack the elusive and highly-competitive American market? (②) Not just crack it; smashed it to the tune (no pun intended) of 1.6 million song downloads, over a billion online streams, and a veritable army—literally "ARMY" as their fan base is known—of screaming admirers at each and every appearance on their recent U.S. circuit. (③) That hasn't stopped BTS devotees from singing along in phonetic approximation, from screaming the band members' names in unison with their patented "fan chants", and, perhaps most crucially, from buying their record. (④) The group's latest album, 2017's Love Yourself: Her, sold nearly 1.5 million physical copies, according to South Korea's Gaon chart. (⑤)

112

글의 흐름으로 보아 주어진 문장이 들어가기에 가장 적절한 곳을 고르시오.

Rather, givers and takers differ in their attitudes and actions toward other people.

In the workplace, givers are a relatively rare breed. They tilt reciprocity in the other direction, preferring to give more than they get. Whereas takers tend to be self-focused, evaluating what other people can offer them, givers are other-focused, paying more attention to what other people need from them. (①) These preferences aren't about money: givers and takers aren't distinguished by how much they donate to charity or the compensation that they command from their employers. (②) If you're a taker, you help others strategically, when the benefits to you outweigh the personal costs. (③) If you're a giver, you might use a different cost-benefit analysis: you help whenever the benefits to others exceed the personal costs. (④) Alternatively, you might not think about the personal costs at all, helping others without expecting anything in return. (⑤) If you're a giver at work, you simply strive to be generous in sharing your time, energy, knowledge, skills, ideas, and connections with other people who can benefit from them.

113 글의 흐름으로 보아 주어진 문장이 들어가기에 가장 적절한 곳을 고르시오. 난이도 중

Only from the late 1950s onward did protective devices like earplugs and earmuff grow more common.

As early as 1907 the "Ohropax" earplug was introduced, but workers were generally not very eager to use it or similar devices. Many of them regarded the use of ear-plugs as "unmanly" and were not worried about noise-induced hearing loss, which came only slowly and gradually. On a symbolic level, noise in industry also had positive connotations. (①) As American historian Mark Smith has once mentioned, a noisy factory meant that industry was booming and earnings were good. (②) Besides, wearing a hearing-protection device made workers insecure about where the noise came from while also causing communication problems. (③) Listening to machine noise or sound gave workers a feeling of security; they would hear it when something was wrong. (④) Furthermore, wearing ear protection could even be dangerous because one could also fail to hear particular warning signals. (⑤) Employers and liability-insurance associations insisted on their use mainly because they faced rapidly increasing compensation claims for employees' hearing losses.

글의 흐름으로 보아, 주어진 문장이 들어가기에 가장 적절한 곳을 고르시오. 난이도 상

Yet it was the bare body that was man's first weapon, and all instruments of violence are extensions of the human body.

The body is the first instrument of violence, the first weapon. Here the "first" doesn't indicate a priority, but the beginning of an anthropological and ultimately a technical development that is still in full force. (①) Three things are constantly increasing: the power of weapons, the skills needed to use them, and the distance to the target. (②) Needless to say, it is the deadly ingenuity of the human mind that devised most weapons and optimized the skills needed to use them and to build them. (③) Examples of simple weapons such as a club, a knife, or a sword, can help illustrate this unity between user and instrument. (④) Martial artists trained in the delicate techniques of fencing or kendo, a Japanese form of sword-fighting will intuitively understand that the purpose of intensive training, mental as well as physical, is to make the weapon's use as natural as the use of one's arms or legs, and vastly more efficient. (⑤) Hence expressions such as "going into the weapon," "becoming one" with it, or "feeling" it.

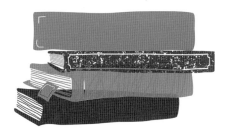

12

글의 순서

글의 도입부가 주어지고 이후 세 개의 문단이

자연스럽게 이어지도록 내용을

논리적으로 배열하는 능력을 묻는 유형이다.

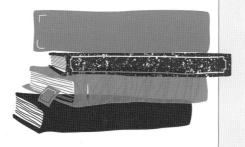

▶ 먼저 주어진 글이나 각 지문에 의문문이나 따옴표가 있는지 보라. 의문문이 있으면 이에 대한 답을, 따옴표가 있으면 같은 따옴표 있는 문장을 각각 찾는다.

▶ 지시사(지시대명사, 지시형용사, 지시부사)는 단독으로 쓰이지 못하고 반드시 지칭 대상이 있어야 한다. 문장의 선후 관계를 파악하는 데 이를 100% 활용하라.

▶ 확실한 것 위주로 가라(애매하면 살려라!)
  • 머리가 확실하면 머리를 고정시킨 채 나머지 두 지문을 비교하고
  • 머리가 아닌 게 확실하면 머리가 아니게 하는 요인을 나머지 두 지문에서 찾는다.

▶ 지문 (A)를 주시하라. 문제 해결의 키는 (A)가 쥐고 있는 경우가 많다. (A)는 머리로 오지 않는다고 전제하고 머리에 못 오게 하는 요인을 나머지 두 지문에서 찾아라. 이 방법이 실전에서 가장 실용적이다.

▶ 머리의 단서는 꼬리에서 찾아라(수미상응).

• 같은 색(논조)은 같은 색(논조)을 부르고, 꺾이면(역접의 연결사가 오면) 색(논조)이 바뀐다.

▶ 같은 색(논조)이면 꺾이는 쪽, 즉 역접의 연결사 있는 지문이 먼저다.

▶ 신정보 vs 구정보를 이용하라.

글의 순서 파악에 자주 쓰이는 지시사, 형용사, 부사

▶ 지시사: • 지시대명사(형용사) – this, these, that, those, it, such(정도를 나타내는 경우 제외)
  • 인칭대명사 – he, she, his, her, him, hers, they, their, them
  • 정관사(대표단수 시 제외) – the

▶ 형용사: the same, another, the other, other, similar

▶ 부사: there, then, too, either, also, 비교급 표현[ex) a century later(earlier), more advanced microscopes]

연결사를 통한 글의 흐름 파악의 예

▶ first, second, then, lastly: 시간이나 절차상 순서를 보여준다.

▶ for example, for instance: 앞의 주장을 뒷받침하는 예가 나온다.

▶ but, however, nevertheless: 글의 흐름의 반전이 이뤄진다.

▶ in addition, additionally, furthermore, besides: 앞의 주장에 내용을 추가한다.

▶ likewise, similarly, namely, that is (to say), in other words: 앞의 말을 부연 설명한다.

▶ as a result, accordingly, therefore, consequently: 원인에 대한 결과가 이어진다.

신정보 vs 구정보에 의한 선후 관계 파악

▶ 신정보(new information): 처음 언급되는 것으로 앞에 나옴
  ⓐ 일반 명사의 경우 부정관사 a(n)이 사용됨.[ex) I bought a red cap.]
  ⓑ 사람 이름의 경우 full name을 쓰며 소개 문구가 따라 나올 때도 있다.
    [ex) She is Jung Mina, a junior at Sewon Highschool.]

▶ 구정보(old information): 되풀이 언급되는 것으로 나중에 나옴
  ⓐ 정관사 the가 쓰인다. [ex) The cap is made in China.]
  ⓑ 사람 이름의 경우 first name 또는 last name만 쓴다. [ex) Mina(Ms. Jung) is very popular with her classmates.]

Traditionally, Kuhn claims, the primary goal of historians of science was 'to clarify and deepen an understanding of contemporary scientific methods or concepts by displaying their evolution'.

(A) Some discoveries seem to entail numerous phases and discoverers, none of which can be identified as definitive. Furthermore, the evaluation of past discoveries and discoverers according to present-day standards does not allow us to see how significant they may have been in their own day.

(B) This entailed relating the progressive accumulation of breakthroughs and discoveries. Only that which survived in some form in the present was considered relevant. In the mid-1950s, however, a number of faults in this view of history became apparent. Closer analysis of scientific discoveries, for instance, led historians to ask whether the dates of discoveries and their discoverers can be identified precisely.

(C) Nor does the traditional view recognise the role that non-intellectual factors, especially institutional and socio-economic ones, play in scientific developments. Most importantly, however, the traditional historian of science seems blind to the fact that the concepts, questions and standards that they use to frame the past are themselves subject to historical change.　[3점]

① (A) - (C) - (B)　　② (B) - (A) - (C)　　③ (B) - (C) - (A)

④ (C) - (A) - (B)　　⑤ (C) - (B) - (A)

[한번에 정리하는 문제 해설]

[지문 해석] Kuhn이 주장하기를, 전통적으로 과학 사학자의 주요 목표는 '당대의 과학적 방법이나 개념의 점진적 발전을 보여 줌으로써 그것에 대한 이해를 분명히 하고, 깊게 하는 것'이다.

(B) 이것은 획기적인 발전과 발견의 점진적인 축적을 거론하는 것을 수반했다. 현재에 어떤 형태로 살아남은 것만이 유의미한 것으로 여겨졌다. 하지만 1950년대 중반에, 역사에 대한 이러한 관점에서 많은 결함이 분명해졌다. 예를 들어, 과학적 발견에 대한 더 면밀한 분석은 역사가들로 하여금 발견의 시기와 그러한 발견을 한 사람들이 정확하게 확인될 수 있는지를 묻게 했다.

(A) 몇몇 발견은 무수한 단계와 발견자들을 수반하는 것처럼 보이는데, 그 중 어느 것도 확정적인 것으로 확인될 수 없다. 게다가, 현재의 기준에 따라 과거의 발견들을 평가하는 것은 그것이 당시에 얼마나 중요했는지를 우리가 알 수 없게 한다.

(C) 전통적인 관점은 또한 비지성적인 요인들, 특히 제도적 요인과 사회경제적 요인이 과학 발전에서 하는 역할을 인식하지 못한다. 하지만 가장 중요한 것은 전통적인 과학 사학자가 과거의 틀을 잡기 위해 자신이 사용하는 개념, 질문, 기준 자체가 역사적 변화의 영향 하에 있다는 사실을 알지 못하는 것처럼 보인다는 것이다.

[글의 소재] 전통적인 과학사관의 맹점

[주요 어휘] clarify 분명히 하다, entail 수반하다, numerous 무수한, phase 단계, identify 확인하다, definitive 확정적인, 최종적인, evaluation 평가, accumulation 축적, breakthrough 획기적인 발전, 돌파구, relevant 유의미한, 관련성 있는, apparent 분명한, precisely 정확하게, institutional 제도적인, blind to ~을 알지 못하는, ~를 못 보는, frame 구상하다, 표현하다, be subject to ~의 영향 하에 있다

[정　답] ②

[정답 해설] 접속사 Nor로 시작되는 문장은 반드시 앞에 부정어를 포함한 문장이 와야 한다. 따라서 (C)가 가야 할 자리는 (A) 뒤뿐이다. (A)와 (C)가 결정됐으니 (B)의 위치만 정해주면 된다. ('머리의 단서는 꼬리에서 찾아라!'라는 말을 생각해 보았을 때) (A) 첫 문장의 'Some discoveries ~'는 문맥상 (B)의 맨 마지막 행 '~discoveries and their discoverers can be identified precisely.'에 연결되는 게 자연스럽다. 따라서 올바른 글의 순서는 ②의 (B) - (A) - (C)이다. 글의 내용의 흐름으로 봐도 주어진 글에서 전통적인 과학사학자들의 관점이 제시된 다음(통념) (B)에서 이런 관점(통념)이 이어진다. 한편 역접의 연결사 however와 함께 그에 대한 문제가 제기되면서 흐름이 꺾이고 (A)에서 추가적인 문제점이 제기된 다음 (C)로 넘어와 가장 중요한 문제점이 제기되며 마무리되는 구조이므로 자연스러운 글의 순서는 (B) - (A) - (C)이다.

주어진 글 다음에 이어질 글의 순서로 가장 적절한 것은?

Darwin justly observed that the struggle between two organisms is as active as they are analogous. Having the same needs and pursuing the same objects, they are in rivalry everywhere.

(A) The dentist does not struggle with the psychiatrist, nor the shoemaker with the hatter. Since they perform different services, they can perform them parally.

(B) As long as they have more resources than they need, they can live side by side, but if their number increases to such proportions that all appetites can no longer be sufficiently satisfied, war breaks out. It is quite different if the coexisting individuals are of different species or varieties.

(C) As they do not feed in the same manner, and do not lead the same kind of life, they do not disturb each other. Men submit to the same law. In the same city different occupations can coexist without being obliged mutually to destroy one another, for they pursue different objects.

① (A) - (C) - (B)
② (B) - (A) - (C)
③ (B) - (C) - (A)
④ (C) - (A) - (B)
⑤ (C) - (B) - (A)

[한번에 정리하는 문제 해설]

지문 해석 두 유기체 간의 경쟁은 그들이 유사한 만큼 활발하다는 다윈의 말은 옳다. 필요로 하는 것이 같고 같은 대상을 추구하기 때문에 그들은 어디서나 경쟁 관계에 있다.

(B) 그들이 필요로 하는 것보다 더 많은 자원이 있는 한 그들은 공존할 수 있지만 그들의 숫자가 증가해 식욕을 충분히 충족시키지 못할 정도가 되면 전쟁이 일어난다. 공존하는 개체가 종이 다를 경우는 상황이 전혀 다르다.

(C) 그들은 같은 방식으로 먹이를 구하지 않고 생활 방식도 같지 않기 때문에 서로를 방해하지 않는다. 인간도 같은 법칙을 따른다. 같은 도시에는 서로 다른 직업이 서로를 파괴할 필요 없이 공존할 수 있는데 이는 그들이 다른 대상을 추구하기 때문이다.

(A) 치과의사는 정신과 의사와 다투지 않고 구두 만드는 사람은 모자 만드는 사람과 다투지 않는다. 그들은 서로 다른 일을 하므로 각자의 일을 간섭 없이 할 수 있다.

글의 소재 유사 종간의 경쟁

주요 어휘 justly 정당하게, 타당하게, analogous 유사한, active 활발한, rivalry 경쟁, struggle 투쟁하다, psychiatrist 정신과 의사, parally 동시에, 간섭 없이, proportion 비율, 정도, sufficiently 충분히, submit to ~에 복종하다, ~에 따르다, be obliged to 어쩔 수 없이 ~하다

정 답 ③

정답 해설 주어진 글은 두 종간의 경쟁 관계를 언급하는 데 반해 (A)와 (C)는 경쟁이 아닌 평화 공존의 관계를 말하고 있으므로 (A), (C)는 주어진 글 다음에 올 수 없다. (B)는 유사종 간의 경쟁으로 시작해 이종 간 평화 공존으로 끝맺기 때문에 주어진 글 다음에 와야 한다. (C)는 이종의 유기체 간 평화 공존으로 시작해서 서로 다른 직업을 가진 사람 사회의 평화 공존으로 넘어가고, (A)는 이 직종 간 평화 공존의 구체적인 예를 제시하므로 (C) - (A) 순서가 돼야 한다. 따라서 이어지는 글의 순서는 (B) - (C) - (A)이고, 정답은 ③이다.

34 주어진 글 다음에 이어질 글의 순서로 가장 적절한 것을 고르시오.

"National forests need more roads like farmers need more drought." We heard somebody say this who was trying to persuade an audience that more roads would be bad for our national forests.

(A) An argument attempts to prove or support a conclusion. When you attempt to persuade someone, you attempt to win him or her to your point of view; trying to persuade and trying to argue are logically distinct enterprises. True, when you want to persuade somebody of something, you might use an argument.

(B) But not all arguments attempt to persuade, and many attempts to persuade do not involve arguments. In fact, giving an argument is often one of the least effective methods of persuading people—which, of course, is why so few advertisers bother with arguments. People notoriously are persuaded by the weakest of arguments and sometimes are undisturbed by even quite good arguments.

(C) The remark, however, is not an argument; it's just a statement that portrays road building in the forests in a bad light. Now, some writers define an argument as an attempt to persuade somebody of something. This is not correct.

① (A) - (C) - (B)　　　② (B) - (A) - (C)　　　③ (B) - (C) - (A)
④ (C) - (A) - (B)　　　⑤ (C) - (B) - (A)

[한번에 정리하는 문제 해설]

지문 해석 "농부가 더 많은 가뭄을 필요로 하는 것처럼 국유림은 더 많은 도로를 필요로 한다." 우리는 어떤 사람이 더 많은 도로는 국유림에 나쁘다는 것을 청중에게 설득하려고 이 말을 하는 것을 들었다.

(C) 하지만 이 말은 논증이 아니다. 그것은 숲에 도로를 건설하는 것을 부정적으로 표현하는 진술일 뿐이다. 어떤 작가들은 논증을 누군가에게 무엇을 설득하려는 시도로 정의한다. 이것은 옳지 않다.

(A) 논증은 결론을 입증하거나 뒷받침하려는 시도다. 당신이 누군가를 설득하려 할 때 당신은 그/그녀를 당신의 관점으로 끌어오려고 시도한다. 설득하려 하는 것과 논증하려는 것은 논리적으로 차이가 분명한 일이다. 실제로 당신이 누군가에게 무엇을 설득할 때 당신은 논증의 방법을 쓰기도 한다.

(B) 그러나 모든 논증이 설득을 시도하는 것도 아니고 설득하려는 시도에 논증이 따르지 않는 경우도 많다. 사실 논거를 들이대는 것은 흔히 사람을 설득하는 가장 비효율적인 방법 중 하나다. - 이것이 물론 논증에 신경 쓰는 광고주들이 드문 이유다. 사람들이 가장 약한 논증으로 설득당하면서 종종 가장 훌륭한 논증으로도 마음이 움직이지 않는 것은 유명하다.

글의 소재 설득에서 논증의 불필요성

주요 어휘 drought 가뭄, persuade 설득하다, distinct 다른, 각별한, argument 논증, 논거, 주장, effective 효율적인, notoriously 악명 높게, undisturbed 마음이 움직이지 않는, 방해받지 않는, remark 발언, statement 진술

구조 분석 People notoriously are persuaded by the weakest of arguments and sometimes are undisturbed by even quite good arguments.
→ notoriously는 문장 전체 수식부사로 'It is notorious that ~'으로 패러프레이즈할 수 있다.

정답 ④

정답 해설 먼저 (C)의 the remark가 눈에 들어온다. 여기서 the는 대표단수의 the가 아니기 때문에 지칭 대상, 즉 '누가 한 발언'이 있어야 한다. 이것은 주어진 글 안의 인용부호 문장에서 쉽게 찾을 수 있다. 따라서 주어진 문장에 이어질 단락은 (C)다. (C)는 일부 작가는 argument를 누군가에게 무엇을 설득하는 것으로 정의하는데 이것은 옳지 않다고 끝맺는다. 그렇다면 이어지는 문장에는 'argument의 쓰임이 설득이 아닌 다른 것'이라는 내용이 들어있어야 한다. 이 말은 'argument는 결론을 증명하거나 뒷받침하기를 시도한다.'는 (A)의 첫 문장에 제시되고 있다. 따라서 글의 순서는 (C) - (A) - (B)이다.

12. 글의 순서

| 해설 420쪽 |

115 주어진 글 다음에 이어질 글의 순서로 가장 적절한 것은?

난이도 중

Have you ever tried to communicate with someone from another culture, and to develop a relationship, maybe as a workmate, a friend, or a partner? It's not only the fact that there is a different spoken language to break through, but also differences in non-verbal communication, belief systems, and values.

(A) And then there are differences in beliefs and values which can be a source of confusion or distress. Take something as basic as our belief in democracy and compare that to attitudes around the world, and you can see how difficult it can be to relate to someone with very different ideas.

(B) For example, in Japan, people use laughter and smiles to conceal anger or grief because it is inappropriate to display these emotions in public. In Asian countries, it is disrespectful to make eye contact with a superior, whereas in white western culture avoiding eye contact may be taken to suggest boredom, ignorance or dishonesty.

(C) Differences in the meaning of non-verbal behaviors are a good example of how not knowing the significance of a particular gesture, action or facial expression can cause misunderstanding and possibly offence.

① (A) – (C) – (B)
② (B) – (A) – (C)
③ (B) – (C) – (A)
④ (C) – (A) – (B)
⑤ (C) – (B) – (A)

116

주어진 글 다음에 이어질 글의 순서로 가장 적절한 것은?

Lend money to a friend, and you are liable to lose both. Many people say the best policy is not to lend any money to those close to you if you can help it. You can be the lender or borrower, they warn, but chances are neither situation will work out well. There are several reasons why loaning money to someone close to you can be troublesome.

(A) If you must lend money to a family member or friend nevertheless, provide them with a timeline and a schedule for repaying the loan. The timeline provides a final deadline for total repayment of the loan and the schedule provides them with guidelines for making monthly payments.

(B) This leaves both parties in limbo, and doesn't set any expectations. The uncertainty can lead to stress as the borrower may worry that the lender expects payment and the lender worries about when he or she will be repaid, a situation that should be avoided at any cost.

(C) First, loans to family and friends tend to be open-ended. The parties don't reach an agreement for a timeline for repayments, and don't include interest on the loan. Lenders don't know when their money will be returned, and borrowers don't know when to repay the loans.

* in limbo 불안정한

① (A) – (C) – (B)
② (B) – (A) – (C)
③ (B) – (C) – (A)
④ (C) – (A) – (B)
⑤ (C) – (B) – (A)

117 주어진 글에 이어질 글의 순서로 가장 알맞은 것을 고르시오. 난이도 중

It is a general phenomenon, and not one confined to music, that words and images rarely, if ever, express quite what they are meant to. They distort the experiences that they are intended to represent, either through carrying false or unintended meanings with them or through leaving unexpressed the finer shades of what was intended.

(A) And it is not only theorists who have such doubts. People who go to concerts must sometimes be upset by the lack of correspondence between the manner in which they experience a piece of music and the manner in which it is described in the programme-note; for programme-notes often dwell on the aesthetic importance of large-scale tonal structures that are in practice inaudible to most listeners.

(B) They have done so on the grounds that there is a basic incompatibility between words and rational reflection on the one hand, and the experiencing of music on the other—an incompatibility whose source lies in the quite distinct logical structures of verbal and musical consciousness.

(C) But in the case of music the problem of experience and its representation is so pressing and so specific that some theorists like the ethnomusicologist Charles Seeger, have questioned the degree to which words can be regarded as capable of expressing musical experiences at all.

*ethnomusicologist 민속음악학자

① (A) - (C) - (B)
② (B) - (A) - (C)
③ (B) - (C) - (A)
④ (C) - (A) - (B)
⑤ (C) - (B) - (A)

주어진 글 다음에 이어질 글의 순서로 가장 적절한 것을 고르시오. 난이도 중

Contemporary research has shown that greater identification with one's ethnicity is related to a host of positive outcomes, including greater self-esteem, ego-identity, and school involvement.

(A) The protection comes from accepting that racism exists and affects all blacks, that negative outcomes are because of a racist system and not the self, and that one can use various strategies to deal with racism (withdrawal, assertion, avoidance, passivity).

(B) Other functions that a strong identity may serve include providing purpose, meaning, and affiliation, often expressed in celebration of accomplishments of the black community.

(C) For example, in a study of Afro-American students, N. Gonzales and A. Cauce found that ethnic pride was positively related to boys' and girls' confidence as potential dating partners and boys' grade point averages. W. Cross Jr., discussing blacks in the United States, views a strong ethnic identity as serving the protective function of filtering one's social worldview so as to make it less dehumanizing.

① (A) – (C) – (B)
② (B) – (A) – (C)
③ (B) – (C) – (A)
④ (C) – (A) – (B)
⑤ (C) – (B) – (A)

119

주어진 글 다음에 이어질 글의 순서로 가장 적절한 것을 고르시오.

난이도 중

No one has successfully quantified the amount of attention that a person has at his or her disposal. Lately, the limits of attention have often been expressed in terms of the "bits" of information that a person can process at any given moment in time.

(A) Expert players, however, have no trouble placing each piece on the right square—not because their attention-span is greater, but because with experience they have learned to recognize likely positions, involving many pieces, as one unit, a single bit of information.

(B) For example, if novices at chess are shown a board with pieces on it from an actual game, and then after a few seconds are asked to reproduce the position of the pieces on another board, very few can remember where the pieces had been.

(C) However, it is not clear what counts as a bit. Also, starting from the earliest studies in information processing in the 1950s, it became apparent that with experience it is possible to "chunk" several bits of information in a single Gestalt that then can be processed as if it were a bit.

* Gestalt: 사물의 인식 단위로서의 포괄적 형태 또는 구조, 게슈탈트

① (A) – (C) – (B)
② (B) – (A) – (C)
③ (B) – (C) – (A)
④ (C) – (A) – (B)
⑤ (C) – (B) – (A)

120 주어진 글에 이어질 글의 순서로 가장 알맞은 것을 고르시오. 난이도 중

Striving to attain majority status in the group we belong to is evident even when the group is itself in the minority. Think about a complex business organization with many factions vying for influence.

(A) Members of peripheral divisions strive to attain status in their group so that they can maneuver themselves into the division's leadership and ultimately control the group's directions. From there, the move to the top becomes feasible, or at least imaginable.

(B) Top management holds the power and by definition runs the show. Subordinate groups within the organization may have considerable control within their respective divisions, but they may well be removed from the power brokers, the executives who hold overall control.

(C) Even so, those who belong to an 'outside' division work hard to attain membership in their division's leadership, to belong to the 'majority within the minority.' It's a safe bet that every middle manager has thought about what it would be like to be the boss and enjoy the power and prestige that go with the job—and probably more than once.

① (A) – (C) – (B)
② (B) – (A) – (C)
③ (B) – (C) – (A)
④ (C) – (A) – (B)
⑤ (C) – (B) – (A)

121

주어진 글에 이어질 글의 순서로 가장 알맞은 것을 고르시오.

난이도 중

In many instances, an animal's responsiveness to specific releasers is innate or inborn. But in many other instances, the animal is born with a gap in his or her knowledge. The animal is innately equipped with all the patterns of an instinct but lacks some information about the releasing stimulus.

(A) Ordinarily, this object is the real mother, but when orphan goslings were raised by Konrad Lorenz, an Austrian ethologist, they took him for their "mother." They energetically followed him about in single file wherever he went, ignoring other geese. They had imprinted on him.

(B) When this information is filled in during an early critical period, the process is called imprinting. Many species of young birds and mammals enter the world with incomplete knowledge about the stimuli that will release their following response.

(C) It's as if a gosling, for example, were to say, "I know I have an instinct to follow, I know I'm supposed to get into single file, and I know something about the releaser—it's my mother when she departs. But what does she look like?" This is the information the gosling acquires when she follows the first moving object she sees during an early critical period.

*releaser 사람이나 동물에게 특정 행동을 유발하는 자극, ethologist 생태학자

① (A) – (C) – (B)
② (B) – (A) – (C)
③ (B) – (C) – (A)
④ (C) – (A) – (B)
⑤ (C) – (B) – (A)

122 다음 주어진 글에 이어질 글의 순서로 가장 알맞은 것을 고르시오. 난이도 중

A medium is any social or technological procedure or device that is used for the selection, transmission, and reception of information. Every civilization has developed various types of media, transmitted through social elements such as territory, dwelling units, dress and fashion, language, clocks and calendars, dance, and other rituals.

(A) But in the modern world, these types of media have been overshadowed by newspapers, radio, and television. Although social scientists tend to focus on the latter when discussing media, we could expand this application to show how other types of media may be regarded as basic features of social life.

(B) Groups aspiring to power seek to gain leverage and legitimacy through media. In addition, select media promote a public portrayal of everyday life and political power according to the logic of the dominant institutions.

(C) It is valuable to examine how media differ from one epoch to another and from one culture to another; every historical period is marked by the dominance of some media over others, and the dominance affects other areas of social life.

① (A) – (C) – (B)
② (B) – (A) – (C)
③ (B) – (C) – (A)
④ (C) – (A) – (B)
⑤ (C) – (B) – (A)

123 주어진 글 다음에 이어질 글의 순서로 가장 적절한 것은?

난이도 상

Much of what you read in school will have an informative purpose where the writer'g goal is to tell readers what's generally known or believed about the topic under discussion. Thus, little or no attempt is made to convey a personal point of view. In fact, writers with an informative purpose go out of their way to avoid expressing any personal opinions, carefully using denotative language, or language that packs little or no emotional punch.

(A) However, even academic writers sometimes write with a persuasive purpose. They convey an opinion that they want readers to share or at least seriously consider.

(B) When the writer's purpose is informative, you are more likely to get supporting details that provide illustrations, convey facts, or describe studies. If the supporting details take the form of reasons, they will be ascribed to other people, rather than to the author.

(C) When persuasion is the writer's intent, you are likely to see more supporting details that take the form of reasons explaining why readers should think the same way the author does. You may also find personal anecdotes, or stories, that are meant to touch readers' emotions and thereby persuade them to share the author's point of view.

① (A) - (C) - (B)
② (B) - (A) - (C)
③ (B) - (C) - (A)
④ (C) - (A) - (B)
⑤ (C) - (B) - (A)

124 주어진 글 다음에 이어질 글의 순서로 가장 적절한 것은? 난이도 상

It's extremely difficult to bring dinosaurs back from extinction. A few scientists, however, have reportedly made successful approaches to finding out clues.

(A) Modern birds are the dinosaur's closest relatives. They first appeared about 150 million years ago and managed to survive through the period when many other species went extinct. Scientists believe reverse engineering birds to look like their prehistoric ancestors is a possibility.

(B) One such approach is working backwards from modern DNA. As scientists gain a better understanding of genetics, there is a good chance they will eventually have what they need to fill in the gaps and rearrange DNA in ways that could be used to create new creatures. They might not be dinosaurs, but certainly could look the part.

(C) In 2006, scientists discovered that chicken embryo can grow rudimentary teeth. Genetic modification can be used to make birds develop jaws instead of beaks and feet similar to those of their non-avian ancestors. A dinosaur-like creature may one day be developed using these methods.

① (A) – (C) – (B)
② (B) – (A) – (C)
③ (B) – (C) – (A)
④ (C) – (A) – (B)
⑤ (C) – (B) – (A)

125 주어진 글 다음에 이어질 글의 순서로 가장 적절한 것은?

난이도 상

David (Bruce) Reimer's life was a tragic and unintentional experiment that shed light on the complexity of gender identity. After the boy's genitals were badly burned during circumcision, his parents took him to the renowned psychologist and sexual identity expert John Money. Dr. Money advised Reimer's parents to raise him as a girl.

(A) It was at this point that his parents informed the boy of his medical history. Reimer responded by taking the name David and assuming the life of a man. Although he married and adopted his wife's children, he was plagued by depression and rage. In May 2004, David Reimer took his own life.

(B) By the time he turned fourteen years old, Bruce, despite two years of estrogen therapy, was still fantasizing about being a boy rather than being a girl. Plagued by these dreams, he refused to continue his life as a female.

(C) The boy was then named Brenda and started life as a female. Although Dr. Money soon reported that the boy had developed a female identity, independent follow-ups of the case have suggested a much different view.

① (A) - (C) - (B)
② (B) - (A) - (C)
③ (B) - (C) - (A)
④ (C) - (A) - (B)
⑤ (C) - (B) - (A)

⑬ 요약문 완성

전체 지문을 한 문장으로 압축한
요약문의 빈칸에 들어갈 적절한 말을 추론해
요약문을 완성하는 유형이다.

가이드라인

▶ 제시된 요약문은 핵심 단어 한두 개가 빠진 주제문 또는 요지라 할 수 있다. 따라서 요약문을 먼저 읽어 글의 전반적인 내용에 대한 윤곽을 잡은 후에 지문을 읽는다.

▶ 주제문의 파악은 글의 주제, 요지 · 주장, 글의 제목 유형에서 제시된 방법을 따른다.

▶ 글의 요지나 주제문이 파악되면 이를 요약문에 비교 · 적용해 빈칸을 추론한다.

▶ 이때 요약문은 동의어나 대체 표현을 사용해 지문의 요지나 주제문을 변형한다는 점을 명심하라.

▶ 사건이나 일화, 우화처럼 주제문이 뚜렷이 드러나지 않을 때는 글의 교훈이 요약문으로 제시될 수 있으므로 글의 성격에 맞게 지문을 읽는다.

▶ 요약문을 완성한 후에는 글의 내용을 정확하게 반영하는지 확인한다.

40 다음 글의 내용을 한 문장으로 요약하고자 한다. 빈칸 (A), (B)에 들어갈 말로 가장 적절한 것은?

수능 기출문제 유형보기

From a cross-cultural perspective the equation between public leadership and dominance is questionable. What does one mean by 'dominance'? Does it indicate coercion? Or control over 'the most valued'? 'Political' systems may be about both, either, or conceivably neither. The idea of 'control' would be a bothersome one for many peoples, as for instance among many native peoples of Amazonia where all members of a community are fond of their personal autonomy and notably allergic to any obvious expression of control or coercion. The conception of political power as a coercive force, while it may be a Western fixation, is not a universal. It is very unusual for an Amazonian leader to give an order. If many peoples do not view political power as a coercive force, nor as the most valued domain, then the leap from 'the political' to 'domination' (as coercion), and from there to 'domination of women', is a shaky one. As Marilyn Strathern has remarked, the notions of 'the political' and 'political personhood' are cultural obsessions of our own, a bias long reflected in anthropological constructs.

* coercion 강제, autonomy 자율, anthropological 인류학의

⬇

It is ____(A)____ to understand political power in other cultures through our own notion of it because ideas of political power are not ___(B)___ across cultures.

	(A)	(B)		(A)	(B)
①	rational	flexible	②	appropriate	commonplace
③	misguided	uniform	④	unreasonable	varied
⑤	effective	objective			

[한번에 정리하는 문제 해설]

지문 해석 비교문화적 관점에서 볼 때 공적 지도력을 지배와 동일시하는 것은 의문의 여지가 있다. 지배라는 것의 의미는 무엇인가? 그것은 강제를 의미하는가? 아니면 가장 가치 있는 것에 대한 통제를 의미하는가? 정치 체계는 둘 모두에 관한 것일 수도 있고, 둘 중 하나에 관한 것일 수도 있으며 아마도 둘 중 어느 것과도 관련이 없을 수도 있다. 지역사회의 모든 구성원이 개인적 자율을 좋아하고 통제나 강제의 어떤 명백한 표현에도 심한 알레르기 반응을 보이는 아마존 원주민의 예에서도 보듯이 많은 국민들에게 통제라는 개념은 성가신 것이다. 강제하는 힘으로서의 정치력의 개념은 서구적 고정관념일 수는 있어도 보편적인 것이 아니다. 아마존 지도자가 무엇을 명령하는 것은 매우 드물다. 많은 국민들이 정치력을 강제하는 힘으로나 가장 가치 있는 영역으로 간주하지 않는다면 정치적인 것에서 지배로(강제로서의), 그리고 거기에서 여성에 대한 지배로 도약하는 것은 불안한 도약이다. Marilyn Strathern이 언급한 대로, 정치적인 것과 정치적 개성의 개념은 우리 자신의 것에 대한 문화적 강박관념으로 이는 인류학적 틀 속에 오래 반영돼 온 편견이다.

글의 소재 정치력의 비교문화적 고찰

주요 어휘 **coercion** 강제, **conceivably** 아마도, **autonomy** 자율, **fixation** 고정, 고정관념, **obsession** 강박관념, **anthropological** 인류학의

정 답 ③

정답 해설 지문 중간 부분에서 '정치력의 컨셉은 서구적 고정관념일 수는 있어도 보편적이지는 않다(The conception of political power as a coercive force, while it may be a Western fixation, is not a universal.)'라고 했으므로 필자의 정치력에 대한 생각은 글의 내용으로 보았을 때 문화권마다 같지(uniform) 않다고 볼 수 있다. 그렇기 때문에 다른 문화권의 정치력을 우리식 개념으로 이해하는 것은 잘못됐다(misguided)고 볼 수 있다. 따라서 (A)는 uniform, (B)는 misguided이다.

24 다음 글의 내용을 한 문장으로 요약하고자 한다. 빈칸 (A), (B)에 들어갈 말로 가장 적절한 것은?

| 사관 2025년 |

The great myth of American culture, then and now, is that democracy is built on free expression, both spoken and printed. Though wrapped up in shibboleths from the marketplace of ideas, such a myth is not without its advantages. There is wisdom in the notion that free expression is its own justification, as a matter of principle and as a check on power. The price, however, is sometimes high. Truth won't always win out, and the public sphere can't be contained. This is a lesson perpetually relearned when novel media technologies flood the information space. In 1938, Orson Welles and his Mercury Theater troupe broadcast a live radio performance of the H. G. Wells novel *The War of the Worlds*. While there is not much evidence that the program touched off an actual panic—and Welles was clear, at both the beginning and the end of the broadcast, that it was a dramatic performance, not a news report of real events—we do know that the broadcast garnered major newspaper coverage. The radio was already under regulations by the Federal Communications Commission, which had been formed in 1934, but one medium confronted another.　　　* shibboleth: 상투적인 어구 ** garner: 모으다

⬇

While it is commonly believed that the free and open exchange of ideas is a ___(A)___ of American democracy, the cost can be the unintended and uncontrollable ___(B)___ of untruth via new media, as in the case of a live radio performance broadcast in 1938.

	(A)	(B)		(A)	(B)		(A)	(B)
①	pillar	elusion	②	highlight	censorship	③	foundation	concealment
④	reflection	disclosure	⑤	cornerstone	circulation			

[한번에 정리하는 문제 해설]

지문 해석 　미국 문화의 위대한 신화는 그때나 지금이나 민주주의는 언어를 통한 것이든 인쇄된 것이든 자유로운 표현 위에 세워진다는 것이다. 아이디어 시장에서 나온 상투어들로 포장돼 있지만 그런 신화에는 장점이 없지 않다. 원칙의 문제로나 권력에 대한 견제로나 자유로운 표현은 스스로를 정당화시킨다는 생각에는 지혜가 담겨있다. 하지만 종종 그 대가가 크다. 진실이 항상 성취되지는 않고 공공 영역은 통제할 수 없다. 이것이 새로운 미디어 기술이 정보 공간에 밀려들 때마다 다시 배우는 교훈이다. 1938년 Orsen Welles와 그의 Mercury Theater극단은 H. G. Wells의 소설 *The War of the Worlds*의 라디오 버전을 생방송했다. 이 프로그램이 실제 공포를 불러일으켰다는 증거는 많지 않지만—Welles는 방송의 서두와 말미에서 프로그램은 드라마이고 실제 사건의 뉴스 보도가 아니라는 것을 명백히 했다.—그 방송은 신문의 비중 있는 보도 대상이 됐음을 우리는 안다. 라디오는 이미 1934년 설립된 연방통신위원회의 규제 하에 있었지만 한 매체는 다른 매체와 맞섰다.

⬇

사상의 자유롭고 공개적인 교류는 미국 민주주의의 초석이라 일반적으로 믿어지지만 1938년 라디오 생방송의 경우에서 보듯 그 대가는 새로운 미디어를 통한 허위사실의 의도치 않은, 그리고 통제할 수 없는 유포일 수 있다.

글의 소재 　자유로운 표현의 장점과 위험성

주요 어휘 　shibboleth 상투적인 어구, justification 정당화, win out 성취하다, contain 담다, 통제하다, perpetually 끊임없이, touch off 불러일으키다, garner 얻다, coverage 보도, regulation 규제, confront 맞서다

구조 분석 　• There is wisdom in the <u>notion</u> <u>that</u> free expression is its own justification, as a matter of principle and as a check on power.
　　➜ that는 동격의 that이며 명사절을 유도하고 notion을 부연 설명한다.

정　답 　⑤

정답 해설 　본문 전반부에서 미국 민주주의가 자유로운 표현에 기반을 둔다는 신화는 장점이 있고 또 자유로운 표현은 스스로 정당화시킨다고 했으므로 자유로운 표현이 미국 민주주의의 중요한 역할을 하는 것이 분명하다. 따라서 요약문 (A)에는 초석, 기둥, 기반 같은 말이 와야 한다. 한편 글 후반부는 당시 새로운 매체인 한 라디오가 전쟁 드라마를 생방송했는데 이 프로그램이 패닉을 불러일으킨 증거는 많지 않지만 신문이 이를 비중 있게 보도했음을 지적해 이를 실제 상황으로 오인한 적지 않은 동요가 있었음을 암시한다. 이는 라디오 매체의 진의가 왜곡 전달된, 즉 허위 사실이 유포돼 과장을 일으킨 사례로 볼 수 있다. 따라서 (B)에 들어갈 말은 유포가 적절하다.

40

다음 글의 내용을 한 문장으로 요약할 때, 빈칸 (A), (B)에 들어갈 말로 가장 적절한 것을 고르시오.

| 경찰 2024년 |

Theory and practice are often at odds. Yet there is something particularly strange in the way in which the received theory and the presumed practice of toleration in contemporary societies seem to go their separate ways. Theoretical statements on toleration assume at the same time its necessity in democratic societies, and its impossibility as a coherent ideal. In her introduction to a comprehensive collection on tolerance and intolerance in modern life, Susan Mendus appropriately makes the point that the commitment that liberal societies have to toleration 'may be more difficult and yet more urgent than is usually recognised'. In contrast with the urgency insisted on by the theory, the practice can appear contented: liberal democratic societies seem to have accepted the need for the recognition and accommodation of difference without registering its depth. So much so that 'practical' people often just dismiss such toleration as an excess of permissiveness. The success of 'zero tolerance' as a slogan for a less forgiving society bears witness to the spread of such a mood in public opinion.

* coherent: 통일성 있는

↓

Theoretically, tolerance is regarded ___(A)___ in democratic societies, but in reality, some people frequently overlook it as a(n) ___(B)___ of permissiveness.

	(A)	(B)		(A)	(B)		(A)	(B)
①	fundamental	overflow	②	fundamental	lack	③	radical	balance
④	customary	luxury	⑤	customary	shortage

[한번에 정리하는 문제 해설]

지문 해석 이론과 실제는 자주 상충한다. 하지만 현대 사회에서 관용에 대한 수용된 이론과 추정된 실제가 각자 자기 길을 가는 방식에는 특별나게 이상한 뭔가가 있다. 관용에 대한 이론적 진술들은 민주 사회에서 그것의 필요성과 일관성 있는 이상으로서는 불가능하다는 두 가지를 동시에 전제한다. 현대적 삶에서의 관용과 불관용에 관한 종합 모음집 서문에서 Susan Mendus는 자유 사회가 관용에 대해 하는 약속은 '일반적으로 인식되는 것보다 더 어렵고 시급할지 모른다.'는 점을 적절히 지적한다. 이 이론이 주장하는 시급함과는 대조적으로 실제는 만족스러운 것으로 나타날 수 있다. 자유 민주주의 사회들은 그 깊이를 재보지도 않고 차이를 인정하고 받아들여야 할 필요성을 이미 수락한 듯 보인다. 그 정도가 너무 심해 '실제적인' 사람들은 그러한 관용을 지나친 방임으로 치부하기도 한다. 덜 관용적인 사회의 '에서 무관용'이 구호로 성공하는 것은 여론 안에 그런 분위기가 확산되고 있음을 입증한다.

↓

이론적으로는 관용이 민주 사회에서 <u>근본적인</u> 것으로 여겨지지만 실제로 어떤 사람들은 흔히 그것을 방임의 <u>과잉</u>으로 보아 넘긴다.

글의 소재 관용에 대한 이론과 실제의 괴리

주요 어휘 at odds 충돌하는, presumed 추정된, toleration 관용, contemporary 현대의, 동시대의, assume 가정하다, 전제하다, coherent 일관성 있는, comprehensive 포괄적인, 종합의, commitment 약속, 책무, urgent 긴급한, in contrast with ~와 대조적으로, contented 만족한, accommodation 수용, 숙박, dismiss A as B A를 B로 치부하다, excess 과잉, permissiveness 방임, bear witness to ~를 입증하다

구조 분석 Susan Mendus appropriately makes <u>the point</u> <u>that</u> <u>the commitment</u> <u>that</u> liberal societies have <u>to toleration</u> 'may be more difficult and yet more urgent than is usually recognised'.
→ 'the point that ~'의 that은 동격의 that으로 point를 부연설명하고 the commitment that의 that은 목적격 관계대명사다. 'to toleration'은 the commitment를 수식한다. the commitment to toleration=관용을 베푼다는 약속

정답 ③

정답 해설 관용이 민주 사회에서 꼭 필요하지만 실천하기는 불가능하다고 이론적으로는 생각하면서 실제로는 과잉 내지는 방임으로 치부될 정도로 관용을 베푸는, 관용에 대한 이론과 실제의 괴리가 민주 사회에 만연함을 지적하는 글이다. 따라서 (A)에는 fundamental, (B)에는 overflow가 적절하다. 본문 중 'Theoretical statements on toleration assume at the same time its <u>necessity</u> in democratic societies'에서 necessity를, ''practical' people often just dismiss such toleration as an <u>excess</u> of permissiveness.' 중 excess를 각각 주목하라.

13. 요약문 완성

| 해설 426쪽 |

126

다음 글을 읽고 지시문의 빈칸에 들어갈 숫자로 적절한 것을 고르시오. 난이도 중

On June 5th, 1895, James Smith of Denver, Colorado, had a great fall. Some say that he injured his left thigh. Others mention his right hip. Being a young man of modest means, Smith tried to outlast the pain, but after three weeks with no improvement he gave up and sought medical help. In 1895, patients still expected their doctor to make house calls, the cost of which ranged from two to five dollars. If the doctor had to travel more than a mile, an extra dollar was added for each mile, two dollars at night. Some doctors had a meter-like device attached to the wheel of their buggy to measure the mileage.

According to the rate mentioned above, a patient owes a maximum _____ dollars to the doctor who had travelled 3 miles for treatment at around midnight.

① 6
② 7
③ 8
④ 9
⑤ 11

다음 글의 내용을 한 문장으로 나타낼 때, 빈칸 (A)와 (B)에 들어갈 가장 적절한 것은?

난이도 중

Simply put, gaslighting is a form of brainwashing that is meant to make one doubt one's own beliefs, thoughts, and perceptions. It is a method that narcissists employ with great success to control those close to them. Gaslighting, however, is somewhat difficult to execute successfully because it essentially demands that others change their basic core beliefs and replace them with those of the gaslighter. Most people vigorously defend their beliefs and become quite resistant unless properly conditioned beforehand. Therefore, to be effective, gaslighting usually starts off gradually and grows slowly and incrementally over time as each new hurdle of resistance is in turn overcome. The gaslighters must be consistent and regular in reinforcing their message that you are wrong and they are right. In order to successfully gaslight someone narcissists will carefully pick and then groom their target for some time before actually initiating the techniques needed to sway their intended target.

⬇

Successful gaslighters are usually ___(A)___ with the pace at which they gaslight, consistent in delivering their message and ___(B)___ in selecting the target.

	(A)	(B)
①	pertinent	cautious
②	pertinent	agile
③	patient	agile
④	patient	cautious
⑤	patient	crafty

128 다음 글을 한 문장으로 요약하고자 한다. 빈칸에 들어갈 말로 가장 적절한 것은?

난이도 중

Individuals often respond differently in a group context than they might if they were alone. Social psychologist Irving Janis examined group decision making among political experts and found that major blunders in US history can be attributed to this pressure to conform, or fit in. To describe the phenomenon, Janis coined the term "groupthink"—the process by which members of a group arrive at a decision that many individual members privately believe is unwise. Why don't they speak up at the time? They don't want to be the ones who undermine the group's sense of agreement or who challenge group leaders. Consequently, members of a group often limit or withhold their opinions and focus on agreement rather than on exploring all possible options and determining the best course of action.

People tend to "groupthink" because they want to avoid a situation where _____.

① it takes two to tango
② praise makes even a whale dance
③ a cornered stone meets the mason's chisel
④ two heads are better than one
⑤ when one dog barks another will join it

129

다음 글의 내용을 한 문장으로 요약하고자 한다. 빈칸 (A), (B)에 들어갈 말로 가장 적절한 것은? 난이도 중

Whether a development research project influences public policy depends decisively, but not only, on the context of its time and place. Influence is easiest to achieve where policymakers' receptivity to research is high and where their capacity to apply research is adequate. Where receptivity is minimal and adaptive capacity is weak, influence is much harder to achieve. What the cases tell us, however, is more complicated than that and more hopeful. Indeed, two striking conclusions emerge from these case studies. The first conclusion is that research can make a difference in policy even where receptivity in the beginning appears unpromising. Researchers can maximize their influence in almost any circumstance by conducting their work, and communicating their results to decision makers and the public, according to a coherent and context-appropriate strategy. The second inescapable conclusion is that things change, both in research and in policymaking. Research projects can, and should, adapt to their changing surroundings. The policy context, meanwhile, often changes while the research is under way. In some cases, research itself seems to have changed policymakers' minds, thereby opening the policy community to the value of research, building trust between researchers and policymakers, and enhancing receptivity.

⬇

Development researchers can _____(A)_____ their chance of success by working in a more communicative, consistent and context-appropriate way while coping with changing policy environment in a more _____(B)_____ manner.

	(A)		(B)
①	jeopardize	⋯⋯	aggressive
②	compromise	⋯⋯	hesitant
③	enhance	⋯⋯	malleable
④	boost	⋯⋯	rigorous
⑤	heighten	⋯⋯	conservative

130 다음 글을 한 문장으로 요약하고자 한다. 빈칸에 들어갈 말로 가장 적절한 것은?

난이도 중

In Darwin's day, biologists had been debating the views of Jean Baptiste Lamarck, who proposed that evolution occurred through the inheritance of acquired characteristics. Lamarck's theory, however, turned out to be wrong. In the Darwin-Wallace theory, no new characteristics need be acquired during an individual's lifetime. The essence of Darwin's theory has it that, among the members of a species, there is endless variation; and among the various members, only a fraction of those who are born survive to reproduce. There is a "struggle for existence" during which the fittest members of a species live long enough to transmit their characteristics to the next generation. Over countless generations, then, nature "selects" those who can best adapt to their surroundings. Take the wolf for example. During seasons when prey is scarce, the swiftest and strongest wolves have the best chances for survival. They are therefore more likely than the others to live long enough to reproduce and pass on their traits to the next generation. After many such seasons, the traits of speed and strength will become increasingly prevalent in the population of the species.

According to Darwin's theory, a species evolves not by passing on its acquired traits, but by having its traits selected through a process of _____.

① rallying its friendly forces available
② battling unfavorable living conditions
③ invoking supernatural powers
④ conforming to its surroundings
⑤ avoiding various natural disasters

다음 글을 한 문장으로 요약하고자 한다. 빈칸 (A), (B)에 들어갈 말로 가장 적절한 것은? 난이도 중

Some of the most innovative research I've come across suggests that task-oriented athletes value practice and commit to it, whereas ego-oriented athletes are more likely to take the easy route and prefer simply to compete. Those who have a high task orientation seek personal feedback and use it to develop their skills, while those high in ego orientation don't care for feedback about the quality of their performance; they only want to know if they've won. Ego-involved athletes might come across as not that interested in learning, even if the information and support is available to help them improve. Even if they lose, they may still reject the information and coaching that could help them to perform better. Research also shows that athletes with a task orientation use the feedback they get and consistently process information that will help them perform better in the next few seconds or minutes of task or contest. They appear to spend that time thinking in a proactive task-focused manner. On the other hand, ego-oriented athletes simply think about how they compare to others and the consequences of winning or losing, leaving little mental capacity to process information about how to improve the task and learn.

Under a competitive situation, task-oriented athletes are more concerned with ____(A)____, while ego-oriented athletes tend to be more preoccupied with ____(B)____.

	(A)	(B)
①	the feedback on their performance	information sharing and learning
②	the feedback on their performance	the result of the competition itself
③	the result of the competition itself	the feedback on their performance
④	the result of the competition itself	information sharing and learning
⑤	information sharing and learning	the feedback on their performance

132

다음 글을 한 문장으로 요약하고자 한다. 빈칸 (A), (B)에 들어갈 말로 가장 적절한 것은? 난이도 중

I have a relative named Jack who's a true example of health fad. He puts like 15 different ingredients in his salad. All those different seeds, the greens, the lemon, the olive oil, what an "antioxidant bomb!" He's so proud of his healthy eating he often brags that "no one eats as healthy as me." And yet he doesn't exercise. He's overweight, and when I asked him to perform a squat, he actually couldn't. He has mobility issues. And he's weak. Of course, he can't do a push-up. Yet he considers himself to even be a teacher of healthy living. One day he said, he wished his father were still alive, so he could teach him all the things he's learned about health!

Do you know that exercise, can, for example, drop your heart disease risk by almost half? And it also helps with cancer, diabetes, depression, and weight management, just to name a few? I'm not saying that to underestimate diet. Diet is important. But there are limits to what diet can do. Diet has reached a level where we see it as a health "god." And if you think "god" is on your side, then why do the other things that you know are healthful—like exercise? You feel you're covered! If only we ate the right foods, we'd live forever! That's what my relative says. I honestly don't see how he'll live a prolonged, energetic life without exercise(unless he has amazing genes).

⬇

The writing above warns against those who refuse to _____(A)_____ and think they are Okay because they have _____(B)_____.

	(A)	(B)
①	move	mobility issues
②	exercise	superior diet
③	play	health fad
④	eat	inborn health
⑤	study	learned enough

133 다음 글을 한 문장으로 요약할 때 밑줄 친 부분에 들어갈 가장 적절한 말은? 난이도 중

The reasons for desiring the international government are two: first, the prevention of war, secondly the securing of economic justice as between different nations and different populations. Of these the prevention of war is the more important, both because war is more harmful than injustice, and because the grosser forms of injustice will not often be inflicted upon civilized nations except as the result of war. It would not be common, for example, in a time of profound peace to deprive a nation of its means of livelihood and at the same time prevent its population from emigrating, as we have done in Austria. If peace can be preserved, it is probable that some degree of justice will ultimately result. Even if a considerable measure of injustice were to remain, it is probable that the least fortunate population in a time of secure peace would be better off than the most fortunate in a period of frequent wars. We have therefore to consider internationalism primarily from the point of view of preventing war, and only secondarily from the point of view of justice between nations. This is important because, as we shall see, some of the most probable approaches to the international government involve considerable injustice for long periods of time.

⬇

_____ is what the establishment of the international government is essentially about.

① The creation of permanent peace
② The securing of economic justice
③ The prevention of war
④ The eradication of all forms of injustice
⑤ The realization of lasting human values

134 다음 글을 아래와 같이 한 문장으로 요약할 때 빈칸에 들어갈 가장 적절한 말은?

난이도 상

News is about what happens, not what doesn't happen, so it features sudden and upsetting events like fires, plant closings, rampage shootings and shark attack. Most positive developments are not camera-friendly, and they aren't built in a day. You never see a headline about a country that is not at war, or a city that has not been attacked by terrorists. The bad habits of media in turn bring out the worst in human cognition. Our intuitions about risk are driven not by statistics but by images and stories. People rank tornadoes (which kill dozens of Americans a year) as more dangerous than asthma (which kills thousands), presumably because tornadoes make for better television. It's easy to see how this cognitive bias could make people conclude the worst about where the world is heading.

The above article criticizes media's news policy that stresses _____.

① "If it bleeds, it leads"
② "No news is good news"
③ "Misinformaton is better than no information"
④ "Bury the lead when necessary"
⑤ "News told, truth implied, facts buried"

135 다음 글을 읽고 지시문의 빈칸에 들어갈 어구로 알맞은 것을 고르시오. 난이도 상

How and why are so many advertisements flooding beauty magazines of all sorts published across the world? A Hong Kong dermatologist explains the trick simply: "Week after week manufacturers' claims, accompanied by glossy photographs, land on the desks of beauty editors around the world. These heavily biased, subjective blurbs, with the photographs captioned, then appear unedited in the magazines as virtually unpaid advertisements masquerading as independent editorial copy." This is cheap for the magazine and even cheaper for the companies. The only losers are those of us who expect a more critical analysis and those who believe everything they read. Once you know how the trick works, you can cast a much more critical eye over the 'new products' columns, the beauty stories, the make-overs, and your local newspaper's ads for beauty salons and weight treatments as well.

* blurb 안내문

The writer of the above paragraph warns consumers against _____.

① side effects caused by some medicines
② infectious skin diseases
③ secret advertizing
④ impulse buying
⑤ any rash subscriptions to magazines

136 다음 글을 한 문장으로 요약할 때, 빈칸 (A)와 (B)에 들어갈 말로 가장 적절한 것은?

난이도 상

According to a study conducted by the Australian Institute of Sport, which echoes international findings, the self-confidence levels of boy and girl athletes at about age 13 and 14 are pretty much identical, and after that they drop off, but the female level drops off quicker and to a greater extent than the male level. The study adds, "For both sexes it seems to bottom out or reach its lowest levels at around 19, 20, 21 years of age and then it bounces back out again, but interestingly the males actually end up higher than when they started, and the female athletes never reach the same level as at 13 and 14 again." This research suggests that even the female 'winners' in our society—the study was of 1,798 athletes over six years, who were physically fit and still winning—will reach a peak of self-esteem before puberty and never again reach that level as young people or adults.

According to a study, the level of self-esteem, which usually hits the bottom at around 20 for both sexes, ends up _____(A)_____ than at puberty for men while never _____(B)_____ the level at puberty for women.

	(A)	(B)
①	higher	missing
②	lower	missing
③	higher	recapturing
④	lower	recapturing
⑤	different	renouncing

137 다음 글을 한 문장으로 나타낼 때, 빈칸 (A)와 (B)에 들어갈 말로 가장 적절한 것은?

난이도 상

Every input to our senses is a stimulus, available for us to interpret as information, and from which we can derive further information. Our physical sensory receptors—our ears, eyes, etc.—can be thought of as information "transducers" which convert external stimuli—changes in air pressure, light, etc.—into nerve impulses recognized by the brain. Scientists and philosophers have advanced many conceptual models of what the brain does with these nerve impulses to derive knowledge and meaning. Regardless of the mechanism by which our brain accomplishes it, it is clear that we generate information ourselves, stimulated by external information. For example, when we hear a lion's roar, our brain, by means largely unknown to us, evaluates those time-varying frequencies and amplitudes as a lion's roar. Our brain then derives further information about the actual source of the sound and its meaning. A person in one time or place might interpret the sound to mean "My life is in danger. I must run away from the sound source immediately as fast and as far as I can." Another who had never learned to associate that sound with any particular source, meanwhile, might attempt to compare it with other known sounds, or might even remain unconcerned as to what produced the sound.

⬇

Irrespective of the specific functions of the brain, we are bound to produce _____(A)_____ information once we are spurred by _____(B)_____ stimulants.

	(A)	(B)
①	subjective	internal
②	subjective	external
③	objective	internal
④	objective	external
⑤	neutral	external

138 다음 글을 한 문장으로 요약할 때 빈칸 (A), (B)로 들어갈 말로 가장 적절한 것은?

난이도 상

The terms "adaptation" and "mitigation" are two important terms that are fundamental in the climate change debate. The International Panel on Climate Change (IPCC) defines mitigation as an anthropogenic intervention to reduce the sources or enhance the sinks of greenhouse gases. Namely, mitigation means any action taken to permanently eliminate or reduce the long-term risk and hazards of climate change to human life and property. Meanwhile, the IPCC defined adaptation as adjustment in natural or human systems in response to actual or expected climatic stimuli or their effects, which moderate harm or exploit beneficial opportunities. In general the more mitigation there is, the less will be the impacts to which we will have to adjust, and the less the risks for which we will have to try and prepare. Conversely, the greater the degree of preparatory adaptation, the less may be the impacts associated with any given degree of climate change.

* anthropogenic = 인위적인

⬇

While mitigation tries to tackle the _____(A)_____ of climate change, adaptation concerns our efforts to adjust the _____(B)_____ so we can better cope with any climatic stimuli.

	(A)	(B)
①	causes	sources
②	causes	systems
③	effects	sources
④	effects	systems
⑤	processes	systems

139

다음 글은 마키아벨리의 군주론의 일부다. 다음 글을 한 문장으로 나타낼 때, 빈칸 (A)와 (B)에 들어갈 가장 적절한 말은? 난이도 상

Let no one be surprised if, in speaking of entirely new principalities as I shall do, I adduce the highest examples both of prince and of state; because men, walking almost always in paths beaten by others, and following by imitation their deeds, are yet unable to keep entirely to the ways of others or attain to the power of those they imitate. A wise man ought always to follow the paths beaten by great men, and to imitate those who have been supreme, so that if his ability does not equal theirs, at least it will savour of it. Let him act like the clever archers who, designing to hit the mark which yet appears too far distant, and knowing the limits to which the strength of their bow attains, take aim much higher than the mark, not to reach by their strength or arrow to so great a height, but to be able with the aid of so high an aim to hit the mark they wish to reach.

* principality 공국, adduce 제시하다

Rulers are encouraged to follow in the footsteps of great men and to _____(A)_____ them, like an archer who, by _____(B)_____, can hope to reach the target.

	(A)	(B)
①	defeat	shooting straight
②	defeat	aiming high
③	emulate	shooting straight
④	emulate	aiming high
⑤	defeat	flexing muscles

140

다음 글을 한 문장으로 요약하고자 한다. 빈칸 (A), (B)에 들어갈 말로 가장 적절한 것은? 난이도 상

The question of whether people should be moderately or totally forgiving is one piece of the larger controversy between Aristotelian moderation and Stoic/Christian extremism. Aristotle's doctrine of the mean is triadic; each sphere of human life is governed by a single virtue which is medial, bracketed by two vices which are extremes. The competing doctrine is dyadic: each virtue lies on one end of a continuum and its one corresponding vice lies on the other end. The fact that many people profess admiration for unconditional forgiveness should not blind us to the fact that they are applauding an extreme. While Aristotle says that the virtue governing insult and injustice is a disposition to retaliate moderately or angrily, the advocates of unconditional forgiveness say that the virtue governing insult and injustice consists in getting as far away in the vice of irascibility as possible. Irascibility is bad; forgiveness is good—so the more forgiving a person is, the better. The right way to be lies on the extreme end of a continuum.

* triadic 삼원적인, dyadic 이원적인, irascibility 화를 잘 냄

While Aristotle's doctrine of the mean urges us to govern insult and injustice through   (A)   , Stoic/Christian extremists claim the virtues lies in achieving   (B)   .

	(A)	(B)
①	retaliation	punishment
②	forgiveness	self-denial
③	retaliation	forgiveness
④	self-denial	forgiveness
⑤	forgiveness	punishment

다음 글을 한 문장으로 요약하고자 한다. 빈칸에 들어갈 말로 가장 적절한 것은?

난이도 상

Coming from a Catholic background, it is surprising that JFK needed the Bay of Pigs to alert him to the terrible consequences of groupthink. He had centuries of Church history to draw upon. From 1587 until recently, the Roman Catholic Church, arguably one of world's most successful organizations, appointed a special skeptic when deciding whether or not to elevate a person to sainthood. Officially, this professional skeptic was known as the Promotor Fidei, the Promoter of the Faith. Unofficially, he was known as the Advocatus Diaboli, 'the devil's advocate.' It was the advocate's job to punch holes in cases that argued for canonization, to question all evidence that attested to the holiness of the nominee for sainthood. Whenever possible, the devil's advocate cross-examined available witnesses, scrutinized testimony of the contender's saintliness, and advanced all reasonable arguments against canonization. The Church instituted this role as insurance against groupthink—though they did not call it that in 1587. The devil's advocate's job was to force consideration of all points of view, thereby enhancing the quality of these important decisions. Not everyone, after all, should be sainted.

* groupthink 집단사고, canonization 성인 반열에 올림, 시성

The devil's advocate was commissioned to play the role of ＿＿＿＿＿＿ by advancing all reasonable arguments against canonization of sainthood nominees.

① a promoter of collective wisdom
② a groupthink stifler
③ a sainthood contender
④ a benevolent canonizer
⑤ a divine troubleshooter

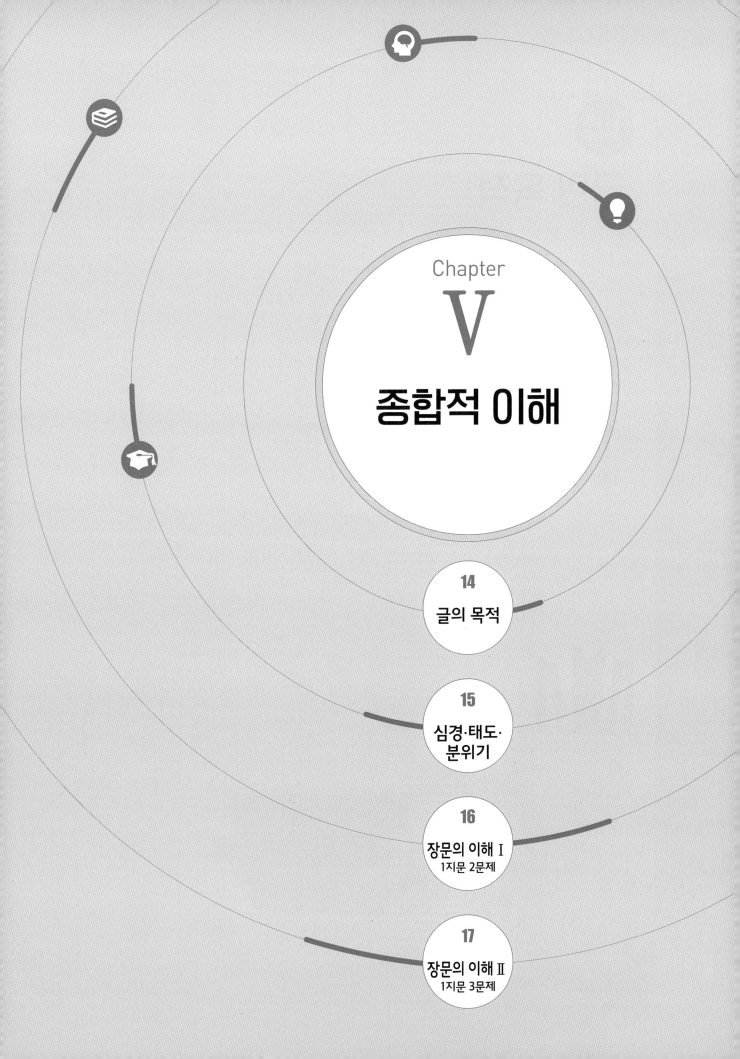

Chapter

V

종합적 이해

14

글의 목적

주어진 글에서 필자가 전달하고자 하는
의도나 목적을 추론하는 유형이다.

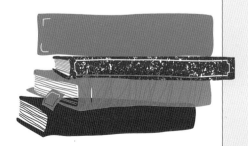

가이드라인

▶ 광고, 신문 기사, 편지, 항의문, 안내문 등 일상에서 흔히 접하는 실용문이 지문으로 제시된다.

▶ 의도를 갖고 쓴 실용문이므로 해석이 비교적 수월하다. 따라서 지문을 신속하게 읽고 누가 누구를 대상으로 무슨 목적으로 쓴 글인지를 파악하는 것이 관건이다.

▶ 단순하고 실제적인 목적을 빙빙 돌려 추상적으로 말하는 경우가 많다. 그런 유도성 딕션이나 '함정'에 빠지지 말아야 한다.

▶ 글의 흐름에 반전이 있을 때 반전 이후의 내용에 주목하라. 예를 들어, 항의문의 경우 글의 앞부분은 의례적인 인사나 감사 표시로 시작하나 however나 but 같은 역접 · 반전의 연결사로 반전시킨 후 글을 쓴 진짜 목적을 밝히는 경우가 일반적이다.

▶ 글의 시작과 끝 부분에 주목하라. 특히, 글의 마무리 부분에 정답의 단서가 드러날 경우가 많다.

▶ 지문 중 ask나 request 같은 단어나 명령법 문장에는 글을 쓴 목적이 직접 드러나는 경우가 많다.

▶ 글의 종류에 따른 표현상의 특징이나 상투어들을 익혀둔다.

글의 목적을 나타내는 말

▶ 위로(to comfort, to console), 격려(to encourage), 칭찬(to praise), 인사(to greet), 알림 · 통보(to inform, to notify), 감사(to appreciate), 주문(to order), 보고 · 신고(to report), 추천(to recommend), 충고(to advise), 사과(to apologize), 불평 · 이의제기(to complain), 취소(to cancel), 비판(to criticize), 광고(to advertize, to promote, to publicize), 확인(to confirm)

목적에 따른 상투어

▶ 알림 · 통보: notice, confirm, let ~ know
▶ 요구 · 요청: call for, ask, demand, require, must, have to, should
▶ 이의제기: unfair, regrettable, angry, afraid, disappointed, dissatisfied
▶ 충고 · 조언: advise, suggest, had better, why don't you?
▶ 광고 · 선전: introduce, come up with, present

18 다음 글의 목적으로 가장 적절한 것은?

I'm Charlie Reeves, manager of Toon Skills Company. If you're interested in new webtoon-making skills and techniques, this post is for you. This year, we've launched special online courses, which contain a variety of contents about webtoon production. Each course consists of ten units that help improve your drawing and story-telling skills. Moreover, these courses are designed to suit any level, from beginner to advanced. It costs $45 for one course, and you can watch your course as many times as you want for six months. Our courses with talented and experienced instructors will open up a new world of creativity for you. It's time to start creating your webtoon world at https://webtoonskills.com.

① 웹툰 제작 온라인 강좌를 홍보하려고
② 웹툰 작가 채용 정보를 제공하려고
③ 신작 웹툰 공개 일정을 공지하려고
④ 웹툰 창작 대회에 출품을 권유하려고
⑤ 기초적인 웹툰 제작 방법을 설명하려고

[한번에 정리하는 문제 해설]

지문 해석 저는 Toon Skills Company의 부장인 Charlie Reeves입니다. 만약 여러분이 새로운 웹툰 제작 기술이나 기법에 관심 있다면 이 게시물은 여러분의 것입니다. 올해 저희는 특별 온라인 강좌를 개설했는데 그것들은 웹툰 제작에 대한 다양한 콘텐츠를 담고 있습니다. 각각의 강좌는 여러분의 그리기와 스토리 작법 개선을 도울 10개의 단원으로 구성돼 있습니다. 더구나 이 강좌들은 초보에서 고급에 이르기까지 어떤 레벨에도 적합하도록 설계돼 있습니다. 강좌 당 수강료는 45 달러인데 여러분은 6개월 동안 원하는 만큼 여러 번 강좌를 시청할 수 있습니다. 재능 있고 숙련된 저희 강사들이 여러분에게 창의성의 새로운 세계를 열어 드릴 것입니다. https://webtoonskills.com에서 여러분의 웹툰 세계 만들기를 시작할 때입니다.

글의 소재 온라인 웹툰 수강생 모집 광고문

주요 어휘 launch 발사하다, 개설하다, contain 담다, 포함하다, consist of ~로 구성되다, be designed to ~하도록 고안되다, suit ~에 맞다, 어울리다, advanced 고급의, instructor 강사, creativity 창조성

구조 분석 • Each course consists of ten units that help improve your drawing and story-telling skills.
→ that 이하는 5형식 문장이다. help는 준사역동사라 목적격 보어 자리에 동사 원형이나 to 부정사가 모두 올 수 있다. 또 전후 문맥 상 명백할 때 목적어는 생략할 수 있다. 여기서는 help와 improve 사이에 you (to)가 생략됐다.

정 답 ①

정답 해설 이 글의 필자는 소속 회사가 올해 온라인 웹툰 제작을 위한 특별 강좌를 개설했음을 알리고 강좌 내용, 수강료, 시청 방법 등을 언급하는 것으로 보아 강좌 수강 희망자들에게 이를 홍보할 목적임을 알 수 있다. 따라서 이 글의 목적은 ① '웹툰 제작 온라인 강좌를 홍보하려고'가 적절하다.

14 다음 글의 목적으로 가장 적절한 것은?

I received a letter from your office, saying that my recent claim for additional compensation had been denied. It appears that the letter is a form letter and does not disclose the reason that I was denied the additional bonus pay for having completed the 14-month language training program with a passing grade. Therefore, I am requesting a review of this claim and a full, specific explanation about the reasons for the denial. If I do not receive a reversal of this decision, I plan to file an appeal within the required time frame to follow up on my rightful claim to this bonus. All appropriate documentation is enclosed (service letter explaining the language bonus, grades, my original letter to you, your form letter to me). I expect to hear from you immediately about this review and to receive the full compensation due me under this recruitment arrangement.

① 언어 연수 프로그램 수료를 보고하려고
② 연수 대상으로 선발되었는지 알아보려고
③ 보너스 수령을 위해 필요한 서류를 확인하려고
④ 추가 보너스 지급 거부에 대한 번복을 요구하려고
⑤ 언어 연수 프로그램 지원 절차에 대해 문의하려고

[한번에 정리하는 문제 해설]

[지문 해석] 저는 최근 귀하의 사무실로부터 저의 추가 보상 요구가 거절됐다는 한 통의 편지를 받았습니다. 그 편지는 (일괄적으로 배포된) 같은 내용의 편지처럼 보였고, 14개월의 언어 연수를 이수하고 합격점을 받은 데 대해 주어지는 추가 보너스가 저에게 거절된 이유를 밝히지 않았습니다. 따라서 귀하가 이 요구를 검토하고 그것의 거절 이유에 대한 완전하고도 구체적인 설명을 해줄 것을 요청드립니다. 만약 이번 결정을 번복받지 못하면 저는 보너스에 대한 저의 정당한 요구를 관철하기 위해 지정된 시간 내에 항소를 계획하고 있습니다. 모든 관련 서류(언어 보너스를 설명하는 안내문, 성적표, 귀하에게 보낸 저의 최초 편지, 귀하가 저에게 보낸 같은 내용의 편지)를 동봉합니다. 이번 검토에 대해 제가 즉시 듣게 될 것과 신규 채용 약정에 따라 저에게 주어지는 완전한 보상을 받을 수 있기를 바랍니다.

[글의 소재] 추가 보너스 지급이 거절된 데 대한 재고 요청

[주요 어휘] claim 요구, 주장, additional 추가적인, compensation 보상, disclose 밝히다, deny 거절하다, reversal 번복, appeal 항소, appropriate 적절한, immediately 즉각적으로, recruitment 신규 채용, arrangement 약정

[구조 분석] • and to receive the full <u>compensation due me</u> under this recruitment arrangement.
→ compensation과 due 사이에 that(which) is가 생략됐다. due는 due to에서 to가 생략된 형태로 '~에게 지급돼야 하는'을 뜻한다.

[정답] ④

[정답 해설] 이 글은 언어 연수 프로그램을 이수한 데 대해 추가 보너스를 신청했으나 거절당하자 지급 거부 결정에 대한 재검토와 번복을 요청하는 서한이다. 따라서 글의 목적으로 가장 적절한 것은 ④ '추가 보너스 지급 거부에 대한 번복을 요구하려고'이다.

32 다음 글의 목적으로 가장 적절한 것은?

What could be more comforting than seeing your dog or cat curled up in blissful sleep? Both species spend almost half their day engaged in some form of sleep. But not all find it restful: older animals, those with muscular or joint issues, or very active dogs often pace or relocate frequently. If your companion fits into one of these categories, he might benefit from a therapeutic bed. These specialized products offer support and comfort unlike regular beds or an impromptu sleeping spot. Regardless of age and health, a good bed promotes muscular-skeletal health and offers additional rejuvenating and healing benefits.

① to prevent domestic animal abuse
② to promote specialized pet furniture
③ to explain the benefits of good sleep
④ to inform pet owners of furniture hazards
⑤ to warn pet owners of poor pet sleep habits

[한번에 정리하는 문제 해설]

[지문 해석] 개나 고양이가 웅크리고 누워 행복한 잠에 빠진 모습을 보는 것보다 당신을 더 편안하게 해주는 것이 어디 있는가? 두 동물은 하루의 거의 절반을 어떤 형태로든 잠자면서 보낸다. 그러나 모두에게 잠이 편한 것은 아니다. 나이가 들었거나 근육이나 관절에 문제가 있는 동물이거나 매우 활동적인 개는 종종 서성거리거나 자리를 자주 옮긴다. 당신의 반려동물이 이 범주의 어느 하나에 든다면 치료용 침대의 도움을 받을 수 있다. 이 특수 제작된 제품은 일반 침대나 임의의 수면 시설과는 다른 지지력과 안락함을 제공해 준다. 나이나 건강 상태와 관계없이 좋은 침대는 근육과 뼈의 건강을 증진하고 활력을 되찾게 하거나 힐링 효과를 가져다준다.
① 가정 내 동물 학대를 방지하기 위해
② 특수 제작된 반려동물용 가구를 홍보하기 위해
③ 숙면의 좋은 점을 설명하기 위해
④ 반려동물 키우는 사람에게 가구의 해악을 알려주려고
⑤ 반려동물 주인에게 동물의 나쁜 수면 습관을 경고하려고

[글의 소재] 반려동물용 특수 침대 홍보

[주요 어휘] curled up 웅크린, restful 편안한, issue 문제 =problem, pace 서성거리다, relocate 자리를 옮기다, therapeutic 치료 목적의, impromptu 임시방편의, rejuvenate 활기를 되찾게 하다

[정 답] ②

[정답 해설] 개나 고양이 등 반려동물이 편안한 잠을 잘 수 있도록 특수 제작된 침대를 홍보하는 글이다. 따라서 정답은 ②다. therapeutic bed나 specialized products, promote 같은 시그널을 놓치지 말아야 한다.

142 다음 글을 쓴 목적으로 알맞은 것은?　난이도 중

Most security systems are created to keep intruders out. Nost, a Washington-based start-up, built its security system "the complete other way around," says chief product officer Jill Patterson, choosing to focus just as much on making it simpler for its users to get in. Case in point: the security hub can be disarmed by waving a key fob instead of typing a pass code, and those key fobs can be programmed to work within certain frames—so babysitter, for example, could access your home only while she's working. A smartphone app also lets users manage their system from afar. Of course, the security hub is plenty capable of guarding a home: if an intruder tries to break or unplug the hub, it will sound an 85-decibel alarm, and companion motion sensors can alert users when a door or window has been opened.

* key fob 열쇠 주머니

① 가정 보안의 중요성을 일깨우려고
② 새로 출시된 보안 제품을 소개하려고
③ 가정이 침입당했을 때 응급처치를 알려주려고
④ 보안 추세 강화를 보도하려고
⑤ 현 보안시스템의 맹점을 지적하려고

143 다음 글을 쓴 목적으로 가장 적절한 것은?

난이도 중

Mr. Chairman. Thank you for holding this hearing. This is exactly the type of oversight and accountability we need to have to make sure our service members get the services they need when they come home. From the veterans I have talked to, it is clear that we do not offer them a seamless transition from the battlefront to the home front, and that has really got to change. If we have a seamless transition, why are so many veterans coming home without jobs? Why are so many veterans unable to get housing? Why are veterans having to wait 6 months to see a Veterans Affairs doctor for primary care? We do not need a hearing to discover if we have a seamless transition. I know that we do not. And we do not need this hearing to find out if the Pentagon and Veterans Affairs are working together enough. I do not think they are. We do need to use this hearing to find out from our witnesses what they are doing about it and how they are going to fix it.

① 공무원들의 근무 자세 확립을 촉구하려고
② 영세민에 대한 복지 확대를 청원하려고
③ 재향군인에 대한 처우 개선을 촉구하려고
④ 정부 부서 간 소통 부족을 지적하려고
⑤ 지역구민의 불만 사항을 전달하려고

144 다음 글을 쓴 목적으로 가장 알맞은 것은?

Who ever thought we'd be nostalgic for a President who had a fondness for barking orders to aides from the john? Rob Reiner's *LBJ*, starring Woody Harrelson, is Lyndon B. Johnson 101, roughly covering the period from 36th President swearing-in ceremony following the JFK assassination to his signing of the Civil Rights Act of 1964. As is well known, President Johnson was notoriously coarse and ill-mannered. But it's also true that his political acumen and innate decency changed the country for the better. His indifference was also a kind of grace, a contradiction that Harrelson conveys beautifully, with a scowl that sometimes hides a smile—or the other way around.

* the john 화장실

① to celebrate the production of a TV documentary
② to publicize a recently published book
③ to eulogize the hidden merits of a late president
④ to recall a historic presidential achievement
⑤ to introduce the release of a new film

다음 글을 읽고 지시문의 빈칸에 들어갈 어구로 알맞은 것을 고르시오. 난이도 중

Our recently-released customizable metabolism-boosting routine will help you shed up to 8 pounds in just 4 weeks. Most important, you'll have a lean, strong physique and energy to spare—for life. At the heart of the plan is the High-Metabolism Workout, five supereffective strength moves that build firm, lean muscle tissue—the key to a robust metabolism. Muscle burns up to 7 times as many calories at rest as fat does, so the more muscle you have, the higher your metabolism. That's just the beginning. Each stage of your life presents special metabolism-slowing risks, including disrupted sleep and even seismic hormone shifts. So we've included a decade-by-decade, fat-fighting prescription guaranteed to keep your metabolism in high gear. And to really make it soar, there's also a High-Metabolism Diet. Start today and you'll sleep better, have more energy, feel firmer, and notice your clothes are looser in as little as 2 weeks.

The above passage was written _____.

① to announce a government package designed to boost public health
② to publicize the result of major academic research on metabolism
③ to advertise a fitness program released by a health firm
④ to warn the public against the adverse effects of excessive exercise
⑤ to educate people about the important function of metabolism

146 다음 글을 쓴 목적으로 가장 적절한 것은?

난이도 중

Dear Mr. Fraser:

I have just received your letter informing me that my insurance policy will not cover my daughter's surgery because you consider the surgery to be "elective" and we did not obtain authorization in advance. It never entered my mind that anyone would consider surgery that would prevent her paralysis and eventual death by suffocation to be "elective." Surely someone made a mistake in writing us this letter, or in defining what is "elective." I trust you have copies of her medical records in your possession. If not, I will have the neurosurgeon send them to you. I request that you review her case to see that her condition clearly was "life-threatening" and therefore not "elective." She now has a chance to lead a relatively normal life, for which we are grateful. To say we have no claim to insurance coverage for her surgery is to add severe insult to injury. I am confident that you will agree once you have seen the documentation. I will await your response before taking other action.

Sincerely,
Mark Davidson,
Dept., of English, Salt Lake University

① to file a life insurance claim
② to protest a surgical mismanagement
③ to complain about a rejected insurance claim
④ to inform about an incorrect corporate image
⑤ to criticize unfair practices rampant in the insurance community

15

심경·태도·분위기

글의 전체적인 분위기나 필자 · 등장인물의
심경이나 태도, 또는 글의 전반적인 분위기나
어조를 묻는 유형이다.

▶ 주로 소설이나 수필 같은 문학 작품이나 전기나 일화 등이 지문으로 제시된다.

▶ 세부 내용에 초점 맞추기보다는 글 전체를 재빨리 읽고 전체적인 분위기를 파악하는 것이 중요하다.

▶ 필자나 주인공의 심경을 넌지시 알려주는 어휘나 표현이 있는지 살핀다. 특히, 감정 표현의 형용사나 부사, 동사에 유의한다.

▶ 필자나 주인공이 어떤 상황에 처했고, 그로 인해 어떤 감정을 갖게 되는지에 초점을 맞춰 읽어 나간다.

▶ 글의 흐름이 반전되어 분위기나 주인공의 심경 또한 크게 바뀌는 부분이 있는지 유의한다.

▶ 선택지에서 빈번히 나오는 어휘들은 반드시 익힌다.

선택지에 자주 나오는 어휘

▶ 심경 관련 어휘: 기쁨(amused, entertained), 흥미 · 관심(intrigued, absorbed, interested), 만족(satisfied, gratified, contented), 고무됨(inspired, animated, heartened, stimulated), 좌절(discouraged, frustrated, disheartened), 두려움 (terrified, horrified), 무서움(scared, frightened), 놀람(surprised, astonished, dumfounded, alarmed, astounded), 앙심 (revengeful, retaliatory), 당황(puzzled, perplexed, embarrassed, bewildered, baffled), 안도(relieved), 불안(unstable, anxious, uneasy, disturbed, restless), 초조(edgy, tense, uptight), 분노(furious, indignant, resentful, infuriated, enraged, inflamed, outraged, incensed)

▶ 태도 · 분위기 관련 어휘: 긍정 · 확신(affirmative, positive), 부정(dissenting), 의심(dubious, doubtful), 비판(disparaging, critical), 냉소(sarcastic, cynical, scornful, satirical), 동감 (sympathetic), 편견(biased, partial), 냉담 · 무관심(callous, indifferent), 성급 (rash, impatient, reckless), 우울(depressed, gloomy, melancholy), 황량(desolate, bleak) 활기(exuberant, vigorous, high-spirited), 단호(stern, strict, rigorous), 해학(humorous, witty), 단조로움(monotonous, prosaic), 명료(articulate), 엄숙 (solemn)

▶ 논조 관련 어휘: 설명(explanatory), 묘사(descriptive), 감탄(exclamatory), 가정(hypothetical), 이야기체(narrative), 설득(persuasive), 유익(informative, instructive, didactic)

다음 글에 드러난 Jamie의 심경 변화로 가장 적절한 것은? | 수능 2023년 |

Putting all of her energy into her last steps of the running race, Jamie crossed the finish line. To her disappointment, she had failed to beat her personal best time, again. Jamie had pushed herself for months to finally break her record, but it was all for nothing. Recognizing how she felt about her failure, Ken, her teammate, approached her and said, "Jamie, even though you didn't set a personal best time today, your performances have improved dramatically. Your running skills have progressed so much! You'll definitely break your personal best time in the next race!" After hearing his comments, she felt confident about herself. Jamie, now motivated to keep pushing for her goal, replied with a smile. "You're right! Next race, I'll beat my best time for sure!"

① indifferent → regretful
② pleased → bored
③ frustrated → encouraged
④ nervous → fearful
⑤ calm → excited

[한번에 정리하는 문제 해설]

(지문 해석) 그녀의 모든 에너지를 달리기 대회의 마지막 발걸음에 쏟아 부으며 제이미는 결승선을 통과했다. 실망스럽게도 그녀는 또 다시 개인 최고 기록을 깨지 못했다. 그녀는 기필코 자신의 기록을 깨려고 여러 달 동안 자신을 몰아붙였지만 모두가 수포로 돌아갔다. 그녀가 자신의 실패에 대해 어떤 느낌인지 알아차린 팀 동료 켄이 그녀에게 다가와 말했다. "제이미야, 너는 비록 오늘 개인 최고 기록을 세우지 못했지만 네 실력은 극적으로 향상됐어! 네 달리는 기량이 무척 많이 발전했어. 다음 경주에서는 네 개인 기록을 확실히 깰 수 있을 거야." 그의 말을 들은 후 그녀는 스스로에 대해 자신감을 느꼈다. 목표를 위해 계속 밀고 나갈 의욕을 느낀 제이미는 웃으며 대답했다. "네 말이 맞아! 다음 경주에서 나는 확실히 내 최고 기록을 깰 거야!"

(글의 소재) 달리기 대회에서 자신감을 되찾은 제이미

(주요 어휘) disappointment 실망, beat 때리다, 물리치다, ~을 능가하다, dramatically 극적으로, progress 발전하다, definitely 확실히, 분명히, confident 자신감 있는, motivate 동기를 부여하다, 자신감을 갖게 하다

(구조 분석) • Recognizing how she felt about her failure, Ken, her teammate, approached her and said, ~

➜ 분사구문으로 'As he recognized how she felt about her failure'로 바꿔 쓸 수 있다. 현재분사(~ing)로 시작되는 분사구문은 주절의 주어를 능동으로 수식하고, Being(또는 Having been)이 생략된 과거분사(pp) 형태면 주절의 주어를 수동으로 수식한다는 점도 알아두자.

(정 답) ③

(정답 해설) 자신의 최고 개인 기록을 깨는 데 실패한 제이미가 크게 실망했으나 팀 동료 켄의 격려의 말을 듣고 자신감을 되찾았다는 내용이므로 제이미의 심경 변화는 '좌절된'에서 '용기를 얻은'으로 적절하다. 지문 전반부에 나오는 'disappointment' 'failed' 'for nothing' 부정적인 어휘와 글 후반부의 'confident' 'with a smile' 같은 긍정적 표현들에서 심경 변화의 단서를 찾을 수 있다.

다음 글의 분위기로 가장 적절한 것은?

| 사관 2009년 |

An elderly couple with memory problems are advised by their doctor to write notes to help them remember things. One morning, while watching TV, the wife asks her husband to get her a bowl of ice-cream. "Sure," he says. "Write it down," she suggests. "No," he says, "I can remember a simple thing like that." "I also want strawberries and whipped cream," she says. "Write it down," she shouts. "I don't need to write it down," he insists, heading to the kitchen. Twenty minutes later, he returns bearing a plate of bacon and scrambled eggs. "I told you to write it down!" his wife exclaims, "I wanted fried eggs."

① scary

② touching

③ urgent

④ romantic

⑤ humorous

[한번에 정리하는 문제 해설]

지문 해석 건망증이 심한 노부부가 무엇을 기억하려면 메모를 하라는 충고를 주치의에게서 듣는다. 어느 날 아침 부인이 남편에게 아이스크림 한 통만 가져다 달라고 부탁한다. 남편이 "알았다"라고 하자 아내가 "받아 적어요."라고 말한다. "그 정도 간단한 건 기억할 수 있다오."라고 남편이 말을 받는다. "딸기하고 거품 크림도 좀 가져다 줘요. 좀 적으라니까요."라고 아내가 소리친다. 이 말에 남편은 고집스럽게 "글쎄 적을 필요 없다니까."라고 말하며 부엌으로 간다. 20분 후 그가 베이컨과 스크램블 계란 한 접시를 들고 나타나자 아내가 소리친다. "거봐요 내가 적으라고 했잖아요. (누가 그거 가져다 달라고 했어요?) 계란프라이 달라고 했지."

① 무서운

② 감동적인

③ 긴박한

④ 낭만적인

⑤ 유머러스한

글의 소재 건망증 노부부의 일화

주요 어휘 **whipped cream** 제과용 생크림

정 답 ⑤

정답 해설 부인은 남편에게 아이스크림을 부탁했는데 정작 남편 가져온 것은 베이컨과 스크램블 계란이다. 그것을 보고 부인은 "(내가 언제 그거 달랬어요?) 계란프라이 갖다 달랬지!"라고 외친다. 남편은 고집 속에 망각하고, 부인은 남편에 대한 원망 속에 망각하는, 피차일반의 건망증 부부의 유머러스한 일화다. 따라서 정답은 ⑤이다.

30 다음 글에 나타난 Dave의 심경으로 가장 적절한 것은?

경찰 2016년

Dave was never quite sure how it happened. He only knew that he awoke as he was being hurled from his bed and, mingled with the startled awakening, there was a terrific explosion. For a moment or more he lay absent-mindedly on the deck of his room, struggling to regain his senses. Then slowly he realized the steady throb of the engines, to which he had grown so accustomed in the week since boarding the ship, had abruptly ceased. What happened? He got up and, feeling his way to the light switch, gave it a turn with a trembling hand. Nothing happened, and he tried it again. The lights did not come on.

① distracted and angry
② confused and nervous
③ overjoyed and proud
④ indifferent and bored
⑤ irritated and stimulated

[한번에 정리하는 문제 해설]

지문 해석 그런 일이 어떻게 일어났는지 데이브는 도저히 알 수 없었다. 그가 아는 거라고는 침대에서 떨어져 잠이 깼다는 사실과 놀라 잠이 깨는 와중에 큰 폭발이 있었다는 것뿐이었다. 그는 잠시 방바닥에 멍하니 누워 감각을 되찾으려고 안간힘을 썼다. 그러다가 승선 후 한 주일 동안 늘 들어 친숙해진 배의 엔진 소리가 갑자기 멈춰버렸음을 그는 서서히 알게 됐다. 무슨 일이 있었지? 그는 일어나 더듬거리며 스위치 쪽으로 가서 떨리는 손으로 스위치를 돌렸다. 반응이 없었다. 그는 다시 한 번 시도했다. 불은 들어오지 않았다.

① 산만하고 화난
② 혼란스럽고 초조한
③ 기쁘고 뿌듯한
④ 무관심하고 지루한
⑤ 짜증 나고 고무된

글의 소재 Dave의 해상 조난

주요 어휘 hurl 세게 잡아 던지다, mingle 섞다, startle 놀라게 하다, terrific 끔찍한, absent-minded 멍한, board 승선하다, feel one's way to 더듬거리며 ~쪽으로 가다, tremble 떨게 하다

정답 ②

정답 해설 이 글은 큰 폭발에 놀라 잠에서 깨어 보니 배의 엔진은 꺼지고 불도 들어오지 않는 가운데 주인공 Dave가 의아스러워하는 상황을 묘사하고 있다. Dave의 심경은 혼란(confused)과 초조(nervous)다. 'never quite sure how it happened', 'startled', 'absent-mindedly', 'abruptly', 'What happened?' 등이 Dave의 심경을 나타내는 단서다.

15. 심경·태도·분위기

| 해설 436쪽 |

147 다음 글의 분위기로 가장 어울리는 것은?

난이도 중

In the spring and summer of 1999, I was hospitalized in Sacramento and in Austin for the treatment of tuberculosis, the first time for a few days and the second time for three weeks. During those months, my dreams often took me back to Beijing. I would be standing on top of a building—one of those gray, Soviet-style apartment complexes—or I would be lost on a bus travelling through an unfamiliar neighborhood. Waking up, I would list in my journal images that did not appear in my dreams: a swallow's nest underneath a balcony, the barbed wires at the rooftop, the garden where old people sat and exchanged gossip, the mailboxes at street corners—round, green, covered by dust, with handwritten collection times behind a square window of half-opaque plastic.

① pastoral
② romantic
③ spell-bound
④ educative
⑤ reminiscent

다음 글의 분위기로 가장 적절한 것은?

Hope in Somalia has always been a fragile thing, uplifted by the waves of refugees who have returned to make something of their homeland after decades of civil war and discouraged by the attacks from Islamic extremist group al-Shabab. Hope had flared this year by the violence-free election in February of President M. A. Mohamed, a returning refugee with U.S. citizenship. With Mohamed and his commitment to rule of law came foreign investment to the capital of Mogadishu—a new hospital, banking systems, even a peace park. Global efforts to rebuild the police and army were paying off. Photographer Brent Stirton, who has documented a renaissance there, said, "Somalia conjures up cliches of the worst of Africa: famine, civil war, tyrants. It hasn't really been fair to Somalis."

① frustrated
② desolate
③ rejuvenating
④ ambiguous
⑤ festive

149

다음 글에 나타난 Maria의 성격을 나타낸 말로 가장 적절한 것은?

난이도 중

Maria wanted to attend a technical school. The technical schools were a little more modern than the classical schools. The courses they offered included modern languages, mathematics, and some science, which most people believed girls would never be able to understand. Furthermore, they were not thought to be proper for girls to study. Maria did not care if it was proper or not. Math and science were the subjects that interested her most. But before she could sign up for the technical school, she had to win her father's approval. She finally did, with her mother's help. For many years after, though, there was tension in the family. Maria's father continued to oppose her plans, while her mother helped her. In 1883, at age 13, Maria entered the "Regia Scuola Tecnica Michelangelo Buonarroti" in Rome. Her experience at this school is difficult for us to imagine. Though the courses included modern subjects, the teaching methods were very traditional. Teachers believed in strict discipline in the classroom and they sometimes used severe punishments. Maria was strong enough to survive these methods. After all, she succeeded brilliantly.

① persistent
② presumptuous
③ considerate
④ affectionate
⑤ self-absorbed

150

다음 글의 중심인물인 Mr. Darcy에 대한 분위기 변화를 옳게 나타낸 것은? 난이도 중

And when the party entered the assembly room it consisted only of five all together,—Mr. Bingley, his two sisters, the husband of the eldest, and another young man. Mr. Bingley was good-looking and gentlemanlike; he had a pleasant countenance, and easy, unaffected manners. His sisters were fine women, with an air of decided fashion. His brother-in-law, Mr. Hurst, merely looked the gentleman; but his friend Mr. Darcy soon drew the attention of the room by his fine, tall person, handsome features, noble mien, and the report which was in general circulation within five minutes after his entrance, of his having ten thousand a year. The gentlemen pronounced him to be a fine figure of a man, the ladies declared he was much handsomer than Mr. Bingley, and he was looked at with great admiration for about half the evening, till his manners gave a disgust which turned the tide of his popularity; for he was discovered to be proud; to be above his company, and above being pleased; and not all his large estate in Derbyshire could then save him from having a most forbidding, disagreeable countenance, and being unworthy to be compared with his friend.

① fascinating   → disgusting
② unassuming   → flamboyant
③ docile   → stubborn
④ reserved   → temperamental
⑤ accomplished   → unsophisticated

151 다음 글의 주된 논조로 가장 적절한 것은? 난이도 상

Quitting opioid addiction is no easy job in itself. Finding a way out will be a lot more difficult, particularly at a time of partisan division when national will is so hard to muster. But the need to act is urgent, and the map is increasingly clear: first, we need to recognize that opioid addiction is a disease. The opioid epidemic must be seen as a public-health crisis rather than a moral failure. That means expanding access to medically assisted treatment and counseling, which is widely considered to be the most effective method of getting people off of opioids for good, yet is available to far fewer people than all those who need it. We must enhance efforts to reduce the supply, through the work of law enforcement, by regulating lawful prescriptions and by encouraging other strategies for managing pain. And, finally, we need to confront problems such as the growing economic divide, unaffordable health care and the diminished employment opportunities for those without a college degree who are helping fuel demand in the first place.

* opioid 오피오이드. 아편 비슷한 작용을 하는 합성 진통 · 마취제

① sentimental
② vindicative
③ bitter
④ pleading
⑤ sympathetic

다음 글의 주된 논조로 가장 적절한 것은?   난이도 상

What characterizes almost all Hollywood pictures is their inner emptiness. This is compensated for by an outer impressiveness. Such impressiveness usually takes the form of a truly grandiose realism. Nothing is spared to make the setting, the costumes, all of the surface details correct. These efforts help to mask the essential emptiness of the characterization, and the absurdities and trivialities of the plots. The houses look like houses; the streets look like streets; the people look and talk like people; but they are empty of humanity, credibility, and motivation. Needless to say, the disgraceful censorship mode is an important factor in predetermining the content of these pictures. But the code does not disturb the profits, nor the entertainment value of the films; it merely helps to prevent them from being credible. It isn't too heavy a burden for the industry to bear. In addition to the impressiveness of the settings, there is a use of the camera which at times seem magical. But of what human import is all this skill, all this effort, all this energy in the production of effects, when the story, the representation of life is hollow, stupid, banal, childish?

① hypothetical
② persuasive
③ accommodating
④ deploring
⑤ inquisitive

⑯ 장문의 이해 I
- 1지문 2문제

200~250단어 정도의 단일 장문을 제시하고

글의 전체적인 흐름과 세부 내용을 파악하고 있는지를

묻는 유형 중 1지문 2문제 형이다.

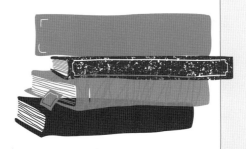

▶ 먼저 제시된 문제와 선택지를 읽고 글에서 어떤 부분에 중점을 두고 읽어야 할지를 결정하여 빠르게 읽어 나간다.

▶ 글의 전체적인 이해를 묻는 문제(주제, 제목, 요지)와 세부 내용을 묻는 문제(빈칸 추론, 어휘, 연결사, 일치ㆍ불일치)가 함께 출제된다.

▶ 문제 유형에 따라 각 유형별로 제시된 가이드라인을 통해 접근하면 된다. 가령, 요지를 묻는 문제는 주제문을 먼저 파악하고, 빈칸 추론의 경우는 빈칸 전후의 문장을 반복적으로 읽어 단서를 찾는 식이다.

▶ 지문의 길이에 주눅 들지 말라. 장문이지만 해석이 수월하거나 문제가 평이한 경우가 얼마든지 있을 수 있다.

▶ 평소에 200~300단어 이상의 장문을 읽는 훈련을 하여 장문에 대한 공포감과 부담감을 줄이자.

For quite some time, science educators believed that "hands-on" activities were the answer to children's understanding through their participation in science-related activities. Many teachers believed that students merely engaging in activities and (a) manipulating objects would organize the information to be gained and the knowledge to be understood into concept comprehension. Educators began to notice that the pendulum had swung too far to the "hands-on" component of inquiry as they realized that the knowledge was not (b) inherent in the materials themselves, but in the thought and metacognition about what students had done in the activity. We now know that "hands-on" is a dangerous phrase when speaking about learning science. The (c) missing ingredient is the "minds-on" part of the instructional experience. (d) Uncertainty about the knowledge intended in any activity comes from each student's re-creation of concepts—and discussing, thinking, arguing, listening, and evaluating one's own preconceptions after the activities, under the leadership of a thoughtful teacher, can bring this about. After all, a food fight is a hands-on activity, but about all you would learn was something about the aerodynamics of flying mashed potatoes! Our view of what students need to build their knowledge and theories about the natural world (e) extends far beyond a "hands-on activity." While it is important for students to use and interact with materials in science class, the learning comes from the sense-making of students' "hands-on" experiences.

* pendulum 추(錘) ** metacognition 초(超)인지 *** aerodynamics 공기 역학

41 윗글의 제목으로 가장 적절한 것은?

① "Hands-on" Activities as a Source of Creativity
② Activity-oriented Learning Enters Science Education!
③ Figure Out What Students Like Most in Science Class
④ Joy and Learning: More Effective When Separated
⑤ Turn "Minds-on" Learning On in Science Class

42 밑줄 친 (a)~(e)중에서 문맥상 낱말의 쓰임이 적절하지 <u>않은</u> 것은?

① (a) ② (b) ③ (c) ④ (d) ⑤ (e)

[한번에 정리하는 문제 해설]

지문 해석 상당한 기간 동안, 과학 교육자들은 '직접 해보는' 활동이 아이들이 과학 관련 활동에 참여하는 것을 통해 이해하게 하는 데 대한 해답이라고 믿었다. 많은 교사들은 학생들이 단지 활동에 참여하고 사물을 조작하는 것만으로 얻게 되는 정보와 이해하게 되는 지식을 개념 이해로 체계화할 것이라고 믿었다. 교육자들은 지식이 자료 자체에 내재해 있는 것이 아니라 학생들이 그 활동에서 한 것에 대한 생각과 초(超)인지에 있다는 것을 깨달으면서 '직접 해보는' 탐구의 요소 쪽으로 추가 너무 많이 기울었다는 것을 알아차리기 시작했다. 이제 과학을 배우는 것을 말할 때 '직접 해보는'이 위험한 문구라는 것을 알게 되었다. 누락된 요소는 교육 경험의 '사고를 요구하는' 부분이다. 어떤 활동에서든 의도된 지식에 대한 불확실성(→ 명료성)은 각 학생의 개념 재창조에서 비롯되는데, 그 활동을 한 뒤에, 사려 깊은 선생님의 지도하에 자신의 선입견에 대해 토론하고, 사고하고, 논쟁하고, 듣고, 평가하는 것을 통해서 이것을 가져올 수 있다. 결국, 음식물 던지기 장난은 직접 해보는 활동이지만, 여러분이 배워야 했던 것은 으깬 감자를 날리는 공기 역학에 관한 것이었다! 자연 세계에 대한 지식과 이론을 구축하기 위해 학생들이 필요로 하는 것에 대한 우리의 견해는 '직접 해보는 활동'을 훨씬 넘어서는 것이다. 과학 수업에서 학생들이 재료를 사용하고 상호 작용하는 것이 중요하기는 하지만, 학습은 '직접 해보는' 학생들의 경험에 대해 의미를 부여하는 것으로부터 나온다.

글의 소재 '직접 해보는(hands-on)' 교육에서 '생각하는(minds-on)' 과학 교육으로의 전환

주요 어휘 hands-on 직접 해보는, 손으로 만지는, manipulate 조작하다, comprehension 이해, pendulum 추, component 요소, inquiry 탐구, 연구, metacognition: 초(超)인지, phrase 문구, ingredient 요소, 성분, instructional 교육의, evaluete 평가하다, preconception 선입견

정 답 41. ⑤

정답 해설 41. 이전의 과학 교육은 학생들이 사물을 직접 해보는 'hands-on' 교육을 강조한 반면 요즘은 학생들이 마음으로 생각하고 깨닫는 'minds-on' 교육의 중요성이 강조되고 있다는 것이 이 글의 주장이다. 따라서 ⑤ '과학 수업에 '생각하는 교육'을 켜라'가 이 글의 제목으로 가장 적절하다. 교육의 한계와 함께 그에 대한 대안으로서의 'hands-on' 교육이 제시되는 'We now know that "hands-on" is a dangerous phrase when speaking about learning science. The missing ingredient is the "minds-on" part of the instructional experience.'와 같은 문장을 유심히 보자. 선택지 중 ①과 ②는 'hands-on' 교육을 강조하기 때문에 안 되고 ③ '과학 수업에서 학생이 가장 좋아하는 것을 알아내라'와 ④ '즐거움과 학습은 분리됐을 때 효과적이다'라는 내용은 글의 주제와 동떨어진 내용이다.

① 창의력의 원천으로서의 "실습" 활동

② 활동 중심의 학습이 과학 교육에 들어온다!

③ 과학 수업에서 학생이 가장 좋아하는 것을 알아내라

④ 즐거움과 학습은 분리됐을 때 효과적이다

⑤ 과학 수업에 '생각하는 교육'을 켜라

정 답 42. ④

정답 해설 42. 이 글의 통념으로 제시된 'hands-on 교육'은 'Educators began to notice ~ done in the activity.' 문장에서 이미 'minds-on 교육' 쪽으로 꺾였기 때문에 글의 흐름상 (d)'Uncertainty'이 속한 문장은 'minds-on' 교육의 중요성이 강조되는 부분이다. 그러므로 'minds-on' 교육의 핵심인 개념 재창조로부터 비롯되는 것은 활동을 통해 얻는 지식의 불확실성 (Uncertainty)이라는 것은 흐름에 어긋난다. 'Uncertainty'는 'Clarity'나 'Certainty'같은 말로 대체돼야 한다. 따라서 정답은 (d)의 ④이다.

As an example of the ability of language to direct our attention, think about the term 'politically correct,' or PC, language. Its proponents argue that we can rid our minds of discriminatory thoughts by removing from our language any words or phrases that could offend people by the way they reference differences and handicaps. Los Angeles County in California asked suppliers to stop using the terms master and slave on computer equipment, even though these are commonly used terms that refer to primary and secondary hard disk drives, because of cultural sensitivity. Other substitutions, such as police officer for policeman, are intended to highlight that such positions are held by both men and women.

Using PC language and being PC have come to be viewed negatively, _____(A)_____, and even ridiculed and satirized because they overcompensate for others' sensitivities. One reason that PC language is fairly easy to ridicule is that its political agenda is not always connected to large social and cultural institutions. _____(B)_____, it is one thing to say that we need to rid the workplace of sexist language in an effort to create equal relationships between men and women, but unless this directive is connected to a broader agenda of fostering gender pay equity and equal opportunity for promotions and advancement, merely ridding the workplace of sexist language may not generate the hoped-for effect.

40 윗글의 주제로 가장 적절한 것은?

① grounds for supporting political correctness
② effects of social progress on language changes
③ pros and cons of using politically correct language
④ differences between male and female language use
⑤ necessity of getting a clear idea with a clear expression

42 윗글의 빈칸 (A), (B)에 들어갈 말로 가장 적절한 것은?

	(A)	(B)
①	however	For example
②	however	In contrast
③	that is	For example
④	thus	In contrast
⑤	thus	For example

[한번에 정리하는 문제 해설]

[지문 해석] 우리의 주의를 환기할 수 있는 언어의 힘의 예로써 '정치적으로 순화된(PC)' 또는 PC 언어라는 용어를 생각해 보자. PC 언어 찬성론자는 차이나 장애를 언급해서 사람들을 불쾌하게 하는 단어나 어구를 제거함으로써 우리는 차별적인 생각을 없앨 수 있다고 주장한다. 캘리포니아주 LA 카운티는 주와 종이 일차와 이차 하드 디스크 드라이브를 지칭하는 흔히 쓰는 표현임에도 불구하고, 문화적 민감성 때문에 공급업자들에게 그 말을 쓰지 말 것을 요청했다. 다른 대체 용어, 가령 policeman 대신 police officer를 쓰는 것도 경찰직은 남녀 모두 수행이 가능하다는 점을 강조하기 위함이다.

하지만 PC 언어 사용이나 PC 자체를 부정적으로 보거나 심지어 조롱과 빈정거림의 대상이 되기도 하는데 이는 PC 언어가 타인의 민감성에 과잉 보상한다고 보기 때문이다. PC 언어가 조롱이 되기 쉬운 한 이유는 그것이 가지는 정치적 의제가 폭넓은 사회 문화적 제도에 늘 맞닿아 있는 것은 아니기 때문이다. 예를 들어, 남녀 사이에 동등한 관계를 이룩하기 위해 직장에서 차별적 언어를 추방하는 것은 있을 수 있지만 그러한 지침이 급료의 평등이나 진급의 기회 평등 촉진이라는 폭넓은 의제와 연관돼 있지 않다면, 단지 차별적인 언어를 제거하는 것만으로는 바라는 효과를 내지 못할 수도 있다는 것이다.

[글의 소재] politically correct(PC) 언어

[주요 어휘] politically correct(PC) 정치적으로 순화된(사회적 약자에 대한 차별적 행동과 언어 사용을 삼갈 것을 권고하는 사회 운동가들이 주장함), proponent 지지자, rid A of B A에서 B를 제거하다, offend 화나게 하다, reference 언급하다, substitution 대체 언어, satirize 빈정대다, overcompensate 과잉보상하다, sexist 남녀차별적인, directive 지침, foster 촉진하다

[정답] 40. ③

[정답 해설] 40. 이 글은 정치적으로 순화된 언어 즉 PC 언어의 순기능과 역기능에 대한 찬반양론을 구체적인 예와 함께 소개하고 있다. 따라서 주제는 ③ PC 언어 사용에 대한 찬반양론이 적절하다.

① PC를 지지하는 이유

② 사회 발전이 언어 변화에 미치는 영향

③ PC 언어 사용에 대한 찬반양론

④ 남녀 간 언어 사용의 차이

⑤ 명확한 표현으로 명확한 사고를 할 필요성

[정답] 41. ①

[정답 해설] 41. PC 언어 찬성론자의 입장에 이어 PC 언어와 PC 자체에 대한 부정적인 견해를 소개하는 단락으로 넘어가고 있으므로 (A)에는 '역접'의 연결사 however가 와야 한다. 또, PC 비판론자들이 PC 언어의 정치적 의제가 폭넓은 사회 문화적 제도에 맞닿아 있지 않다고 보는 구체적인 근거를 (B)에서 예시하고 있으므로 (B)에는 '예시'의 연결사 For example가 적절하다.

경찰 기출문제 유형보기

It is sometimes proposed that direct brain-computer interfaces, particularly implants, could enable humans to exploit the fortes of digital computing—perfect recall, speedy and accurate arithmetic calculation, and high-bandwidth data transmission—enabling the resulting hybrid system to radically outperform the unaugmented brain. But although the possibility of direct connections between human brains and computers has been demonstrated, it seems unlikely that such interfaces will be widely used as enhancements any time soon.

To begin with, there are significant risks of medical complications—including infections, electrode displacement, hemorrhage, and cognitive decline—when implanting electrodes in the brain. Perhaps the most vivid illustration to date of the benefits that can be obtained through brain stimulation is the treatment of patients with Parkinson's disease. The Parkinson's implant is relatively simple: it does not really communicate with the brain but simply supplies a stimulating electric current to the subthalamic nucleus. A demonstration video shows a subject slumped in a chair, completely immobilized by the disease, then suddenly springing to life when the current is switched on: the subject now moves his arms, stands up and walks across the room, turns around and performs a pirouette. Yet even behind this especially simple and almost miraculously successful procedure, there lurk negatives. One study of Parkinson patients who had received deep brain implants showed reductions in verbal fluency, selective attention, color naming, and verbal memory compared with controls. Treated subjects also reported more cognitive complaints. Such risks and side effects might be tolerable if the procedure is used to alleviate severe disability. But in order for healthy subjects to volunteer themselves for neurosurgery, there would have to be some very _____ of normal functionality to be gained.

39 윗글의 제목으로 가장 적절한 것은?

① Full Functionality Gained Via Brain-Computer Interface
② A Breakthrough in Parkinson's Disease Treatment
③ How Best to Augment Brain Power with Implants
④ Direct Brain-Computer Interfaces: Pros and Cons
⑤ Hopes for Success Dwindle Away in Neuroscience

40 윗글의 빈칸에 들어갈 말로 가장 적절한 것은?

① substantial enhancement
② universal application
③ complicated achievements
④ complete deprivation
⑤ authoritative establishment

[한번에 정리하는 문제 해설]

지문 해설 뇌와 컴퓨터 간의 인터페이스 특히 이식은 인간으로 하여금 완벽한 기억이나, 신속 정확한 산술 계산, 고역폭 데이터 전송 등을 하게 하고 그 결과 얻게 되는 혼성 시스템이 증강되지 않은 두뇌를 획기적으로 앞설 수 있을 것이라고 종종 제안된다. 그러나 인간의 뇌와 컴퓨터 간의 직접 연결 가능성이 입증되기는 했지만 그러한 인터페이스가 가까운 장래에 강화 수단으로 폭넓게 사용될 가능성은 낮아 보인다.

우선, 전극을 두뇌에 이식할 때 감염이나 전극 치환, 출혈, 인지 저하 같은 의학적 합병증의 심각한 위험이 있다. 아마 아직까지 두뇌 자극을 통해 얻은 이점의 가장 두드러진 예는 파킨슨씨병 환자의 치료이다. 파킨슨씨병 이식은 비교적 간단해 뇌와 직접 교신하는 것이 아니라 단순히 시상하핵에 자극 전류를 공급하는 것이다. 실험 비디오는 피험자가 병으로 이동이 전혀 불가능한 상태에서 의자에 털썩 주저앉았다가 전류가 흐르자 갑자기 생기를 되찾는 모습을 보여준다. 그러더니 환자는 팔을 움직이고, 일어서서 방을 왔다 갔다 하고, 뒤로 180도 돌고 발레의 돌기 동작까지 한다. 그러나 이 매우 단순하면서 거의 기적적일 정도로 성공적인 수술의 이면에는 부정적인 것들이 숨어있다. 고강도 뇌 이식을 받은 파킨슨씨병 환자를 대상으로 한 연구는 언어 유창성, 선택적 주의, 색 명명 그리고 언어 기억 면에서 통제 집단보다 기능 저하를 보여줬다. 치료받은 피험자들은 또한 인지 상의 불만을 토로했다. 그러한 위험과 부작용들은 그 수술이 심각한 장애를 경감하기 위해 사용된다면 견딜만한 수준에 머무를지 모른다. 그러나 건강한 피험자들이 뇌수술을 자원하도록 하기 위해서는 정상 기능의 상당한 향상이 획득돼야 할 것이다.

글의 소재 뇌-컴퓨터 인터페이스의 장단점

주요 어휘 implant 이식, exploit 이용하다, forte 강점, 장점, high-bandwidth 고대역폭, hybrid 혼성의, outperform ~보다 잘하다, unaugmented 증강되지 않은, enhancement 향상, 강화 수단, complication 복잡화, 합병증, electrode displacement 전극 치환, hemorrhage 출혈, subthalamic 시상하부, nucleus 핵, immobilize 이동을 못 하게 하다, pirouette 피루엣(발레의 돌기 동작), lurk 숨다, 잠복하다, reduction 감소, control 통제 그룹(실험에서 피험자를 판단하기 위한 준거 집단), cognitive 인지적, tolerable 참을 만한, alleviate 경감하다, functionality 기능성

정 답 39. ④

정답 해설 39. 이 글은 뇌와 컴퓨터 간의 인터페이스가 여러 가지 이점에도 불구하고 감염 위험 등 합병증의 위험 때문에 상용화는 아직 시기상조라는 사실을 파킨슨씨병 환자에게 이 기법을 적용했을 때 나타나는 여러 가지 긍·부정적인 효과들을 예를 들어 설명하고 있다. 따라서 윗글의 제목으로는 ④ 직접적 뇌-컴퓨터 인터페이스의 찬반양론이 적절하다.

① 뇌-컴퓨터 인터페이스를 통한 완전한 기능의 획득

② 파킨슨병 치료의 획기적 돌파구

③ 이식으로 두뇌 능력을 최고로 증강하는 법

④ 직접적인 뇌-컴퓨터 인터페이스: 장단점

⑤ 뇌 과학에서 성공 희망 점점 희박해져

정 답 40. ①

정답 해설 40. 정상적인 실험 참가자가 뇌수술을 자원하기 위해서는 정상 기능의 어떤 점이 획득돼야 하는가를 물은 문제다. 같은 단락의 파키슨씨병 환자를 대상으로 한 실험에서 인터페이스가 환자에게 놀라운 행동 장애 개선을 가져다주지만 뇌 이식 환자가 언어 구사력 등에서 기능 저하를 겪는다고 했으므로 뇌 이식에서 무엇보다 중요한 것은 정상 기능을 향상시키는 문제임을 알 수 있다. 그러므로 빈칸에는 ①의 '상당한 향상'이 적절하다. 따라서 정답은 ①이다.

② 보편적 응용

③ 복잡한 성과

④ 완벽한 상실

⑤ 권위적 확립

[153~154] 다음 글을 읽고 물음에 답하시오. 난이도 중

The classical civilizations of Greece and Rome developed sophisticated financial economies based on money and markets. The Greeks invented banking, coinage, and commercial courts. The Romans built on these innovations and added business corporations, limited liability investments, and a form of central banking, Unlike the ancient cities of Mesopotamia, which were primarily organized around the redistribution of local produce and secondarily around long-distance trade, Athens and Rome both (a)<u>outgrew</u> their local agricultural capacity and substituted overseas trade for it. Athens imported much of her wheat from as far away as the Black Sea. Rome depended on rich farmland of the Nile delta for its grain. To make these audacious economic models work (b)<u>required</u> a novel financial structure. Athens and Rome had to make grain flow toward the center. The economy had to motivate farmers (c)<u>overseas</u> to grow grain for export, to motivate sailors and captains to risk their lives to bring the grain, to motivate investment in ships and trade goods, and to create a system of payment that was (d)<u>subject</u> to uncertainties of international commerce. The solutions involved the invisible hand of the market, financial technologies for dealing with the (e)<u>unpredictability</u> of the sea, and a monetary economy that relied on universally accepted measures of value.

153 윗글의 주제로 가장 적절한 것은?

① attempts by Athens and Rome to curb export-oriented economy
② what was behind Athens' and Rome's emergence as ancient powers
③ the ancient power struggle in and around the Mediterranean Sea
④ Athens' and Rome's contributions to the birth of modern capitalism
⑤ the measures Athens and Rome took to address expanding economies

154 밑줄 친 (a)~(e) 중에서 문맥상 낱말의 쓰임이 적절하지 <u>않은</u> 것은?

① (a) ② (b) ③ (c) ④ (d) ⑤ (e)

[155~156] 다음 글을 읽고 물음에 답하시오.　　　난이도 중

Besides eating right and exercising, there are other more surprising ways to prolong your life. Luckily for us, these unexpected methods for extending our longevity are easier and much more enjoyable than chowing down on carrot sticks and fiercely burning calories at the gym.

The first step to living longer is reading more novels. A Yale University study that lasted over a decade found that readers live two years longer than non-readers. This was largely due to the cognitive enhancement linked to reading. Reading more than three and a half hours per week helped individuals in the study improve their memory and creativity, which contributed to their longer lifespan. Even those who are slightly under par in their weekly reading hours had a 17% life expectancy advantage over the non-readers. But before you run to the comic book store or use this as an excuse to read social media posts for hours, it's worth noting that these health benefits are _____(A)_____ only to novels.

If reading isn't your thing, you have another opportunity to extend your life through humor. Researchers in Norway found that both women and men were physically healthier if they could understand humor, or even attempts at humor, well. This is due to the stress-reducing qualities of the ability to turn a negative situation into one you can laugh off. In this case, it seems your mind can help control your body by preventing that excessively negative energy from turning into inflammation. It seems like all those dad jokes may be worth _____(B)_____ after all.

The next time the latest health fad tempts you, just remember there's more than one way to live a healthy life. Pick up a book and laugh freely.

155　윗글의 제목으로 가장 적절한 것은?

① What Aspects of Modern Life Are Stressful?
② Surprising Tips on Improving Your Quality of Life
③ What We Should Do To Improve Our Intellectual Capacity
④ Hidden Secrets to Longevity: Novels and Humor
⑤ Where Will Studying and Laughing Get Us after All?

156　글의 흐름으로 보아 (A)와 (B)에 들어갈 가장 적절한 말로 짝지어진 것은?

	(A)	(B)		(A)	(B)
①	conducive	telling	②	conducive	withholding
③	applicable	telling	④	applicable	withholding
⑤	conducive	showering			

When my mother retired from teaching college, she found herself with a large, empty house and no one to fill it: her children had all ended up living in other cities, some quite distant, and my father had died years before. A former professor of sociology, she made what, in retrospect, seems a smart social move: my mother offered a free room to graduate students from her university, with a preference for those from East Asian cultures, where older people are appreciated and respected. It's been more than thirty years since she retired, and this arrangement still continues. She has had a revolving series of housemates from places like Japan, Taiwan, and currently Beijing—with what seem to be great benefits for her well-being. When one couple had a baby while living with her, their daughter grew up treating my mother like her own grandmother. As a two-year-old, the toddler would go into my mother's bedroom every morning to see if she was up yet and routinely gave her hugs through the day. That baby was born when my mother was almost ninety—and with that bundle of delight roaming the house, my mother actually seemed for a few years to get younger, both physically and mentally. We'll never know how much of my mother's longevity can be attributed to her living situation, but evidence suggests hers was a wise bit of social engineering.

157 윗글의 제목으로 가장 적절한 것은?

① My Mother's Bold Choice for Undisturbed Aging
② The Best Way to Prepare for One's Retirement
③ Socializing: The Secret to My Mother's Comfortable Aging
④ Respect for the Elderly: The Proud Cultural Heritage of East Asia
⑤ The Effects of Frequent Bodily Contacts on Aging

158 어머니에 대한 다음 서술 중 위 글의 내용과 일치하는 것은?

① 퇴직 당시 자녀들이 모두 인근 도시에 살고 있었다.
② 어머니께서 재직했던 대학의 대학원생에게 싼 월세로 방을 제공했다.
③ 일본이나 대만, 북경 출신을 선호한 것은 이국적 호기심 때문이었다.
④ 함께 살던 젊은 부부가 낳은 딸이 어머니를 친할머니처럼 따랐다.
⑤ 장수를 하신 것은 전적으로 노년의 사교 생활 덕분이었다.

[159~160] 다음 글을 읽고 물음에 답하시오. 난이도 중

Despite its origin in Pagan and Christian tradition, the modern American Halloween is often a purely secular celebration centered on candy and costumes. But in fact, one of the most frivolous aspects of the holiday has a serious religious past.

Medieval Christian tradition held that on Hallowtide, the eve of All Saints' Day, the poor went to the home of the wealthy and offered to pray for the recently departed in that household; it was believed that more prayers meant a soul was more likely to be saved. The rich then rewarded the poor with food and beer, explains historian Nicholas Rogers. But after the Protestant Reformation, the idea that souls could be saved <u>in this way</u> began to lose popularity in many of the new denominations. Some people kept up the tradition, but its religious connection faded, even among Catholics.

By the 1840s, when a wave of Irish and Scottish immigrants brought the custom to the US, it was basically a secular pastime. Although the Catholic Irish faced widespread prejudice from nativist forces in their new homeland, the celebration, having been stripped of its Catholic underpinning, quickly proved to be popular. As those immigrants began to assimilate, newspapers reported the custom trending among 19th century college students. By the 1930s, North America had a new term for the old tradition: (A)   .

159 밑줄 친 in this way가 가리키는 것은?

① 가난한 사람이 부잣집 집 떠난 사람의 무사 귀환을 빌어주는 것
② 가난한 사람이 부잣집 죽은 이를 위해 기도해 주는 것
③ 부자와 가난한 사람이 술과 음식을 함께 하는 것
④ 가난한 사람이 부잣집 허드렛일을 도와주는 것
⑤ 부자와 가난한 사람이 만성절 전야를 함께 보내는 것

160 글의 흐름으로 보아 빈칸 (A)에 들어갈 가장 적절한 말은?

① underpin or demolishing   ② celebrate or denouncing
③ conquer or surrendering   ④ save or wasting
⑤ trick or treating

A converted hotel in Ottawa houses an alcohol treatment facility with a vastly different philosophy than most facilities that treat addiction. The Oaks is a permanent home for alcoholics pulled off of the frigid streets to be treated for alcoholism under the Managed Alcoholic Program(MAP). Unlike other alcoholic treatment programs which preach abstinence above all else, residents at the Oaks are treated to an hourly dose of 13 % white wine brewed right there in the building.

Clutching coffee cups, glasses, mugs or anything else they can use, the residents line up every hour for the pour. Beginning with 7 oz at 7:30 in the morning and continuing with 5 oz every hour until 9:30 pm, the Oaks keeps its patients plied with a steady and relatively harmless amount of alcohol. What's the idea behind this unusual approach? "I'd love them all to be abstinent," said Dr. Jeff Turnbull, chief of staff at Ottawa Hospital and one of the creators of the program, "but is that feasible or possible? Perhaps not." Instead, Dr. Turnbull and his staff subscribe to the theory of _____, which is the idea that the negative effects of drug or alcohol use can be limited through practical strategies. Although the MAP program is not without its critics there is no doubt that it is making a positive impact on the Ottawa community. The number of 911 calls, hospital visits and paramedic responses in regards to freezing alcoholics has dropped significantly.

161 윗글의 요지를 한 문장으로 요약할 때 가장 적절한 것은?

① Slow and steady wins the race.
② A drowning man will catch at a straw.
③ God helps those who help themselves.
④ Where there is a will, there is a way.
⑤ Bite off only as much as you can chew.

162 빈칸에 들어갈 말로 가장 적절한 것은?

① harm reduction   ② aggressive treatment
③ positive accommodation   ④ negative healing
⑤ sobriety spreading

When I was a child, I was not enamored with babies. An only child to the bone, I found small children irritating, and babies, with their perpetual drooling and persistent diaper odor, were the worst. My mother and other adults would point out cute specimens, hoping to pique my interest, but I promptly turned up my nose at each one. This trickled down even to my play habits. (A)The idea of playing house was enough to send me running to climb the highest tree in sight.

Animals were different. I cherished my stuffed animals as much as I detested dolls. I might twist the head off a Barbie, but I would swaddle a stuffed bear and rock it to sleep. I loved the real things too; there wasn't a kitty, puppy, hamster, fish or canary alive that I didn't want to "mommy" and play with. Even as a teen and into my early twenties, I would pick a golden retriever over a cute baby any day.

My first child was a Himalayan cat named Margot. She filled the emptiness of my graduate school apartment and life. I adored her and turned into one of those crazy pet people, putting her picture in frames around the house and dressing her up for Halloween. My cat was my baby, and I was her mommy. She was a snuggly sort of cat, so I carried her around the house with me and let her sleep on my bed. She was the perfect child—sweet and loving without the upkeep.

* swaddle 아기를 포대기로 싸다

163 밑줄 친 (A)의 상황을 한 단어로 표현할 때 가장 적절한 말은?

① adventurous
② loathsome
③ frivolous
④ awkward
⑤ eccentric

164 '나'의 어렸을 때 취향에 대해 옳게 말한 것은?

① 아기는 좋아했지만 동물은 싫어했다.
② 동물은 좋아했지만 아기는 싫어했다.
③ 아기도 동물도 좋아했다.
④ 아기도 동물도 싫어했다.
⑤ 아기나 동물에 대한 특별한 호불호가 없었다.

Amidst tightening security throughout France in response to recent acts of terrorism, a group of cities along the French Riviera have banned the "burkini," a women's bathing suit that covers the majority of the body like a burqa, from local beaches. Mayors have justified these laws by claiming that the burkini is a flamboyant display of religion, which counters the French value of secularism and therefore poses a threat to ____(A)____. These new, local bans have caused a bit of an uproar on social media and were suspended by French courts late August for violating fundamental liberties.

Viral images of a recent incident in which a woman was forced to take off the conservative swimwear by a group of armed police were immediately compared to photos of US police enforcing bikini laws on women in the 1920's and 1930's. It seems women especially are under constant strain to find the happy medium between showing too much skin and not showing enough. Despite the ban, vendors of the burkini report more sales than ever before, and not only to Muslim women, but to those with concerns about body image and survivors of skin cancer. For many, it is a matter of choosing what to wear.

Aside from questions of personal freedom, the effectiveness of banning the burkini is yet another pressing issue. France has been in a state emergency since last November's terrorist attacks, resulting in thousands of house raids and arrests as well as the ____(B)____ of numerous mosques reported to be preaching radical Islam. Recently, and former president Nicolas Sarkozy stated that if he is re-elected president, he will change the country's constitution in order to ban the burkini.

* burqa 이슬람 여성이 입는 전통 의상의 하나

165 빈칸 (A)와 (B)에 들어갈 적절한 말로 짝지어진 것은?

	(A)	(B)		(A)	(B)
①	religious practices	dedication	②	public order	retention
③	public order	closure	④	public order	dedication
⑤	religious practices	closure			

166 윗글의 내용과 일치하는 것은?

① 시장들은 버키니가 프랑스의 세속주의 가치에 부합한다고 보았다.

② 1920년대와 1930년대 미국에서도 버키니 착용이 크게 논란이 된 적이 있다.

③ 당국의 버키니 단속으로 버키니 매출이 급감했다.

④ 현 프랑스 총리는 외국인의 모스크 지원을 찬성하였다.

⑤ 사르코지는 대통령에 재선되면 버키니를 금지하는 쪽으로 개헌하겠다고 말했다.

One short route to the substantive core of interdisciplinary problems is to ask why the social sciences should be sought by professions that hitherto saw little need of them. Why, for example, should the once sacrosanct schools of medicine have any interest at all in the social sciences? The medical profession certainly has its own prestige, to the point (a) <u>where</u> it is ridiculous to think that the social sciences could add to it. The medical profession is supported by the rapidly developing physical and biological sciences. Why social scientists? Why the behavioral science departments in many medical schools?

The answer is that the medical profession deals with man, and (b) <u>what</u> even man's anatomy and physiology are not an insulated, self-contained subject matter for study. Most medical specialties today are highly technical, (c) <u>requiring</u> mastery in depth of a great deal more theory and technique than most social sciences can offer their students. For example, the measurement and treatment of metabolic disorders (d) <u>is</u> a highly technical affair these days. Yet when Dr. William Schottstaedt and his colleagues studied the detailed biochemical and physiological records of patients in a metabolic ward, they found that variations in these (e) <u>strictly</u> physiological measures of metabolism were significantly related to the vicissitudes of interpersonal relationships among patients, with nurses and doctors, and with visitors.

* sacrosanct: 신성불가침의, vicissitude 변화의 추세

167 윗글의 제목으로 알맞은 것은?

① Independence between Individual Sciences: A Must
② A Proposal To Promote the Prestige of Medical Professionals
③ Specialization: A Viable Option for Contemporary Medicine
④ Why Is Interdisciplinary Collaboration a Necessity in Medicine?
⑤ Merging and Integration: An Irreversible Trend for Scientific Studies

168 윗글의 밑줄 친 (a)~(e) 중, 어법상 틀린 것은?

① (a)　　　② (b)　　　③ (c)　　　④ (d)　　　⑤ (e)

On Feb. 5th 2018, people on Wall Street had to watch the stock market crash with panic and extreme anxiety. The Dow Jones average plummeted 1,175 points, the largest point drop in its history—before stabilizing Feb 6th. Practical-minded business people may be tempted to dismiss these market collapses the same way they dismiss technical corrections which usually happen to a bullish market. After all, the fundamentals of the economy are good, earnings are strong, inflation and interest rates are low, so why worry? But there's probably a signal in there somewhere. Yes, algorithmic trading of volatility-related derivatives had a lot to do with the market's roller-coaster ride. But so did legitimate uncertainty about the future. For the past decade, the world has been awash in easy money—the result of an unprecedented experiment in monetary policy. As flood recedes, rocks will emerge. To quote a famous American investor, "You only learn who has been swimming naked when the tide goes out." There was no great harm done in the recent swoon. Market indexes ended up close to where they had been when the year began. But the Federal Reserve Board(FRB), whose mission it is to instil confidence in money, markets and the economy, should consider this a warning. There will be rough swimming ahead.

169 윗글의 제목으로 가장 적절한 것은?

① Easy Money: A Potential Threat to Wall Street
② Too Much Fear in the Market Is Good for Nothing
③ We Better Believe in the Resilience of the Market
④ Prosperity Never Lasts Forever
⑤ Don't Be Too Susceptible to Market Fluctuations

170 다음 중 윗글의 내용과 일치하지 않는 것은?

① 2018년 2월 5일 다우존스지수는 사상 최대치 폭락했다.
② 변동성 높은 파생상품의 알고리즘식 매매가 주식 급등락에 영향을 끼쳤다.
③ 미래에 대한 불안 또한 이번 주식 급등락과 관계가 있다.
④ 실험적 통화정책의 결과로 지난 10년간 전 세계는 이지머니로 넘쳐났다.
⑤ FRB는 이번 폭락 사태를 너무 심각하게 받아들이지 말아야 한다.

There is plenty to complain about when it comes to flying: long lines in the airport, confusing rules at security gates, tight quarters in regular economy class, and the ever-present stench of your neighbor's shoeless toes. You may also have a couple of uncomfortable memories from the taste of airline food or the lack of it. Although the rubbery noodles and not-so-sticky rice truly lack appeal, there are valid explanations for the disappointment of airline food.

According to a study conducted by Lufthansa in 2010, as a plane ascends to its cruising altitude of 10.6 km, pressure inside the cabin drops and humidity levels plummet to less than 12%, which is drier than most deserts. Due to these factors, your sensitivity to sweet and salty flavors is reduced to about 30% of your taste buds' typical capacity. But taste isn't everything. Nearly 80% of what we think of as taste should really be attributed to our sense of smell, which unfortunately also suffers in flight. Our odor receptors need evaporating mucus in order to pick up the aromas of our goods, but the cabin air parches our nostril.

Furthermore, recent psychological studies have shown that taste and smell aren't the whole story when it comes to enjoying our food. The deafening jet engines also seem to negatively affect people's ability to taste salty and sweet flavors, while others like cardamon, lemongrass and curry become stronger. Taking into account these reasons, and remembering that airline chefs mass produce food for thousands of customers each day, maybe you'll add a wedge of patience to your in-flight beverage, be it a rehydrating glass of water or a rejuvenating soda pop.　　* mucus 코의 점액

171　윗글의 제목으로 가장 적절한 것은?

① Several Inconveniences Forced on All Air Travellers
② The Case for the Poor Taste of Airline Food
③ Poor Airline Food as a Major Source of Customer Complaint
④ Proposals to Improve the Quality of Airline Food
⑤ Airline Food Causing Unpleasant Memories for Air Travellers

172　윗글의 내용과 일치하는 것은?

① 기체가 순항 고도에 이르면 기내 압력이 급격히 상승한다.
② 운항 중인 기내에서는 단맛과 짠맛을 더 잘 느낄 수 있다.
③ 우리가 미각이라 생각하는 것의 80%는 사실 후각 때문이다.
④ 콧속의 점액이 증발할 때는 음식의 냄새를 맡기 어렵다.
⑤ 비행기 소음은 모든 음식 맛을 떨어뜨린다.

The revolution of the human mind is a single process, revealed, with different intensity, different clarity, and different timing, in its various manifestations—art, science, philosophy, social and political thought. It is like a fugue, or an oratorio, in which different instruments, or different voices, enter in turn. The voice of the artist is often the first to respond. The artist is the most (a) sensitive individual in society. His or her feeling for change or apprehension of new things to come, is likely to be more (b) acute than that of the slower moving, rational, scientific thinker. It is in the artistic production of a period, rather than in its thinking, that one should search for shadows cast in advance by coming events, for prophetic anticipation. I do not mean the forecast of future events, but rather the revelation, in the framework of artistic production, of the mental attitudes which only later will become (c) apparent in other fields of human endeavor. Thus, the impending breakdown of the existing order of things, of the generally accepted system of values, should be—and often is—first (d) recognizable in a revolt against the values and canons that had dominated artistic creation; a revolution in art precedes the revolution of society. In the same way the stabilization of a new political regime, or social order, is often (e) followed by the acceptance of new canons in art—be it the glorious neoclassicism of the French revolution, or the drab "socialist realism" of the Russian one.

173 윗글의 제목으로 가장 적절한 것은?

① Who Leads Social Integration, the Artist or the Thinker?
② The Artist: the Herald of an Impending Social Change
③ Social Revolutions: Their Causes, Agents and Patterns
④ Does Art Drive the Birth of a New Political Order?
⑤ Hidden Forces behind Major Social Changes in History

174 밑줄 친 (a)～(e) 중에서 문맥상 낱말의 쓰임이 적절하지 않은 것은?

① (a)　　　② (b)　　　③ (c)　　　④ (d)　　　⑤ (e)

Information-rich traditions might become quite important without any change in individual cognitive equipment. The social environment changes as a result of innovation or environmental change, and as a consequence, parental capacities are reliably regained in the next generation. But they are regained through adults shaping juvenile learning environments as a by-product of the adults' own ecological activities. They are not regained as a result of adaptations for social learning or teaching. No feedback loop yet. But clearly, once information-rich traditions are established, _____. The initial shift to a stone-tool-based lifestyle may well have depended on preexisting mechanisms of adaptive plasticity, preexisting potentials for manual dexterity, and preexisting foraging patterns. But once established, the new lifestyle will select for genetic variants that enable these new skills to be acquired with high reliability and low cost (it is easy to lose eyes and fingers while flint knapping). There will be selection in favor of mutations that increase the reliability and accuracy of learning from the parental generation (unless these mutations come with other unaffordable costs). Such mutations can adapt morphology as well as mind to the new technology. As archeologist Stanley Ambrose notes, our hands, wrists and arms are better suited than those of chimps for flint knapping. Likewise, if traditions are transmitted vertically from parent to offspring, mutations that alter parental behavior in ways that increase transmission reliability will be favored.

* flint knapping 부싯돌을 쳐서 불을 붙이는 것

175 윗글의 주제로 가장 적절한 것은?

① parental capacities successfully regained but lacking any feedback loop
② information-rich traditions and mutations resulting in transmission of learning
③ parental capacities transmitted through adaptations for social learning
④ the changing environment that might have expedited the coming of the stone age
⑤ the benefits and costs involved in acquiring favorable genetic variants

176 글의 흐름으로 보아 빈칸에 가장 알맞은 말은?

① the innovative move tapers off   ② such a feedback loop loosens
③ the quest for social learning persists   ④ society in general stabilizes fast
⑤ selective environment changes

Risk portfolios explain why people often become original in one part of their lives while remaining quite conventional in others. T. S. Eliot's landmark work, *The Waste Land*, has been hailed as one of the twentieth century's most significant poems. But after publishing it in 1922, Eliot kept his London bank job until 1925, rejecting the idea of embracing professional risk. As the novelist Aldous Huxley noted after paying him an office visit, Eliot was "the most bank-clerky of all bank clerks." When he finally did leave the position, Eliot still didn't strike out on his own. He spent the next forty years working for a publishing house to provide stability in his life, writing poetry on the side. As Polaroid founder Edwin Land remarked, "No person could possibly be original in one area unless he were possessed of the emotional and social stability that comes from fixed attitudes in all areas other than the one in which he is being original." But don't day jobs distract us from doing our best work? Common sense suggests that creative accomplishments can't flourish without big windows of time and energy, and companies can't thrive without intensive effort. Those assumptions overlook the central benefit of _____. Having a sense of security in one realm gives us the freedom to be original in another. By covering our bases financially, we escape the pressure to publish half-baked books, sell shoddy art, or launch untested businesses.

* portfolio 포트폴리오(위험을 회피하기 위해 다양한 금융상품에 분산 투자하는 것)

177 윗글의 제목으로 가장 적절한 것은?

① No Risk, No Gain
② To Be Original, Offset Your Risks
③ Strike While the Iron Is Hot
④ You Need to Double Down If Necessary
⑤ Originality Lies in Never Avoiding Risks

178 글의 흐름으로 보아 빈칸에 가장 알맞은 말은?

① a balanced risk portfolio　② an aggressive investment strategy
③ a more comprehensive approach　④ a choice and concentration tactics
⑤ a prioritized investment plan

[179~180] 다음 글을 읽고 물음에 답하시오.   난이도 상

The process of human unification has taken a distinct form; establishing links between distinct groups. Links may be formed even between groups that continue to behave very differently. In fact, links may form even between sworn enemies. War itself can generate some of the strongest of all human bonds. Historians often argue that globalization reached a first peak in 1913, then went into a long decline during the era of the world wars and the Cold War, and recuperated only after 1989. This may be true of economic globalization, but it ignores the different but equally important dynamic of military globalization. War spreads ideas, technologies and people far more quickly than commerce does. In 1918 the US was more closely linked to Europe than in 1913; the two then drifted in the interwar years, only to have their fates meshed together inextricably by the Second World War and the Cold War. War also makes people far more interested in one another. The US had never been more closely in touch with Russia than during the Cold War, when every cough in a Moscow corridor sent people scrambling up and down Washington staircases. People care far more about their enemies than about their trade partners. For every American film about Taiwan, there are probably fifty about Vietnam.

179 윗글의 주제로 적절한 것은?

① regretable heritage from the Cold War era
② war as the creator of powerful human bonds
③ economic globalization vs military globalization
④ ideological and technological exchanges between enemies
⑤ a shift in emotions caused by turbulent human experiences

180 밑줄 친 부분이 의미하는 바는?

① 미국은 베트남보다는 대만을 중시한다.
② 미국의 일차적 관심사는 교역이다.
③ 베트남은 미국이 선호하는 영화 소재가 아니다.
④ 미국의 대만보다 베트남과의 영화 교류가 훨씬 활발하다.
⑤ 미국인들은 경제 파트너보다는 적에 관심이 많다.

Writing can be daunting, frustrating, and even frightening—yet then, somehow, magically fulfilling. That's why having a writing routine is so important. If there's a single defining trait among most successful writers, it's that they all show up to write (a) <u>regularly</u>. Whether they write at midnight, dawn, or after a two-martini lunch, they have a routine. "A goal without a plan is just a wish," said Antoine Saint Exupéry. And a routine is a plan. A plan of dedication. A routine helps (b) <u>obliterate</u> any obstacle hindering you from writing, whether it's a psychological block or a tantalizing party invitation.

But it's even more than that. When you write during a certain time each day, and in an environment designated solely for rumination, you (c) <u>experience</u> creative benefits. The regularity of time and place serves as an invitation for your mind to walk through the doorways of your imagination and fully concentrate on your story. Routines help to (d) <u>trigger</u> cognitive cues that are associated with your story, cloaking you in the ideas, images, feelings, and sentences that are swirling in your subconscious. If you anoint a specific time and place for writing and make it sacred and regular, it's (e) <u>harder</u> to transcend the intrusive fretfulness of life and rise above its cacophony. Regularity and repetition are like guides who lead you deeper into the realm of your imagination.

181　윗글의 주제로 알맞은 것은?

① the importance of having a routine in writing
② the risk of repeating the same old routine in writing
③ goal-keeping as the decisive factor of career success
④ confusion and frustration caused by a change of routine
⑤ imagination and concentration needed for all literary writing

182　밑줄 친 (a)~(e) 중에서 문맥상 낱말의 쓰임이 적절하지 <u>않은</u> 것은?

① (a)　　　　② (b)　　　　③ (c)　　　　④ (d)　　　　⑤ (e)

장문의 이해 Ⅱ
– 1지문 3문제

250~350단어 정도의 단일 장문을 제시하고

글의 전체적인 흐름과 세부 내용을 파악하고 있는지를

묻는 종합 유형 중 1지문 3문제 형이다.

가이드라인

▶ 먼저 제시된 문제와 선택지를 읽고 글에서 어떤 부분에 중점을 두고 읽어야 할지를 결정하여 빠르게 읽어 나 간다.

▶ 장문을 소화하는 데 시간이 부족할 수 있으므로 핵심 소재와 주제문을 중심으로 읽어 불필요한 정보를 걸러 가며 독해의 시간을 단축할 필요가 있다.

▶ 글의 전체적인 이해를 묻는 문제(주제, 제목, 요지)와 세부 내용을 묻는 문제(빈칸 추론, 연결사, 어휘, 일치 · 불일치)가 함께 출제된다.

▶ 문제 유형에 따라 각 유형별로 제시된 가이드라인을 통해 접근하면 된다. 가령, 제목을 묻는 문제는 주제문을 먼저 파악한 후에 이를 압축하거나 상징적으로 제시한 선택지가 있는지 살피고, 일치 · 불일치를 묻는 문제는 선택지를 먼저 읽고 지문을 접하면 전체 내용의 파악이 한결 수월하다.

▶ 평소에 300단어 이상의 장문을 읽는 훈련을 하여 장문에 대한 공포감과 부담감을 줄인다.

▶ 지문에 대한 이해가 완전하지 않아도 정답의 추론이 가능한 경우가 얼마든지 있을 수 있으므로 끝까지 포기 하지 않는 자세가 중요하다.

(A) The colors of the trees looked like they were on fire, the reds and oranges competing with the yellows and golds. This was Nina's favorite season, but she remained silent for hours while Marie was driving. Nina had been heartbroken after losing her championship belt. Now a former champion, she was thinking of retiring from boxing. Marie, her long-time friend and trainer, shared her pain. After another silent hour, Marie and Nina saw a sign: Sauble Falls. Marie thought this would be a good place for (a) <u>them</u> to stop.

(B) Then, with a great push, a small one turned a complete circle and made it over the falls. "He made it!" Nina shouted at the success with admiration. More salmon then followed and succeeded. She felt ashamed to be looking at (b) <u>them</u>. After a moment, she turned to Marie and said, "Giving up is not in my vocabulary. Marie, I'll get my championship belt back." Marie nodded with a bright smile. "Our training begins tomorrow. It's going to be tough. Are you ready?" Walking up the path and back to the car, (c) <u>they</u> could still hear the fish splashing in the water.

(C) Marie pulled over into the parking lot. Marie and Nina went down a path to watch the falls. Another sign: Watch Your Step. Rocks Are Slippery. (d) <u>They</u> found the falls spilling out in various layers of rock. No one was there except them. "Look at them!" Marie pointed to movement in the water moving toward the falls. Hundreds of fish tails were flashing and catching light from the sun, moving upstream. Beneath them in the water, they saw salmon slowly moving their bodies.

(D) While Marie and Nina kept watching the salmon, a big one suddenly leapt. It threw itself up and over the rushing water above, but in vain. (e) <u>They</u> were standing without a word and watching the fish struggling. Another jumped, its body spinning until it made it over the falls. Another one leapt and was washed back by the power of the water. Watching the salmon, Marie noticed Nina fixing her eyes on their continuing challenge. Nina's heart was beating fast at each leap and twist.

* splash 물을 튀기다

43 주어진 글 (A)에 이어질 내용을 순서에 맞게 배열한 것으로 가장 적절한 것은?

① (B) – (D) – (C)　　　　② (C) – (B) – (D)　　　　③ (C) – (D) – (B)

④ (D) – (B) – (C)　　　　⑤ (D) – (C) – (B)

44 밑줄 친 (a)~(e) 중에서 가리키는 대상이 나머지 넷과 <u>다른</u> 것은?

① (a)　　　　② (b)　　　　③ (c)　　　　④ (d)　　　　⑤ (e)

45 윗글에 관한 내용으로 적절하지 <u>않은</u> 것은?

① Marie가 운전하는 동안 Nina는 말이 없었다.
② Marie는 Nina의 오랜 친구이자 트레이너였다.
③ 폭포에서 Nina는 Marie에게 권투를 그만두겠다고 말했다.
④ 폭포에 있는 사람은 Marie와 Nina뿐이었다.
⑤ Nina는 폭포 위로 뛰어오르는 연어를 유심히 바라보았다.

[한번에 정리하는 문제 해설]

지문 해석 (A) 나무들의 색깔이 마치 불이 붙은 것처럼 보였으며, 빨간색과 오렌지색이 노란색 및 황금색과 다투고 있었다. 이때가 Nina가 가장 좋아하는 계절이었지만, 그녀는 Marie가 운전하는 중에 몇 시간 동안 침묵을 지키고 있었다. Nina는 챔피언 벨트를 잃은 뒤 상심해 있었다. 이제 전 챔피언이 된 그녀는 권투에서 은퇴하는 것을 생각하고 있었다. 오랜 친구이자 트레이너인 Marie는 그녀의 고통을 함께 나누었다. 침묵의 한 시간이 또 지난 후 Marie와 Nina는 'Sauble 폭포'라는 표지판을 보았다. Marie는 이곳이 그들이 멈추기에 좋은 장소라고 생각했다.

(C) Marie는 주차장으로 들어가 차를 댔다. Marie와 Nina는 폭포를 구경하기 위해 길을 내려갔다. '발걸음 조심하세요. 바위가 미끄럽습니다.'라는 또 다른 표지판이 있었다. 그들은 겹겹의 다양한 바위에서 폭포가 쏟아져 내리는 것을 발견했다. 거기에는 그들 말고는 아무도 없었다. "저것들 좀 봐!" Marie는 폭포를 향해 이동하는 물속의 움직임을 가리켰다. 수백 마리의 물고기 꼬리가 번쩍거리고 태양으로부터 빛을 받으며, 상류로 이동하고 있었다. 자신들 발밑 물속에서, 그들은 연어들이 천천히 몸을 움직이고 있는 것을 보았다.

(D) Marie와 Nina가 계속 연어를 지켜보고 있는 동안, 커다란 연어 한 마리가 갑자기 뛰어올랐다. 그것은 빠르게 흐르는 물 위로 몸을 솟구쳐 넘어가려고 했지만, 소용없었다. 그들은 말 한마디 없이 선 채 물고기들이 온 힘을 다하는 것을 지켜보았다. 또 다른 한 마리가 뛰어올랐고, 몸이 빙글빙글 돌더니 마침내 폭포를 넘어가는 데 성공했다. 또 다른 한 마리가 뛰어올랐으나 물의 힘에 의해 다시 쓸려갔다. 연어를 지켜보던 Marie는 Nina가 그들의 계속된 도전에 눈을 고정하는 것을 보았다. 매번의 도약과 회전을 볼 때 Nina의 심장은 빠르게 고동쳤다.

(B) 그때 한 마리의 작은 연어가 크게 박차고 올라 완전히 한 바퀴를 돌더니 폭포를 넘어가는 데 성공했다. "쟤가 해냈어!"라며 Nina는 그 성공에 감탄하며 외쳤다. 그런 다음 더 많은 연어가 뒤따랐고 성공했다. 그녀는 그것들을 바라보고 있는 것에 창피함을 느꼈다. 잠시 후 그녀는 Marie를 향해 말했다. "포기하는 것은 내 어휘에는 없어. Marie, 나는 내 챔피언 벨트를 되찾을 거야." Marie는 밝게 미소를 지으며 고개를 끄덕였다. "내일 우리의 트레이닝 시작이다. 쉽지 않을 거야. 준비는 됐니?" 길을 걸어 올라가 차로 돌아가며 그들은 여전히 물고기들이 물속에서 첨벙거리는 소리를 들을 수 있었다.

글의 소재 챔피언 벨트를 빼앗긴 좌절의 극복

주요 어휘 compete 다투다, 경쟁하다, heartbroken 상심한, retire 은퇴하다, admiration 감탄, 탄복, make it 해내다, 성공하다, tough 쉽지 않은, 힘든, splash 첨벙거리다, pull over 차를 대다, path 길, spill out 쏟아져 나오다, upstream 상류로, salmon 연어, leap 뛰어오르다, in vain 소용없는, struggle 발버둥 치다, 애쓰다, spin 빙글 돌다, fix 고정하다, twist 회전, 선회

정답 43. ③

정답 해설 43. 'Marie와 Nina가 Sauble 폭포 안내판을 발견한다'라는 내용으로 끝나는 주어진 글과 '그때 작은 것 한 마리가 힘차게 폭포 너머로 뛰어올랐다'라는 말로 시작하는 (B)는 전혀 논리적 연결 관계가 성립하지 않는다. 따라서 (B)는 주어진 글 다음에 올 수 없다. (D)의 첫 문장에 나오는 'the salmon'이 주어진 글에는 전혀 언급되지 않기 때문에 (D) 또한 주어진 글 다음에 올 수 없다. 따라서 주어진 글 다음에 올 수 있는 것은 (C) 뿐이다. 그리고 (D)는 Nina와 Marie가 연어들이 분투적으로 폭포를 뛰어오르는 것을 지켜보는 내용이고, (B)는 성공적으로 뛰어오르는 연어를 보고 권투 포기 직전 마음을 되돌린다는 내용이므로 흐름상 (D)가 (B)보다 앞에 오는 것이 자연스럽다. 따라서 옳은 글의 순서는 (C) - (D) - (B)이다.

정답 44. ②

정답 해설 44. (a), (c), (d), (e)는 Nina와 Marie를 가리키고 (b)는 폭포를 뛰어오르는 연어들을 가리킨다. 따라서 정답은 ②이다.

정답 45. ③

정답 해설 45. 차 안에서 Nina는 권투에서 은퇴하겠다는 생각을 했지만(~she was thinking of retiring from boxing ~) 폭포를 뛰어오르는 연어를 지켜본 뒤 '포기하는 건 내 어휘에 없어. 챔피언 벨트를 되찾을 거야'(Giving up is not in my vocabulary. Marie, I'll get my championship belt back)라며 권투에 다시 도전하는 쪽으로 마음을 고쳐먹는다. 따라서 ③은 본문의 내용과 부합하지 않는다.

(A) "Are you carrying any fruit or handguns?"

"Sure, I've got three kilos of kiwis in the trunk, and she has a .44 magnum in her purse."

No, that's not what I say to the border guard. It's best not to joke with these guys. They don't have much of a sense of humor, and they like to tear cars apart. Border guards make me nervous. I feel better as soon as I'm beyond those expressionless eyes and frozen faces.

(B) The rain slashes sideways, driving me back inside under an awning I try to use for cover. The ferry is starting to sway. Margaret tells a story of a ferry ride she once took from Sicily to Malta when she got seasick from diesel fumes and waves. Some kids are running toy cars up and down the plastic seats. Through rain mottle windows the mountaintops are obscured in mist. Soon we're pulling into the dock on the far side. Cars file off the ferry, and we heard the last nine miles to the hot springs. Admission is $4.00 Canadian.

(C) It winds along Kootenai Lake for fifty miles with only about three spots for cars to pass the whole way. We're the last car to board. Nautical looking workers in navy blue direct us to a parking space on the lower deck. We climb steep stairs to the passenger level. The wind and rain gain intensity as the ferry pulls away from the dock and heads across the lake. I step outside on the deck, but only for a minute.

(D) But a trip to Ainsworth is worth facing a hundred border guards. Ainsworth Hot Springs. I've been wanting to go for years now. Everyone I know has been there. It's gotten to the point where I feel deprived whenever anyone starts talking about Ainsworth. So off my friend Margaret and I go on a cold, rainy November Tuesday—not a bad day for hot spring. A few miles into Canada the road changes.

(E) There aren't any locker; each of us gets a plastic bag to put our clothes in, which we check with a clerk who gives out velcro wristbands with claim numbers on them. Mine is 38. Rain dots my body as I head out to the pool. The big pool is warm—a good place to get psyched-up for the hotter pool above and the caves. The caves! That's what makes Ainsworth so unique. We paddle back into the mountainside following the hot water to its source. Dim lights reveal an incredible scene.

43 주어진 글 (A)에 이어질 내용을 순서에 맞게 배열한 것으로 가장 적절한 것은?

① (B) - (D) - (C) - (E)
② (B) - (D) - (E) - (C)
③ (D) - (C) - (B) - (E)
④ (D) - (C) - (E) - (B)
⑤ (E) - (C) - (D) - (B)

44 윗글에 나타난 Ainsworth에 대한 화자의 심경 변화로 가장 적절한 것은?

① relieved → tensed
② determined → excited
③ frightened → amazed
④ regretful → committed
⑤ dejected → uninterested

45 윗글의 내용과 일치하지 <u>않는</u> 것은?

① The narrator did not have a casual talk with the border guard.

② Ainsworth was nine miles away from the Canadian border.

③ The travelers faced heavy rain and wind on the ferry.

④ Margaret went to the trip with the narrator.

⑤ The cave was the point that made Ainsworth distinctive from other hot springs

[한번에 정리하는 문제 해설]

지문 해석 (A) "과일이나 총을 소지하고 계신가요?"

"네, 저는 3킬로의 키위가 트렁크에 있고, 저 여자는 44밀리 매그넘을 지갑 속에 가지고 있습니다."

설마, 그런 말은 국경수비대원에게 할 말이 아니다. 이 친구들과는 농담하지 않는 게 상책이다. 그들은 유머 감각이 보잘것없고 차분해하는 것을 좋아한다. 그런 무표정한 눈과 굳은 얼굴을 벗어나자마자 나는 기분이 나아진다.

(D) 그러나 Ainsworth 여행은 국경수비대원 백 명을 마주칠 가치가 있다. Ainsworth 온천. 몇 년 동안 가고 싶었던 곳이다. 내가 아는 사람은 모두 거기 가본 적이 있다. 나는 누군가가 Ainsworth 얘기를 꺼내면 박탈감을 느끼는 지경까지 이르렀다. 그래서 내 친구 마가렛과 나는 어느 춥고 비 오는 11월 화요일에 - 온천 여행에는 그다지 나쁘지 않은 - 떠난다. 캐나다 안으로 몇 마일 들어서자 길이 바뀐다.

(C) Kootenai 호숫가를 따라 50마일을 굽이굽이 길이 나 있는데 차를 추월할 수 있는 곳은 전 도로를 통틀어 세 군데뿐이다. 우리 차는 마지막 승선 차량이다. 짙은 감색 해군 병사 차림의 직원들이 우리를 아래층 갑판의 주차장으로 안내한다. 우리는 급경사 계단을 따라 승객 층으로 오른다. 페리 선이 부두를 떠나 호수를 가로지르자 비바람이 거세진다. 나는 갑판으로 나와 보지만 단 일 분 동안뿐이다.

(B) 비가 비스듬히 내리치고 비는 내가 차양으로 쓸 덮개 밑으로 나를 다시 밀어 넣는다. 페리 선이 흔들리기 시작한다. 마가렛이 언젠가 시칠리아에서 몰타로 가는 페리 선을 탔다가 디젤 연기와 파도 때문에 뱃멀미를 했던 이야기를 한다. 몇몇 아이들이 장난감 차를 플라스틱 좌석 위로 굴리고 있다. 빗방울로 얼룩진 유리창 너머로 산꼭대기가 안갯속에 흐릿하다. 차들이 페리 선에서 줄지어 내리고 우리는 온천까지 9마일 남았다는 말을 듣는다. 입장료는 4 캐나다 달러다.

(E) 라커는 없고 우리는 옷을 담을 비닐봉투를 하나씩 받아 그것을 종업원에게 보여주면 그가 청구 번호가 적힌 끈끈이 팔찌를 나눠준다. 내 번호는 38번이다. 풀장으로 향할 때 비가 한두 방울씩 몸에 떨어진다. 대형 풀장은 따뜻하고 위에 있는 고온 풀장이나 동굴 가기에 앞서 마음을 가다듬기에 알맞은 곳이다. 동굴! Ainsworth를 독특한 곳으로 만드는 것은 바로 그것이다. 우리는 온천물을 따라 그것의 근원인 산기슭으로 다시 노를 저어 간다. 희미한 불빛이 믿기 어려운 장면을 드러낸다.

글의 소재 Ainsworth 온천 여행

주요 어휘 magnum 탄약통, tear apart 분해하다, sideways 비스듬히, awning 차양, sway 흔들리다, mottle 얼룩, file 줄지어 가다, wind(v) 구불구불하다, nautical 해상의, intensity 강도, wristband 팔찌, psych up 마음을 가다듬게 하다, paddle 노를 젓다, incredible 믿기 어려운

정 답 43. ③

정답 해설 43. (A)에서 입국절차를 밟으며 국경수비대원들의 무표정하고 굳은 표정을 경험하는 장면은 그럼에도 Ainsworth 온천은 백 명의 그런 수비대원을 마주칠 가치가 있다고 말하는 (D)로 자연스럽게 이어진다. (D)의 마지막 행에서 캐나다에 들어서자 길이 바뀐다고 했으므로 이는 그것(길)이 Kootenai 호수를 따라 굽이굽이 나 있는 사실이 언급되는 (C)와 자연스럽게 연결된다. 또, 비바람이 점점 세지는 와중에 갑판으로 나가는 (C) 말미는 비가 거세 다시 안으로 몸을 피하는 (B)로 이어지는 것이 매끄럽다. 또 (B) 말미에서 입장료가 4 캐나다 달러라고 한 것으로 보아 필자는 온천에 도착한 것이므로 이는 온천 입장이 상술되는 (E)로 이어지는 것이 논리적이다.

정 답 44. ②

정답 해설 44. (A)에서 유머 감각이 없고 무표정한 얼굴을 하는 국경수비대원들과는 농담을 주고받지 않는 것이 상책이라며 결연한 자세를 보이던 필자가 온천에 도착해 대형 풀장이 '좋고', 동굴이 '독특하며' '믿기 어려운 장면'을 연출한다고 말하는 등 만족을 드러내므로 필자는 심경 변화를 표현할 말은 determined→excited가 적절하다.

정 답 45. ②

정답 해설 45. 온천까지 9마일이 남았다는 말을 들었을 때 필자 일행은 이미 국경을 지나고 호수를 건너온 후이므로 캐나다 국경에서 온천까지는 9마일이라는 ②는 윗글의 내용과 일치하지 않는다.

17. 장문의 이해 Ⅱ – 1지문 3문제

| 해설 450쪽 |

[183~185] 다음 글을 읽고 물음에 답하시오. 난이도 중

In large cities around the world, (a) taller and taller buildings are constantly being constructed. Building upward instead of outward has become a common theme of construction because it allows people to live and work closer together. This might seem like an ideal solution, but it also creates some problems. The top floors of most high-rise buildings usually command a fantastic view, but, at the same time, they are leaving many residents living in (b) their shadows.

These new buildings are not only changing the city's skyline, but they have other unintended effects on the city. (c) The massive structures darken the streets below and cast their shadows over public areas such as parks. The construction of these increasingly large structures is sparking debate in many growing cities. In some cases, there is no room for the city to expand, and in other cases, there is a demand for additional residential and office space near the city center. Either way, many residents are not happy. The arguments often focus on the placement of new buildings, the necessity for natural light, or the negative effects it will have on the city. There are real concerns about how these structures change the atmosphere of the area and influence the value of other properties.

(d) The skyscrapers are often a reminder that the growth of cities can have unintended consequences for longtime residents. In some ways, the shadows cast by new construction can turn access to sunlight into a sign of inequality. Natural light in some areas has become a luxury that only the rich can afford, and it is often taken without the public's permission. It happens as a result of the growth that provides additional employment and business opportunities, but the issue is location and what the effect will be on the streets, residences, and public spaces below. Should the demand for housing and office space _____(A)_____ the concerns of citizens? Some argue that new buildings add more value to a city than they take away from it. Without large buildings and evolving architectural styles, many of the world's cities wouldn't have the same appeal (e) they do today. Others, however, question how much residents benefit from this.

183 윗글의 제목으로 가장 적절한 것은?

① Ever-Expanding Demands for Inner-city Skyscrapers
② The Lights and Shadows Caused by Modern High-Rise Buildings
③ Dazzling Evolution in Modern Architectural Design
④ Contributions Skyscrapers Make to Urban Aesthetics
⑤ Conditions for Sustainable Urban Development

184 글의 흐름으로 보아 빈칸 (A)에 들어갈 가장 적절한 말은?

① forgo
② override
③ create
④ replace
⑤ incite

185 밑줄 친 (a)~(e) 중에서 의미하는 바가 나머지와 <u>다른</u> 것은?

① (a)
② (b)
③ (c)
④ (d)
⑤ (e)

The baseball world was shocked by what happened to Tonya Carpenter at a Boston Red Sox game last month. She was sitting in the second row on the third-base side when a broken bat flew into the stands. The broken bat struck her head, causing life-threatening injuries. She was rushed to the hospital where she underwent a series of surgical procedures that ultimately saved her life.

This has brought up many questions about safety and responsibility at sporting events. Is the team responsible for keeping the spectators safe? Should the whole field have netting like most fields have behind home plate to catch foul balls? Although there is a warning printed on the tickets telling spectators to be aware, is it enough to place the responsibility on the ticket holder? What if there were no tickets to be purchased and,   (A)   , no warning label? Tracey DeBriga got hit by a baseball while watching her son's little league baseball game. She was setting up a blanket to sit on when an errant throw went over the fence and struck her in the face. DeBriga suffered serious injuries which resulted in a hefty medical bill.

To help pay for her bills, DeBriga sued both the baseball team and the baseball league to get them to pay for the damages. She claims that the organizers have a responsibility to provide a safe area for spectators to watch the game without fear of injury. Her basis for this claim was supported by the fact that there were not enough bleachers at the field for the number of fans in attendance. She argues that if she had a safe place to watch the game, she would not have been injured. In the end, the court ruled against DeBriga, stating that the responsibility falls on the spectator at a baseball game. The court said that the organizers are not liable for injuries because spectators are expected to be cautious when attending these kinds of events.   (B)   , it added, the organizers have no obligation to provide safe viewing areas.

* bleacher 외야석

186 윗글의 제목으로 가장 적절한 것은?

① Refrain from Visiting Baseball Parks Unprepared
② Watch Baseball Games at Your Own Risk
③ Misfortunes Never Come Singly
④ What Makes Baseball So Popular?
⑤ Bad Things Could Happen Anytime, Anywhere

187 윗글의 빈칸 (A), (B)에 들어갈 말로 가장 적절한 것은?

	(A)	(B)
①	otherwise	In contrast
②	otherwise	Moreover
③	therefore	In contrast
④	therefore	Moreover
⑤	however	In contrast

188 다음 중 윗글의 내용과 일치하지 <u>않는</u> 것은?

① Tonya Carpenter는 관중석으로 날아든 부러진 배트에 맞아 큰 부상을 입었다.
② 대부분 구장에는 홈 플레이트 뒤에 보호망을 쳐놓았다.
③ Tracey DeBriga는 타자의 빗맞은 공에 얼굴을 맞아 크게 다쳤다.
④ 사고 구장에는 외야석이 충분하지 않았다.
⑤ 법원은 Tracey DeBriga에게 패소 판결을 내렸다.

Traditionally, mothers are viewed by society as better caretakers for their children. Mothers are typically more caring and more connected with their child's emotion. Fathers are more interested in play and are better at "being silly." For example, one study shows that mothers interacting with five-month-old infants are more likely to look into the child's eyes during playtime and mirror their movements. Fathers, ____(A)____, tend to stimulate the babies with actions and movements to get them to laugh. According to new research, both these parenting styles are good for the child's emotional well-being and beneficial for the child's overall development.

In the past, researchers have scored fathers lower on parental evaluation. When researchers interviewed children in the studies, however, the children spoke highly of their fathers and said their relationships were positive. This led researchers to question the validity of their previous experiment. They discovered that the reason the initial evaluations were wrong was because they were based on skills that mothers were typically better at. These skills included being affectionate and providing feelings of comfort, which are not typically a father's strong suit.

Fathers tend to be better at encouraging children and making them feel confident. When researchers added these elements to their evaluation criteria, fathers' scores improved significantly. It turns out that a father's boisterous and somewhat random style of play helps children learn to take risks and do more exploring. Mothers, on the contrary, are less likely to encourage their children to challenge themselves physically during play. ____(B)____, what researchers have learned is that a father's style of parenting and play helps a child develop in a different way than their mother's style does. Fathers use physicality and play to bring out laughter and elevate levels of emotion, but the key is that they also help the children control these emotions in their heightened state. During playtime with fathers, children often get excited or even upset, but they manage their emotions to complete the challenging activity. This ability not to let one's emotions control the situation is part of how fathers help their children feel more confident.

189 윗글의 주제로 가장 적절한 것은?

① similarities between fathers' and mother' parenting styles
② the competitive edge of fathers' parenting rediscovered
③ the importance of balanced parenting between fathers and mothers
④ fathers' parenting as a supplement to mothers'
⑤ the reason why fathers' parenting has been undervalued

190 빈칸 (A), (B)에 들어갈 말로 가장 적절한 것은?

	(A)	(B)
①	likewise	In the end
②	likewise	In addition
③	on the other hand	In addition
④	on the other hand	In the end
⑤	however	In addition

191 윗글의 내용과 일치하는 것은?

① 엄마들은 갖가지 행동으로 얘기들을 자극해 웃긴다.
② 과거 연구자들은 아빠의 자녀 교육에 후한 평가를 내렸다.
③ 초기의 교육 평가는 아빠가 잘하는 솜씨를 중심으로 이루어졌다.
④ 아이의 모험심을 키우는 데는 엄마의 부드러운 교육이 효과적일 수 있다.
⑤ 아빠는 아이 감정이 최고조에 도달했을 때 그 감정을 조절하도록 돕는다.

Tomb Raider isn't just a movie but a real thing happening throughout China as a part of an unusual, ancient custom. Single, deceased women are being dug up and their corpses are being sold to families interested in having a ghost wedding for their single, deceased son. Once such a wedding is completed, the women's remains are reburied in the groom's family tomb.

Traditionally in China, ghost weddings were just for ghosts. However, now it's not uncommon to have a living "husband" and a dead "wife." Living relatives perform these weddings to prevent their family members from being lonely in the afterlife. It's also the family's way of making amends for the deceased's unfulfilled wishes. The living family members believe that if they fail to satisfy the needs of a son who passed away, he will become an angry or agitated spirit.

While the concept of a ghost wedding may sound simple, it's not easily carried out. The same criteria that are adopted for real life are also applied to ghosts. Fengshui masters help families choose suitable ghost brides and also arrange for a bride price and a dowry, which can include jewelry, servant and a mansion. This exchange of goods and money is just a formality, though, as the money isn't actually paid out in real life, and the gifts are just paper decorations.

Unfortunately, with Chinese men outnumbering women due to the recently abandoned one-child policy and a traditional preference for sons, there just aren't enough living or ghost brides to go around. This has led people to illegally robbing graves and selling the remains. Other people desperate to make a quick buck even resort to murder. This uncomfortable truth was brought to light this past August when a Chinese man murdered two mentally disabled women while posing as a match-maker. Whether ghost weddings are seen as touching tributes to deceased family members, or as grisly rituals contributing to a rise in crime rates, tradition is tradition. Since there is no end in sight for this custom in China, one can only hope that it doesn't continue in a violent and illegal manner with the death of one person to satisfy the _____(A)_____ of another.

192 Discussions above are focused on _____.

① the ghost wedding as a means of healing the deceased
② the ghost wedding practices prevalent in China
③ the importance of compensating for the deceased's unfulfilled wishes
④ the complicated procedures required for any ghost wedding
⑤ the significance of keeping age-old traditions alive

193 글의 흐름으로 보아 빈칸 (A)에 들어갈 가장 적절한 말은?

① demand
② interest
③ self-esteem
④ well-being
⑤ ghost

194 다음 중 윗글의 내용과 일치하는 것은?

① 영혼 결혼은 살아있는 신랑과 죽은 신부 사이에도 이뤄진다.
② 영혼 결혼이 끝나면 파내진 여성의 시신은 원래 있던 곳에 갖다 놓는다.
③ 영혼 결혼은 생전 결혼과 달리 간소하게 치러진다.
④ 영혼 결혼에서도 신부 지참금이 실제로 지불된다.
⑤ 영혼 결혼의 관습은 머지않아 사라질 전망이다.

It was 1973, and Stephen King's pockets were empty. He lived in a mobile home and drove a shabby Buick held together with wire and adhesive tape. King's wife, Tabby, worked second-shift at Dunkin' Donuts while he taught English at Hampden Academy, a private high school in eastern Maine. To scrape by, King worked summers at an industrial laundry and moonlighted as a janitor and gas pump attendant. With a toddler and a newborn to feed, money—and time to write fiction—were hard to come by.

King couldn't even afford his own typewriter; (a) <u>he</u> had to use Tabby's old brand from college. She set up a makeshift desk in the laundry room, fitting it snugly between the washing machine and the dryer. Each evening, while Tabby changed diapers and cooked dinner, King ignored the ungraded papers in his briefcase and locked himself in the laundry room to write.

The early returns weren't promising. King mailed his short stories to men's magazines like Cavalier and Penthouse. When (b) <u>he</u> was lucky, every once in a while, a small check would turn up in the mailbox. It was just enough money to keep the King family off of welfare.

One day, the head of Hampden's English department gave King an offer (c) <u>he</u> thought he couldn't refuse. The debate club needed a new faculty advisor, and the job was his for the taking. It would pay an extra $300 per year—not much, but enough to cover the family's grocery bill for 10 weeks.

The lure of extra income enticed King, and when (d) <u>he</u> came home, he thought Tabby would share his enthusiasm about the news. But she wasn't so convinced. "Will you have time to write?" she asked.

"Not much," King said.

Tabby told him, "Well, then you can't take it."

So King turned down the job. It was a good call. Within a year, (e) <u>he</u> would write his way out of that trailer with a bestseller called Carrie.

195 윗글을 아래와 같은 요약할 때 밑줄 친 부분에 들어갈 가장 적절한 말은?

King's strenuous effort to write amid financial hardship ended up with

_____ .

① a further deepening misery

② a serious marital discord

③ the birth of an overnight millionnaire

④ a successful academic achievement

⑤ a dramatic turnaround

196 윗글의 내용과 일치하는 것은?

① 아내가 가사 일을 돌보는 동안 킹은 학교에서 가져온 잔무 처리에 열중했다.

② 킹의 작품 활동 초기에는 벌이가 변변치 않아 정부의 복지 혜택에 의존해야 했다.

③ 고교 토론회 지도교사가 되는 데는 까다로운 자격 심사를 거쳐야 했다.

④ 여분의 수입에 대한 기대감을 아내 태비도 크게 반겼다.

⑤ 지도교사 직을 거절한 지 일 년이 안 돼 킹은 글을 써서 트레일러 신세를 면할 수 있었다.

197 밑줄 친 (a)~(e)의 he가 가리키는 대상이 나머지 넷과 다른 것은?

① (a)

② (b)

③ (c)

④ (d)

⑤ (e)

Any list of the most important figures in the history of chemistry includes Mendeleev, a Russian chemist who developed the periodic table of elements in the 19th century. But he never won a Nobel, despite being alive when the first few prizes were awarded. The key problem was that Alfred Nobel's 1895 will said the prizes were to recognize "those who, during the preceding year, shall have conferred the greatest benefit to mankind." So the early prizes, beginning with the first in 1901, went to work done roughly contemporaneously. But in 1900, statutes that embodied an official interpretation of the will by the Nobel Foundation, which administers the prize, stated that the awards should primarily honor recent achievements but could also be granted for earlier work whose significance had recently become apparent. Mendeleev supporters pointed to that latter interpretation after the inert gas elements were the subject of chemistry and physics Nobel Prizes in 1904. They thought those discoveries made Mendeleev's 19th-century periodic table work Nobel-eligible. Mendeleev was therefore nominated for the 1905 prize but didn't win. He was nominated again for the 1906 prize, and the Nobel committee, which recommends winners, voted 4 to 1 in his favor. However, the Royal Swedish Academy, which makes the final prize decisions, did not accept the vote. Instead, it packed the committee with four more members and made the committee vote again. This subsequent vote was 5 to 4 in favor of Henri Moissan for isolating elemental fluorine and developing an electric furnace. The Royal Swedish Academy accepted that vote. Scholars believe Svante Arrhenius, a prominent member of the Royal Swedish Academy, may have helped block Mendeleev's selection because he was unhappy about the Russian's long-standing and open criticism of Arrhenius's ionic dissociation theory, the idea that electrolytes dissociate in water to form ions. Arrhenius may also have believed that Mendeleev's achievement was just too old. Mendeleev died in 1907 and therefore never got another chance because of another stipulation in Alfred Nobel's will: _____.

* inert gas 불활성 기체, ionic dissociation theory 이온해리이론, electrolyte 전해질

198 윗글의 제목으로 가장 적절한 것은?

① Loopholes Found in the Selection Process for the Nobel Prize
② Luck: No Small Factor in Winning the Nobel Prize
③ Mendeleev's Unrivaled Contributions to Modern Chemistry
④ What Kept Mendeleev from Becoming a Nobel Prize Winner
⑤ Feuds and Enmities Prevalent in the Scientific Community

199 밑줄 친 빈칸에 들어갈 가장 적절한 말은?

① Any scientists whose backgrounds raise concerns can not receive the prize
② Scientists' achievements must transcend all ideological differences
③ Scientists' work shall be unique and creative to win the prize
④ Scientists must still be alive to win the prize
⑤ The Nobel Committee voting shall override all other decisions

200 다음 중 윗글의 내용과 일치하지 않는 것은?

① 노벨상 초기의 수상자 선정은 선정 당시의 업적이 주된 고려 대상이었다.
② 선정 당시 이전의 업적도 수상할 수 있다는 노벨 유언에 대한 해석이 나왔다.
③ 멘델레예프는 1905년 처음으로 노벨상 후보에 올랐다.
④ 노벨상 수상작에 대한 최종 결정은 노벨상위원회가 내린다.
⑤ 당시 멘델레예프의 수상을 방해한 인물이 있었다고 보는 견해도 있다.

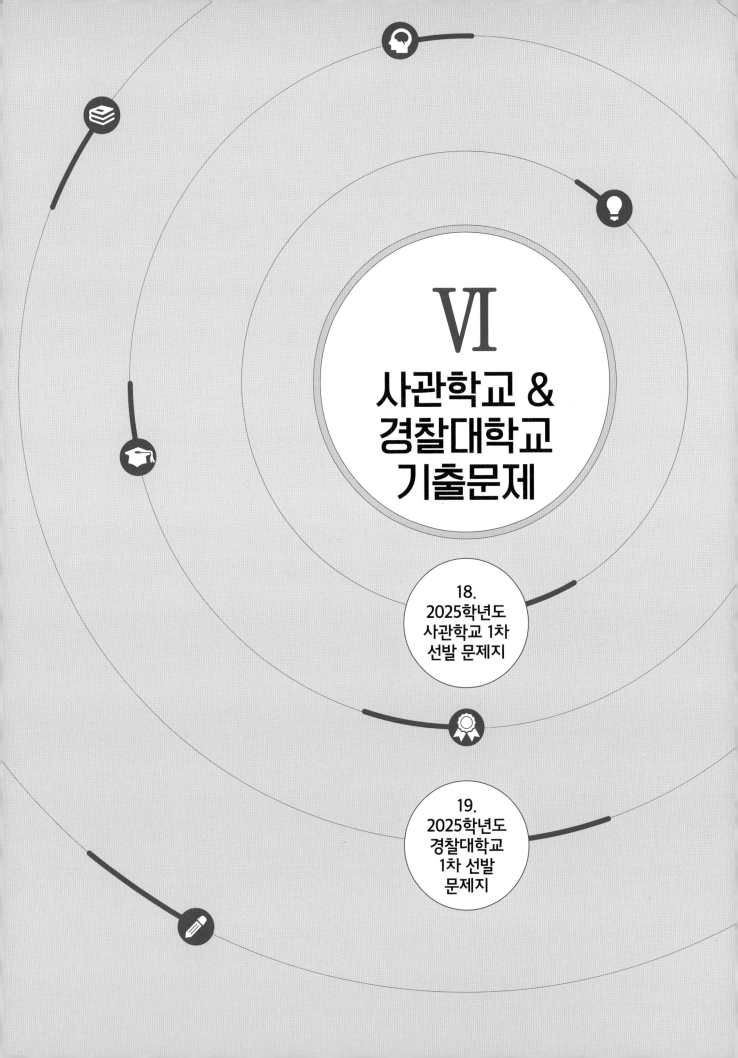

VI

사관학교 &
경찰대학교
기출문제

18.
2025학년도
사관학교 1차
선발 문제지

19.
2025학년도
경찰대학교
1차 선발
문제지

2025학년도 사관학교 1차 선발시험 문제지

영어 영역 공통

성명		수험번호							

○ 먼저 문제지에 성명과 수험번호를 기입하시오.

○ 답안지에 성명과 수험번호를 정확하게 표기하시오.

○ 문제는 3점 20문항, 4점 10문항 총 30문항입니다.

  (4점 문항에만 점수가 표시되어 있고, 나머지는 모두 3점 문항입니다.)

※ 시험 시작 전까지 표지를 넘기지 마시오.

공 란

| 해설 456쪽 |

[1~2] 다음 글의 밑줄 친 부분 중, 어법상 틀린 것을 고르시오.

01

Illuminance quite simply describes the quantity of light emitted by a light source that lands on a given surface area, ① measured in footcandles or, in the metric system, lux. In the built environment, illuminance is the feature that brings shape and clarity to a nuanced spatial composition. ② What is capable of controlling the intensity of visual extremes, crescendos of light and dark that can both reveal and hide layers of a complex space. This principle is of great practical and phenomenological importance in architectural lighting design, as it allows us to navigate our way through, or ③ perform tasks within, a space. Illuminance, moreover, plays a critical role in our emotional response to a space: our intrinsic fear of the dark or gravitation toward light has influenced the ways ④ in which our society places faith in light as a means to establish safety and provide emotional reassurance. Finally, one must not forget that the term "illuminance" describes a quantity of light or energy that, when administered at the appropriate levels, ⑤ ensures the sustenance of life, but when pushed to extremes, can cause physical damage to its recipient.

[3점]

* crescendo: 크레센도(점점 세어짐)

02

Karl Popper is sometimes said to have claimed that no theory can be proved definitively to be true. But he held a far more radical view than this: he thought that of the theories that have not yet been positively disproved, we have absolutely no reason ① to believe one rather than another. It is not that even our best theory cannot be definitively proved; it is rather that there is no such thing as a "best theory," only a "surviving theory," and all surviving theories are equal. Thus, in Popper's view, there is no point in trying to gather evidence that supports one surviving theory over the others. Scientists should consequently devote ② themselves to reducing the size of the pool of surviving theories by refuting as many ideas as possible. Scientific inquiry is ③ essentially a process of disproof, and scientists are the disprovers, the debunkers, the destroyers. Popper's logic of inquiry ④ is required of its scientific personnel a murderous resolve. Seeing a theory, their first thought must be to understand it and then to liquidate it. Only if scientists throw themselves single-mindedly into the slaughter of every speculation will science ⑤ progress.

[4점]

* liquidate: 폐지하다

[3~4] 다음 글의 밑줄 친 부분 중, 문맥상 낱말의 쓰임이 적절하지 않은 것을 고르시오.

03

　　The mindset that mindfulness needs strong mind control to clean up all your thoughts is not correct because by doing so, you take your own thoughts as your ① enemy in your conscious and unconscious mind and want to get rid of them. However, your thoughts are actually the exact reflection of your physical and mental states. If your physical and mental states do not ② change, your thought patterns remain the same. In fact, the right effort and appropriate control are the key to efficient mindfulness learning and practice. We often put ③ considerable effort into a target such as breathing, thought process, and body feeling or sensation whenever we practice mindfulness. However, intensive and effortful practice makes our mind fatigue easily and even ④ decreases the stress hormone (cortisol) that can deteriorate and damage our body and brain/mind states. Some studies have shown that adverse events can occur with intensive mindfulness meditation during a retreat period. Therefore, only ⑤ using mind control for mindfulness is not a natural method for our minds and for mindfulness practice.

[3점]

04

There is a wonderful game at my local science museum called Mindball. Two players sit at opposite ends of a long table. Each wears a headband equipped with electrodes, designed to pick up general patterns of electrical activity on the surface of the brain. Between the players is a metal ball. The goal is to mentally ① <u>push</u> this ball all the way to the other end of the table, and the player who does so first wins. The motive force—measured by each player's electrodes, and conveyed to the ball by a magnet hidden underneath the table—is the ② <u>combination</u> of alpha and theta waves produced by the brain when it's relaxed: the more alpha and theta waves you produce, the more force you mentally exert on the ball. Essentially, Mindball is a contest of who can be the most ③ <u>active</u>. It's fun to watch. The players visibly struggle to relax, closing their eyes, breathing deeply, adopting vaguely yogic postures. The panic they begin to feel as the ball approaches their end of the table is usually balanced out by the ④ <u>overeagerness</u> of their opponent, both players alternately losing their cool as the big metal ball rolls back and forth. You couldn't wish for a better, more condensed illustration of how ⑤ <u>difficult</u> it is to try not to try.

[4점]

* electrode: 전극

[5~6] 다음 글의 요지로 가장 적절한 것을 고르시오.

05

    In today's techno-lifeworld we can no longer make such a sharp distinction between real and virtual. What does this mean for gaming? It means that gaming is as real as any other technology-mediated practice today. The gamer exercises agency and personality in the new world. Her experience and actions are real. Gaming is also social: contemporary gaming often involves many players, is interactive, and requires role playing. Gamers meet new people and develop friendships and romantic relationships. They thus have real social experiences, including emotional experiences. These experiences are not a mere response to what happens on the screen or on stage, but are the result of the interaction of the gamer with others in the game environment. Gamers' thinking, interaction, engagement, and feelings are not fictional or virtual; they are totally real. Thus, phenomenologically, gamers do not leave this world for another world.   [3점]

① 가상 게임은 실제 현실과 같은 사회적 활동이다.
② 가상 게임은 다양한 최신 기술이 집약된 결과물이다.
③ 가상 게임은 현실보다 더욱 실감나는 경험을 제공한다.
④ 개인은 온라인 게임에 참여하여 개성을 드러낼 수 있다.
⑤ 게임 속 교류를 통해 인간관계의 갈등을 해소할 수 있다.

06

If we humanists have much to learn from the natural sciences, the reverse is also true: humanists have a great deal to contribute to scientific research. As discoveries in the biological and cognitive sciences have begun to blur traditional disciplinary boundaries, researchers in these fields have found their work bringing them into contact with the sort of high-level issues that traditionally have been the domain of the core humanities disciplines, and often their lack of formal training in these areas leaves them groping in the dark or attempting to reinvent the wheel. This is where humanist expertise can and should play a crucial role in guiding and interpreting the results of scientific exploration—something that can occur only when scholars on both sides of the humanities-natural science divide are willing to talk to one another. It is becoming increasingly evident that the traditionally sharp divide between the humanities and natural sciences is no longer viable, and this requires that researchers on both sides of the former divide become radically more interdisciplinary.

[4점]

* grope: 더듬어 찾다.

① The speculative theories of humanities can be demonstrated by empirical studies.

② Natural sciences and humanities should focus on their own fields and paths respectively.

③ Natural scientists should reinforce their philosophical contents through the study of humanities.

④ True integration of natural sciences and humanities is possible by embedding one in the other.

⑤ The contribution of humanities to scientific discoveries can be achieved through interdisciplinary

07 다음 글에서 밑줄 친 부분이 의미하는 바로 가장 적절한 것은?

Compared to other primates, we are freakishly social and cooperative; not only do we sit obediently on airplanes, we labor collectively to build houses, specialize in different skills, and live lives that are driven by our specific role in the group. This is quite a trick for a primate to pull off, considering our most recent evolutionary history. Hive life is (literally) a no-brainer for ants: They share the same genes, so sacrificing for the common good is not really a sacrifice—if I'm an ant, the common good simply is my good. Humans, though, are apes, evolved to cooperate only in a limited way with close relatives and perhaps fellow tribe members, acutely alert to the dangers of being manipulated, misled, or exploited by others. And yet we march in parades, sit in obedient rows reciting lessons, conform to social norms, and sometimes sacrifice our lives for the common good with an enthusiasm that would put a soldier ant to shame. Trying to hammer a square primate peg into a circular social insect hole is bound to be difficult. [4점]

* freakishly: 이상할 정도로 ** no-brainer: 쉽게 할 수 있는 일

① downgrade humans' superiority over apes and ants
② enforce the collaboration between apes and social insects
③ manipulate hive insects into adopting ape-like characteristics
④ suppress our traits as apes in order to pursue communal benefits
⑤ maximize apes' physical capabilities in contributing to the common good

08 다음 글에서 전체 흐름과 관계 없는 문장은?

The law of large numbers is one of the foundations of probability theory and statistics. ①It guarantees that, over the long term, the outcomes of future events can be predicted with reasonable accuracy. ②This, for example, gives financial companies the confidence to set prices for insurance and pension products, knowing their chances of having to pay out, and ensures that casinos will always make a profit from their gambling customers—eventually. ③That, however, is the "gambler's fallacy"—where a person assumes that the outcomes of each trial are connected. ④According to the law, as you make more observations of an event occurring, the measured probability (or chance) of that outcome gets ever closer to the theoretical chance as calculated before any observations began. ⑤In other words, the average result from a large number of trials will be a close match to the expected value as calculated using probability theory—and increasing the number of trials will result in that average becoming an even closer match.   [3점]

[9~10] 다음 글의 제목으로 가장 적절한 것을 고르시오.

09

Business ethics was born in scandal. It seems to regenerate itself with each succeeding wave of scandal. And, there are two problems here. The first is that our world is so interconnected that we can no longer afford to see business as a separate institution in society, subject to its own moral code. Business must be thoroughly situated in society. This means that we can no longer accept the now rather commonplace narrative about businesspeople being economic profit-maximizers and little else. Business is a deeply human institution set in our societies and interconnected all over the world. The second problem is that business ethics, by being reborn in scandal, never escapes the presumption that business starts off by being morally questionable. It never seems to get any credit for the good it brings into the world, only questions about the bad. In fact, capitalism may well be the greatest system of social cooperation that we have ever invented. But, if it is, then it must stand the critical test of our best thinkers, if for no other reason than to make it better. Simply assuming that capitalism is either unquestionably morally good or unquestionably morally problematic violates both scholarly and practical norms. [3점]

① Forget Scandals, Let's Innovate!
② Innate Challenges of Business Ethics
③ Unavoidable Obstacles of Human Institutions
④ Business Ethics: An Emerging Scholarly Norm
⑤ Business Ethics as A Magic Bullet for Success

10

The European Mediterranean Seismological Centre (EMSC) has recently implemented a method for rapidly collecting in situ observations on earthquake effects from eyewitnesses. This is extremely important because it certainly contributes to reducing uncertainties in rapid impact assessment of earthquakes. Social media (e.g., Facebook, Twitter, etc.) can be considered as useful networks for the purpose of earthquake detection. Data mining from social networks has been employed to detect and determine the area of an earthquake and led to the development of the Twitter Earthquake Detector (TED), developed by United States Geological Service. The early detection of earthquakes using such media represents a radical change in basic seismological detection paradigms. Information carried by social networks travels much faster than seismic waves, allowing a fast and reliable detection within a few minutes of an earthquake's origin. For the Italian region a software system named TwiFelt has been available since 2012. Its aim is to provide real-time earthquake perception maps through an analysis of Twitter streams.

[3점]

* in situ: 원래 장소의

① Use Social Media in Disaster Relief!
② Social Media: Quick Earthquake Detectors
③ Data Mining in Seismology Is Yet to Come
④ Citizens as Instruments for Top-down Information
⑤ Earthquake-related Rumors Spreading via Social Media

11 다음 글의 주제로 가장 적절한 것은?

Experts say that if you feel drowsy during the day, even during boring activities, you haven't had enough sleep. If you routinely fall asleep within five minutes of lying down, you probably have severe sleep deprivation, possibly even a sleep disorder. Microsleeps, or very brief episodes of sleep in an otherwise awake person, are another mark of sleep deprivation. In many cases, people are not aware that they are experiencing microsleeps. The widespread practice of "burning the candle at both ends" in Western industrialized societies has created so much sleep deprivation that what is really abnormal sleepiness is now almost the norm. Many studies make it clear that sleep deprivation is dangerous. Sleep-deprived people who are tested by using a driving simulator or by performing a hand-eye coordination task perform as badly as or worse than those who are intoxicated. Sleep deprivation also magnifies alcohol's effects on the body, so a fatigued person who drinks will become much more impaired than someone who is well rested.

[3점]

① troublesome manifestations of sleep deprivation
② effects of severe sleep deprivation on commuting drivers
③ similarities between the intoxicated and the sleep-deprived
④ conventional sleep habits of Western industrialized societies
⑤ higher rates of alcohol dependency among the sleep-deprived

12 다음 글의 목적으로 가장 적절한 것은?

Happy Veteran's Day! I hope this message finds you well. As the Director of the Military Library, I am very happy to announce that the last book giveaway event was a huge success. I take great pride in representing the library that has been instrumental in many community cultural activities. Also, I am delighted to inform you of our library's latest event. We have planned a free movie showing every Saturday at 6 P.M., starting this weekend until the end of the year. The movie showing will take place at the Eisenhower Community Room on the third floor. It is open to the public. The movie list will be uploaded on our website on the first day of every month. The first movie, which will be shown this Saturday, is *Black Hawk Down*. So come on out and enjoy free movies! [3점]

① 새로 개봉하는 전쟁 영화를 홍보하려고
② 퇴역 군인을 위한 정기 후원을 요청하려고
③ 홍보 영상 촬영으로 인한 휴관을 알리려고
④ 도서관의 무료 영화 상영 행사를 안내하려고
⑤ 책 나눔 행사를 도울 자원봉사자를 모집하려고

13 다음 글에서 필자가 주장하는 바로 가장 적절한 것은?

Knowing the importance of language interaction can shape parental behavior and decisions. When infants are alert, it is vital to interact with them and to respect that they are interacting in return and working on finding meaning in what we say. One way to do this is to acknowledge their contributions (however meager) to the conversation. Parents might also look for evidence that caregivers and baby-sitters engage in this kind of interaction. It is not unusual for sitters to watch television when they are with infants or to spend a lot of time on the telephone even when babies are awake. More than a bottle and a clean diaper is needed. The new view of the interactive infant means that caregiving involves more than custodial care. The new job description for caregiving might add "caregiver stimulation required in the form of sensitive and responsive behavior." Parents should look for empathic and encouraging caregivers who are eager to converse with babies. Research shows that language stimulation from a television set does not prepare infants for language learning. Only conversations with people will.

[3점]

① 부모는 유아의 보모를 찾을 때 정서적 수용력을 우선 고려해야 한다.
② 부모와의 애착을 강화하기 위해 유아의 기본 요구를 세심하게 살펴야 한다.
③ 부모는 유아와 공감하며 언어적 상호작용에 적극적인 양육자를 찾아야 한다.
④ 또래 아이와의 지속적인 상호작용을 통해 유아의 언어 발달을 촉진해야 한다.
⑤ 부모는 유아의 언어 학습 능력을 향상시키기 위해 텔레비전 시청을 줄여야 한다.

14 Maurice Wilkins에 관한 다음 글의 내용과 일치하지 <u>않는</u> 것은?

Maurice Wilkins was born in New Zealand, where his father was a medical doctor. The Wilkinses moved to Birmingham, England when he was 6. He went to St. John's College, Cambridge in 1935 to study physics and received a Bachelor of Arts degree in 1938. During World War II, he participated for two years in the Manhattan Project at the University of California, Berkeley. After the War, horrified by the effects of the atomic bomb, Wilkins decided to move into another branch of science. Upon his return to Great Britain, Wilkins lectured at the University of St. Andrews in Scotland. In 1946 he joined the Biophysics Unit at King's College and served as the unit's director from 1970 to 1980. There he began the series of investigations that led to his X-ray diffraction studies of DNA. With James Watson and Francis Crick, he received the Nobel Prize for Physiology or Medicine for his contribution to the determination of DNA's molecular structure.

[3점]

* diffraction: 회절

① 뉴질랜드에서 의사의 아들로 태어났다.
② 1935년에 St. John's College에서 학위를 받았다.
③ 2차 세계대전 중 2년간 Manhattan Project에 참여했다.
④ University of St. Andrews에서 강의했다.
⑤ DNA 분자구조 연구로 노벨상을 공동 수상했다.

[15~19] 다음 빈칸에 들어갈 말로 가장 적절한 것을 고르시오.

15

To reduce the challenge of the Northwest Passage to that of a hostile environment is to _____ . A challenging environment can take many forms: from a highly competitive market to a battlefield. In comparing one challenge context to another, one can differentiate along a number of dimensions: the variability, predictability, and seriousness of the hazards, the availability of external help, and the duration of exposure. It is rare to find a leadership environment in which all of these variables are high. Fighting a fire is dangerous business, but to a trained firefighter, fire moves in predictable ways and the duration of exposure to its risks is relatively short. Launching a fin-tech start-up involves facing a highly variable and unpredictable environment, but there is always the option of appealing for more investment. Navigating the Northwest Passage was a challenge along every dimension: the threats came in many forms, were of a highly unpredictable nature, and were all potentially lethal, while outside intervention was ruled out and exposure long-term. Leading expeditions in this environment was thus a multi-dimensional challenge.

[4점]

* lethal: 치명적인

① nullify

② induce

③ confront

④ resolve

⑤ oversimplify

16

In the 1830s and 1840s, several European countries _____.
It made things visible that had previously been hidden or taken for granted. The poor appeared as a social entity only when they were counted, and the resulting emergence of "poverty" as an abstract concept helped to arouse a moral commitment. Statistical societies and journals were founded, and government offices were called into being to gather, evaluate, and store social data. Politics rested more than ever before on exact information. In France, the systematic and regular collection of data was instituted at the prefecture level in 1801. Seeking to make deep inroads into civil society, the Napoleonic state needed as much accurate information as possible about it. In Britain too, despite its much less developed regional bureaucracy, the parliamentary government made extensive use of empirical facts about all manner of things—from sanitation in workers' districts to the medical condition of soldiers in the army. The collection of these was entrusted to ad hoc royal commissions, whose conclusions were publicly available both to the government of the day and to its critics. [3점]

* prefecture: 도청 ** inroad: 침입 *** ad hoc: 임시의

① were gripped by a passion for statistics
② instituted the regulation of data collection
③ gave citizens free access to state-owned data
④ were terror-stricken by overwhelming statistics
⑤ were dedicated to overcoming economic inequality

17　　There was plenty of evidence about _____ . The Russian troops who thought they were on "exercises" in Belarus and inside Russia were using their own cellphones—on Ukrainian networks—to call home to express their angst to family members and girlfriends that they had been deceived and were suddenly in a real battle. Others were posting on TikTok or Instagram. Again, the Ukrainians were in a position to exploit such amateurism: New recruits tucked away in hidden monitoring centers were busy geolocating the calls and social media phones and sharing that information with the military to launch precision attacks. As Pentagon officials watched the invasions unfold, they were also struck by the evidence that Russian supply and logistics operations were hopelessly snarled and backlogged. Not only had the Russians failed to bring along enough food to sustain a battle of more than a few days, but the column of Russian troops marching down to Kyiv had stalled out entirely. [3점]

* snarl: 교란하다

① how new recruits fled the battlefield
② how unprepared the Russian troops were
③ why Russia failed in its logistical operations
④ what Ukraine's handicap was in information warfare
⑤ how serious the tension was between Russia and Ukraine

18

In several ways, uncertainty can be understood as pervasive and written into the very script of life. Due to this, the craving for certainty has only become a means of stemming a perceived tide of phenomena that cannot yet be grasped and, to an even lesser extent, controlled. Consequently, the interplay between the desire to overcome uncertainty and instead strive towards certainty became inscribed into humans and society as a way of influencing the present and the future. This interplay is as old as the hills and is rooted in the human hope for security and the material, technological and social protection regarded as necessary for survival, comfort, and wellbeing. Mokyr shows how Western capitalist societies are indebted to all the systematic attempts to _____.
According to Mokyr, the strong belief in technical progress and the continuous improvement of various aspects of life are rooted in the reasoning that emerged and developed in the philosophical movement of the Enlightenment and which created a "space" for humans' "desire to know" and practically experiment with a wide range of activities.

[4점]

* stem: 저지하다

① reduce insecurity in terms of uncertainty
② outdo their forerunners in scientific areas
③ negate errors in interpretation of certainty
④ minimize the potential of human reasoning
⑤ survive the overloaded world of information

19

So many accounts of democracy emphasize legislative processes or policy outcomes, but these often miss the depth of connection between communication and political culture. When culture is discussed, it's often in the context of liberal-democratic values. But the question we're asking is: What determines the valence of those values? If a democracy stands or falls on the quality of the culture propping it up, then we ought to know under what conditions those values are affirmed and rejected. We believe those conditions are determined by a society's tools of communication, facilitated through media, to persuade. Indeed, _____ . If a democracy consists of citizens deciding, collectively, what ought to be done, then the manner through which they persuade one another determines nearly everything else that follows. And that privileges media ecology as the master political science. Some of its foremost practitioners, like Marshall McLuhan and Neil Postman, sensed, far better than political scientists or sociologists, that our media environment decides not just what we pay attention to but also how we think and orient ourselves in the world. [4점]

* valence: 결합가

① media will soon solve communication issues in democracy
② democracies are defined by their cultures of communication
③ conflicts between individuality and collectivity are inevitable
④ democracy thrives on order rather than endless public discourse
⑤ democracies can be sustained by valuing socioeconomic dynamics

[20~21] 주어진 글 다음에 이어질 글의 순서로 가장 적절한 것을 고르시오.

20

On January 26, 2013, a band of al-Qaeda militants entered the ancient city of Timbuktu on the southern edge of the Sahara Desert.

(A) The mayor of Bamako, who witnessed the event, called the burning of the manuscripts "a crime against world cultural heritage." And he was right⬛or he would have been, if it weren't for the fact that he was also lying.

(B) There, they set fire to a medieval library of 30,000 manuscripts written in Arabic and several African languages and ranging in subject from astronomy to geography, history to medicine. Unknown in the West, this was the collected wisdom of an entire continent, the voice of Africa at a time when Africa was thought not to have a voice at all.

(C) In fact, just before, African scholars had collected a random assortment of old books and left them out for the terrorists to burn. Today, the collection lies hidden in Bamako, the capital of Mali, moldering in the high humidity. What was rescued by ruse is now once again in jeopardy, this time by climate. [3점]

* ruse: 책략

① (A) – (C) – (B)   ② (B) – (A) – (C)   ③ (B) – (C) – (A)
④ (C) – (A) – (B)   ⑤ (C) – (B) – (A)

21

The need for trust in transactional human relationships is obvious. It is also clear in other non-transactional relationships that are driven by commitment and interdependence—classically, parent-child relationships, and those between the sick and their caregivers.

(A) This is also why the occasional discovered violation of one of these items of background faith is so scandalous: Dog meat in local vendor's hot dogs! Local father passing funny money at the park! Lurid tabloid headlines merely reinforce how deeply we trust these fundamental background assumptions, and how rarely they are violated.

(B) What is less commonly realized is the degree to which even interactions that seem purely transactional on the surface can occur only against a deeper background of implicit trust. When I pay $4 for a hot dog from a street vendor, the money-for-wiener trade rests upon a set of assumptions so long it would be impossible to exhaustively list.

(C) The hot dog is properly cooked. It has not been deliberately contaminated. The dollar bills I am handing over are not counterfeit. The hot dog contains (at least mostly) beef or pork, not dog meat. None of this is explicitly spelled out, but it is all nonetheless firmly taken for granted. [3점]

* lurid: 선정적인 ** wiener: 소시지

① (A) - (C) - (B)   ② (B) - (A) - (C)   ③ (B) - (C) - (A)

④ (C) - (A) - (B)   ⑤ (C) - (B) – (A)

[22~23] 글의 흐름으로 보아, 주어진 문장이 들어가기에 가장 적절한 곳을 고르시오.

22

And reading, as neurosciences are showing, connects parts of our brain that are otherwise normally separated.

A new world has been born, where images have killed words simply because they are easier to use and do not require complex thoughts. The evolution of means of communication, from letter to e-mail; from e-mail to Facebook; finally, from Facebook to Instagram, is quite paradigmatic. (①) The shift from written words, which require time, to pictures, videos and emoticons, tools that even a child can handle, has been a process characterised not only by unbelievable rapidity but also by lack of precedents. (②) As a matter of fact, in the last millennia the progress of mankind has been based on complex thoughts: and these require words, and words require reading. (③) But reading is not innate, it is a cultural product. (④) The end of reading and of written words means the vanishing of these connections, and the emergence of a different brain, maybe speedier and multitasking, but destined to remain on the surface since deeper thought and understanding require words and time. (⑤) It is impossible to write a poem, a novel, or a scientific paper using pictures, selfies, emoticons, or simple sentences!

[3점]

* paradigmatic: 계열적

23

> But what society really needs right now is new vaccines and more efficient lithium-ion batteries.

As the creative primate, humans are crucially dependent on lateral thinking. We require a continuous stream of novel insights and a constant reorganization of existing knowledge. (①) Children, with their underdeveloped prefrontal cortices, are superstars in this regard. (②) But the very thing that makes them so creative renders most of their creations useless, at least from the pragmatic perspective of goal-oriented adults. (③) Bizarrely distorted Lego worlds featuring post-apocalyptic, scavenged-parts vehicles driven by Lego people with Barbie-doll heads, or menageries of superhero figurines and stuffies organized into formal English tea parties, reflect impressive out-of-the-box thinking. (④) If your goal is to maximize implementable cultural innovation, your ideal person would be someone with the body of an adult but, for a brief period, the mind of a child. (⑤) Someone with downregulated cognitive control, heightened openness to experience, and a mind prone to wander off in unpredictable directions.

[4점]

* prefrontal cortices: 전전두피질 ** menagerie: 전시장

24

다음 글의 내용을 한 문장으로 요약하고자 한다. 빈칸 (A), (B)에 들어갈 말로 가장 적절한 것은?

The great myth of American culture, then and now, is that democracy is built on free expression, both spoken and printed. Though wrapped up in shibboleths from the marketplace of ideas, such a myth is not without its advantages. There is wisdom in the notion that free expression is its own justification, as a matter of principle and as a check on power. The price, however, is sometimes high. Truth won't always win out, and the public sphere can't be contained. This is a lesson perpetually relearned when novel media technologies flood the information space. In 1938, Orson Welles and his Mercury Theater troupe broadcast a live radio performance of the H. G. Wells novel *The War of the Worlds*. While there is not much evidence that the program touched off an actual panic—and Welles was clear, at both the beginning and the end of the broadcast, that it was a dramatic performance, not a news report of real events—we do know that the broadcast garnered major newspaper coverage. The radio was already under regulations by the Federal Communications Commission, which had been formed in 1934, but one medium confronted another.

* shibboleth: 상투적인 어구 ** garner: 모으다

⬇

While it is commonly believed that the free and open exchange of ideas is a ___(A)___ of American democracy, the cost can be the unintended and uncontrollable ___(B)___ of untruth via new media, as in the case of a live radio performance broadcast in 1938.

	(A)		(B)		(A)		(B)
①	pillar	……	elusion	②	highlight	……	censorship
③	foundation	……	concealment	④	reflection	……	disclosure
⑤	cornerstone	……	circulation				

[25~26] 다음 글을 읽고, 물음에 답하시오.

Natural evolution _____ which even today are of great interest. The bats are the subject of continuing studies; they emit with their mouth (some, with the nose) short ultrasonic signals (with frequencies well above 100 kHz) called *chip* or *click* and listen to the echo due to the presence of objects up to some meters away. Their brain reconstructs the precise position of the object on the basis of the delay of the echo perceived by each ear, its frequency and its intensity. A great sensitivity is required to locate insects, the main food of bats, even at distances of several meters. The emitted signal has both narrow-band i.e. *constant frequency* (CF), and broadband (*frequency modulated*, FM, or *Chirp*) components. The linearly frequency modulated signal called *Chirp* (including its evolutions with non-linear modulation) is one of those emitted by bats, and has been studied for radar applications by both the Germans and the Allied powers since 1942–43. It is remarkable that the first analyses of the signals emitted by bats date back to just four or five years before these years. With respect to a normal rectangular pulse of equal duration and energy, this type of signal allows a dramatic improvement in the capacity of *range resolution*, i.e. of discrimination in the distance measurement. Not only signals, but also the processes by which the bats locate obstacles and their prey are of great interest from the radar point of view. According to tradition, the name *chirp* (which identifies the chirping of a bird) is due to one of the U.S. experimenters who developed the *pulse compression* in the 1950s, i.e. B. M. Oliver, who stated that radar should emit "not with a bang, but with a chirp."

25 윗글의 제목으로 가장 적절한 것은? [3점]

① When Bats Chirp, We Learn about Radar
② Arms Competition: Mother of Radar Technology
③ Too Bad! We Bypassed What Bats Showed Us about Radar
④ Bat Echolocation: Adaptations for Prey Detection and Capture
⑤ Chip, Click, and Chirp: Use of Animals for Military Intelligence

26 윗글의 빈칸에 들어갈 말로 가장 적절한 것은? [4점]

① emphasized the value of air units in the aviation sector
② taught us depth perception, navigation, and visual resolution
③ revealed the use of passive receptors to detect electric signals
④ introduced the true definition and proper functions of technologies
⑤ produced signal types and techniques of detection and localization

[27~28] 다음 글을 읽고, 물음에 답하시오.

Cultural heritage can be understood in the narrow sense as the reservoir of cultural elements that are recognized as being significant and worthy of preservation and transfer to succeeding generations. Cultural heritage in the wide sense, however, is understood as a dynamic discursive area within which the cultural resources of the past, and their significance, are constructed through social interaction. Once (a) extracted from this discursive area, the reservoir becomes just an empty and meaningless collection of artefacts and ideas embedded in various forms. Such an understanding of cultural heritage is rooted in the idea of (b) collective memory introduced by Maurice Halbwachs. He argues that our memory about the past is socially constructed. To some extent, social conditions determine what and how we remember. The phenomenon of tradition and cultural heritage being socially determined is emphasized by Eric Hobsbawn and Terence Ranger, who consider that tradition is not reproduced but rather (c) invented. Belief in the discursive nature of cultural heritage is based on the conviction that the criteria for determining which artefacts and behavioural patterns should be transmitted to posterity are (d) stable. On the one hand, a reservoir of cultural heritage is subject to selection and is determined by global flows, new technology, economics, cultural policy, or the sentiments of decision-makers. On the other hand, such a reservoir is the object of continual reinterpretation, which is influenced by the social position, background, biography, and cultural competences of the individuals who participate in a culture. Social interaction is the (e) essence of transition in cultural heritage.

* posterity: 후대

27 윗글의 주제로 가장 적절한 것은?   [3점]

① the significance of cultural heritage preservation
② procedures to build a reservoir for cultural heritage artefacts
③ cultural heritage's discursive characteristic as a social construct
④ discursive efforts by social organizations to designate world heritages
⑤ established criteria for categorizing artefacts based on historical values

28 밑줄 친 (a)~(e) 중에서 문맥상 낱말의 쓰임이 적절하지 <u>않은</u> 것은?   [3점]

① (a)   ② (b)   ③ (c)   ④ (d)   ⑤ (e)

[29~30] 다음 글을 읽고, 물음에 답하시오.

(A)

Sarah dreamed of becoming a doctor. Since elementary school, she had known, without a sliver of doubt, that she would become a doctor of medicine. One day, a childhood friend, Amanda, was visiting (a) her home. She also had dreams of pursuing a career in medicine, so together they hatched a plan to attend the same Ivy League school. Though Sarah and Amanda's parents agreed the two friends should go to college, they had quite different attitudes towards their daughters' chosen paths.

(B)

Amanda still wasn't convinced by (b) her reasoning. If she could flunk such a basic test, wasn't it obvious that she wasn't cut out to be a doctor? She considered changing courses, and even thought about dropping out altogether. Sarah refused to be perturbed. Her personal values protected her from absorbing the dangerous cultural message that she wasn't performing academically as well as her peers simply because (c) she was 'bad at science.' This was a small bump in the road and Sarah knew that in a few years' time, both friends would achieve their dream of becoming a medical doctor.

* perturbed: 혼란스러운

(C)

Sarah's parents were supportive. They encouraged her to identify and understand her own personal values rather than connecting success in life with school grades and accolades. Sarah asked Amanda what her parents thought about their plan. She revealed they had expressed concern on more than one occasion. This surprised (d) her, as Amanda was academically talented. Raising their daughter in a culture with stereotypes such as 'girls are bad at science,' Amanda's parents questioned whether or not she was cut out for such a career path.

(D)

After they entered university, the friends experienced their first minor setback. They received a bad grade on the midterm biology test. Amanda was upset. She felt the bad grade proved what her parents had been saying all along. Sarah was disappointed but simply shrugged it off. She reminded her friend that (e) she was in a new place, juggling classes, social events, sorority obligations and living away from family for the first time in her life.

29 주어진 글 (A)에 이어질 내용을 순서에 맞게 배열한 것으로 가장 적절한 것은? [3점]

① (B) − (D) − (C) ② (C) − (B) − (D) ③ (C) − (D) − (B)
④ (D) − (B) − (C) ⑤ (D) − (C) − (B)

30 밑줄 친 (a)~(e) 중에서 가리키는 대상이 나머지 넷과 다른 것은? [3점]

① (a) ② (b) ③ (c) ④ (d) ⑤ (e)

공 란

2025학년도 경찰대학교 1차 선발시험 문제지

영어 영역

성명		수험번호							

○ 먼저 문제지에 성명과 수험번호를 기입하시오.

○ 답안지에 성명과 수험번호를 정확하게 표기하시오.

○ 문제는 3점 20문항, 4점 10문항 총 30문항입니다.

   (4점 문항에만 점수가 표시되어 있고, 나머지는 모두 3점 문항입니다.)

※ 시험 시작 전까지 표지를 넘기지 마시오.

| 해설 469쪽 |

공 란

[1~5] 밑줄 친 단어의 뜻으로 가장 적절한 것을 고르시오.

01

He has violated one of the profession's most <u>sacred</u> rules.

① holy   ② weird   ③ demanding
④ practical   ⑤ uncommon

02

Ask them to send you information on how to <u>assess</u> the value of your belongings.

① upgrade   ② evaluate   ③ maximize
④negotiate   ⑤ overestimate

03

She was filled with <u>despair</u> at the conditions under which miners were forced to work.

① anger   ② regret   ③ hopelessness
④ sympathy   ⑤ contentment

04

The fresh tire tracks in the snow were <u>obvious</u> proof that someone had recently driven down this country road.

① abstract   ② invisible   ③ evident
④ plentiful   ⑤ unruly

05

The company provided <u>valid</u> reasons for the delay in delivering the product to customers.

① reasonable   ② unsound   ③ multiple
④ invaluable   ⑤ incredible

06

A: Hey, have you ever thought about picking up a new hobby?

B: I don't know. I feel like I'm too old to start something new.

A: Not at all! What's something you've always wanted to try?

B: Well, I've always wanted to learn how to play the piano.

A: That's a fantastic idea! There are plenty of resources for adult beginners. You could start with online lessons or find a local class.

B: I guess you're right. I'll think about it.

A: I've seen people of all ages learn new things. It's very inspiring. Remember, _____.

B: Thanks for the encouragement! I'll give it a shot!

① practice makes perfect
② it's never too late to learn
③ two heads are better than one
④ never judge a book by its cover
⑤ there is no royal road to learning

07

A: What are you up to this weekend?

B: Probably just chilling at home. What about you?

A: I'm thinking of going hiking. It's been a while.

B: Where are you headed?

A: I found a great spot in the mountains with awesome views.

B: Nice! Are you going by yourself?

A: Yeah, I need some time to clear my head.

B: Understood. Besides hiking, do you have any other plans?

A: Maybe I'll catch up on some reading. There's a new thriller I've been waiting for.

B: Sounds like a perfect weekend! _____ .

A: I will.

① Let's play outside more often

② Hiking is my favorite activity

③ I'll meet you up in the mountains

④ Let me know how the book turns out

⑤ I'll try to make some other plans tomorrow

[8~9] 밑줄 친 부분 중, 어법상 <u>틀린</u> 것을 고르시오.

08

Growing up in India, I would spend summer breaks visiting my grandparents in Kolkata. Each afternoon, my grandmother ① <u>settling down</u> on a floor mat, facing the family's worship room, where stone idols of Hindu gods sat on little wooden thrones. For half an hour, she would sit still, her eyes closed, fingers rolling her prayer beads, chanting Krishna's name in a whisper. It's impossible to know, objectively, ② <u>whether</u> those meditation sessions helped my grandmother achieve some sort of communion with a higher power, but a growing body of scientific evidence suggests she benefited from it in multiple ways. The practice was ③ <u>likely</u> an effective approach for her to manage her stress. It may have also helped slow down aging-related cognitive decline. It also probably enhanced her ability to cope with pain. ④ <u>Defined</u> most broadly as the exercise of focusing one's attention on the current moment, meditation in some form has been practiced for millennia by religious traditions around the world—most rooted in a quest for spiritual enlightenment. Today, the popularity of meditation ⑤ <u>has grown</u> in parallel with awareness about the importance of mental health and stress relief.

* throne: 왕좌

09

Anger is clearly related to aggression but they are not one and the same. It is possible to be aggressive without being angry and it is ① <u>equally</u> possible to be angry without becoming aggressive. However, the two (the emotion of anger and the behaviour of aggression) are linked and are biologically based, with obvious survival value. Anger always results in a much increased burst of energy and, ② <u>although</u> biologically based, is seen by some psychologists as largely socially constructed. That is, some people might be temperamentally more prone to anger than others, but the extent ③ <u>to which</u> they express this is probably socially determined. In our culture, for example, boys are encouraged to express their anger more openly than girls and a far greater proportion of men than women are made ④ <u>take</u> anger management courses. These are ⑤ <u>learned</u> differences, not differences of biology.

[3점]

[10~11] (A), (B), (C)의 각 네모 안에서 문맥에 맞는 낱말로 가장 적절한 것을 고르시오.

10

As a result of the political and social changes of recent decades, cultural pluralism is now generally recognized as an organizing principle of this society. In (A) addition / contrast to the idea of the melting pot, which promised to erase ethnic and group differences, children now learn that variety is the spice of life. They learn that America has provided a shelter for many different groups and has allowed them to (B) maintain / reform their cultural heritage or to assimilate, or —as is often the case—to do both; the choice is theirs, not the state's. They learn that cultural pluralism is one of the norms of a free society; that differences among groups are a national resource rather than a problem to be solved. Indeed, the unique feature of the United States is that its common culture has been formed by the interaction of its subsidiary cultures. It is a culture that has been influenced over time by immigrants, American Indians, Africans (slave and free), and by their descendants. American music, art, literature, language, food, clothing, sports, holidays, and customs all show the effects of the blending of (C) similar / diverse cultures in one nation. Paradoxical though it may seem, the United States has a common culture that is multicultural.

* subsidiary: 부차적인

	(A)	(B)	(C)
①	addition	maintain	similar
②	addition	reform	similar
③	contrast	maintain	similar
④	contrast	maintain	diverse
⑤	contrast	reform	diverse

11

　　Popular understanding of the interrelationship between knowledge and power is frequently expressed through the phrase "Knowledge is power." Foucault, in his genealogical studies, (A) confirms / reverses the logic of this expression. He contends that it is not the acquisition of knowledge that gives one power. Instead, knowledge is already always deeply invested with power in such a way that it must be said that "power is knowledge." Thus, in Foucault's analysis, knowledge is never separate from power but is instead a specific means for (B) exercising / resisting power. In this way, power is not simply something embodied within an individual or a social structure and expressed by brute coercion or punishment. Power appears in its most potent form when successfully translated into systems of "knowledge" and thus removed from reflection under the veil of obvious truths. The (C) inseparability / separability of power and knowledge is so thoroughgoing, according to Foucault, that he often conjoins the two into the term power/ knowledge.

* coercion: 강제

	(A)	(B)	(C)
①	confirms	exercising	inseparability
②	confirms	resisting	inseparability
③	reverses	exercising	inseparability
④	reverses	resisting	separability
⑤	reverses	exercising	separability

[12~13] 밑줄 친 부분 중, 문맥상 낱말의 쓰임이 적절하지 않은 것을 고르시오.

12

Every economics textbook will tell you that competition between rival firms leads to innovation in their products and services. But when you look at innovation from the long-zoom perspective, competition turns out to be less ① central to the history of good ideas than we generally think. Analyzing innovation on the scale of individuals and organizations—as the standard textbooks do—② broadens our view. It creates a picture of innovation that overstates the role of proprietary research and "survival of the fittest" competition. The long-zoom approach lets us see that openness and connectivity may, in the end, be more ③ valuable to innovation than purely competitive mechanisms. Those patterns of innovation deserve recognition—in part because it's intrinsically important to understand why good ideas emerge historically, and in part because by ④ embracing these patterns we can build environments that do a better job of nurturing good ideas, whether those environments are schools, governments, or social movements. We can think more creatively if we open our minds to the many ⑤ connected environments that make creativity possible.

[3점]

* proprietary: 독점의

13

    The great American author Edgar Allan Poe, who needs no ① <u>lengthy</u> introduction, is one of the writers who invented the modern short story. A modern short story is different from earlier forms of tales and fables not only in that it sets the story on a modern realistic background but also in the way its form ② <u>concentrates</u> on a single dramatic event. In Poe's case, this single event very often has to do with some ③ <u>abnormal</u> act typically involving death and murder. It was Poe's innovation to narrate such disturbing event from the viewpoint of the murderer himself, so that the reader of Poe's short story has to hear the vivid voice of the ④ <u>aggressor</u> who takes great care to give a detailed account of how he committed the act. The ⑤ <u>disadvantage</u> of such mode of storytelling is that it allows the writer to explore that mysterious thing, the human mind, in a most intimate and extreme fashion.

14 Virgil에 관한 다음 글의 내용과 일치하지 <u>않는</u> 것은?

Virgil's masterful poetry earned him a legacy as the greatest poet in the Latin language. Throughout the Middle Ages and the Renaissance, his fame only grew. Before the invention of the printing press, when classical texts, transmitted by the hands of scribes, were scarce, Virgil's poetry was available to the literate classes, among whom he was regarded as the most significant writer of the ancient time. He inspired poets across languages, including Dante in Italian, Milton in English, and an anonymous French poet who reworked the *Aeneid* into the medieval romance *Le Roman d'Eneas*. In what became a Christian culture, Virgil was viewed as a pagan prophet because several lines in his works were interpreted as predictions of the coming of Christ. Among writers of the Renaissance, Virgil was appreciated for his vivid portrayals of human emotion. Modern critics, on the other hand, have been less kind. Virgil's poetry is often judged in relation to that of his Greek predecessors, especially the *Iliad* and the *Odyssey*, epics attributed to Homer that also portray the Trojan War. Most contemporary scholars hold that Virgil's poetry pales in comparison to Homer's.

* pagan: 이교도의

① His skillful poems in Latin made him a noted poet.
② His reputation fell into a decline during the Renaissance.
③ He influenced the poems of different languages.
④ His poetry clearly expressed human emotion.
⑤ His poetry was valued less than Homer's by modern critics.

15

Alice James에 관한 다음 글의 내용과 일치하는 것은?

Alice James is always classified as some famous person's sister or brother. Both of her brothers, Henry James the novelist and William James the philosopher, are important figures in their fields. Her family itself was a famous and respected household in Cambridge, MA. Yet Alice, the youngest daughter, was something of a problem, ever since she had her first mental breakdown at sixteen. She also suffered from numerous health problems. The brothers, in the meantime, were becoming more and more successful in their public career. Alice James died at the age of forty-four, yet she left behind a most interesting record of her thoughts during the last three years of her life. She was, however, too weak even to write. Her close friend K. P. Loring wrote down her words for her. Loring also printed a copy of her diary for Alice's brothers and herself. The challenge in reading her journal is to appreciate the mixture of anger, self-pity, and, of course, the pain the writer feels. One should also remember that hers was a uniquely feminine experience, as women in those times were very often considered to be a "case" or "problem" to be studied and treated by male doctors.

① She came from a lower-class family in Cambridge.
② She was the oldest child in her family.
③ Her brothers failed to gain a reputation.
④ She left a dictated writing of her thoughts.
⑤ Her journal was full of her pity for other women.

16 다음 글의 내용과 일치하는 것은?

The American transition to analytic philosophy was mediated by several important figures, institutions, and events. One such figure was Morris Cohen (1880-1947). Born in Russia, he was educated at City College of New York. With a 1905 Harvard Ph.D., he taught at City from 1912 to 1938, and at the University of Chicago from 1938 to 1941. Known for his interest in logic and the philosophy of science, he was a committed naturalist who recognized no non-scientific methods capable of attaining knowledge in philosophy. One of his students was the Czechoslovakian-born Ernest Nagel, who, after earning his B.A. at City, got his Ph.D. in 1931 from Columbia University. With the exception of a year at Rockefeller University in the 1960s, he spent his career at Columbia University teaching and writing about the philosophy of science and explaining the centrality of logic to philosophy.

① Cohen was born in Czechoslovakia.
② Cohen taught at City College of New York until 1941.
③ Cohen was known for his interest only in logic.
④ Nagel earned his Ph.D. from Harvard University in 1931.
⑤ Nagel spent most of his career at Columbia University.

[17~21] 다음 글의 빈칸에 들어갈 말로 가장 적절한 것을 고르시오.

17

In terms of education, history has not always received a good press. Advising his son in 1656, Francis Osborne was far from enthusiastic about the subject. His experience of hearing contradictory reports about the Civil Wars of his own time (contemporary history), led him to be doubtful about the _____ of records of less recent events. Such historical records, he concluded, were likely to present a 'false, or at best but a contingent beliefe'; and as such they hardly warranted serious study. Osborne's anxiety about his son potentially wasting his time by studying history that is unreliable, implies an understanding of history as being ideally of a certain kind—the kind that yields certain, 'factual' knowledge about the past. Now, although that model was already under challenge in Osborne's day, it has persisted to some extent up to our own time.

* contingent: 부수적인

① continuity
② reliability
③ rediscovery
④ conciseness
⑤ predictability

18

Every intelligence has to _____. A human brain, which is genetically primed to categorize things, still needs to see a dozen examples as a child before it can distinguish between cats and dogs. That's even more true for artificial minds. Even the best-programmed computer has to play at least a thousand games of chess before it gets good. Part of the AI breakthrough lies in the incredible amount of collected data about our world, which provides the schooling that AIs need. Massive databases, self-tracking, web cookies, online footprints, terabytes of storage, decades of search results, and the entire digital universe became the teachers making AI smart. Andrew Ng explains it this way: "AI is akin to building a rocket ship. You need a huge engine and a lot of fuel. The rocket engine is the learning algorithms but the fuel is the huge amounts of data we can feed to these algorithms."

① be taught
② exceed itself
③ think by itself
④ be governed by rules
⑤ calculate all possibilities

19

Etymology is the study of the root or origin of a word: it derives from the Greek root etymos, meaning 'true'. The importance and the implications of etymology are considerable. Generally speaking, there are two contradictory processes at work in the relation between etymology and meaning. The first is a gradual erosion of the original link: words tend to move steadily away from their original meanings. Contrary to this is a desire to revive the link, to get words 'to make sense' with their past. People _____, and even invent them if they do not exist. Some words do indeed have such striking origins. Few of us ever forget (once we are told) that the sandwich derives from the Earl of Sandwich, a compulsive gambler who, in order not to leave the gaming table during a twenty-four-hour bout, sustained himself in part with slices of cold beef between slices of toast. Thus was born the sandwich, first recorded in 1762. [3점]

* erosion: 침식

① prefer memorable or logical origins for words
② pay little attention to the implications of etymology
③ consider the original meanings of words unimportant
④ are unaware of the contradictory processes of etymology
⑤ dislike any association between use and meaning of words

20

Our intuition is that in chess experts, the parsing of board games becomes a reflex. Indeed, research proves that a single glance is enough for any grand master to evaluate a chessboard and to remember its configuration in full detail, because he automatically parses it into meaningful chunks. Furthermore, a recent experiment indicates that this segmenting process is truly unconscious: a simplified game can be flashed for 20 milliseconds, sandwiched between masks that make it invisible, and still influence a chess master's decision. The experiment works only on expert chess players, and only if they are solving a meaningful problem, such as determining if the king is under check or not. It implies that the visual system takes into account the identity of the pieces (rook or knight) and their locations, then quickly binds together this information into a meaningful chunk ("black king under check"). These sophisticated operations _____ _____.

[3점]

* parsing: 분석

① happen only when the master's consciousness is working
② unfold consciously with meaningful awareness
③ occur entirely outside conscious awareness
④ succeed through careful analysis and repetition
⑤ prove that multisensory information can be bound together

21

The industrial (and associated agricultural) revolution which occurred in Europe during the eighteenth and nineteenth centuries not only changed the nature of work, but also dramatically transformed the organization of society, gender and kinship relationships, and ＿＿＿＿＿＿＿＿＿＿＿＿＿＿＿. In particular, the composition of, and link between, the rural and the urban was completely overturned as a result of the large-scale migration of potential industrial workers from the countryside to the cities where the factories of the emerging manufacturing bourgeoisie were located. The scope of the demographic change that occurred at this time is underlined by research showing that at the beginning of the nineteenth century only 15 British towns had populations of more than 20,000 but by its end there were 185. Indeed, it has been estimated that in 1800 only 2.2 percent of the population of Europe lived in cities of more than 100,000— today that geopolitical space is predominantly urbanized and highly industrialized.

* kinship: 친족 ** demographic: 인구학의

① the geographical features of some nations
② the system of the manufacturing industry
③ the concept of social justice and equality
④ the dominant form of human settlement
⑤ the definition of the working class

22 다음 글의 빈칸 (A), (B)에 들어갈 말로 가장 적절한 것은?

Are you the type of person who sees the proverbial glass as half full or as half empty? People with more optimistic attitudes—who see the glass as half full— tend to be more resilient than others to the effects of stress, including stress associated with physical disorders. _____(A)_____, investigators link optimism to lower levels of emotional distress among heart disease and cancer patients and to lower levels of reported pain among cancer patients. Optimism in pregnant women even predicts better birth outcomes, as measured, for instance, by higher infant birth weights. Optimism in coronary artery bypass surgery patients is also associated with fewer serious postoperative complications. _____(B)_____, people with more pessimistic attitudes tend to report greater emotional distress in the form of depression and social anxiety.

* resilient: 탄력 있는

	(A)		(B)
①	For instance	······	Hence
②	For example	······	On the other hand
③	In addition	······	Nevertheless
④	However	······	Therefore
⑤	In fact	······	As a result

[23~26] 다음 글의 제목으로 가장 적절한 것을 고르시오.

23

One of the most daring deep-space missions NASA has ever planned is turning out to be one of the least publicized. The target is a large asteroid named 1992KD, which orbits the sun millions of km from Earth. But that destination is almost incidental to the performance of the spacecraft that will make the trip. Though it looks little different from countless other unmanned spaceships NASA has launched, the ship will be navigated by an electronic brain that has been likened to HAL, the independent-minded computer in the film *2001 Space Odyssey*, and will move through space under power of a system that has long been the stuff of technological fantasies: an ion propulsion engine. If all goes as planned, Deep Space 1, scheduled for launch later this month, will be the forerunner of a new generation of spacecraft. While flight planners hope the ship will make some interesting observations about the target asteroid, including its composition and the structure of its surface, DS1's prime assignment is to validate a host of new technologies NASA had always considered too risky to try on a high-profile mission.

[3점]

* asteroid: 소행성 ** propulsion: 추진

① A Smart New Kind of Spacecraft
② The Launch of Unmanned Rockets
③ Failure of DS1's Risky Technologies
④ Performance of Computerized Engine System
⑤ New Mission to Navigate a Larger Asteroid

24

Cattle are sensitive creatures. They have evolved a suite of sensory adaptations to detect predators at long distances. They have a keen sense of smell and hearing at least as good as a dog's or cat's. People often say that elephants never forget, but neither do cattle. Cattle can recognize pictures of herd mates as well as humans they know. Charles Darwin argued that both humans and animals possess a similarity in the expression of emotions. We can, of course, discern basic emotions, like pleasure and fear. But what endears dogs to us is their apparent capacity for what we take as their version of love—the longing in their eyes to be with their people and their overall willingness to please. How do you know cattle love you? Pretty much the same way you do with dogs. My bull, Ricky Bobby, happily lies down next to me and puts his horned head in my lap. He loves for me to brush him, and he'll even roll over for a belly rub.

① Cattle Can Be Our New Pets
② Pets Express Emotional Change
③ How to Domesticate Wild Animals
④ Ways to Drive the Cattle Home Safe
⑤ Darwin's Discovery of Animal Behaviors

25

Because of the goals of protecting life and property and maintaining order, and because the police are open for business 24 hours a day in all kinds of weather, it is inevitable that the police are called upon to look after people who cannot or will not properly care for themselves. This includes young children, elderly citizens, the mentally ill, and the homeless. Police assistance to these people can only go so far, of course—police cannot raise other people's children, cure the mentally ill, or build houses for all the homeless people in this country. However, police can and often do provide or arrange for temporary shelter and transportation for those in need. They also make referrals and provide information so that people can take advantage of programs and services available to them. During times when the economy is struggling, when social programs are underfunded, and when many citizens turn a cold shoulder to those less fortunate, police assistance is often the only option for those who cannot properly care for themselves.

① Police Always on the Lookout for Potential Problems
② A Key Objective of the Police: To Prevent Serious Crimes
③ Police Are Here for Those Who Cannot Care for Themselves!
④ Who Is in Charge of Resolving Various Kinds of Conflicts?
⑤ Patrol as the Backbone of the Police Service

26

Although there had been a long tradition of religious and morally enlightening dramas (termed respectively the miracle and morality plays) the first public playhouse in England was built only in 1576. This proved the catalyst for what Gamini Salgado has rightly called 'the greatest efflorescence of dramatic writing England has ever seen'. The conditions of the Elizabethan stage, though difficult to reconstruct with total accuracy now, were generally primitive. To compensate for these inadequacies, a whole new linguistic medium was created. On a bare stage with minimal properties and effects with which to build up a sense of theatrical illusion, the great dramatists, Shakespeare especially, created an extraordinary diversity of experience and range of characters exclusively through the medium of individuated language, worlds of words in which their creations could philosophize, agonize, laugh, suffer and die.   [3점]

* catalyst: 촉매 ** efflorescence: 전성기

① Technological Advancements of Elizabethan Theaters
② The Elizabethan Stage and Its Linguistic Innovation
③ Shakespeare's Effective Use of the Primitive Stage
④ The Decline of Religious Drama in England
⑤ The Rise of Medieval Morality Plays

27 다음 글의 주장으로 가장 적절한 것은?

Behind every anhedonic choice that keeps you stuck is the belief that you (or your life) will fall apart if you challenge the rules. This is a powerful myth! It can keep you absolutely paralyzed! The only way to rid yourself of it is to put your psychological strengths to the test. Few people realize how strong they really are until they stop putting up with the problems in their lives and take some steps toward change. It won't be easy. You may get knocked down a few times, but you won't fall apart. On the contrary, the more you assert your ability to take control over your life, the stronger you'll become. Developing psychological strengths is just like developing physical abilities. The more you exercise, the stronger you become.

* anhedonic: 쾌락을 추구하지 않는

① Do not feel you always have to have a realistic plan.
② Identify the conditions that help you become a success.
③ Choose one of your bigger dreams and make it a reality.
④ Set attainable goals and enjoy each small step of progress.
⑤ Stop thinking of yourself as fragile and be mentally strong.

28 다음 글의 주제로 가장 적절한 것은?

No clear-cut category can encompass all jazz. Each performer's idiom is a style unto itself; if it were not so, the music would hardly be jazz. Jazz, like almost all other music, comprises three artistic activities: creating, performing, and listening. In traditional Western European music, these three activities are not always performed by the same individual, although they quite often are. In jazz, however, it is necessary for the performer to combine all three at the same time. Musical creation is an active part of any jazz performance and depends on the performers' understanding of the developing creation, an understanding gained only by their ability to listen well. They must react instantaneously to what they hear from their fellow performers, and their own contribution must be consistent with the unfolding themes and moods. Every act of musical creation in jazz is, therefore, as individual as the performer creating it.

① traits of jazz reflecting performers' individuality
② how to compose jazz for a great performance
③ similarities between jazz and Western music
④ celebrated figures in the modern jazz scene
⑤ influences of traditional music on jazz

[29~30] 다음 글에서 전체 흐름과 관계 <u>없는</u> 문장을 고르시오.

29

Computer-aided instruction is changing the very nature of the educational process at the college level. An increasingly large number of students want a college education, yet they work during the day and may not have a university nearby that offers evening instruction. A solution to this problem is called *distance learning*, meaning that students can enroll in college courses yet not be physically present at the college. ① Course lectures offered at the college are recorded and made available for viewing by students on their personal computers, at whatever time the students have available. ② Thus a course can be offered without regard to time or space because computer technology delivers the course to the student. ③ Some universities are now offering entire degree programs to students through this technology. ④ Hence, distance learning cannot be a good option for students who keep delaying things or those who aren't able to stick to deadlines. ⑤ A student can earn a degree from a university without ever having physically attended the university.

30

It is common knowledge that Descartes was a Cartesian Dualist. (Perhaps it's nothing more than common sense!) ① As everyone knows, he held that there are two worlds, one of mental objects and one of material things, including animals and human bodies. ② The mental objects are 'states of consciousness' (e.g. pains, visual experiences, beliefs and desires, fear and joy); the material objects are more or less complex bits of 'clockwork'. ③ The items in the 'inner world' are understood through the exercise of a special faculty called 'introspection'; objects in the 'outer world' are perceived by the five senses. ④ Like most items of 'common knowledge', the importance of reading is often taken for granted without critical examination. ⑤ Mental states and states of the body are logically independent but causally interrelated: causal interaction is, as it were, the glue bonding mind to body in each individual person.

[31~33] 글의 흐름으로 보아, 주어진 문장이 들어가기에 가장 적절한 곳을 고르시오.

31

> But AI promises to transform all areas of human experience.

Humanity has experienced technological change throughout history. Only rarely, however, has technology fundamentally transformed the social and political structure of our societies. (①) More frequently, the preexisting frameworks through which we order our social world adapt and absorb new technology, evolving and innovating within recognizable categories. (②) The car replaced the horse without forcing a total shift in social structure. (③) The rifle replaced the musket, but the general paradigm of conventional military activity remained largely unaltered. (④) Only very rarely have we encountered a technology that challenged our prevailing modes of explaining and ordering the world. (⑤) And the core of its transformations will ultimately occur at the philosophical level, transforming how humans understand reality and our role within it.

32

Seeking refuge, the pair transformed themselves into fish, tied together for safety, and leapt into the river Euphrates.

The constellation Pisces is most often imagined as a pair of fish that are joined together by a rope. This image has been recorded in ancient Egypt of the 2nd millennium BCE and later Babylonian texts. Why these two fish happen to be tied together is not recorded by these earliest sources but later Greek and Roman myths offer some explanations. (①)When the gods were facing the terrible monster Typhon, it is said that Aphrodite and Eros were far away from the battle. (②) Being gods of love and lust, these two had little they could do in the face of such a world-crushing threat. (③) This is the moment that was captured in the form of this constellation. (④) An alternative version has the two fish of Pisces rescuing the gods who rode away on their backs. (⑤) As a reward for their help the fish were placed in the night sky.

33

A principal vehicle of this enterprise was educational reform and specifically the building of a university system dedicated to the ideals of science, reason, and humanism.

Writing just after the end of World War I, an acute observer of the French philosophical scene judged that "philosophical research had never been more abundant, more serious, and more intense among us than in the last thirty years." (①) This flowering was due to the place of philosophy in the new educational system set up by the Third Republic in the wake of the demoralizing defeat in the Franco-Prussian War. (②) The French had been humiliated by the capture of Napoleon III at Sedan and wasted by the long siege of Paris. (③) They had also been terrified by what most of the bourgeoisie saw as seventy-three days of anarchy under the radical socialism of the Commune. (④) Much of the new Republic's effort at spiritual restoration was driven by a rejection of the traditional values of institutional religion, which it aimed to replace with an enlightened worldview. (⑤) Albert Thibaudet highlighted the importance of this reform when he labeled the Third Republic "the republic of professors."　　　[3점]

* siege: 포위　** anarchy: 무정부

[34~36] 주어진 글 다음에 이어질 글의 순서로 가장 적절한 것을 고르시오.

34

"National forests need more roads like farmers need more drought." We heard somebody say this who was trying to persuade an audience that more roads would be bad for our national forests.

(A) An argument attempts to prove or support a conclusion. When you attempt to persuade someone, you attempt to win him or her to your point of view; trying to persuade and trying to argue are logically distinct enterprises. True, when you want to persuade somebody of something, you might use an argument.

(B) But not all arguments attempt to persuade, and many attempts to persuade do not involve arguments. In fact, giving an argument is often one of the least effective methods of persuading people—which, of course, is why so few advertisers bother with arguments. People notoriously are persuaded by the weakest of arguments and sometimes are undisturbed by even quite good arguments.

(C) The remark, however, is not an argument; it's just a statement that portrays road building in the forests in a bad light. Now, some writers define an argument as an attempt to persuade somebody of something. This is not correct.

[3점]

① (A)-(C)-(B) ② (B)-(A)-(C) ③ (B)-(C)-(A)
④ (C)-(A)-(B) ⑤ (C)-(B)-(A)

35

Good critical thinking is a cognitive skill. In general, developing a skill requires three conditions—learning the theory, deliberate practice, and adopting the right attitudes.

(A) However, your attitudes make a big difference as to whether your practice is effective and sustainable. If you hate playing the piano, forcing you to practice is not productive in the long run.

(B) However, knowing the theory is not the same as being able to apply it. You might know in theory that you should balance the bike when you are cycling, but it does not mean you can actually do it. This is where practice comes in, because it translates your theoretical knowledge into actual ability.

(C) By theory we mean the rules and facts we have to know in order to possess the skill. For example, one cannot be a good basketball player without knowing the rules of the game—for example, kicking the basketball is not allowed. Likewise, thinking critically requires knowing a certain amount of logic.

① (A)-(C)-(B)　　② (B)-(A)-(C)　　③ (B)-(C)-(A)
④ (C)-(A)-(B)　　⑤ (C)-(B)-(A)

36

In regard to problem solving, imagery can be used to help solve problems that one could not easily solve using verbal reasoning.

(A) She then realizes that after driving to Washington, traveling to Chicago and then to Buffalo before returning to New York City will save her many hours of driving.

(B) For example, a salesperson who lives in New York City has to drive to three cities, Washington, DC; Buffalo; and Chicago. If she plans to travel to the cities in that order and then return to New York City, she might not be traveling the shortest route.

(C) Hence, she might image a map of the United States and make several virtual trips in her mind's eye. She realizes if she travels to Buffalo after visiting Washington and then after visiting Buffalo travels to Chicago and back to New York, she would be partially retracing her path.

① (A)-(C)-(B)   ② (B)-(A)-(C)   ③ (B)-(C)-(A)
④ (C)-(A)-(B)   ⑤ (C)-(B)-(A)

[37~38] 다음 글의 내용을 한 문장으로 요약하고자 한다. 빈칸 (A), (B)에 들어갈 말로 가장 적절한 것은?

37

To be really smart, an online group needs to obey one final rule—and a rather counterintuitive one. The members can't have too much contact with one another. To work best, the members of a collective group ought to be able to think and work independently. This rule came to light in 1958, when social scientists tested different techniques of brainstorming. They posed a thought-provoking question: If humans had an extra thumb on each hand, what benefits and problems would emerge? Then they had two different types of groups brainstorm answers. In one group, the members worked face-to-face; in the other group, the members each worked independently, then pooled their answers at the end. You might expect the people working face-to-face to be more productive, but that wasn't the case. The team with independently working members produced almost twice as many ideas. Traditional brainstorming simply doesn't work as well as thinking alone, then pooling results.

⬇

In brainstorming, group members who have direct contact produce ___(A)___ ideas than those who work physically separately from one another, which is against our ___(B)___ .

	(A)		(B)		(A)		(B)
①	fewer	·····	intuition	②	fewer	·····	benefit
③	more	·····	conclusion	④	more	·····	intuition
⑤	smarter	·····	benefit				

38

Soon after the first computers appeared, their blunders became the subjects of jokes. The tiniest errors in programming could wipe out clients' bank accounts, or send out bills for outlandish amounts, or trap the computers in cyclical loops that kept repeating the same mistakes. This maddening lack of common sense led most of their users to conclude that machines could never become intelligent. Today, of course, computers do better. Some programs can beat people at chess. Others can diagnose heart attacks. But no machine yet can make a bed, or read a book, or babysit. What makes our computers unable to do the sorts of things that most people can do? Do they need more memory, speed, or complexity? Do they use the wrong kinds of instruction-sets? Or do machines lack some magical attribute that only a human brain can possess? I will argue that none of those are responsible for the deficiencies of today's machines; instead, all those limitations come from the out-of-date ways in which programmers have chosen to program them.

* blunder: 큰 실수

⬇

Although early computers had significant errors, modern machines ___(A)___ at tasks like chess and medical diagnosis but struggle with basic human activities due to outdated programming rather than inherent technological ___(B)___ .

	(A)		(B)		(A)		(B)
①	fail	‥‥‥	problems	②	excel	‥‥‥	limitations
③	malfunction	‥‥‥	problems	④	succeed	‥‥‥	advances
⑤	stare	‥‥‥	limitations				

[39~40] 다음 글을 읽고, 물음에 답하시오.

Pompeii was destroyed by the catastrophic eruption of Mount Vesuvius in 79 A.D., entombing residents under layers of volcanic ash. But there is more to this story of an ancient Roman city's doom. Research published in the journal *Frontiers in Earth Science* offers proof that Pompeii was simultaneously wrecked by a massive earthquake. The discovery establishes a new timeline for the city's collapse and shows that fresh approaches to research can (a) reveal additional secrets from well-studied archaeological sites. Researchers have always had an idea that seismic activity contributed to the city's destruction. The ancient writer Pliny the Younger reported that the eruption of Vesuvius had been accompanied by violent shaking. But, until now, no evidence had been discovered to (b) support this historical account. A team of researchers led by Domenico Sparice from Italy decided to investigate this (c) gap in the record. Dr. Sparice said that excavations of Pompeii to date had not included experts in the field of archaeoseismology, which deals with the effects of earthquakes on ancient buildings. Contributions from (d) specialists in this area were key to the discovery, he said. "The effects of seismicity have been speculated by past scholars, but no factual evidence has been reported before our study," Dr. Sparice said, adding that the finding was "very exciting." The team focused on the Insula of the Chaste Lovers. This area encompasses several buildings, including a bakery and a house where painters were evidently interrupted by the eruption, leaving their paintings (e) colored. After excavation and careful analysis, the researchers concluded that walls in the insula had collapsed because of an earthquake.

* seismic: 지진의 ** excavation: 발굴

39 윗글의 제목으로 가장 적절한 것은?

① Who Found Pompeii Covered with Volcanic Ashes
② Mt. Vesuvius's Influence on the Scenery of Pompeii
③ The Eruption of Mt. Vesuvius Triggered by Earthquake
④ Seismic Timeline by Archaeological Discovery in Pompeii
⑤ The Eruption of Mt. Vesuvius Wasn't Pompeii's Only Killer

40 밑줄 친 (a)~(e) 중, 문맥상 낱말의 쓰임이 적절하지 않은 것은?   [3점]

① (a)　　② (b)　　③ (c)　　④ (d)　　⑤ (e)

[41~42] 다음 글을 읽고, 물음에 답하시오.

Personality is one of those parts of the human condition that is obvious in everyday life. Each of us is unique and it is the study of personality that stresses this uniqueness, whereas much of the remainder of psychology emphasises similarities between people. Some parts of personality appear to be built in and others appear to be learned. Certainly, personality is also influenced by culture, either through environmental necessity or through beliefs, values, opinions and judgements.

Whichever way that personality is looked at or theorised about, it is clear that it does not exist in a vacuum. A person may be made up of an id, an ego and a superego, or of an actualising self, or of a series of learned social behaviours, or of a set of traits. Whichever of these it might be occurs within a context or a series of situations or experiences, no two of which are the same. So the best way to look at personality in general, or at someone's personality in particular, is through the eyes of _____. People cannot exist without their environment, each influencing the other. It is therefore best to make sense of personality as it exists in its particular environment. Personality cannot exist in isolation.

41 윗글의 제목으로 가장 적절한 것은?

① How Does Personality Develop as One Grows Older?
② Gender Differences in Personality and Social Behaviour
③ Understanding Personality: Uniqueness, Culture, and Context
④ Personality, One Factor That Determines Your Social Behaviours
⑤ What Are the Similarities between Personality and Characteristics?

42 윗글의 빈칸에 들어갈 말로 가장 적절한 것은? [3점]

① emotion　　　　② creativity　　　　③ usefulness
④ interaction　　　⑤ productivity

[43~45] 다음 글을 읽고, 물음에 답하시오.

(A)

Sophia leaned against the brick wall of North High, tracing the graffiti with her fingers. The final bell had rung, and students were leaving quickly. She looked around for her older sister Sara but couldn't find her. With a sigh, (a) she started walking home. Next week was the school talent show, and she had signed up to sing. She loved singing but had never sung in front of a big audience before.

(B)

Sophia's eyes widened. "Really? That'd be amazing!" They spent the next hour planning and practicing. When they finally said goodbye, Sophia felt more confident because Janet helped her a lot. As she walked home, the evening sun made the town look golden. She realized that unexpected moments and new friends could make everything better. The talent show was no longer something to be scared of but a chance for (b) her to shine.

(C)

As Sophia walked, she was lost in thought and didn't notice Janet, the senior class president, until she was right in front of her. Janet and Sara knew each other, but Sophia had never talked to her before. "Hey, Sophia," Janet said with a big smile. "Hi, Janet. What's up?" (c) she replied, feeling surprised. "I heard you signed up for the talent show," Janet said. "What are you going to sing?" Sophia felt nervous. "I'm not sure yet," (d) she said. "I'm still deciding." Janet smiled again. "Want to grab a coffee and talk about it?"

(D)

They walked to a local café and talked about school and music. Janet was easy to talk to, and Sophia felt more relaxed with (e) her. "What kind of music do you like?" Janet asked. "I love classic rock," Sophia said. "So, I'm thinking about doing an acoustic version of classic rock." Janet's eyes lit up. "That sounds perfect. I play a bit of guitar; maybe I could play with you?"

43 주어진 글 (A)에 이어질 내용을 순서에 맞게 배열한 것으로 가장 적절한 것은?

① (B)-(D)-(C) ② (C)-(B)-(D) ③ (C)-(D)-(B)
④ (D)-(B)-(C) ⑤ (D)-(C)-(B)

44 밑줄 친 (a)~(e) 중, 가리키는 대상이 나머지 넷과 다른 것은?

① (a) ② (b) ③ (c) ④ (d) ⑤ (e)

45 윗글에 관한 내용으로 적절하지 <u>않은</u> 것은?

① Sophia signed up to sing in the school talent show.
② Sophia felt more confident after practicing with Janet.
③ Sophia's sister and Janet knew each other.
④ Sophia was thinking about singing a classic rock song.
⑤ Sophia taught Janet how to play the guitar.

사주만에 다끝내는 리얼 문제집 [국영수]

수능/사관학교/경찰대학/1등급 대비

영어 독해 고난도 200제

정답 및 해설

국순엄 저

씨마스

목 차

Chapter I

글의 핵심 이해

1. 글의 주제

정답

001 ④	002 ①	003 ②	004 ③	005 ⑤
006 ④	007 ④	008 ②	009 ④	010 ⑤
011 ⑤				

001

정답 ④

[지문 해석] 가치라는 말에 두 가지 의미가 있음을 언급할 필요가 있다. 그것이 때로는 특정 물건의 효용성을 나타낼 때도 있고 그 특정 물건을 소유함으로써 가지게 되는, 다른 물건의 구매력을 의미할 때도 있다. 전자를 '사용가치' 후자를 '교환가치'로 각각 부를 수 있다. 사용가치가 아주 큰 물건이 교환가치가 거의 없거나 전혀 없는 경우도 많고 반대로 교환가치가 아주 큰 물건이 사용가치가 거의 없거나 전혀 없는 경우도 많다. 물보다 효용이 큰 물건은 없지만 물을 팔아 구매할 수 있는 것은 거의 없다. 그것을 주고 손에 넣을 수 있는 것이 거의 없다는 말이다. 반면에 다이아몬드는 효용성 면에서 가치가 없지만 그것을 팔면 엄청나게 많은 다른 상품을 살 수 있다.

① 상품의 본질적 효용성에 값하는 가치
② 구매력에 해당하는 가치
③ 상품의 효용성과 가치의 관계
④ 사용가치와 교환가치의 비교
⑤ 상품의 실질 가치를 높이기 위한 제안

[글의 소재] 사용가치와 교환가치

[주요 어휘] observe 관찰하다, 언급하다, utility 효용성, scarcely 거의 ~하지 않다

[구조 분석] ⊙ sometimes the power of purchasing other goods which the possession of that object conveys.

➜ that object는 앞 문장의 some particular object를 가리키고 which의 선행사는 power이다.

⊙ Nothing is more useful than water

➜ 부정의 비교급으로 최상급을 표시한 문장이다. 원급 비교나 최상급 비교 구문으로 바꾸면 Water is as useful as any other things=Water is the most useful of all things이 된다.

[정답 해설] 'The things which have the greatest value in use have frequently little or no value in exchange; and, on the contrary, those which have the greatest value in exchange have frequently little or no value in use.'로 보았을 때, 이 글은 상품 가치의 두 가지 의미 즉, 사용가치와 교환가치의 차이점을 비교 설명하고 있음을 알 수 있다. 따라서 정답은 ④이다.

002

정답 ①

[지문 해석] 비버가 설치류, 즉 쥐과에 속하는데도 대부분의 사람들은 비버를 귀엽고 심지어 매력적인 동물로 생각한다. 개나 박쥐처럼 비버도 포악해져서 접근하면 누구든 공격할 수 있다는 사실을 많은 사람들이 모른다. 2013년도에 동유럽의 벨라루스 출신의 한 어부가 시골 길가에 비버 한 마리가 서 있는 것을 발견했다. 사진을 찍으려고 접근하자 비버는 어부의 넓적다리를 물어 버렸다. 안타깝게도 그는 친구들의 지혈을 받지 못해 과다출혈로 사망했다. 역시 2003년 벨라루스에서 포악한 비버가 그를 헛간에서 쫓아내려던 농부 두 명을 물었다. 포악한 비버는 고향 가까이에(즉 미국 국내에서) 나타나기도 한다. 2012년도에 83세의 할머니가 워싱턴의 한 호수에서 수영하다가 포악한 비버의 공격을 받았다. 비버는 2피트 길이에 몸무게는 34파운드였다. 두 명의 젊은 여자도 버지니아 호수에서 수영하다가 비버의 공격을 받기도 했다.

① 사람을 공격하는 포악한 동물 비버
② 비버의 공격을 피하는 최선의 방법
③ 비버가 포악한 동물로 변한 이유
④ 설치류 동물의 일반적 특징
⑤ 비버를 무해한 동물로 생각하는 사람들의 오해

[글의 소재] 비버

[주요 어휘] beaver 비버, appealing 매력적인, rodent 설치류의, rabid 포악한, spot 발견하다, stem 지혈하다, bleed to death 과다출혈로 숨지다, chase 쫓다, barn 헛간

[글의 흐름] ⊙ 주제문은 'beavers can become rabid and attack anyone who come near them.'이고 두괄식 구조이다.

[구조 분석] ⊙ the beaver bit him on the thigh.

➜ bite A on the B 구문이다. A는 무는 대상, B는 구체적인 신체 기관이 온다.

⊙ And rabid beavers can turn up closer to home as well.

➜ 여기서 home은 독자인 미국인의 home 가까이, 즉 미국 내에서도 일어난다는 말이다.

[정답 해설] 'Many people just don't realize that, like dogs and bats, beavers can become rabid and attack anyone who come near them.'에서 알 수 있듯이, 이 글은 비버가 일반의 상식과는 달리 포악하고 사람을 공격할 수 있는 동물이라는 사실을 전달하고 있다. 이어지는 내용은 이러한 사실에 대한 구체적인 사례들이다. 따라서 정답은 ①이 타당하다.

003

지문 해석 시베리아의 수렵채취인인 Kitoi족들은 개를 귀하게 여겼음이 확실하다. Kitoi족과 그들이 키웠던 개들은 같은 음식을 먹고 같은 기생충을 가졌을 뿐만 아니라 바이칼 호숫가의 공동묘지에 함께 묻혔다. "Kitoi족은 정교한 매장 전통을 가지고 있었고 그것을 개에게까지 적용했다. 그들은 개를 사람처럼 대우했다"라고 앨버타대학의 고고학자 Robert Losey씨는 말한다. 과연 어떤 곳에서는 사랑하는 개의 공간을 마련하기 위해 무덤 파는 인부가 사람의 유해를 한 쪽에 치워놓는 일도 있었다. "개 한 마리가 네 개의 고라니 이빨로 엮어 만든, Kitoi족들이 이용하던 같은 목걸이를 건 채로 매장됐고 다른 개는 숟갈을 찔러 넣은 채로, 그리고 어떤 개들은 석기와 함께 발견됐다"고 Losey씨는 말한다. 개들의 자세도 세심하게 배려됐다. 머리를 앞발 위에 조아린 채 웅크린 자세를 하고 있는 개가 있는가 하면 옆으로 돌돌 말아 잠자는 자세를 취한 개들도 있었다. 두 마리는 성인 남자와 함께 매장됐는데 그중 하나는 오른쪽에 돌린 채로 다른 하나는 왼쪽에 각각 위치했다. "사람이 동물과 밀접한 정서적 유대를 느낄 때만이 이런 식으로 행동하는데 Kitoi족은 키우던 개들에 대해 이런 식이었다. 개도 가족 구성원이었으며 죽어서도 그렇게 대우받았다"라고 Losey씨는 말한다.

① 한 시베리아 부족의 개를 이용한 생존 전략
② 시베리아 한 종족의 매장 풍습에 나타난 인간과 개의 밀접한 관계
③ 시베리아 종족에서 유일하게 발견되는 개 매장 풍습
④ 같은 음식 전통을 공유하는 인간과 개에 대한 고찰
⑤ 인간과 개를 함께 매장하는 시베리아 풍습 분석

글의 소재 키토이족의 지독한 개 사랑

주요 어휘 red deer 고라니, hunter-gatherer 수렵채취인, prize 귀하게 여기다, parasite 기생충, mortuary 매장의, gravedigger 무덤 파는 인부, make room for ~를 위한 공간을 마련하다, pendant 늘어뜨린 장식, tuck 찔러 넣다, crouch 웅크리다, rest on ~에 기대다, paw 앞발, curl 돌돌 말다

글의 흐름 ⊙ 시베리아 키토이 부족과 개 사이의 밀접한 관계를 매장 풍습을 통해 예증하는 글이다. 'Certainly, the Kitoi hunter-gatherers of Siberia prized their dogs.'이 주제문이며 두괄식 구조다. 주제문과 이에 대한 뒷받침 진술의 형식을 취하고 있다.

구조 분석 ⊙ Some were placed in a crouching pose with their heads resting on their paws

➡ with는 부대 상황을 나타내며 their heads가 with의 목적어, resting on their paws가 목적격 보어이다. 그들의 머리를 앞발에 조아린 채로.

⊙ and the Kitoi clearly did with their dogs.

➡ did는 대동사로 앞의 'have close emotional bonds'를 받

는다.

정답 해설 글의 흐름 분석에서도 살폈듯이 이 글은 시베리아 키토이 부족과 개 사이의 밀접한 관계를 매장 풍습을 통해 예증하는 글이다. 따라서 정답은 ②이다.

004

지문 해석 E-Marketer에 의하면 1999년 휴가기간 동안 약 3천 4백만 명이 적어도 한 번은 온라인상에서 구매했다. 웹 사용자들은 종종 인터넷 정보 검색이 익명의 프로세스라는 잘못된 믿음에 빠진다. 실제로 폭발적인 전자상거래에는 갈수록 정교해지는 정보 수집 기술이 따른다. 고객 보호를 위한 적절한 안전장치가 마련된다면 고객 정보 수집이 본질적으로 비윤리적인 것은 아님이 확실하다. 상업이 시작된 이래로 재래식 가게의 주인들은 단골손님들에 대한 정보를 수집해 왔다. 그러나 정교한 기술 발달로 고객에 대한 세부 정보가 전례 없는 규모로 수집, 전파, 결합되는 것이 가능해짐에 따라 정보 수집 과정이 돌이킬 수 없게 바뀌었다.

① 잠재적 과소비 원인으로서의 e 마케팅
② 인터넷 검색을 조장하는 익명성
③ e 마케팅에서 정보 수집의 심각성
④ 전자상거래를 촉진시키는 기술 발전
⑤ 전통적 마케팅에 나타난 정보 수집

글의 소재 e 마케팅에서의 정보 수집

주요 어휘 lull ~ into 안심시켜 ~하게 만들다, anonymous 익명의, be accompanied by ~이 따르다, inherently 태생적으로, 본질적으로, safeguard 안전장치, bricks-and-mortar 실제 매장이 존재하는, 오프라인의, 재래식의, regular customer 단골손님, irrevocably 돌이킬 수 없게, sophisticated 정교한, 복잡한, dissemination 전파, unprecedented 전례 없는

글의 흐름 ⊙ 주제문은 맨 마지막 문장 'However, what has irrevocably altered this information gathering process is the growth of sophisticated technology that enables the collection, dissemination, and combination of detailed information on customers at previously unprecedented levels.'으로 미괄식 구조이다. 일반적으로 however같은 역접의 연결사로 이어질 경우 그 이어지는 문장이 주제문일 가능성이 크다.

구조 분석 ⊙ Clearly there is nothing inherently unethical in gathering information on customers

➡ Clearly는 문장 전체 수식 부사이다. It is clear that~로 바꿀 수 있다.

정답 해설 글의 흐름 분석에서 제시한 주제문에서 알 수 있듯이 이 글은 전자 상거래에서의 고객 정보 수집이 기술 발달과 함께 점점 심각한 수준에 이르고 있음을 지적한 글이므로 주제는 ③이 타당하다.

005

지문 해석 "노동 계급을 만족시키는 것은 정부의 의무이므로 정당화시킬 수 없는 건... 에~.."(긴 침묵)

1904년 4월 22일 윈스턴 처칠은 영국 하원에서 연설하고 있었다. 그는 노동조합에 대해 한 시간 가까이 연설하고 있었는데 갑자기 생각의 흐름이 끊겼다. 그는 시간을 끌며 생각해 보았으나 연설을 끝마칠 수 없었다. 그는 연설을 경청해 준 데 대해 좌중에 감사의 인사를 하고 자리에 앉아 얼굴을 손으로 감쌌다. 그때까지 그는 연설을 통째로 암기하는 버릇이 있었다. 그러나 이 일이 있은 뒤부터 처칠은 방대한 양의 주석과 여러 번의 수정을 가한 연설 작성법을 만들기로 마음먹었다. 이 연설 작성법은 수필집 'The Scaffolding of Rhetoric'에 적힌 대로 스물세 살의 처칠이 꿈꿔 왔던, 그리고 후에 그의 명성을 높여 준 바로 그 힘 있고 장엄한 웅변술이 세상에 나오는 데 도움을 주었다. 그래서 여러 면에서 처칠의 놀라운 웅변술의 탄생은 그날 하원에서의 작은 실수에서 비롯된 것이다. 당시 그는, 종종 간과되기는 하지만 그의 인생에서 가장 중요한 연설로 추앙받는 연설을 하고 있었다.

① 젊은 처칠이 경험한 좌절의 순간
② 처칠의 캐리어를 날릴 수도 있었던 치명적 연설
③ 대중 앞에서 큰 봉변을 당하고도 무사할 수 있는 비결
④ 망친 의회 연설에서 처칠이 얻어낸 것
⑤ 처칠을 명연설가로 바꾼 끔찍하지만 고마운 실수

글의 소재 처칠을 명연설가로 재탄생시킨 '망친' 연설

주요 어휘 lie with ~의 의무이다, address ~에게 연설하다, House of Commons 영국 하원, trade union 노동조합, for a better part of =almost, train 죽 이어진 것, stall 시간을 끌다, be in the habit of ~ing ~한 버릇이 들다, from this point forward =from then on, 그때부터 내내, forge 구축하다, copious 방대한, awe-inspiring 경외심을 불러일으키는, oratory 웅변술, envision 꿈꾸다, 바라다, scaffolding 비계, 뼈대, overlook 간과하다, revere 숭앙하다

구조 분석 ⊙ when he suddenly lost his train of thought.

➔ 이때 when =and then이며 결과로 해석한다.

⊙ It was this system which helped create the powerful and awe-inspiring oratory which Churchill had envisioned as a 23-year-old in 'The Scaffolding of Rhetoric' and for which Churchill has become famous.

➔ It was this system which helped는 It that 강조 구문에서 that 대신 which를 쓴 경우이다. as a 23-year-old에서 'a 23-year-old'는 명사구로 쓰여 '23살의 청년'을 뜻한다. 'The Scaffolding of Rhetoric'는 처칠이 쓴 수필집 제목이다. for which Churchill has become famous에서 which의 선행사는 oratory다.

정답 해설 이 글은 처칠이 젊은 시절 의회에서 경험한 연설 실수가 후일 명연설가로 탄생하는 데 결정적인 역할을 했다는 게 주 내용이므로 ⑤가 정답에 가장 가깝다.

006

지문 해석 많은 미국 교도소에서 장기적인 독방 수감이 일반적인 관행이 된 것은 징역형에 관한 한 사회적 고립이 특별히 가혹하거나 고통스럽지 않다고 여겨지기 때문이다. 그러나 일군의 정신병학자들은 이와는 다른 견해를 갖는데 그들은 장기간 독방 수감이 파괴적이고 지속적인 심리적 효과를 가져오는 참을 수 없는 고문이라고 생각한다. 2011년 캘리포니아주 하원 안전위원회의 한 청문회에서 테리 쿠퍼스 박사는 교도소에서 일어나는 모든 자살의 절반이 최고의 보안시설에서 장기간 홀로 수감된 죄수들에 의해 저질러진다고 지적했다. 그의 시각에서 봤을 때 이런 자살은, 죄수들이 화장실 크기의 방에서 사람과의 접촉 없이 하루 23시간을 보내야 하는 유독한 환경이 빚은 결과다. 장기간 고립의 정신병리학적 영향을 10년 동안 연구해 온 매사추세츠의 정신병학자 스튜어트 그라시안은 이런 관행에 대한 쿠퍼스 박사의 평가에 동의한다. 장기간 고립이 징역형 리스트에서 사라져야 할 고문의 일종이라고 그라시안은 주장한다.

① 사회적 고립이 유효한 대안이 될 수 있는 이유
② 교도소 내 자살을 효과적으로 예방하기 위한 제안
③ 징역형 폐지에 대한 옹호
④ 장기 독방 수감의 유독성 부작용
⑤ 사회적 고립의 치유 효과

글의 소재 장기 독방 수감의 폐해

주요 어휘 extended 장기적인, solitary confinement 독방 수감, prison punishment 징역형, social isolation 사회적 고립, psychiatrist 정신병학자, unbearable 참을 수 없는, devastating 황폐화시키는, perspective 시각, 관점, toxic 유독성의, echo 맞장구치다, 동의하다, assessment 평가, eliminate 제거하다

글의 흐름 ⊙ 주제문은 'solitary confinement for extended periods of time is unbearable torture, bound to have devastating and long lasting psychological effects' 중괄식 구조로 볼 수 있다. 역접의 접속사 however를 포함하는 문장이 주제문일 경우가 많다.

구조 분석 ⊙ as prison punishments go

➔ as far as prison punishments are concerned나 when it comes to prison punishments로 바꿀 수 있다.

⊙ in cells the size of the closets

➔ A the size of B 구문이다. =A which is as big as B. 'B 크기의 A'의 뜻이다. A와 the size 사이에 아무 전치사가 없음을 유의하라.

정답 해설 이 글은 장기간의 독방 감금이 죄수들에게 미치는 부정적인 영향을 관련 학자 두 명의 증언과 함께 지적하고 있다. 그러므로 이 글의 주제로는 ④가 타당하다.

007
정답 ④

지문 해석 교육에는 적극적인 목적이 있어서는 안 되고 단지 자발적인 발달에 적합한 환경을 제공하는 데서 그쳐야 한다고 말하는 사람들이 있다. 나는 지나치게 개인주의적이고 지식의 중요성에 무관심한 그들에게 동의하지 않는다. 우리가 사는 공동체는 협력을 필요로 하는데 모든 필수적인 협력이 자발적 충동에서 나오리라고 기대하는 것은 지나치게 낙관적이다. 제한된 면적 안에 많은 인구가 거주하는 것이 가능한 것은 과학과 기술 덕분이다. 따라서 교육은 필요한 최소한의 과학과 기술을 전수해야 한다. 최대한의 자유를 허용하자는 교육자들은 선행과 자제, 훈련된 지성에 성공을 의존하지만 충동이 억제되지 않는 상태에서 그런 것들이 생성되기 어렵다. 그러므로 그들이 강경한 입장을 고수하는 한 그들의 강점은 오래 지속되기 어렵다. 교육은 단지 성장의 기회를 제공하는 것 이상의 적극적인 것이어야 한다. 물론 성장의 기회를 제공해야 하지만 어린이들이 스스로 얻지 못하는 정신적, 도덕적 자질 또한 제공해야 한다.

- ① 교육에서 자연스러운 충동의 역할
- ② 성공의 기회를 제공하는 도구로서의 교육
- ③ 자유에 근거한 교육의 장점
- ④ 보다 적극적이고 목적이 분명한 교육의 필요성
- ⑤ 확대일로의 과학 기술 시대에 걸맞은 교육

글의 소재 보다 적극적인 교육의 필요성

주요 어휘 suitable for ~에 적합한, spontaneous 자연발생적인, unduly 과도하게, undiluted 희석되지 않은, 강경 입장을 고수하는, equipment 장치, 소양, 자질

글의 흐름 마지막 두 문장 'Education must be something more positive than a mere opportunity for growth. It must, of course, provide this, but it must also provide a mental and moral equipment which children cannot acquire entirely for themselves.'이 주제문인 미괄식 구조이다.

구조 분석 ⊙ Education must be something more positive than a mere opportunity for growth. It must, of course, provide this,

→ this는 근칭대명사로서 앞 문장에서 가까운 것, 즉 a mere opportunity for growth를 가리킨다.

정답 해설 마지막 두 문장에서 알 수 있듯이 이 글은 자유와 자연스러운 충동에 근거한 교육의 한계점을 지적하고 교육은 보다 적극적이고 목적이 분명해야 한다고 주장하고 있다. 따라서 ④가 주제에 가장 가깝다.

008
정답 ②

지문 해석 인구가 많은 사회일수록 그리고 현대로 내려올수록 종교의 위로 기능이 커져 갔다. 그런 사회일수록 우리에게 더 많은 나쁜 일들이 가해져 위로를 구할 수밖에 없기 때문이다. 이러한 종교의 위로 기능은, 불행이 보다 많은 사람들을 종교적이게 한다든지 사회적 빈곤층이나 빈곤한 지역이나 국가가 부유한 집단보다 더 종교적인 경향이 있다는 빈번한 언급을 설명하는 데 도움을 준다. 그들이 위로를 더 필요로 한다는 것이다. 오늘날 세계 국가 중 GDP 1만 달러 미만의 대부분 나라에서는 종교가 그들의 일상 삶의 중요한 일부라고 말하는 시민의 비율이 80~99%에 이르지만 GDP 3만 달러 이상의 나라에서 그 숫자는 17~43%에 불과하다. 미국 국내만 보더라도 부유한 지역에는 교회를 세우고 다닐 수 있는 자원과 자유 시간이 풍부한데도 불구하고 가난한 지역에 교회가 더 많고 교회 다니는 사람이 더 많은 것으로 나타난다. 미국 사회에서 최고의 종교적 헌신과 급진적인 기독교 종파가 발견되는 곳은 소외되고 불우한 사회그룹이다.

- ① 언제 어디서든 위로를 구하는 인간의 본능적 욕구
- ② 종교의 중요한 모티브로서의 불행과 위로
- ③ 종교 성향에 부정적 영향을 주는 경제적 풍요
- ④ 종교적 기회 부족에 시달리는 빈곤 지역
- ⑤ 빈곤국과 부유국의 대조적인 종교 현실

글의 소재 종교적 모티브로서의 인간 불행

주요 어휘 crave 갈망하다, strata stratum의 복수, 계층, marginalize 소외시키다, affluence 풍족함, destitute 궁핍한

글의 흐름 ⊙ 주제문은 'This comforting role of religion helps explain the frequent observation that misfortune tends to make people more religious, and that poorer social strata, regions, and countries tend to be more religious than richer ones : they need more comforting.'이다.

구조 분석 ⊙ the frequent observation that misfortune tends to make people more religious,

→ 'the frequent observation that ~'는 '~라는 빈번한 언급'이라는 뜻으로, 여기서 that은 동격의 that이다.

정답 해설 이 글은 인간에게 닥친 불행이 위로를 구하게 하고 그런 노력이 종교 귀의로 나타난다는 사실을 구체적 사례와 함께 논증하고 있다. 따라서 이 글의 주제는 ② 종교의 중요한 모티브로서의 불행과 위로라고 말할 수 있다.

009
정답 ④

지문 해석 사건으로서의 교육에서 개인적 만남은 교육적 경험의 정중앙에 위치한다. 카라바조의 그림 '성마테오의 부름'에서

교육은 곤경에 처한 사람들이 만날 때 시작된다. 스승은 모방의 영감을 불어넣고 평생 동반자가 된다. 카라바조는 그의 걸작에서 교육적 만남의 본질을 스승을 따르도록 부름을 받았을 때의 놀라움, 믿기 어려움, 그리고 즐거움으로 묘사한다. 그것은 미지의 세계로 향하는 통로이고 이 통로는 진리의 드러남으로 나타난다. 이런 만남을 의도적으로 애매모호함의 영역에 위치시키면서 카라바조는 부름을 받은 사람에게 스스로 한계를 넘어가며 부름에 응하게 하는 그런 개인적 만남의 의미를 강조한다. 이런 부름에 직면했을 때 요청되는 것은 대답인데 그것은 가장 직접적인 책임의 표현이다. 스승은 제자의 세계에 진정한 빛을 가져다준다. 서로 다른 세계가 부딪치며 새로운 삶의 방식이 약속되는 것이다. 이러한 새로움은 상상해서 이론적으로 세워지는 것이 아니라 철저하게 실행되는 것이다.

[글의 소재] 교육에서 만남의 중요성

[주요 어휘] situate 위치하게 하다, depict 묘사하다, disbelief 불신, 믿기 어려움, opening 통로, deliberate 의도적인, relevance 관련성, 의미, transgress 한계를 넘다, 어기다, in the face of ~에 직면하여, collision 충돌, live out 실행하다

[글의 흐름] 첫 문장 'Education as an event situates personal encounter in the very center of the educational experience.'가 주제문이고 Caravaggio의 그림을 예로 들어 주제를 뒷받침하는 두괄식 구조다.

[구조 분석] ⊙ In his masterpiece, Caravaggio depicts the essence of the educational encounter as a surprise, disbelief, and overwhelming joy of being called to follow the teacher.

→ 'depict A as B'는 'A를 B로 묘사하다'를 의미하며 'of being called to follow the teacher'는 surprise와 disbelief, overwhelming joy에 모두 걸리는 공통 전치사구이다.

[정답 해설] 이 글은 교육에 있어서 개인적 만남, 스승과 제자와의 만남의 중요성을 카라바조의 그림을 예로 들어 설명하고 있다. 따라서 정답은 ④의 '교육에서 개인적 만남의 중요성'이다. 주제문인 첫 문장에서 개인적 만남의 중요성의 힌트를 얻을 수 있다.
① 교육의 영역에서 발견되는 기쁨
② 종교적 회화에 숨어있는 교육적 모티브
③ 스승과 제자와의 이상적 관계
④ 교육에서 개인적 만남의 중요성
⑤ 교육에서 종교적 영감의 의미

010
[정답 ⑤]

[지문 해석] 유아는 서로 다른 정서 반응도를 가지고 태어나며 그것은 그들의 돌봄 환경에 영향을 미친다. 사람들은 흔히 반응도가 높은 아기를 시끄럽고 어렵다고 말하고 반응이 크지 않은 아기는 다루기 쉽다고 말한다. 시끄러운 아기는 좀처럼 울지 않는 아기보다 돌보미에게게 더 많은 좌절을 이끌어낼 수 있다.

또한, 시끄러운 아기가 울면 그 아기는 좀처럼 울지 않는 아기와는 다른 반응을 그의 돌보미로부터 이끌어낼 수 있다. 톰슨과 캐시디 등이 가정한 기질에 대한 동적인 견해에 의하면, 아기의 정서적 표현 능력에 대한 돌보미 반응의 양과 질의 차이가 아기의 다음 정서적 표현을 결정지을 가능성이 있다고 한다. 결국, 아기가 감정을 표현하는 방식이 부모로부터 더 큰 정서적 사회화를 이끌어내는 것이다. 따라서 시끄러운 아기는 부모로부터 더 큰 개인적 고통의 표현을 이끌어내고 이것은 아기의 부정적 정서성을 높일 수 있는 반면 아기의 울음에 위로 섞인 반응을 하는 다른 부모는 아기의 부정적 정서성을 낮출 수 있다.
① 유아 각자에게 고유한 서로 다른 정서 반응도
② 크게 우는 아기가 더 좋은 대우를 받는다는 사실
③ 돌보미가 개인적 고통을 표현하는 데 따르는 위험성
④ 돌보미가 유아와 적정 거리를 유지하는 데 따르는 장점
⑤ 정서적 영향을 주고받는 유아와 돌보미

[글의 소재] 유아와 돌보미의 상호 영향

[주요 어휘] reactivity 반응, fussy 시끄러운, 까다로운, elicit 이끌어내다, posit 가정하다, expressivity 표현성, 표현 능력, subsequent 차후의, 다음의, in turn 차례차례로, 결국, distress 고통, 스트레스, emotionality 정서성, keep ~ at arm's length 거리를 두고 지내다

[글의 흐름] ⊙ 주제문은 'Thus, a fussy infant might elicit greater expression of personal distress from a parent, which may increase the infants' negative emotionality over time, whereas another parent who responds to the infants' crying with comforting may decrease the infants' negative emotionality.'이고 미괄식 구조이다. Thus 같은 결론/요약의 연결사가 들어있는 문장이 주제문일 가능성이 크다.

[구조 분석] ⊙ People often refer to highly reactive infants as fussy or difficult and (refer to) infants who are not reactive as easygoing.

→ refer to A as B 구문으로, 'A를 B라 말하다'라는 뜻이다. 이 구문이 두 번 연속해서 나온다.

⊙ a fussy baby might elicit a different response from his or her caregiver upon crying than an infant who rarely cries.

→ from ~은 response에 걸려 '~에서 나오는 반응'으로 해석한다. than은 different와 연동된다. 원래는 different ~ from 이지만 최신 영어에서는 from 대신 than을 쓰는 경우가 많다.

[정답 해설] 이 글은 유아와 돌보는 사람이 서로의 감정적 표현에 따라 반응하며, 따라서 정서 형성에 상호 영향을 주고받는다는 내용이므로 정답은 ⑤가 타당하다.

011
[정답 ⑤]

[지문 해석] 명상은 야비한 트윗과 얼빠진 부족주의 정신을 치료

하는 만병통치가 결코 아니다. 나는 수년째 명상을 해오고 있지만 최근 대선 후보 토론을 보다가 스트레스를 받아 패밀리 사이즈 팝콘 한 통을 그만 다 먹어 버렸다. 얼마나 몰입했는지 나중에 발 주변에 팝콘 부스러기가 어지럽게 떨어진 것을 보고서야 내가 무슨 짓을 했는지 알 정도였다. 그럼에도 불구하고 나는 명상이 이 불만과 분열의 계절을 견디는 데 도움이 된다는 것을 확신한다. 분노에 눈이 멀면 당신은 당신이 동의하지 않는 사람의 견해를 이해하기 어렵다. 일관성 있는 명상 수련은 당신의 편견을 알아채는 데 도움이 된다. 뮬러 특별검사의 수사가 백악관으로 한발 한발 다가설수록 당신의 가슴이 벅차지는 않은지, 또는 '진보의 눈물'이라는 문구를 아로새긴 머그잔을 가지고 있지는 않은지 알게 된다. 부족의 본능을 좀 더 깨달을수록 당신은 이념의 좁은 방에서 과감히 벗어나 반대 의견을 주의 깊게 들을 수 있다. 자기도 모르게 고약한 트윗을 자제하게 되고 당신 삼촌과 공손한 대화를 주고받기까지 한다(세대 간 갈등을 극복할 수 있다는 말). 부질없이 감정에 휘둘리는 일을 줄이면 자원봉사 같은 정말 의미 있는 것을 하는 쪽으로 에너지를 발산시킬 수 있다. 충분히 많은 사람이 이 일에 동참하면 미국이 직면한 유독성 간극에 의미 있는 빛을 비춰줄 수도 있을 것이다.

① 명상을 통해 깨달음으로 인도하기 위한 제언
② 정치 이념적 양극화 시대를 살아남는 방법들
③ 명상 수행에 꾸준함이 필요한 이유
④ 심한 정치적 편견과 그것이 사회에 끼치는 악영향
⑤ 이념적 편견을 극복하기 위한 효과적 수단으로서의 명상

[글의 소재] 이념적 편견을 극복하기 위한 수단으로서의 명상

[주요 어휘] tribalism 부족주의, stress-eat 스트레스를 먹는 거로 풀다, kernel 견과류의 알맹이, emblazon 아로새기다, inch 조금씩 다가가다, Liberal Tears 진보주의자의 눈물, 마시는 물을 보수 진영이 경멸적으로 이르는 말, next thing you know 자기도 모르게, 부지불식간에, cut down on ~을 줄이다, make a difference 중요하다, 의미 있다, churn 휘저음, chasm 간극, toxicity 유독성

[글의 흐름] ⊙ 주제문은 'Nevertheless, I really do believe meditation can help you survive this season of discontent and division.'이며 중괄식 구조이다. 반전의 연결사 nevertheless로 시작하고 'I really do believe ~'와 같은 강한 표현이 들어있는 문장이기 때문에 주제문일 가능성이 크다.

[구조 분석] ⊙ Next thing you know
→ '문득 깨닫고 보니', '어느 틈엔가', '부지불식간에'를 뜻하는 부사구이다. 놀라운 일이 갑작스레 일어날 때 쓴다. out of the blue나 out of nowhere로 바꿔 쓸 수 있다.

[정답 해설] 필자는 명상을 통해 자신의 편견을 바로 보고 마침내 이념적 틀에서 벗어날 수 있음을 주장하고 있다. 따라서 주제는 ⑤의 '이념적 편견을 극복하기 위한 효과적 수단으로서의 명상'이 알맞다.

2. 요지·주장

정답

012 ④	013 ③	014 ③	015 ③
016 ②	017 ③	018 ②	019 ②	020 ①

012　　　　　　　　　　　　　　정답 ④

[지문 해석] 휘발유값이 오르면 성난 미국인들이 의회나 백악관, OPEC를 비난하는 일이 주기적으로 일어난다. 미국 지역 신문의 한 논설에 의하면 고유가를 정말로 책임져야 할 사람이 누군지 알고 싶으면 미국인 스스로 거울을 들여다봐야 한다고 한다. "놀라울 정도로 비싼 주유소 기름값의 진짜 이유는 미국 소비자들의 자동차 중독과 그로 인한 생활 방식 때문이다."라고 논설은 말한다. 너무나 많은 미국인이 마치, 미국에서 팔리는 차량의 상당 부분을 차지하는, 연료 소모가 많은 대형차나 픽업트럭을 소유할 권리가 있는 것처럼 행동한다고 논설위원은 계속 지적한다. 그 결과는? 미국이 기름에 대해 채워지지 않은 탐욕을 가지게 되고 OPEC은 우리의 석유 의존을 이용하는 것이다. 미국인들은 저유가를 요구하기보다는 가급적 차를 적게 몰고, 대중교통이 보다 이용이 편하고, 믿을 만하고, 저렴하게 되도록 그들의 지도자에게 요청해야 한다고 논설은 말한다.

[글의 소재] 미국의 고유가의 원인

[주요 어휘] soar 급등하다, infuriate 격노하게 하다, editorial 사설, 논설, gas-pump 주유 펌프, sticker shock 비싼 가격에 놀람, be entitled to ~할 자격이 있다, gas-guzzling 연료를 많이 소비하는, oversized 특대의, account for ~를 차지하다, insatiable 만족을 모르는, take advantage of ~를 이용해 먹다(부정적 뉘앙스), affordable 저렴한

[글의 흐름] ⊙ 주제문은 'The real cause of gas-pump sticker shock is American consumers' addiction to the automobile and the life style it allows.'이다.

[구조 분석] ⊙ they should look in the mirror.
→ 거울을 들여다봐야 한다고 함은 그 속에 비친 자신들이 문제를 일으킨 장본인임을 깨달으라는 말이다.

⊙ The editorialist goes on to point out that far too many Americans act as if they are entitled to own big, ~ this country.
→ as if 이하는 가정법이 아닌 직설법을 써서 '현실적 실현가능성'을 강조했다.

⊙ Americans should be driving as little as possible and insisting that ~
→ driving과 insisting이 병렬 구조이다.

정답 해설 주제문인 'The real cause of gas-pump sticker shock is American consumers' addiction to the automobile and the life style it allows.'를 통하여, 고유가의 근본 원인이 미국인들의 과도한 자동차 사랑에 있다는 이 글의 요지를 확인할 수 있다. 따라서 정답은 ④가 가장 가깝다. 이 문제를 통해서도 요지문을 찾는 문제는 언제나 주제문을 찾는 것이 관건임을 알 수 있다.

013

정답 ③

지문 해석 본질적으로 전투는 적대적 감정의 표현이다. 그러나 우리가 전쟁이라 부르는 대규모 전투에서는 이 적대적 감정이 종종 적의(敵意)로 약화돼 왔다. 어찌 됐든 일반적으로 각 개인 간의 적대적 감정은 없다. 그러나 전쟁에서 그런 감정이 완전히 사라질 리는 만무하다. 현대의 전쟁은 국가 간의 증오심 없이 치러지는 경우가 거의 없다. 국가 간 증오가 개인 간 증오를 어느 정도 대체해 주기 때문이다. 처음에는 자발적 증오나 반감이 없다가도 싸움 그 자체가 적대 감정을 불러일으킨다. 상부의 지시로 폭력을 가했을 경우 그 폭력을 지시한 권력이 아닌 그 폭력을 행사한 당사자에게 복수나 보복 욕구를 불러일으킨다. 그것은 지극히 인간적일 뿐이지만 – (동물적이라 해도 좋다) – 그러나 사실이다.

① 전투에서는 적대 감정이 기승을 부리지만 전쟁에서는 그렇지 않다.
② 현대의 전쟁은 국가 간 증오를 뿌리 삼는다.
③ 적대 감정은 결국 모든 전쟁의 근본 요소다.
④ 국가 간 증오가 개인 간 증오를 대체한다.
⑤ 적대 감정은 실제 전투 과정에서 생기기도 한다.

글의 소재 클라우제비츠의 전쟁론

주요 어휘 animosity 반감, superior order 상관의 명령, stir up 흥기시키다, 발기시키다, retaliation 보복, perpetrator 가해자

글의 흐름 주제문은 'Yet such emotions can never be completely absent from war.'이다. 역접의 연결사 Yet이 주제문을 이끄는 경우이다.

정답 해설 적대적 감정은 전쟁보다는 전투의 주된 모티브지만 대규모 전쟁에서도 이는 완전히 배제할 수 없고 특히 전쟁의 과정에서 없던 적대 감정도 생기는 것은 물론 권력에 대한 증오가 개인 간 증오로 발전하는 게 인지상정이라 했으므로 이 글의 요지는 '적대 감정은 모든 전쟁의 근본 요소'로 보는 게 타당하다.

014

정답 ①

지문 해석 의사나 다른 전문 의료인들은 체크리스트의 사용을 강하게 반대해왔다. 그것은 그들의 전문적 능력에 대한 모욕으로 여겨졌다. "다른 사람들은 체크리스트가 필요할지 모르나 나는 아니다."라고 그들은 불평한다. 유감스러운 일이다. 인간은

잘못을 저지르게 돼 있다. 스트레스를 받거나 시간이나 사회적 압력을 받을 때, 또는 저마다 나름대로 불가피한 여러 번의 중단을 겪은 후라면 우리는 누구나 크고 작은 실수를 할 수밖에 없다. 인간적인 것은(실수하는 것은) 전문적 능력에 대한 위협이 아니다. 특정 체크리스트에 대한 정당한 비판이 체크리스트의 개념에 대한 비난의 근거로 (잘못) 사용되고 있다. 다행히 의료계에서 체크리스트는 서서히 용인되기 시작하고 있다. 고위직원이 체크리스트 사용을 고집하면 그것은 그들의 권위나 직업적 위상을 높인다. 체크리스트가 가령 상업 항공계에 용인되는 데는 수십 년이 걸렸다. 의사나 다른 전문 의료인은 좀 더 빨리 변하기를 희망해 보자.

글의 소재 의료계에도 필요한 체크리스트

주요 어휘 competence 능력, err 잘못을 저지르다, subject ~ 할 수밖에 없는(형), ~할 수밖에 없게 하다(동), interruption 중단, in its own right 나름대로, legitimate 정당한, indictment 기소, 비난의 근거, enhance 높이다, authority 권위

글의 흐름 ⊙ 맨 마지막 문장 'let us hope that doctors and other medical professionals will change more rapidly.'에 나타난 필자의 희망 속에 글 쓴 의도가 숨어 있다.

구조 분석 ⊙ ~ after being subjected to multiple interruptions, each essential in its own right.
→ each는 multiple interruptions를 가리키고 each와 essential 사이에 being이 생략된 분사구문으로 'as each is essential in its own right.'로 바꿔 쓸 수 있다. '각각의 중단이 나름대로 불가피한 채로'의 뜻이다.

정답 해설 필자가 인간은 누구나 실수하고 인간적인 실수는 전문적 능력에 대한 위협이 아님을 밝힌 데다 마지막 문장에서 의료계가 체크리스트 사용 쪽으로 빠르게 변화하기를 바란다고 한 것으로 보아 윗글의 요지는 ① '의료인에게도 체크리스트가 필요하다.'가 적절하다.

015

정답 ③

지문 해석 시일이 흐르면서 잡스는 제품 출시를 지휘하는 거장으로 성장해 갔다. 매킨토시의 경우, Ridley Scott이 연출한 놀랄 만한 광고는 단지 여러 가지 요소 중 하나일 뿐이었다. 또 다른 중요한 요소는 언론 보도였다. 잡스는 폭발적인 홍보에 불을 붙여 열광적 반응이 마치 연쇄반응처럼 자가 증식하는 방법을 알아냈다. 그것은 1984년 매킨토시에서 2010년 아이패드에 이르기까지 거대 제품 출시 때마다 그가 재현해 낸 인기몰이였다. 마술사처럼 그는 관중을 속이고 또 속였다. 기자들이 같은 수법을 여러 번 경험해 이미 비법을 알아버린 후에도 말이다. 때론 거만한 기자들과 교분을 쌓고 그들을 다루는 데 능숙했던 Regis McKenna로부터 한 수 배우기도 했다. 하지만 잡스는 관심을 불러일으키고, 기자들의 경쟁 본능을 이용해 독점 취재를 주는 대신 큰 지면을 보장받는 데 대해 그만의 직관력을 갖

추고 있었다.

글의 소재 S. Jobs의 미디어 감각

주요 어휘 coverage 보도, frenzy 광분 광란, feed on oneself 자가 증식하다, conjurer 마술사, pull something off ~를 해내다, move 장기 · 바둑의 수, stoke 불을 지피다, intuitive 직관력을 갖춘, trade A for B A와 B를 교환하다, lavish treatment 융숭한 대우(여기서는 보다 큰 지면을 보장받는다는 의미)

글의 흐름 ⊙ 주제문은 'Another part of the recipe was media coverage.'이고, 이하는 이에 대한 뒷받침 진술이다.

구조 분석 ⊙ even after journalists had seen it happen a dozen times,

→ happen이 had seen의 목적격 보어이고, seen이 지각동사이므로 원형으로 일치시켰다.

⊙ Some of the moves he had learned from Regis McKenna,

→ 이 문장의 주어는 he, 목적어는 Some of the moves이다. Some of the moves를 주어 자리로 도치해 강조의 효과를 노린 구문이다.

정답 해설 주제문 'Another part of the recipe was media coverage.'에서 알 수 있듯이 잡스가 제품 홍보를 위해 media coverage를 이용할 줄 알았다는 것이 이 글의 핵심 내용이다. 따라서 ③이 정답이다.

016
정답 ②

지문 해석 초기 빅토리아 시대 의상은 여성들을 약하고 무력해 보이게 했을 뿐만 아니라 실제로 약하고 무력하게 만들었다. 무기력의 주된 원인은 코르셋 때문이었는데 당시 이것은 단순히 패션뿐 아니라 의료용품으로 고안되었다. 여성의 골격은 극도로 허약하고, 외부 도움이 없으면 여성의 근육은 몸을 지탱할 수 없다는 것이 일반적인 생각이었다. 가정교육을 제대로 받은 여자애들의 몸에는 서너 살 무렵부터 어린이용 코르셋이 꽉 조인 채로 입혀졌다. 코르셋 스테이는 길어졌고 딱딱해졌고 꽉 조여졌다. 사춘기에 이를 무렵이면 그들은 무거운 철심을 박은 무거운 천막을 새장처럼 두르게 되고, 등 근육이 위축돼 지지대 없이 오랫동안 앉거나 서 있지 못하는 지경에 이르렀다. 코르셋은 또한 내부 장기를 변형시키고 숨을 깊게 들이 마실 수 없게 만들었다. 따라서 멋지게 차려입은 여성들은 걸핏하면 졸도했고 소화 장애를 앓았고 힘든 일을 하고 나면 무력감과 피곤함을 호소했다.

글의 소재 코르셋

주요 어휘 debility 무기력, frame 골격, delicate 허약한, well-brought-up 가정교육을 제대로 받은, lace ~ into 끈

을 꽉 조여 입히다, juvenile 청소년의, stay 스테이, 버팀줄, canvas 천막, reinforce 강화하다, atrophy 위축되다, unsupported 지지대 없는 deform 변형시키다, fashionably 최신 유행대로, 멋지게, faint 졸도하다, digestive complaint 소화 장애, strenuous 격렬한, exertion 수고, 노력

글의 흐름 ⊙ 주제문은 'The main agent of the debility was the corset, which at the time was thought of not as a mere fashion item but as a medical necessity.'이다.

구조 분석 ⊙ their back muscles had often atrophied to the point where they could not sit or stand for long unsupported.

→ to the point where는 결과로 해석하는 게 자연스럽다. 등 근육이 위축돼 ~하는 지경에 이르렀다. unsupported는 주격 보어로 쓰였고 주어가 처한 상태를 나타낸다. 여기서 could not sit or stand for long을 be 동사로 바꿔도 말이 됨을 알 수 있다.

정답 해설 주제문 'The main agent of the debility was the corset, which at the time was thought of not as a mere fashion item but as a medical necessity.'로 알 수 있듯이, 이 글의 주장은 빅토리아 시대의 코르셋은 주 용도가 의료 목적이었으나 아이러니하게도 많은 여성을 허약 체질로 만들었다는 것이다. 따라서 요지는 ②가 타당하다. 필자의 논조가 코르셋에 대하여 시종일관하여 비판적인 입장을 취하고 있음을 놓치지 말아야 한다.

017
정답 ③

지문 해석 충돌의 위험을 줄이기 위한 절박한 시도의 하나로 대부분의 주가 운전자 교육 프로그램을 제공한다. 몇몇 주는 심지어 운전자 교육을 성공적으로 이수하면 주에서 주관하는 이론 및 실기시험을 치르지 않고 자동으로 면허를 교부하는 인센티브를 제공하기까지 한다. 하지만 1996년에 실시된 '오토바이 운전자 교육이 충돌 위험에 미치는 영향' 평가에 의하면 운전자 교육이 충돌 감소와 관계가 있다는 어떤 유력한 증거도 없다. 뉴욕주 차량관리부는 1981년과 1985년 사이 오토바이 운전자 교육에 대해 방대한 조사를 실시한 바 있다. 미도로교통안전국(NHTSA)이 후원한 이번 연구에서 오토바이 면허증 신청자들은 임의로 네 그룹으로 분류되었다. 한 그룹은 주가 이미 실시 중인 이론 및 실기시험을 치렀고 다른 그룹은 NHTSA이 개발한 기술시험을 봤다. 나머지 두 그룹은 운전자 교육과 기술시험을 치렀다. 뉴욕 주가 실시 중인 이론 및 실기시험을 치른 그룹이 나머지 세 그룹보다 그 후 2년 동안 오토바이 충돌 사고를 덜 당했다. 2010년 실시된 국제적 조사에 대한 평가에서도 오토바이 운전자 교육과 충돌 위험 사이에는 이렇다 할 관계가 없는 것으로 드러났다.

① 운전자 교육 프로그램은 충돌을 감소시키는 효과적 수단으로 크게 장려돼야 한다.
② 운전자 교육 프로그램은 정식 면허시험을 효과적으로 대체할 수 있다.
③ 운전자 교육 프로그램이 충돌 위험을 줄인다는 단서는 아직 발견되지 않았다.
④ 충돌 위험을 줄이기 위해 운전면허 발급에 대한 엄격한 정책이 필요하다.
⑤ 충돌을 방지하는 데 이론과 실기시험의 역할을 과소평가해서는 안 된다.

글의 소재) 운전자 교육과 교통사고의 연관성

주요 어휘) licensure 면허 교부, in lieu of~ ~대신에, compelling evidence 유력한 증거

글의 흐름) ⊙ 주제문은 'A 1996 review of the effects of motorcycle rider training on crash risk, however, concluded that there is "no compelling evidence that rider training is associated with reductions in collisions."'로 중괄식 구조이다. 이 경우, 도입부에 기존 통념이 제시되고, 이 주장 이후 however와 같은 전환 연결사와 함께 뒤집히면서 주제문이 나온다.

구조 분석) ⊙ In a desperate move to reduce ~
➜ '~ 하는 절박한 노력의 일환으로'의 뜻으로 많이 쓰는 표현이다. In a desperate effort to reduce로 바꿔 쓸 수 있다.

⊙ Some states even provide the incentive of automatic licensure in lieu of a state-administered written knowledge test or road test once riders successfully complete a rider education course.
➜ road test까지가 주절이고 once 이하가 때를 나타내는 종속절이다.

정답 해설) 이 글은 오토바이 운전자 교육이 실제 충돌 사고 방지에는 별로 도움이 되지 않는다는 점을 3가지 연구 결과를 근거로 들어 주장하고 있다. 따라서 요지에 가장 가까운 것은 ③이다. ⑤의 이론과 실기시험을 과소평가해서는 안 된다는 내용은 본문에 없다. 이는 주관 개입이 매력적인 오답을 낳는 경우이다.

018
정답 ②

지문 해석) 유명한 과학자들의 전기가 그들의 실수를 편집해서 빼는 경향이 있기 때문에 우리는 그들이 거는 모험의 정도를 과소평가한다. 그리고 과학자가 한 일 중에서 실수가 아닌 것이 아마도 오늘날 전통적 지혜가 됐기 때문에 그런 선택은 모험적이지 않은 것처럼 보인다. 예를 들어 뉴튼의 전기가 연금술이나 신학보다는 물리학에 초점 맞추는 것은 이해할 만하다. 그래서 그의 완전무결한 판단이 그를 어느 누구도 보지 못한 진리로 이끌었다는 것이 우리가 갖게 되는 인상이다. 그러나 그가 연금술이나 신학에 바친 모든 시간을 우리는 어떻게 설명할 수 있나? 외견상 우리에게는 물리학이 더 유망하고 신학은 분명히 시간 낭비처럼 보인다. 그러나 그것은 사태가 어떻게 판명됐는지를 우리가 알기 때문이다. 뉴튼 시대에는 세 가지 문제가 거의 비슷하게 유망했다. 우리가 물리학이라 부르는 것을 발명한 데 따른 결실이 어떨지 아직 아는 사람들이 없었다. 만일 그들이 그것을 알았다면 더 많은 사람들이 그것을 연구했을 것이다. 당시에는 연금술이나 신학이 Marc Andreessen의 표현대로 '사실이면 대박인' 분야였던 것이다. 뉴튼은 세 군데에 베팅을 했고 그 중 하나가 맞았다. 그러나 셋 다 모험이었다.

글의 소재) 과학자와 모험

주요 어휘) edit out 편집에서 빼다, underestimate 과소평가하다, alchemy 연금술, theology 신학, unerring 잘못이 없는, 완전무결한, apparently 외견상, 명백히, payoff 결실, 소득

글의 흐름) 글의 첫 두 문장이 주제문이다. 일반적으로 예시의 연결사 for example은 구체 진술로 이어지고 그 앞 문장(들)이 일반 진술, 즉 주제문일 경우가 많다.

구조 분석) ⊙ And because anything a famous scientist did that wasn't a mistake has probably now become the conventional wisdom~
➜ anything과 a famous scientist 사이에 목적격 관계대명사가 생략됐고 뒤이어 나오는 that도 anything을 꾸며주는 관계대명사다. 따라서 anything은 두 개의 관계대명사에 의해 동시에 수식되고 있는데 이럴 경우 '~한 것 중에서 ~한 것은'으로 해석하면 자연스럽다.

정답 해설) 이 글은 오늘날의 우리에게 크게 부각되지 않아서 그렇지 사실 과학자들의 업적 중 많은 부분이 모험의 소산이었다는 점을 뉴튼의 예를 들어 설명하고 있다. 따라서 이 글의 요지는 ②다.

019
정답 ②

지문 해석) 지각과 판단이 열정을 낳고 만든다는 것은 아무도 놀래지 않을 것이다. 아마 더 놀라운 것은 반대의 인과관계 즉 열정 또한 지각과 판단을 형성한다는 사실이다. '감정은 사람들을 변화시켜 그들의 판단에 영향을 주고, 고통과 쾌락이 따르는 모든 느낌'이라고 아리스토텔레스는 말한다. 지각은 순전히 이성적이고 객관적이고 초연한 방식으로 일어나지 않는다. 대신 지각은 열정과 그들의 이웃 기분의 풍부한 영역에 의해 채색된다. 열정은 한 상황 내에 몇몇 요인을 전면에 두는 한편 다른 것들을 배경에 둔다. 특히 화는 희생자들로 하여금 그들이 부당하게 취급됐거나 되고 있다는 사실을 감지하고, 집착하고, 거기에 의미를 부여하도록 부추긴다. 화를 느끼지 못하면 사람들

은 부정에 충분히 주의하지 않을 것이고 그래서 그것을 알아차리거나, 그것을 심각하게 받아들이지 못하기 쉽다. 그들은 종종 그런 부정을 부당한 취급이나 해악으로 여기지도 않는다. 일반적으로 열정은 두드러짐과 가치의 투사기이다(두드러진 곳과 가치 있는 곳을 비춰준다). 그것은 상황을 밝은 부분과 어두운 부분으로 칠한다(상황의 중요한 부분과 그렇지 않은 부분을 구분 짓는다).

① 열정은 늘 우리가 너무 성급하게 반응하도록 추동한다.
② 열정은 우리가 지각하고 판단하는 방식에 영향을 준다.
③ 감정은 종종 건전한 추리에 방해가 된다.
④ 지각은 열정의 탄생에 책임이 있다.
⑤ 화는 부당하게 행사된 부정을 감지하는 데 도움을 준다.

[글의 소재] 아리스토텔레스 윤리학

[주요 어휘] converse 역의, 반대의, causal 인과의, detached 초연한, foreground ~를 전면에 두다, hold onto 집착하다, wrong(v) 부당하게 취급하다, salience 돌출 부분

[글의 흐름] 주제문은 'Perhaps more surprising is the converse causal relationship: the fact that passions also shape perceptions and judgments.'이고 두괄식 문단이다.

[구조 분석] ⊙ That perceptions and judgements produce and shape passions should surprise no one.
→ 'That ~passions'로 이뤄진 명사절이 이 문장의 주어이다.
⊙ The emotions are all those feelings that so change men as to affect their judgments,
→ 'so ~ as to R' 구문으로 '~해서 ~하다'로 해석하며 이때 as to R은 결과의 부사구다. '~하기 위하여'로 해석되는 목적의 부사구 'so as to R'와 구분된다.
⊙ ~ anger helps victims to recognize, hold onto, and attach importance to the fact that they have been, or are being wronged.
→ the fact가 recognize, hold onto, attach importance to의 공동 목적어이다.

[정답 해설] 이 글은 아리스토텔레스 윤리학에서 열정이 어떻게 지각이나 판단 형성에 영향을 미치는지를 주장한 글이다. 따라서 정답은 ②의 '열정이 우리가 지각하고 판단하는 방식에 영향을 준다.'이다. 주제문(2~3행)을 참조하라.

020 정답 ①

[지문 해석] 개인이 자신에게 저지르는 비행은 동정을 통해 그리고 이해를 통해 주변 사람에게 큰 영향을 미치고, 정도는 덜하지만 사회 전반에도 영향을 준다는 점을 나는 충분히 인정한다. 한 개인이 이런 행위로 타인 또는 타인들에 대한 분명하고 확실한 의무를 저버리면 그 사건은 자기애의 차원을 떠나 진정한 의

미에서 도덕적 지탄의 대상이 된다. 만일 한 사람이 방탕한 생활로 자신의 빚을 갚지 못하거나 가족을 부양해야 하는 도덕적 책무가 있음에도 같은 이유로 자녀를 부양하거나 교육을 시키지 못한다면 그는 비난받는 것이 마땅하고 또 처벌받아 마땅할 것이지만 그것은 가족과 채권자들에 대한 의무를 저버렸기 때문이지 방탕함 때문은 아니다. 그들을 위해 써야 마땅한 재산을 그들에게서 빼내, 가장 신중한 투자라 해도 어쨌든 투자를 했다면 도덕적 과실은 마찬가지일 것이다. 그 대상이 개인이든 공공이든 간에 분명한 피해가 발생하거나 발생할 위험성이 있을 때 해당 사건은 자유의 영역에서 벗어나 도덕이나 법의 영역에 놓이게 된다.

[글의 소재] 자유와 책무

[주요 어휘] mischief 비행, assignable 책임 소재를 가릴 수 있는, self-regarding 자기애적인, amenable to ~에 해당하는, disapproval 반감, 지탄, extravagance 방탕, 사치, deservedly 마땅히, breach 어김, 위반, culpability 과오, 과실, province 영역

[글의 흐름] ⊙ 개인의 자유가 허용될 수 있는 조건을 다루는 글이다. 주제문은 'Whenever there is a definite damage, or a definite risk of damage, either to an individual or to the public, the case is taken out of the province of liberty, and placed in that of morality or law.'이고 미괄식 구조이다.

[구조 분석] ⊙ both through their sympathies and their interests, those nearly connected with him and, in a minor degree, society at large.
→ 밑줄 친 두 their는 뒤에 오는 those를 받는다.
⊙ having undertaken the moral responsibility of a family, becomes from the same cause incapable of supporting or educating them,
→ 밑줄 친 분사 구문은 양보의 의미를 갖는다. =even though they undertook the moral ~.
⊙ and might be justly punished
→ justly는 문장 전체를 수식하는 부사이다. It is just that they might be punished로 바꿔 쓸 수 있다.

[정답 해설] 개인의 비행으로 타인에 대한 의무를 저버리면 개인 자유의 영역을 벗어나 도덕적 지탄의 대상이 된다는 주장에서 개인의 자유는 도덕적 책임을 다하는 한도 내에서만 허용된다는 글쓴이의 입장을 추론할 수 있다. 따라서 정답은 ①이다. 두 번째 문장인 'When, by conduct of this sort, ~ proper sense of the term.'과 마지막 문장인 'Whenever there is a definite damage, or a definite risk of damage, ~ in that of morality or law.'에서 단서를 찾을 수 있다.

3. 글의 제목

정답

021 ②	022 ③	023 ②	024 ①	025 ④
026 ③	027 ①	028 ⑤	029 ⑤	

021

<정답 ②>

지문 해석 영국의 한 대학은 최근 돈과 사랑 사이의 관계 가능성을 보여주는 조사 결과를 발표했다. 영국 스완지대학의 심리학자들은 75명의 남성과 76명의 여성에게 데이트 상대가 될 만한 50명의 사진을 보여주고 각각의 상대와 장/단기적인 관계를 맺고 싶은지, 아니면 아무 관계도 맺고 싶지 않은지 물었다. 그러고 나서 조사자들은 몇몇 참여자들에게는 고급 차와 보석, 대저택 또는 현금 사진을 보여주고 이것들이 데이트 상대 선택에 영향을 주는지 여부를 살폈다. 과연 그러했다. 그 참여자들이 호화로운 물건들 사진을 보고 나서 다시 데이트 상대의 사진을 보게 했다. 호화로운 물건들을 보지 않은 그룹에 비해 그것들을 본 참여자들은 단기간 즐기는 사랑을 선호했다. 단기적인 애정 파트너를 선택하는 경우가 16% 더 많았다.

① 사랑 자체를 위한 사랑이 오래 지속될 수 있다
② 사치는 애정 욕구에 영향을 미치나?
③ 단기적인 관계는 해볼 가치가 있나?
④ 사치를 피해라. 그러지 않으면 사랑에 실패한다.
⑤ 심각한 관계에는 사치가 끼어들 자리가 없다.

글의 소재 돈과 사랑

주요 어휘 release 발표하다, potential 잠재적인, love interest 데이트 상대, preference 선호, fling 한바탕 즐기기

구조 분석 ⊙ It did.

→ It did는 It affected how they felt about dating을 말한다.

⊙ Compared with the group that was not shown any luxury images,

→ compared with는 '~와 비교했을 때'의 의미이다. When they were compared with ~에서 When they were가 생략된 구문이다.

정답 해설 이 글은 돈이나 물질적 사치가 우리의 애정 행각에 영향을 끼친다는, 영국 한 대학의 심리학자들(Psychologists at Swansea University in the UK)이 발표한 조사 결과를 설명하고 있다. 따라서 사치가 애정 욕구에 영향을 미치는지를 묻는 ②가 제목으로 가장 적절하다.

022

<정답 ③>

지문 해석 2007년 1월과 5월 사이 양봉업자들은 전체의 4분의 1에 달하는 엄청난 수의 벌을 잃었다. 이런 정보가 따분하다고 생각하는 사람이 있다면 다시 생각해 보기 바란다. 왜냐하면 꿀벌은 단지 꽃가루 수정에 벌이 필요한 정원사에게만 중요한 게 아니기 때문이다. 정반대로 꿀벌의 실종은 훨씬 큰 의미를 지닌다. 사실, '서식지 붕괴 증후군'으로도 불리는 꿀벌의 실종은 식량 위기마저 부를 수 있다. 꿀벌은 견과류, 아보카도, 사과, 셀러리, 호박, 오이, 체리, 블루베리를 수분시킨다. 이마저도 완전한 리스트가 아니다. 전문가에 의하면 인간이 먹는 음식의 3분의 1이 곤충의 수분에 의한 것이고, 이런 수분의 80퍼센트는 꿀벌에 의해 이뤄진다. 꿀벌은 고기가 식탁에 오르는 과정의 일부분을 맡기도 한다. 소의 주식인 알팔파가 다 자라려면 벌의 수분이 필요하기 때문이다. 과학자들이 꿀벌의 실종 이유를 찾아내지 못하면 육식주의자들은 어쩔 수 없이 채식해야 한다. 채소마저 부족한 이 판국에 말이다.

① 식량 위기에 가장 잘 대처하는 방법
② 꿀벌이 수분을 못 하는 이유
③ 꿀벌의 실종, 잠재적 식량 위기의 원인
④ 최상의 꽃가루 매개자, 꿀벌
⑤ 육류 생산의 한 축을 맡은 꿀벌

글의 소재 벌의 실종과 식량 위기

주요 어휘 beekeeper 양봉업자, ho-hum 따분해하다, pollinate 수분(受粉)하다, celery 셀러리, figure out 생각해 내다, 80 percent of the time 80퍼센트의 경우에, of choice 최선호의, alfalfa 알팔파, figure out 알아내다

글의 흐름 ⊙ 주제문은 'The truth is the disappearance of honeybees, also known as "Colony Collapse Disorder," could cause a food crisis.'로 중괄식 구조이다. The truth is ~처럼 필자의 의견이 강하게 들어가 있는 문장이 주제문일 가능성이 크다.

구조 분석 ⊙ The truth is the disappearance of honeybees, also known as "Colony Collapse Disorder," could cause a food crisis.

→ The truth is (that) the disappearance(S) + could cause(V) + a crisis(O)의 구조이다. S + V + C의 구문에서 C가 다시 S + V + O 형식을 취하고 있다.

정답 해설 주제문 'The truth is the disappearance of honeybees, also known as "Colony Collapse Disorder," could cause a food crisis.'에서 알 수 있듯이, 이 글은 꿀벌이 사라지면 수분이 어려워져 식량 위기가 올 수 있음을 주장하고 있다. 그러므로 ③이 제목으로 타당하다. 이와 같이 글의 주제문을 파악하면 문제 해결을 쉽게 할 수 있다.

023

지문 해석 건강과 질병은 하나의 연속체의 극단적으로 서로 다른 두 모습으로 볼 수 있다. 한 극단에는 극심하고, 생명을 위협하며, 장애를 유발하는 질병이 있어 환자의 신체적 정서적 건강에 심대한 영향을 끼친다. 다른 극단은 이상적인 건강 상태로 이는 완전한 육체적 정신적 안녕으로 정의할 수 있다. 건강한 사람은 정서적으로나 육체적으로나 완전하고, 행복하고 생산적인 삶을 영위할 수 있고 근심이나 혼란 그리고 활동을 제한하는 육체적 장애가 없다. 이 두 극단 사이에는, 어느 정도 활동을 제한하는 가벼운 단기 질병에서 이상적인 상태는 아니지만 괜찮은 건강 상태에 이르기까지 많은 등급이 있다. 이 연속체의 중간지점은 아프지도 건강하지도 않은 "중립적" 위치라 볼 수 있다. 이 연속체에서 우리들 대부분은 이 중간지점과 이상적인 건강 상태 사이 어디쯤 존재한다.

① 건강과 질병의 상호 의존성
② 하나의 연속체로서의 건강과 질병
③ 삶의 질의 양극단
④ 인간의 건강에서 왜 중립적 위치를 점유하는 게 중요한가?
⑤ 환자의 육체적 정신적 안녕이 갖는 의미

글의 소재 하나의 연속체로서의 건강과 질병

주요 어휘 continuum 연속체, turmoil 혼란, gradation 등급

글의 흐름 ⊙ 주제문이 'Health and disease may be considered two extremes of a continuum.'인 두괄식 구조이다.

구조 분석 ⊙ Between these two extremes are many gradations of health and disease, ranging from mild or short-term illness that limit activities to some extent through moderate good health that falls short of the ideal state.

➔ many gradations 이하가 주어인 1형식 문장으로, 주어가 길어 뒤로 뺀 도치 구문이다. 무거운 것은 뒤로 돌린다는 영어의 이른바 'end weight' 원칙이 적용된 경우이다. ranging from ~ through(~에서 ~에 이르는)는 many gradations를 수식한다.

정답 해설 주제문인 'Health and disease may be considered two extremes of a continuum.'을 통해 이 글이 건강과 질병이 하나의 연속체라고 주장함을 알 수 있다. 따라서 글의 제목으로는 ②가 알맞다.

024

지문 해석 네덜란드 학생들은 대학생 주택 문제에 대한 하나의 새로운 해결책을 가지게 됐다. 이제 그들은 늘 보던 비좁고 우중충한 공동주택이나 기숙사 대신 노인 장기 요양 시설의 하나인 Humanitas에서 무료로 생활할 수 있다. 이웃에 90세 노

인이 산다는 게 좀 이상해 보일 테지만 주거비용이 이를 벌충해준다. 평균적인 네덜란드 학생이 매달 집세로 쓰는 돈이 366유로인데 반해 휴마니타스에 살면 한 달에 30시간의 봉사활동만 하면 끝이다. 노인들에게 학생은 새로운 세계를 내다보는 창이다. 봉사활동 시간에는 이메일 쓰기나 소셜미디어를 배울 수 있다. 그 시간은 노년의 특징이기도 한 단조로움과 외로움에서 벗어나는 시간이다. 이제 그들은 관절이 아프다는 말 대신에 재미있는 대학 과목이나 데이트에 대한 이야기를 나눌 수 있다. 학생들로서는 경제적 이득이 자명하다. 이득도 이득이지만 사회의 현자들과 관계함으로써 삶의 애환에 대한 독특한 시각을 얻을 수 있다. 많은 학생들이 교회나 클럽의 일회적 활동에서 웃음을 나누는 것 이상으로 연로한 이웃과 가깝고 지속적인 관계를 발전시켜 나가고 있다.

① 누이 좋고 매부 좋고
② 어려울 때 친구가 진짜 친구
③ 제때 한 땀이 아홉 땀을 덜어준다(때를 잘 고르면 큰 이득을 본다는 뜻).
④ 다른 사람이 너에게 해줬으면 하는 그것을 그들에게 해줘라(역지사지하라).
⑤ 백지장도 맞들면 낫다.

글의 소재 네덜란드의 대학생 기숙사/양로원 겸용 시설

주요 어휘 cramped 비좁은, dingy 우중충한, make up for 벌충하다

구조 분석 ⊙ Now they can replace conversations about aching bones with gossip about interesting college courses and even dating.

➔ replace A with B 구문으로, 'A를 안 하고 대신 B를 하다'의 의미이다.

정답 해설 이 글은 학생들과 노인들이 함께 살면서 학생들은 주거비용에서 이익을 보고 노인들은 단조로움과 외로움에서 벗어날 수 있어서 서로에게 도움을 주는 상생의 삶을 살아간다는 내용이다. 그러므로 이 글의 제목으로는 '누이 좋고 매부 좋고'를 뜻하는 ①이 가장 적절하다.

025

지문 해석 개인 간 지속적인 정서적 유대는 우정을 정의하는 것이며 이는 짝짓기 상대가 결합하는 것과 유사하다. 이 개별적인 불변성은 집단적인 불변성에 그대로 반영된다. 우리가 검토한 사회적 종의 개체들은 오고 간다. 그들은 태어나고 죽는다. 그리고 우정은 시작이 있고 끝이 있다. 하지만 종의 전반적인 사회 구조는 변하지 않는다. 집단 내에서 일어나는 어떤 사회적 유대의 재편은 관계망이 지속하는 데 필요하기까지 하다. 그것은 배의 널빤지를 교체하는 것과 같다. 그것은 배를 항해할 수 있게 하는 데 필요하다. 그러나 모든 개별 널빤지들을 교체해

도, 사회관계망의 위상이 그러하듯, 배의 항해 계획은 그대로다. 즉, 모든 2원적 우정의 유대와 우리 안의 유전자에서 나오는 사회관계망의 구조는 우리 종의 특질 그 자체다. 놀랍게도 인간은 이 신생 구조를 다른 사회적 포유류들과 공유하는데 이 점은 문화와 무관하게 이 속성이 인간에게 얼마나 본질적인지를 잘 보여준다.

[글의 소재] 인간 사회의 버팀목, 사회관계망

[주요 어휘] enduring 지속적인, sentimental 정서적인, analogous 유사한, overall 전반적인, turnover 재편, seaworthy 항해에 적합한, topology 위상, dyadic 2원적인, emergent 신생의, highlight 잘 보여주다, fundamental 근본적인, property 속성

[글의 흐름] 주제문은 'That is, the structure of social networks—arising from all the dyadic friendship ties and the genes within us—is a feature of our species itself.'이며 대체로 미괄식 구조를 취하고 있다.

[구조 분석] ⊙ humans share this emergent structure with other social mammals, which highlights how fundamental this property is to all humans, regardless of their culture.

→ which는 관계대명사의 계속적 용법으로 선행사는 앞 문장 전체다. how ~ 이하는 highlights의 목적어인 의문사절(명사절)이며 의문사(how fundamental) + 주어(this property) + 동사(is)의 어순을 취하고 있다.

[정답 해설] 사회 구성인자가 바뀌어도 사회관계망은 여전히 지속되고 이것이 인간 사회의 본질적인 속성이라는 것이 이 글의 일관된 논지이므로 윗글의 제목으로 가장 적절한 것은 ④ '사회관계망: 인간 사회의 불변적 버팀목'이다.

① 세대가 교체돼도 우정은 살아남는다
② 사회관계망이 결핍된 사회도 종종 번영한다
③ 인간의 문화 규범은 축소되는 사회관계망을 반영한다
⑤ 집단적 불변성: 인간 진화의 제1차적 결정 요소

026

[정답 ③]

[지문 해석] 임박한 변화에 대한 예술의 반응은 열렬한 기대가 아니라 혐오감이다. 과학이 처음 인간의 삶을 변화시키기 시작했을 때 많은 예술가들이 미래가 돌이킬 수 없이 과학에 바쳐질 것이라는 전망 앞에 격렬하게 반발했다. 그러나 과학은 진전이 이론의 여지가 없고 불가피한 유일한 인간의 활동 영역이기 때문에 이것은 부질없는 반발이다. 예술가나 정치인, 철학자들은 과거 역사의 이런저런 시기를 – 그것이 고전적 그리스건 르네상스 시기의 이탈리아건, 로마제국의 시민적 질서건, 빅토리아조 영국의 튼실함이든 아니면 인도나 중국의 역사 예술적 황금기건 간에 – 인류가 쌓은 업적의 최고봉이라 회상할 수 있다. 그러나 과학에서 그런 향수는 불가능하다. 그것의 최고점은

현재이고 이어지는 모든 해는 이전 해를 넘어서는 진보다. 이런 끊임없는 발전을 받아들이고 그것에 적응하기를 거부하는 문명은 거기에 따르는 위험을 스스로 감수해야 한다. 현재로서 그 위험은 너무도 끔찍하다.

① 과학에 맞서는 예술, 헛된 시도
② 예술과 함께 성공을 구가하는 과학
③ 과학은 진보할 뿐 결코 뒤돌아보지 않는다
④ 영광된 과거는 예술의 영원한 양식
⑤ 퇴보에 따르는 책임은 본인 스스로 져라

[글의 소재] 과학의 속성

[주요 어휘] revulsion 혐오감, revolt 반발하다, irrevocably 돌이킬 수 없이, incontrovertible 이론의 여지가 없는, inevitable 불가피한, successive 계속되는, appalling 끔찍한

[글의 흐름] 주제문은 'Its highest point is the present, and every successive year is bound to be an advance beyond the preceding one.'이고 미괄식 구조다.

[구조 분석] ⊙ A civilization that refuses to accept this constant progress, and to adjust itself to it, ~

→ 'to adjust ~'는 '~ to accept'와 병렬구조를 이루고 있다.

[정답 해설] '과학은 여타 정신 활동 영역과 달리 과거를 돌아보지 않으며 진보를 거듭할 뿐'이라는 것이 이 글의 요지이므로 적합한 제목은 ③이다.

027

[정답 ①]

[지문 해석] 철새들의 굴절적응의 또 하나의 부류에 에너지 저장, 즉 피하지방 비축이 포함된다. 산발적 음식이 풍부하거나 생물체가 긴급한 (음식) 수요에 직면했을 때 에너지를 저장하는 능력은 많은 저자들에 의해 철새 이동을 위한 적응으로 간주됐지만, 이 능력은 대부분은 아니지만 많은 텃새들에게서도 발견된다. 예를 들어 날기를 시작하기 전에 어린 새끼들에게 집중적으로 먹이를 줘 그들이 둥지를 떠날 때 상당한 지방을 축적하도록 하는 것은 정주형 새나 텃새, 만성조의 흔한 전략이다. 또한 적어도 몇몇 텃새종의 새끼들이 둥지를 떠나기 전 많은 양의 피하지방을 축적하는 것은 잘 알려져 있다. 어떤 텃새종의 암컷들은 산란의 준비 과정에서 지방을 축적하고 또 다른 텃새들은 털갈이나 춘궁기 수요를 위한 준비 과정으로 지방을 축적한다. 또 일시적 자원 집중을 활용하는 월동 열대종이나 텃새 열대종 개체들을 포획해 보니 몸에서 보통에서 상당 수준에 이르는 피하지방이 나왔다.

① 에너지 저장은 많은 텃새들에게 중요하다
② 에너지 저장의 주요 원천인 피하지방
③ 새를 보호하고 싶으면 그들의 서식지를 먼저 보존하라.
④ 왜 철새에게 적절히 먹이를 줘야 하는지
⑤ 텃새 생존에 위협인 식량 부족

글의 소재 텃새의 생존 전략

주요 어휘 exaptation 굴절적응, subcutaneous 피하의, adaptation 적응, patchy 여기저기 흩어져있는, imminent 긴급한, sedentary 정주형의, altricial 만성조(晩成鳥)의, nestling 갓깬 새끼 새, fledgling 부등깃이 나기 시작하는 새끼 새, prior to ~이전에, dispersal 분산, preparatory to ~에 대한 준비 작업으로, molt 털갈이, lean season 춘궁기, exploit ~을 활용하다

글의 흐름 ◉ 주제문은 'the capacity to store energy at times when patchy foods are abundant ~ is found in many if not most resident birds as well.'이다. 이 문장이 예시의 연결사 For instance 바로 앞 문장이라는 점, 그리고 양보절 (Although ~)에 의해 꺾이고 있음을 주목하라.

구조 분석 ◉ Females of some resident species lay down fat reserves preparatory to egg-laying, and many also lay down fat reserves preparatory to undergoing molt ~
➡ 'preparatory to'는 '~에 대한 준비 과정으로'의 뜻으로 부사적으로 쓰였고 to는 전치사이다.

정답 해설 이 글은 피하지방 축적을 통한 에너지 저장이 그간 철새들의 적응 방식으로 알려졌으나 사실 많은 텃새들이 생존 전략을 위해 활용하고 있음을 다양한 예와 함께 보여주고 있다. 따라서 정답은 ① '에너지 저장은 많은 텃새들에게 중요하다'가 적절하다. 에너지 저장(혹은 피하지방 축적)과 텃새의 두 요소가 들어간 선지를 찾아야 한다.

028
정답 ⑤

지문 해석 나는 최근 '사랑'이라는 제목의 새로운 그림책 하나를 펴냈다. 그 책을 집필한 지 서너 주가 지났을 때 아내와 나에게 좀 나쁜 소식이 전해져 아내가 드러내놓고 우는 모습을 딸애가 처음 보게 됐다. 이것이 딸애의 작은 세계를 흔들었는지 그 애는 울음보를 터뜨리며 아내의 다리를 잡고 무슨 일인지 알려 달라며 보챘다. 우리는 아이를 진정시키고 설득해 잠자리에 들게 했다. 아내가 딸에게 모자를 만난 거북이 두 마리 동화를 읽어줄 때 나는 딸의 눈물로 얼룩진 얼굴을 유심히 들여다봤다. 나는 그날 딸이 순수함의 일부를 잃었다는 생각을 안 할 수 없었다. 그러나 이러한 상실의 사건이 기쁨의 순간 못지않게 어린이의 정서 안정과 발달에 중요할지 모른다. 우리의 일은 아마도 애들을 온갖 상처와 심적 고통으로부터 지키려고만 하지 않고 애들이 그런 경험을 잘 해내도록 돕는 것인지도 모른다. 그들에게 말을 붙이고 그들을 붙잡아 주는 것인지도 모른다.

① 회초리를 아끼면 아이를 버린다.
② 상심한 동심은 쉽게 낫지 않는다.
③ 애들 앞에서 눈물을 보이지 말라.
④ 부모 노릇 잘하려면 감정 조절부터 배우라.
⑤ 애들은 기쁨 못지않게 고통 속에서도 큰다.

글의 소재 애환과 어린이의 성장

주요 어휘 settle down 진정시키다, stumble across 우연히 발견하다 =come across, study 자세히 들여다보다, tear-stained 눈물로 얼룩진, fraction 조각, 부분

글의 흐름 ◉ 주제문은 'But maybe these episodes of loss are as vital to the well-adjusted child's development as moments of joy.' 역접의 접속사가 들어있는 문장은 주제문일 경우가 많아 주의 깊게 봐야 한다.

구조 분석 ◉ A few weeks into the writing of the book,
➡ 시간부사 + into + 사건이나 행위를 나타내는 명사구가 나올 경우 '~한 지 ~가 지나서'의 뜻이다. (e.g. A few days into the summer vacation, I had to visit my aunt's[여름방학이 시작된 지 며칠 안 돼 나는 숙모 댁을 방문해야 했다].)
◉ To talk to them. To hold.
➡ 각각 앞에 'Our job is'가 생략됐다.

정답 해설 이 글의 필자는 기쁨의 순간 못지않게 상실의 경험 역시 어린이들의 정서 발달에 필수적일 수 있다는 입장이다. 따라서 ⑤가 제목으로 가장 적절하다.

029
정답 ⑤

지문 해석 의식 또는 기도와 불확실한 결과의 연관성을 잘 설명해 주는 두 가지 구체적인 예가 있다. 운(이 좌우하는) 게임인 주사위 게임을 하는 도박사는 주사위를 던지기 전에 종종 개인적인 의식을 치르지만 체스기사는 말을 움직이기 전에 그런 일을 하지 않는다. 이것은 주사위 게임은 운에 좌우되는 게임이지만 체스에서는 운의 여지가 없기 때문이다. 당신이 실착으로 게임에서 진다면 변명의 여지가 없다. 상대의 반응을 예견하지 못한, 전적으로 당신의 잘못이기 때문이다. 마찬가지로 서부 뉴멕시코에서는 복잡한 지질 구조로 지하수 층의 깊이와 지하수 양이 측정할 수 없을 정도로 편차가 심해 전문 지질학자조차 표면 지형을 보고 지하수의 위치와 양을 정확히 짚어내지 못하기 때문에 지하수 관정을 원하는 농부는 종종 수맥 탐사가를 찾는다. 그러나 텍사스 팬핸들에서는 수맥의 깊이가 125피트로 일정하기 때문에 농부는 단지 물이 필요한 장소 가까이 한 곳을 골라 그 깊이까지 파 내려가기만 하면 된다. 수맥 탐사가 널리 알려져 있지만 어느 누구도 이를 이용하지 않는다. 요컨대, 뉴멕시코 농부나 주사위 도박사는 의식에 의존해 예측불허의 상황에 대처하려 하는 반면 텍사스 팬핸들 농부나 체스기사는 그런 의식이 없는 채로 지낸다.

① 운이 다하면 기댈 것은 능력뿐이다
② 의식과 기도가 때로는 기적을 부른다
③ 상심한 이들의 조용한 치료자, 의식과 기도
④ 기도해서 손해 안 본다. 많이 할수록 좋다
⑤ 불확실성이 의식과 기도의 가능성을 높인다

글의 소재 기도와 불확실성의 연관성

주요 어휘 game of chance 운에 좌우되는 게임, move 장기나 바둑의 수(手), dowser 수맥 탐사가, dispense with ~ 없이 지내다

글의 흐름 ⊙주제문은 'Two specific examples illustrate for us the association between rituals or prayers and uncertain outcome.'으로, 두괄식 구조이다.

구조 분석 ⊙ if your move costs you the game, you have no excuses.

➡ your move(S) costs(V) you(IO) the game(DO)의 4형식 구문이다.

⊙ ~ water, such that not even professional geologists can predict accurately from surface features the location and depth of underground water.

➡ 여기서 such 이하는 a big unpredictable variation을 수식하는 형용사절이다. 해석은 결과로 하는 것이 자연스럽다. 이 문장은 'He is a big liar, such that even his wife doesn't trust him.'과 같은 구조이다.

정답 해설 주제문에서 보듯 이 글은 불확실성과 의식이나 기도의 관계를 주사위 도박과 체스, 그리고 수맥 탐사의 경우를 예를 들어 논증하고 있다. 불확실성이 높을수록 의식이나 기도의 가능성이 커진다는 것이 이 글의 요지이므로 이에 가장 가까운 제목은 ⑤이다.

Chapter II
어법·어휘·세부 내용 파악

4. 어법

정답

				030 ④
031 ⑤	032 ⑤	033 ①	034 ②	035 ③
036 ④	037 ⑤	038 ②	039 ②	

030
정답 ④

지문 해석 실질적인 이타주의자들은 자기 자식들이 모르는 사람의 자식에 우선하는 특별한 책무라는 것을 인정한다. 이에 대해서는 다양한 근거를 댈 수 있다. 대부분의 부모는 자식을 사랑해서 그들에게 자기 자식과 남의 자식을 똑같이 대하라고 요구하는 것은 비현실적일 것이다. 또한 우리는 그런 편견을 막지도 않을 것인데 왜냐하면 아이들은 친밀하고 사랑이 넘치는 가정에서 잘 자라고 남보다 그들의 행복을 위해 더 큰 관심을 보이지 않으면 우리는 사람들을 사랑할 수 없기 때문이다. 어쨌든, 최상의 선을 행하는 것이 모든 실질적 이타주의자의 중요한 삶의 일부이기는 하지만 실질적 이타주의자들도 성인이 아닌 일반 사람인 이상 일 년 365일 하는 일마다 선을 극대화하려 하지는 않는다. 전형적인 실질적 이타주의자들은 편안한 상태에서 자기가 하고 싶은 것을 할 수 있도록 시간과 자원을 스스로 확보한다. 우리 대부분에게 있어 자식과 식구들과 가깝게 지내는 것은 시간 보내기의 중심 고려사항이다. 그럼에도 불구하고 실질적인 이타주의자들은 다른 사람들의 보다 큰 어려움 앞에서 자식들을 위해서 하는 것에는 한계가 있다는 점을 인정한다.

글의 소재 실질적 이타주의자들의 이타행

주요 어휘 effective 실질적인, 효과적인, altruist 이타주의자, ahead of ~에 앞서, impartial 공평한, maximize 극대화하다, 24/7 일 년 365일 내내, typical 전형적인, given ~을 고려할 때

글의 흐름 ⊙ 실질적 이타주의자들도 자기 가족에 관심을 두지만 분수껏 챙긴다는 것이 필자의 주장으로 마지막 두 문장에 이런 입장이 담겨 있다.

구조 분석 ⊙ Nonetheless, effective altruists recognize that there are limitations to how much they should do for their children, given the greater needs of others.

➡ how much 이하가 전치사 to의 목적어인 의문사절이자

명사절이다. given은 전치사로 '~를 고려해 볼 때'의 뜻이고 considering이나 in consideration of로 바꿔 쓸 수 있다.

정답 해설 뒤 문장이 완전하기 때문에 ④의 자리에는 what이 올 수 없다(관계대명사든, 의문사든). 의문부사 how가 와야 how ~이하가 전치사 to의 목적어인 의문사절(명사절)을 유도할 수 있다.

① 가정법 과거 주절의 동사로 적절하다.

② '~도 아니다'(and not)의 상관접속사로 적절하게 쓰였다.

③ 동명사구 doing the most good이 while 절의 주어로 쓰였다.

⑤ '~를 고려할 때'를 뜻하는 전치사 given의 쓰임은 적절하다.

031

정답 ⑤

지문 해석 어린이들과 놀이하는 어른들은 심각한 갈등에 빠진 기분을 느낄 수 있다. 어린이는 필사적으로 이기고 싶어 하는데 이는 그 또는 그녀가 이기는 것이 매우 중요하다고 배웠기 때문이다. 만약 부모가 아이에게 지거나 경쟁하는 법을 가르치기 위해 전력을 다해 경기하면 아이는 종종 좌절의 눈물을 흘리며 쓰러진다. 만약 부모가 져주려고 하면 아이는 일부러 봐준다는 느낌을 갖거나 그(어린이)가 이기면, 일부 부모들이 참기 힘든, 일종의 조롱하는 듯한 태도를 보인다. 아빠들은 그들이 여전히 아이들을 장악할 수 있음을 입증하기 위해 종종 게임에서 이기려 한다. 영화 The Great Santini에서는 아빠가 우월적 위치를 주장하고 젊음을 유지하기 위해 아들과의 게임에서 격렬한 경쟁을 벌이는데 이는 이런 종류의 갈등이 주는 고통의 예를 보여준다.

글의 소재 아이들과 경기할 때 부모가 느끼는 갈등

주요 어휘 conflict 갈등, desperately 필사적으로, collapse 무너지다, 쓰러지다, frustration 좌절, patronize 후원하다, 어린애 취급하다, taunt 조롱하다, dominate 지배하다, 장악하다, intense 격렬한, assert 주장하다, illustrate 예증하다

글의 흐름 ⊙ 주제문은 'Adults playing with children can find themselves in a terrible conflict.'이며 두괄식 구조다.

구조 분석 ⊙ the child feels patronized or, when he wins, engages in a kind of taunting behavior that may be difficult for some parents to tolerate.

➔ engages는 feels와 병렬구조이고, when he wins는 삽입의 부사절이다. 'to tolerate'는 difficult를 수식하는 부사적 용법으로 쓰였고 'for some parents'는 'to tolerate'의 의미상 주어다.

정답 해설 마지막 문장의 주어는 The film이고 'in which ~'는 주어를 꾸며주는 수식절이므로 ⑤에는 준동사가 아니라 동사가 와야 하고 따라서 illustrating이 아니라 illustrates가 적절하다.

① 목적어 themselves가 주어 adults와 같기 때문에 재귀대명

사 themselves는 적절하게 쓰였다.

② that가 명사절을 유도해 동사 has been taught의 목적어로 쓰였기 때문에 접속사 that의 쓰임은 적절하다.

③ 'how to lose or compete'는 의문사 + to 부정사의 명사적 용법으로 동사 teach의 직접목적어로 쓰인 것은 적절하다.

④ 문장에서 when he wins는 삽입의 부사절이고 engages는 feels와 병렬구조이기 때문에 engages는 문법적으로 옳다.

032

정답 ⑤

지문 해석 오래전에 우리 조상들은 어떤 식물을 먹거나 동물의 신체 기관을 섭취하는 것이 불쾌하거나 심지어는 치명적인 효과를 가져왔다는 것을 알아냈다. 이러한 물질에 대한 언급이 죽어가는 사람을 위한 위로의 기도문집에 나타난 적이 있고 당시 pharmakon이라고 불리던 일종의 영적 치료제를 지칭했는데 그것은 주로 임종의 고통을 완화하기 위해 사용되었다. 간단히 말하면 pharmakon은 독이었다. 원래 pharmakos라는 용어는 인간 희생양을 뜻했는데 그는 그 지역 사회에서 자신보다 훨씬 중요한 어떤 다른 사람의 병을 위한 치료제로 종종 글자 그대로 독살에 의해 희생됐다. 그 후 기원전 600년경에 그 용어는 병자를 치료하기 위해 사용된 물질을 지칭하게 됐다. 그것은 물론 오늘날 사용되고 있는 두 용어와 관련이 있는데, 약이 인체에 미치는 영향을 연구하는 약리학과 약이 뇌에 미치는 영향, 즉 "정신 활성"이라 정의되는 영향을 연구하는 정신약리학이 그것들이다.

글의 소재 약리학이라는 용어의 탄생 배경

주요 어휘 ingest 섭취하다, lethal 치명적인, substance 물질, alleviate 완화하다, simply put 간단히 말하면, scapegoat 희생양, pharmacology 약리학, psychopharmacology 정신약리학, psychoactive 정신 활성의

구조 분석 ⊙ Originally, the term pharmakos referred to a human scapegoat, who was sacrificed, sometimes literally by poisoning, as a remedy for the illness of another person, usually someone far more important in the local society.

➔ who는 관계대명사 계속적 용법으로 선행사는 a human scapegoat이고 'sometimes literally by poisoning'는 삽입의 부사구이며 another person과 someone은 동격이다.

정답 해설 ⑤ which 다음 문장이 완전하기 때문에 ⑤의 자리에는 관계부사나 전치사 + 관계대명사가 와야 한다. 여기서는 which 대신 by which가 와야 한다.

① 여기서 동명사 ingesting은 that절의 주어로 쓰였기 때문에 적절하다.

② 이 문장은 병렬구조로 appeared와 문법적 형태가 같은

referred의 쓰임은 적절하다.

③ 'to alleviate'는 to 부정사의 부사적 용법으로 동사 원형 alleviate가 쓰인 것은 옳다.

④ 부정대명사 someone을 뒤에서 수식하고 있는 형용사 important의 쓰임은 적절하다.

033
정답 ①

[지문 해석] 어떻게 하면 실천적으로 지혜롭게 될 수 있는가? 제조 비법이나 공식, 일련의 기법은 없다. 기술은 경험을 통해 학습되고 실천의 목표에 전념하는 것도 그러하다. 그래서 우리는 지혜를 경험과 연관시킨다. 그러나 아무 경험이라고 다 효과가 있는 건 아니다. 어떤 경험은 실천적 지혜를 기르고 가르치지만 그것을 부식시키는 것도 있다. 바로 이 점에서 아리스토텔레스는 우리의 관심을 정말 중요한 것에 집중시키는데, 성격과 실천적 지혜는 우리가 종사하는 기관에 의해 함양돼야 한다는 사실이다. 아리스토텔레스가 윤리학 책을 쓴 것은 단지 실천적 지혜가 더 나은 삶과 사회에 중요하다는 것을 강조하기 위해서뿐 아니라 시민들이 실천적 지혜를 배우도록 장려하는 기관을 건립할 것을 아테네 도시국가 시민과 정치인에게 촉구하기 위해서이기도 했다. 오늘날의 지혜 부족, 즉 우리의 일상생활과 직장에서 성공하기 위해 필요한 지혜의 부족에 직면한다면 그는 우리에게 기관들이 전문직 종사자의 지혜를 억누르지는 않는지, 그렇다면 그런 부족을 메꾸기 위해 무엇을 해야 하는지 조사해 보라고 촉구할 것이다.

[글의 소재] 아리스토텔레스의 실천적 지혜

[주요 어휘] commitment 전념, associate A with B A를 B와 연관시키다, nurture 기르다, corrode 부식시키다, underline 강조하다, urge 촉구하다, practitioner 전문직 종사자

[글의 흐름] ⊙ 주제문은 'character and practical wisdom must be cultivated by the major institutions in which we practice.'이며 중괄식 구조를 취하고 있다.

[구조 분석] ⊙ he would urge us to examine whether our institutions are discouraging the wisdom of practitioners and, if so, what can be done to make up the deficit.

➡ urge가 동사, 'to examine ~'가 목적격보어인 5형식 문장이며 whether 이하와 what 이하는 examine의 공동목적어절이다.

[정답 해설] 이 문장은 병렬구조이기 때문에 ①의 자리에 올 대동사는 does가 아니라 are learned와 문법 형태가 같은 is라야 한다. 따라서 정답은 ①이다.

② 여기서 do는 자동사로 쓰여 '효과가 있다'는 뜻이므로 적절하다.

③ 'it ~ that' 강조구문으로 부사 here가 강조됐으므로 that의

쓰임은 적절하다.

④ 'not only(simply) to R but also to R'의 상관 표현으로 '단지 ~만을 ~하기 위해서가 아니고 ~도 ~하기 위해서'라는 의미이므로 'to urge'의 쓰임은 적절하다.

⑤ whether 이하가 명사절을 유도해 타동사 examine의 목적어가 되고 있으므로 접속사 whether의 쓰임은 타당하다.

034
정답 ②

[지문 해석] 일반적으로 귀는 정기적인 청소를 필요로 하지 않는다. 귀는 자동으로 세척되는 오븐과 같다. 중력과 체열의 도움으로 귀지는 서서히 저절로 밖으로 나온다. 귀지가 외이에 발견되면 면봉이 사용될 수 있다. 만약 어쩔 수 없이 더 안쪽으로 들어가야 한다면 이구경색(귀지 막힘)이나 상처의 위험을 유발할 수 있다. 만일 귀 안에 귀지가 들어차게 되면 당신은 고통을 느끼거나 반 귀머거리가 된다. 귀지 막힘을 완화해 주는 데는 의사 처방 없이 살 수 있는 약이 있지만 따뜻한 물을 주사기로 주입하면 종종 효과를 볼 수 있다. 최후 수단으로 충분한 세척을 위해 귀 전문 의사나 응급실을 찾을 수 있다. 이런 규칙을 어기고 귀 안에 빠진 면봉 끝을 제거하기 위해 환자가 의사를 찾는 일은 비일비재하다. 걱정 말라. 의사들은 준비돼 있다. 그들은 바퀴벌레나 구슬, 볼펜 뚜껑 같은 것들도 제거하는데 그들은 그 모두를 귀에서 꺼내 주었다.

[글의 소재] 귀지 처리 요령

[주요 어휘] gravity 중력, earwax 귀지, cotton swab 면봉, wax impaction 이구경색(귀지 막힘), over-the-counter 의사 처방 없이 살 수 있는, preparation 조제 약품, blockage 막힘, syringe 주사기, ER(Emergency Room) 응급실, cockroach 바퀴벌레, bead 구슬

[구조 분석] ⊙ If you can't help but to go in farther, ~

➡ ② cannot help but + 동사 원형은 '~하지 않을 수 없다'의 뜻으로 cannot help ~ing와 같다. 따라서 to go가 아닌 go를 써야 맞다.

[정답 해설] 구조 분석을 참조하라.

① like는 전치사로 쓰여 목적어 a self-cleaning oven을 취했으므로 적절하다.

③ 귀지가 막히는 것이므로 수동의 의미를 가진 과거분사 impacted가 쓰인 것은 타당하다.

④ have violated의 violated와 병렬구조를 이루므로 come(과거분사)이 쓰인 것은 적절하다.

⑤ which는 관계대명사의 계속적 용법으로 cockroaches, beads, and pen caps를 선행사로 받으므로 문법적으로 적절하다.

035

지문 해석 1898년 영국 출신 이집트학 학자인 James Quibell과 Frederick Green은 Hierakonpolis 상(上) 이집트 폐사지에서 조각된 경사암 석판—녹회색 점판암—을 발굴했다. 20년 후 발견된 Tutankhamun 무덤과는 달리 이번 발견이 전 세계 언론인들을 현장으로 달려가게 하지는 못했지만 발굴자들은 거의 즉각적으로 그 중요성을 알아차렸다. 이 석판 조각, 즉 Narmer Palette는 로제타석처럼 Hierakonpolis에 국한된 의미를 크게 벗어나 고대 이집트 연구에 강한 영향을 미치게 됐다. 다음 한 세기 동안, 그것은 이집트 국가의 정치적 기원에서 이집트 예술과 문자의 성격에 이르는 많은 문제들을 풀려는 이집트학 학자들에 의해 다양하게 해석됐다. 한 가지 물건이 전체 문화를 대표할 수는 없지만 Narmer Palette는 고대 이집트 문화의 특정 측면 전체에 대한 축소판 역할을 할 정도로 상징적이고 정보가 풍부한 몇 개의 현존하는 나일 계곡산(産) 공예품들 중 하나다.

글의 소재 Narmer Palette의 문화사적 의미

주요 어휘 Egyptologist 이집트학 학자, uncover 발견하다, repercussion 반향, 영향, typify 대표하다, artefact 공예품, iconic 상징적인, microcosm 소우주, 축소판

글의 흐름 ⊙ 맨 마지막 문장 'the Narmer Palette is one of a few surviving artefacts ~ certain aspects of ancient Egyptian culture as a whole.'에 글쓴이의 주장이 집약돼 있다.

구조 분석 ⊙ Unlike the discovery of Tutankhamun's tomb twenty-four years later this find would not bring the world's journalists racing to the scene,

➜ bring(V), the world's journalists(O), racing to the scene(OC)인 5형식 문장으로 '전 세계 언론인들을 현장으로 달려가게 했다'는 말이다.

정답 해설 (A) 동사 bring의 목적격보어 역할을 할 race의 알맞은 형태는 현재분사 racing이다. race는 '달려가다'를 뜻하는 자동사로 여기서는 과거분사 형태를 취할 수 없다.

(B) 앞 문장이 이미 완결됐기 때문에 또다시 동사가 나올 수 없다. 준동사(현재분사)가 나와 분사구문을 이뤄야 한다.

(C) 'so 형용사/부사 that' 용법이다. '너무 ~해서 ~하다'의 뜻으로 (C)에는 결과의 부사절을 유도하는 접속사 that이 와야 한다. 뒤 문장이 완전하므로 관계대명사 which는 올 수가 없다. 따라서 정답은 ③이다.

036

지문 해석 사회과학자들이 전통 사회 연구로부터 학문적 중요성을 지닌 결론을 분명히 이끌어낼 수 있지만 이외의 우리들도 마찬가지로 실제적 중요성을 가진 것들을 배울 수 있다. 전통 사회는 사실상 인간 사회를 어떻게 구성하는지에 대한 수천 개의 자연 실험의 표본이다. 그들은 우리 현대 사회가 채택한 것과는 다른, 인간적 문제에 대한 수천 개의 해결책을 제시해 왔다. 그들 해결책 중 몇몇은—가령, 전통 사회가 애들을 교육하고, 연장자를 대우하고, 건강을 유지하고, 말하고, 여가를 보내고, 분쟁을 해결하는 몇몇 방법들은—나에게 그랬듯 여러분에게도 제1 세계의 일반적 관행보다 우월하다고 여겨질 것이다. 우리는 그런 전통적인 관행을 선택적으로 채택함으로써 도움을 받을 수도 있다. 우리 중 몇몇은 이미 그렇게 해서 건강과 행복에 입증된 혜택을 누리기도 했다(혜택을 누린 사례가 되기도 했다). 어떤 면에서 우리 현대인들은 부적응자들이다. 지금 우리의 몸과 관행은 그것이 진화하고 적응해 온 여건과는 다른 여건에 직면해 있다.

글의 소재 전통 사회 연구에서 배울 점

주요 어휘 in effect 사실상, come up with ~를 생산하다, 제시하다, dispute 분쟁, selectively 선택적으로, demonstrate 입증하다, 본보기를 보이다. misfit 부적응자, adapt 적응시키다

글의 흐름 ⊙ 첫 문장 'While social scientists can surely draw conclusions of academic interest ~ be able to learn things of practical interest.'가 주제문인 두괄식 구조다.

구조 분석 ⊙ We shall see that some of those solutions … may strike you, as they do me, as superior to normal practices in the First World.

➜ strike A as B 구문으로 'A에게 B의 인상을 주다'는 뜻이다. do는 대동사로 strike를 받는다.

정답 해설 (A) 앞에 나온 명사의 반복을 피한 대명사가 수식구—이 경우는 준동사구—에 의해 제한될 경우 지시대명사 that(those)를 써야 하므로 those가 적절하다.

(B) benefits가 입증되는 것이므로 수동의 의미의 과거분사 demonstrated가 적절하다.

(C) 뒤 문장이 완전하기 때문에(1형식) 앞에는 관계부사나 전치사+관계대명사가 와야 한다. 따라서 which가 적절하다.

037

지문 해석 현명한 광고주들은 잠재의식적 광고가 효과를 낼 수 있는 방법을 생각해낼 수도 있다. 하지만, 그렇다 하더라도 그들의 광고 효과는 의식적인 수준에서 제시되는 매일 매일의 광고만큼 강력할 가능성이 낮다. 사람들이 TV에서 보고, 라디오에서 듣고, 인쇄 매체에서 보는 광고에 대한 심드렁한 태도에도 불구하고 이런 광고들은 그들의 태도 형성에 강한 영향을 미칠 수 있다. 아마도 이에 대한 최상의 증거는 분할된 케이블 시장 조사법을 사용하는 연구에서 나올 것이다. 광고주들은 케이블 TV 회사와 식료잡화점과 공동 작업하에 무작위로 선택한 케이

블 가입자군에게 서로 다른 버전의 광고를 보여준다. 가입자들은 쇼핑할 때 특수 ID 카드를 사용하고 그럼으로써 식료잡화점이 그들이 구매하는 것들을 정확하게 추적하게 하는 데 동의한다. 그래서 광고주들은 특정 광고를 보는 사람들이 실제로 광고된 제품을 살 가능성이 큰지 아닌지를 알 수 있다. 이에 대한 답은 그럴 가능성이 큰 경우가 자주 있다는 것이다.

글의 소재 잠재의식 광고보다 큰 일상 광고 효과

주요 어휘 figure out 생각해내다, subliminal 잠재 의식적인, blasé 심드렁한, in conjunction with ~와 공동으로, subscriber 가입자, keep track of 추적하다

글의 흐름 ⊙ 주제문은 'Even if they do, however, the effects of their ads are unlikely to be as powerful as every day ads presented at conscious levels.'이다.

구조 분석 ⊙ The subscribers agree to use a special identification card when they shop, allowing the grocery stores to keep track of exactly what they buy.

→ 분사구문으로 부대 상황을 나타내며 'as they allow the grocery ~'로 바꿔 쓸 수 있다.

정답 해설 (A) 다음에는 ads를 꾸며주는 수식구가 와야 하고 수동 의미를 가져야 하므로 present의 과거분사인 presented가 적절하다. ads와 presented 사이에는 which(that) are가 생략됐다.

(B) 'working ~'는 삽입의 부사구(분사구문)에 불과하므로 이 문장의 주어 Advertisers에 이어지는 (B) 자리에는 준동사가 아닌 동사가 와야 한다. 따라서 show가 적절하다.

(C) 앞 문장 'people who see a particular commercial are in fact more likely to'로 보아 (C)의 대동사는 are가 적절하다. 따라서 정답은 ⑤다.

038

정답 ②

지문 해석 과학자들은 멸종을 살아있는 생물과 끊임없이 변하는 그들의 물리적 환경 사이에 벌어지는 복잡한 상호작용의 자연스러운 결과로 본다. 한 종이 환경과 너무 맞지 않아 그것이 음식과 생활공간을 위해 성공적으로 경쟁할 수 없을 때 그것은 멸종할 가능성이 크다. 위기는 그 종 자체 내의 진화론적 변화나 환경 변화 또는 같은 지역에 새로운 종의 출현으로 비롯될 수 있다. 대규모 환경 변화는 지질학적으로 짧은 시간 내에 다수의 종을 전멸시키는 "대량 멸종"을 초래할 수 있다. 과학적 관점에서 봤을 때 단일 종의 멸종은 인상주의 그림에서 한 점의 색깔처럼 보다 큰 패턴의 한 부분으로서 의미 있다. 이에 반해 대중문화는 개별 종의 멸종에 심오한 의미를, 그리고 멸종에 얽힌 이야기에 강한 설교 논조를 각각 부여한다. 현재를 배경으로 하는 사람들은 위협받는 종을 귀엽고 순진한 인간 무지와 탐욕의 희생자로 묘사한다. 과거를 배경으로 하는 사람들은 멸종된

종을 불행한 자기 약점의 희생자로 묘사한다. 두 묘사는 자연에 대한 폭넓은 문화적 태도에 뿌리를 두고 있다.

글의 소재 멸종을 보는 과학적, 문화적 시각

주요 어휘 extinction 멸종, interaction 상호작용, ill-suited 맞지 않는, wipe out 전멸시키다, geologically 지질학적으로, moralize 설교하다, greed 탐욕, hapless 불행한

글의 흐름 ⊙ 주제문은 'Scientists see extinction as a natural result ~ and their continually changing physical environment.'와 'Popular culture, on the other hand, invests ~ with a strong moralizing tone.'인 병렬식 구조다.

구조 분석 ⊙ Popular culture, on the other hand, invests the extinction of individual species with deep meaning and (invests) its stories about extinctions with a strong moralizing tone.

→ invest A with B는 'A에게 B를 부여하다'의 뜻이고 and와 its 사이에는 invests가 생략됐다.

정답 해설 ②의 what 앞에 선행사(mass extinctions)가 있고 뒤 문장이 불완전하기 때문에 what의 자리에는 관계대명사 that이나 which가 와야 한다.

① 의 it은 a species를 받기 때문에 맞다.

③ '설교하는'의 능동의 뜻을 가진 현재분사가 온 것은 적절하다.

④ '위협받는'의 수동의 뜻을 가진 과거분사가 쓰인 것은 타당하다.

⑤ 주어인 those에 복수로 수 일치시킨 것은 적절하다.

039

정답 ②

지문 해석 고고학자와 인지과학자들이 선사시대 예술의 의미와 목적에 대해 다양한 이론을 제시했지만 예술이 완전히 인간적이 되는 의미의 본질을 구현하는 진화론적 발전의 한 과정이라는 데 그들 모두는 동의한다. 더구나, 대부분의 이론가들은 구석기시대 예술과, 비슷한 시기 선사 기록에 나오는 추상적인 상징이나 기호를 구분한다. 예술의 본질적인 모방 특성은—상징이나 기호 체계의 추상적 성격과는 대조적으로—캐나다 신경심리학자인 Merlin Donald에 의해 강조됐는데 그는 그것의 의미를 심도 있게 밝혀주는 이론을 제시한다. 그의 *Origins of the Modern Mind*에서 Donald는, 모방은 언어와 상징적 사고가 태동하기 바로 전에 호모 사피엔스의 직전 조상들 사이에서 현실을 그려내는 일차적 수단으로 기능하며 인간의 인지 발전에 중요한 역할을 했다는 설득력 있는 주장을 편다. Donald에게 "모방"이라는 용어는 목소리 톤, 얼굴 표정, 몸동작, 손짓과 다른 비언어적 수단을 이용해 의도적으로 현실을 그려내는 수단을 지칭한다. 그의 견해로는 그것(모방)은 흉내 내기나 모사

와는 본질적으로 다르다.

글의 소재 선사 예술의 주 특징으로서의 모방

주요 어휘 archaeologist 고고학자, prehistoric 선사시대의, embody 구현하다, Paleolithic 구석기 시대의, mimetic 모방의, notational 기호의, highlight 강조하다, profoundly 심오하게, persuasively 설득력 있게, crucial 중요한, manual 손의, mimicry 흉내 내기

글의 흐름 ⊙ 'mimesis played a crucial role in human cognitive evolution, ~ just prior to the emergence of language and symbolic thought.'에 필자의 주장이 들어있다.

구조 분석 ⊙ all agree that the arts are among the evolutionary developments that "embody the very essence of <u>what</u> <u>it</u> means to be fully human."

➡ what 이하는 전치사 of의 목적어인 명사절이고 it는 가주어, 'to be fully human'이 진주어이다.

정답 해설 ②는 선행사가 있고 뒤 문장이 불완전하기 때문에—emerged의 주어가 없다—관계부사가 아니라 관계대명사 which나 that이 와야 한다.

①에서 what 앞에 선행사가 없고 뒤 문장이 불완전하기 때문에—타동사 means의 목적어가 없다—관계대명사 what가 쓰인 것은 옳다.

③에서 부사 profoundly가 준동사 illuminating을 수식한 것은 적절하다.

④ 문장에서 이미 주어(mimesis)와 동사(played)가 나왔으므로 동사가 나오지 못하고 준동사(현재분사)가 나와 분사구문을 이룬 것은 옳다.

⑤ utilize는 선행사 means(복수)에 맞춰 수 일치시켰으므로 옳다.

5. 어휘

정답

				040 ⑤
041 ③	042 ⑤	043 ④	044 ②	045 ①
046 ①	047 ⑤	048 ④		

040

정답 ⑤

지문 해석 학습공동체에서 신뢰는 깨지기 쉽다. 증가할 수도 있고 감소할 수도 있다는 점에서 그것은 다른 정신적 자산과 같다. 이를테면 모든 사람을 즐겁게 만드는 식으로 반응하기는 어려워서 교육자들은 쉽게 동료의 선의를 오해할 수 있다. 더군다나, 리더십은 다수의, 때로는 상충하는 요구에 답하여 결정 내리기를 수반해서, 지배적인 요구가 교사들의 현재 욕구를 처리하지 못하면 그들은 교장에 대한 신뢰를 잃을 수 있다. 신뢰 없이는 진정한 공동체 의식이 발전할 수 없고 협조 문화가 존재할 수도 없다. 이런 상황에서 사람들은 공식적인 규칙과 규정의 체계 아래서만 협력한다. 본질적으로 신뢰의 부족은 관리자들이 규정과 표준 절차에 의존해 맹종과 협조를 구하는 보다 관료적인 학교를 탄생시킬 가능성이 크다. 신뢰가 적을수록 학습이 이뤄질 가능성이 적은데 이는 관료화된 환경에서는 공동체 구축이 가능하기(➡ 어렵기) 때문이다. 이런 환경에서 사람들은 제도적 요구 준수에 필요한 최소한의 것만 하는 경향이 있다. 이런 분위기에서 학교는 제대로 기능하지 않는다.

글의 소재 학습공동체에서 신뢰 부족으로 인한 부작용

주요 어휘 fragile 깨지기 쉬운, enhance 높이다, 고양하다, diminish 줄이다, misinterpret 오해하다, entail 수반하다, dominant 지배적인, address 처리하다, collaborative 협조하는, compliance 준수, bureaucratize 관료화하다, feasible 실현 가능성이 있는, comply 따르다

글의 흐름 ⊙ 주제문은 'Without trust, a true sense of community cannot be developed, nor can a collaborative culture exist.'이고 중괄식 구조의 글이다.

구조 분석 ⊙ Without trust, a true sense of community cannot be developed, <u>nor</u> <u>can</u> a collaborative culture <u>exist</u>.

➡ 부정의 접속사 nor 때문에 조동사 + S + 본동사 어순의 도치 구문이 되었고 '~도 ~하지 않다'는 뜻이다.

정답 해설 신뢰가 없으면 관료적인 학교가 탄생하고 관료화된 환경에서는 공동체 구축이 어려워 학습이 이뤄질 가능성이 작다는 것이 글의 전체적인 흐름이므로 ⑤는 difficult 등의 다른 말로 바꿔야 한다. feasible은 실현 가능성이 있다는 말이다.

041

지문 해석 만약 당신이 비행기를 탔는데 기장이 기내 방송에서 "오늘 밤 7시 30분 클리블랜드에 안전하게 도착하기를 바랍니다."라고 말했을 때 당신의 반응을 생각해 보라. 아직 이륙하지 않았다면 당신은 비행기에서 내릴 것이다. 왜냐고? "바랍니다"라는 기장의 어휘 선택이 안전한 도착에 대한 일말의 의구심을 드러내기 때문이다. 그런 불확실한 언어는 항공기 조종실이나 제품 소개에 어울리지 않는다. 만일 당신이 "우리 제품이 ~하다는 것을 당신은 알게 될 거 같은데요."라고 말하는 버릇이 있다면 당신은 지나치게 머뭇거리는 것이다. 성공 가능성은 "당신이 동의할 거로 압니다." 같은 보다 유연한(➡ 적극적인) 접근을 선호한다. 자신 없는 언어는 공손한 대화의 정상적인 일부여서 조심하지 않으면 제품소개에 쉽게 끼어들 수 있다. 만일 당신의 언어 선택이 적극적이지 않고 머뭇거린다면 그런 머뭇거림은 당신이나 당신 제품의 일부로 연상될 것이다. 영업 발표에 단정적이고 적극적인 어휘를 사용하고 "아마도," "어쩌면," "그럴 거 같은데요." 등은 아껴 두었다가 공손한 대화에나 써라.

글의 소재 단정적이고 적극적인 어휘 사용의 필요성

주요 어휘 reaction 반응, intercom 구내 방송(= intercommunication system), tentative 임시의, 머뭇거리는, cockpit 비행기 조종실, flexible 유연한, definite 단정적인, save 아끼다

글의 흐름 ⊙ 맨 마지막 문장 "Use definite positive phrases within your presentation and save the "maybe's," "might be's," and "I think so's" for polite conversation."이 주제문이고 미괄식이다. 명령문 같은 강한 표현이 들어간 문장이 주제문이 된 경우다.

구조 분석 ⊙ If you hadn't taken off yet, you'd get off the plane.

➡ 조건절에는 가정법 과거완료가, 주절에는 가정법 과거가 각각 쓰인 혼합형 가정법 문장이다. "이륙하지 않았다면"(과거 사실) "내릴 텐데"(현재 사실)를 각각 가정한 것이다.

정답 해설 머뭇거리는 말보다는 좀 더 적극적이고 단정적인 표현이 영업 발표에 효과적이라는 맥락이므로 밑줄 친 ③의 '유연한'은 어색하다. 'positive'나 'definite' 같은 보다 단호한 뉘앙스의 말로 대체돼야 한다.

042

지문 해석 만일 당신이 과거에 어떤 다른 위기를 극복한 경험을 이미 가지고 있다면 그것은 당신에게 새로운 위기도 해결할 수 있다는 자신감을 준다. 그것은 이전 위기가 극복되지 않은 데서 오는, 당신이 무엇을 하든 성공하지 못할 것이라는 절망감과 대조된다. 이전 경험의 중요성은 왜 위기가 나이 든 사람들보다 청소년이나 젊은 성년들에게 더 큰 상처를 주는지에 대한 이유를 말해준다. 친밀한 관계의 단절은 어떤 나이에도 상처를 주지만 첫 번째 긴밀한 관계의 단절은 특히 파괴적이다. 초기의(➡ 나중의) 단절 시에는 그것이 아무리 고통스러워도 우리는 전에 비슷한 고통을 겪었고 이겨냈음을 기억한다.

글의 소재 과거의 위기 극복 경험의 중요성

주요 어휘 cope with 극복하다, confidence 자신감, contrast 대조되다, traumatic 상처를 주는, adolescent 청소년, break-up 단절, devastating 파괴적인, 황폐화하는, recall 기억하다

글의 흐름 ⊙ 'If you have already had the experience of coping successfully with some different crisis in the past, ~ that you can solve the new crisis as well.'을 주제문으로 볼 수 있으며 두괄식 구조다.

구조 분석 ⊙ That contrasts with the sense of helplessness, growing out of previous crises not mastered, that, whatever you do, you won't succeed.

➡ that은 helplessness를 보충 설명해주는 동격의 that으로 that 다음에 완전한 문장이 오고 있다. 'growing ~ mastered'는 현재분사 + α로 이뤄진 삽입구로 helplessness를 수식하고 있다.

정답 해설 처음 위기를 맞으면 큰 상처를 받을 수 있지만 과거에 위기를 극복한 경험이 있으면 그 극복의 기억 때문에 상처가 덜하다는 맥락이므로 ⑤의 earlier는 later 등의 낱말로 대체돼야 한다.

043

지문 해석 바닷속 소금의 기원을 설명하기 위한 첫 번째 과학적 시도는 영국계 아일랜드 과학자인 Robert Boyle에 의해 1670년대에 이뤄졌다. 대기 화학과 색채 현상에 관한 자신의 연구를 활용해 그는 강물이 바다로 흘러 들어가면서 미세한 양의 소금을 실어 나른다는 것을 보여주는 몇 가지 측정을 했다. 이것이 바닷속 소금의 기원 관(觀)으로 이어져 수 세기 동안 표준적인 설명 역할을 했다. 그것은 빗물에 의해 바위와 토양으로부터 광물질이 끊임없이 떨어져 나오고 땅 위의 빗물과 합류해 지방 하천을 이뤄 강으로 나아간 다음 바다로 흘러 들어간다는 것이다. 바다로 들어가는 물방울은 육지로부터 몇몇 광물질을 가져오고 물방울이 마침내 증발하고 다시 비가 될 때 이 광물질들은 사라진다(➡ 남는다). 이 그림에서 지구의 수계(水系)는 물질을 바다로 유입시키고 물이 증발-강수 사이클을 시작할 때 그것들을 뒤에 남기는, 일종의 끊임없는 컨베이어 벨트를 만든다.

글의 소재 바닷물이 짠 이유에 대한 한 이론

주요 어휘 draw on ~을 활용하다, measurement 측정,

minute 미세한, standard 표준적인, discharge 방출하다, runoff 땅 위를 흐르는 빗물, vanish 사라지다, evaporate 증발하다, precipitation 강수

글의 흐름 ⊙ 바닷물이 짠 이유는 마지막 문장 'the river systems of earth form a kind of continuous conveyor belt, ~ its evaporation precipitation cycle again.'에 집약돼 있으므로 이것을 주제문으로 봐도 무방하다.

구조 분석 ⊙ the river systems of earth form a kind of continuous conveyor belt, <u>washing</u> materials into the sea and <u>leaving</u> them behind as the water starts its evaporation precipitation cycle again.

→ washing과 leaving은 병렬구조이면서 동시에 분사구문이다. 이 문장은 'as they wash materials into the sea and leave them ~'으로 바꿀 수 있다.

정답 해설 마지막 문장에서 광물질을 바다로 유출시켜 그것들을 바다에 남겨둔 상태에서(leaving them behind) 증발-강수 사이클을 시작한다고 했으므로 ④의 vanish는 remain이나 linger 같은 단어로 바뀌어야 한다.

044
정답 ②

지문 해석 정보와 의미를 분리하기는 어려운데 이는 우리가 메시지를 계속 해석할 수밖에 없기 때문이다. 우리는 자동적으로 메시지에 의미를 주입하고 그럼으로써 메시지의 의미가 메시지 안에 실린다고 믿도록 스스로를 기만한다. 그러나 그렇지 않다. 그것은 착각일 뿐이다. 의미는 맥락과 사전 지식에서 나온다. 의미는 인간 같은 지식의 주체가 메시지에 부여하는 해석이지만 그것은 메시지를 실어 나르는 물리적 질서와 다르고 메시지 그 자체와도 다르다. 의미는 메시지가 생물체나 정보 처리 능력을 가진 기계를 만날 때 발생한다. 그것은 정보를 전달하는 잉크 흔적이나 음파, 광선, 또는 전기 펄스에 실리지 않는다. 9.11이라는 어구를 생각해보자. 내가 이 말을 하면 대부분의 미국인들은 자동적으로 2001년 트윈 타워 테러를 생각할 것이다. 칠레인들은 1973년 쿠데타를 생각한다. 그러나 내가 9.11이라는 말을 쓰면 나는 그날 MIT에 복귀한다는 말을 학생들에게 하는 것이다. 따라서 메시지의 의미는 당신이 구성하는 어떤 것이다. 겉으로는 그렇게 보일지 모르나 그것은 메시지의 일부가 아니다.

글의 소재 메시지가 아닌 맥락의 소산으로서의 의미

주요 어휘 interpret 해석하다, infuse 주입하다, illusion 착각, emerge 나타나다, 발생하다, life-form 생물체, coup d'état 쿠데타

글의 흐름 ⊙ 주제문은 'Meaning is derived from context and prior knowledge.'이며 중괄식 구조다.

구조 분석 ⊙ But it is not.

→ it은 the meaning of a message를 가리키고 not 다음에는 'carried in the message'가 생략됐다.

정답 해설 (A) 다음 문장에서 의미는 맥락과 사전 지식에서 나온다고 했으므로 이것, 즉 의미가 메시지에 실린다고 믿는 것은 착각일 뿐이라는 식으로 이야기가 전개돼야 하므로 (A)에는 illusion이 적절하다.

(B) 바로 앞에서 의미는 생물체나 정보처리 능력을 가진 기계를 만났을 때 발생한다고 했으므로 그에 해당하지 않는 잉크 흔적이나 음파 따위에는 의미가 실리지 않는다는 식으로 논리가 전개돼야 한다. 따라서 (B)에는 carried가 적절하다. not에 주의하라.

(C) 의미는 맥락에서 나오는 것이며 메시지의 일부가 아니라는 것이 이 글의 일관된 논지이므로 (C)에는 message가 옳다. 역시 not에 주의하라. 정답은 ②이다.

045
정답 ①

지문 해석 동물계에서는 큰 두뇌가 왜 그렇게 드문가? 사실은 큰 두뇌가 몸을 크게 고갈시킨다는 것이다. 특히 큰 두개골 안에 둘러싸여서 그것을 가지고 다니기란 쉽지 않다. 그것에 연료를 공급하는 것은 한층 더 어렵다. 호모 사피엔스의 경우 두뇌는 전체 체중의 2~3퍼센트를 차지하지만 휴식 중 몸의 에너지의 25퍼센트를 소비한다. 이에 비해 다른 유인원의 두뇌는 휴식 중 에너지의 8퍼센트만을 요구한다. 고대 인류는 큰 두뇌 때문에 두 가지 방식으로 고생했다. 첫째, 그들은 음식을 찾는 데 더 많은 시간을 소비했다. 둘째, 그들의 근육이 위축됐다. 돈을 방위에서 교육으로 전용하는 정부처럼 인간은 에너지를 이두박근에서 신경세포로 전용했다. 이것이 사바나에서 바람직한 전략이라는 것은 필연적인 결론이라 하기 어렵다. 침팬지는 호모 사피엔스와의 논쟁에서 이길 수 없지만 유인원은 인간을 봉제인형(rag doll)처럼 박살 낼 수 있다.

글의 소재 인간의 큰 두뇌의 역기능

주요 어휘 drain 고갈, 소모, encase 감싸다, skull 두개골, fuel 연료를 공급하다, account for 차지하다, ape 유인원, atrophy 위축되다, divert 전용하다, biceps 이두박근, neuron 신경세포, 뉴런, foregone 기정의, 필연적인, savannah 대초원, 사바나, argument 논쟁, rip apart 산산조각 내다

글의 흐름 ⊙ 'The fact is that a jumbo brain is a jumbo drain on the body.'가 주제문인 두괄식 구조다. 글의 도입 부분에서 의문문이 나오면 그에 대한 답이 주제문일 경우가 많다.

구조 분석 ⊙ It's not easy to carry around, especially when encased inside a massive skull.

→ when과 encased 사이에 'it is'가 생략됐다. when, while, if, though 등의 시간이나 조건, 양보의 부사절에서는 흔히 S + be 동사가 생략된다.

정답 해설 (A) 두뇌는 몸에 지니거나 에너지 공급이 쉽지 않다는, 이어지는 부정적 내용으로 보아 두뇌는 몸에 고갈 요인임이 명백하다. 따라서 (A)에는 drain이 적절하다.

(B) 인간이 음식 찾기에 더 많은 시간을 소비하고 근육이 줄어들었다고 했으므로 고대인은 큰 두뇌로 이익을 본 것이 아니고 그것 때문에 고생했다고 해야 맞다. 따라서 (B)에는 suffered가 적절하다.

(C) 역시 이어지는 내용이 '유인원이 인간을 박살 낸다.'는 것이기 때문에 이것 — 이두박근을 신경세포로 전용한 것 — 은 바람직한 전략이라고 결론 내리기 어렵다. 따라서 (C)에는 desirable이 타당하다. 부정어 hardly 때문에 반대 내용을 골라야 한다는 점에 주의하라. 정답은 ①이다.

046

정답 ①

지문 해석 후 과도기의 다극화 세계에서는 국제 공조로부터 많은 잠재적 이득을 얻을 수 있다. 하지만 그러한 이득의 존재는 공조가 실제로 이뤄질 것을 의미하지는 않는다. 한 가지 장애는 맺게 될 조약의 준수를 보장하기가 어렵다는 것이다. 두 핵 강국이 원자탄을 포기한다면 그들은 더 잘 살 수 있을 것이다. 그러나 그들이 그렇게 하기로 원칙적인 합의에 이른다 해도 상대방이 속일지 모른다는 서로 간 두려움 때문에 군비 축소는 결국 달성하기 어려울 것이다. 이 두려움을 완화하기 위해서는 검증 메커니즘의 설치가 필요하다. 무기 프로그램이 복원되지 않았음을 확실히 하기 위해 기존 핵 저장고의 폐기를 감독하고 원자로와 기타 시설을 모니터할 감독관들이 있어야 할 것이다. 치러야 할 첫 번째 대가는 이 감독관들에게 드는 비용이다. 또 다른 대가는 감독관들이 스파이 활동으로 상업적 또는 군사 비밀을 빼낼 위험이다. 무엇보다 중요한 것은 쌍방이 상대가 비밀리에 핵 능력을 보유할지 모른다고 두려워하는 것이다. 준수 여부를 검증하기가 너무 어려워서 많은 잠재적 이익 거래가 실현되지 못한다.

글의 소재 국제 공조 실현의 어려움

주요 어휘 potential 잠재적인, collaboration 공조, 협력, imply 함축하다, 의미하다, compliance 준수, relinquish 포기하다, disarmament 군비 철폐, evasive 달성하기 어려운, allay 완화하다, verification 확인, oversee 감독하다, stockpile 핵무기 저장고, reconstitute 복원하다, make off with ~를 빼돌리다, clandestine 비밀의, capability 능력, consensus 합의

글의 흐름 ⊙ 국제 공조가 어려운 이유를 두 핵 강국의 경우를 예로 들어 설명하고 있다. 예시가 시작되기 바로 전 문장 'One obstacle is the difficulty of ensuring compliance with any treaty that might be agreed.'이 주제문이고, 주제문은 글 마지막에 다시 한 번 반복된다.

구조 분석 ⊙ One cost is paying for these inspectors.

→ paying은 동명사로 paying 이하가 is의 보어다.

정답 해설 (A) 역접의 연결사 however 때문에 앞 문장과 반대로 공조가 이뤄지지 않는다는 내용이 돼야 하므로 achieved가 적절하다. 주절의 not을 주의하라.

(B) 원칙 합의가 이뤄져도 서로 간 의심 때문에 군축이 실현되기 어렵다는 식으로 내용이 전개돼야 하기 때문에 네모 안 어휘는 elusive가 적절하다.

(C) 쌍방이 상대방 핵 시설을 감독하는 과정에서 가장 두려워하는 것은 상대방이 은밀한 핵 보유 능력을 유지하는 것이기 때문에 네모 안에는 preserve가 적절하다. 따라서 정답은 ①이다.

047

정답 ⑤

지문 해석 기억에 대한 많은 문제들 중 가장 근본적인 것은 기억의 형태와 다양성에 관한 것이다. 최근 몇 년 사이 심리학과 신경생물학 연구들은 기억이 근본적으로 다른 과정이나 시스템으로 분리된다고 제시했다. 예를 들어 뇌 손상이나 뇌병이 있는 기억상실 환자들은 최근 사건을 기억하고 인지하는 데 심각한 무능력을 보이고, 새로운 사실이나 다른 종류의 정보를 학습하는 데 어려움을 겪는다. 그러나 이 환자들은 비교적 온전한 몇몇 학습 및 기억 능력을 가진다. 예를 들어 손의 기민성 실험 과제에서 그들은, 비록 방금 과제를 수행한 것을 의식적으로 기억하지는 못하지만 건강하고 뇌가 손상되지 않은 사람들 못지않은 수행능력을 보여준다. 의식적인 기억을 전달하는 뇌 구조물이 손상을 입어도 몇몇 종류의 학습은 정상적으로 진행됨을 보여주는 이런 증거는 별도의 분리된 형태의 기억이 존재한다는 일반 명제를 뒷받침한다.

글의 소재 기억의 차별성과 다양성

주요 어휘 fundamental 근본적인, neurobiological 신경생물학적, dissociate 분리시키다, amnesic 기억상실의, intact 온전한, 손상되지 않은, dexterity 기민함, mediate 중재하다, 전달하다, contradict ~와 상충하다, proposition 명제, distinct 별도의

글의 흐름 ⊙ 주제문은 'In recent years, both psychological and neurobiological work have suggested that memory is dissociated into processes or systems that are fundamentally different.'로 예시의 연결사 For example이 주제문을 암시하는 경우다.

구조 분석 ⊙ Of the many questions about memory, one of the most fundamental concerns the types or varieties of memory.

→ fundamental 다음에 questions가 생략됐다. 이 문장의 주어는 one, 동사는 concerns이고 one에 맞춰 단수로 수 일치시켰다.

⊙ This evidence—that some kinds of learning can proceed

normally even when the brain structures that mediate conscious remembering are damaged—supports the general proposition that there are distinct, dissociated types of memory.

→ 삽입절 안의 첫 번째 that은 evidence를 부연 설명하는 동격의 that이고, 두 번째 that은 선행사 brain structures를 수식하는 관계대명사, 그리고 마지막 that 역시 proposition과 동격 관계다.

정답 해설 (A): 이어지는 예시에서 기억 상실 환자는 최근 사건을 기억하는 데는 어려움이 있지만 몇몇 온전한 기억 능력을 가진다고 했고 이는 기억이 서로 다른 시스템으로 분리되는 것을 의미하므로 (A)에는 dissociated가 적절하다.

(B) 역시 다음 예시에서 기억 상실 환자가 자기가 한 일을 기억하지는 못하지만 손의 기민성은 정상인 못지않고 했고, 이는 환자가 온전한 학습 능력을 가짐을 의미하므로 (B)에는 intact가 오는 것이 타당하다.

(C) '뇌 손상을 입어도 어떤 학습들은 정상 진행된다'함은 기억이 다 똑같은 게 아니라 차별화된 다양한 기억이 존재한다는 명제를 뒷받침하는 것이므로 (C)에 들어갈 말은 supports가 적절하다. 따라서 정답은 ⑤이다.

048
정답 ④

지문 해설 고고학자들은 종종 과거를 연구한다는 말을 한다. 실제로는 그렇지 않다(그들은 과거를 연구하지 않는다). 그들은 현재, 즉 살아남은 과거의 현대판 조각들, 오늘의 그들이 접근할 수 있으며 어제 일어난 일에 대한 추론을 가능하게 하는 영속적인 증거의 방식들을 연구한다. 고고학 큐레이터직에 관한 문제를 다루는 주요 저술가 중 한 명인 Susan Pearce는 모호해진 과거 해석의 복잡성을 예증하기 위해 Ferdinand Saussure의 랑그와 빠롤의 차이점을 이용한다. 체계화되지 않은 광범위한 가능태로부터 한 사회의 의사전달 체계, 물질적 문화와 기타 문화 형태가 취하는 일련의 형상을 뽑아낸다. 문화적으로 이해되기 위해 이 형상들은 문화적으로 체계화된 규칙에 기반한 적절한 방식으로 사용돼야 한다. 행동을 유발하는 이 체계화되고 의미 있는 사용 규칙들이 랑그다. 빠롤은 발화(發話)나 연장 만들기, 요리하기 같은 일상 행동들을 표현하고 이는 랑그로부터 나오는, 기호 체계를 표현하는 육체적 행동을 의미한다. 민족지적인 경우에조차 고고학자들은 랑그를 직접 관찰하지 않고 관찰된 빠롤, 즉 사람들이 일상생활에서 보이는 체계화된 실제 행동에 근거해 그것(랑그)을 추론할 수 있다.

글의 소재 랑그와 빠롤의 차이를 이용한 고고학적 과거 추론

주요 어휘 latter-day 현대판의, perduring 영속적인, accessible 접근할 수 있는, inference 추론, curatorship 큐레이터직, langue 사회 관습적인 의사소통 체계로서의 언어, parole 개개인의 언어 사용 측면에서의 언어, obscured 모호해진, intelligible 이해할 수 있는, appropriate 적절한, represent 표현하다, utterance 발화(發話), semiotic 기호의, ethnographic 민족지(誌)적인

글의 흐름 ⊙ 주제문은 'Susan Pearce, one of the major authors addressing issues of archaeological curatorship ~ to illustrate the complexity of interpreting that obscured past.'이며 중괄식 구조다.

구조 분석 ⊙ From the wide range of unstructured possibilities are drawn a set of forms that a society's communication systems, material culture, and other cultural forms may take.

→ 이 문장의 주어는 a set of forms이며 주어가 길어 도치시켰고 a set of forms의 forms를 개별자(복수)로 취급하여 동사를 복수로 일치시켰다.

정답 해설 (A) 고고학자들이 모호한 과거를 해석할 때 두 가지 상반된 개념, 즉 parole—사람들의 구체적인 일상적 활동—과 langue—그런 행동을 유발하는 사용 규칙—를 이용한다는 맥락이므로 distinction이 타당하다.

(B) 문화적으로 이해되기 위해서 이 형상들은 적절한 방식으로 사용돼야 한다는 맥락이기 때문에 intelligible이 적절하다. 'To be culturally ~'의 의미상 주어인 these forms는 의미상 intelligent(똑똑한)를 보어로 받을 수 없다.

(C) 앞 문장에서 빠롤은 일상 행동이나 육체적 행동을 의미한다고 했으므로 빠롤을 동격으로 부연·설명하는 (C) 자리에 들어갈 수식어는 실제(actual)가 적절하다. 따라서 정답은 ④이다.

6. 세부 내용 파악

정답

			049 ③	050 ⑤
051 ③	052 ③	053 ⑤	054 ③	055 ③
056 ②	057 ④	058 ⑤	059 ④	060 ①
061 ③	062 ③			

049

정답 ③

(지문 해석) 홈오피스에서 일할 때 가장 중요하게 고려해야 할 한 가지가 안전과 보안이다. 업무에 컴퓨터를 사용한다면 컴퓨터 시스템을 바이러스나 해킹으로부터 끊임없이 보호해줘야 한다. 바이러스나 해킹 피해가 점증하는 추세임을 감안하여 항상 최신의 방어벽이나 컴퓨터 백신을 갖춰야 한다. 더욱 중요한 것은 홈오피스의 물리적 안전에 만전을 기하는 것이다. 무단침입이나 절도, 이에 따른 혼란으로부터 홈오피스를 지켜야 한다. 보안시스템 설치와 별도로 홈오피스 보호를 위해 몇 가지 조치를 취해야 한다. 세간의 이목을 피하고 컴퓨터나 고가 장비 설치 시 되도록 공개된 장소를 피하라. 출타 시 커튼이나 블라인드를 치고 특히 밤에 조도를 낮춰라. 사무실과 모든 장비를 보험 가입하는 것도 매우 중요하다.

(글의 소재) 홈오피스의 안전과 보안

(주요 어휘) paramount 최고의, firewall 방화벽, break-in 침입, aside from ~와는 별도로, implement 설치하다, keep a low profile 저자세를 취하다, 세간의 이목을 피하다

(글의 흐름) ⊙ 첫 문장 'One important issue of working in a home office that you should give paramount importance is its safety and security.'이 주제문인 두괄식 구조이다.

(구조 분석) ⊙ Given the increasing amount of threat and damage caused by viruses and hackers,

➜ Given은 '~을 고려할 때'라는 뜻의 preposition으로, 'In consideration of', 'Considering'으로 바꿔 쓸 수 있다.

⊙ More importantly, you should give the physical safety of your home office its due consideration.

➜ More importantly가 문장 전체 수식 부사로서 What's more important로 바꿔 쓸 수 있다.

(정답 해설) 'Keep a low profile, making sure that your computer systems and other expensive equipment are hidden from public view.'에서 알 수 있듯이, 세간의 이목을 피하기 위해 컴퓨터나 고가 장비 설치 시 되도록 공개된 장소를 피하라고 했다. 그러므로 ③은 사실이 아니다.

050

정답 ⑤

(지문 해석) 물론 지칠 줄 모르는 의욕을 가진 많은 다른 박식가가 있었고 르네상스는 다른 인문주의자를 산출했다. 그러나 어느 누구도 모나리자를 그리지 못했을 뿐만 아니라 타의 추종을 불허하는 다층절단 해부도를 그리고, 강의 수로(水路) 변경을 계획하고, 지구에서 달로 빛이 반사되는 현상을 설명하고 막 도살된 돼지의 뛰는 심장을 절개해 심실의 작동을 보여주고, 악기를 디자인하고, 야외극 안무를 창작하고 화석을 이용해 성경 속의 대홍수 기록을 반박하고 홍수를 그림으로 남기는 일을 동시에 한 사람은 더욱 없다. 다빈치는 분명 천재이지만 이는 그가 단지 똑똑하기 때문은 아니었다. 중요한 건 그가 역사상 어느 누구보다 호기심이 많았던 우주정신의 표상이었다는 점이다.

(글의 소재) 레오나르도 다빈치의 위대성

(주요 어휘) insatiable 만족할 줄 모르는, polymath 박식가, unsurpassed 타의 추종을 불허하는, dissection 절단, come up with ~을 제안하다, divert 방향을 바꾸게 하다, ventricle 심실, choreograph 안무하다, the Deluge 성경의 대홍수, epitome 표상, most important =most importantly 가장 중요한 것은

(글의 흐름) ⊙ 주제문은 마지막 문장 'He was, more important, the epitome of the universal mind, the person most curious about more things than anyone else in history.'이다. 따라서 이 글은 구체적 진술이 앞서 나온 뒤에 일반 진술로 마무리되는 미괄식 구조의 형식을 가지고 있다.

(구조 분석) ⊙ But none painted the Mona Lisa, much less did so at the same time as producing unsurpassed anatomy drawings, coming up with ~, explaining ~, opening ~

➜ 부정문 다음에 오는 much less는 '하물며 ~는 더더욱 아니다.'라는 뜻이다. 여기서 did so는 painted Mona Lisa를 가리키고, 'coming ~', 'explaining ~', 'opening ~' 등은 producing과 병렬 구조를 이룬다. '어느 누구도 모나리자를 그리지 않았으며, 하물며 ~도 동시에 하면서 그린 사람은 더더욱 없다.'의 뜻이다.

(정답 해설) 'using fossils to dispute the biblical account of the Deluge and then drawing a deluge.'로 보았을 때, 다빈치는 화석을 이용해 성경의 사실(史實)을 입증한 게 아니라 성경 기록이 잘못됐다며 이를 반박했다. 따라서 ⑤는 틀린 내용이다. '성경 사실 입증'이 상식적으로 개연성이 있다고 해서 성급하게 정답으로 단정하지 말아야 한다. 일치·불일치 유형의 문제에서 중요한 것은 지문에서 언급된 fact이지 상식이 아니다.

051

정답 ③

(지문 해석) 어떤 사람들은 이를 대수롭지 않게 여기지만 차(茶)

에는 소중한 플라보노이드, 즉 효과적인 항산화제로 알려진 천연 물질이 들어있다. 하루 차 한 잔이면 세포 변형이나 염증을 유발하는 유해 물질인 유리기로부터 우리 몸을 더 잘 보호할 수 있다. 이런 유리기는 세포 손상을 일으켜 암이나 심장병의 원인이 된다. 차 두 잔에 들어있는 항산화 물질은 사과 네 개 또는 오렌지 주스 열 잔과 맞먹는다. 티백을 물에 몇 분 담가 놓으면 우러나는 항산화제의 양은 최고에 이른다. 차는 또한 식도암의 발병 가능성을 남성의 경우 20%, 여성의 경우 40%나 낮춘다. 차가 이미 발병한 종양의 크기를 줄일 가능성마저 있다. 차는 심장병의 또 다른 흔한 원인인 혈액 응고를 감소시킬 수 있다. 우리에게 큰 도움을 주는 것은 차의 플라보노이드 성분뿐이 아니다. 차에는 소량이지만 건강을 위해 꼭 필요한 몇몇 미네랄 즉 망간이나 칼륨, 아연 등이 내포돼 있다.

글의 소재 차(茶)의 효능

주요 어휘 flavonoid 플라보노이드(토마토 등에서 발견되는 물질로 항암에 효과가 있는 것으로 알려져 있다.), antioxidant 항산화 물질, free radical 유리기, deformation 변형, inflammation 염증, steep 담가두다, go a long way in ~ing ~에 큰 도움을 주다, esophageal 식도의, clot 응고시키다, cardiovascular 심혈관계의, potassium 칼륨

글의 흐름 ⊙ 차에 들어있는 여러 가지 우리 몸에 좋은 성분을 예시하는 병렬식 구조이다.

정답 해설 'With a cup of tea a day our protection is improved against free radicals, harmful substances that can cause problems, such as cell deformation and inflammation.'을 보면 차는 유리기로부터 우리 몸을 보호해 준다. 그러므로 '유리기 분비를 촉진한다.'라는 ③은 이 글의 내용에 어긋난다.

052
정답 ③

지문 해석 그녀 또래 애들처럼 Ulmer도 처음엔 벌을 싫어했다. "윙윙거리는 건 뭐든지 정말 싫었어요."라고 그녀는 말한다. 그러다 2009년에 벌에 두 번 쏘인 뒤 얼마 안 돼 이 텍사스 토박이는 벌에 푹 빠졌다. 꿀벌이 멸종 위기를 맞고 있음을 안 것도 그때였다. 그래서 Ulmer는 레몬 음료를 가지고 돕기로 결심했다. Ulmer는 증조할머니의 조리법을 모태로 토종꿀을 가미한 혼합 음료를 만들어 지역 사업 시연회에서 판매했고 수익의 10%는 꿀벌 후원 단체에 기부했다. 부업으로 시작한 일이 2014년 무렵에는 당당한 사업체가 되었다. 이제 Ulmer의 Me & the Bees Lemonade는 웨그먼스를 포함한 슈퍼마켓 체인은 물론 300개 이상의 홀 푸드 매장에 입점했고 그녀는 꿀벌 위기에 대한 대중의 인식을 제고하기 위해 비영리 재단 Healthy Hive Foundation을 운영하고 있다. 계획 중인 사업으로는 아동의 창업을 돕기 위한 첫 번째 책을 발간하는 일과 사세를 확장하는 일이 있다. 그럴 목적으로 "방금 아빠를 직원으로 채용

했다"고 Ulmer는 말한다.

글의 소재 어린이 사업가이자 꿀벌 생태 후원자 Mikaila Ulmer

주요 어휘 lemonade 레몬 탄산음료, full-blown 완전히 갖춘, nonprofit 비영리 단체, to that end 그럴 목적으로, 그런 취지로

구조 분석 ⊙ Like most kids her age
→ her age가 kids를 꾸며주는 형용사구이다. kids와 her age 사이에 전치사를 쓰지 않음에 주의하라. e.g. She liked to befriend boys her age. 그녀는 또래의 소년들과 교제하기를 좋아했다.

⊙ (a)Using her great grandmother's recipe, Ulmer made a blend, (b)sweetened with local honey, (c)to sell at community business fairs, (d)donating 10% of her profits to honeybee-advocate groups.
→ 조금 복잡해 보이지만 (a)는 분사 구문으로 As she used her great grandmother's recipe의 준말이고, (b)와 (c)는 모두 blend를 수식하는 형용사구로 (b)와 (c) 사이에 콤마를 사용하여 둘이 대등한 수식 관계에 있음을 분명히 하고 있다. (d) 또한 분사 구문으로 and donated로 바꿔 쓸 수 있다.

정답 해설 'Ulmer made a blend, sweetened with local honey, to sell at community business fairs, donating 10% of her profits to honeybee-advocate groups.'로 보았을 때 ③의 내용이 이 글의 내용과 일치함을 알 수 있다.
① → 벌에 두 번 쏘인 후 벌에 매료됐다.
② → 증조할머니의 조리법을 모태로 했다.
④ → 이미 입점해 판매하고 있다.
⑤ → 계획 중인 사업이다.

053
정답 ⑤

지문 해석 암의 역학 역사에서 가장 중요한 발견은 담배의 암 유발 가능성을 밝힌 일이다. 담배를 계속 피우는 사람들 사이의 폐암 발생률은 급격히 증가하지만 담배를 끊은 사람의 암 발생률은 큰 변화 없이 대체로 일정하다. 따라서 어려서 담배를 피우기 시작해 평생 계속 피우는 사람이 제일 위험하다. 2차 흡연 또는 간접흡연 역시 암을 유발하지만 위험의 정도를 계량화하기는 쉽지 않다. 20세기 전반 선진국에서 있었던 급격한 남성 흡연 증가는 수십 년 후 사상 유례없이 높은 폐암 발생률로 나타났다. 담배에서 타르 성분을 낮추고 흡연율이 감소하자 많은 선진국에서 폐암 발생률이 줄어들었다. 대부분 서구 국가에서 여성은 남성보다 담배를 늦게 시작했고 금연자의 수도 적어서 폐암 발생률은 여전히 증가하고 있거나 줄어드는 속도가 남성보다 더디다.

글의 소재 흡연과 폐암

epidemiology 역학, carcinogenic 발암성의, incidence 발생률, constant 일정한, second tobacco smoking 간접흡연, quantify 계량화하다, magnitude 강도, 정도, unprecedented 전례 없는, subsequently 후에, 나중에

글의 흐름 ⊙ 도입문 'The most important discovery in the history of cancer epidemiology is the carcinogenic effect of tobacco'이 주제문인 두괄식 구조다. 일반 진술이 구체 진술로 전개되는 연역적 구조다.

구조 분석 ⊙ fewer have stopped, so their lung cancer rates are either still increasing or falling less rapidly.

→ fewer (women)에서 women이 생략됐다. either still increasing or falling less rapidly는 either A or B 구문으로 '여전히 증가하고 있거나 떨어지더라도 그 속도가 (남성보다) 더디다'는 뜻이다.

정답 해설 'Women in most Western countries began smoking later than men and fewer have stopped, so their lung cancer rates are either still increasing or falling less rapidly.'에서 알 수 있듯이 서구에서 여성의 폐암 발생률은 여전히 증가하고 있거나 줄어드는 속도가 남성보다 더디다. 그러므로 ⑤는 사실과 다르다. 불일치를 묻는 문제 유형은 선택지를 먼저 훑어본 뒤에 본문을 읽는 것이 빠르게 내용을 파악하는 데 도움이 된다.

054
정답 ③

지문 해석 테니스는 이집트인들이 처음 시작한 것이 거의 확실하다. 사원의 벽 조각에는 구기 경기 모습이 새겨져 있다. 테니스는 무어인들과 함께 유럽으로 건너왔는데 수사들은 이를 라술이라 부르며 크게 반겼다. 12~13세기 테니스는 수도원 밖으로 나왔고 맨손으로 경기하던 손에 장갑과 손잡이가 들려졌다. 공은 이제 나무가 아닌 쌀겨를 채운 가죽으로 만들어졌고 16~18세기 중 프랑스인들은 테니스를 Jeu de Paume 즉, 손바닥 게임이라 부르며 아주 좋아했다. 경기가 시작될 때는 '테네즈!'를 외쳤다. 테니스는 궁정 안에서도 인기 게임이어서 벽을 치는 실내 테니스가 성행했다(햄프튼 궁정에는 실내 테니스장이 있다). 제1회 윔블던 대회에서는 22명의 선수와 200명의 관중이 참여했다. 1939년은 남자 선수가 경기 중 긴 바지를 입도록 허용된 마지막 해였다.

글의 소재 테니스의 기원

주요 어휘 arguably 거의 틀림없이, frieze 프리즈, 띠 모양의 조각, supplant ~을 대신하다, bran 쌀겨, real tennis 실내 테니스, off the walls 벽을 맞고 튕겨 나가는

정답 해설 'In the 12th and 13th centuries it came out of the monasteries and a glove and handle supplanted the bare hand.'으로 ③의 내용이 이 글의 내용과 일치함을 알 수

있다. 이러한 문제 유형을 해결할 때는 먼저 선택지를 훑어보아 본문이 '테니스의 역사'에 대한 내용의 글임을 파악한 뒤에 본문을 읽어나가면 본문의 내용을 파악하는 데 도움이 된다.

① → 첫 문장에서 이집트에서 시작된 것이 거의 틀림없다고 (arguably) 말하고 있다.

② → 수사들을 매혹시켰다(fascinated the monks).

④ → 궁정의 테니스 경기는 '벽에 대고 치는(played off the walls)' real tennis, 즉 '실내경기'를 말한다.

⑤ → 긴 바지가 허용된 마지막 해가 1939년이라고 했으므로 이전에는 허용됐음을 알 수 있다.

055
정답 ③

지문 해석 오 헨리의 삶의 우여곡절이 본격적으로 시작된 건 이때부터였다. 특히 은행은 그의 천직이 아니었다. 그는 장부 정리에 허술해 은행으로부터 해고됐고 1894년 횡령 혐의로 기소됐다. 그의 장인은 그의 보석을 신청했지만 그는 재판 하루 전 도망쳐 처음에는 뉴올리언스로 나중에는 온두라스로 피신했다. 당시엔 온두라스와 범죄인 인도 협정이 없었다. 거기서 알 제닝스라는 악명 높은 철도 강도 한 명을 알게 됐는데 제닝스는 후에 그들의 우정을 책으로 출간하기도 했다. 오 헨리는 아내와 딸을 오스틴으로 되돌려 보내고 자신은 호텔에 틀어박혀 Kings and Cabbages를 집필했다. 아내가 폐결핵으로 사경을 헤매 온 두라스에서 합류할 수 없게 되자 오 헨리는 오스틴의 그들 곁으로 돌아가 법원에 자진 출두했다. 그의 장인이 다시 한 번 보석을 신청해 그는 1897년 아내 사망 때까지 그녀 곁에서 지낼 수 있었다. 그는 5년 형을 언도받아 1898년 3월 오하이오 교도소에 수감됐다.

글의 소재 오 헨리의 굴곡진 삶

주요 어휘 twists and turns 우여곡절, charged with ~로 기소된, embezzlement 횡령, extradition 범죄인도, hole up in ~에 틀어박히다, tuberculosis 폐결핵, penitentiary 교도소

정답 해설 'He befriended a notorious train robber there, Al Jennings, who later wrote a book about their friendship.'로 O. Henry가 철도 강도와 나눈 우정을 후에 책으로 쓴 사람은 철도 강도인 Al Jennings임을 알 수 있다. 따라서 정답은 ③이다. 이와 같은 불일치를 묻는 문제 유형은 본문보다 먼저 선택지를 읽고 시작하는 것이 시간을 절약하고 정확도를 높일 수 있다.

056
정답 ②

지문 해석 참치는 고등어과의 한 계통인 참치족에 속하는 염수어이다. 참치족은 5개 속, 15개 종으로 구성되는데 크기가 제각각이어서 성어의 길이가 50cm, 1.8kg인 몽치다래에서 4.6m에

684kg에 달하는 대서양 참다랑어까지 다양하다. 참다랑어는 평균 길이가 2m이고 50살까지 사는 것으로 전해진다. 참치와 악상어는 주변 수온보다 높은 체온을 유지하는 유일한 어종이다. 활동적이고 민첩한 포식자로 참치는 날렵한 유선형 몸매를 지니며 수영속도가 매우 빠른 표층어에 속한다. 가령 황다랑어는 시속 75km까지 속도를 낼 수 있다. 따뜻한 바다에 서식하는 참치는 상업 용도로 많이 잡고 낚시 시합용으로도 인기가 많다. 남획의 결과 남부 참다랑어 같은 일부 참치 어종은 멸종의 위기에 직면해 있다.

글의 소재 참치의 생태적 면모

주요 어휘 genera genus속(屬)의 복수, bullet tuna 몽치다래, Atlantic bluefin tuna 대서양 참다랑어, mackerel shark 악상어, agile 민첩한, sleek 미끈한, pelagic fish 표층어, yellowfin tuna 황다랑어, game fish 낚시 시합용 물고기, overfishing 남획

글의 흐름 참치의 다양한 생태를 나열하며 소개하는 병렬적 구조의 글이다.

구조 분석 ⊙ An active and agile predator, the tuna has a sleek, streamlined body
→ An active and agile predator와 the tuna는 동격이다.

정답 해설 'Tuna and mackerel sharks are the only species of fish that can maintain a body temperature higher than that of the surrounding water.'에서 알 수 있듯이, 참치와 악상어는 주변 수온보다 높은 체온을 유지하는 유일한 어종이다. 따라서 ②는 이 글과 일치하지 않는다. 이 글을 독해하다 ②가 정답이라는 확신이 들면 독해를 멈추고 과감하게 다음 문제로 넘어가 시간을 절약해야 한다.

057
정답 ④

지문 해석 새들이 번식지에 접근할수록 이동은 가속화되지만 새들의 동작은 점점 산발적이 되는데 이는 적합한 번식지 탐색 때문으로 보인다. 하지만 몇몇 새들은 새로운 번식지를 찾을지 모르나 대부분의 철새들은 그들이 이전에 번식기나 유년기를 경험했던 번식지로 귀환하고 그럼으로써 흩어짐이 아닌 높은 장소 충실도를 보여준다. 많은 철새에게 번식지 선택은 종종 전해에 짝짓기를 했던 곳으로 다시 돌아가는 것을 포함한다. 귀환율은 당연히 종에 따라 혹은 해마다 차이가 있는데 다 자란 작은 연작류의 경우 평균 50%에서 갈매기 같은 몇몇 장수종은 90%를 넘는 높은 귀환율을 보이기도 한다. 전 해에 성공적으로 번식했던 많은 종의 성인 철새는 생존율에 비교되는 비율로 다시 그 번식처로 귀환하고 있음을 조류표지법에 따른 연구는 보여준다.

글의 소재 철새의 이동

주요 어휘 migration 철새의 이동, suitable 적절한, habitat 서식지, fidelity 충실도, dispersal 확산, 흩어짐, passerine 연

작류, banding study 조류표지법에 의한 연구, demonstrate 보여주다, 입증하다

글의 흐름 주제문은 'However, whereas some birds may be searching for ~and thereby display site fidelity rather than dispersal.'로, 역접의 연결사가 이 주제문을 이끄는 경우이다.

구조 분석 ⊙ Return rates vary naturally from species to species and year to year but average around 50 percent for adult small passerines
→ 여기서 average는 '평균 ~에 이르다'의 뜻으로 동사로 쓰였고 vary와 병렬구조를 이룬다.

정답 해설 다 자란 작은 연작류의 귀환율은 평균 50%이고 갈매기 같은 몇몇 장수종이 90%를 넘는 귀환율을 보인다고 했으므로 ④는 사실과 다르다.

058
정답 ⑤

지문 해석 2008년의 어느 서늘한 가을 저녁 네 명의 학생이 업계를 혁명하는 일에 착수했다. 빚에 허덕이던 그들은 안경을 잃어버리거나 깨뜨렸는데 그것을 교체하는 데 드는 비용이 상당하다는 데 분개했다. 그들 중 한 명은 망가진 안경을 오 년째 끼고 있었다. 안경 틀을 클립으로 고정한 채 말이다. 안경 도수가 두 번이나 바뀐 후에도 그는 비싼 새 렌즈를 사기를 거부했다. 업계의 시장 지배적 강자인 Luxottica는 안경 시장의 80퍼센트 이상을 점유하고 있었다. 안경값을 보다 저렴하게 만들기 위해서 학생들은 거대기업을 무너뜨려야만 했다. 최근 Zappos가 신발 온라인 판매로 신발 시장을 뒤바꾼 것을 보고 그들은 안경에 대해서도 같은 것을 할 수 있지 않을까 생각했다. 그들의 생각을 친구들에게 우연히 꺼냈을 때 그들은 번번이 통렬한 비난 세례를 받아야 했다. 안경을 인터넷으로 사려는 사람은 아무도 없을 거라고 친구들은 주장했다. 사람들은 먼저 껴봐야 한다는 거였다. Zappos가 신발에 대해 (인터넷 판매) 컨셉을 성공한 것은 확실하지만 안경은 그럴 수 없는 데는 이유가 있었다. "그 아이디어가 괜찮다면 누군가가 이미 했을 거야"라는 말을 그들은 되풀이해서 들었다.

글의 소재 사회통념에 반하는 행태의 위험성

주요 어휘 set out to 착수하다, revolutionize 혁신하다, outrage 화나게 하다, the 800-pound gorilla 업계의 시장 지배적 강자, affordable 감당할 수 있는, 알맞은, topple 무너뜨리다, scorching 무더운, 통렬한, pulled ~ off ~을 해내다, 성공하다

구조 분석 ⊙ Buried in loans, they had lost and broken eyeglasses and were outraged at how much it cost to replace them.
→ Buried 앞에 Being이 생략된 분사 구문으로 'If they had been buried~'로 바꿀 수 있다. how~ 이하는 전치사 at의 목

적어인 의문사절로서 의문사 + S + V의 어순을 취한다. It는 가격의 비인칭 It이다.

⊙ To make glasses more affordable, the students would need to topple a giant.

→ to 부정사로 시작하는 문장은 대부분 목적의 부사적 용법으로 해석한다. 이때 to 부정사의 의미상 주어는 주절의 주어와 일치한다.

정답 해설 When they casually mentioned their idea to friends, time and again they were blasted with scorching criticism에서 알 수 있듯이 주변 사람들은 온라인으로 안경을 파는 그들의 생각에 우호적이 아니라 비판적이었다. 따라서 정답은 ⑤이다.

059

정답 ④

지문 해설 매년 시험 전날 밤 자정 무렵이면 하버드 학생들은 이른바 '원초적 외침'에 참여하는데, 그것은 몇몇 사람들이 그다지 청교도적이 아닌 조상들 때문에 생겼다고 주장하는 존경할 만한 전통이다. 건국의 아버지 존 아담스가 독립선언서에 서명함으로써 역사에 이정표를 남기는 동안 그의 아들 찰스는 하버드 마당에서 친구들과 스트리킹을 하는 것으로 탁월한 점수를 따고 있었다. 그들은 퇴교당했으나 나중에 복교됐고(아빠가 건국의 아버지면 분명 당신은 적어도 한 번 감옥에서 풀려날 기회가 있다) 이러한 냉랭한 전통은 오늘날까지 계속된다. 300년 이상 지난 지금 가장 용감하고 술 취한 학생들이 Mower Hall 앞에 모여 옷을 벗는다. 그리고 나서 수백 명의 구경꾼이 기숙사에서 쏟아져 나오는 가운데 몸이 반쯤 얼어붙은 완전 나체의 학생들은 온기를 유지하려고 빽빽이 무리를 지어 옛 하버드 마당의 언 땅을 달리기 시작한다. 그리고 시험에서 실력 발휘를 못 할지도 모른다는 불안감은, 잠간 동안이나마, 동상이 걸릴지도 모른다는 현실적 불안감으로(동료들 앞에서 창피당할 수도 있다는 불안은 물론이고) 대체된다.

글의 소재 하버드대생들의 스트리킹 전통

주요 어휘 primal 원초적인, venerable 존경할 만한, puritanical 청교도적인, forebear 선조, distinction 우수함, 탁월함, streaking 벌거벗고 대중 앞을 달리는 행위, intoxicated 술 취한, disrobe 옷을 벗다, huddle 모이다, onlooker 구경꾼, frostbite 동상, embarrassment 창피스러운 일

구조 분석 ⊙ Every year, on the midnight before exams begin, Harvard students take part in what's called the Primal Scream, a venerable tradition that some attribute to our clearly not-so-puritanical forebears.

→ the Primal Scream과 a venerable tradition는 동격이고, 'attribute A to B'는 'A를 B의 탓으로 돌리다'의 뜻이다.

정답 해설 '가장 용감하고 술 취한 학생들이 스트리킹에 참여

한다'라고 말할 뿐 '수줍은 학생들이 참가한다'라는 언급은 없다. 따라서 정답은 ④이다.

060

정답 ①

지문 해설 조사기관마다 편차가 있지만 회사원들은 근무 중 1~3시간가량을 개인적인 일로 인터넷 검색을 한다. 대부분의 조사가 직원들이 직접 작성한 자료를 근거로 하기 때문에 사업주들은 직원들의 인터넷 사용을 감시할 수밖에 없는데, 이는 생산성 상실이나 그들의 검색 내용에 대한 우려 때문이다. 직원들은 쇼핑, 온라인 뱅킹, 스포츠 사이트 방문, 각종 납부, 페이스북, 트위터 등 많은 것을 검색한다. 대부분 직원들에게 인터넷 검색은 휴식이나 점심시간에 잠깐씩 하는 여가 활동이다. 그들은 검색으로 까먹은 근무시간을 집에 와서 애들 재워놓고 이메일 등을 통해 벌충할 것이다. 그러나 개중에는 이런 혜택을 악용하는 부류도 있다. 회사에 앙심을 품은 한 회사의 관리자는 6~7시간을 구직이나 조리법을 검색하고 쿠폰을 다운로드 받는 데 소비하기도 했다. 또 다른 회사에서는 한 직원이 자기 이외에 어느 누구도 화면을 볼 수 없게 컴퓨터 위치를 바꿔놔 IT 부서의 의심을 샀다. 그 직원은 성인영화를 다운받아 시청한 것으로 드러났다. 따라서 때로는 사업주들의 큰 우려가 정당화되기도 한다.

글의 소재 직장인들의 인터넷 사적 이용

주요 어휘 depending on ~에 따라 (결과가 제각각이다), occasional 가끔씩 있는, make up for 벌충하다, disgruntled 앙심을 품은

구조 분석 ⊙ Employees spend between one and three hours a day surfing the web on personal business at work, depending on the study reviewed.

→ depending on A는 'A에 따르면'의 뜻이다. 이때 A에 따라 주절의 내용이 변하는데, A의 내용과 상관없이 주절의 내용이 항상 같은 According to와는 구별된다. 이 문장의 경우 어떤 연구를 인용했냐에 따라 '서핑 시간이 1~3시간으로 다양하게 나타난다.'는 말이다.

⊙ this productivity loss, combined with the concerns employers have for where their employees are surfing the web at work, causes more employers to monitor employee use of the Internet.

→ this productivity loss ~ causes(V) more employers(O) to monitor(OC)의 5형식 문장이다.

정답 해설 이 글의 첫 문장 'Employees spend between one and three hours a day surfing the web on personal business at work'로, ①은 '회사원들은 개인적인 일로 인터넷 검색을 하는 데 평균 1~3시간을 소비한다.'는 본문의 내용에 어긋남을 알 수 있다.

061

지문 해석) 중앙은행장들이 젊거나, 미남이거나 매력적인 경우는 별로 없지만 Mark Carney는 이 세 가지에 모두 해당되며 게다가 매우 영리하기까지 하다. 캐나다 중앙은행인 45세의 카니는 부도 위기를 맞은 은행이 단 하나도 없는 금융시스템의 수장이 되는 행운까지 누렸다. 세계 선진국들이 새로운 금융 규칙을 마련하느라 바쁜 요즘 카니는 대중의 인기 영합적 열기에 휘둘리지 않고, 은행이 불충분한 자본 확충이나 서구인의 과소비와 같은 위기의 원인에 집중하라고 소리 높여 외치고 있다. 농담도 잘하고 싫으면 싫은 표정도 잘 짓는 이 골드만삭스 출신 은행가는 국가 상황이 심각해지고 있으므로 개인 빚을 너무 많이 지지 말라고 캐나다 국민들에게 경고하고 있다. 경제에 활력을 불어넣는 게 주 업무인 인사에게서 쉽게 듣기 어려운 직설적인 발언이다.

글의 소재) 캐나다 중앙은행장 Mark Carney

주요 어휘) bailout 구제 금융, clamor 소리 높여 외치다, crack a joke 농담하다, roll one's eyes 못마땅해 눈을 굴리다, take on (빚을) 지다, juice 원활하게 하다

글의 흐름) 캐나다 중앙은행장 Mark Carney의 여러 리더적 면모를 소개하는 글로, 병렬식 구조를 하고 있다.

구조 분석) ⊙ one rarely hears from a person whose job it is to juice the economy.

➔ (a) one rarely hears from a person과 (b) It is his job to juice the economy 두 문장이 관계대명사로 이어진 것이다. It는 가주어이고, his가 소유격 관계대명사 whose로 바뀌어 선행사 다음으로 이동하면서 두 문장이 연결되었다.

정답 해설) 'instead of getting distracted by populist zeal' 즉, '인기 영합적 열기에 휘둘리지 않는다'고 했기 때문에 민간의 요구에 호락호락하지 않음을 짐작할 수 있다. 따라서 ③ 민간의 금융 수요에 호의적이라는 말은 옳지 않다.

062

지문 해석) 미국에서 초창기 엑스레이 사업은 "아무한테도 맞지 않는 요셉의 채색옷처럼 일종의 얼룩무늬 사업"으로 묘사되었다. 1896년 초 시작된 미국의 엑스레이 사업은 거의 20년 동안 많은 사진사, 전기기사, 물리학자, 수련의나 투기꾼들이 득실거리는 규제되지 않는 영역이었다. 1920년대가 돼서야 조직적인 의료 전문가 집단 즉 방사선 전문의가 엑스레이 개업에 독점권을 따냈다. 미국 의료계가 이 새로운 발명에 대해 굼뜬 반응을 보인 점을 역사가들은 의아해했다. 어떤 이들은 이것을 엑스레이라는 신기술이 맞닥뜨린 이론적 기술적 난제가 낳은 결과라고 설명했다. 또 어떤 역사학자는 사진사, 전기기사, 의사의 전문지식을 형틀에 부어 새로운 직업을 만드는 과정에 수반되는 사회적 제도적 복잡성에 초점을 맞추기도 했다. 한편 촉각과 언어에서 시각으로의 전환을 가로막는 인식론적 장벽을 숙고하는 부류도 있었다.

글의 소재) 초기 미국 방사선업계

주요 어휘) piebald 얼룩무늬의, Joseph's coat of many colors 요셉이 아버지 야곱에게서 물려받은 채색옷, 영욕의 상징, welter 엄청난 양, medical novice 수련의, speculative soul 투기꾼, radiologist 방사선 전문의, warming 데워지는 것, 몸이 풀리는 것, intricacy 복잡한 일, mold A into B A를 틀에 부어 B로 만들다, epistemological 인식론적인, tactile 촉각의

구조 분석) ⊙ The early years of X-ray practice in America were described as "a piebald proceeding, a sort of Joseph's coat of many colors, which fitted no one."

➔ 초기 엑스레이 사업에 관심을 가졌던 다양한 전문가 집단을 'many colors'로, 주인이 없었음을 'fitted no one'으로 각각 비유하고 있다.

⊙ It was only in the 1920's that an organized community of medical specialists, the radiologists, successfully claimed monopoly over the X-ray practice.

➔ it that 강조 구문이다. only in the 1920's 부분이 강조되고 있다.

⊙ The slow warming of the American medical community to the new discovery

➔ 준동사 warming의 의미상 주어는 American medical community이며, 이 명사구는 명사절 That the American medical community slowly warmed to the new discovery로 바꿔 쓸 수 있다.

정답 해설) 'The slow warming of the American medical community to the new discovery has posed a puzzle to historians.'로 알 수 있듯이, 엑스레이에 대한 미 의료계의 굼뜬 반응을 역사가들은 의아해했다. 따라서 ③은 사실과 다르다.

Chapter Ⅲ
추론적 이해

1. 지칭 추론

정답

		063 ⑤	064 ①
065 ②	066 ④	067 ②	

063

정답 ⑤

지문 해석 직업 무용가로서 이사도라 덩컨은 공연의 상업적 측면을 좋아하지 않아서 투어나 계약, 기타 실무를 아름다움의 창조와 젊은이 교육이라는 그녀 본연의 임무로부터 일탈로 간주했다. 파격적이긴 하나 천부적 재능이 있는 교육자로서 덩컨은 어린 여자애들에게 — 사내애들 교육도 잠시 시도했지만 성공하지 못했다 — 그녀의 철학을 심어줄 목적으로 세 개의 학교를 설립했다. 독일 그루네발트에 세워진 첫 번째 학교는 이사도라블즈라 불리는 그녀의 가장 유명한 문하생 그룹을 탄생시켰는데 이곳 학생들은 덩컨이라는 성姓을 사용했고 그녀와 합동 공연을 하거나 혹은 단독 공연했다. 두 번째 학교는 1차 세계대전 발발 전 파리 교외의 대저택에 잠깐 설치 운영됐고 셋째 학교는 러시아 혁명을 겪은 그녀의 격동적인 모스크바 경험을 반영한 것이었다. 덩컨의 교육과 그녀의 제자들은 그녀에게 자부심과 근심을 동시에 안겨줬다. 그녀의 언니인 엘리자베스 덩컨은 독일학교를 인수해 그것을 독일인 남편이 가지고 있던 게르만 민족 철학에 맞춰나갔다. 이사도라블즈들이 상업적인 공연 의도를 드러낼 때마다 덩컨의 호통을 감수해야 했고 이윽고 그중 하나인 리사 덩컨이 나이트클럽에서 공연했다는 이유로 영구 제명됐다.

글의 소재 이사도라 덩컨의 교육관

주요 어휘 practicality 실무적인 면, inculcate ~ into 반복 학습을 통해 ~에게 주입하다, chateau 대저택, tumultuous 격동적인, in the wake of ~이 끝난 후에, Teutonic 게르만족 특유의, ostracize 추방하다, hector 괴롭히다

글의 흐름 ⊙ 도입문 'Throughout her career, Isadora Duncan did not like the commercial aspects of public performance, regarding touring, contracts, and other practicalities as distractions from her real mission : the creation of beauty and the education of the young.'이 주제문인 두괄식 구조이다.

구조 분석 ⊙ A gifted if unconventional pedagogue, she was the founder of three schools

→ A gifted if unconventional pedagogue와 she는 동격이다. if는 even if의 양보의 의미로 '파격적이기는 하나 천부적 재능이 있는'의 뜻이다.

⊙ The Isadorables were subject to ongoing hectoring from Duncan over their willingness to perform commercially ~.

→ be subject to A from B over C 구문이다. C라는 이유로 B로부터 A를 감수해야 했다. over는 이유의 over이다.

정답 해설 (a)~(d)는 모두 Isadora Duncan을 가리킨다. 하지만 (e) 문장은 Isadora의 언니인 Elizabeth가 처음 언급되고, 그녀 남편의 학교 운영이 소개되는 상황이다. 그러므로 (e)는 명백히 언니인 Elizabeth Duncan을 가리킨다.

064

정답 ①

지문 해석 오늘날 세계의 보조어는 만들어진 어떤 대체 언어가 아니라 바로 영어다. 영어를 모국어로 쓰는 사람보다 제2 공용어로 쓰는 사람이 더 많다. 통계 수치가 제각각이지만 보수적으로 잡아도 영어를 제2 공용어로 사용하는 사람은 5억 명에 이른다. 이보다 훨씬 많은 세계인들이 이러한 추세를 거스르기보다는 그에 편승하려고 애쓴다. 그러한 열정이 종교적으로 보이는 경우도 있고, 외부인들이 보기에는 고행의 모습으로 비치는 경우도 있다. 마트 애블리에 의하면, 몇몇 부유한 한국인들은 좀더 유창한 영어 구사를 위해 애들에게 혀를 늘리는 수술을 해준다고 한다. 그래야 r과 l 발음을 잘 할 수 있다는 계산이지만, 영국이나 미국에 거주하는 영어에 능숙한 한국 이민자들의 실례를 보면 그 절차가 과연 필요하거나 유용한지 고개를 갸우뚱하게 한다. 하지만 이것은 사람들이 언어 자산이 곧 경제적 자산이라는 믿음에 빠져 영어를 배우기 위해 갖은 노력도 마다하지 않는 구체적 실례를 보여준다.

① 혀를 늘리는 수술을 하는 것
② 미국이나 영국에서 영어를 공부하는 것
③ 영어 과외 선생을 집으로 초청하는 것
④ r과 l 발음을 잘하게 하는 것
⑤ 사교육에 많은 비용을 쓰는 것

글의 소재 영어 학습 광풍

주요 어휘 self-mortification 고행

구조 분석 ⊙ Far more of the world's citizens are eagerly jumping on board than trying to resist its progress.

→ its progress는 jumping on board와 trying to resist의 공동 목적어이다.

⊙ devotion can involve what (to outsiders) looks a lot like self-mortification.

→ 삽입구 to outsiders를 ( )에 넣으면 involve what looks

like A 구문임이 드러난다. 이때 what는 복합관계대명사이다.

⊙ Still, it is a powerful example of the lengths people will go to in order to learn English

→ the lengths와 people 사이에 목적격 관계대명사 that(which)가 생략됐다. people will go to the lengths in order to ~에서 the lengths 부분이 관계대명사 that(which)으로 바뀌어 문두로 이동한 구문이다. go to the lengths in order to ~ =~하려고 갖은 노력을 다하다.

[정답 해설] 'the procedure'가 포함된 문장은 '그래야 "r"과 "l" 발음을 잘 할 수 있다는 계산이지만, 영국이나 미국에 거주하는 영어에 능숙한 한국 이민자들의 실례를 보면 그 절차 (the procedure)가 과연 필요한지 고개를 갸우뚱거리게 한다.'는 내용이다. 이때 'the procedure'는 바로 앞 문장에 쓰인 'an operation that lengthens the tongue because it helps them speak English convincingly.'를 말한다. 필자는 그런 혀 늘리는 수술 안 받아도 "l"과 "r" 발음을 포함해 영어를 능숙하게 잘만 하더라고 말한다. 따라서 정답은 ①이다.

065 　　　　　　　　　　　　　　　　　　[정답 ②]

[지문 해석] 처칠의 강인한 면모는 1911년 1월 런던에서 경찰이 두 명의 강도가 은신 중인 한 건물을 포위하고 있었던 현장을 그가 방문했을 때 드러났다. 이날 처칠의 관여 정도는 아직도 논란거리다. 어떤 기록에 의하면 그가 현장에 간 것은 단지 무슨 일이 벌어지는지 보기 위해서였다는 말이 있는가 하면 그가 건물에 급습해 범인을 잡도록 경찰에게 구체적 지시를 내렸다고 주장하는 기록도 있다. 알려진 바로는 포위 작전 시 건물에 불이 났고 처칠은 인명 손실을 무릅써 가며 안에 갇힌 사람을 구조하느니 차라리 건물이 불타도록 놔두는 것이 더 낫다며 소방대원들에게 불을 끄지 못하도록 했다. 두 강도의 시신은 타 버린 건물 잔해에서 발견됐다.

[글의 소재] 윈스턴 처칠의 강인한 면모

[주요 어휘] allegedly 주장에 의하면, controversial 논란이 있는, siege 포위, hole up 숨다, account 진술, storm 급습하다

[글의 흐름] ⊙ 처칠이 강인한 성격을 지녔음을 주장하고 이를 구체적 일화로 예시하는 두괄식 구조이다. 주제문은 'In January 1911, Churchill showed his tougher side when he made a controversial visit to a police siege in London, with two robbers holed up in a building.'이다.

[정답 해설] (a), (b), (e)는 강도를, (c), (d)는 소방관을 각각 가리킨다. (b)는 경찰의 체포 대상(targets)인 강도를 말하고, (e)는 건물 안에 있는 소방관의 구조 대상인 강도를 지칭한다. (d)는 인명 손실을 무릅쓰고 구조 활동을 벌이는 소방관의 목숨을 가리킨다.

066 　　　　　　　　　　　　　　　　　　[정답 ④]

[지문 해석] 프레더릭스버그 전투가 있던 다음 날 아침 Marye's Heights 고지의 석벽 앞 공터는 부상당해 죽어가는 북군으로 넘쳐났다. 이윽고 양측 군인들이 물을 달라, 도와달라는 외침소리를 듣기에 이르렀다. 결국 젊은 남군 Richard Kirkland 병장은 더 참을 수 없었다. 그가 지휘관 Joseph Kershaw 준장에게 다가가 말했다. "장군님, 더 이상 못 참겠습니다." "뭘 말인가, 병장?" 장군이 대답했다. "하루 종일 저 불쌍한 사람들의 물 달라는 소리를 들었습니다. 이제 도저히 더 못 참겠습니다." Kirkland가 말했다. "저 사람들한테 가서 물 좀 주려 합니다. 허락해 주십쇼." "Kirkland, 자네가 벽을 넘어서는 순간 머리에 총 맞게 된다는 거 몰라서 그러나?" 장군이 말했다. "아뇨, 압니다. 하지만 허락해 주시면 한번 해보고 싶습니다." 이 말에 감명을 받은 장군은 Kirkland의 요청을 받아들였다. 그러나 그가 안전을 도모할 수 있도록 휴전의 백기를 지니는 것은 허락하지 않았다. 몸에 지닐 만큼 최대한 물통을 챙겨 든 Kirkland가 위험을 무릅쓰고 벽을 넘었다. 북군의 총탄 세례를 받으며 그는 가장 가까운 부상자에게로 가서 물을 전했다. 그의 의도를 알아차린 적군이 사격을 멈췄고 Kirkland는 한 시간 반 동안 무사히 부상자들을 돌볼 수 있었다.

[글의 소재] 미국 남북 전쟁 당시의 영웅담

[주요 어휘] brigadier general 준장, white flag of truce 휴전의 백기, canteen 식당, 수통

[구조 분석] ⊙ and for an hour and a half Kirkland tended the wounded unharmed.

→ unharmed는 주격 보어로 쓰였다. 커크랜드가 부상자를 돌봤는데 unharmed한 상태에서 돌봤다는 말로, Kirkland tended the wounded와 Kirkland was unharmed 두 문장을 합쳐놓은 것과 같다.

[정답 해설] 지금 전장에는 교전 중인 북군과 남군, 그리고 석벽 앞에서 죽어가는 북군 패잔병의 세 무리의 군인들이 있다. (d)는 전투 중인 적군(북군)을 말하고 나머지는 석벽 앞에서 부상당해 죽어가는 북군 군인들을 말한다. 따라서 (d)가 정답이다.

067 　　　　　　　　　　　　　　　　　　[정답 ②]

[지문 해석] 이끌림에 의한 가장 간단한 이주는 농지나 풍요로운 계곡 근처의 척박한 초원이나 고지에 사는 사람들이 하는 경우다. 농경민족은 대체로 전쟁을 싫어하고 전쟁 준비가 서툴다. 생활이 윤택해질수록 그들은 자신의 문명에 의해 기력이 쇠해질 가능성이 크다. 그들은 따라서 주변 약탈자의 공격을 받기 쉬운데 약탈자들은 전리품을 챙겨 척박한 고향으로 되돌아가기도 하지만 피정복민 속에 그대로 남아 그들에 동화되고 더욱 문명화된 다음 또다시 국경의 야만인 동족으로부터 침략을 받

는다. 그래서 한편으로는 야만인들을 교화하고 다른 한 편으로는 수월한 환경에 의해 섬약해진 사람들에게 원기를 불어넣어 주는 자동적인 사회적 체계가 형성된다.

글의 소재 이끌림에 의한 이주

주요 어휘 enervate 약화시키다, brigand 산적, 약탈자, kinsman 친척, 일가, invigorate 원기를 불어넣다

글의 흐름 ⊙ 'The simplest cases of migration by attraction are those of a people living on poor steppes or plateaus adjoining cultivated land or rich valleys.'가 주제문으로, 두 괄식 구조이다. 이끌림에 의한 이주가 구체적으로 어떻게 이뤄지는지 약탈자의 예를 들어 설명하고 있다.

정답 해설 (a), (b), (d)는 농경민족을, (c), (e)는 약탈자를 각각 가리킨다. (d)는 약탈자가 동화되는 대상을 가리키기 때문에 농경민족을, (e)는 국경의 야만인과 동족이기 때문에 약탈자를 각각 지칭한다.

8. 빈칸 추론

정답

068
정답 ②

지문 해석 프로이트 심리학은 인간 정신에 대한 유일한 체계적 설명인데 그 설명은 미묘함이나 복잡성, 흥미와 비극적 힘의 측면에서 문학이 수 세기 동안 쌓아온, 혼돈으로 가득 찬 다량의 심리적 통찰과 비견되는 것이다. 위대한 문학 작품을 읽다가 학구적인 심리학 논문으로 넘어가는 것은 하나의 지각 체계에서 또 다른 지각 체계로 넘어가는 것이지만 프로이트 심리학이 다룬 인간성은 시인이 늘 자신의 예술을 행사해온 바로 그 재료다. 따라서 심리분석이 문학에 큰 영향을 끼친 것은 놀라운 일이 아니다. 하지만 둘의 관계는 상호적이어서 프로이트가 문학에 끼친 영향은 문학이 프로이트에 끼친 영향보다 적으면 적었지, 크지 않았다. 70세 생일을 축하하는 자리에서 '무의식의 발견자'라고 소개받고 프로이트는 사회자를 시정하고 그 타이틀이 자기에게 해당하지 않는다며 거절했다. 그는 "나보다 앞선 시인과 철학자들이 무의식을 발견했다. 내가 발견한 것은 무의식을 연구할 수 있는 과학적 방법론이었다."라고 프로이트는 말했다.

① 추방했다
② 거절했다
③ 받아들였다
④ 소중히 했다
⑤ 의절했다

글의 소재 프로이트 심리학과 문학

주요 어휘 in point of ~면에서, =in terms of, stand beside 비견하다, 대등하다, treatise 논문, order 질서, 체계, reciprocal 상호적인, ostracize 도편추방하다, disclaim 거절하다, disown 의절하다

글의 흐름 ⊙ 주제문은 'Yet the relationship is reciprocal, and ~ upon Freud.'이며, 중괄식 구조로 볼 수 있다.

구조 분석 ⊙ the only systematic account of the human mind which, in point of subtlety and complexity, of interest and tragic power, deserves to stand beside the chaotic mass of psychological insights which literature has accumulated through the centuries.

→ 수 세기 동안 쌓여온 문학적 성과와 비견될 만한 것은 systematic account이지 human mind가 아니다. 따라서 which의 선행사는 systematic account이다.

⊙ the effect of Freud upon literature has been no greater than the effect of literature upon Freud.

→ 부정의 비교급. 여기서 no greater than은 '~보다 작거나 같은' 상태를 말한다. 즉, 적으면 적었지 크지 않다는 뉘앙스다.

정답 해설 빈칸이 있는 문장은 프로이트가 '무의식의 발견자라는 타이틀이 제 것이 아니라고 거절'하는 상황을 말하고 있다. 그러므로 빈칸에 들어갈 말은 disclaimed가 타당하다.

069 정답 ②

지문 해석 신경과학자들은 신피질의 설정이 놀라울 정도로 유연하다는 것, 즉 그것 안으로 흘러들어 오는 입력 정보의 종류에 따라 스스로 변하고 재설정한다는 것을 알아냈다. 예를 들어 갓 태어난 흰족제비의 뇌를 수술해 조작해 눈의 신호를 평소 청각 작용이 일어나는 피질 구역으로 보낼 수 있다. 그 결과 놀랍게도 흰족제비들은 청각을 담당하는 뇌 구역에서 정상 작동하는 시각 경로를 만들어낸다. 달리 말하면 그들은 평소 소리를 듣는 뇌 조직을 통해 볼 수 있다. 비슷한 실험이 다른 감각과 뇌 구역을 대상으로 실시됐다. 가령, 출생 시 쥐의 시각 피질 조각이 통상적으로 촉각에 해당하는 구역에 이식될 수 있다. 쥐가 성장해 가면서 이식된 조직은 시각이 아닌 촉각을 처리한다. 세포들은 시각이나 촉각, 청각만을 전문으로 다루도록 태어나지 않았다.

글의 소재 뇌 조직의 놀라운 유연성

주요 어휘 wire ~성향을 띠도록 만들다, 설정하다, neo-cortex 신피질, ferret 흰족제비, surgically 외과적으로, 수술로, function 정상적으로 작동하다, auditory 청각의, tissue 조직, transplant 이식하다, represent ~에 해당하다, specialize ~를 전문으로 다루다

글의 흐름 ⊙ 주제문은 'Neuroscientists have found that the wiring of the neo-cortex is amazingly "plastic," meaning it can change and rewire itself depending on the type of inputs flowing into it.'이고 두괄식 구조다.

구조 분석 ⊙ For example, newborn ferret brains can be surgically rewired so that the animals' eyes send their signals to the areas of cortex where hearing normally develops.

→ so that ~이하는 목적의 부사절로 '~하도록'으로 해석하는 것이 원칙이나 이 경우는 결과의 부사절로 보고 '~해서 ~하다' 식으로 해석해도 무방하다.

정답 해설 대뇌 신피질 세포는 매우 유연해 입력 정보의 종류에 따라 속성이 변한다는 것이 필자의 주장이고, 이는 특정 세포가 특정 기능만을 담당하지는, 즉 전문으로 다루지는 않는다는 것을 의미하므로 빈칸에 들어갈 적절한 말은 specialize이다. 따라서 정답은 ②이다.

070 정답 ⑤

지문 해석 가장 낮은 단계의 감각 과정부터 다른 사람들을 대하는 것에 이르기까지 사물을 그루핑하는 것이 인간 두뇌의 기본적인 활동 중 하나다. 많은 시각적 환상이 보여주듯이, 시간적으로 동시에 발생하는 것 또는 공간적으로 가까운 것만으로도 충분할 수 있다. 우리가 어떤 사물을 보는 것과 비슷한 시간에 어떤 소리를 듣는다면, 그렇지 않다고 배운 적이 없다면 우리는 당연히 그 사물이 그 소리를 내는 거라고 생각한다. 우리는 무리로 모으고 분류하며 평생 동안 무수한 범주 개념을 습득한다. 우리는 이것을 사용하여 세상에 대한 우리의 해석에 속도를 높인다. 내가 새로운 사물이 '고양이' 범주의 구성원이라고 판단할 수 있으면 나는, 새로 찾아내려 할 필요 없이 즉시 새로운 사물에 대한 모든 종류의 저장된 정보(고기를 먹는다든지 할퀸다든지 주방에서 마음대로 휘두를 수 없다든지 하는)에 접근할 수 있다. 이것은 상당한 시간과 에너지 절약, 그리고 명백한 생존력을 나에게 준다.

글의 소재 인간의 그루핑 본능

주요 어휘 sensory 지각의, temporal 시간의, coincidence 동시 발생, 우연의 일치, spatial 공간의, proximity 근접성, assume 가정하다, 전제하다, classify 분류하다, innumerable 무수한, interpretation 해석, immediately 즉시, have access to ~에 접근하다, survival edge 생존력

구조 분석 ⊙ If I can judge a novel object to be a member of the category 'cat,' I immediately have access to all sorts of stored information about the new object

→ judge가 불완전타동사로 쓰였고 'to be a member of the category 'cat''가 목적격보어다.

정답 해설 본문은 인간은 사물에 대한 정보를 모으고 분류하며 평생 동안 무수한 범주 개념을 습득하고 또 이 과정을 통해 세상에 대한 해석에 속도를 높인다는 인간의 그루핑 본능에 대해 설명하고 있다. 따라서 인간 두뇌의 기본 활동을 묻는 빈칸에는 '사물을 그루핑하기'가 적절하다.

071 정답 ③

지문 해석 나는 지난 몇 년간 해고 노동자들의 수많은 불만을 들어왔는데 그들의 말은 전혀 알지도 못하는 사이에 일 처리를 제대로 못 한다고 버림을 받아 가슴이 아프다는 것이다. 연

말 근무 평정에서 수차례 빛나는 성과를 거뒀는데 갑자기 보스의 방으로 불려 들어가 그만두라는 통보를 받았다고 그들은 주장한다. 사람들은 자기들과는 무관한 회사의 곤경—(대개는 사실이 아니다)—때문에 해고당한 거라면 그다지 분개하지 않는다. 그들이 정말 화나는 건 보스가 분명히 자신들 마음에 들지 않는 구석이 있었음에도 숨기고 있다가 해고 당일에야 이를 언급할 때이다. 이런 경험을 가진, 내가 아는 한 사람은 "사전 경고를 해줬더라면 그쪽 방면에 내가 좀 더 잘하도록 노력했을 텐데…."라며 아쉬워했다.

┌ ① 해고 통지서
│ ② 친절한 안내문
│ ③ 사전 경고
│ ④ 계약 갱신
└ ⑤ 책임 회피 조항

(글의 소재) 갑작스러운 해고

(주요 어휘) toss aside 내던지다, let go 해고하다, drive someone up the wall ~를 화나게 하다, heads up 사전 경고

(구조 분석) ⊙ A little heads up would have been nice so ~
➡ 가정법 과거완료 구문이다. 주어 A little heads up에 조건절이 숨어있다.

(정답 해설) 이글은 상사로부터 해고에 대한 어떤 암시도 받지 못하고 황당하게 해고당한 사람이 이를 complain 하는 상황이다. 그러므로 빈칸에는 사전 경고를 뜻하는 a little heads up이 가장 적절하다.

072 정답 ②

(지문 해설) 종간의 및 종 내의 비교 연구는 협력적 행동에 관련된 인지적 메커니즘의 폭과 미묘함을 이해하는 데 결정적이다. 예를 들어 Brian Hare의 작업은, 사회적 생활에서 영장류의 일관된 패턴이 부족하기 때문에 우리가 영장류 협력에 대해서도 일반화할 수 없음을 보여준다. Hare는 같은 협력 과제에 참여하는 보노보와 침팬지를 비교했다. 한 접시의 음식을 주면 보노보 한 쌍은 서로 장난치며 반응한다. 그들은 과실을 나누는 경향이 있다. 침팬지 한 쌍은 보통 나누지 않고 서로의 접촉을 피한다. 두 명으로 구성된 팀이 과일 접시를 가져오기 위해 밧줄을 당겨야 하는 협력 과제에서 음식이 나눌 수 있는 작은 조각으로 잘려 제시되면 침팬지와 보노보 팀은 서로 협력했다. 그러나 과일이 큰 조각으로 제시되었을 때 침팬지들은 덜 협력했고, 작업을 함께 한 경우 어느 한 쪽이 보상을 독점하려 했다. 이것은 우리에게 행동이 종에 따라 다를 것이라는 것을 다시 한번 상기시켜준다.

(글의 소재) 유인원의 차별화된 협력 행태

(주요 어휘) crucial 중차대한, 결정적인, subtlety 미묘함, cognitive 인지적인, generalization 일반화, react 반응하다, behavioral 행동의, collaborative 협력의, retrieve 되찾다, 회수하다, monopolize 독점하다, species-specific 종에 따라 다른

(구조 분석) ⊙ When given a plate of food, a pair of bonobos will react by playing with each other.
➡ When과 given 사이에 'they are'가 생략됐다. 시간. 조건, 양보의 부사절에서 주어와 시제가 주절과 같으면 '주어 + 동사'는 생략할 수 있다.

(정답 해설) 실험에서 보노보는 파트너와 음식을 나누거나 협력에 적극적이지만 침팬지는 음식을 나누지 않고 협력에 소극적이다. 이는 같은 영장류지만 보노보와 침팬지는 사회생활에서 서로 다른 행동 양태를 보임을 의미한다. 따라서 무엇의 부족 때문에 유인원의 협력을 일반화하기 어려운지를 묻는 빈칸에는 ② '사회생활에서 유인원의 일관성 있는 패턴'이 적절하다.

073 정답 ④

(지문 해설) 디자이너가 산업 주류로 이동함에 따라 디자이너는 누구이고 무엇을 하는가에 대한 폭넓은 논란에 불이 붙었다. 실리콘 밸리의 디자인 권위자인 존 마에다 씨는 디자이너를 세 가지로 분류한다. 특정 그룹의 사람을 위해 물품이나 상품을 만드는 고전적인 디자이너와 고객이 상품이나 서비스와 소통하는 방식에 대해 깊이 통찰함으로써 개혁하는 상업 디자이너, 그리고 프로그래밍 기술과 자료를 이용해 수백만에서 많게는 수십억 사용자를 동시에 만족시키는 컴퓨터 디자이너가 그들이다. 캠프들은 항상 사이가 좋은 건 아니다. 고전적인 훈련을 받은 디자이너는 다른 그룹 출신의 디자이너의 예술적 능력을 미심쩍은 눈으로 바라보기 쉽다. 상업 디자이너들은 컴퓨터 디자이너가 만나본 적도 없는 수백만 명과 어떻게 공감할 수 있는지에 대해 의문을 품는다. 컴퓨터 디자이너는 다른 두 부류의 방법은 규모를 키울 수 없다고 불평한다. 그러나 많은 사람들이 미래의 가장 가치 있는 디자이너는 세 부류의 디자이너에게 통용되는 기술과 안목을 결합할 수 있는 이들이라고 믿고 있다.

┌ ① 캠프들은 항상 서로의 빈 곳을 메워주려 한다.
│ ② 캠프들은 서로에게 무관심하다.
│ ③ 캠프들은 대체로 우호적인 분위기다.
│ ④ 캠프들은 항상 사이가 좋은 건 아니다.
└ ⑤ 캠프들이 정면충돌하는 경우는 거의 없다.

(글의 소재) 세 부류의 디자이너

(주요 어휘) spark 불을 지피다, guru 구루, 권위자, instantaneously 동시에, get along 사이좋게 지내다, be apt to ~하기 쉽다, askance 미심쩍은 눈으로, empathize 공감하다, scale

규모를 키우다

⊙ 주제문은 'in the future, the most valuable designers will be those who combine skills and perspectives from all three categories.'로 미괄식 구조이다.

정답 해설 빈칸 문장에 이어지는 문장에서 세 부류의 디자이너들은 서로를 비판적으로 보고 있다. 그러므로 빈칸 문장에는 '서로 사이가 안 좋다'는 의미의 내용인 ④가 적절하다.

074
정답 ②

지문 해석 체형 변화를 선전하는 사람들이 가장 열성적으로 외치는 것이 몸만들기, 즉 특이하면서 부자연스러운 보디빌더 체형을 가져오는 과도한 운동이다. 만약 당신이 몇몇 근육을 집중적으로 단련한다면 크고 확실한 근육을 얻을 수 있을 것이다. 스케이트 선수들 허벅지가 굵어지고 역도 선수들의 팔뚝이 굵어지는 건 이런 이유다. 그 반대로 가는 것, 즉 특정 부분이 살이 빠져 작아지는 것은 입증된 바 없다. 얼마나 많은 체형이 있는지에 대해 의사들도 의견이 엇갈림을 명심하라. 주변을 돌아보라. 사람 수만큼의 체형이 있지 않은가. 적어도 837가지는 된다. 당신이 체형을 바꿀 수 있다고 말하는 사람들의 한 가지 공통점은 그들이 당신에게 무엇을 팔려고 한다는 점이다. 돈 때문이 아니라면 얻을 수 없는 것에 대해 그렇게 장광설을 늘어놓을 이유가 없을 테니까.

┌ ① 당신에게 뭔가를 가르치려 든다.
│ ② 당신에게 뭔가를 팔려고 한다.
│ ③ 당신에게 운동을 더 하게 한다.
│ ④ 당신에게 뭔가를 경고하려 한다.
└ ⑤ 선택적 살빼기는 사실상 불가능하다는 말을 하려 한다.

글의 소재 체형 변화

주요 어휘 propagandist 선전원, defined 확실한, undocumented 입증되지 않는, money-driven 돈이 목적인, elaborate on 상술하다

구조 분석 ⊙ the phrase 'body sculpting', heavy exercise of the kind
→ the phrase 'body sculpting'와 heavy exercise는 동격이다.
⊙ That's why ~
→ For the reason의 부사구로 바꿀 수 있다.

정답 해설 빈칸이 있는 문장 바로 다음 문장 'Unless they are money-driven, they have no reason to elaborate on something unattainable(돈 때문이 아니라면 얻을 수 없는 것에 대해 그렇게 열성적일 이유가 없을 테니까).'에서 빈칸에는 'they are trying to sell you something(당신에게 뭔가를 팔려고 한다.)'가 와야 함을 알 수 있다. 따라서 정답은 ②이다.

075
정답 ②

지문 해석 아마존은 거침없는 혁신을 통해 번창했고 사업 영역을 무차별적으로 확대해 왔다. 이 소매와 기술의 거인이 최근 건강보험업에 진출한다고 발표했다. 아마존이 건강보험업에 뛰어든다는 소식이 전해지자 전통적인 보험회사의 기업 가치가 급락했다. 둘 중 어느 한 곳의 고객이었던 사람이라면 그 이유를 안다. 미국의 건강보험업계는 실리콘밸리와는 정반대다. 엄청나게 비효율적이고 사용자에 대한 배려가 없으며 기업이 불투명하기가 크렘린을 제외하면 세계 제일 수준에 돈도 그(크렘린)에 못지않게 넘쳐난다. 미국인들이 2016년 건강 비용으로 사용한 3조3천억 달러는 그해 독일의 전체 GDP와 맞먹는다. 그것은 미국 국내 총생산의 18%에 이르는 엄청난 액수로 다른 선진국들의 통상 건강 비용의 두 배에 달하지만, 미국인의 평균 수명이 사실상 짧아지고 있다는 사실에 잘 나타나 있듯이 투자 대비 수익이 너무 적어 어떤 CEO라도 해고시킬 수 있을 정도다.

┌ ① 2016년 무수한 건강 서비스 체인이 문을 닫았다
│ ② 미국인의 평균 수명이 사실상 짧아지고 있다
│ ③ 건강 관련 주식 투자자들이 큰 손해를 봤다
│ ④ 미국인들의 생활 수준이 크게 낮아졌다
└ ⑤ 미국인들의 건강지수가 상당히 좋아지고 있다

글의 소재 미국의 건강 산업의 비효율성

주요 어휘 omnivorously 닥치는 대로, dominion 영토, 영역, word 소문, old-school 구식의, 전통적인, antithesis 정반대되는 것, awash ~이 넘쳐나는

구조 분석 ⊙ Anyone who has been a customer of either knows why.
→ either는 Amazon과 old-school health-insurance companies 둘 중 하나를 가리킨다.
⊙ the least transparent enterprise outside the Kremlin
→ 크렘린 밖에서 투명성이 가장 적다고 함은 기업이 불투명하기가 크렘린을 제외하면 세계 제일 수준이라는 뜻이다.
⊙ and just as awash in money.
→ and just as awash in money (as in Kremlin). 크렘린만큼이나 돈이 넘쳐나는

정답 해설 미국인들이 건강관리에 엄청난 돈을 쏟아부었지만 그 결과 어떤 CEO도 해고할 만큼 형편없는 수익을 거뒀다고 함은 미국인들의 건강이 오히려 나빠졌다는 말이다. 따라서 미국인의 평균 수명이 짧아지고 있다는 내용의 ②가 정답이다. 'return on investment'나 'CEO' 같은 말에 현혹되지 않아야 한다.

076
정답 ①

지문 해석 모든 뉴미디어는 이것을 공통으로 가지고 있다. 시공간과 우리의 관계를 크게 변화시킨다는 것이다. 이것들은

현재 인간 존재의 기본 틀을 형성한다. 공간을 통해 우리는 우리 밖에 있는 모든 사물을 감지하고 시간을 통해 외부와 내부의 사물을 감지한다. 우리가 사물과 다른 사람과 우리 자신을 보는 방식은 이러한 관계에 크게 의존한다. 우리와 대상물 간에 떨어진 거리와 시간의 정도에 따라 있기도 하고 없기도 하거나 강하거나 약해지는 우리의 의지와 기분, 감정도 역시 마찬가지다 (이런 관계에 의존한다). 대체로 뉴미디어는 우리와 사람, 사물과 떨어진 시간과 공간을 축소한다. 우리는 그들이 세상 어디에 있건 그들을 즉각적으로 알아차리고, 듣고 볼 수 있다. 부분적으로는 가상적이고 부분적으로는 실재하는 방식에 따라 우리는 다양한 관련 제약이 따르는 거리를 이동하거나 기다릴 필요 없이 그들을 만날 수 있다.

[글의 소재] 우리와 시공간의 관계를 크게 변화시킨 뉴미디어

[주요 어휘] profoundly 심대하게, perceive 감지하다, overall 대체로, shrink 축소하다, immediately 즉각적으로, virtual 가상의, constraint 제약, involve 관련되다

[글의 흐름] ⊙ 'All the new media have this in common: they alter profoundly our relationships with space and time.'이 주제문이며 두괄식 구성을 하고 있다.

[구조 분석] ⊙ Through space, we perceive all things that are outside ourselves, and through time, both things outside ourselves and those within.

→ 밑줄 친 time과 both 사이에는 we perceive가 생략됐다.

[정답 해설] 우리는 시간과 공간을 통해 우리 내부와 외부의 사물을 인식하고 양자 관계에 의존해 자신과 타인을 보는데 뉴미디어가 우리와 사람, 사물의 거리를 좁혀 그들을 즉각적으로 보게 한다고 했으므로 양자 관계에 큰 변화를 가져다준 것이다. 따라서 빈칸에 알맞은 말은 ① '시공간과 우리의 관계를 크게 변화시킨다'가 적절하다.
② 우리가 시공간에 대한 기본 개념을 확립하는 데 도움을 준다
③ 시공간상에 심각한 제약을 가하는 쪽으로 나아간다
④ 시간과 공간이 지각 학습에서 차지하는 역할을 강화한다
⑤ 우리의 시공간적 인식이 언제까지고 굳어지도록 한다

077 정답 ①

[지문 해석] 몇몇 범죄 전문가들은 대규모 총기 난사 사건이 범인의 가정 폭력과 관계있다고 주장한다. 그들의 주장은 Omar Mateen이 49명을 살해한 올란도 펄스 나이트클럽 난사 사건 같은 최근 발생한 일련의 대형 참극에서 여실히 입증되고 있다. 당시 Mateen은 전처를 학대한 것으로 알려졌다. 그러나 과학적 견지에서 이런 연관성은 입증되지 않았다. 총기 난사범이 종종 학대 전력이 있다고 해서 반드시 학대 전력자가 난사범이 될 가능성이 높은 것은 아니다. 그래서 위험 신호는 일이 다 끝난

후에야 나타난다. 연구자들이 사전에 둘의 상관성을 입증할 증거가 부족한 것이다. 펜실베이니아대 Susan Sorenson 교수는 "지금 현재 우리는 자료가 충분하지 못해 일정한 패턴을 얻을 수 없다"라고 말한다.

[글의 소재] 총기 난사범의 가정 학대 전력 관련성

[주요 어휘] forensic 법의학의, mass shooting 대형 총기 난사 사건, underscore 밑줄 긋다, 분명히 보여주다, a host of 일련의, anecdotal 일화적인, 입증되지 않은, red flag 위험 신호

[구조 분석] ⊙ Just because mass shooters are often abusers doesn't mean abusers are more likely to be mass shooters.
→ Just because A does not (necessarily, always) mean B 구문으로, 'A하다고 반드시 B한 것은 아니다.'는 뜻이다. 경우에 따라서 necessarily, always 등의 부사를 끼워 넣기도 한다.

[정답 해설] 글의 흐름상 가족 학대 전력자 중에 총기 난사범이 있을 수 있다는 '위험 신호'는 사후적으로(in hindsight) 알 수 있을 뿐 양자 간의 관계를 사전에(ahead of time) 알기는 어렵다는 내용이 이어져야 한다.

078 정답 ①

[지문 해석] 경제학에서 결핍은 도처에 산재해 있다. 우리 모두는 제한된 액수의 돈을 가지고 있다. 가장 부유한 사람들조차도 모든 것을 살 수는 없다. 그러나 우리는, 물질적 결핍은 어디에나 있지만 결핍에 대한 느낌은 그렇지 않다고 생각한다. 당신의 일정표에 몇 개의 모임이 표시돼 있고 해야 할 일 목록을 그런대로 관리할 수 있는 직장에서의 하루를 상상하라. 당신은 일정이 빈 시간을 점심이나 미팅 후 뭉그적거리거나 동료에게 안부 전화하는 데 사용한다. 자, 이제는 당신의 일정표가 꽉 찬 직장에서의 또 다른 하루를 상상하라. 당신의 자유 시간은 아무리 작은 것이라 하더라도 밀린 프로젝트에 모조리 쏟아부어야 한다. 두 경우 모두 시간은 물리적으로 부족하다. 직장에서 당신에게 주어진 시간은 똑같았고 그 시간을 채울 활동도 넘쳐났다. 그러나 한 경우에 당신은 결핍, 즉 시간의 유한성을 뼈저리게 깨달았다. 다른 한 경우에는 설사 당신이 그것(결핍)을 느꼈다 해도 그것은 현실과 동떨어진 생각이었다. 결핍의 느낌은 그것의 물리적 현실과는 별개다.

[글의 소재] 결핍의 경제학

[주요 어휘] scarcity 결핍, ubiquitous 어디에나 있는, sprinkle 뿌리다, linger 뭉그적거리다, catch up 안부를 묻다, chock-full 꽉 찬, overdue 기한이 지난, acutely 통렬하게, 뼈저리게, finiteness 유한성, distinct 별개의

[글의 흐름] ⊙ 주제문은 'The feeling of scarcity is distinct from its physical reality.'이고 미괄식 구조다.

[구조 분석] ⊙ What little free time you have must be sunk into a project that is overdue. In both cases time was physically scarce.

→ What은 복합관계형용사로 명사절을 유도하며 'Any little free time that(which) you have'로 바꿔 쓸 수 있다.

[정답 해설] 직장의 예에서 업무가 많을 때나 그렇지 않을 때나 항상 '할 일'이 있다는 점에서 시간이 부족한 것은 마찬가지지만 시간 부족에 대한 압박은 업무가 많을 때 훨씬 크다고 했으므로 시간 부족에 대한 느낌은 시간의 현실과는 관계가 없다. 즉 결핍에 대한 느낌은 결핍의 물리적 현실과는 별개이고 따라서 빈칸에 적합한 것은 ①이다.

① 그것의 물리적 현실과 별개다
② 그것의 수치를 정확하게 반영한다
③ 우리가 하지 못한 일에 대해 걱정하게 만든다
④ 우리가 상대적 박탈감에 시달리게 한다
⑤ 그것의 물리적 수치에 비례한다

079
[정답 ⑤]

[지문 해석] 빅데이터는 우리 주변 세계를 이해하기 위한 새로운 기회를 만들어내지만 그것은 또한 새로운 과학적 문제들을 창출하기도 한다. 하나의 주요한 문제는 빅데이터가 우리가 통상 과학적 방법이라 생각하는 것에 잘 들어맞지 않는다는 것이다. 과학자들은 구체적인 가설을 확인하거나 그들이 학습한 것을 조합해 인과적 이야기, 그리고 궁극적으로 수학적 이론을 만들기를 좋아한다. 적절히 흥미로운 데이터세트 주변을 어슬렁거리다 보면 당신은 필연적으로 공해상의 해적 행위 빈도와 대기 온도의 상관관계 같은 발견을 할 것이다. 당신이 무엇을 발견할지 모른다는 점에서 이런 종류의 탐험적 연구는 종종 무가설이라 불린다. 그러나 빅데이터는 이러한 상관관계를 인과의 측면에서 설명하는 것에 관한 한 (가설을 세우는 과학적 방법보다) 훨씬 예리하지 못하다. 해적들이 지구온난화를 불러오는가? 더운 날씨가 더 많은 사람들로 하여금 해적질을 하게 하는가? 빅데이터는 우리에게 이런 것을 생각하게 한다.

① 해적 활동과 지구온난화의 가능한 관계를 밝히는 것
② 가설과 입증된 사실을 구분하는 것
③ 과거에 일어난 일을 근거로 해서 미래를 예측하는 것
④ 두 개의 임의의 변수 사이의 관계를 밝히는 것
⑤ 이러한 상관관계를 인과의 측면에서 설명하는 것

[글의 소재] 빅데이터의 문제점

[주요 어휘] fit into ~에 맞아떨어지다, hypothesis 가설, causal 인과관계의, correlation 상관관계, blunder about 어슬렁거리고 돌아다니다, high-seas 공해상의, incisive 예리한, when it comes to ~로 말하면, ~에 관한 한, pirate 해적

[글의 흐름] 'But big data is much less incisive when it comes to explaining these correlations in terms of cause and effect.'이 주제문인 중괄식 구조다. 역접의 연결사와 함께 사회 통념이 깨지면서 필자의 주장이 나오는 구조다.

[구조 분석] ⊙ Scientists like to confirm specific hypotheses, and to gradually assemble~

→ to confirm과 to gradually assemble가 병렬구조를 이룬다.

⊙ Blunder about in any reasonably interesting big dataset and you will inevitably make ~

→ 명령문 + and S V 구문으로 If you blunder about ~, you will inevitably make ~ 구문으로 바꿀 수 있다.

[정답 해설] 빅데이터는 둘 간의 상관관계는 말해줄 수 있으나 인과관계는 설명해줄 수 없다는 것이 이 글의 주장이다. 따라서 빈칸에 들어갈 말은 ⑤의 '이러한 상관관계를 인과의 측면에서 설명하는 것'이 적절하다. 해적 활동과 대기 온도의 인과관계를 묻는 빈칸 다음의 두 문장에서 단서를 찾을 수 있다.

080
[정답 ③]

[지문 해석] 어떤 생각이 얼마나 쉽게 떠오르는지 그 수월성이 관련 사건의 빈도, 그리고 더 중요하게는 사건의 중요성에 관한 우리의 판단에 영향을 미친다. 한 연구에서 피험자들은 여섯 개의 단어로 이루어진 목록을 받고 그 단어들이 한 사람을 묘사하기 위한 것이라는 말을 들었다. 그들은 이 사람이 어떤지를 그들이 이미 받은 단어를 사용해 좀 더 구체적으로 묘사하라고 요청받았다. 모든 피험자들은 같은 단어의 조합을 받았지만 그들의 절반에게는 단어들이 배열된 순서가 정반대였다. 한 그룹은 그 사람이 지적이고, 근면하고, 충동적이고, 비판적이고, 고집이 세고, 시샘이 많다는 말을 들었고 나머지 피험자들은 그 사람이 시샘이 많고, 고집이 세고, 비판적이고, 충동적이고, 근면하고, 지적이라는 말을 들었다. 긍정적 수식어가 앞에 나오는 목록을 받은 피험자들은 상당히 낙관적 묘사를 내놓았다. 이런 결과에 대해 할 수 있는 설명은 목록에서 앞서 나온 말들이 피험자에게는 가용성이 크기 때문에 목록의 뒤에 나온 말들에 대한 태도를 결정한다는 것이다.

[글의 소재] 가용성 휴리스틱

[주요 어휘] frequency 빈도, subject 피험자, given ~를 고려해서, reverse 뒤바꾸다, industrious 근면한, impulsive 충동적인, plausible 그럴듯한

[글의 흐름] 첫 문장이 주제문인 두괄식 문단이다. 예시와 마찬가지로 연구, 실험, 조사 등의 reference가 나오면 구체 진술이 시작된 것이고 일반 진술 즉 주제문은 한두 문장 전에서 이미 언급됐을 가능성이 크다.

[구조 분석] ⊙ given the six words they'd already been given~

→ 앞의 given은 전치사로 considering으로 바꿔 쓸 수 있고 '~를 고려해서'를 뜻한다.

⊙ One group was told that the person was intelligent, industrious, impulsive, critical, stubborn and envious~

→ 4형식 문장이 수동태로 전환돼 간접목적어가 주어로 나간 문장으로 was told는 heard로 바꿀 수 있다. 4형식 문장을 수동태로 만들 때 동사가 give, tell, teach면 간접목적어가 주어로 나갈 수 있다.

정답 해설 목록의 앞에 나오는 말들이 가용성이 크기 때문에 다음에 나오는 말들에 대한 태도를 결정한다는 것이 이 실험의 요지이다. 따라서 빈칸에는 가용성, 즉 '생각이 쉽게 떠오르는 그 수월성'이 적절하다. 마지막 문장에 주제가 다시 한 번 요약돼 있는데 예시, 연구, 실험, 조사 등으로 이뤄진 구체진술 파트는 흔히 요지를 마무리하는 문장으로 끝맺을 경우가 많다.

081
정답 ④

지문 해석 학습은 실제 세계로부터 오는 정보에 우리 사고의 도식을 적응시키는 데 있다. 피아제에 의하면 이런 적응은 동화나 수용 둘 중 한 방법으로 일어난다. 동화는 기존의 사고의 도식으로 새로운 사건을 해석하는 데 있다. 예를 들어 아기는 자기가 좋아하는 딸랑이를 한 손의 손가락으로 잡고 그것을 던지면 그것이 내는 소리를 들을 수 있다는 것을 안다. 그녀는 아빠의 섬세한 시계 같은 새로운 물건을 만난다면 스스럼없이 그녀가 이미 알고 있는 운동 도식을 새 물건에 적용해 땅바닥으로 던질 것이다. 수용은 반대 과정이다. 그것은 새로운 물건이나 현상에 의미를 부여하기 위해 내적 인지 구조를 바꾸는 것이다. 같은 아기가 비치볼을 마주친다고 가정해 보자. 그녀는 처음에는 딸랑이를 잡을 때처럼 한 손으로 그것을 잡으려 할 것이다. 그러나 곧 이것이 효과가 없다는 것을 깨닫고 마침내 볼을 두 손으로 잡는 법을 발견할 것이다.

- ① 언제 더 이상의 시도를 포기할지
- ② 어떻게 한 손 사용을 고집할지
- ③ 어떻게 공을 효과적으로 피할지
- ④ 어떻게 공을 두 손으로 잡을지
- ⑤ 어떻게 공을 한 손으로 던질지

글의 소재 피아제 인지 발달

주요 어휘 adapt 적응시키다, schema 틀, 도식, assimilation 동화, accommodation 수용, consist in ~에 있다, internal 내부의, cognitive 인지의, incorporate ~와 통합하다, ~와 한 몸이 되다, encounter 만나다, 조우하다

글의 흐름 피아제의 발달론의 대표적 인지 방식인 동화와 수용을 설명하는 병렬식 구조를 취하고 있다. 주제문은 'Assimilation consists in interpreting new events in light of pre-existing thought schemas.'과 'Accommodation is the opposite process ~a new object or phenomenon.'이다.

구조 분석 ⊙ ~ she has no trouble in transferring this motor schema that she already knows to this new object~

→ transfer A to B 구문. = A를 B로 전환하다

⊙ ~ the way she does her rattle.

→ '~한 대로'를 의미하며 the way 앞에 전치사(in)를 쓰지 않는다. the way와 she 사이에 관계부사가 생략됐다.

정답 해설 수용은 새로운 '물건이나 현상과 통합하기 위해 자신을 사고의 틀을 바꾸는 데 있다고 했으므로 아기가 비치볼과 통합할 수 있는 합리적인 방법은 한 손으로는 잡는다는 기존의 생각을 버리고 두 손으로 사용하는 것이다. 따라서 정답 ④이다.

082
정답 ⑤

지문 해석 쇼핑에서 결혼이나 감정 표현에 이르기까지 거의 모든 인간 행동은 학습된다. 예를 들어 캐나다인들은 결혼을 사랑의 감정에 기반을 둔 두 사람 간의 선택이라고 본다. 다른 나라 다른 시기에 사랑은 전 가족 간의 면담이나 협상 같은 복잡한 과정을 통해, 또는 편지 왕래를 통해 신부를 정하는 직접 방식을 통해 중개돼 왔다. 캐나다 위니펙에서 자란 사람에게 나이지리아식 결혼 관습은 이상하거나 심지어 잘못돼 보일 수 있다. 반대로, 전통적인 나이지리아 가정에서 자란 사람은 연애 감정을 결혼이라는 평생 약속의 근거로 삼는다는 생각에 당혹할지도 모른다. 달리 말해 사람들이 결혼을 보는 방식은 그들이 학습된 바에 크게 의존한다. 글로 써지거나 그렇지 않은 문화 규칙에 길듦으로써 사람들은 안정감과 '정상적'인 느낌이 든다. 대부분의 사람들은 그들의 행동이 도전받거나 방해받지 않는다는 것을 확신하면서 생활을 영위하고 싶어 한다. 이런 점에서 학습된 관행에 근거한 행동은 그리 나쁜 게 아니지만 그것은 필히 <u>문화적 차이에 어떻게 반응하는가</u> 하는 문제를 불러일으킨다.

- ① 문화적 통합 문제를 어떻게 다룰 것인지
- ② 세계화를 통한 문화적 통일을 어떻게 추구할지
- ③ 고유한 지역문화를 어떻게 보존할지
- ④ 문화적 양극화를 어떻게 방지할지
- ⑤ 문화적 차이에 어떻게 반응할지

글의 소재 학습된 문화의 순기능과 역기능

주요 어휘 mutual 상호간의, intricate 복잡한, conversely 역으로, perplex 당혹스럽게 하다, disrupt 방해하다

글의 흐름 맨 마지막 문장이 주제문인 미괄식 구조를 취하고 있다.

구조 분석 ⊙ Most people want to live their daily lives <u>confident</u> that their behaviors will not be challenged or disrupted.

→ confident 앞에 being이 생략된 분사 구문으로 보라. 분사 구문을 'as they are confident that ~' 같은 절로 바꿀 수 있고 '~를 확신하면서'의 뜻이다.

정답 해설 문화는 기본적으로 학습되는 속성이 있고 그런 학습을 공유하는 사람의 생활을 안정시킨다는 긍정적 측면이 있지

만 문화 간 소통의 문제가 있을 수 있음을 시사한 글이다. 따라서 빈칸에는 ⑤가 적절하다. 자국 문화에 길든 캐나다인과 나이지리아인이 상대방의 결혼 풍습에 대해 서로 당혹스러워한다는 대목에 주목하라.

083

[지문 해석] 이 책 '주요 역사 사상가 50인'은 다양한 역사 사상가들이 지녔던 믿음이나 가정에 대한 소개서이다. 그것은 인기도를 근거로 선정한 표준적인 역대급 50인이 아니다. 내가 선정한 사상가들 중 많은 이가 확실히 그런 리스트에 오를 수 있지만(예를 들면 Gibbon, Ranke, Thucydides 같은 이들) 다른 이들이 포함된 점은 아마 놀라움을 줄 것이다. 이 책은 또한 독자들이 존경하거나 닮고 싶은 모범적인 사상가들을 모아놓은 컬렉션이 아니다. 내가 사상가들을 선정하는 방식으로는 어느 누구도 그런 시도를(존경하거나 닮는 것) 하는 것이 불가능하다. 가령, Niall Ferguson과 Emmanuel Le Roy Ladurie, 또는 G. W. F. Hegel과 William H. McNeill의 견해 사이에 화해를 시도해 보라(아마 어려울 것이다). 더군다나 내 생각에 주요 사상가로 확실히 인정받을 수 있는 사람은 역사학계에 무시할 수 없는 도전으로 널리 간주되는 사상을 가진 자이다. 따라서 나로서는 '주요 역사 사상가 50인'이 제안이기도 하지만 또한 도발이기도 하다.

① 제안이기도 하지만 또한 도발
② 알려지지 않은 역사 인물을 재발견하려는 접근
③ 역사에 대한 상반된 의견들을 화해시키려는 시도
④ 전통적인 학문적 방법을 이용하려는 시도
⑤ 역사적 극단주의자들을 배척하기 위한 책략

[글의 소재] 역사서 *Fifty Key Thinkers on History*의 발간 취지

[주요 어휘] assumption 가정, canonical 정전의, 표준적인, inclusion 포함, exemplary 모범적인, revere 존경하다, reconcile 화해시키다, hallmark 보증 각인

[글의 흐름] 이 글은 마지막 문장 '*Fifty Key Thinkers on History* is as much about provocation as it is about suggestion'이 주제문인 미괄식 구조다. 인과의 연결사 Thus가 주제문을 유도한 경우이다.

[구조 분석] ⊙ Nor <u>is</u> <u>it</u> a collection of exemplary thinkers that I expect readers to revere or imitate.

➜ 부정어 Nor가 문두에 나와서 주어(it)와 동사(is)가 뒤바뀐 도치 구문이다.

⊙ My choice of thinkers would make <u>it</u> impossible <u>for</u> <u>anyone</u> to do so.

➜ it는 가목적어, to do so가 진목적어, for anyone은 to do so의 의미상 주어이다. to do so는 to revere or imitate를 가리킨다.

[정답 해설] 필자가 소개하는 책에는 독자가 존경할 만한 모범적인 사상가들뿐만 아니라 그렇지 못할 인물이 뒤섞여 있고, 필자가 생각하는 핵심 사상가란 역사학계에 무시할 수 없는 도전 (a challenge to be reckoned with)으로 널리 간주되는 사상을 가진 자들이라 했으므로 필자의 책의 성격을 묻는 빈칸에는 ①의 '제안이기도 하지만 또한 도발'이기도 하다는 내용이 와야 한다.

084

[지문 해석] 어떤 것이든 존재하든지 존재하지 않든지 하지 둘 사이에 중간지점은 없다. 내 책상 위의 램프는 정말 거기 있거나 있지 않거나 둘 중 하나이다. 다른 가능성은 없다. 되어 가는 것이 있지 않냐, 혹은 있는 것과 없는 것 사이에 되어가는 상태가 있지 않냐고 우리는 물을지 모른다. 그에 대한 대답은 '아니오'다. 그냥 '되어가는' 그런 것은 없다. '된' 것이 있을 뿐이다. 되어가는 상태는 이미 존재의 영역 안에 들어와 있다. 만들어지는 과정에 있는 램프는 아직 램프가 아니다. 하지만 그것을 구성하게 될 부품들은 실제 존재하고 램프의 '되어 감'은 전적으로 그 부품들의 존재에 의존한다. 그래서 절대적 의미에서의 '되어 감', 즉 없음에서 있음으로의 전이는 일어나지 않는다. 엘레인은 꾸준한 연습으로 매일 점점 기량이 뛰어난 음악가가 돼 가지만 그녀가 이미 엘레인이 아니라면 그녀는 음악가가 돼 갈 수 없다. 인간이라는 바로 그 존재 면에서 '돼 가는 것'은 없다. 그녀는 절대적이 아닌, 상대적으로 돼 가는 것이다. 즉, 그녀는 엘레인이 돼 가는 것이 아니라 기량이 뛰어난 음악가가 엘레인이 돼 가는 것이다. 다시 말하건대 중간 배제의 원칙 바탕에 깔린 기본 생각은 존재에는 틈이 없다는 것이다. 이른바 '돼 가는 것'은 비존재에서 존재자로 전이가 아니라 이미 존재하는 사물 또는 사물들 안에서 일어나는 변화를 의미한다.

① 변화
② 퇴행
③ 고착
④ 도약
⑤ 통합

[글의 소재] 'becoming'의 의미

[주요 어휘] realm 영역, entirely 전적으로, transition 전이, assiduous 근면한, 꾸준한, relatively 상대적으로, absolutely 절대적으로, exclude 제외하다

[글의 흐름] 마지막 문장 'What we call "becoming" is not a passage from nonbeing to being, but an alteration in a thing or in things already in existence.'가 주제문인 미괄식 구조를 하고 있다.

[구조 분석] ⊙What we call "becoming" is <u>not</u> a passage from nonbeing to being, <u>but</u> an alteration in a thing or in things already in existence.

→ not A but B 구조로 'A가 아니라 B'의 뜻이다.

정답 해설 빈칸 위 Elaine의 예에서 '되어가는 것'이란 상대적이지 절대적이 아니라 밝히고, 상대적 의미는 Elaine은 그대로 있고 음악가적 속성이 더해진 것이라고 주장하고 있다. 그러므로 becoming의 의미는 비존재에서 존재자로 전이되는 과정을 말하는 게 아니라 존재의 본질은 그대로 있고 그 속성이 변화하는 것임을 알 수 있다. 따라서 빈칸에 들어갈 말은 변화(alteration)가 적절하다. 따라서 정답은 ①이다

085

정답 ①

지문 해석 수십 년 동안 우리는 지능을 창의력이나 참여도, 투지를 측정할 때와 같이 개인적 차원에서 측정해왔다. 그러나 우리는 훨씬 더 중요한 어떤 것을 측정하지 못했음이 드러났다. MIT나 Union College, Carnegie Mellon 연구자들은 개인과는 대조되는 집단의 지능을 체계적으로 측정하는 방법을 마침내 발견해 냈다. 한 개인이 성공적으로 문제를 해결하는 정도를 평가하는 것처럼 한 집단이 문제 또는 문제들을 얼마나 성공적으로 해결할 수 있는지 우리는 이제 예측할 수 있다. 높은 IQ를 가진 사람들 집단을 모을 수 있다면 그들은 당연히 높은 집단 지능을 보여 줄 것이라고 쉽게 생각할 수 있다. 그러나 사실은 그렇지 않다. 그들의 연구는, 각 구성원이 개별 능력은 평균에 불과했으나 집단 지성을 가진 집단이 개별적 천재로 이루어진 집단보다 지속해서 높은 성공률을 보여준다는 것을 알아냈다. 연구자들은 "폭넓은 과제에 대한 집단의 수행 능력을 설명해 주는 일반적 집단 지능 요인은 집단 자체의 속성이며 단지 그에 속한 개인들의 그것만은 아니"라고 결론 내렸다. 달리 말하면 전체는 부분의 합보다 크다.

┌ ① 전체가 부분의 합보다 크다.
│ ② 부분은 전체 중 일부로서만 의미가 있다.
│ ③ 부분과 전체는 따로따로 봐야 한다.
│ ④ 개별적인 재능이 집단 지성에 우선한다.
└ ⑤ 개인은 종종 집단보다 문제 해결 능력이 우수하다.

글의 소재 집단 지능의 중요성

주요 어휘 measure 측정하다, grit 투지, assume 가정하다, 전제하다, collective 집단적인

글의 흐름 주제문은 맨 마지막 문장인 'In other words, the whole is greater than the sum of its parts.'이다. 연구, 조사, 실험으로 이뤄진 구체 진술은 흔히 연구 성과를 아우르는 요약문으로 끝맺는 경우가 많다.

구조 분석 ⊙ Indeed, their research found that a <u>team</u> on which each person <u>was merely</u> average in their individual abilities <u>but</u> <u>possessed</u> a collective intelligence <u>would</u> continually exhibit higher success rates than a team of

individual geniuses.

→ that절의 주어는 team이고 동사는 would~이다. 'on which ~intelligence'가 team을 수식하는 관계대명사절이고 was merely ~와 possessed는 병렬구조다.

정답 해설 빈칸 앞의 앞줄에 천재들로 이뤄진 집단보다 개별 능력은 평균이나 집단 지능을 가진 집단이 성공률이 높다고 했으므로 '전체가 부분의 합보다 크다'라는 취지의 ①이 빈칸에 적절하다.

086

정답 ④

지문 해석 물건의 크기를 늘릴 때 그것의 부피는 면적보다 훨씬 빠른 비율로 증가한다. 예를 들어 당신이 집의 모양을 그대로 둔 채 모든 길이를 두 배로 늘린다면 부피는 2의 세제곱 즉 8배로 증가하는 반면 집의 표면적은 2의 제곱 즉 네 배로 증가한다. 이것은, 우리 주변에 있는 많은 것들의 – 그것이 우리가 사는 건물이건 자연계의 동식물이건 – 디자인과 기능에 큰 의미를 지닌다. 가령, 대부분의 난방, 냉방, 조명은 각 히터, 에어컨, 창문이 가지는 해당 (기능의) 표면적에 비례한다. 따라서 그것들의 효율성은 냉·난방되거나 조명될 생활공간의 부피보다 훨씬 느리게 증가하고 따라서 건물 규모를 늘릴 때 이런 기기들의 크기를 불균형적으로 키울 필요가 있다. 이와 유사하게 몸집이 큰 동물의 경우 신진대사나 신체 활동으로 발생하는 열을 발산하는 데 문제가 있는데, 이는 큰 동물들의 경우 작은 동물과 달리, 열이 발산되는 피부 면적이 그들의 몸집에 비해 비례적으로 훨씬 작기 때문이다. 가령 코끼리는 불균형적으로 큰 귀를 진화시킴으로써 이 문제를 해결해 왔는데 이는 <u>피부 면적을 획기적으로 늘려 열을 식히기 위함</u>이다.

┌ ① 주변에서 일어나는 일을 보다 잘 듣기 위해
│ ② 파리나 해충을 쫓기 위한 부채로 사용하기 위해
│ ③ 넓적하게 펴서 잠재적 위협을 겁주기 위해
│ ④ 피부 면적을 획기적으로 늘려 열을 식히기 위해
└ ⑤ 실제보다 커 보임으로써 동료들에게 뽐내려고

글의 소재 규모를 키울 때 나타나는 부피와 면적의 불균형성

주요 어휘 scale up 일정 비율로 키우다, dimension 치수, 차원, by a factor of ~배만큼, implication 함축, 의미, functionality 기능, 성능, proportional 비례하는, corresponding 상응하는, effectiveness 효율, disproportionately 불균형적으로, dissipate 발산하다, metabolism 신진대사

글의 흐름 주제문은 'When an object is scaled up in size, its volumes increase at a much faster rate than its areas.'이고 주제문 다음으로 예시의 연결사와 함께 구체 진술이 펼쳐지는 두괄식 구조이다.

구조 분석 ⊙ For example, if you double the dimensions of every length in your house <u>keeping</u> its shape the same, ~

→ 분사 구문으로 '~하면서'로 해석한다.

⊙ Their effectiveness therefore increases much more slowly than the volume of living space needed to be heated, cooled or lit, so these need to be disproportionately increased in size when a building is scaled up.

→ space와 needed 사이에는 which(that) is가 생략됐다.

⊙ Similarly, for large animals, the need to dissipate heat generated by their metabolism and physical activity

→ for는 '~의 경우에'의 뜻이고 with, as for, in terms of, when it comes to ~ 등으로 바꿔 쓸 수 있다.

[정답 해설] 부피의 증가 속도는 면적의 증가 속도보다 빠르고 이런 둘 사이의 증가 속도의 차이는 인공 구조물이나 자연계를 이해하는 데 중요하다는 게 이 글의 요지다. 그런데 큰 동물들은 몸집에 비해 표면적이 상대적으로 작기 때문에 열의 체외 발산에 어려움을 겪는데 코끼리는 이런 문제를 큰 귀로 표면적을 늘리는 쪽으로 진화해서 해결한다고 해야 이 글의 논지에 부합하므로 정답은 ④가 알맞다.

087
정답 ①

[지문 해석] Edgar Allan Poe는 분열된 마음을 이해했음이 틀림없다. 그의 단편소설 중 하나인 *The Imp of the Perverse*에서 Poe의 주인공은 살인을 완벽하게 저지르고, 죽은 이의 토지를 물려받아 부정하게 손에 넣은 소득을 여유 있게 즐기면서 여러 해를 산다. 살인에 대한 생각이 의식의 주변에 나타나면 그는 '나는 안전해'라고 중얼거린다. 모든 게 잘 돼가다가 어느 날 그가 주문 내용을 '나는 안전해. 바보처럼 죄를 공개적으로 고백하지 않는다면'으로 바꾸자 상황이 달라진다. 그런 생각과 함께 그는 무너진다. 그는 고백한다는 생각을 억누르지만 그렇게 하면 할수록 그 생각은 더욱 끈질기게 그에게서 떠나지 않는다. 그는 공포에 빠져 달리기 시작하고 사람들이 그를 뒤쫓고, 그는 의식을 잃고 의식을 되찾았을 때 그는 이미 모든 것을 고백했다는 말을 사람들에게서 전해 듣는다.

  ① 분열된 마음
  ② 위약 효과
  ③ 만트라 명상
  ④ 범죄 심리
  ⑤ 몸과 마음의 통합

[글의 소재] Poe 작품 속에 나타난 '분열된 마음'

[주요 어휘] protagonist 주인공, inherit 상속하다, 물려받다, estate 사유지, fringe 주변, murmur 중얼거리다. mantra (기도의) 주문 come undone 무너지다, 실패하다, suppress 억제하다, insistent 끈질긴, panic 공포에 빠지다, chase 추격하다, black out 의식을 잃다

[글의 흐름] 주제문은 'Edgar Allan Poe must have understood the divided mind'이고 Poe의 작품을 예로 들어 주제문의 주장을 뒷받침하는 두괄식 문단이다.

[구조 분석] ⊙ With that thought, he comes undone.

→ With는 이유를 나타내는 전치사로 Because of나 Due to로 바꿔 쓸 수 있다.

⊙ but the harder he tries, the more insistent the thought becomes.

→ 'the +비교급 S + V, the + 비교급 S + V' 구문으로 '~할수록 ~하다'의 뜻이다.

⊙ he is told that he has made a full confession.

→ 능동태로 바꾸면 'They tell him that he ~'이 되고 4형식 문장이 수동태로 바뀌면서 간접목적어가 주어로 나가고 3형식 문장이 된 경우다.

[정답 해설] 포우의 소설 속 주인공이 살인을 저지른 후 스스로 괜찮다고 위로하며 잘 지내다가 갑자기 암시의 내용을 바꾸면서 갈등을 겪고 마침내 스스로 무너진다는 내용이므로 주인공이 경험한 것은 분열된 마음이라 할 수 있다. 따라서 작가 Poe가 이해한 것은 ①의 '분열된 마음'이다.

088
정답 ④

[지문 해석] 칸 영화제에서 12일을 보내는 것은 영화 애호가들에게는 낙원이나 다를 바 없어서 매년 바깥세상을 완전히 잊고 지내지만, 올해는 달랐다. 거의 모든 평론가나 기자들은 의무상 시사회 동안엔 핸드폰을 껐지만, 끝나기가 무섭게 핸드폰을 켜고 새로 들어온 뉴스가 없는지 확인하지 않을 수 없었다. 어둠 속에 있어도 세상일은 멈추지 않고 일어난다. 더구나 올해는 보안이 그 어느 때보다 삼엄하다. 언론 시사회나 영화 최초 개봉 때면, 엠마 필이 좋아했을 법한 몬드리안 스타일의 옷을 미끈하게 빼입은 여직원들이 축 처진 배낭이나 보석으로 치장한 핸드백을 철저하게 검사했다. 종업원들의 유니폼을 포함해 칸에서는 모든 것이 좀 화려하다. 그것은 불확실하고 무서운 세계를 피하기 위한 방법이 아니라 그것에 당당히 맞서는 행위다.

[글의 소재] 변화된 올해의 칸 영화제 분위기

[주요 어휘] lose track of ~을 잊다, press screening 언론 시사회, premiere 개봉, 초연, saggy 축 처진, bejeweled 보석으로 치장한, sleek 맵시 있는, bulwark 방어벽

[구조 분석] ⊙ most of us couldn't resist powering up

→ can not resist ~ing는 '~하고 싶은 유혹을 참기 어렵다'는 뜻으로, 반드시 동명사를 목적어로 쓰인다.

⊙ World events don't stop happening

→ stop ~ing은 '~함을 멈추지 않는다', '계속 ~한다'는 뜻이다. 역시 동명사를 목적어로 쓰인다.

⊙ That's less a way of avoiding an uncertain, scary world than an act of standing as a bulwark against it.

→ less A than B 구조로, 'A라기보다는 B'의 뜻이다. B rather than A 형식으로 바꿔 쓸 수 있으며, 이때 A와 B가 뒤바뀜을 유의해야 한다.

정답 해설 보통 때에는 칸에 참가하면 바깥세상을 잊고 지내기 쉽다는 문맥이므로 (A)에는 lose track of가 적절하다. 칸의 분위기가 화려한 것은 테러에 위축되지 않은 당당함의 표현, 즉 무서운 세상을 '피하지' 않고 맞서는 행위라 했으므로 (B)에는 avoiding이 타당하다.

089
정답 ①

지문 해석 지금은 고전이 된 '기획의 일반 이론상의 딜레마'라는 글에서 Rittel과 Weber는 이른바 온순한 문제와 사악한 문제의 중요한 차이점을 도출한다. 꼭 쉬운 것은 아니지만 온순한 문제는 일반적으로 전문 기술 지식으로 해결할 수 있는 상대적으로 단순한 해결책을 가지고 있다. 예를 들어 인간을 달에 착륙시키는 것은 매우 복잡한 일이었지만 목표를 명확히 밝히고 기존 과학 지식을 응용해 그것을 달성하는 것이 가능했다. 이런 문제들은 그들의 해결 가능성을 높이는 명확한 인과의 메커니즘을 가지고 있다. 반면 사악한 문제들은 통제가 어렵고 구조가 엉성해 일시적이고 불확실한 해결책만이 가능하다. 사악한 문제의 경우는 그들의 해결 여부를 판단할 명확한 기준이 없다. 사실, 이런 문제들은 보통 표준적인 기준이나 경험적 조건과 상황이 꼬인 경우가 많기 때문에 애초에 정의 내리기가 쉽지 않다.

① 그들의 해결 여부를 판단할 명확한 기준
② 그들의 원천을 설명할 모호한 메시지
③ 그들의 성격을 정의할 불명확한 용어
④ 입증된 사실과 견해 사이의 불분명한 경계
⑤ 그들에 대한 정의의 근거가 되는 역사적 배경

글의 소재 문제의 종류와 해결책

주요 어휘 distinction 차이, straightforward 똑바른, 단순한, amenable ~로 해결할 수 있는, ~가 용이한, undertaking 일, 과제, articulate 명확히 밝히다, enhance 높이다, intractable 고집 센, 통제할 수 없는, in the first place 애초에, intertwined 꼬인, 뒤얽힌, normative 표준적인, empirical 경험적인

글의 흐름 온순한 문제와 사악한 문제 두 종류의 문제를 대비해 설명하는 병렬식 구조를 하고 있다. 주제문은 'While not necessarily simple, tame problems generally have a relatively straightforward solution that is amenable to expert, technical knowledge.'와 'Wicked problems, by contrast, are intractable, poorly structured and have only temporary or uncertain solutions.'이다.

구조 분석 ⊙ While not necessarily simple, tame problems generally have ~

→ While과 not 사이에 they are가 생략됐다. 시간과 조건의

부사절에서 주어가 주절의 주어와 같으면 주어와 be 동사는 흔히 생략된다.

⊙ there are clear cause and effect mechanisms that enhance the likelihood that they can be solved.

→ 앞의 that는 주격관계대명사, 뒤의 that는 동격의 접속사이다.

정답 해설 사악한 문제는 통제하기 어렵고 구조가 엉성하다고 정의됐고 빈칸 문장은 부정어 no를 포함하고 있으므로 정의와 같은 뜻이 되기 위해서 빈칸에는 '명확하고 분명한' 취지의 수식어가 들어간 문장이 와야 한다. 이를 만족시키는 것은 ①뿐이다.

090
정답 ②

지문 해석 비대칭적 지배 효과는 비대칭적으로 열등한 제3의 선택지가 제시됐을 때, 소비자들은 두 개의 선택 사이에서 특정한 선호도의 변화를 겪게 된다는 인지 편향이다. 간단히 말해 전략적으로 중요한 제3의 선택지가 있을 때 소비자들은 두 개의 선택지 중 더 비싼 것을 선택할 가능성이 크다는 것이다. 하나의 선택지가 다른 하나보다는 모든 면에서 열등할 때 비대칭적으로 지배된다. 그러나 다른 선택지와 비교했을 때 그것은 어떤 면에서는 열등하지만 다른 면에서는 우월하다. 달리 말해서 그것은 한 선택지에게는 완전히 지배당하지만(즉 그것보다 열등하지만) 다른 선택지에게는 부분적으로만 지배당한다. 비대칭적으로 지배당하는 선택지가 있을 때 소비자들은 그것이 없을 때보다 지배적인 선택지를 선택한다. 따라서 비대칭적으로 지배되는 선택지는 지배적 선택지에 대한 선호도를 증가시키기 위한 미끼이다.

① 소비자의 관심을 지배되는(열등한) 선택지로 끌기 위한
② 지배적인(우월한) 선택지에 대한 선호도를 증가시키기 위한
③ 소비자의 관심을 우월한 선택지로부터 멀어지게 하기 위한
④ 소비자들이 되도록 많은 선택지를 접하도록 돕는
⑤ 원 플러스 원 전략을 은밀히 홍보하기 위한

글의 소재 소비자의 인지 편향

주요 어휘 asymmetric 비대칭적인, dominated 지배되는(열등한), dominating 지배하는(우월한), cognitive 인지의, bias 편향, simply put 간단히 말해, in comparison to ~과 비교해, partially 부분적으로, decoy 미끼, 유인책

글의 흐름 첫 문장이 일반 진술, 즉 주제문이고, 이에 대한 구체적인 설명이 구체 진술로 이어지는 두괄식 문단이다.

구조 분석 ⊙ Simply put, when there is a third strategically important choice ~

→ Being simply put에서 being이 생략된 분사 구문이지만, 'simply put=간단히 말해'를 숙어로 알아두는 게 좋다.

정답 해설 빈칸 바로 앞 문장에서 비대칭적으로 지배되는 선택지가 없을 때보다는 그런 선택지가 있을 때 소비자들은 더 지배

적인(우월한) 선택지를 선호한다는 말이 있으므로 비대칭적으로 지배되는(열등한) 선택지는 지배적인 선택지에 대한 선호도를 증가시키기 위한 미끼라는 추론이 가능하다. 따라서 정답은 ②이다.

091

지문 해설 진화생물학자인 Jessica Flack과 그녀의 동료들은 조지아주 Lawrenceville에 있는 Yerkes National Primate Research Center에서 84마리의 아프리카 원숭이 집단의 관계 구조를 조작했다. 그들은 먼저 원숭이들이 누구 털을 다듬고 누구와 노는지를 근거로 친소관계를 측정했다. 그들은 평화 시 원숭이들이 누구에게 조용히 이빨을 드러내 보이는지 – 이 원숭이 종이 경의를 표하는 방식임 – 그 횟수를 셈으로써 조직의 리더를 확인했다. 그리고 과학자들은 최고위 리더들을 제거한 다음 그로 인한 사회관계 변화를 조작되지 않은 통제 상태와 비교했다. 고위 리더들을 제거하자 혼란이 이어졌다. 갈등과 공격 횟수가 치솟았다. 이런 분석은 리더가 집단 전체의 상호교류에 영향력을 행사함을 보여준다. 먼저, 리더들이 제거되자 집단 내 털을 다듬고 놀이를 하는 횟수가 전반적으로 줄었다. 즉 남은 원숭이들 사이에 관계가 덜 친밀해진 것이다. 이것은 안정된 리더십이 리더와 추종자들 간은 물론 추종자들 사이의 평화로운 상호교류 증진에도 기여함을 보여준다. 인기 있는 리더의 존재는 집단 내 사회 질서 확립에 도움을 주는 것처럼 보인다. 그리고 이런 상호교류가 유익한 상호 지원의 기회를 만든다는 사실을 고려할 때 자연도태가 왜 위계질서에 대한 개인적 관심과 존중의 진화를 선호하는지 쉽게 그 이유를 알 수 있다.

① 동료애
② 평등
③ 격변
④ 위계질서
⑤ 훈육

글의 소재 macaque 원숭이 실험을 통해 드러난 hierarchy의 중요성

주요 어휘 evolutionary 진화의, manipulate 조작하다, groom 털을 다듬다, deference 존경, 경의, unperturbed 방해받지 않은, ensue 잇따라 일어나다, skyrocket 폭발적으로 증가하다, shed light on ~를 밝히다, facilitate 촉진하다

글의 흐름 맨 마지막 문장 'And given that these interactions create opportunities for beneficial mutual support ~ and respect to hierarchy.'이 이 글의 주제문이다. 연구 조사 실험의 구체진술은 흔히 전체 내용을 요약하면서 즉 주제문으로 끝맺는다.

구조 분석 ⊙ They first measured connections based on whom the monkeys groomed or played with.

→ based on은 '~에 근거해'라는 뜻의 부사구이다. whom 이하는 전치사 on의 목적어가 되는 의문사절이며 의문사 + S + V의 어순을 취하고 있다.

⊙ And given that these interactions create opportunities for beneficial mutual support

→ given that ~은 '~을 고려할 때'를 의미하는 관용적 표현이다. 여기서 given=considering이다.

정답 해설 안정된 리더십이 조직의 상하 관계는 물론이고 상호 간의 관계 활성화에 기여한다는 점이 원숭이 실험으로 드러났으므로 어떤 것을 선호하는 쪽으로 진화가 이뤄질 것인가를 묻는 빈칸에는 leadership과 관련된 말이 와야 한다. 따라서 정답은 ④이다.

092

지문 해설 경험이나 경험의 이해가 어떻게 언어에 영향을 미치는지는 Galili와 Hazan이 광학 현상과 관련해 관찰한 바가 있다. 역사적으로 언어는 시각의 영향 아래, 그리고 시각에 대한 오늘날 우리의 이해가 있기 오래전부터 발전돼 왔다고 그들은 주장한다. 그 결과 많은 언어적 구조물이 오늘날 과학 지식에 부합하지 않는다. '시선을 던지다' '시선을 주다'와 같은 일상 언어 표현들은, 시각이 눈에 의한 빛의 수용보다는 발산 쪽에 더 가깝다는 고대의 잘못된 엠페도클레스식 생각과 관련이 있을 것이라고 그들은 주장한다. 이와 마찬가지로, Eshach는 우리가 일상생활에서 그림자에 대해 얘기하는 방식은 그림자에 대한 언어와 생각 사이의 밀접한 관련성을 보여준다고 밝힌 바 있다. 그에 따르면 '무서운 내 그림자를 봐'나 '내 그림자가 나를 따라오네'라는 표현처럼 우리는 그림자를 하나의 존재하는 실체로 본다는 것이다. 그런 표현들은 학생이나 성인으로 하여금 그림자를 단지 빛의 부재의 결과물로 보는 것이 아니라 그것에 물질적 실체의 속성을 부여하게 할지 모른다.

① 오늘날의 변화하는 언어 패턴을 반영하지
② 현재의 과학적 지식에 부합하지
③ 현대 과학 규범을 거스르지
④ 유구한 과학 전통을 존경하지
⑤ 소통 촉진자의 역할을 수행하지

글의 소재 비과학적인 언어 표현의 예

주요 어휘 optical 광학의, conform to 적응하다, 부합하다, attribute ~ to ~를 ~에게 돌리다, ~에게 ~를 부여하다

글의 흐름 빈칸 문장 'many linguistic constructions do not conform to present-day scientific knowledge'이 주제문이고 이후 두 가지 비과학적인 언어 표현의 예가 주제문에 대한 뒷받침 진술로 제시되는 구조다.

구조 분석 ⊙ Such phrases may lead students, and adults as well, to attribute the properties of material substances to shadows, rather than to understand them as the product merely of the absence of light.

→ lead(V) + student, and adults(O) + to attribute(OC)의 5형식 구문이고 'rather than to understand'는 'to attribute'와 병렬구조를 이룬다.

정답 해설 이 글은 우리가 일상에서 쓰는 언어 표현들이 오늘날의 과학적 지식을 반영하지 못한다는 점을 광학의 경우를 예로 들어 설명하고 있으므로 빈칸에 들어갈 표현은 ② '현재의 과학적 지식에 부합하지'가 적절하다(부정어 not에 유의하라). 빈칸 다음에 소개되는 두 가지 에피소드(시선과 그림자)는 모두 언어가 비과학적으로 쓰이는 예다. 그리고 빈칸 다음 문장의 incorrect가 정답 추론의 단서가 될 수 있다.

093
정답 ②

지문 해석 경계가 포스트휴머니즘에 필수불가결한 요소라는 주장은 직관에 반하는 것처럼 보일지 모른다. 결국 경계를 모호하게 하고 허무는 것이 많은 포스트휴먼 작업의 주요한 특징이다. 가령 포스트휴먼 이론의 공통된 출발점은 자연과 문화적 연속성에 대한 비이원론적 이해이며, 달리 말해 이들 두 영역 사이의 경계를 모호하게 함으로써 포스트휴머니즘은 시작된다고 Braidotti는 주장한다. 포스트휴머니즘은 역동적이고 규정하기 어려운 세계를 확연하게 상정한다. 전형적으로 인간적인 것이 인조인간이 되고 전형적인 동물이 의식과 인간과 동급의 주관성을 부여받고 전형적인 무정물 기계가 생명이 있고 아마 지각 있는 것이 된다. 이러한 경계 모호하게 하기는 인문학의 ─ 이는 포스트휴머니즘 이전 시기를 상기시키는 용어다. ─ 경계를 넘어서는데 이는 과학에서도 또한 이전 규범의 경계선이 과도기를 맞고 있기 때문이다. 예를 들어 사상과 의식의 경계는 점점 더 모호해지고 의문시되고 있다. Andy Clark은 과학에서의 이 새로운 인지관을, 뇌와 몸과 세계의 경계를 어지럽게 교차하는 피드백과 피드포워드, 피드어라운드의 고리가 뒤엉킨 혼돈 상태를 반영하는 관점이라고 표현하고 있다.

┌ ① 안정의 조짐을 보이고 있다.
│ ② 현재 과도기 상태에 있다.
│ ③ 그들의 애매모호성을 제거했다.
│ ④ 이전의 활력을 아직 되찾지 못했다.
└ ⑤ 그들이 처음 그려진 대로 남아있다.

글의 소재 포스트휴머니즘

주요 어휘 post-humanism 포스트 휴머니즘, 유전자 변형이나 AI와의 융합 등을 통해 신 인간을 지향하는 새로운 정신 사조, counterintuitive 직관에 반하는, blur 흐리게 하다, break down 허물다, non-dualistic 비이원론적, continuum 연속성, conspicuously 확연하게, posit 상정하다, indeterminate 규정하기 어려운, invested with ~을 부여받아, subjectivity 주관성,

inanimate 무정물의, sentient 지각 있는, paradigmatic 규범적인, inextricable 뒤엉킨, tangle 혼돈, promiscuously 난잡하게, 어지럽게, criss-cross 교차하다

글의 흐름 'blurring and breaking down boundaries is a major feature of much post-human work.'이 주제문인 두괄식 문단이다.

구조 분석 ⊙ ~ as in the sciences, too, previously paradigmatic boundary lines are now in a state of transition.

→ as 절의 주어는 previously paradigmatic boundary lines, 동사는 are이고, in the science와 too는 모두 부사(구)다. 복잡한 문형에서는 뼈(문장 성분)와 살(수식어구)을 잘 구분하는 게 중요하다.

⊙ Andy Clark describes this new view of cognition in the sciences as that which takes into account "inextricable tangles of feedback,~

→ that은 view of cognition을 받고 that which는 관계대명사 what으로 대체할 수 있다.

정답 해설 경계를 모호하게 하고 허무는 것이 많은 포스트휴먼의 특징이고 이는 인문학뿐 아니라 과학에서도 마찬가지라고 했으므로 빈칸에는 (과학에서 이전 패러다임의 경계가) 변한다는 계통의 내용이 와야 한다. 따라서 정답은 ②이다. 빈칸 다음 문장의 'blurred and called into question' 부분에서 힌트를 얻을 수 있다.

094
정답 ⑤

지문 해석 사회 기간시설을 개발하고 관광의 섬에 미치는 영향을 낮추기 위한 계획은 관련 사전 연구와 생태환경에 대한 감시를 필요로 한다. 예를 들어 서호주의 주요 관광명소인 Rottnest Island에는 관광 성수기가 바닷가 새의 최고 도래 시기와 맞물린다. 관광과 새의 서식지 보호의 상관관계에 관해 환경학자 A. Morrison-Saunders는 예방적 감시 시스템으로 관광과 보존이 상충하는 곳, 가령 매년 번식지를 바꾸는 흰제비갈매기가 번식하는 곳을 찾아내 울타리를 칠 수 있었다고 보고했다. 또 Saunders는 염수호 주변에 도로를 건설해 섭금류의 먹이 활동에 영향을 준다든지 염수호 사이에 전선을 설치해 이를 오가다 충돌로 인해 많은 새들이 목숨을 잃는 것과 같은 과거의 관광 관련 활동의 강도를 감시를 통해 경감할 수 있었다고 보고했다. Saunders는 이어서, 전선줄에 경고 장치를 부착하는 데 15년이 걸렸는데 이 같은 상황은 적응형 관리와 연계된 관광 영향 감시 시스템이 가동됐더라면 피할 수 있었을 거라고 보고했다.

┌ ① 지방 정부가 이끄는 획기적인 관광 진흥 드라이브
│ ② 초현대 21세기에 걸맞은 거대한 기술적 진보
│ ③ 생태 발자국을 줄이기 위한 효율적인 봉사활동 프로그램
└ ④ 환경을 파괴하는 시도를 엄하게 단속하는 정부의 의지

⑤ 적응형 관리와 연계된 관광 영향 감시 시스템

글의 소재 섬 관광지의 환경 보호 전략

주요 어휘 infrastructure 사회 기간시설, mitigate 경감하다, relevant 관련된, baseline 기초선의, 사전의, coincide 동시에 일어나다, nexus 관계, proactive 선제적인, magnitude 강도, fairy tern 흰제비갈매기, wader 섭금류, mortality 사망자 수, collision 충돌

글의 흐름 주제문은 'Plans to develop infrastructure and mitigate tourism impact on islands requires relevant baseline studies and monitoring of ecological conditions.' 로 주제문이 예시의 연결사와 함께 구체 진술로 이어지는 구문이다.

구조 분석 ⊙ and the construction of a power line within the flight path of birds moving between salt lakes which resulted in significant mortality arising from collisions.

→ which의 선행사는 construction of a power line이고 'within ~ salt lakes'는 power line을 수식하는 형용사구이다.

⊙ ~ with warning devices, a situation which could have been avoided if a tourism impact monitoring system linked to adaptive management had been in place.

→ 'a situation which ~' 이하는 앞 문장 '~with warning devices'와 동격으로 앞 문장을 부연 설명한다.

정답 해설 이 글은 환경 감시를 통해 관광이 섬 지역 생태계에 미치는 부정적 영향을 경감할 수 있음을 호주의 Rottnest 섬의 경우를 예로 들어 설명하고 있다. 따라서 빈칸에는 ⑤의 '적응형 관리와 연계된 관광 영향 감시 시스템'이 알맞다. '~ and monitoring of ecological conditions~'나 'a proactive monitoring system could identify areas~', 'monitoring could have mitigated~' 같은 구절의 monitor가 핵심 단어다.

095
정답 ①

지문 해석 불확실성은 삶의 기본적인 사실이고 기술도 예외가 아니다. 기술적 불확실성의 첫 번째 원천은 특정 과제를 수행하는 데는 언제나 다양한 해결책이 있다는 다행스러운 사실에서 나온다. 기술적 기준, 경제적 기준, 그리고 사회적 기준을 고려해야 하므로 어떤 것이 최선인지 결정하는 것은 늘 불확실하다. 초기 디자인의 선택이나 시장에서의 성공 또는 실패에서 최종적 환경적 영향이나 파급 효과에 이르기까지 불확실성은 기술 발전의 모든 단계에서 위세를 떨친다. 기술이나 경영학 서적은 그런 불확실성을 "뱀 소굴" 문제라고 부른다. 그것은 비슷해 보이는 수백 마리의 뱀 소굴에서 특정 한 마리를 골라내는 것과 유사하다. 기술적 불확실성은 기술적 변화를 예측하려는 노력을 계속 큰 곤경에 처하게 한다. 그러나 "하늘이 맑을 때까지 기다리자"라는 전략으로는 아무것도 얻을 수 없다. 날씨는 맑아지

지 않고, 불확실성은 지속되어 옳은 전략은 기술적 다양성을 실험하는 것이다. 이것은 "비효율적인" 발전 전략으로 보일 수도 있다. 그런 정도로 그것은 작가들이 기술과 생태의 유용한 유추를 이끌어낸 많은 분야 중 하나이다(비효율적일수록 작가들이 기술과 생태의 유사성을 즐겨 다뤘다는 말).

┌ ① 기술적 다양성에 대한 실험
│ ② 기존의 과학적 원칙에 충실하기
│ ③ 기술적 단일성에 대한 확고한 믿음
│ ④ 성급한 기후적 접근에 대한 경계
└ ⑤ 무관한 학문적 교류에 대한 제약

글의 소재 삶과 기술의 숙명적인 불확실성

주요 어휘 uncertainty 불확실성, derive from ~에서 파생하다, criteria 기준, prevail 위세를 떨치다, spin-off 파급, 파생, literature 문학, 서적, pit 구덩이, 소굴, notorious 악명 높은, inefficient 비효율적인

글의 흐름 주제문은 'Uncertainty is a basic fact of life and technology is no exception.'이며 두괄식 문장이다.

구조 분석 ⊙ Uncertainty prevails at all stages of technological evolution, from initial design choices, through success or failure in the marketplace, to eventual environmental impacts and spin-off effects.

→ from A through B to C로 연결되는 구문이다. 이는 'A에서 B를 거쳐 C로 이르기까지'의 뜻이다.

⊙ To the extent that it is, it is one of the many areas in which writers have drawn useful analogies between technology and biology.

→ it는 앞 문장의 this(the correct strategy is experimentation with technological variety)를 받고 앞의 'it is' 다음에는 inefficient가 생략됐다. 이 문장은 '그것이 비효율적일수록 작가들이 기술과 생태의 유사성을 즐겨 다뤘다'라는 뜻이다.

정답 해설 지문 두 번째 문장에서 기술적 불확실성의 원천은 문제 해결의 다양성에서 온다고 했는데 이 말은 기술적 불확실성은 기술적 다양성 때문이라는 의미이기 때문에 불확실성에 대처하는 옳은 전략은 기술적 다양성을 인정하고 이를 실험하는 것이라고 추론할 수 있다. 따라서 정답은 ①이다.

9. 함축적 의미 추론

정답

096 ④	097 ④	098 ③	099 ③	100 ①

096

정답 ④

지문 해석) 결정과 결정들. 우리 모두는 수백 개 심지어는 수천 개의 결정을 매일 내린다. 그것은 쌓여서 한 사람을 쇠약하게 할 수 있다. 그러나 당신이 그것을 끝낼 수 있는 적어도 하나의 간단한 방법이 있다. 바바라 쇼 씨는 사실상 같은 옷을 거의 매일 입는다. 홍보 이사인 그녀의 옷장은 똑같은 옷으로 가득 차 있어서 매일 출근할 때 입을 옷을 고를 필요가 전혀 없다고 말한다. 그것은 같은 결정을 매일 되풀이하는 데서 오는 피로감을 줄이고 스스로를 해방시켜 보다 중요한 일에 집중하게 하는 전략이라고 그녀는 말한다. 마크 저커버그도 같은 이유로 매일 똑같은 옷을 입는다. 심지어는 오바마 대통령도 청색과 회색 정장만을 입는데 "내려야 할 결정이 너무 많아서 입는 것 결정하는 데까지 신경 쓰고 싶지는 않다"고 그는 말한다.

- ① 옷값을 절약하기 위해
- ② 수월하고 단순한 삶을 살기 위해
- ③ 시간을 낼 수 없어서
- ④ 의사결정의 피로감을 줄이기 위해
- ⑤ 최신 유행을 따르기 위해

글의 소재) 의사결정의 피로감

주요 어휘) on a daily basis 매일, add up 쌓이다, wear down 마모시키다, 쇠약하게 하다, free up 해방하다, outfit 의상, 단團, guesswork 짐작, 추측, fatigue 피로감

정답 해설) 밑줄 바로 앞 문장 'to decrease fatigue from making the same decision over and over again'에서 같은 결정을 되풀이하는 데서 오는 피로감, 즉 의사결정의 피로감을 줄이기 위해 한 가지 옷만을 고집함을 알 수 있다. 따라서 정답은 ④이다.

097

정답 ④

지문 해석) 교육자들 역시 스마트폰 관련 딜레마와 씨름하고 있다. 대부분 학교가 수업과 수업 사이 또는 자유시간에 학생들의 스마트폰 사용을 허용하고 있지만 수업 시간에 폰 사용을 못 하게 하는 것 또한 큰 부담이라고 교사들은 말한다. 이런 딜레마를 풀려고 캘리포니아의 한 고등학교가 아이디어를 하나 냈다. 이 학교는 최근 한 지역 IT 회사와 협력해 수업 시간 동안 아이들의 스마트폰 접근을 제한하는 기술을 개발했다. 회사가 개발한 잠금장치가 있는 작은 주머니를 평소 아이들이 가지고 다니되 일과가 끝나기 전에는 열 수 없는 그런 장치였다. 이 고교 교

장인 Alison Silvestri는 이미 큰 변화가 있다고 말한다. 학생들 수업 집중도와 참여도가 높아졌을 뿐만 아니라 교지에 의하면 고등학생들이 스트레스도 덜 받는다는 것이다. 이번 학기에는 학생들 간 싸움이 줄었는데 이는 소셜미디어 차단이 준 혜택이라고 그녀는 말한다. '나도 하나 사서 집에서 사용하려면 어떻게 해야 하나요?'라는 학부모들의 문의 전화를 얼마나 받았는지 모를 지경이라고 Silvestri는 덧붙인다.

글의 소재) 교내 스마트폰 사용

주요 어휘) grapple with ~와 씨름하다, come up with 제안하다, pouch 주머니

구조 분석) ⊙ but teachers say keeping students off their phones during class has become a tremendous burden.
→ keep A off B 구문으로 'A를 B로부터 접근 금지하다.'는 뜻이다.

정답 해설) 밑줄 친 문장은 문맥상 학교 측이 성공한 스마트폰 잠금장치를 가정에서도 사용하려고 학부모들이 문의한 내용이다. 따라서 정답은 ④이다.

098

정답 ③

지문 해석) 아카데미 시상식이 생중계되는 돌비극장에서 중간 광고 시간이 되면 영화업계 인사나 업계 밖의 초청 인사들은 식장의 자리에서 일어나 공짜 술과 음료를 마시며 서로 다른 좌석 층을 오간다. 식장은, 2019년 최고의 화제작 기생충과 제작자인 한국의 봉준호가 무대 위로 불려 나갈 때마다 열광적으로 박수를 치며 환호하는 백인들이 대부분 차지했으나 아카데미 측이 다양성 문제를 어떻게 접근해야 하는지에 대한 의견은 다양했다. 쿠엔틴 타란티노 감독과 *Once Upon a Time in Hollywood*를 잠시 협업한 적이 있는 컨설턴트 Scott Michaels씨는 "포용적이 되는 것은 매우 좋은 일이지만 그것을 작품 선정의 기준으로 삼는 데에는 동의하지 않는다."라고 말한다. BuzzFeed News에서 올해 연기 부문에서 백인 배우들이 과도하게 지명받은 데 대해 질문 받고 Michaels는 "다양성은 찬성하지만 작품은 그와는 별개"라고 말했다. 그는 "나는 작품은 작품을 대표하고 상은 상이라는 말을 엄청 신봉하는 사람이고 인구 비례로 적당히 상을 나눠주는 건 옳지 않다고 생각한다"라고 덧붙였다.

글의 소재) 봉준호의 영화 Parasite의 Academy 시상식

주요 어휘) mill about ~주변을 오가다, acclaimed 칭송받는, mastermind 주도자 제작자, inclusive 포용적, standing point 입점, 기준점, stand-alone 독립된, overrepresentation 과잉대표됨, stand for 대표하다

글의 흐름) 주제문은 'views on how the Academy should navigate diversity were varied.'이다.

구조 분석) ⊙ views on how the Academy should navigate diversity were varied.

→ 'how ~diversity' 의문사절이 전치사 on의 목적어이고 이절은 의문사 S + V의 어순을 취하고 있다.

⊙ base merit on demographic.

→ base A on B는 'A를 B에 근거하게 하다'의 뜻이다.

정답 해설 밑줄 친 부분은 '공훈의 근거를 인구학적 요소에 두는 것', 즉 상을 인구 비례로 적당히 나눠주는 것을 의미한다. 작품 평가에 작품 이외의 요소가 개입하는 데 회의적인 화자의 입장을 근거로 추론할 수도 있다.

099 정답 ③

지문 해석 T.S. Eliot의 유명한 시 황무지는 공동 저작된 시가 끈질기게 단일 저자로 귀착되는 주목할 만한 예다. 엘리어트의 원고에는 그가 발간한 시에 에즈라 파운드가 상당히 기여했다는 증거 서류가 발견된다. 파운드는 황무지가 출간되기 전 시의 다양한 양상에 주요한 수정을 가하는 것은 물론 황무지 초고 1000행 중 434행을 삭제하는 데 도움을 주었다. 엘리어트는 파운드의 상당한 기여를 늘 고마워했다. 1938년에 그가 말한 대로 파운드는 "좋은 글귀와 나쁜 글귀가 뒤섞인 잡동사니를 시로 탈바꿈시켰다." 그러나 이런저런 반대 증거에도 불구하고 많은 엘리어트 학자들은 파운드의 기여를 최소화하려는 노력을 고집해오고 있다. 파운드가 엘리어트의 황무지 저술에 대한 기여를 부인하는 것이 명백히 함축하는 것은 이 시가 어떤 식으로든 지금보다 덜 위대한 것으로 받아들여질 수 있다는 점이다.

① 단일 저자주의에 대한 엘리어트의 확고한 믿음
② 파운드의 기여에 대한 엘리어트의 감사
③ 파운드가 황무지 저술에 기여한 것
④ 작품에 영향을 미치려는 파운드의 시도를 엘리어트가 거부한 점
⑤ 엘리어트 지지자들이 그의 작품을 지나치게 편애하는 것

글의 소재 T.S. Eliot의 황무지의 공동 저작 논란

주요 어휘 notable 저명한, consistently 끈질기게, attribute to ~ (공적이나 비난을) ~의 탓으로 돌리다, substantially 상당히, carve out 잘라내다, 삭제하다, alteration 변경, acknowledge 인정하다, 고마워하다, jumble 잡동사니, contingent(n) 분견대, 한 무리의 사람들

글의 흐름 주제문은 첫 문장 'T. S. Eliot's famous poem *The Waste Land* stands as a notable instance of a co-authored poem that is consistently attributed to one author alone.'이고 두괄식 구조이다. 주제문(일반 진술)에 이어 증거 제시와 인용 등의 구체 진술로 주제문의 주장을 뒷받침하는 구성을 하고 있다.

구조 분석 ⊙ There is documentary evidence from Eliot's manuscript that Ezra Pound contributed substantially to the published poem.

→ that은 동격의 that으로 evidence와 연결되는데 'from Eliot's

manuscript'가 형용사구로 삽입되는 바람에 둘 사이가 떨어졌다. 동격의 that이기 때문에 that 다음에 완전한 문장이 왔다.

⊙ ~ despite this and other evidence to the contrary.

→ to the contrary는 evidence를 꾸며주는 형용사구이고 '그와 반대되는'의 뜻이다. 'to the contrary'는 부사구로 쓰일 때도 있다. (e.g. No matter what they say to the contrary, I am positive that he was present[그들이 무슨 반대 얘기를 하건 나는 그가 출석했다고 확신한다].)

정답 해설 그와 반대되는 증거란 파운드의 기여를 최소화하려는 엘리어트 추종자들의 시도에 반하는 증거, 즉 파운드가 엘리어트의 황무지 저술에 기여한 것을 말한다. 따라서 정답은 ③이다.

100 정답 ①

지문 해석 교육부 장관 Betsy DeVos는 전임 오바마 대통령의 논란성 규제 조치 중 하나인 2011년 성폭행 피의자 학생에 대한 학내 징계 조치를 문제 삼았다. 당시 오바마 행정부는 성폭행 피해자에 대한 정의가 거부됐다며 무죄 추정이나 고소인 반대 신문권 같은 전통적 피의자 보호 장치를 약화시켰다. 조지메이슨대학 연설에서 DeVos는 "그러한 시스템은 부끄럽고 비미국적이며 240년 전 건국의 아버지들이 목숨 바쳐 지키려 했던 자치 제도에 정면으로 배치된다."고 말했다. 놀랄 것도 없이, DeVos는 즉각적으로 공격받았다. 그녀가 인사청문회에서 보잘것없는 성적을 거둔 데 이어 공립 교육보다 자립형 공립학교를 선호하는 점, 장애 학생의 권리에 관한 72개의 정책 문서를 폐기한 것에 이르기까지 그녀는 잦은 비난의 표적이 돼 왔다.

① 비난의 표적
② 관심의 초점
③ 매력의 원천
④ 분쟁의 원인
⑤ 정말 보기 좋은 것

글의 소재 비난의 표적이 된 교육부 장관 DeVos

주요 어휘 take on 공격하다, presumption of innocence 무죄 추정, cross-examine 반대 신문하다, anathema 파문, 저주, 정면으로 배치되는 것, charter school 미국의 자립형 공립학교, rescind 폐지하다, lightning rod 피뢰침, 잦은 비난의 표적

구조 분석 ⊙ From her poor performance at her nomination hearing to her preference for charter schools over public education

→ From ~ to 구문으로, '~에서 ~에 이르기까지'의 뜻이다.

정답 해설 lightning rod는 피뢰침을 말하지만 비유적으로 '잦은 비난의 표적'의 의미로 쓰인다. 이 말을 모르더라도 전 문장 'DeVos was immediately attacked.'에서 공격 · 비난의 의미를 추론할 수 있다.

글의 흐름 이해

10. 무관한 문장 파악

정답

101 ④	102 ④	103 ④	104 ②	105 ④
106 ④				

101
정답 ④

지문 해석 좋은 신문을 만들기 위해 최근 많은 일을 하고 있지만 좋은 신문 독자를 만들기 위해서는 아직 할 일이 많다. 신문은 독자에 의해 감독이 된다. ① 신문의 수준을 높이거나 끌어내리는 것은 신문 독자다. ② 신문은 신문 독자층이 원하거나 허용하는 것 이상으로 좋아질 수 없다. ③ 독자가 민주주의를 제대로 이해하지 못하면 어떤 신문도 자유민주주의의 버팀목이 될 수 없다. ④ 자유민주주의는 그 구성원들이 진정한 평등사회를 구현할 충분한 의지가 있을 때만 꽃피울 수 있다. ⑤ 따라서, 신문의 역할에 대한 일반 대중의 날카로운 의식이 민주사회의 성공적인 유지에 필수조건이다.

글의 소재 좋은 독자와 좋은 신문

주요 어휘 raise up 고양하다, pull down 끌어내리다, constituent 구성원, committed to ~에 헌신하는, egalitarian 평등의, prerequisite 선결 조건

구조 분석 ⊙ It is newspaper readers who raise up the newspaper and pull it down.

➡ it that 강조 구문에서 that 대신 who가 쓰였다.

⊙ It can hardly be any better than the reading public wants it to be or allows it to be.

➡ it은 모두 newspaper를 가리킨다.

정답 해설 이 글은 좋은 독자가 좋은 신문을 만들고 좋은 신문이 성공적인 민주사회의 버팀목이라는 것이 주된 내용이다. '자유민주주의와 구성원들의 평등사회 구현 의지'를 강조한 ④는 이러한 글의 주된 내용의 흐름에 맞지 않는다. 따라서 정답은 ④이다.

102
정답 ④

지문 해석 비트코인은 사토시 나카모토라는 가명을 쓰는 정체 불명의 인물이 2009년에 처음 발명한 새로운 통화다. 이것은 중개자 없이 즉 은행을 통하지 않고 직접 거래된다. 거래수수료도 없고 실명을 밝힐 필요도 없다. ① 비트코인을 받아들이는 상인의 수가 늘고 있어서 비트코인으로 웹호스팅 수수료를 내거나 피자나 심지어 매니큐어도 살 수 있다. ② 비트코인으로 물건을 사는데 이름을 밝힐 필요도 없다. ③ 더구나 비트코인은 어떤 국가나 어떤 규제에도 묶여있지 않으므로 국제 결제가 쉽고 저렴하다. ④ 비트코인은 '디지털 지갑'에 보관되는데 이는 클라우드나 사용자 컴퓨터에 저장된다. ⑤ 신용카드 수수료가 없어서 중소기업이 선호할 수 있다.

글의 소재 비트코인의 결제 상의 장점

주요 어휘 alias ~라는 가명으로 알려진, transactions 거래, middle man 중개인, anonymously 익명으로, subject to ~에 매여있는

글의 흐름 ⊙ 비트코인의 결제 상의 장점들을 열거한 병렬식 구조의 글이다.

정답 해설 이 글은 비트코인의 통화 결제 상의 장점들에 대해 서술하고 있다. 따라서 비트코인의 보관 방법을 언급한 ④는 이러한 글의 흐름과는 거리가 멀다. 따라서 정답은 ④이다.

103
정답 ④

지문 해석 광고업에 종사하는 대부분의 사람들은 텔레비전 광고 구매가 인쇄 매체 구매보다는 여러 면에서 더 정확하고 복잡하다는 데 의견을 같이하는데 이는 독서 패턴보다는 시청자들의 시청 행태에 대해 알려진 것이 훨씬 많기 때문이다. ① TV 시청자 구성을 나이나 성별, 직업, 지역, 가족 구성, 구매 습관이나 여타 기준으로 세분해서 끊임없이 분석할 수 있다. ② 예를 들어 시청자가 채널 돌리는 것을 저녁 내내 추적할 수 있고 한 집에 TV가 여러 대일 경우 각각의 수상기의 서로 다른 시청 패턴을 측정할 수 있다. ③ 이 모든 것이 표적 시청자의 TV 시청을 정확히 짚어낼 수 있게 한다. ④ 따라서 시청자들은 그들이 볼 것으로 예상됐던 프로그램을 종종 보지 않으며 채널 간 경쟁은 시청자 수를 예측하기가 어렵게 만든다. ⑤ 그래서 광고 구매자는 어떤 프로그램이, 또는 어떤 프로그램 내의 어떤 광고 시간대가 가장 비용 효율적으로 목표 시청자층에 다가갈 수 있는지 정확하게 평가할 수 있다. 가령 황금 시간대와 비인기 시간대 광고는 가격 면에서 큰 차이가 있고 이런 가격 차이는 대개 시청자의 수와 시청자의 구성 요소를 반영한다.

글의 소재 TV 광고 경쟁력의 원천

주요 어휘 accurate 정확한, inter-channel 채널 간, unpredictable 예측할 수 없는, cost-effectively 비용 효율적으로, 싸게, approximately 대략적으로, off-peak 비인기 시간대의, spot 스폿 광고

글의 흐름 'Most people engaged in the advertising

industry ~ because far more is known about the ways viewers watch than is known about reading patterns.'가 주제문인 두괄식 구조다.

[구조 분석] ⊙ because far more is known about the ways viewers watch than is known about reading patterns.

➔ the way와 viewers 사이에는 관계부사가 생략됐고, than은 more ~ than에 연결돼 있는 유사관계대명사다.

⊙ The media buyer will then be able to evaluate precisely which programs and even which breaks in which programs will reach the target market most cost-effectively.

➔ 밑줄 부분이 전체 문장의 목적어절이다. 목적어절의 주어는 which programs와 which breaks in which programs(어떤 프로그램 안의 어떤 광고 시간대)의 두 개다.

[정답 해설] 이 글은 텔레비전 광고 구매가 매우 엄밀하고 정확한 시청자 조사에 근거해 이뤄지고 있고 이를 통해 광고주가 효율적인 광고를 할 수 있음을 주장하고 있다. 시청자가 예상 밖의 프로그램을 시청한다든지 채널 간 경쟁이 심해 시청자 수를 예측할 수 없다는 ④의 주장은 이러한 흐름과 무관하다. 따라서 정답은 ④이다.

104
정답 ②

[지문 해석] 의도적이든 우연히든 정상적인 환경 밖으로 도입된 포식자들은 매우 해로운 영향을 미칠 수 있다. 특히 도서(섬) 환경에서는 문제가 심각해지는데 거기서는 다양한 자연발생적 포식자나 복잡한 먹이 그물이 일반적으로 존재하지 않기 때문이다. ① 따라서 도서 종은 새로운 포식자의 갑작스러운 출현으로 인한 '방해'에 특히 민감하다. ② 섬 고유종의 필사적인 생존 노력이 침입 포식자와 평화공존을 이끌어낸다. ③ 개나 고양이처럼 외래 포식자들이 섬과 같은 다른 생태계에 도입됐을 때 그들의 영향력은 고유종의 심각한 감소나 심지어는 멸종까지도 초래할 수 있다. ④ 이는 고립된 섬 고유의 동물들은 포식의 공진화 압력이 없어서 회피나 도피 기제를 발달시키지 못했기 때문이다. ⑤ 그래서 섬 동물들은 도입 포식자들의 손쉬운 먹잇감이 된다. 호주 대륙에서 바로 그런 일이 있었는데 도입된 고양이와 여우가 국립공원이나 자연보호구역 내 토종 유대동물의 현 개체 수에 심각한 위협이 되고 있다.

[글의 소재] 외래종이 도서 지역의 동물 서식 환경에 미치는 영향

[주요 어휘] deliberately 의도적으로, detrimental 해로운, acute 첨예한, 심각한, susceptible 민감한, disturbance 방해, alien 외래의, extinction 멸종, co-evolved 공진화의, fauna 동물군, endemic 고유의, evasion 회피, marsupial 유대동물

[글의 흐름] 처음 두 문장 'Predators which are deliberately or accidentally introduced ~ predators and complex food webs are typically absent.'가 주제문이고 두괄식 구조다.

[구조 분석] ⊙ The problem is particularly acute in island settings, where a wide variety of naturally occurring predators and complex food webs are typically absent.

➔ '~, where'는 관계부사의 계속적 용법으로 'because a wide variety ~ there.'로 바꿔 쓸 수 있다.

⊙ Desperate efforts for survival by the island species usually ends up generating peaceful coexistence

➔ 'end up ~ing'는 '결국 ~하다'를 뜻하는 관용적 표현이다.

[정답 해설] 이 글은 포식자가 도서 지역(섬)에 도입되면, 외부 침입에 취약한 섬 고유종은 생존에 심각한 위협을 받는다는 내용이다. 섬 고유종의 필사적인 생존 노력이 침입 포식자와 평화 공존을 이끌어낸다는 ②는 전체 논지에 반한다. 따라서 정답은 ②이다.

105
정답 ④

[지문 해석] 성찰적 불신자들은 초월이라는 말을 기본적으로 이해할 수 없고 심지어 무의미하다고 봤으며 이것이 그들이 자신들을 회의론자라고 말하는 이유다. 좀 더 신랄하게 말하면 만일 그들이 신의 존재를 입증하기 위해 역사적으로 제시된 논거를 검증한다면 그들은 그것들이 근거 없고 따라서 설득력이 없다고 본다. 그들은 소위 경험에 대한 호소를 근거 없는 것으로 본다. 신비주의도 기적이나 계시에 대한 호소도 초월적 존재의 실존을 입증하지 못한다는 것이다. 더군다나 그들은 신에 대한 믿음 없이도 도덕성이 가능하다고 주장한다. 불신자들은 초자연적 주장에 대한 비판자이고 그것들을 미신으로 여긴다. 사실 그들은 신의 가설을, 실현 가능성이 없고 (신으로부터) 해방된 남녀가 자세하게 조사할 만한 가치가 없는 인간 상상력의 산물이라고 보았다. (그래서 그들은 신의 개념이 모든 인간사에서 고려해야 할 가장 본질적인 요소로 확립되는 데 크게 기여하게 됐다.) Baron d'Holbach, Denis Diderot, Karl Marx를 포함한 많은 고전적 무신론자들이 이런 부류에 속하는데 이는 그들이 애초에 유물론자였고 그들의 유물론적 형이상학에서 종교적 회의론과 불신이 나왔기 때문이다.

[글의 소재] 성찰적 불신자가 회의론에 빠지는 이유

[주요 어휘] reflective 성찰적인, 사색적인, transcendence 초월, unintelligible 이해하기 어려운, pointedly 신랄하게, 통렬하게, argument 논거, invalid 근거 없는, 부당한, unwarranted 부당한, mysticism 신비주의, revelation 계시, maintain 주장하다, supernaturalistic 초자연적인, superstition 미신, hypothesis 가설, fanciful 공상의, emancipate 해방시키다, go a long way towards ~에 크게 기여하다, atheist 무신론자, materialist 유물론자, metaphysics 형이상학

[글의 흐름] ⊙ 'Reflective unbelievers find the language of transcendence basically unintelligible, even meaningless, and that is why they say they are skeptics.'가 주제문이고 두 괄식 구조다.

구조 분석 ⊙ neither mysticism nor the appeal to miracles or revelation establishes the existence of transcendental realities.

→ neither A nor B 구문에서 동사는 B에 맞춰 일치시키기 때문에 여기서는 establishes는 the appeal에 맞춰 수 일치시켰다.

정답 해설 불신자는 초자연적인 것을 인정하지 않고 따라서 신의 개념에 대해 비판적이라는 것이 이 글의 주된 논조이므로 '그들이 인간사에서 신의 개념을 확립하는 데 기여했다'는 ④의 주장은 전체 흐름에 반한다. 따라서 정답은 ④이다.

106
정답 ④

지문 해석 고의적이건 우발적이건 사람들은 전 영역의 유기체를 이동해 왔고 그 과정에서 자연적 분포 경계를 깨거나 지역사회의 구조에 장애를 초래했다. 이들 불청객 편승자들은 몸을 잘 숨기거나 너무 작아 평생 또는 당분간 발견되지 않는다. ① 개방적인 해양 환경은 대부분의 해안종에게 우호적이지 않아 그것이 멀리 떨어진 유사한 서식 환경으로 흘러 들어가는 것을 허용하지 않는다. ② 두 서식 환경을 가르는 거리가 너무 멀어 능동적인 수영을 통해서건 수동적으로 해류에 몸을 실어서건 이를 극복하기 어렵다. ③ 인간이 외래종의 수입을 돕는 메커니즘을 도입 수단(vectors of introduction)으로 부르는데 이는 주로 선적 활동, 해양 재배, 관상용 종의 거래와 연관돼 있다. ④ 바다 양식은 야생에서 잡은 표본의 공급을 효율적으로 보충하거나 대체할 수 있기 때문에 야생 채취에 대한 실용적인 대안으로 인정받고 있다. ⑤ 다른 도입 수단으로는 살아있는 미끼나 해산물, 또는 연구나 교육용의 살아있는 유기체의 국제적 운송이나 판매가 있다.

글의 소재 해양 생물의 이동

주요 어휘 inhospitable 우호적이지 않은, vector 벡터, 매개체, 수단, aquaculture 바다 양식, ornamental species 관상용 종, viable 실용적인, specimen 표본

글의 흐름 ⊙ 주제문은 'Whether deliberately or accidentally, people have been transporting whole range of organisms, breaking natural distribution boundaries and interfering with community structures.'로 두괄식 구조이다.

정답 해설 이 글은 해양 생물의 이동에 인간이 직간접적으로 개입할 수밖에 없는 현실을 논하고 있다. 따라서 해양 생물을 가두어 기르는 '바다 양식의 효용'을 설명하는 ④는 이러한 글의 논지와 직접적인 관련이 없다. ④를 소거하면 도입 수단(vectors)을 설명하는 ③에서 ⑤로의 글의 흐름이 자연스럽다.

11. 문장 삽입

정답

	107 ③	108 ⑤	109 ④	110 ④
111 ③	112 ②	113 ⑤	114 ③	

107
정답 ③

지문 해석 1991년 이그노벨상이 처음 제정된 이래 많은 특이한 업적에 대해 상이 수여됐다. (①) 이를테면 영국 킬레대학의 한 연구팀은 고통과 비속어 사용에 관한 연구로 이 상을 수상했다. (②) 그들은 비속어가 고통에 대한 공통적인 반응일 뿐만 아니라 유용한 반응이라는 것을 발견했다. (③) 구체적으로 비속어가 사람들이 높은 수준의 고통과 불편함을 참아내는 데 도움을 준다는 것을 알아냈다. 그들의 한 실험에서 실험 대상자들은 찬 얼음물 속에 손을 넣고 되도록 오랫동안 견디도록 요청되었다. (④) 욕을 하도록 허용된 피험자들은 그렇지 않은 피험자들보다 거의 50퍼센트나 더 오래 견딜 수 있었다. (⑤) 연구자들은 후속 연구에서 어쩌다 한 번씩 욕하는 사람이 가장 큰 수혜자이며 빈번하게 욕하는 사람은 거의 또는 전혀 차이가 없었다는 사실을 발견했다.

글의 소재 Ig Nobel 프라이즈

주요 어휘 inception 시작, 개시, issue 발행하다, specifically 구체적으로, profanity 불경스러움, 비속한 말, 욕, withstand 견디다, test subject 실험 대상자, 피험자, swear 욕하다, follow-up 후속, infrequent 잦지 않은, 어쩌다 한 번씩 하는, whereas ~인 반면

글의 흐름 ⊙ 주제문은 첫 문장인 'Since the inception of the Ig Nobel Prizes in 1991, prizes have been issued for a number of unusual achievements.'이다. 이 글은 이처럼 첫 문장에서 일반적인 진술이 나온 뒤에 구체적인 진술이 이어지는 연역적 형태의 두괄식 구조를 이루고 있다.

구조 분석 ⊙ For example, a research team from the UK's Keele University was awarded an Ig Nobel

→ 수여 동사의 수동태로 was awarded는 was given이나 received로 바꿔 쓸 수 있다.

정답 해설 'Specifically, they found ~'로 보았을 때, 주어진 문장은 어떤 발견 사실을 보다 구체적으로 부연 진술하고 있는 것임을 알 수 있다. 따라서 이 문장은 무엇을 발견했다는 취지의 문장 'They discovered that profanity ~' 다음인 ③의 자리에 와야 한다.

108

지문 해석 미국의 교육학자 Edward L. Thorndike는 테스트 방식과 교육을 철학과 완전히 분리해 그것을 경험적 심리학 쪽으로 옮기는 방식을 채택했다. 삶의 모든 것은 측정할 수 있다는 믿음이 그랬던 것처럼 통계학의 활용이 이 방식의 중심에 있었다. (①) 당시 그것은 이런 식으로 표현됐다. "무릇 존재한다고 하는 것은 양(量)으로 존재하고 양으로 존재하는 것은 측정할 수 있고 교육에서 측정은 자연과학에서의 측정과 대체로 같다." (②) Thorndike는 학습을 연구하는 데 주도면밀한 실험적 절차들을 도입했다. (③) 그의 가장 유명한 공헌은 효과의 법칙이다. (④) 이 법칙에 따르면 반응에 대한 효과가 똑같은 반응을 반복하는 경향이 강해지거나 약해지는 것을 결정한다. (⑤) 요컨대 적절한 보상이 동물이나 인간으로 하여금 어떤 행동을 더 신속하게 보여주는 결과를 낳는 것이다. 이리하여 통계학은 학문의 한 분야인 동시에 교육과 학교 수업을 체계화하기 위한 폭넓은 교육 개발의 일부가 되었다.

글의 소재 교육학에서 통계학 도입의 배경

주요 어휘 embrace 껴안다, 채택하다, empirical 경험적인, procedure 절차, inclination 성향, 경향, discipline 규율, 학문의 분야

구조 분석 ⊙ The use of statistics was central for this, as was the belief that everything in life can be measured.
→ as는 유사관계대명사로 쓰였고 선행사는 'central for this'이다. that 이하의 동격의 명사절이고 belief를 부연 설명한다.

정답 해설 주어진 문장이 '적절한 보상이 ~ 신속하게 보여주는 결과를 낳는다'는 보상의 효과를 언급하고 있고 이것이 요약 재진술의 연결사 'In short'로 연결되고 있으므로 이 문장은 효과와 관련된 표현이 들어있는 문장 다음에 올 가능성이 크다. ⑤ 바로 앞 문장이 '반응 효과가 반응의 지속 성향의 강약을 결정한다.'는 내용이므로 이곳에 주어진 문장이 오는 것이 적절하다.

109

지문 해석 판다는 큰 덩치치고는 요리조리 잘도 피해 다니기 때문에 숫자 파악이 어렵기로 정평이 나 있다. 1970년대 첫 공식 개체 조사 후 조사 방법이 바뀌었다. 조사원들은 이제 더 이상 판다의 흔적을 찾아 숲을 헤매기만 하지 않고 판다 배설물에서 DNA를 분석하거나, 먹다 남은 대나무 길이로 식사량을 추정한다. 현재 판다 수는 새끼를 포함해 2,060마리에 빠르게 접근하고 있다. (①) 2014년 조사에서 밝혀진 대로 10년간 17% 증가는 밀렵 감소와 판다 서식지 증가 두 가지 요인으로 귀결된다. (②) 판다는 전에만 해도 남중국, 미얀마, 베트남의 대나무 밀림 지역에 살았다. (③) 그러나 요즘 그들의 서식지는 서부 중국 삼림지역이 유일하다. (④) 그 결과 중국은 중국인이 숭

배하는 '거대한 곰 고양이' ─ 판다를 한자로는 이렇게 부른다. ─ 의 수를 유지하는 데 주도적 역할을 담당해야 했다. 중국은 지난 30년 동안 만4천 제곱킬로미터에 이르는 67개의 판다 보호 구역을 지정해 환경 보호국의 이미지를 제고한 바 있다. (⑤) 판다는 또한 중국과 국제 사회 간 외교의 중요한 상징이 돼왔다.

글의 소재 중국의 판다 보존 노력

주요 어휘 elusive 요리조리 잘 피해 다니는, fecal 배설물의, cub 사자나 호랑이, 곰의 새끼, habitat 서식지, inhabit ~에 거주하다, lush 우거진, encompass 포함하다, reserve 보호구역

정답 해설 주어진 문장은 어떤 계기 때문에 중국이 판다의 수를 유지하는 데 주도적인 역할을 해야 했음을 강조하고 있다. 따라서 이는 판다 생태계가 위기를 겪고 있다는 내용 다음인 ④에 오는 것이 자연스럽다. 그래야 중국의 적극적인 역할로 67개의 판다 보호구역이 새로 생겼다는 다음 문장으로 매끄럽게 연결될 수 있다.

110

지문 해석 물자를 소비하는 속도도 빨라졌을 뿐 아니라 우리가 소비하는 물자의 종류도 다양해졌다. (①) 내화금속이나 경합금, 플라스틱, 합성섬유 등 폭넓은 신물질들이 20세기 인간 사용의 문을 열었다. (②) 이 중에는 이전 것들의 기능을 더 잘, 더 싸게 수행하는 것도 있고, 속성을 적절히 결합해 이전과는 전혀 다른 기기를 만들거나 새로운 효과를 내는 것도 있다. (③) 우리는 현재 자연 상태에서 존재하는 주기율표 상의 92개 원소의 대부분을 산업 처리 과정에서 사용한다. (④) 그러나 1세기 전만 해도 그나마 알려진 20여 개만이 화학적 호기심의 대상이었다. 더 많은 자연 상태의 물질이 사용될 뿐 아니라 완전한 신소재가 실험실에서 합성되고 있다. (⑤) 인류의 고도 물질문명 달성 여부는 우리가 이런 다양한 신소재를 얼마나 확장적으로, 그리고 거의 사치스러울 정도로 활용할 수 있느냐에 달렸다.

글의 소재 신소재

주요 어휘 refractory 내화성의, alloy 합금, synthetic fiber 합성섬유, periodic table 주기율표, all but =nearly, synthesize 합성하다, extravagant 사치스러운

글의 흐름 ⊙ 주제문은 'A great new range of materials has opened up for the use of 20th-century man'이며, 두괄식 구조이다.

구조 분석 ⊙ Not only are we consuming materials more rapidly, but we are using an increasing diversity of materials.
→ Not이라는 부정의 부사구 때문에 'are we'가 도치돼 있다.

정답 해설 주어진 문장이 '~ 20여 개만이 관심의 대상이었다.'고 말하고 있으므로 바로 앞에는 숫자가 제시된 문장이 올 가능성이 크다. 이를 ④의 자리에 놓으면 '지금은 92개 원소를 대부

분 사용하지만 한 세기 전만 해도 겨우 20여 개만이 호기심의 대상이었다'는 식으로 자연스럽게 연결된다.

111

지문 해석 2017년에 대부분 미국인에게 한국 연예인 한 명을 꼽으라고 한다면 그 대답은 대단한 BTS이었을 가능성이 크다. 이 일곱 명의 청년 그룹은 한 지역적 돌풍에서 전 세계적 현상으로 커 나갔고 K-pop을, 한국이 지구 어느 곳에 붙었는지 모르는 사람들 사이에서조차 모르는 사람이 없게 만들었다. (①) 이 불가능한 일을 그들은 어떻게 할 수 있었고 공략이 까다롭고 경쟁이 심한 미국 시장을 어떻게 뚫을 수 있었을까? (②) 그들은 단지 그것을 뚫은 게 아니라 무려 160만 노래 다운로드(말장난 의도 없음), 10억 스트리밍 그리고 최근 미국 순회에서 나타날 때마다 소리치는 열성 팬 군단-그들의 팬층을 말 그대로 ARMY(군단)로 부른다-으로 미국 시장을 박살내다시피 했다. (③) 팬들이 DNA나 Mic Drop 같은 히트작의 한국어 가사를 대개는 제대로 이해하지 못한다는 것을 중요하지 않다. 그것이 BTS 열성 팬이 대충 비슷한 발음으로 따라 부르고, 그들의 전매특허인 연호 방식으로 그룹 멤버의 이름을 일제히 부르며, 그리고 무엇보다 중요하게 그들의 앨범을 사는 것을 막지 못하기 때문이다. (④) 한국의 가온차트에 의하면, 이 그룹의 최근 앨범인 '2017's Love Yourself: Her'는 약 150만 장의 하드카피가 팔렸다. (⑤)

글의 소재 미국에서의 BTS의 인기

주요 어휘 resounding 대단한, phenomenon 현상, 비범한 사람, 누구나 아는 유명한 이름, elusive 까다로운, highly-competitive 경쟁이 심한, smash 박살내다, to the tune of ~의 엄청난 수의(tune이 BTS의 곡조를 의미할 수도 있어 말장난으로 언급했다), veritable 진정한, lyrics 가사, devotee 신봉자, 열성 팬, phonetic 음성 상의, approximation 근사치, in unison 일제히, crucially 매우 중요하게

구조 분석 ⊙ That hasn't stopped BTS devotees from singing along in phonetic approximation, from screaming the band members' names in unison with their patented "fan chants", and, perhaps most crucially, from buying their record.

→ stop A from ~ing 구문이다. from screaming과 from buying이 from singing과 병렬구조를 이루고 있다.

정답 해설 ③ 다음 문장의 주어 That가 받을 말이 바로 앞 문장에 없다. 그래서 That의 지칭 대상은 주어진 문장에서 찾아야 하고(that=that those fans, for the most part, don't actually understand the Korean lyrics of major hits like "DNA" and "Mic Drop".), 따라서 주어진 문장이 들어갈 곳은 ③이다.

112

지문 해석 직장에서 주는 사람은 비교적 희귀한 부류다. 그들은 상호성을 다른 쪽으로 즉, 얻기보다는 주기를 선호하는 쪽으로 기울인다. 받는 사람이 다른 사람들이 그들에게 줄 것을 평가하는 자기중심적인 사람인데 반해 주는 사람은 다른 사람이 그들에게 필요한 것이 무엇인지에 주의를 기울이는 타인 중심적인 사람이다. (①) 이런 선호는 돈에 대한 것이 아니다. 주는 사람과 받는 사람은 그들이 얼마나 많이 자선에 기부하는지 혹은 그들의 고용인으로부터 얼마나 많은 보상을 받아내는지에 의해 구분되지 않는다. (②) 오히려 주는 사람과 받는 사람은 다른 사람에 대한 태도나 행동에서 차이가 난다. 만일 당신이 받는 사람이라면 당신은 당신에게 돌아오는 이득이 개인적 비용을 초과할 때 전략적으로 다른 이를 돕는다. (③) 당신이 주는 사람이라면 당신은 다른 비용-이득 분석법을 사용한다. 다른 사람들에 대한 이득이 개인적 비용을 초과할 때 당신은 돕는다. (④) 혹은 당신은 비용을 전혀 생각하지 않고 보상에 대한 고려 없이 다른 이들을 도울 수도 있다. (⑤) 당신이 직장에서 주는 사람이라면 당신은 당신의 시간과 에너지, 지식, 기술, 아이디어 그리고 인간관계를 그것들로부터 혜택을 받을 만한 사람들과 함께 나누는 데 관대하도록 힘쓸 것이다.

글의 소재 givers vs takers

주요 어휘 rare 희귀한, breed 혈통, 부류, tilt 기울이다, reciprocity 상호성, 호혜, evaluate 평가하다, preference 선호, distinguish 구분하다, charity 자선, outweigh ~보다 무게가 더 나가다, analysis 분석법, exceed 초과하다, alternatively 혹은, 그렇지 않으면

글의 흐름 주제문은 'Rather, givers and takers differ in their attitudes and actions toward other people.'이다.

구조 분석 ⊙ ~ when the benefits to you outweigh the personal costs.

→ outweigh는 목적어를 취하는 타동사이기 때문에 outweigh than으로 쓰지 않는다. 이런 동사에는 outlive, outdo, outperform, outgrow, outshine, outwit 등이 있다.

⊙ Alternatively, you might not think about the personal costs at all, helping others without expecting anything in return.

→ helping 이하는 분사 구문으로 순차 진행을 나타낸다. 'helping others~'는 'and you help others~'로 바꿔 쓸 수 있다.

정답 해설 주어진 문장은 주는 자와 받는 자는 다른 사람을 대하는 태도나 행동이 다르다고 말하고 있으므로 그 '다른 태도와 행동'이 어디에서 언급되기 시작하는지를 찾으면 된다. 아울러, 대조의 연결사 Rather로 시작하는 문장 앞에는 예외 없이 부정어를 사용한 문장이 온다는 사실도 알아두자.

113

지문 해석 오로팍스 귀마개는 일찍이 1907년에 도입됐지만 근로자들은 대체로 그것이나 유사 기구를 사용하는 데 그다지 열성적이지 않았다. 그들 중 많은 수는 소음용 귀마개를 사용하는 것을 '남자답지 못하다'라고 생각했고 느리고 서서히 진행되는 소음성 청력 상실을 걱정하지 않았다. 또한 상징적 차원에서 산업 현장의 소음은 긍정적 의미를 지녔다. (①) 미국 역사학자 Mark Smith가 언급한 것처럼 공장이 소란스러운 것은 산업이 호황이고 수익성이 좋다는 것을 의미했다. (②) 게다가 근로자들이 청력 방지용 기구를 끼면 소음이 어디서 나는지 몰라 불안해하고 또 그것은 의사소통에 문제를 일으켰다. (③) 그들은 기계 소음을 듣고 있어야 편안함을 느꼈다. 그 소리를 듣고 기계에 문제가 있다는 것을 알았기 때문이다. (④) 더군다나, 귀 보호 장치를 끼는 것은 특정 경고 시그널을 듣지 못하기 때문에 위험하기까지 했다. (⑤) <u>귀마개나 귓집 같은 보호 장구들이 일반화된 것은 1950년대 후반에 이르러서였다.</u> 근로자들의 청력 손실로 보상 요구가 급증하자 고용주나 책임보험 기관들이 그들(보호 장구)의 사용을 주장하고 나선 것이다.

글의 소재 상업적 earplug 도입의 역사적 배경

주요 어휘 eager 열성적인, unmanly 남자답지 않은, connotation 의미, 함축, insecure 불안해하는, liability 책임, compensation 보상, claim 요구

글의 흐름 earplug 도입 초기만 해도 산업 현장에서 earplug 착용에 대해 미온적인 반응을 보이다가 1950년대 들어서 청각 상실로 인한 보험 청구가 급증하자 earplug 착용이 본격화됐다는 내용이다. 'Only from the late 1950s~'부터 글의 흐름이 반전되고 있다.

구조 분석 ⊙ Besides, <u>wearing</u> a hearing-protection device made <u>workers</u> <u>insecure</u> about where the noise came from while also causing communication problems.

→ 이 문장은 주어가 wearing, 목적어는 workers이고 insecure가 목적격보어인 5형식 문장이며, 'where ~from'은 전치사 about의 목적어인 의문사절로서 '의문사 + S + V'의 어순을 취하고 있다. 그리고 while과 also causing 사이에는 it was가 생략됐다.

⊙ <u>Only</u> from the late 1950s onward <u>did</u> protective devices like earplugs and earmuff <u>grow</u> more common.

→ 제한을 나타내는 부사 only가 문장 맨 앞에 나오는 바람에 조동사(did) + 주어(protective devices like earplugs and earmuff) + 동사(grow)의 도치 구문이 됐다.

정답 해설 ⑤ 다음 문장의 their use의 their를 받을 말이 바로 앞 문장에는 없다(의미상 warning signals는 their의 지칭 대상이 될 수 없다). their는 주어진 문장의 earplugs and earmuff를 지칭하는 것이 확실하므로 주어진 문장이 들어갈 곳은 ⑤이

다. 또 ⑤ 전 문장은 ear plug를 끼지 않는 쪽(-)을 옹호하다가 다음 문장에서 갑자기 끼는 쪽으로(+) 흐름이 바뀌었기 때문에 그 사이에 주어진 문장이 와야 전환이 자연스럽다(± 전략).

114

지문 해석 몸은 첫 번째 폭력의 도구, 즉 첫 번째 무기이다. 여기서 첫 번째라 함은 우선적인 것이 아니라 아직도 엄존하고 있는 인류학적인, 그리고 궁극적으로 기술적인 발전의 시작을 가리킨다. (①) 끊임없이 증가하는 것이 세 가지 있는데 무기의 힘, 그것들을 사용하는 데 필요한 기술 그리고 목표물에 이르는 거리가 그것들이다. (②) 말할 것도 없이 대부분의 무기를 발명하고 그것들을 사용하고 짜 맞추는 데 필요한 기술을 최적화하는 것은 인간 정신의 치명적인 재능이다. (③) <u>그러나 인간의 첫 번째 무기는 맨몸이었고 모든 폭력의 도구들은 인간의 몸의 연장이다.</u> 곤봉이나 칼, 검 등 간단한 무기의 예들은 사용자와 도구 간의 이러한 통일성을 예증한다. (④) 펜싱이나 일본식 칼싸움의 한 형태인 검도의 섬세한 기술을 훈련받은 격투기 선수들은, 육체적은 물론 정신적으로인 격렬한 훈련의 목적이 무기의 쓰임을 팔다리의 쓰임만큼 자연스럽게 만들고 그보다 훨씬 더 효율적으로 만드는 데 있다는 것을 직감적으로 알고 있다. (⑤) 그래서 "무기 속으로 들어간다" 그것과 "하나가 된다" 또는 그것을 "느낀다"는 표현이 생겼다.

글의 소재 첫 번째 무기로서의 인간의 몸

주요 어휘 anthropological 인류학의, ultimately 궁극적으로, deadly 치명적인, ingenuity 재능, illustrate 예증하다, delicate 섬세한, intuitively 직감적으로, intensive 격렬한, 효율적인

글의 흐름 ⊙ 주제문은 'Yet it was the bare body that was man's first weapon, and all instruments of violence are extensions of the human body.'이고 역접의 연결사가 주제문을 이끄는 경우다.

구조 분석 ⊙ ~ is to make the weapon's use as natural as the use of one's arms or legs, and <u>vastly more efficient.</u>

→ 밑줄 친 부분은 생략 구문으로 완전한 문장으로 만들면 'and to make the weapon's use vastly more efficient than the use of one's arms and legs.'이다.

정답 해설 ③ 다음 문장에 나오는 '사용자와 도구 사이의 이러한 통일성'을 받을 말이 바로 앞 문장에는 없기 때문에 ③에서 글의 흐름이 끊어진다. 주어진 글에서 '인간의 몸이 첫째 무기이고 모든 폭력의 도구는 인간 몸의 연장'이라 했는데 이는 인간 몸과 도구 사이의 연관성, 즉 양자 간 통일성을 의미하고 그래서 'this unity'의 지칭 대상이 된다. 따라서 주어진 글이 들어갈 곳은 ③이다.

12. 글의 순서

정답

				115 ⑤
116 ⑤	117 ⑤	118 ④	119 ⑤	120 ③
121 ③	122 ①	123 ②	124 ②	125 ⑤

115
정답 ⑤

지문 해석 다른 문화권 사람과 소통을 시도하거나, 직장 동료나 친구, 파트너로 관계 맺기를 시도한 적이 있는가? 극복해야 할 것은 말하는 언어가 서로 다르다는 사실 뿐만이 아니라, 비언어적 소통이나 신념 체계, 가치관의 차이도 극복해야 한다. (C) 비언어적 태도의 의미 차이는 우리가 특정 제스처나 행동, 얼굴 표정의 의미를 모르면 상대방에게 오해와 불쾌함을 부를 수 있다는 것을 잘 보여주는 예다. (B) 가령 일본인들은 화나 슬픔을 숨기기 위해 웃거나 미소 짓는다. 대중 앞에 그런 감정을 드러내는 게 부적절하기 때문이다. 아시아 국가에서는 어른과 눈을 마주치면 불손하게 여겨지지만 서양 백인 문화에서 눈을 피하는 것은 따분함이나 상대 무시, 또는 부정직함으로 받아들여질 수 있다. (A) 그리고 혼동과 스트레스를 부를 수 있는 것으로 신념과 가치관의 차이가 있다. 민주주의에 대한 믿음처럼 기본적인 것을 예로 들어 그에 대한 전 세계인의 태도와 비교해 보면 사상이 다른 사람과 공감하는 게 얼마나 어려운지 알 수 있다.

글의 소재 원활한 소통을 위해 극복돼야 할 비언어적 소통, 신념 체계, 가치관

주요 어휘 workmate 직장 동료, break through 돌파하다, 극복하다, offence 화, 불쾌, inappropriate 부적절한, disrespectful 불손한, superior 상급자, relate to 이해하다, 공감하다

글의 흐름 ⊙ 질문 형식의 도입문에 대한 답변 'It's not only the fact that there is a different spoken language to break through, but also differences in non-verbal communication, belief systems, and values.'이 주제문이며, 두괄식 구조이다.

구조 분석 ⊙ It's <u>not only</u> the fact that there is a different spoken language to break through, <u>but also</u> differences in non-verbal communication, belief systems, and values.

→ not only ~ but also 구문으로, a different spoken language와 differences가 모두 break through의 목적어다. to break through는 that we should break through로 바꿔 쓸 수 있다.

116
정답 ⑤

지문 해석 친구에게 돈을 빌려주면 돈도 친구도 모두 잃는다. 할 수만 있다면 가까운 사람에게는 돈을 빌려주지 않는 것이 최상의 정책이라고 많은 사람들은 말한다. 당신은 돈을 빌릴 수도 빌려줄 수도 있지만 어느 경우든 일이 잘 풀릴 가능성은 없다고 그들은 경고한다. 가까운 사람에게 돈 빌려주는 것이 왜 골칫거리인가에는 몇 가지 이유가 있다. (C) 우선 친척이나 친구에게 빌려주는 돈은 개방적이다. 양측이 채무 상환의 시한이나 이자를 약정하지 않는다. 빌려주는 사람은 돈을 언제 회수할지 알 수 없고 빌리는 측은 언제 갚아야 할지 모른다. (B) 이런 상황은 양측을 불안하게 하고 어떤 기대도 못 하게 한다. 이런 불확실성으로 채무자는 채권자가 상환을 기대하고 있다는 점을 걱정하고 채권자는 언제 상환이 이뤄지는지를 걱정하게 돼 스트레스를 유발하는 데 어떤 일이 있어도 이런 상황은 막아야 한다. (A) 그럼에도 불구하고 가족이나 친구에게 돈을 빌려줘야 한다면 빚을 갚을 시한과 일정을 제시하라. 시한이라 함은 빚을 완전하게 갚을 데드라인을 말하고 일정이라 함은 매달 분할 상환할 가이드라인을 말한다.

글의 소재 가까운 사람과의 금전 거래

주요 어휘 work out well 일이 잘 풀리다, open-ended 제약을 두지 않는, 개방적인, timeline 시한, in limbo =unstable, 불안정한

글의 흐름 ⊙ 가까운 사람 간의 돈거래는 가급적 피하라는 것이 이 글의 요지이다. 주제문은 'Many people say the best policy is not to lend any money to those close to you if you can help it.'이고, 두괄식 구조이다.

구조 분석 ⊙ The uncertainty can lead to stress as the borrower may worry that the lender expects payment and the lender worries about when he or she will be repaid, a <u>situation</u> that should be avoided at any cost.

→ a situation 이하는 앞 문장 전체와 동격이다. he or she는 the lender를 말한다.

정답 해설 주어진 글에서 가까운 사람과의 돈거래가 바람직하

정답 해설 주어진 글에서 비언어적 소통이나 신념 체계, 가치관을 언급하고 있다. 그런데 (A)에서 다시 '신념과 가치관의 차이'를 되풀이해서 언급하는 것은 어색하므로 (A)는 주어진 글 다음에 올 수 없다. (C)에서 특정 몸짓을 모르면 오해를 부른다고 했으므로 다음에는 그 구체적인 사례가 나오는 (B)로 이어지는 것이 논리적이고, 그런 다음 또 다른 극복 대상인 신념 체계와 가치관의 차이를 말하는 (A)로 넘어가는 것이 적절하다. 따라서 주어진 글 다음의 순서는 (C) - (B) - (A)가 알맞다.

지 않은 데는 몇 가지 이유가 있다고 했으므로 그 이유가 처음으로 언급되는 (C)가 먼저 오는 것이 자연스럽다. (A)는 그 이유가 아닌 돈을 빌려줄 때 주의할 점을 언급하기 때문에 주어진 글에 이어지기에는 무리가 있고, (B)는 '이것(This)이 양측을 불안하게 한다.'에서 이것(This)이 받을 말이 주어진 글에 없기 때문에 그 다음에 올 수 없다. (C)에서 돈을 빌린 사람이나 빌려준 사람이나 모두 갚을 계획이 없다고 했으므로 '이런(This) 상황이 양측을 불안하게 한다'라는 (B)로 이어지는 것이 자연스럽다. 따라서 정답은 (C) - (B) - (A)이다.

117 정답 ⑤

[지문 해석] 말과 이미지가 그들이 표현하도록 의도된 바를 좀처럼 표현하지 못한다는 것은 음악에만 한정되지 않는 일반적인 현상이다. 그릇된, 또는 의도하지 않은 의미를 전하거나 의도된 보다 섬세한 색조를 표현되지 않은 상태로 남겨 놓음으로써 그들은 그들이 표현하려는 경험을 왜곡한다.
(C) 그러나 음악의 경우 경험과 표현의 문제는 너무도 절박하고 구체적이어서 민속음악학자 Charles Seeger 같은 이론가들은 말이 음악적 경험을 어느 정도까지 표현할 수 있는지에 대해 의구심을 나타내왔다.
(B) 말과 합리적 사유와 음악적 경험 사이에는 기본적으로 불일치가 존재하며 그 불일치는 말과 음악적 인식 사이의 상이한 논리적 구조 때문이라는 점을 들어 이론가들은 그런 주장을 해왔다.
(A) 그리고 그런 의구심을 가지고 있는 것은 이론가뿐만이 아니다. 콘서트에 가는 사람들은 종종 그들이 음악 작품을 경험하는 방식이 프로그램 해설지에 소개되는 방식과 일치하는 점이 없어 언짢아하곤 한다. 해설서는 흔히 광역 음 체계의 미학적 중요성에 주안점을 두는데 대부분 청중들의 귀에는 그런 음 체계가 들리지 않기 때문이다.

[글의 소재] 음악적 표현과 언어적 표현의 다른 점

[주요 어휘] confine 제한하다, distort 왜곡하다, ethnomusicologist 민속음악학자, incompatibility 불일치, distinct 다른, theorist 이론가, dwell on 숙고하다, 주안점을 두다, aesthetic 미학적

[글의 흐름] 꺾이는 (C) 문장이 주제문이다. 주어진 글에 나타난 통념-음악과 언어적 표현의 공통점-이 역접의 연결사와 함께 깨지면서 필자의 주장-음악적 표현의 독특함-이 제시된다. 이하 문장은 이를 뒷받침하는 부연 진술이다.

[구조 분석] ⊙ But in the case of music the problem of experience and its representation is so pressing and so specific that some theorists ~
→ so ~ that 용법이다. so 형용사나 부사 that S V=너무 ~해서 ~하다.

⊙ And it is not only theorists who have such doubts.
→ it ~ that 강조 구문인데 강조 대상이 사람이기 때문에 that 대신 who를 썼다.

[정답 해설] 먼저 주어진 글에는 (A)의 such doubts를 받을 말이 없기 때문에 (A)는 머리로 올 수 없다. (B)의 they(=사람) 주어진 글의 they(words and images)이 아닌 것이 분명하기 때문에 이 또한 머리로 올 수 없다. 따라서 머리로 올 수 있는 것은 (C)뿐이다. 그리고 (B)의 they는 내용상 학자임이 분명하므로 청중을 논하는 (A) 뒤에 이어질 수 없다. 따라서 글의 순서는 ⑤의 (C) - (B) - (A)이다.

118 정답 ④

[지문 해석] 최신의 연구는 민족성에 대한 더 큰 귀속의식이 더 큰 자존심과 자아정체성, 학교 관련 활동 등 다수의 긍정적인 성과와 관련됐음을 보여주었다.
(C) 예를 들어, 아프리카계 학생들을 대상으로 한 연구에서 N. Gonzales와 A. Cauce는 민족적 자부심이 남녀 학생이 잠재적 데이트 파트너로서 느끼는 자신감이나 남학생의 평균 점수와 긍정적으로 관련이 있음을 발견했다. 미국의 흑인을 논하면서 W. Cross Jr.는 강한 민족적 정체성이 한 사람의 사회적 세계관을 덜 비인간적인 것으로 만들도록 걸러내는 보호 기능을 수행한다고 본다.
(A) 그런 보호는 인종차별이 존재하고 또 모든 흑인에게 영향을 미친다는 것, 부정적 결과는 인종차별적 시스템 때문이지 자신 때문이 아니라는 것, 그리고 차별에 대처하기 위해 다양한 전략(물러남, 주장, 회피, 수동적임)을 쓸 수 있다는 것을 인정하는 데서 나온다.
(B) 강한 정체성이 수행할 수 있는 다른 기능에는 목적의식, 의의, 연대감 등을 제공하는 것이 있고 이런 것들은 종종 흑인 사회의 성취를 기리는 식으로 표현된다.

[글의 소재] 민족적 귀속의식의 순기능

[주요 어휘] contemporary 현대의, 최근의, identification 동일시, 귀속의식, ethnicity 민족성, a host of 다수의, self-esteem 자존심, ego-identity 자아정체성, withdrawal 물러남, assertion 주장, avoidance 회피, passivity 수동적임, affiliation 유대감, filter 여과하다, 거르다, dehumanize 비인간화하다

[글의 흐름] ⊙ 주제문은 'Contemporary research has shown that ~ including greater self-esteem, ego-identity, and school involvement.'이며 일반 진술(주제문)이 먼저 주어지고 예시의 구체 진술이 이를 뒷받침하는 두괄식 구조다.

[구조 분석] ⊙ W. Cross Jr., discussing blacks in the United States, views a strong ethnic identity as serving the protective function of filtering one's social worldview so as to make it less dehumanizing.

→ view A as B 구문으로 A를 B로 여기다의 뜻이다. of는 function과 'filtering ~'를 동격으로 연결해주는 동격의 of다.

[정답 해설] 주어진 글에서 언급되는 민족적 귀속의식의 긍정적 성과가 (C)에서 미국 내 흑인 사회의 구체적인 예로 제시되고, (C)에서 언급되는 긍정적 '보호 기능'의 뿌리가 (A)로 넘어가서 밝혀진 다음, 민족적 귀속의식이 수행하는 다른 긍정적 기능들이 언급되는 (B)로 마무리되는 것이 자연스럽다. 기술적인 면에서 (A)의 'the protection'의 the는 대표단수가 아니므로 반드시 지칭 대상이 있어야 하는데 주어진 글에는 이에 대한 언급이 없으므로 주어진 글 다음에 올 수 없고 protective function이 언급되는 (C) 뒤에 와야 한다. (B)의 'other functions' 역시 주어진 글에 function에 대한 언급이 없으므로 머리로 올 수 없고 갈 곳은 (A) 뒤뿐이다. 따라서 정답은 ④ (C) - (A) - (B)이다.

119
[정답 ⑤]

[지문 해석] 한 사람이 마음대로 사용할 수 있는 주의력을 양으로 나타내는 데 성공한 사람은 아무도 없다. 최근 주의력의 한계는 종종 한 사람이 주어진 시간에 처리할 수 있는 정보의 비트 단위로 표현되고 있다.

(C) 하지만 비트의 정의가 분명하지 않다. 또, 경험이 쌓이면 단일 형태(게슈탈트) 안에 있는 여러 개의 정보 비트를 덩어리로 묶어 그것을 하나의 비트처럼 처리하는 게 가능하다는 것이 1950년대 초기 정보 처리 연구 단계부터 분명해졌다.

(B) 예를 들어 실제 게임에서 가져온, 말들이 있는 기보를 체스 초보자에게 보여주고 몇 초 후 말들의 위치를 다른 체스판에 복기하라고 요청받는다면 말들이 있었던 자리를 기억할 수 있는 사람은 극히 일부에 불과할 것이다.

(A) 그러나 노련한 플레이어들은 큰 어려움 없이 각각 말들을 정확히 원래 위치에 갖다 놓는데 이는 그들의 주의력 지속 기간이 길어서가 아니라 경험을 통해 그들이 여러 개의 말들이 있어야 할 자리들을 하나의 단위, 즉 단일 정보 비트로 인식하는 법을 익혔기 때문이다.

[글의 소재] 주의력을 양으로 측정하는 어려움

[주요 어휘] quantify 양을 측정하다, at one's disposal 마음대로 사용할 수 있는, in terms of ~ 단위로, novice 초보자, chunk 덩어리로 묶다, Gestalt 형태, 게슈탈트

[글의 흐름] ⊙ 주의력을 양으로 측정하는 일의 어려움을 체스 선수들의 복기 능력을 예로 들어 설명하고 있다. 주제문은 'No one has successfully quantified the amount of attention that a person has at his or her disposal.'이고 두괄식 구조다.

[구조 분석] ⊙ but because with experience they have learned to recognize likely positions, involving many

pieces, as one unit, a single bit of information.

→ recognize A as B=A를 B로 인식하다 구문이다. involving ~은 positions을 꾸며주는 현재분사고 unit와 a single bit of information은 동격이다.

⊙ it is not clear what counts as a bit.

→ it는 가주어, 진주어는 의문사절 'what ~ a bit.'이고 count는 자동사로 '~로 간주되다'(be considered)의 뜻이다.

[정답 해설] 주어진 글에서 최근 주의력 양으로 측정하려는 시도가 이뤄져 왔으나 이런 시도가 한계가 있음을 먼저 지적하고 (C), 체스 플레이어 초심자(B)와 숙련자(A)를 예로 들어 설명하는 글의 흐름이 가장 자연스럽다. 기술적으로 (A)는 느닷없이 Expert players가 언급되므로 주어진 글에 연결될 수 없고 체스 플레이어가 처음 언급되는 (B) 다음에 와야 한다. (B)에서 언급되는 체스 플레이어 역시 주의력 계량 시도를 언급하는 주어진 글 다음에 이어지기에는 무리가 있다. 주어진 글 다음에 올 수 있는 것은 측정 시도의 한계를 지적한 (C)뿐이다. 따라서 올바른 글의 순서는 ⑤ (C) - (B) - (A)이다.

120
[정답 ③]

[지문 해석] 우리가 속한 집단 내에서 다수의 위치를 차지하기 위한 노력은 그 집단이 소수일 경우에도 분명하다. 많은 부서들이 영향력을 행사하려고 다투는 복잡한 기업 조직을 생각해 보라.

(B) 최고 경영층은 권한을 쥐기 때문에 당연히 주도적으로 이끈다. 조직 내 하위 집단들은 각 부서 내에서는 상당한 영향력을 가지지만 실세 즉 전체를 총괄하는 임원 명단에서는 당연히 제외된다.

(C) 하지만 외곽부서에 속하는 직원들은 자기 부서의 지도부에 합류하려고, 즉 '소수 속의 다수'에 속하려고 노력한다. 모든 중간 관리자는 조직의 장이 되어 그 직이 주는 권력과 위엄을 맛보면 어떨까 하고 한 번 이상은 생각해봤을 것이 확실하다.

(A) 주변부서의 구성원들은 조직 내에서 위치를 차지해 부서의 지도부에 합류하고 궁극적으로 조직의 방향을 좌지우지하려고 온갖 공작을 편다. 그런 다음에 최고에로의 이동이 가능해지거나 적어도 상상이라도 할 수 있다.

[글의 소재] 하위 그룹의 주류 합류 노력

[주요 어휘] strive 분투 노력하다, faction 당파, 부서, vie 경쟁하다, by definition 당연히, even so 하지만, it's a safe bet that~ ~는 확실하다, feasible 실행 가능한

[글의 흐름] 첫 문장 'Striving to attain majority status in the group we belong to is evident even when the group is itself in the minority.'가 주제문인 두괄식 구조다.

[구조 분석] ⊙ but they may well be removed from the power brokers, the executives who hold overall control.

→ may well은 '당연히 ~하다'라는 의미의 숙어이고 the power brokers와 the executives는 동격이다.

⊙ ~ every middle manager has thought about what it would be like to be the boss and enjoy the power and prestige that go with the job—and probably more than once.

→ 'what ~once'는 전치사 about의 목적어가 되는 명사절로서 의문사(what) S + V의 어순을 취하고 있다. enjoy는 to be와 병렬구조를 이루고 있다.

정답 해설 먼저 (C)는 '하지만 외곽부서 직원은 자기 부서의 지도부에 합류하려고 노력한다'라는 내용이므로 주어진 글에 이어지기에는 논리적 비약이 따르고, '하위 부서들이 회사의 실세 그룹에서 제외된다는 (B)에 이어지는 것이 자연스럽다(대조의 연결사 Even so를 주목하라). (B)-(C). 주변부서 직원들의 지도부 합류 노력을 다루는 (A)는 내용상 (C)의 부연 진술이므로 (C) 다음에 와야 한다. 따라서 정답은 ③의 (B) - (C) - (A)이다.

121 {정답 ③}

지문 해석 많은 경우에 특정 자극에 대한 동물의 반응은 타고난다, 즉 선천적이다. 그러나 많은 다른 경우에 그 동물은 자신의 지식에 틈을 가지고 태어난다. 그 동물은 본능의 모든 패턴을 갖추고 태어나지만 특정 행동을 유발하는 자극에 대한 정보는 빠질 수 있다.

(B) 이런 정보가 초기 중요한 시기에 채워질 때 그 과정은 각인이라 불린다. 많은 종의 어린 새나 포유류가 그들의 다음 반응을 유발할 자극에 대해 불충분한 지식을 가지고 세상에 온다.

(C) 예를 들면 마치 거위 새끼가 "나는 따라야 할 본능이 있다는 걸 알아. 난 한 줄로 서야 되고 그 자극이 무엇인지도 알아. 바로 엄마가 출발할 때야. 근데 엄마가 어떻게 생겼지?"라고 말하려는 것과 같다. 이 정보를 거위 새끼는 초기 중요한 시기에 처음으로 움직이는 물체를 보면서 얻는다.

(A) 이 물체는 보통 그의 실제 어미이지만 고아 거위 새끼들이 오스트리아 생태학자인 로렌츠씨의 손에 키워졌을 때 그들은 그를 자기들의 '어미'로 여겼다. 그들은 다른 거위들은 아랑곳하지 않고 로렌츠가 가는 곳 어디든 힘차게 한 줄로 따라다녔다. 그들은 그를 각인한 것이다.

글의 소재 동물의 각인(imprinting)

주요 어휘 releaser 사람이나 동물에게 특정 행동을 유발시키는 자극, innate 타고난, gosling 거위 새끼, ethologist 생태학자, energetically 힘차게, imprint 인쇄하다, 각인하다, critical 매우 중요한

글의 흐름 주제문은 'Many species of young birds and mammals enter the world with incomplete knowledge

about the stimuli that will release their following response.'으로 예시의 연결사 for example이 나오기 바로 전, 즉 구체 진술이 시작되기 바로 전 문장이다.

구조 분석 ⊙ They had imprinted on him.

→ 그들이 이미 어미를 각인한 상태이므로 기준 시제(과거)보다 한 시제 빠른 과거완료를 썼다.

⊙ It's as if a gosling, for example, were to say,

→ as if 다음에는 보통 가정법 구문이 오기 때문에 is나 was가 아닌 were를 썼다(가정법 과거). 여기서 be to~는 intend to ~와 같이 '~하려 하다'의 뜻이다.

정답 해설 (B)는 글의 주제부인 동물의 각인에 대한 설명, 즉 일반 진술의 일부이므로 주어진 글 다음에 와야 한다. 'this information'은 주어진 글의 'some information'을 지칭하는 것으로 보는 것이 자연스럽다. (A)와 (C)는 거위 새끼를 예를 들어 설명하는 구체 진술 부분인데 구체 진술에서는 예시의 연결사(for example)가 있는 부분이 앞에 오기 때문에 (C)-(A) 순으로 이어져야 한다. 따라서 정답은 ③의 (B) - (C) - (A)이다.

122 {정답 ①}

지문 해석 미디어는 정보의 선택, 전송, 수용을 위해 사용되는 모든 사회적 기술적 절차나 장치다. 모든 문명은 영토나 거주 단위, 옷과 패션, 언어, 시계와 달력, 춤이나 다른 의식과 같은 사회적 요소를 통해 전달되는 다양한 형태의 미디어를 발전시켜 왔다.

(A) 그러나 현대 세계에서 이 같은 형태의 미디어들은 신문이나 라디오, 텔레비전에 의해 완전히 무색해졌다. 미디어를 논할 때 사회과학자들은 후자(신문 라디오 TV)에 초점 맞추는 경향이 있지만 우리는 이 적용을 확대해 다른 형태의 미디어가 어떻게 사회생활의 기본 특질로 간주될 수 있는지 보여줄 수 있다.

(C) 미디어가 시대별로 또 문화권별로 어떻게 다른지 검토하는 것은 매우 중요하다. 모든 역사적 시기는 한 미디어가 다른 미디어를 지배하는 특징이 있고 이런 지배는 사회생활의 다른 영역에 영향을 미친다.

(B) 권력을 열망하는 집단은 미디어를 통해 영향력과 합법성을 추구한다. 게다가 엄선된 미디어는 지배 체제의 논리에 따라 일상생활과 정치력에 대한 공적 묘사를 선전한다.

글의 소재 미디어의 다양한 종류와 역할

주요 어휘 procedure 절차, transmission 전송, territory 영토, dwelling 거주, ritual 의식, 제례, overshadow 무색케 하다, 그늘지게 하다, application 적용, 응용, leverage 힘, 영향력, legitimacy 합법성, dominant 지배적인, institution 제도, 체제, epoch 시기, 시대

글의 흐름 주제문은 'we could expand this application to show how other types of media may be regarded as basic features of social life.'이다. 양보절(Although~)에 의해 글의 흐름이 꺾이고 사회 통념이 깨지면서 필자의 주장(주제문)이 제시되는 구조이다.

구조 분석 ⊙ these types of media have been overshadowed by newspapers, radio, and television. Although social scientists tend to focus on the latter when discussing media, we could expand this application to show how other types of media may be regarded as basic features of social life.

→ the latter는 'newspapers, radio, and television'을 가리키고 this application은 'to focus on the latter'를 지칭한다, to 부정사의 부사적 용법 중 결과로 보는 것이 자연스럽다.

정답 해설 먼저 지시사가 들어있는 단락을 주목하라. (A)의 these types of media가 받을 수 있는 말은 주어진 글의 various types of media뿐이다. 또 (A) 둘째 문장의 'the latter(=newspapers ~ television)'는 주어진 글의 'territory ~ other rituals.(=the former)'을 전제로 했을 때 성립하는 말이기 때문에 (A)가 머리로 와야 한다. 또, (B)의 Groups aspiring to power는 내용상 the dominance affects other areas of social life에 이어지는 것이 자연스럽다. 따라서 글의 순서는 (A) - (C) - (B)이다.

123
정답 ②

지문 해석 학교에서 읽는 글의 상당수가 정보 전달의 목적을 갖는데 거기서 필자는 토론 주제에 대해 일반적으로 알려지거나 믿어지는 바를 독자에게 말한다. 따라서 개인적인 관점을 전달하려는 시도는 아예 없거나 거의 없다. 사실 정보 전달 글의 필자는 외연적 언어, 즉 감정적 호소력이 거의 또는 전혀 없는 언어를 사용함으로써 개인적 견해를 드러내기를 피하려고 각별히 노력한다.

(B) 필자의 목적이 정보 전달에 있을 경우 당신은 실례를 들고, 사실을 전달하고, 연구 조사를 인용하는 부연 진술 구문과 맞닥뜨리게 된다. 이 부연 진술이 이유의 형태를 띤다면 그 이유는 필자가 아닌 다른 사람에 기인할 것이다(이유가 주관적이 아니고 객관적이라는 의미).

(A) 그러나 학문적 글쓰기를 하는 사람조차도 때로는 설득을 목적으로 하는 글을 쓴다. 그들은 독자가 공감하거나 적어도 심각하게 생각해 보기를 원하는 견해를 전달하려 한다.

(C) 필자의 목적이 설득일 경우, 당신은 독자가 왜 필자와 같은 생각을 공유해야 하는지 그 이유를 설명하는 많은 부연 진술을 보게 된다. 또 당신은 독자의 감정선을 건드려 필자의 견해에 공감하도록 설득하는 여러 개인적 일화나 이야기를 만나게 된다.

글의 소재 정보 전달 글과 설득 글

주요 어휘 go out of one's way to ~하려고 각별히 노력하다, denotative language 외연적 언어, emotional punch 감정적 호소력, supporting details 글의 뒷받침 진술, 부연 진술

글의 흐름 ⊙ 글의 두 부류 즉, 정보 전달 목적의 글과 설득 목적의 글의 일반적 성격을 소개하는 병렬식 구조의 글이다. 'Much of what you read in school will have an informative purpose where the writer'g goal is to tell readers what's generally known or believed about the topic under discussion'과 'However, even academic writers sometimes write with a persuasive purpose' 두 문장에 주제가 들어있다.

구조 분석 ⊙ They convey an opinion that they want readers to share or at least seriously consider.

→ 관계대명사 구문으로 선행사 opinion은 share와 consider의 공동 목적어다.

⊙ You may also find personal anecdotes, or stories, that are meant to touch readers' emotions and thereby persuade them to share the author's point of view.

→ that are meant to touch의 to touch와 (to) persuade가 병렬 구조이다.

정답 해설 주어진 문장이 정보 전달 목적의 글에 대해 말하고 있으므로 이를 부연 설명하는 (B)가 뒤이어 나와야 하고 정보 전달과 대(對)가 되는 설득 목적의 글인 (A)로 넘어간 다음 - 전환의 연결사 however를 주의하라. - 설득 목적의 글에 관한 뒷받침 진술이 나오는 (C)로 이어지는 것이 논리적으로 타당하다.

124
정답 ②

지문 해석 공룡을 멸종 위기로부터 살려내는 것은 극도로 어렵다. 하지만, 몇몇 과학자들은 복원을 위한 단서를 얻는 데 성공적으로 접근한 것으로 전해졌다.

(B) 그 한 접근은 현대의 DNA로부터 거슬러 올라가면서 작업하는 것이다. 과학자들이 유전학을 좀 더 잘 이해함에 따라, 시간의 격차를 메우고 DNA를 재배열해 새로운 생명체를 탄생시키는 데 필요한 것을 마침내 갖게 될 가능성이 커졌다. 그것이 꼭 공룡이 아닐 수도 있지만 공룡이 가장 제격이다.

(A) 오늘날의 공룡에 가장 가까운 친척은 새다. 그들은 1억5천만 년 전에 처음 출현해 많은 다른 종들이 멸종한 기간에도 어떻게든 생존해왔다. 새의 유전자를 역설계해 그들의 머나먼 조상과 같은 모습을 재현하는 게 가능하다고 과학자들은 믿는다.

(C) 2006년에 과학자들은 닭의 배아에서 미발달 치아가 날 수 있음을 발견했다. 유전자를 조작하면 새에게서 부리가 아닌 턱이나 '그들의 비조류 조상,' 즉 공룡의 발과 유사한 발이 나게 할 수 있다. 이 방법을 쓰면 언젠가 공룡 같은 생물체를 탄생시킬 수 있는 것이다.

글의 소재 공룡 복제

주요 어휘 extinction 멸종, genetics 유전학, rearrange 재배열하다, look the part 제격이다, reverse engineer 역설계하다, 분해하여 모방하다, prehistoric 선사의, embryo 배아, rudimentary 초보의, 미발달의, modification 수정, 조작, non-avian 조류가 아닌

글의 흐름 ⊙ 주제문은 'A few scientists, however, have reportedly made successful approaches to finding out clues.'이다. 주제문에서 과학자들이 얻은 단서가 무엇인지 구체적인 뒷받침 진술을 통해 부연되는 두괄식의 연역적 구조이다.

구조 분석 ⊙ Scientists believe reverse engineering birds to look like their prehistoric ancestors is a possibility.

→ S + V (that) S + V + C 구문으로, 밑줄 친 부분이 목적어절의 S이다.

⊙ Genetic modification can be used to make birds develop jaws instead of beaks and feet similar to those of their non-avian ancestors.

→ those는 feet를 가리킨다.

정답 해설 주어진 문장이 '공룡 복제의 성공적인 접근법'으로 끝났으므로 그 접근의 한 예(One such approach)를 언급한 (B)가 다음에 오는 것이 자연스럽다. (B)에서 현재 생존 동물의 DNA를 역추적해 공룡을 복제한다고 했으므로 살아있는 동물 중 공룡의 가장 가까운 친척인 새를 말한 (A)로 넘어가는 것이 적절하고, 새를 가지고 공룡을 복원하는 구체적인 방법이 제시된 (C)로 마무리되는 것이 논리적이다.

125

지문 해석 데이빗 (브루스) 라이머의 삶은 성 정체성의 복잡성을 보여주는 비극적이고도 의도치 않은 실험극이었다. 할례 도중 소년의 생식기가 불에 타버리자 그의 부모는 그를 저명한 심리학자이자 성 정체성 전문가인 존 머니씨에게 데려갔다. 그는 라이머 부모에게 그를 여자로 키울 것을 권했다.

(C) 그리하여 그 소년은 브렌다라는 이름으로 개명돼 여자의 삶을 살기 시작했다. 이 사내애는 이미 여자로서의 정체성을 보여줬다고 머니씨는 이내 보고했지만 별도의 후속 보고에 의하면 이후 진행과정은 사뭇 다른 면모를 보였다.

(B) 열네 살 무렵이 될 때까지 브루스는 2년에 걸친 에스트로겐 치료에도 불구하고 아직도 자신이 여자가 아닌 남자인 꿈을 꿨다. 이런 꿈에 시달린 나머지 그는 계속 여자로 살기를 거부했다.

(A) 바로 이 시점에 부모가 소년에게 그의 지난 치료 기록에 대해 알려줬다. 이에 대해 라이머는 이름을 데이비드로 고치고 다시 남자로 사는 것으로 응수했다. 그는 결혼하고 아내의 애를

글의 소재 성 정체성에 시달린 David (Bruce) Reimer의 삶

주요 어휘 shed light on 비추다, 밝히다, genital 생식기, circumcision 할례, sexual identity 성 정체성, follow-up 후속 조치, 후속 처방, plague 역병, 시달리게 하다, rage 분노, respond by ~ing ~로 응수하다, take one's own life 자살하다

글의 흐름 ⊙ 주제문은 'David (Bruce) Reimer's life was a tragic and unintentional experiment that shed light on the complexity of gender identity.'로 두괄식 구조이다.

구조 분석 ⊙ It was at this point that his parents informed the boy of his medical history.

→ It that 강조 구문으로 at this point를 강조한다. 또 inform A of B는 'A에게 B를 알리다.'는 뜻이다.

정답 해설 주인공이 성 정체성으로 혼란을 겪다가 비극적으로 삶을 마감했다는 첫 문장을 상기하면서 이 글을 읽으면 전체적인 이해에 도움이 된다. 주어진 글이 의사가 라이머를 여자로 키울 것을 권하는 것으로 끝나므로 여자로서의 새 삶을 시작하는 내용인 (C)가 이어져야 한다. (C)에서 주인공이 여성으로 보고됐음에도 다른 면모를 보였다고 했으므로 그 다른 면모, 즉 여자임도 불구하고 계속 남자에 대한 꿈을 꾼다는 내용의 (B)가 그다음에 온 다음, 뒤바뀐 성 때문에 악몽에 시달리다가 마침내 여자를 포기하고 다시 남자로 되돌아오는 (A)로 이어지는 것이 논리적이다.

13. 요약문 완성

정답

126 ④	127 ④	128 ③	129 ③	130 ④
131 ②	132 ②	133 ③	134 ①	135 ③
136 ③	137 ②	138 ②	139 ④	140 ③
141 ②				

126

정답 ④

[지문 해석] 1895년 6월 5일 콜로라도 덴버에 사는 제임스 스미스씨는 크게 낙상을 당했다. 혹자는 그가 왼쪽 넓적다리를 다쳤다고 말하고 혹자는 오른쪽 엉덩이라고 말한다. 넉넉지 않은 형편에 스미스는 상처를 그럭저럭 버텨보려 했지만 3주가 지나도 차도가 없자 포기하고 의사의 도움을 청했다. 1895년까지만 해도 환자가 의사를 집으로 부를 수 있었고 비용은 2달러에서 5달러 선이었다. 만약 의사가 1마일 이상을 움직일 경우는 1마일을 초과할 때마다 1달러를, 밤일 경우에는 2달러를 추가 지불해야 했다. 어떤 의사들은 미터기 같은 기구를 마차 바퀴에 달아 왕진 거리를 측정하기도 했다.

[글의 소재] 19세기 말 미국의 민간 의료와 왕진비

[주요 어휘] have a great fall 크게 낙상하다, man of modest means 재산이 넉넉지 않은 사람, outlast ~보다 오래가다, ~를 버티다, buggy 이륜마차, rate 요율

[구조 분석] ⊙ Being a young man of modest means, Smith tried to outlast the pain.

→ 분사 구문으로, 축약 전 문장은 'Since(As) he was a man of modest means, Smith tried to outlast the pain.'이다.

[정답 해설] 이 글은 1895년경 미국인들이 왕진을 온 의사에게 지불한 비용을 설명하고 있다. 이 문제는 이 글에 언급된 왕진비 요율에 따라 환자가 자정 무렵에 3마일을 왕진 온 의사에게 최대 몇 달러까지 지불해야 하는가를 묻고 있다. 왕진비 요율은 기본 왕진 거리인 1마일까지는 2~5달러, 이후 추가 1마일 당 1달러(야간에는 2달러)이다. 그러므로 지불해야 할 최대 비용은 '5달러(기본료 중 최고액) + [2마일(추가 마일) × 2달러(야간 시 마일당 추가 요금)] = 9달러'이 된다. 따라서 정답은 ④이다.

127

정답 ④

[지문 해석] 간단히 말해 가스라이팅은 사람으로 하여금 자기 자신의 믿음, 사상, 지각을 의심하게 만드는 일종의 세뇌다. 그것은 자아도취자들이 주변 사람들을 통제하기 위해 사용해 크게 성공하기도 하는 방법이다. 그러나 가스라이팅은 다른 사람에게 자신의 기본적인 핵심 신념을 버리고 가스라이터의 신념으로 바꿀 것을 요구하기 때문에 성공하기가 다소 어렵다. 대부분의 사람들이 사전에 적절히 조건 지어진 경우라면 모를까 자신의 신념을 맹렬히 지키고 거세게 저항한다. 따라서 가스라이팅이 효과를 보려면 서서히 시작해, 새로운 저항의 장애물이 극복되는 정도에 따라 시간을 두고 점차 강도를 늘려나가야 한다. 가스라이터는 당신이 그르고 그들이 옳다는 메시지를 일관성 있게 주기적으로 보내야 한다. 누군가를 성공적으로 가스라이트하기 위해서 자아도취자는 상대를 조심스럽게 선택해 일정 기간 길들인 다음 그를 조종하는 데 필요한 기법을 실제로 활용한다.

↓

성공적인 가스라이터는 보통 가스라이팅이 이뤄지는 속도를 조급해하지 않고, 전달하는 메시지에 일관성이 있으며 상대를 조심스럽게 선택한다.

[글의 소재] Gaslighting

[주요 어휘] gaslighting 마음에 스스로에 대한 의심을 불러일으켜 현실감과 판단력을 잃게 만듦으로써 그 사람을 정신적으로 황폐화시키고 그 사람에게 지배력을 행사하여 결국 그 사람을 파국으로 몰아가는 것을 의미하는 심리학 용어, incrementally 증가하여, reinforce 강화하다, groom 길들이다, initiate 착수하다, 개시하다, agile 재빠른, crafty 술수에 능한

[글의 흐름] ⊙ 도입문 'Simply put, gaslighting is a form of brainwashing that is meant to make one doubt one's own beliefs, thoughts, and perceptions.'이 주제문이고, 뒷받침 진술이 이어지는 연역적 형태의 두괄식 구조이다.

[구조 분석] ⊙ It is a method that narcissists employ with great success ~

→ with great success는 결과적으로 해석하여 '크게 성공하는'의 의미이다.

⊙ Therefore, to be effective, gaslighting usually starts off gradually and grows slowly and incrementally over time as each new hurdle of resistance is in turn overcome.

→ to be effective의 의미상 주어는 gaslighting인데 이 경우 to infinitive의 의미상 주어와 주절의 주어는 반드시 일치해야 한다. 서로 다른 주어를 쓰려면 to infinitive 앞에 'for + S'를 추가해야 한다.

[정답 해설] 이 글의 'Therefore'로 시작되는 문장과 그 다음 문장을 보면 가스라이팅이 효과를 보려면 단계적으로 서서히 진행돼야 하고, 전달하는 메시지에 일관성이 있어야 하며, 상대를 조심스럽게 골라야 한다고 했다. 그러므로 (A)와 (B)에 들어갈 적절한 말은 patient와 cautious이다.

128

지문 해석 개인이 특정 그룹에 속하면 혼자 있을 때와는 종종 다른 반응을 보인다. 사회심리학자 어빙 재니스는 정치전문가들의 집단적 결정 과정을 조사한 적이 있는데 미국 역사에서 주요한 큰 실책은 이렇듯 함께 행동해야 하는 압박감에 기인한다는 것을 알아냈다. 이런 현상을 설명하기 위해 재니스는 '집단 사고(groupthink)'라는 신조어를 만들어냈는데 이는 한 집단의 구성원이, 개별적으로는 그것이 현명하지 않다고 생각하면서도 하나의 결정에 동의하는 과정을 가리킨다. 그때 그들은 왜 자신의 생각을 말하지 않나? 이는 그들이 집단의 일체감을 약화시키고 리더에 도전하는 사람이 되고 싶지 않기 때문이다. 그래서 집단 구성원들은 모든 가능한 대안을 찾고 최선의 방책을 결정하기보다는 자신의 의견을 굽히거나 숨기고 합의에만 열중하는 것이다.

↓

사람들은 '모난 돌이 정 맞는 상황'을 피하고 싶기 때문에 집단적으로 사고하는 경향이 있다.
- ① 손뼉도 마주 쳐야 소리가 난다
- ② 칭찬은 고래도 춤추게 한다
- ③ 모난 돌이 정 맞는다
- ④ 머리는 맞댈수록 좋다
- ⑤ 친구 따라 강남 간다

글의 소재 집단적 사고(groupthink)

주요 어휘 blunder 대실수, fit in 어울리다, speak up 자기 의견을 솔직히 말하다, withhold 억제하다

글의 흐름 ⊙ 주제문은 'Consequently, members of a group often limit or withhold their opinions ~ the best course of action.'으로 미괄식 구조이다.

정답 해설 이 글의 요지는 개인은 집단의 일체감을 약화시키고 리더에 도전하는 사람이 되고 싶지 않기 때문에 대중의 의견에 따른다는 것이다. 그러므로 사람들이 집단 사고를 하는 이유로 '모난 돌이 정 맞는 상황'을 피하고 싶은 마음을 들 수 있다. 따라서 정답은 ③이다.

129

지문 해석 연구 개발 프로젝트가 공공 정책에 영향을 미치는지 여부는 그것의 시기와 분야의 상황에 결정적으로—유일한 것은 아니지만—의존한다. 연구에 대한 정책 결정자들의 수용성이 높고 연구를 수용할 능력이 충분할 때 영향력은 성취하기 쉽다. 수용성이 최소이고 적응 능력이 약할 때 영향력은 얻기가 훨씬 어려워진다. 하지만, 사례들이 우리에게 전하는 것은 이보다 훨씬 복잡하고 희망적이다. 이들 사례 연구로부터 두 가지 주목할 만한 결론이 나온다. 첫 번째 결론은 초기 수용성이 희망적이지 않은 경우에도 연구가 정책 변화를 끌어낼 수 있다는 것이다.

연구자들은 일관성 있고 상황에 합당한 전략에 따라 과업을 수행하고 그 결과를 의사 결정권자나 대중과 소통함으로써 거의 어떤 상황에서도 영향력을 극대화할 수 있다. 두 번째 필연적인 결론은 연구에서나 정책 결정에서 상황은 변한다는 것이다. 연구 프로젝트는 변화하는 상황에 적응할 수 있고 또 그래야 한다. 한편, 연구가 진행되는 도중에 정책 상황이 종종 변하기도 한다. 어떤 경우에는 연구 그 자체가 정책 결정자의 심경에 변화를 일으켜 정책 커뮤니티로 하여금 연구의 가치를 깨닫게 하고 연구자와 정책 결정자 간에 신뢰를 구축해 수용성을 높인 것처럼 보이는 경우도 있다.

↓

연구 개발자들은 보다 소통 원활하고 일관성 있으며 맥락에 입각한 전략에 따라 작업하는 한편 변화하는 정책 환경에 보다 선제적 방식으로 대처해 성공 가능성을 높일 수 있다.

글의 소재 연구 개발의 정책 수용성을 높이는 방법

주요 어휘 receptivity 수용성, adequate 충분한, adaptive 적응의, striking 주목할 만한, emerge 나오다, unpromising 전망이 좋지 않은, coherent 일관성 있는, context-appropriate 상황에 합당한, inescapable 필연적인, surroundings 상황, under way 진행 중인, enhance 높이다

글의 흐름 ⊙ 두 개의 결론이 나오는 부분(The first conclusion is ~, The second inescapable conclusion is~)이 주제문으로 병렬식 구조를 하고 있다.

구조 분석 ⊙ In some cases, research itself seems to have changed policymakers' minds, thereby opening the policy community to the value of research, building trust between researchers and policymakers, and enhancing receptivity.

→ opening과 building, enhancing은 분사구문이며 동시에 병렬구조를 이루고 있다.

정답 해설 본문에 나오는 첫 번째 결론에서 '연구자들은 일관성 있고 상황에 합당한 전략에 따라 과업을 수행하고 그 결과를 의사 결정권자나 대중과 소통함으로써 영향력을 극대화한다'고 했으므로 (A)에는 enhance가 적절하다. 또 두 번째 결론에서 연구나 정책은 늘 변하기 때문에 연구는 변화하는 정책 상황에 잘 적응할 수 있어야 한다고 필자는 말한다. 이는 상황에 유연하게 대처하는 것을 의미하므로 (B)에 들어갈 적절한 말은 malleable이다.

130

지문 해석 다윈 당시 생물학자들은, 진화는 획득 형질의 유전을 통해 이뤄진다는 Jean Baptiste Lamarck의 이론에 대해 이런저런 토론을 벌여오고 있었다. 하지만 라마르크 이론은 옳지 않은 것으로 판명됐다. Darwin-Wallace 이론에 의하면 개

체의 일생동안 어떤 새로운 형질도 획득될 필요가 없다. 다윈 이론의 핵심은 종의 개체 중에는 끊임없이 변종이 발생하는데 그 다양한 개체 가운데 태어난 것들 중 일부만이 생존해서 번식한다. 생존을 위한 투쟁이 있고 그 기간 동안 가장 적합한 개체만이 오래 살아남아 후세에 자기 형질을 전한다는 것이다. 수많은 세대가 흐르는 동안 자연은 주변 환경에 가장 잘 적응하는 개체를 선택한다. 늑대를 예로 들면 먹이가 궁한 계절에는 가장 민첩하고 강한 늑대들이 살아남을 가능성이 가장 크다. 그들이 다른 늑대에 비해 오래 살아 번식하고 자신의 형질을 후손에 전할 가능성이 큰 것이다. 그런 계절을 여러 번 겪다 보면 그 종의 개체들 사이에 민첩함과 강함의 형질이 점점 우세적이 될 것이다.

↓

다윈의 이론에 의하면 좋은 획득 형질을 물려줌으로써가 아니라 <u>주변 환경에 적응 과정</u>을 통해 형질을 선택받게 함으로써 진화한다.

- ① 가능한 우호적인 세력을 불러 모으는
- ② 비우호적인 생활환경과 싸우는
- ③ 초자연적인 힘을 부르는
- ④ 주변 환경에 적응하는
- ⑤ 여러 가지 자연재해를 피하는

[글의 소재] 다윈 진화론

[주요 어휘] characteristic 특징, 형질, variation 변종, adapt 적응하다, trait 특질, 형질, prevalent 우세한

[글의 흐름] 주제문은 'Over countless generations, then, nature "selects" those who can best adapt to their surroundings.'이고 중괄식 구조다. 예시 문장 바로 앞에서 일반 진술이 이뤄지는 경우다.

[구조 분석] ⊙ The essence of Darwin's theory has it that, among the members of a species, there is ~
➡ '~ have it that ~' 구문은 관용적 표현으로 '~에 의하면 ~'으로 해석한다.

⊙ They are therefore more likely than the others to live long enough to reproduce and pass on their traits ~
➡ be likely to(~할 가능성이 크다) 구문에 than the others가 비교를 위해 삽입됐다. enough가 형용사나 부사를 수식할 경우 '형/부 enough to~' 어순을 취한다. pass는 to reproduce와 병렬구조를 이루고 있다.

[정답 해설] 다윈의 진화론에 의하면 종의 진화는 획득 형질을 후손에 물려줌으로써가 아니라 다양한 변종 중에 주변 환경에 성공적으로 적응한 개체만이 살아남아 그의 형질을 후손에 남기는 방식으로 이뤄진다. 따라서 빈칸에 적당한 말은 ④의 '주변 환경에 적응하는'이다. 예시문이 시작하기 전 문장 'Over countless generations, then, nature "selects" those who can best adapt to their surroundings.'에서 단서를 얻는다.

131

[지문 해석] 내가 맞닥뜨린 가장 혁신적인 연구 중 몇몇은 과제지향적인 선수는 연습을 중시하고 그것에 전념하는 반면 자아지향적인 선수는 보다 쉬운 길을 택해 경기에 임하는 경향이 있다고 제안한다. 높은 과제지향성을 가진 사람들은 개인적인 피드백을 구하고 그것을 기술 개발을 위해 사용하는 반면 자아지향도가 높은 사람들은 기량의 질에 관한 피드백에 신경 쓰지 않는다. 그들은 단지 그들이 이겼는지를 알고 싶어 할 뿐이다. 자아지향적 선수들은 그들을 향상시키는 데 사용할 수 있는 정보와 지원이 있어도 학습에는 그다지 관심이 없는 것으로 이해될 수 있다. 설령 실패하는 한이 있어도 그들은 그들의 기량 향상에 도움을 줄 수 있는 정보나 지도를 거절할지 모른다. 과제지향적 선수들은 그들이 받는 피드백을 활용하고 과제나 경기의 몇 분 또는 몇 초라도 그들의 경기력을 향상시켜 줄 정보가 있으면 이를 구준히 처리해 나간다고 연구자들은 주장한다. 그들은 그 시간을 선제적인 과제 중심적인 방식으로 생각하는 데 쓰는 것 같다. 반면, 자아지향적 선수들은 과제 개선을 위해 정보를 처리하거나 학습하는 데는 거의 정신력을 쓰지 않고 자신들이 다른 선수들과 어떻게 비교되는지와 승패의 결과만을 생각한다.

↓

경쟁 상황에서 과제지향적 선수들은 그들의 수행에 대한 피드백에 더 관심이 많은 반면 자아지향적 선수들은 경기의 결과 자체에 더 관심을 두는 경향이 있다.

[글의 소재] 과제지향형 선수와 자아지향형 선수

[주요 어휘] come across 우연히 만나다(1행), ~한 인상을 주다(7행), task-oriented 과제 지향적인, ego-oriented 자아지향적인, proactive 선제적인

[글의 흐름] 주제문은 'Those who have a high task orientation seek personal feedback and use it to develop their skills, ~ if they've won.'이며 다음에는 주제문의 주장에 대한 부연 설명이 이어지는 두괄식 구조다.

[구조 분석] ⊙ Ego-involved athletes might come across as not that interested in learning, even if the information and support is available to help them improve.
➡ come across as는 '~로 이해되다'라는 뜻으로 come across는 자동사로 쓰였고 that는 부사로서 so의 의미다. 또 여기서 as는 전치사로 not와 that 사이에 as의 목적어인 동명사 being이 생략됐다.

⊙ how they compare to others and the consequences of winning or losing ~
➡ compare는 '비교되다'의 뜻으로 자동사로 쓰였다.

[정답 해설] 과제 지향형 선수는 자신의 기량에 대한 주변의 피드백을 적극 활용하고 정보 공유나 학습에 적극적인 반면 자아지향

428 정답 및 해설

형 선수는 이들에 대해 소극적이고 경기의 결과에만 관심을 둔다는 것이 이 글의 요지이므로 빈칸에 알맞은 순서쌍은 ②이다.

132
정답 ②

(지문 해석) 유행 건강법을 믿는 적절한 예가 될 만한 책이라는 친척이 한 명 있다. 그는 샐러드에 자그마치 15가지 재료를 섞어 먹는다. 각종 씨와 채소, 레몬, 올리브오일, 가히 산화방지제 폭탄이라 할 만하다. 자신의 건강식에 자부심이 대단한 그는 종종 "나보다 건강하게 먹는 사람 나와 보라고 해!"라고 떠벌린다. 하지만 그는 운동을 안 한다. 그는 과체중이라 내가 스쿼트를 하라고 권해도 그는 할 수 없다. 거동이 불편하고 힘이 없다. 푸쉬업도 할 수 없다. 그런 그가 스스로를 건강한 삶의 스승이라고 생각한다. 하루는 '아버지가 아직 살아계셨으면 건강에 대해 배운 것을 모두 가르쳐 드릴 텐데' 하는 말을 한 적도 있다.
운동이 심장병의 위험을 거의 절반이나 낮춘다는 것을 아는가? 이외에도 운동은 몇 가지 예만 들어도 암, 당뇨, 우울증, 비만 예방에 좋다. 이 말은 다이어트를 과소평가하려고 하는 게 아니다. 다이어트는 중요하다. 그러나 다이어트가 할 수 있는 것에는 한계가 있다. 다이어트는 이미 건강 '신(神)'의 단계에 이르렀다. 그 '신'이 당신 편인데 왜 굳이 다른 건강 수단 이를테면 운동 같은 것을 하려 드는가? 당신은 이미 보호받는 몸인데. 음식만 올바르게 먹으면 우리는 영생할 수 있다. 이는 내 친척의 말이다. 근데 솔직히 나는 운동 안 하고 그가 과연 오래 활기차게 살 수 있을지 모르겠다(그가 탁월한 유전자를 가졌다면 모를까).

⬇

필자는 운동하기를 거부하고 자기들은 훌륭한 식단을 가져서 괜찮다고 생각하는 사람들을 경고한다.

(글의 소재) 다이어트

(주요 어휘) fad 유행, antioxidant 산화방지제, brag 자랑하다, mobility issue 거동하는 데 문제가 있음, 즉 거동이 불편함, just to name a few 몇 가지 예만 들어도

(글의 흐름) ⊙ 친척 한 명의 예를 들어 다이어트 과신 풍조에 일침을 가하는 글로 주제문은 'But there are limits to what diet can do.'이다. 중괄식 구조로 볼 수 있다.

(구조 분석) ⊙ And if you think "god" is on your side, then why do the other things that you know are healthful—like exercise? You feel you're covered!

➡ why (do you) do the other things에서 do you가 생략됐다. the other things that you know are healthful에서 you know는 삽입절이다. 이 두 문장은 빈정거리는(sarcastic) 반어적(ironic) 말투이다.

(정답 해설) 이 글은 운동은 안 하면서도 자신의 다이어트가 훌륭하기 때문에 문제가 없다고 생각하는 사람인 친척을 예로 들어 비판한 내용이다. 따라서 글의 요지인 문장의 빈칸 (A)와

(B)에는 exercise와 superior diet가 들어가야 맞다.

133
정답 ③

(지문 해석) 국제 정부를 희망하는 이유는 두 가지인데 첫째는 전쟁의 방지이고 둘째는 다른 나라 다른 민족 사이에서 지켜지는 것과 같은 경제 정의를 구현하는 일이다. 이 중에 전쟁 방지가 더 중요한데 그 이유는 전쟁이 불의보다 해롭기 때문이기도 하고, 보다 중대한 불의가 문명국에 저질러지는 경우는 전쟁의 결과로 인한 경우가 아니면 거의 없기 때문이기도 하다. 가령 예를 들어 완벽한 평화의 시기라면, 오스트리아에서 그랬듯이 국민의 생계 수단을 빼앗고 그와 동시에 국민들의 이민을 불허하는 그런 경우는 흔치 않을 것이다. 평화가 유지될 수 있다면 어느 정도의 정의가 필연적으로 남아있을 가능성이 크다. 설사 상당한 불의가 남는다 하더라도 확고한 평화의 시대에 가장 덜 행복한 국민이 빈번한 전쟁의 시기에 가장 행복한 국민보다 더 잘 살 가능성이 높다. 따라서 우리는 국제주의를 일차적으로 전쟁 방지의 관점에서 봐야 하고 단지 이차적으로만 국가 간 정의라는 시각에서 봐야 한다. 이것은 중요한데 왜냐하면, 앞으로도 보듯이, 국제정부를 이루기 위한 몇몇 가장 가능성 있는 접근법에는 장기간에 걸친 상당한 불의가 따를 것이기 때문이다.

⬇

국제 정부 설립의 핵심 목표는 전쟁의 방지이다.
- ① 영원한 평화의 구현
- ② 경제 정의의 확보
- ③ 전쟁의 방지
- ④ 모든 형태의 부정의 추방
- ⑤ 지속적인 인간 가치의 실현

(글의 소재) 국제 정부 설립 목적

(주요 어휘) emigrate 이민 가다, primarily 일차적으로, probable 개연성이 있는, 가능성이 있는 eradication 근절

(글의 흐름) ⊙ 주제문은 'Of these the prevention of war is the more important.'인데, 이런 취지는 문미에 'We have therefore to consider internationalism primarily from the point of view of preventing war.'라고 다시 한 번 반복되어 양괄식 구조를 취하고 있다.

(구조 분석) ⊙ economic justice as between different nations and different populations

➡ as exists between에서 exists가 생략됐다. '서로 다른 나라 서로 다른 민족 사이에 지켜지는 것과 같은 경제 정의'를 뜻한다.
⊙ It would not be common, for example, in a time of profound peace to deprive a nation of its means ~

➡ 가정법 문장이며, in a time of ~에 가정의 의미가 들어있다. it는 가주어고 진주어는 'to deprive a nation of its means ~'이다.

정답 해설 국제 정부의 일차적인 설립 목적은 전쟁의 방지라는 것이 이 글의 일관된 논지이므로 빈칸에 들어갈 말은 The prevention of war이다. 요약문은 'A is what B is about(B의 핵심은 A이다.)' 구조의 문장이다.

134

정답 ①

지문 해석 뉴스는 일어나는 일을 다루고 일어나지 않는 일을 다루지 않는다. 그래서 화재나 공장 폐쇄, 총기 난사, 상어의 공격처럼 갑작스럽고 속상한 사건을 집중적으로 다룬다. 대부분의 긍정적인 사건들은 카메라 친화적이지도 않고(화면이 잘 안 받고) 하루아침에 이뤄진 게 아니다. 전쟁을 벌이지 않는 나라나 테러 공격을 당하지 않은 도시는 결코 헤드라인을 장식할 수 없다. 미디어의 못된 버릇은 결국 인간의 인지 능력 중 최악의 것을 불러일으킨다. 우리가 위험을 직감하는 것은 통계치가 아닌, 이미지나 이야기를 통해서다. 사람들은 일 년에 수십 명의 목숨을 앗아가는 토네이도가 수천 명을 앗아가는 천식보다 위험하다고 여기는데 이는 토네이도가 TV의 시각적 호소력에 더 적합하기 때문으로 추정된다. 우리는 이러한 편향된 인지 능력이 사람들로 하여금 세상이 나아갈 바를 최악으로 결론 내리게 할 것이라는 것을 쉽게 알 수 있다.

↓

위 기사는 '피를 흘리면 머리기삿감이다.'라고 강조하는 언론의 뉴스 정책을 비판한다.

- ① '피를 흘리면 머리기삿감이다'
- ② '무소식이 희소식'
- ③ '아예 보도 않는 것보다는 오보가 낫다'
- ④ '필요할 때는 논점을 흐려라'
- ⑤ '뉴스는 말해지고 진실은 추측되고 사실은 묻히는 것'

글의 소재 뉴스의 역기능

주요 어휘 camera-friendly 카메라 친화적인, 화면이 잘 받는, in turn 결국, intuition 통찰력, asthma 천식, presumably 추정컨대, make for ~에 도움이 되다, ~에 적합하다

글의 흐름 ⊙ 인간의 편향된 인지 능력을 교묘히 이용하는 TV의 그릇된 관행을 비판하고 있는 글이다. 주제문은 'The bad habits of media in turn bring out the worst in human cognition.'이다.

구조 분석 ⊙ People rank tornadoes (which kill dozens of Americans a year) as more dangerous than asthma

➡ rank A as B, 즉 regard A as B와 같은 구문이다.

⊙ presumably because tornadoes make for better television.

➡ '추정컨대 ~ 때문에'라는 종속절이지만, '~인데 이는 ~ 때문인 것으로 추정된다'와 같이 결과로 해석하는 것이 좋다.

⊙ tornadoes make for better television.

➡ 여기서 television은 물리적인 텔레비전이 아니라 텔레비전의 시각적 호소력을 가리킨다. 토네이도가 TV의 시각적 호소력에 더 적합하다는 말이다.

정답 해설 이 글은 폭력적이고 자극적일수록 시청자의 시선을 끈다는 미디어 정책을 비판하고 있으므로 빈칸에 적절한 말은 '피를 흘리면 머리기삿감이다.'이다.

135

정답 ③

지문 해석 전 세계에서 발행되는 다양한 미용 잡지에 왜 그리고 어떻게 해서 그렇게 많은 광고가 쇄도하는가? 홍콩의 한 피부과 의사가 이러한 농간을 명쾌하게 설명한다. "매주 제조사들의 주장이 화려한 사진과 동봉되어 전 세계로부터 미용 편집자의 데스크로 답지합니다. 이런 심하게 편향되고 주관적인 안내문은 설명이 곁들인 사진과 함께 편집되지 않은 채 독립된 기사로 위장한 사실상 무료 광고로 잡지 지면에 모습을 드러냅니다." 이것이 잡지사에는 비용이 덜 들고 제조사에는 한층 덜 든다. 유일하게 손해 보는 측은 좀 더 비판적인 분석을 기대하는 우리들 중 누구이거나 읽는 것을 모두 믿어버리는 사람들뿐이다. 당신이 일단 이러한 농간이 어떻게 부려지는지 알게 되면 당신은 신제품 칼럼이나 미용담, 변신, 지역 신문의 미용실이나 살빼기 치료 광고를 훨씬 비판적인 눈으로 보게 될 것이다.

- ① 의료 부작용
- ② 전염성 피부병
- ③ 은밀한 광고
- ④ 충동구매
- ⑤ 성급한 잡지 구독

글의 소재 미용 잡지의 은밀한 광고

주요 어휘 flood ~에 쇄도하다, dermatologist 피부과 의사, trick 장난, 농간, glossy 화려한, blurb 안내문, biased 편향된, subjective 주관적인, masquerade as ~로 가장하다, cheap 비용이 덜 드는, cast a critical eye over ~을 비판적인 눈으로 보다, make-over 변신, weight treatment 살빼기 치료

구조 분석 ⊙ These heavily biased, subjective blurbs, with the photographs captioned, then appear unedited in the magazines as virtually unpaid advertisements masquerading as independent editorial copy.

➡ 이 문장의 '뼈대'만 보면 blurbs(S), appear(V) unedited(C)로 이루어진 2형식 문장이다. 나머지는 모두 형용사구나 부사구로 이루어진 수식구, 즉 '살'이다.

정답 해설 이 글의 작자가 독자들에게 무엇을 경고하고 있는지를 묻는 문제이다. 이 글은 미용 잡지에 성행하는 기사를 가장한 광고 행위에 속지 말라는 경고를 전하고 있다. 따라서 정답은 ③이다.

136

지문 해설 호주 체육협회가 실시한 조사에 의하면 - 이는 국제적인 조사 결과와 다르지 않다 - 13, 14세 무렵 남녀 선수의 자존심은 엇비슷한 수준을 보이다가 이후 감소하지만 여성의 감소 속도와 정도가 남성보다 훨씬 급격한 것으로 나타났다. 또 이 연구는 남녀 모두 자존심이 19, 20, 21세 무렵 바닥을 쳤다가, 즉 최저 수준에 이르렀다가 이후 반등하지만 재밌게도 남성은 처음 보다 높은 수치를 보이며 끝나는 데 반해 여성은 13-14세 수준을 결코 회복하지 못한다는 것을 보여줬다. 이것은 우리 사회의 여성 "승리자"들조차도 — 이 연구는 육체적으로 건강하고 아직도 승리하고 있는 1,798명의 여자 선수를 6년 넘게 조사했다 — 사춘기 전에 자존심이 최고조에 이르렀다가 성년이 된 후에 그 수준을 결코 회복하지 못함을 보여준다.

자존심은 남녀 모두 20세 무렵 최저 수준을 보이고 남자는 사춘기 수준보다 높게 끝나는 데 반해 여자는 사춘기 수준을 다시 회복하지 못한다.

글의 소재 호주 남녀 선수의 자존심 변화

주요 어휘 echo ~를 그대로 반영하다, ~와 다르지 않다, findings 조사 결과, bottom out 바닥을 치다, end up ~한 상태로 끝나다, 결국 ~하다, puberty 사춘기

글의 흐름 ⊙ 주제문: 'the males actually end up higher than when they started, and the female athletes never reach the same level as at 13 and 14 again.'으로, 중괄식 구조이다.

정답 해설 이 글은 남녀 공히 자존심이 20세 무렵 바닥을 치다 남자는 사춘기 수준보다 높게 끝나 이를 회복하지만 여자는 사춘기 수준을 회복하지 못한다는 것이 요지이다. 그러므로 (A)와 (B)의 빈칸에는 각각 higher와 recapturing이 들어가야 맞다.

137

지문 해설 우리의 감각으로 들어오는 모든 인풋은 자극인데 이것을 우리는 정보로 해석할 수 있고 또 그로부터 더 많은 정보를 얻을 수 있다. 귀, 눈 등 우리 몸의 감각 기관은 공기압이나 빛의 변화 같은 외부 자극을 우리 뇌가 인식할 수 있는 신경 충동으로 바꾸는 정보 변환기로 볼 수 있다. 우리 뇌가 지식과 의미를 얻기 위해 이들 신경 충동을 가지고 무슨 일을 하는지에 대해 과학자와 철학자들이 많은 개념 모델을 개발해 왔다. 우리 뇌가 그 일을 성취하는 메커니즘에 관계없이 우리가 외부 정보에 자극받아 스스로 정보를 생산하는 것은 확실하다. 가령, 우리가 사자의 포효를 들으면 뇌는 알려지지 않은 수단을 통해 이들 시변(時變) 주파수와 파장을 사자의 포효로 평가한다. 그리고 나서 뇌는 실제 음원에 대해 더 많은 정보와 의미를 얻게 된다. 어느 한 시공간의 개인은 그 소리가 "내 생명이 위험해. 음원으로부터 가급적 빨리 그리고 멀리 도망가야 해"를 의미하는 것으로 해석할 수 있다. 한편, 그 소리가 특정 출처와 연관이 있다는 것을 전혀 알지 못하는 또 다른 개인은 그것을 다른 알려진 소리와 비교해 보거나 아니면 그 소리를 낸 물체에 대해 태연하거나 할 것이다.

두뇌가 작동 방식과 관계없이 일단 외부 자극이 우리를 추동하면 우리는 주관적인 정보를 생산하게 돼있다.

글의 소재 외부 자극과 주관적 정보 형성

주요 어휘 sensory receptor 감각 수용기, transducer 변환기, nerve impulse 신경 충동, time-varying 시변時變의

글의 흐름 ⊙ 'Regardless of the mechanism by which our brain accomplishes it, it is clear that we generate information ourselves, stimulated by external information' 이 주제문으로, 중괄식 구조이다. For example 같은 예시의 연결사 바로 앞의 문장이 주제문일 경우가 많다. 'it is clear that'과 같은 단정적인 표현도 주제문의 가능성을 높인다.

구조 분석 ⊙ our brain, by means largely unknown to us, evaluates those time-varying frequencies and amplitudes as a lion's roar.

→ 'by means largely unknown to us'는 삽입의 부사구이고, 'evaluate A as B' 구조이다.

정답 해설 일단 외부 자극이 우리 안에 들어오면 두뇌가 그것을 어떻게 처리하는지에 상관없이 우리는 정보를 생산하는데 그 정보는 주관적이라는 게 이 글의 요지이다. 따라서 괄호 안에는 subjective와 external이 적절하다. 중간 부분 예시의 연결사 For example ~이 나오기 전 문장인 'Regardless of the mechanism ~ by external information'이 주제문인데, 이를 참조하면 추론이 가능하다.

138

지문 해설 적응과 경감은 기후변화 논의에서 빠질 수 없는 두 용어다. 국제기후변화패널(IPCC)은 경감을 온실가스원을 줄이거나 저감을 촉진하기 위한 인위적 개입으로 정의한다. 즉, 경감이란 기후변화가 인간의 생명과 재산에 가져올 장기적인 리스크나 위험을 영구 제거하거나 줄이기 위해 취하는 행동을 말한다. 한편 IPCC는 적응을, 자연적 또는 인위적 시스템을 현재적 또는 예상되는 기후 자극이나 결과에 따라 조절함으로써 피해를 줄이고 유익한 기회를 활용하는 것이라 정의한다. 일반적으로 경감 조치가 많을수록 조절해야 할 충격과 우리가 대비해야 하는 리스크가 줄어든다. 역으로 예방적 적응 조치가 많을수록 특정 기후변화 정도에 따르는 충격은 작아진다.

경감은 기후 변화의 <u>원인</u>을 해결하기 위해 힘쓰는 것이고, 적응은 <u>시스템</u>을 조절해 기후 자극에 좀 더 잘 대처하는 것을 말한다.

[글의 소재] 기후 변화 대책으로서의 경감과 적응

[주요 어휘] mitigation 경감, anthropogenic 인위적인, intervention 개입, adjustment 조절, exploit 활용하다, try and prepare = try to prepare, conversely 역으로

[구조 분석] ⊙ The International Panel on Climate Change (IPCC) defines mitigation as an anthropogenic intervention to reduce the <u>sources</u> or enhance the <u>sinks</u> of <u>greenhouse gases</u>.

→ of greenhouse gases는 sources와 sinks를 모두 꾸며준다.

⊙ Namely, mitigation means any action taken <u>to</u> <u>permanently</u> <u>eliminate</u> or reduce the long-term risk

→ to permanently eliminate는 분리부정사이다. 분리부정사에서는 to와 infinitive 사이에 낀 부사가 다른 동사가 아닌 해당 infinitive만을 수식한다. 여기서 permanently는 eliminate만을 수식한다.

⊙ In general the more mitigation there is, the less will be the impacts to which we will have to adjust

→ will be(V)와 the impacts to which we will have to adjust(S)가 도치되었다. 주어부가 길어서 뒤로 뺀 경우로 end weight 원칙이 적용됐다. 다음 문장 Conversely, the greater the degree of preparatory adaptation, the less may be the impacts associated with any given degree of climate change도 마찬가지다.

[정답 해설] mitigation은 기후 변화의 요인을 사전에 제거하는 것이고 adaptation은 인적 물적 시스템을 조절해 기후 변화에 보다 슬기롭게 대처하는 것이다. 따라서 정답은 ②다.

139 [정답 ④]

[지문 해석] 전혀 새로운 공국들을 언급함에 있어 내가 최고의 군주, 최고의 국가를 예로 들더라도 어느 누구도 놀라서는 안 된다. 왜냐하면 사람은 늘 다른 사람이 걷던 길을 걷고 그들의 행위를 모방해 따르면서도 그들의 방식을 완전히 고수하지도 못하고 모방하려는 사람들이 가진 권력을 얻지도 못하기 때문이다. 현자는 반드시 위대한 사람이 걷던 길을 따라 걷고 최고의 자리에 있던 사람을 모방해서, 설사 그의 능력이 위대한 사람의 능력에는 못 미친다 하더라도 적어도 흉내라도 낼 수 있어야 한다. 너무 멀리 떨어져 보이는 과녁을 맞히려 하지만 활의 힘으로 도달할 수 있는 한계를 알기 때문에 과녁보다 훨씬 높은 곳을 겨냥하는 - 이는 힘이나 화살로 그런 높이에 도달하려는 게 아니라 그런 높은 조준의 도움을 받아 목표하는 과녁을 맞히려는 것인데 - 영리한 궁사와 같이 행동하라.

↓

높은 곳을 조준해야 과녁에 도달하기를 희망할 수 있는 궁사처럼 군주는 위인의 발자국을 따라 그들을 모방하기를 권한다.

[글의 소재] 현명한 군주의 조건, 모방

[주요 어휘] principality 공국, adduce 제시하다, savor of ~의 기미가 있다, 흉내 내다, design to =intend to, 의도하다, defeat 물리치다, emulate 흠모의 대상을 모방하다, flex muscles 겁주다

[글의 흐름] ⊙ 'A wise man ought always to follow the paths beaten by great men, and to imitate those who have been supreme.'이 주제문이다. ought to 같은 강한 표현은 주제문일 경우가 많다.

[구조 분석] ⊙ so that <u>if</u> his ability does not equal theirs, at least it will savour of it.

→ if는 even if로 양보의 의미다. '그의 능력이 그들의 능력에 필적하지는 못해도 적어도 흉내는 낼 수 있도록'의 의미이다.

⊙ take aim much higher than the mark, <u>not to</u> reach by their strength or arrow to so great a height, <u>but to</u> be able with the aid of so high an aim to hit the mark they wish to reach.

→ not to infinitive but to infinitive 구문으로, to infinitive는 부정사의 부사적 용법(목적)이다. by their strength or arrow와 with the aid of so high an aim은 부사구이다.

[정답 해설] 마치 궁사가 먼 과녁에 도달하기 위해 일부러 높은 곳을 조준하는 것처럼 군주는 반드시 위인을 닮도록 노력해야 그들에게 조금이라도 가까워질 수 있다는 것이 이 글의 요지이므로 정답은 ④이다. 'to imitate those who~'나 'with the aid of so high an aim'이 시그널이다.

140 [정답 ③]

[지문 해석] 사람들이 적당히 용서해야 하는지 아니면 완전히 용서해야 하는지 하는 문제는 아리스토텔레스의 절제와 스토아/기독교의 극단주의 사이에 벌어지는 보다 큰 논란의 일부다. 아리스토텔레스의 중용의 교리는 3원적이다. 인간 삶의 각 영역은, 양극단에 두 개의 악이 놓인 상태에서 가운데 있는 단일 덕목에 의해 다스려진다. 이에 맞서는 교리는 2원적인데 각각의 덕은 연속체의 한 끝에 놓여있고 그에 상응하는 악은 다른 끝에 놓여있다. 많은 사람들이 무조건적인 용서에 경의를 표한다는 사실이 우리로 하여금 그들이 극단에 갈채를 보내고 있다는 사실을 못 보게 해서는 안 된다. 모욕이나 부정을 다스리는 덕은 적당히 화를 내며 보복하려는 성향이라고 아리스토텔레스는 말하지만 무조건적 용서를 주창하는 이들은 모욕과 부정을 다스리는 덕은 성마름의 악으로부터 가능한 한 멀리 떨어지는 데 있다고 주장한다. 화를 잘 내는 것은 나쁘고 용서는 선하기에 인

간은 더 많이 용서할수록 더 좋다. 존재하는 올바른 방법은 연속체의 극단에 있다.

아리스토텔레스의 중용 교리는 우리가 <u>보복</u>을 통해 모욕과 부정을 다스리기를 권유하지만 스토아/기독교 극단주의자들은 미덕이 <u>용서</u>를 달성하는 데 있다고 주장한다.

〔글의 소재〕 아리스토텔레스 삼원적 미덕관과 기독교/스토아학파의 이원적 미덕관

〔주요 어휘〕 controversy 논란, triadic 삼원적인, dyadic 이원적인, continuum 연속체, corresponding 상응하는, profess 공언하다, 표하다, disposition 성향, retaliate 보복하다, irascibility 화를 잘 냄

〔글의 흐름〕 'Aristotle's doctrine of the mean is triadic; each sphere of human life ~ The competing doctrine is dyadic: each virtue lies on one end of a continuum and its one corresponding vice lies on the other end.'의 두 문장이 주제문이다.

〔구조 분석〕 ⊙ The fact <u>that</u> many people profess admiration for unconditional forgiveness should not blind us to the fact <u>that</u> they are applauding an extreme.

→ 두 that는 모두 동격의 접속사 that이고, 앞의 동격절이 forgiveness까지 이어지며 주어부를 구성한다.

〔정답 해설〕 아리스토텔레스의 중용의 관점에서 불의나 모욕에 대한 미덕은 적당한 보복을 가하는 것인 반면에 스토아나 기독교 학파는 화라는 악으로부터 최대한 떨어진 곳, 즉 무조건적인 용서를 통해 선을 이룰 수 있다고 주장한다. 따라서 정답은 ③이다. 'While Aristotle says~'에서 시작되는 글 후반부에서 단서를 찾을 수 있다.

141
〔정답 ②〕

〔지문 해석〕 가톨릭 집안 출신의 JFK에게 집단사고의 끔찍한 결과에 대한 주의를 환기시키는 데 피그만 침공 사건이 필요했다는 점은 놀랍다(침공 사건을 당하고서야 ~를 주의했다는 점은 놀랍다). 그는 수 세기의 교회사를 이용할 수 있었다. 1587년부터 최근까지, 세계에서 가장 성공적인 조직 중 하나임이 거의 틀림없는 로마가톨릭교회는 어떤 사람을 성인의 자리에 올리는 결정을 하기 위해 특별한 회의론자 한 명을 임명했다. 공식적으로 이 직업적인 회의론자는 Promotor Fidei, 즉 믿음의 촉진자라고 알려졌다. 비공식적으로 그는 Advocatus Diaboli, 즉 악마의 변호인으로 알려졌다. 악마의 변호인이 하는 일은 성인 반열에 오르기를 신청하는 건에 구멍을 내는 것, 즉 성자 후보자의 신성함을 입증하는 모든 증거를 심문하는 것이었다. 가능할 때마다 악마의 변호인은 동원 가능한 증인들을 대질신문했고, 후보자의 성인됨에 대한 증언을 정밀 조사했고, 시성을 반대하

는 모든 합리적인 주장을 펼쳤다. 교회는 이런 역할을 집단사고에 대한 보호책으로 제정했다-1587년에 그런 이름(집단사고)으로 부르지는 않았지만-. 악마의 변호인이 하는 일은 모든 관점에 대한 고려를 강제하고 그럼으로써 이 중요한 결정의 질을 높이는 것이다. 결국 모든 사람을 성인으로 만들 수는 없으니까.

악마의 변호인은 성자 반열에 오른 후보자들에 대한 모든 합리적인 반대 주장을 개진함으로써 <u>집단사고의 억압자</u> 역할을 맡도록 위촉되었다.

- ① 집단 지혜의 촉진자
- ② 집단사고 억압자
- ③ 성인 후보자
- ④ 자비로운 시성자
- ⑤ 성스러운 해결사

〔글의 소재〕 로마 가톨릭의 Devil's Advocate 전통

〔주요 어휘〕 groupthink 집단사고, draw upon ~에 의존하다, arguably 거의 틀림없이, skeptic 회의론자, canonization 성인 반열에 올림, 시성, attest to ~를 입증하다, cross-examine 대질신문하다, scrutinize 정밀조사하다, institute 제정하다, insurance 보험, 보호책

〔글의 흐름〕 주제문은 'The Church instituted this role as insurance against groupthink—though they did not call it that in 1587.'으로 미괄식 구조의 문단이다.

〔구조 분석〕 ⊙ Coming from a Catholic background, it is surprising that JFK needed the Bay of Pigs to alert him to the terrible consequences of groupthink.

→ 분사 구문으로서 절로 바꾸면 'Though he came from ~'이다.

⊙ It was the advocate's job <u>to punch</u> holes in cases that argued for canonization, <u>to question</u> all evidence that attested to the holiness of the nominee for sainthood.

→ 'It ~ to ~' 가주어 진주어 구문이고 to question은 to punch와 동격으로 to punch ~의 의미를 구체적으로 풀어주고 있다.

〔정답 해설〕 로마 가톨릭은 다수 의견을 견제하기 위한, 즉 집단사고의 폐단을 경계하기 위한 수단으로 devil's advocate를 만들어 시성식 후보자에 대한 보다 엄밀한 사정을 꾀했다는 것이 윗글의 요지이므로 빈칸에 알맞은 말은 ②의 '집단사고 억압자'이다.

Chapter V

종합적 이해

14. 글의 목적

정답

142 ②	143 ③	144 ⑤	145 ③
146 ③			

142

정답 ②

지문 해석 대부분의 보안 시스템은 침입자가 들어오지 못하도록 고안되었다. 워싱턴 소재 스타트업 기업인 노스트는 이와는 완전히 반대되는 개념의, 즉 사용자가 들어가기 쉽도록 고안한 시큐리티를 구축했다고 이 회사의 CPO인 Jill Patterson은 말한다. 적절한 예를 들자면 이 시큐리티의 허브는 비밀번호를 입력하는 게 아니고 전자열쇠를 흔들어 풀 수 있는데 열쇠는 특정 시간대에만 작동하게 돼 있어 가령 베이비시터는 근무 시간에만 집을 출입할 수 있다. 또 사용자는 스마트폰 앱으로 시스템을 원격 조정할 수도 있다. 물론 시큐리티 허브는 집을 잘 지킬 수도 있다. 침입자가 허브를 부수거나 전원을 뽑거나 할 때는 85데시벨의 경고음이 울리고 문이나 창문이 열리면 양쪽의 동작 센서가 사용자에게 경보를 띄울 수 있다.

글의 소재 보안 제품 홍보

주요 어휘 start-up 벤처기업, case in point 적절한 예, fob 주머니, intruder 침입자, companion 양쪽의

구조 분석 ⊙ choosing to focus just as much on making it simpler for its users to get in.

→ get in 다음에 as focusing on keeping intruders out이 생략됐다. focus as much on A as on B의 구문.

정답 해설 이 글은 워싱턴 소재의 벤처기업 Nost가 홍보를 목적으로 최근 출시된 보안 제품의 기능과 특장을 소개하고 있다. 특히, 'a Washington-based start-up, built its security system ~'이나 'chief product officer' 같은 시그널에 유의하면 이 글이 상품 홍보용으로 쓰였음을 알 수 있다. 따라서 정답은 ②이다.

143

정답 ③

지문 해석 위원장님, 이번 청문회 개최에 대해 감사드립니다. 이번 청문회야말로 군인들로 하여금 제대 후 필요로 하는 서비스를 확실히 얻도록 하는 데 우리가 수행해야 할 감독과 책임의 한 형태입니다. 제가 몇몇 재향군인들과 얘기해 본 바에 의하면 우리는 그들에게 전선에서 후방으로의 매끄러운 복귀를 제공하지 못하고 있음이 확실하고 이것은 바뀌어야 합니다. 그들의 복귀가 매끄럽다면 왜 그렇게 많은 군인들이 제대 후 실직돼야 합니까? 왜 그렇게 많은 이들이 무주택자가 돼야 합니까? 왜 그들이 초기진료를 받기 위해 6개월이나 기다려야 합니까? 매끄러운 복귀제도가 있는지 알기 위해서라면 이런 청문회는 필요 없습니다. 그런 제도는 없으니까요. 국방부나 보훈처가 충분히 협업하고 있는지 알기 위해서라면 이런 청문회는 필요 없습니다. 협업을 제대로 안 하고 있으니까요. 이 청문회는 그들이 그것을 위해 무엇을 하고 있고 어떻게 개선할 수 있는지를 증인들로부터 알아내기 위해 필요한 것입니다.

글의 소재 재향군인 복지 탄원

주요 어휘 oversight 감독, accountability 책임, service member 군인, home front 후방, seamless 아주 매끄러운, 끊어지지 않고 이어진, primary care 초기진료

구조 분석 ⊙ This is exactly the type of oversight and accountability we need to have / to make sure ~

→ 여기서 have의 목적어는 관계사절의 선행사인 oversight and accountability이고, to make sure ~는 목적의 부정사구이다. 이때 have to로 잘못 읽지 않아야 한다.

⊙ I do not think they are.

→ they are 다음에 'working together enough'가 생략됐다.

정답 해설 이 글은 청문회에서 재향군인의 복리 증진을 다루도록 탄원하는 내용이다. 'This is exactly the type of oversight and accountability we need to have to make sure our service members get the services they need when they come home.'에 필자가 글을 쓴 목적이 재향군인들의 복리 증진에 있음이 드러나 있다. 따라서 정답은 ③이다.

144

정답 ⑤

지문 해석 화장실에서 보좌관에게 큰소리로 업무 지시하기를 좋아하는 대통령에게 향수를 느낄지 누가 생각했으랴? 우디 해럴슨이 주연을 맡은 Rob Reiner 감독의 LBJ는 린든 존슨 대통령 입문서인데, 대략 JFK 암살에 따른 36대 대통령의 취임과 그의 1964년 공민권법 서명까지를 다룬다. 잘 알려진 대로 존슨 대통령은 거칠고 무례하기로 악명 높았다. 그러나 그의 정치 감각이나 타고난 품격은 국가를 긍정적인 쪽으로 변화시켰다. 그의 냉담함마저 품위가 있었는데 이런 모순된 점을 해럴슨은 날카로운 시선 속에 미소를 숨기며 또는 반대로 미소 속에 노려보면서 훌륭하게 전달하고 있다.

① TV 다큐멘터리 제작을 축하하기 위해
② 최근 발간된 책을 홍보하기 위해

③ 작고한 대통령의 숨은 미덕을 기리기 위해

④ 역사적인 대통령의 치적을 회상하기 위해

⑤ 새 영화 개봉을 소개하기 위해

[글의 소재] 영화 LBJ

[주요 어휘] the john =bathroom, 101 one-oh-one, 기본, 개론, swearing-in ceremony 취임식, acumen 감각, innate 타고난, decency 품위, contradiction 모순, scowl 노려봄, the other way around 앞서 말한 것과 정반대로

[구조 분석] ⊙ roughly covering the period from 36th President swearing-in ceremony following the JFK assassination to his signing of the Civil Rights Act of 1964.

→ covering a period from A to B 구문이다. 중간에 following the JFK assassination은 바로 앞의 ceremony를 꾸며주는 형용사구이다.

⊙ His indifference was also a kind of grace, a contradiction that~

→ a contradiction은 앞의 문장 전체와 동격이다.

[정답 해설] 두 번째 문장인 'Rob Reiner's LBJ, starring Woody Harrelson, is Lyndon B. Johnson 101, roughly covering the period from 36th President swearing-in ceremony following the JFK assassination to his signing of the Civil Rights Act of 1964.'나 마지막 문장인 'His indifference was also a kind of grace, a contradiction that Harrelson conveys beautifully, with a scowl that sometimes hides a smile — or the other way around.'를 통해 이 글이 영화 LBJ를 소개하는 글임을 알 수 있다. 따라서 정답은 ⑤이다.

145
[정답 ③]

[지문 해석] 우리가 최근 출시한 맞춤형 신진대사 증진 프로그램은 단 4주 만에 최대 8파운드까지 살을 빼도록 해드립니다. 무엇보다 군살 없는 튼튼한 체격에 넘치는 에너지를 평생 지니게 합니다. 이 프로그램의 핵심은 '고高대사 운동'인데 이는 튼튼하면서 날렵한 근육조직을 만들어주는 효과 만점의 강화 동작 다섯 가지로 이루어진, 강력한 신진대사에 이르는 열쇠입니다. 휴식 시 근육은 지방보다 7배 많은 칼로리를 태우기 때문에 근육이 많을수록 신진대사가 활발합니다. 이것은 단지 시작일 뿐이죠. 삶에는 매 시기마다 수면 방해나 대규모 호르몬 변화 같은 신진대사를 약화시키는 위험 요소가 있습니다. 따라서 우리는 당신의 신진대사를 최고조로 유지시켜줄 시기별 지방 제거 처방을 포함시켰습니다. 그리고 대사량을 높이기 위한 고대사 식단을 운용합니다. 오늘 시작하세요 그리고 2주일만 있으면 잠이 더 잘 오고 활력이 더욱 넘치고 옷이 더 헐렁해진 것을 알게 될 것입니다.

①공중 보건 증진을 위한 정부 계획을 발표하기 위해

② 신진대사에 관한 주요 학술 조사 결과를 홍보하기 위해

③ 건강관리 회사가 최근 출시한 피트니스 프로그램을 홍보하기 위해

④ 일반 대중에게 과도한 운동의 부작용을 경고하기 위해

⑤ 신진대사의 중요한 기능을 사람들에게 교육하기 위해

[글의 소재] fitness 프로그램 홍보

[주요 어휘] customizable 맞춤형의, metabolism 신진대사, shed 줄이다, =lose, lean 군살 없는, physique 체격, 체형, boost 높이다, supereffective 매우 효율적인, robust 강한, disrupt 방해하다, seismic 지진의, 대규모의, decade-by-decade 시기별, in high gear 최고조로, soar 날아오르다

[구조 분석] ⊙ Most important, you'll have a lean, strong physique and energy to spare—for life.

→ Most important=Most importantly=What's most important

⊙ and notice your clothes are looser in as little as 2 weeks.

→ 여기서 in은 after로 바꿔 쓸 수 있다. '~후', '~만 있으면'의 의미이다. (e.g. I will see you in a couple of days. =이삼일 후 뵙겠습니다.)

[정답 해설] 첫 문장 'Our recently-released customizable metabolism-boosting routine will help you shed up to 8 pounds in just 4 weeks.'와 마지막 문장의 'Start today'로 이 글이 건강관리 회사가 최근 출시한 피트니스 프로그램을 홍보하는 내용임을 알 수 있다.

146
[정답 ③]

[지문 해석] 프레이저님:

제 딸의 수술이 선택적이고 이에 대한 사전 승인을 받지 못해 저의 보험증권으로는 딸의 수술비 지원이 안 된다는 취지의 귀하 편지를 최근 받았습니다. 마비와 이로 인한 질식사를 방지하기 위한 수술을 어느 누가 선택적이라 부를 수 있는지 저로선 상상이 되지 않는군요. 누군가가 저에게 편지를 잘못 보냈거나 '선택적'이라는 정의를 잘못 내린 것이 분명합니다. 귀하는 제 딸의 의료 기록서를 가지고 계시리라 믿습니다. 그렇지 않다면 신경외과의에게 부탁해 한 부 보내라고 하겠습니다. 이번 건을 잘 검토하셔서 제 딸의 상태가 '생명에 위협적이며' 따라서 '선택적'이지 않다는 쪽으로 조치해 주셨으면 합니다. 딸은 이제 정상에 가까운 생활을 할 기회를 얻었고 이 점에 대해 감사드립니다. 딸의 수술이 보험 처리가 안 된다고 말씀하시는 것은 상처에 심한 모욕을 더하는 것과 같습니다. 증빙 자료를 보시면 저희 입장에 동의하시리라 확신합니다. 귀하의 답변을 보고 다른 조치를 취할지 여부를 결정하겠습니다.

솔트 레이크 대학교 영문과

마크 데이비슨 드림

① 생명보험금을 청구하려고
② 잘못된 수술 결과를 항의하려고
③ 보험금 지급 거절에 이의를 제기하려고
④ 잘못된 회사 이미지를 알려주려고
⑤ 보험업계에 만연하는 불공정 관행을 비판하려고

글의 소재 보험금 미지급에 대한 이의신청

주요 어휘 insurance policy 보험증권, elective 선택적인, authorization 승인, in advance 사전에, enter one's mind ~한 생각이 들다, suffocation 질식, neurosurgeon 신경외과 의사, documentation 증거 문서

구조 분석 ⊙ It never entered my mind that anyone would consider surgery that would prevent her paralysis and eventual death by suffocation to be 'elective.'

➡consider 이하에서 surgery ~ suffocation 부분이 목적어, to be 'elective.'가 목적격 보어이다.

⊙ I request that you review her case to see that ~

➡ to see는 결과로 해석하는 것이 좋다.

⊙ She now has a chance to lead a relatively normal life, for which we are grateful.

➡ 관계대명사 which의 선행사는 앞 문장 전체이다.

정답 해설 'To say we have no claim to insurance coverage for her surgery is to add severe insult to injury.'를 보면, 이 글이 딸의 수술이 보험 처리가 안 된데 대해 필자가 보험회사에 이의를 제기하는 내용임을 알 수 있다. 따라서 정답은 ③이다.

15. 심경 · 태도 · 분위기

정답

	147 ⑤	148 ③	148 ①	150 ①
151 ④	152 ④			

147
정답 ⑤

지문 해석 1999년 봄과 여름 나는 Sacramento와 Austin에서 폐결핵 치료를 위해 두 번 입원했는데 처음에는 며칠간 나중에는 3주간 입원했다. 그 몇 달간 종종 꿈을 꿔 북경으로 달려가곤 했는데 회색의 옛 소련식 아파트 지붕 위에 서 있거나 낯선 동네를 달리는 버스에서 길을 잃는 꿈이었다. 꿈에서 깨면 꿈에 나타나지 않은 장면들을 일기장에 기록하곤 했다. 가령, 발코니 밑의 제비집, 지붕 위 철조망, 노인들이 앉아 한담을 나누던 정원, 그리고 먼지 뒤집어쓴 채 거리 후미진 곳에 놓여있던, 둥근 초록색 우체통 - 반투명 창 뒤에 편지 수거 시간이 적힌 — 등속이다.

① 전원적
② 낭만적
③ 귀신에 홀린
④ 교육적
⑤ 회상하는

글의 소재 회상

주요 어휘 tuberculosis 폐결핵, barbed 철조망이 쳐진, half-opaque 반투명의

구조 분석 ⊙ Waking up, I would list in my journal images that did not appear in my dreams:

➡ Waking up은 분사 구문. When I woke up으로 paraphrase 된다. would는 과거의 불규칙적인 습관을 나타낸다. list(V) in my journal(부사구) images(O).

정답 해설 'During those months, my dreams often took me back to Beijing.'이라는 두 번째 문장을 직접적인 단서로 해서, 이 글의 '나'는 과거 병원에 입원했을 때 꿈속에 고향 북경을 방문하던 기억을 회상하고 있음을 알 수 있다. 따라서 정답은 ⑤이다.

148
정답 ③

지문 해석 소말리아에서 희망은, 수십 년 내란을 겪은 난민들이 고국으로 물밀듯이 밀려들어 뭔가를 해보려 할 때는 부풀었다가 이슬람 극단주의자 알 샤밥의 공격을 받으면 좌절되는, 늘 깨지기 쉬운 어떤 것이었다. 귀환 난민으로 미 시민권자인 M.

A. Mohamed 대통령이 올 2월 비폭력으로 치러진 선거에서 당선된 후 희망이 타올랐다. Mohamed와 그의 법의 지배 약속으로 수도 모가디슈에 대한 외국인들의 투자가 이뤄지고 새로운 병원과 은행 기관, 심지어는 평화공원이 들어섰다. 경찰과 군을 재건하려는 국제적 노력이 결실을 맺고 있다. 이곳의 제 2의 전성기를 기록으로 남기고 있는 사진작가 Brent Stirton은 "소말리아 하면 아프리카 최악의 용어들 즉, 기근이나 내전, 폭군을 떠올리는데 소말리아인들로선 정말 억울한 일이다."

┌ ① 좌절된
│ ② 황량한
│ ③ 활기를 되찾은
│ ④ 애매모호한
└ ⑤ 축제의

[글의 소재] 희망적인 소말리아의 정정

[주요 어휘] fragile 깨지기 쉬운, uplift 들어올리다, flare 타오르다, commitment 언질, 확약, pay off 성공하다, 결실을 맺다, conjure up ~를 상기시키다, cliche 상투적인 문구, rejuvenating 활기를 되찾은

[구조 분석] ⊙ Hope in Somalia has always been a fragile thing, uplifted by the waves of refugees who have returned to make something of their homeland after decades of civil war and discouraged by the attacks from Islamic extremist group al-Shabab.

➜ uplifted by ~와 discouraged by ~가 나란히 a fragile thing을 꾸며주는 병렬 구조이다.

⊙ With Mohamed and his commitment to rule of law came foreign investment to the capital of Mogadishu—a new hospital, banking systems, even a peace park.

➜ foreign investment 이하가 주어, 동사는 came으로 주어가 길어서 뒤로 보낸 도치 구문이다. 영어 문장에서는 주어가 길면 가분수처럼 불안정해 뒤로 보내 안정을 찾으려는 경향이 있는데 이것이 'end weight' 법칙이다. 가주어 진주어 구문 또한 이 법칙이 적용된 예다.

[정답 해설] 이 글은 그동안 소말리아의 정정이 불안했지만 대선 이후 외국인 투자가 이뤄지고 군과 경찰이 재건되는 등 활기를 되찾고 있다는 내용이다. 그러므로 이 글의 분위기를 나타내는 데에는 rejuvenating이 알맞다.

149
정답 ①

[지문 해석] 마리아는 기술학교 가기를 희망했다. 기술전수학교는 전통적인 학교보다 조금 더 현대적이었다. 그곳에서 가르치는 과목에는 현대 언어, 수학, 과학 등이 있었다. 대부분의 사람들이 여학생들은 소화하기 어렵다고 본 과목들이었다. 나아가 그 과목들은 여학생들이 배우기에 적절하지 않은 것으로 여겨

졌다. 그것들이 적절하든 말든 마리아는 괘념치 않았다. 그녀에게는 수학과 과학이 제일 재미있었다. 그러나 그녀가 그 기술학교에 등록하기 위해서는 아버지의 허락을 받아야 했다. 엄마의 도움으로 마침내 아버지의 허락을 받아냈다. 하지만 그 후 몇 년 동안 집안에는 긴장감이 흘렀다. 엄마는 그녀를 도왔으나 아버지가 마리아의 계획에 번번이 반대한 것이다. 1883년 13세의 나이로 마리아는 로마의 Regia Scuola Tecnica Michelangelo Buonarroti에 입학했다. 그녀가 이 학교에서 어떻게 지냈는지 상상하기는 어렵다. 수업 과목에는 현대적인 것들이 있었으나 교수 방법이 매우 전통적이었다. 선생들은 엄격한 학습 규율을 신봉했고 종종 가혹한 체벌이 따랐다. 마리아는 강인해 이런 학습 분위기를 이겨냈다. 결국 멋지게 성공한 것이다.

┌ ① 끈기 있는
│ ② 젠체하는
│ ③ 배려하는
│ ④ 다정다감한
└ ⑤ 자기도취의

[글의 소재] 아동 교육자 마리아 몬테소리

[주요 어휘] sign up for ~에 등록하다

[구조 분석] ⊙ Furthermore, they were not thought to be proper for girls to study.

➜ they는 courses를 가리키고 의미상 study의 목적어이다. 이 문장을 가주어 it을 써서 'it was not thought to be proper for girls to study them.'으로 바꿔 쓸 수 있다.

[정답 해설] 전문학교 교과목이 여학생에게는 적절치 않다는 데 전혀 괘념치 않고 진학한 점이나 아버지의 허락을 얻어낸 점, 엄격한 학교 생활을 이겨내고 우수한 성적으로 졸업한 점을 두루 고려하면 마리아의 성격이 persistent함을 알 수 있다.

150
정답 ①

[지문 해석] 일행이 연회실에 들어섰을 때 그들은 Bingley, 그의 두 여동생, 첫째 여동생의 남편, 그리고 또 한 명의 젊은이 이렇게 다섯 명뿐이었다. Bingley는 잘생기고 점잖았다. 밝은 용모에 태도도 너그럽고 꾸밈이 없었다. 그의 여동생들도 유행 감각이 있는 멋쟁이였다. 그의 매제인 Hurst는 단지 점잖아 보일 뿐이었지만 그의 친구인 Darcy는 잘 차려입은 큰 체격에 잘생긴 용모, 당당한 태도 그리고 그가 들어온 후 5분 안에 쫙 퍼지는, 연 수입 만 파운드라는 소문 등으로 방 안의 시선을 끌어들였다. 남자들은 그가 풍채가 좋은 남성이라고 선언했고 여성들도 그가 Bingley보다 미남이라고 단언해서, 저녁 시간 반이 지날 때까지는 누구나 그를 우러러봤으나 이내 그의 예의범절이 혐오감을 불러일으켜 그의 인기의 흐름이 완전히 뒤바뀌었다. 왜냐하면 그가 거만하고 일행을 무시하는 까다로운 사람이라는 것이 드러났기 때문이다. 그래서 더비셔에 있는 그의 광활한 사

유지조차 그가 엄청나게 험악하고 뿌루퉁한 표정을 짓고 그래서 친구와 비교할 가치조차 없는 처지로부터 그를 구제해주지 못할 것이기 때문이다.

① 매력적인 → 역겨운
② 꾸밈없는 → 이색적인
③ 유순한 → 고집이 센
④ 내성적인 → 신경질적인
⑤ 세련된 → 단순한, 촌티 나는

글의 소재 Mr. Darcy에 대한 인상 반전

주요 어휘 party 무리, 일행, consist of ~로 이루어지다, assembly room 연회실, countenance 용모, unaffected 수수한, 꾸밈없는, mien 표정, 태도, pronounce 발음하다, 공개적으로 표명하다, fine figure of a man 풍채가 좋은 남성, turn the tide of ~의 조류를 바꾸다, ~의 흐름을 반전시키다, above being pleased 비위 맞추기가 어려운, 까다로운, estate 사유지, 재산, forbidding 험악한, disagreeable 불쾌한, 뿌루퉁한

구조 분석 ⊙ His brother-in-law, Mr. Hurst, merely looked the gentleman
→ the gentleman이 looked의 보어인 2형식 문장으로 '신사처럼 보였다.'는 의미이다.

⊙ the report which was in general circulation within five minutes after his entrance, of his having ten thousand a year
→ the report of his having~으로 연결되는 구문이다. 동격의 명사구 of his having~과 관계사절 which was~가 동시에 report를 수식하고 있다.

⊙ till his manners gave a disgust which turned the tide of his popularity
→ '~할 때까지 ~했다'의 till의 원래 의미대로 해석하기보다는 '~했으나 이내(곧) ~했다'의 결과적 용법으로 해석하는 게 자연스럽다.

정답 해설 이 글은 중심인물 Darcy가 품격 있고 매력적인 인물에서 거만하고 역겨운 인물로 급반전하는 과정을 묘사하고 있다. 따라서 정답은 ①이 타당하다.

151
정답 ④

지문 해석 오피오이드 중독을 끊는 것은 그 자체로도 쉬운 일이 아니다. 특히 당파가 둘로 갈려 국민적 의지가 모아지기 어려운 이때 해결책을 찾는 것은 훨씬 더 어렵다. 그러나 행동의 필요성이 시급하고 구도는 점점 명확해지고 있다. 먼저 우리는 오피오이드 중독이 병이라는 사실을 인정해야 한다. 오피오이드의 급속한 확산을 도덕적 해이라기보다는 공중보건의 위기로 봐야 한다. 이는 일반의 오피오이드 접근을 영원히 차단하는 가장 효과적인 방법임에도 불구하고 필요한 사람 중 극히 일부에

게만 제공되고 있는 의학적 치료와 상담 기회를 확대함을 의미한다. 우리는 법 집행을 통해, 또는 합법 처방을 규제한다든지 통증 관리를 위한 대체 전략을 장려함으로써 오피오이드 공급을 줄이는 노력을 계속해야 한다. 그리고 끝으로 심화되는 경제 양극화나 부담스러운 수준의 건강보험료, 그리고 오피오이드 수요를 애초에 부채질하는 대학 미졸업자에 대한 고용 기회 감소와 같은 문제에 적극 대처할 필요가 있다.

① 감상적인
② 변명하는
③ 신랄한
④ 호소하는
⑤ 동정적인

글의 소재 오피오이드

주요 어휘 opioid 아편 비슷한 작용을 하는 합성 진통·마취제, find a way out 해결책을 찾다, muster 모으다, 소집하다, epidemic 유행병, enhance 높이다, law enforcement 사정당국, economic divide 경제 양극화, unaffordable 값이 부담스러운 수준의, fuel 부채질하다, in the first place 애초에

글의 흐름 ⊙ 오피오이드 문제를 해결하기 위한 여러 방법을 열거하여 소개하는 병렬식 구조이다.

구조 분석 ⊙ particularly at a time of partisan division when national will is so hard to muster.
→ when 이하는 time을 꾸며주는 관계부사절이다.

⊙ getting people off of opioids for good,
→ get A off of B 구문. A를 B로부터 멀어지게 하다. of는 '~로부터'의 뜻이고 off of 대신 off만 쓸 수도 있다.

⊙ the diminished employment opportunities for those without a college degree who are helping fuel demand in the first place.
→ fuel은 동사로 쓰였다. are helping (to) fuel demand=수요를 부채질하다.

정답 해설 이 글은 오피오이드 문제에 보다 적극적으로 대처할 것을 호소하고 있다. 그러므로 이 글의 논조는 ④가 타당하다.

152
정답 ④

지문 해석 거의 모든 할리우드 영화를 특징짓는 것은 내적 부실함이다. 그런 부실은 번드르한 외관으로 보상받는다. 그러한 외관은 항상 거창한 리얼리즘의 형태를 띤다. 무대 배경과 의상, 모든 외면적 디테일을 똑바로 하기 위해 아무것도 아끼지 않는다. 이러한 노력은 근본적으로 부실한 성격 묘사나 엉터리 같은 또는 경박한 플롯을 가리는 데 도움이 된다. 집은 집처럼 보이고 거리는 거리처럼 보이고 사람은 사람처럼 보이고 말하지만 거기에는 휴머니티와 신뢰감, 동기 부여가 빠져있다. 말할 필요도 없이 부끄러운 검열 제도가 이런 영화들의 내용의 방향

을 사전에 결정짓는 중요한 요소다. 그러나 이런 규정은 영화의 수익이나 오락적 가치를 훼손하지는 않는다. 그것은 단지 영화가 신뢰성을 갖지 못하도록 할 뿐이다. 그것은 영화 산업이 감당하기에 그리 큰 부담이 아니다. 번드르르한 무대 배경 이외에 카메라를 사용하기도 하는데 이것이 종종 마법을 행한다. 그러나 삶을 묘사하는 이야기가 공허하고, 바보 같고, 진부하고 유치하다면 효과 제작에 바치는 이런 모든 기술과 노력과 에너지에 무슨 인간적인 의미가 있겠는가?

① 경박한
② 얼버무리는
③ 수용하는
④ 개탄하는
⑤ 꼬치꼬치 캐묻는

글의 소재 화려함 속에 내적 가치 상실한 할리우드 영화

주요 어휘 characterize 특징짓다, outer impressiveness 외면적 성장(盛裝), 번드르르한 외관, take the form of ~의 형태를 띠다, grandiose 거창한, characterization 성격 묘사, absurdity 불합리함, 말도 안 됨, triviality 시시한 것, motivation 동기 부여, disgraceful 치욕적인, 부끄러운, predetermine ~의 방향을 결정하다, import 의미, 내포, representation 묘사, banal 진부한

글의 흐름 ⊙ 주제문은 'What characterizes almost all Hollywood pictures is their inner emptiness.'이고, 두괄식 구조이다.

구조 분석 ⊙ Nothing is spared to make the setting, the costumes, all of the surface details correct.

→ 수동태를 능동으로 고치면 They spare nothing to ~이다. '그들은 아무것도 아끼지 않고 (전심전력으로) ~한다'는 의미이다.

⊙ But of what human import is all this skill, all this effort, all this energy in the production of effects~

→ Of what human import는 of + 추상명사가 형용사화해 보어로 기능하고 있다. (e.g. Of what use is all this scheme? =How useful is all this scheme?)

정답 해설 이 글은 내실이 없고 외관만 번드르르한 할리우드의 현실을 개탄하는 내용이므로 정답은 ④이다.

16. 장문의 이해 I - 1지문 2문제

정답

		153 ⑤	154 ④	155 ④
156 ③	157 ③	158 ④	158 ②	160 ⑤
161 ⑤	162 ①	163 ②	164 ②	165 ③
166 ⑤	167 ④	168 ②	169 ①	170 ⑤
171 ②	172 ③	173 ②	174 ⑤	175 ②
176 ⑤	177 ②	178 ①	179 ②	180 ⑤
181 ①	182 ⑤			

[153~154]

지문 해석 그리스와 로마 고전 문명은 화폐와 시장에 근거한 정교한 재정 경제를 발전시켰다. 그리스인들은 은행업과 화폐 주조, 상업 법정을 발명했다. 로마인들은 이런 혁신 조치 위에 법인 회사와 유한책임투자, 그리고 일종의 중앙은행 제도를 더했다. 메소포타미아의 고대 도시들이 국내 농산품의 재분배를 주력으로 하고, 원거리 무역을 부수적으로 해서 형성된 것과 달리 아테네와 로마 두 나라는 국내 농업 생산력보다 규모가 커지자 해외 무역으로 그것을 대체했다. 아테네는 많은 양의 밀을 멀리 흑해로부터 수입했다. 로마는 나일 삼각주의 비옥한 농토에 의존해 곡물을 조달했다. 이러한 대담한 경제 모델이 작동하기 위해서는 새로운 재정 구조가 필요했다. 아테네와 로마는 곡물이 중심(자국)을 향해 흐르도록 해야 했다. 경제는 해외 농민들이 수출용 곡물을 경작하고, 선원과 선장이 목숨을 걸고 곡물을 실어 나르며, 배와 교역 상품에 투자하도록 동기를 부여하고, 국제 교역의 불확실성에 취약한(→ 견디는) 지불 시스템을 만들어야 했다. 이에 대한 해결책으로 시장의 보이지 않는 손, 바다의 예측 불가능성을 처리할 재정 기술 그리고 만국이 인정하는 가치 척도에 근거한 화폐 경제 등이 나왔다.

글의 소재 그리스와 로마가 확장하는 경제를 다루기 위해 취한 조치들

주요 어휘 sophisticated 정교한, coinage 화폐 주조, corporation 법인, limited liability 유한 책임, redistribution 재분배, secondarily 부수적으로, outgrow 규모가 ~보다 커지다, substitute 대체하다, audacious 대담한, motivate 동기를 부여하다, vulnerable 취약한, uncertainty 불확실성, unpredictability 예측 불가능성, monetary 화폐의, measure 척도

글의 흐름 ⊙ 마지막 문장 'The solutions involved the invisible hand of the market, ~ a monetary economy that relied on universally accepted measures of value.'을 그리스 로마가 취한, 확장 경제에 걸맞은 구체적인 조치가 언급되어 있는 주제문으로 볼 수 있다.

구조 분석 ⊙ Athens and Rome both <u>outgrew</u> their local agricultural capacity and <u>substituted</u> overseas trade for it.

→ outgrew는 '규모가 ~보다 커지다'라는 뜻의 타동사이고 and 이하는 'substitute A for B' 구문으로 'B를 A로 대체하다'의 뜻이다. it는 their local agricultural capacity를 가리킨다.

153
정답 ⑤

정답 해설 이 글은 경제가 국내 농산물 수준을 넘어 해외 무역으로 확장돼 가자 그리스와 로마가 이에 맞춰 취했던 여러 가지 재정 개혁 조치를 소개하고 있다. 따라서 주제는 ⑤ '아테네와 로마가 확장 경제에 맞춰 취했던 조치들'이 적절하다.

① 수출 지향형 경제를 억제하기 위한 아테네와 로마의 시도들
② 아테네와 로마가 고대 강국으로 부상한 배경
③ 지중해 인근에서 벌어졌던 고대 권력 투쟁
④ 아테네와 로마가 현대 자본주의 탄생에 기여한 점

154
정답 ④

정답 해설 그리스와 로마가 농업 생산 규모의 확대로 국제 교역에 주력하는 상황이므로 양국이 만든 지불 시스템은 국제 교역의 불확실성에 취약한 것이 아니라 불확실성을 견디는 강한 것이라야 의미가 있다. 따라서 (d)는 robust 등의 낱말로 바뀌어야 한다. 'subject to'는 '~를 받기 쉬운' '~에 취약한'의 뜻이다.

[155~156]

지문 해석 제대로 먹고 운동하는 것 이외에 수명을 연장하는 다른 놀라운 방법이 있다. 다행히도 이들 수명 연장 방법은 당근을 마구 먹어치우거나 헬스장에서 맹렬히 칼로리를 태우는 것보다는 훨씬 쉽고 재밌다.

오래 살기 위한 첫 번째 방법은 소설을 많이 읽는 것이다. 예일 대는 10년간의 연구를 통해 책을 읽는 사람이 안 읽는 사람보다 2년을 더 산다는 사실을 알아냈다. 이것은 독서가 인지 능력을 개선해주기 때문으로 알려졌다. 일주일에 세 시간 반 이상의 독서로 실험 참가자들은 기억력과 창의력이 개선됐고 이것이 수명 연장에 기여하였다. 주간 독서량이 평균에 조금 못 미치는 사람조차도 전혀 안 읽는 사람보다는 평균 수명이 17% 정도 길었다. 그러나 만화책 방으로 달려가거나 이것을 몇 시간씩 소셜 미디어 검색을 위한 구실로 쓸 심산이라면 이러한 건강상의 혜택은 소설 읽기에만 해당된다는 점을 기억하는 게 좋다.

독서가 당신의 취향이 아니라 하더라도 수명을 늘일 또 한 번의 기회가 있는데 유머를 통해서다. 노르웨이 연구자들이 유머나 유머 시도를 제대로 이해하기만 하면 남녀 구분 없이 육체적으로 더 건강한 삶을 누릴 수 있다는 사실을 알아냈다. 이는 부

정적 상황을 웃어넘길 수 있는 상황으로 바꾸는 능력이 스트레스를 줄여주기 때문이다. 이 경우 당신의 마음이 몸을 통제해 지나치게 부정적인 에너지가 염증으로 발전해 나가는 것을 막아주기 때문인 것으로 보인다. 그래서 모든 아재 개그도 들려줄 만한 가치가 있는지도 모른다. 다음에 최근 유행하는 건강법이 당신을 유혹한다면 건강한 삶을 도모하는 방법은 여럿이라는 점을 기억하라. 몸과 마음에 좋다고 생각하고 책을 빼들라. 그리고 활짝 웃어라.

글의 소재 수명 연장 수단으로서의 소설 읽기와 유머

주요 어휘 chow down 게걸스럽게 먹다, under par 평균 미만의, inflammation 염증, fad 일시적 유행

글의 흐름 ⊙ 주제문은 'The first step to living longer is reading more novels.'와 'If reading isn't your thing, you have another opportunity to extend your life through humor.'이고, 병렬식 구조이다.

구조 분석 ⊙ The first step to <u>living</u> longer

→ to live가 아니고 to living임을 주의하라. to는 to 부정사의 to가 아니고 전치사다. 여기서 to는 'the key to success'의 to와 성격이 같다.

⊙ it's <u>worth</u> <u>noting</u> that these health benefits are applicable only to novels.

→ it's worth ~ing that 구문이다. it은 가주어이고 that 이하가 진주어이며, ~ing는 worth의 목적어이다. it's worth ~ing that는 '~는 ~할 만한 가치가 있다.'는 뜻이다.

155
정답 ④

정답 해설 둘째 단락의 첫 문장 'The first step to living longer is reading more novel.'과 둘째 단락의 첫 문장 'you have another opportunity to extend your life through humor.'를 통해 이 글이 '효과적인 수명 연장 수단으로서의 소설 읽기와 유머'에 대해 말하고 있음을 알 수 있다. 따라서 이 글의 가장 적절한 제목은 ④이다.

① 현대생활의 어떤 점이 스트레스를 주나?
② 당신의 삶의 질을 향상시킬 수 있는 놀라운 팁
③ 지적 능력을 높이기 위해 우리가 해야 하는 것
④ 장수의 숨겨진 비결 : 소설과 유머
⑤ 공부와 웃음은 결국 우리를 어디로 이끄나?

156
정답 ③

정답 해설 (A)가 있는 구절은 '그런 혜택은 소설에만 해당된다'는 내용이므로 (A)에는 applicable이, (B)가 있는 구절은 '아재 개그도 들려줄 만하다'는 내용이므로 (B)에는 telling이

각각 와야 한다. 선택지의 conducive는 '도움이 되는', withold
는 '억제하다', shower는 '마구 퍼주다'는 의미이다.

[157~158]

지문 해석 어머니가 대학 교직에서 은퇴했을 때 텅 빈 대저택
에 당신 홀로 남았음을 알게 되었다. 자녀들은 이미 장성해서
타 도시에서 살고 있었고 그중 몇은 먼 도시에 살았으며 아버
지는 이미 수년 전에 돌아가신 상태였다. 전직 사회학과 교수
인 어머니는 한 가지 꾀를 냈는데 시간이 지나 돌이켜 생각하니
그것은 사교를 위한 절묘한 수였다. 당신 학교의 대학원생에게
무료로 방을 제공하되 노인들이 존경받는 동아시아 출신들에
게 우선권을 준 것이었다. 어머니가 은퇴한 지 30년이 더 됐지
만 이 방식은 아직 계속되고 있다. 그녀는 일본과 대만 출신의
동거인을 계속 교대로 들여왔으며 현재는 북경 출신과 살고 있
는데 이런 동거는 그녀의 행복한 삶에 크나큰 도움을 주고 있는
것처럼 보인다. 그중 한 부부는 애기를 낳았는데 그 딸이 자라
면서 어머니를 친할머니처럼 따르기도 했다. 두 살배기 아기가
매일 아침 어머니 방으로 들어와 어머니가 깼는지 확인하고 늘
상 포옹으로 하루 인사를 했다. 그 아기가 태어났을 때 어머니
연세가 거의 90이었는데 환희의 다발로 온 집안을 감싸는 바람
에 어머니는 몸과 마음이 실제로 몇 살 젊어지시는 듯했다. 어
머니가 누린 천수 중 얼마가 그녀의 생활환경에 기인하는지는
결코 알 수는 없지만 그것이 그녀의 사려 깊은 사교술의 일부였
음은 증거가 말해준다.

글의 소재 사교와 노년 건강

주요 어휘 in retrospect 되돌아보면, move 장기나 바둑의 수,
preference 선호, housemate 동거인, toddler 걸음마 타는 유
아, roam 배회하다, longevity 장수, social engineering 사교
공학, 사교술

글의 흐름 ⊙ 주제문은 'We'll never know how much of
my mother's longevity can be attributed to her living
situation, but evidence suggests hers was a wise bit of
social engineering.'으로, 미괄식 구조이다.

구조 분석 ⊙ her children had all <u>ended up</u> living in other
cities
➡ end up 전치사(in, with) 또는 ~ing 구문이다. '~한 상태로
끝나다.'의 뜻이다.
⊙ she made what, in retrospect, seems a smart social
move
➡ in retrospect는 삽입구, what은 복합관계대명사이다.
⊙ She has had a revolving series of housemates from
places like Japan, Taiwan, and currently Beijing
➡ 일본과 대만 출신의 동거인 시리즈가 회전됐다는 말은 일본
인 출신과 대만 출신 동거인이 교대로 여러 번 반복해 들어오다
가 현재는 북경 출신과 살고 있다는 말이다.

157 정답 ③

정답 해설 'She has had a revolving series of housemates
from places like Japan, Taiwan, and currently Beijing—
with what seem to be great benefits for her well-being.'
과 my mother actually seemed for a few years to get
younger, both physically and mentally.', 'We'll never know
how much of my mother's longevity can be attributed to
her living situation, but evidence suggests hers was a wise
bit of social engineering.'으로 필자의 어머니가 동거인들을
들여 교제함으로써 노년을 건강하고 편안하게 보낼 수 있었다
는 것을 알 수 있다. 따라서 이 글의 제목으로 ③이 적절함을 알
수 있다.
┌ ① 방해받지 않는 노후를 위한 어머니의 대담한 결정
│ ② 정년 후를 준비하는 최상의 방법
│ ③ 교제, 어머니의 편안한 노후의 비결
│ ④ 노인의 공경, 동아시아의 자랑스러운 문화유산
└ ⑤ 잦은 육체 접촉이 노화에 미치는 영향

158 정답 ④

정답 해설 'When one couple had a baby while living with
her, their daughter grew up treating my mother like her
own grandmother.'로 ④의 내용이 이 글의 내용과 일치함을
알 수 있다.
┌ ① → 몇 자녀는 먼 도시에 살았다.
│ ② → 무료로 제공했다.
│ ③ → 그곳에서는 노인이 공경받기 때문이었다.
└ ⑤ → 노년의 사교 생활이 장수에 얼마나 기여했는지는 알 수
       없다.

[159~160]

지문 해석 그 뿌리가 이교도와 기독교적인 전통에 있음에도 불
구하고 현대 미국의 할로윈은 사탕과 옷을 중심으로 한 순전히
세속적인 축제로 종종 취급된다. 그러나 가장 하찮은 이 휴일의
모습은 사실 심각한 종교적 역사를 가지고 있다.
중세 기독교 전통에 의하면 만성절 하루 전 저녁인 할로우타이
드 날 가난한 사람은 부잣집에 가서 그 집에 최근 유명을 달리
한 사람을 위해 기도를 바친다. 바치는 기도가 많을수록 영혼이
구제받을 가능성은 더 큰 것으로 믿어졌다. 이때 부자는 가난한
이에게 음식과 맥주를 대접했다고 역사가 니콜라스 로저스는
설명한다. 그러나 종교개혁이 끝나자 영혼이 이런 식으로 구제
받는다는 사상은 많은 신흥 교단에서 인기를 잃었다. 일부 주민
들이 이 전통을 이어갔지만 그 종교적 연관성은 가톨릭교도 사
이에서조차 사라져갔다.

일군의 아일랜드와 스코틀랜드 이민자들이 이 관습을 미국에 전파한 1840년 무렵이 되면 할로윈이 완전한 세속적인 놀이가 된다. 비록 아일랜드 가톨릭교도들이 그들의 새 고향에서 배척주의자 세력으로부터 갖가지 편견에 시달렸지만, 이 축제는 가톨릭 뿌리가 제거돼 재빨리 확산돼 갔다. 이민자들이 동화되어 가자 신문은 19세기 대학생들 사이에 유행하는 이 관습을 보도했다. 1930년대 무렵 북미에서는 이 오랜 전통을 지칭하는 새로운 용어가 생겨났다. '사탕 안 주면 장난치기'라는 말이다.

글의 소재) 할로윈의 기원

주요 어휘) frivolous 경박한, All Saints' Day 만성절, the departed =the deceased, 고인, denomination 교단, nativist 배척주의자, underpinning 지주, 토대, trick or treat 할로윈에 어린이들이 외치는 구호로 '사탕 안 주면 장난칠 거예요'의 뜻

구조 분석) ⊙ the celebration, having been stripped of its Catholic underpinning, quickly proved to be popular.

→ having been 이하가 분사 구문으로 'the celebration, as(since) it had been stripped of its Catholic underpinning(가톨릭 뿌리가 제거됐기 때문에, 즉 종교적 색채가 약해졌기 때문에 재빨리 대중적으로 확산될 수 있었다).'이라는 말이다.

159
정답 ②

정답 해설) 둘째 단락의 처음과 다음 문장을 보면 '가난한 사람이 부잣집에 가서 최근 유명을 달리한 사람을 위해 기도하고 그 기도가 많으면 많을수록 망자가 구원받을 가능성이 크다'는 내용을 알 수 있다. 그러므로 밑줄 친 'in this way'가 가리키는 것은 ②이다.

160
정답 ⑤

정답 해설) 할로윈이 미국에 유입돼 빠르게 확산되는 과정에서 탄생한 말은 할로윈의 대표적 구호인 trick or treat이다. '과자를 안 주면 장난칠 거예요'라는 뜻으로 할로윈 때 아이들이 집집마다 다니며 하는 말이다.

[161~162]

지문 해석) 오타와의 한 개조한 호텔 안에는 기존의 시설과는 매우 다른 운영 철학을 가진 알코올 중독 치료 센터가 입주해 있다. Oaks는 MAP 프로그램에 따라 추운 거리에서 방황하는 알코올 중독자들을 거둬들여 치료하기 위한 알코올 중독자들의 영구적 보급자리다. 무엇보다 절제를 우선시하는 다른 알코올 치료센터와 달리 Oaks 거주자들은 바로 그 건물에서 담근 13도 백포도주를 매시간 마실 수 있다.

거주자들은 커피잔이나 물잔, 머그잔 등 마실 수 있는 용기를 들고 매시간 와인 배급을 위해 줄을 선다. 배급은 아침 7시 반에 7온스로 시작해 매시간 5온스로 저녁 9시 반까지 이어지는데 이는 꾸준하나 비교적 해가 적은 양의 알코올 환자에게 권하자는 Oaks의 취지에 따른 것이다. 이런 색다른 접근을 택한 이유는 무엇일까? 오타와병원의 임원이자 Oaks 프로그램의 산파역 중 한 명인 제프 턴벌씨는 "모두가 절제했으면 좋겠지만 그게 가능할까요? 아마 아니겠죠."라고 말한다. 대신 턴벌씨와 스탭들은 손상 감소 이론을 따르는데 이는 실용적 전략을 통해 마약이나 알코올의 부정적 효과를 제한한다는 생각이다. MAP 프로그램을 비판하는 사람이 없는 건 아니지만 그것이 오타와 사회에 긍정적인 영향을 주는 건 틀림없는 사실이다. 동상 걸린 알코올 중독자와 관련된 119 전화나 병원 방문, 응급 출동 횟수가 상당히 줄었으니까.

글의 소재) 실용적인 알코올 중독 치료법

주요 어휘) pulled off of ~로부터 거둬들여진, abstinence 절제, clutch 꽉 잡다, ply ~ with ~에 ~을 계속 공급하다, subscribe to ~을 구독하다, 지지하다, paramedic 응급구조원

구조 분석) ⊙ The Oaks is a permanent home for alcoholics pulled off of the frigid streets to be treated for alcoholism under the Managed Alcoholic Program(MAP).

→ 'to be treated' 이하가 home을 꾸며주는 to 부정사의 형용사적 용법이고, for alcoholics pulled off of the frigid streets가 의미상의 주어다. It's a school for me to go to와 같은 구조이다.

161
정답 ⑤

정답 해설) Oaks에서 시행하는 알코올 관리 프로그램(MAP)은 알코올 중독자가 감당하기 어려운 무조건적인 절제의 수단보다는 중독자에게 일정량의 음주를 허용하는 실용적인 방법을 택했다. 그러므로 '욕심내지 말고 할 수 있는 만큼만 하라.'는 의미의 '씹을 만큼만 물라.'는 말이 이 글의 요지에 가장 가깝다. 따라서 정답은 ⑤이다.

① 천천히 꾸준히 해야 이긴다.
② 물에 빠진 사람 지푸라기라도 잡는다.
③ 하늘은 스스로 돕는 자를 돕는다.
④ 뜻이 있는 곳에 길이 있다.
⑤ 씹을 수 있는 만큼만 물라.

162
정답 ①

정답 해설) 빈칸을 부연·설명하는 관계사절 'which is the idea that the negative effects of drug or alcohol use can be limited through practical strategies.(실용적 전략을 통해

마약이나 알코올의 부정적 효과를 제한한다)'를 가장 잘 반영하는 것은 harm reduction이다.

[163~164]

지문 해석 어렸을 적 나는 아기들을 좋아하지 않았다. 뼛속까지 외동딸이었던 나는 어린애들이 짜증스러웠고 언제나 침 흘리고 기저귀 냄새를 풍기는 아기들은 특히 싫었다. 엄마나 어른들이 귀여운 아기들을 데려와 나의 관심을 끌려했지만 그럴 때마다 나는 이내 각각의 것을 외면했다. 이런 취향은 내 놀이에까지 영향을 미쳤다. 누가 소꿉놀이를 제안만 해도 나는 도망쳐 눈에 보이는 높은 나무로 오르곤 했다.

동물은 달랐다. 나는 사람인형을 싫어하는 만큼이나 동물인형을 좋아했다. 바비인형의 목을 비틀었을 테지만 곰인형은 포대기로 감싸 달래며 잠재우곤 했다. 살아있는 동물도 좋아했다. 고양이나 강아지에서 햄스터, 물고기, 카나리아까지 내가 엄마 노릇을 하며 데리고 놀고 싶지 않은 것은 없었다. 십대에서 이십대 초반까지 나는 언제고 귀여운 아기보다는 골든리트리버를 더 좋아했다. 나의 첫애는 마르고라는 히말라야고양이였다. 마르고는 내 대학원 생활의 공허함을 채워줬다. 마르고에 대한 나의 사랑으로 나는 그녀 사진을 액자에 넣고 할로윈이면 옷을 해 입히는 등 애완동물 마니아로 변해갔다. 나의 고양이가 내 아기였고 나는 그녀의 엄마였다. 마르고는 파고드는 타입이라 나는 그녀를 집 안 어디든 데리고 다니고 내 침대 밑에서 재우기까지 했다. 누가 돌봐주지 않아도 귀엽고 사랑스러운 마르고는 완벽한 아이였다.

글의 소재 동물을 좋아하고 아기를 싫어하던 유년의 취향

주요 어휘 enamor 매혹시키다, drool 침을 질질 흘리다, pique 호기심을 자극하다, trickle down to ~로 번지다, 스며들다, swaddle 아기를 포대기로 싸다, snuggly 파고드는, upkeep 양육

구조 분석 ⊙ An only child to the bone, I found small children irritating.

➡ An only child to the bone은 I와 동격이다.

⊙ I would pick a golden retriever over a cute baby any day.

➡ 여기서 over는 '~보다'의 의미를 지닌다. over는 in favor of와 바꿔 쓸 수 있다.

163
정답 ②

정답 해설 본문에서 '누가 소꿉놀이를 제안만 해도 나는 도망쳐 눈에 보이는 높은 나무로 오른다.'고 했다. 이는 소꿉놀이가 너무 싫어 나무 위로 도망치는 상황이므로 ② loathsome(극도로 싫은)이 맞다.

① 모험적인
② 극도로 싫은
③ 경박한
④ 어색한
⑤ 괴짜인

164
정답 ②

정답 해설 이 글에는 동물은 좋아하지만 아기는 싫어하는 필자의 취향이 잘 나타나 있다. 이는 첫 단락의 첫 문장 'When I was a child, I was not enamored with babies.'와 다음 단락의 'Animals were different. ~ I loved the real things too.' 부분으로 확인할 수 있다. 따라서 정답은 ②이다.

[165~166]

지문 해석 최근 테러로 프랑스 전역에서 보안이 강화되면서 리비에라 지방의 몇몇 도시들이 부르카처럼 신체의 대부분을 가리는 이슬람 수영복인 버키니를 해변에서 착용하지 못하도록 금지 조치를 내렸다. 그곳 시장들은 버키니가 노골적인 종교색을 드러내 프랑스의 세속주의 가치에 반하고 사회 질서를 뒤흔들 수 있다며 금지법이 옳다고 주장했다. 이러한 금지 조치가 소셜 미디어에서 논란이 되었고 급기야 몇몇 프랑스 법원은 8월 말 그 법이 기본 자유를 침해한다며 효력을 중단시키기도 했다.

한 무더기의 무장 경찰이 한 여성에게서 보수적인 수영복(버키니)을 강제로 벗기는 동영상이 유포되자 1920년대와 1930년대 비키니 착용을 단속하던 미국 경찰과 비교하는 사진이 즉각적으로 나란히 게시됐다. 여성들은 지나친 신체 노출과 노출을 지나치게 피하는 노력 사이에서 중용을 찾으려고 늘 중압감을 느끼는 것 같다. 버키니 판매상들은 이번 금지에도 불구하고 버키니 판매가 크게 늘었고 수요가 무슬림 여성은 물론 몸매에 자신이 없거나 피부암 전력이 있는 사람에게까지 다양화됐다고 말한다. 많은 사람에게 이것은 무엇을 입느냐 선택의 문제일 뿐이다.

개인의 자유 문제와 상관없이 버키니를 효과적으로 금지하는 것은 이제 시급히 해결해야 할 문제다. 지난 11월 테러 사태 이후 프랑스는 비상사태가 이어져오고 있다. 수천 건의 가택 급습과 구속, 그리고 급진 이슬람을 전파하는 것으로 추정되는 몇몇 모스크에 대한 폐쇄 조치가 취해졌다. 최근 현 프랑스 총리는 외국인의 모스크 지원을 금지하는 데 지지 의사를 표했다. 또 사르코지 전 대통령은 자신이 대통령에 재선되면 버키니를 금지하는 쪽으로 개헌하겠다고 공언했다.

글의 소재 프랑스에서의 버키니 착용 논란

주요 어휘 flamboyant 대담한, 노골적인, secularism 세속주의, pose a threat to ~에 위협이 되다, uproar 소란, 논란, viral 바이러스성의, 빠르게 확산되는, strain 압박, happy medium

중용=golden means

구조 분석 ⊙ Viral images of a recent incident in which a woman was forced to take off the conservative swimwear by a group of armed police were immediately compared to photos of US police enforcing bikini laws on women in the 1920's and 1930's.

→ 문장이 길고 복잡해 보이지만 Viral images(S)와 were compared(V)로 이뤄진 1형식의 문장이다. 나머지는 모두 S와 V라는 뼈에 붙어있는 살에 불과하다. 뼈와 살을 구분해내는 일은 독해에서 제일 중요하다.

165
정답 ③

정답 해설 프랑스가 세속주의를 옹호하는 상황(the French value of secularism)에서 (A)에 'public order(공공질서)'가 와야지 'religious practices(종교적 관습)'는 적절하지 않다. 또 극단주의 이슬람을 전파하는 모스크에 내려진 조치이므로 (B)에는 'closure(폐쇄)' 같은 부정적인 단어가 와야지 'dedication(헌신)'이나, 'retention(유지)'와 같은 긍정적인 단어는 적절하지 않다.

166
정답 ⑤

정답 해설 마지막 부분인 'former president Nicolas Sarkozy stated that if he is re-elected president he will change the country's constitution in order to ban the burkini.'로 ⑤가 이 글의 내용과 일치함을 알 수 있다.
- ① → 세속주의 가치에 반한다고 보았다.
- ② → 당시에 논란이 된 건 버키니가 아닌 비키니 착용 논란이었다.
- ③ → 버키니 매출이 오히려 늘었다.
- ④ → 외국인의 모스크 지원 금지를 지지했다.

[167~168]
지문 해석 학문 간 문제의 핵심에 이르는 지름길은 왜 사회과학이 아직까지 그것을 별로 필요로 하지 않았던 전문분야의 추구 대상이 돼야 하는지 묻는 것이다. 예를 들어 왜 한때 신성불가침이던 의학이 사회과학에 일말의 관심이라도 갖게 되었는가? 의학 분야는 확실히 나름대로 쌓아온 명성이 있어서 사회과학이 거기에 추가될 수 있다고 생각하는 것이 우스꽝스러울 정도다. 의학은 급속도로 발전하는 물리학과 생물학의 도움을 받고 있다. 왜 사회과학자들인가?(왜 사회과학자들의 도움을 받아야 하는가?) 왜 많은 의과대학에 행동과학 학과들이 설치돼 있는가?

그에 대한 답은 의학은 인간을 다루며 인간의 해부학적 구조와 생리는 단절되고 독립된 연구 주제가 아니라는 것이다. 오늘날 대부분의 의학 전공들은 대부분의 사회과학이 학생들에게 제공할 수 있는 것보다 훨씬 많은 이론과 테크닉에 대한 고도의 숙련을 요하는 매우 전문적인 분야다. 예를 들어 신진대사 장애의 측정과 치료는 요즘 전문성이 높은 업무다. 그러나 Schottstaedt 박사와 그의 동료들은 대사 병동 환자들의 생화학적, 생리학적 세부 기록들을 들여다보고 생리학 고유의 신진대사 수치상 차이들이라 여겨졌던 것들이 환자와 환자들 사이나 환자와 간호사, 의사, 또는 방문객 간에 맺는 관계의 변화와 크게 관련돼 있음을 알아냈다.

글의 소재 의학에서 학문 간 협업의 필요성

주요 어휘 substantive 실질적인, interdisciplinary 학제 간, 학문 간, hitherto 지금까지, sacrosanct: 신성불가침의, ridiculous 우스꽝스러운, behavioral 행동의, anatomy 해부학적 구조, insulated 단절된, self-contained 독립된, specialty 전공, metabolic 신진대사, disorder 장애, biochemical 생화학의, physiological 생리학의, ward 병동, variation 수치상의 차이, strictly 엄밀하게, vicissitude 변화, interpersonal 개인 간

글의 흐름 ⊙ 앞 단락에서 제기하는 질문에 대한 답 즉, 'The answer is that the medical profession deals with man, and what even man's anatomy and physiology are not an insulated, self-contained subject matter for study.'이 주제문이다.

구조 분석 ⊙ Why social scientists? Why the behavioral science departments in many medical schools?

→ 생략 구문으로 원래 문장은 각각 'Why (is the medical profession is supported by) social scientists?'와 'Why (are there) the behavioral science departments in many medical schools?'이다.

167
정답 ④

정답 해설 이 글은 의학이 고도로 전문적인 분야임에도 불구하고 많은 의학적 연구들이 독립적으로 단절돼 수행될 수 없음을 신진대사 환자의 경우를 예로 들어 설명하고 있다. 이는 의학의 학문 간 협업의 필요성을 암시하는 것이므로 윗글의 제목으로 가장 적절한 것은 ④ '의학에서 왜 학문 간 협업이 필요한가?'이다.
① 반드시 지켜져야 하는 개별 과학 간의 독립성
② 의학 전문가들의 명성을 높이기 위한 제언
③ 전문화: 현대의학의 실현 가능한 선택
⑤ 합병과 통합: 과학 연구상의 거스를 수 없는 추세

168

정답 해설 (b)의 'what'은 앞의 that과 병렬구조를 이뤄야 하기 때문에 that이 와야 한다. 또, 다음 문장이 완전하기 때문에 what은 올 수가 없다.

(a) 뒤 문장이 완전하고 선행사가 장소(point)이므로 관계부사 where가 쓰인 것은 적절하다.

(c) 분사구문으로 목적어(mastery)를 취하고 있으므로 현재분사 requiring이 쓰인 것은 적절하다. 이 문장은 'as they require master in depth ~'로 바꿔 쓸 수 있다.

(d) 이 문장의 주어는 'the measurement and treatment'인데 여기서는 측정(measurement)과 치료(treatment)를 하나의 과정으로 봤으므로 동사 is의 쓰임은 문법적으로 하자가 없다.

(e) strictly는 physiological를 수식하는 부사로 쓰였고 '엄밀하게 생리학적인,' 즉 '생리학 고유의'를 뜻하기 때문에 적절하다.

[169~170]

지문 해설 2018년 2월 5일 월가는 주식시장의 붕괴를 공포와 극도의 근심 속에 지켜봐야 했다. 다우존스지수는 사상 최대치인 1,175포인트 폭락했고 이튿날인 2월 6일에야 안정을 되찾았다. 실용적인 사고방식을 가진 실업가들은 이런 시장의 붕괴를, 강세장에 흔히 나타나는 기술적 조정을 무시하듯 그렇게 똑같이 무시하고 싶을 것이다. 어쨌든 경제의 기초가 양호하고 기업의 수익이 견실하며 인플레이션과 이자율이 낮은데 걱정할 이유가 어디 있는가? 그러나 거기 어딘가에는 신호가 있는지도 모른다. 변동성과 관련된 파생상품의 알고리즘식 매매가 시장의 급등락과 관계가 컸던 것은 사실이다. 그러나 미래에 대한 불확실성 또한 그러했다(시장의 급등락과 관계가 컸다). 지난 10년간 세계는 이지머니로 넘쳐났는데 이는 전례 없는 통화정책 상의 실험의 결과물이었다. 범람했던 물이 빠지면 바위가 드러난다. 유명한 미국 투자자의 말을 빌리면 "썰물이 빠질 때 비로소 누가 벌거벗고 수영하는지 알게 된다." 최근의 마비는 큰 해를 끼치지는 않았다. 시장의 지수들은 연초에 근접하는 수준까지 회복했다. 그러나 돈과 시장, 경제에 신뢰를 불어넣어 주는 것이 임무인 연방준비제도이사회는 이를 하나의 경고로 받아들여야 한다. 힘든 수영이 예상된다.

글의 소재 주가 폭락의 의미

주요 어휘 crash 붕괴, plummet 폭락하다, practical-minded 실용적인 사고방식을 가진, business people 실업가, dismiss 대수롭지 않게 생각하다, technical correction 기술적 조정, bullish 상승장의, fundamental 기초, earnings 실적, algorithmic 알고리즘의, trading 거래, 매매, volatility 변동성, 급등락, derivative 파생상품, awash ~이 넘쳐나는, easy money 조달 비용이 낮은 돈, 이지머니, unprecedented 전례 없는, recede 물러가다, 퇴각하다, swoon 졸도, 마비, Federal Reserve Board(FRB) 미 연방준비제도이사회

글의 흐름 ⊙ 주가 폭락의 의미를 살피며 이는 과거 통화 정책이 그 원인일 수 있는 만큼 FRB는 이를 심각하게 받아들여야 한다고 권고하는 글이다. 주제문은 'the Federal Reserve Board(FRB), whose mission it is to instil confidence in money, markets and the economy, should consider this a warning.'이고, 미괄식 구조이다.

구조 분석 ⊙ But so did legitimate uncertainty about the future.

→ 여기서 주어는 legitimate uncertainty about the future 이고 술어는 so did이다. so did는 'had a lot to do with the market's roller-coaster ride'를 가리킨다.

⊙ To quote a famous American investor, "You only learn who has been swimming naked when the tide goes out."

→ To quote는 독립 부정사이기 때문에 To quote의 의미상 주어가 주절의 주어인 You와 꼭 일치할 필요는 없다.

⊙ Market indexes ended up close to where they had been when the year began.

→ end up + 전치사 또는 ~ing 구문으로 '~한 상태로 끝나다' 의 뜻. end up 다음에 being이 생략됐다.

169

정답 해설 이 글은 주가 폭락 사태를 부른 근본 원인이 지난 10년간 실험적 통화정책으로 인해 이지머니가 넘쳐난 결과로 보고 이를 잠재적 위험 요인으로 경고하고 있다. 따라서 제목은 ①이 타당하다.

① 이지머니: 월가의 잠재적 위협
② 시장에서 지나친 두려움은 아무 도움이 안 돼
③ 시장의 힘을 믿자
④ 영원한 호황은 없다
⑤ 시장의 변덕에 너무 민감하지 말라

170

정답 해설 'But the Federal Reserve Board(FRB), whose mission it is to instil confidence in money, markets and the economy, should consider this a warning.'로 필자가 FRB는 이번 사태를 하나의 경고로 생각해야 한다고 했으므로 ⑤는 본문 내용과 다르다.

[171~172]

지문 해설 비행기 여행의 불만거리는 많다. 공항에서의 긴 줄, 보안 검색대의 까다로운 규칙, 이코노미 클래스의 비좁음, 옆

손님의 양말에서 나는 악취 등등. 기내식의 맛, 아니 맛없음과 관련된 불편한 기억도 두어 개 있을 것이다. 질긴 면발이나 찰지지 않은 밥이 도무지 마음이 끌리지 않지만 기내식의 실망스러운 맛에는 그럴 만한 이유가 있다.

루프트한자 항공이 2010년 실시한 연구에 의하면 비행기가 순항 고도 10.6km에 도달하면 기내 압력이 떨어지고 습도가 12% 밑으로 급격히 떨어져 사막보다 건조한 상태가 된다. 이러한 요인으로 단맛과 짠맛에 대한 민감도가 미뢰의 평소 능력의 30% 수준으로 떨어진다. 미각뿐 아니다. 우리가 미각 때문이라 생각하는 것의 80%는 사실 후각 때문이고 비행 중 후각은 둔해진다. 후각 수용체는 점액을 증발시켜 음식 냄새를 맡는데 건조한 공기 속에 콧구멍이 바싹 말라 이 기능에 이상이 생긴다.

또한 최근의 심리학 연구에 의하면 음식 맛에 관한 한 미각과 후각이 전부가 아닌 것으로 드러났다. 과도한 비행기 소음이 인간의 단맛과 짠맛에 부정적인 영향을 주는 반면 카더몬이나 레몬그라스, 카레 향은 더욱 강하게 한다는 것이다. 이런 모든 요인과 기내 요리사가 매일 수천 명분의 요리를 한다는 점 등을 고려하면 수분 섭취를 위한 한잔의 물이건 상큼한 탄산음료건 기내에서 제공되는 기내 음료에 대해 당신은 약간의 인내심을 발휘할 수 있을 것이다(맛이 없어도 참을 수 있다는 말).

글의 소재 기내식이 맛없는 이유

주요 어휘 stench 악취, plummet 급락하다, receptor 수용기, mucus 코의 점액, parch 바싹 마르게 하다, cardamon 카더몬, lemongrass 레몬그라스, soda pop 탄산음료

글의 흐름 ⊙ 기내식이 맛없을 수밖에 없는 몇 가지 이유를 서술한 글로, 주제문은 'Although the rubbery noodles and not-so-sticky rice truly lack appeal, there are valid explanations for the disappointment of airline food.'이다.

구조 분석 ⊙ Nearly 80% of what we think of as taste should really be attributed to our sense of smell,

➜ 여기서 what은 '80% of'의 목적어이자 동시에 'think of'의 목적어인 복합관계대명사다. what은 'the thing that.'으로 바꿔 쓸 수 있다.

⊙ be it a rehydrating glass of water or a rejuvenating soda pop.

➜ 여기서 be it 이하는 양보구문으로 whether it is로 바꿔 쓸 수 있다.

171
정답 ②

정답 해설 이 글은 기내식이 맛이 없을 수밖에 없는 이유를 상술하고 있다. 따라서 ②가 이 글의 제목으로 타당하다.

① → 모든 항공기 승객이 감내해야 하는 몇 가지 불편
② → 맛없는 기내식을 위한 옹호
③ → 고객의 주된 불만 사항인 맛없는 기내식

④ → 기내식의 질 향상을 위한 제언
⑤ → 여행객의 불쾌한 기억을 부르는 기내식

172
정답 ③

정답 해설 둘째 단락의 'Nearly 80% of what we think of as taste should really be attributed to our sense of smell'로 ③이 이 글의 내용과 일치함을 알 수 있다.

① → 기체가 순항 고도에 이르면 기내 압력이 떨어진다.
② → 운항 중인 기내에서는 단맛과 짠맛이 평소 능력의 30% 수준으로 떨어진다.
④ → 음식 냄새는 콧속의 점액이 증발하는 과정에서 맡아진다.
⑤ → 단맛과 짠맛에 부정적인 영향을 주고 카더몬이나 레몬그라스, 카레 향은 더욱 강하게 한다.

[173~174]

지문 해설 인간 정신의 혁명은 예술과 과학, 철학, 사회 정치적 사상 같은 인간 정신이 서로 다른 강도나 명확성, 타이밍을 가진 채로 다양한 표현 수단으로 나타난 단일 과정이다. 그것은 서로 다른 악기와 목소리가 차례로 연주되는 푸가나 오라토리오와 같다. 예술가의 목소리는 종종 첫 번째로 반응한다. 예술가는 사회에서 가장 예민한 구성원이다. 그의 변화 감각이나 다가올 것들에 대한 이해도는 보다 굼뜨고 이성적이고 과학적인 사상가보다 예리하다. 우리가 다가오는 사건이 미리 드리우는 그림자, 즉 예언자적 기대를 탐색할 곳은 한 시대의 사상이라기보다는 예술적 성과에서다. 나는 미래 사건의 예측을 말하는 것이 아니라, 인간 노력의 다른 분야에는 나중에야 나타나는 정신 자세가 예술적 성과의 형태로 드러남을 말하는 것이다. 따라서 기존 질서나 일반적으로 받아들여지는 가치 체계의 붕괴는 예술 창작을 지배했던 가치와 규범에 대한 반란에서 먼저 찾아볼 수 있고 또 실제로 찾아진다. 예술적 혁명은 사회 혁명에 선행한다. 마찬가지로 새로운 정치 체계나 사회 질서의 안정은, 그것이 프랑스 대혁명 이후의 화려한 신고전주의건 러시아 혁명 이후의 단조로운 사회적 리얼리즘이건, 새로운 예술 규범이 먼저 승인된 후에야 올 수 있다.

글의 소재 예술과 사회 변혁

주요 어휘 intensity 강도, manifestation 표현, fugue 푸가, 둔주곡, apprehension 우려, 이해도, acute 예리한, 민감한, breakdown 몰락, 와해, prophetic 예언자적인, revelation 폭로, 드러남, 계시, impending 다가오는, 임박한, recognizable 인지할 수 있는, revolt 반란, canon 규범, 정전, precede ~에 선행하다, drab 단조로운, 재미없는

글의 흐름 주제문은 'It is in the artistic production of a period, rather than in its thinking, that one should search for shadows cast in advance by coming events, for prophetic anticipation.'이고 중괄식 구조를 하고 있다.

구조 분석 ⊙ It is in the artistic production of a period, rather than in its thinking, that one should search for shadows ~

→ It ~that 강조 구문이다. 전치사구 in the artistic production of a period를 강조하고 있다.

⊙ I do not mean the forecast of future events, but rather the revelation

→ not ~ but 구문이다. 'not A but B'는 'A가 아니라 B'라는 뜻이다.

173
정답 ②

정답 해설 사회 변혁의 조짐은 예술 분야에서 가장 먼저 나타난다는 것이 이 글의 요지이므로 제목으로 가장 적절한 것은 ②의 '예술가, 다가올 사회 변화의 전령'이다.

① 누가 사회 통합을 이끄는가? 예술가인가, 사상가인가?
② 예술가, 다가올 사회 변화의 전령
③ 사회 혁명의 원인과 동인과 패턴
④ 예술가는 새 정치질서 탄생을 추동하는가?
⑤ 역사상 주요 사회 변혁을 이끈 숨은 힘

174
정답 ⑤

정답 해설 (e) 바로 앞 문장에서 예술의 변혁이 사회 변혁에 선행한다고 했으므로 새로운 예술적 규범이 새로운 정치체계의 안정에 선행한다는 내용이 와야 하는데 (e)에 followed를 쓰면 앞뒤가 뒤바뀌므로 followed를 preceded나 heralded, presaged 등으로 바꿔 써야 한다. 따라서 정답은 ⑤이다.

[175~176]

지문 해석 풍요로운 정보의 전통은 개별적인 인지 능력의 변화 없이도 매우 중요한 것이 될 수 있다. 혁신이나 환경 변화의 결과로 사회 환경이 바뀌고 다시 그 결과 부모의 능력이 다음 세대에 신뢰할 수 있는 수준으로 회복된다. 그러나 그 능력 회복은 성인이 청소년의 학습 환경을 조성하는 과정에서 성인 자신의 생태학적 활동의 부산물로 생겨난다. 사회 학습이나 가르침에 대한 적응의 결과가 아니다. 아직 피드백의 고리가 없다는 말이다. 하지만 확실한 것은 일단 풍요로운 정보의 전통이 확립되면 자연선택의 환경이 바뀐다는 점이다. 석기시대 생활로의 초기 변화는 기존에 있던 적응형 가소성의 기존 메커니즘이나 기존의 손재주 잠재력, 기존의 채집 패턴에 의존했을 수도 있다. 그러나 새로운 생활 방식이 일단 확립되면 그것은, 확실성은 크고 대가는 적은 상태에서 이 새로운 능력들을 습득하는 유전자 변이를 받아들이는 쪽으로 자연 선택할 것이다(부싯돌로

불을 붙이다가 손가락이나 눈을 잃을 수 있다). 부모 세대에게 받는 학습의 신뢰도나 정확성을 높여주는 돌연변이를 선호하는 쪽으로 선택이 이뤄질 것이다(이런 변이가 다른 값비싼 대가를 치르게 하지 않는다면). 그러한 돌연변이는 마음은 물론 몸의 형태마저 신기술에 적응시킬 수 있다. 고고학자 S. Ambrose가 지적한 대로 우리의 손과 손목, 팔은 침팬지의 그것들보다 부싯돌 불 켜기에 더 적합하다. 마찬가지로 전통이 부모에서 자식으로 수직적으로 전승된다면 전승의 신뢰도를 늘리는 쪽으로 부모의 행동을 변화시키는 돌연변이가 우세할 것이다.

글의 소재 학습의 전승을 추동하는 풍요로운 정보 전통과 돌연변이

주요 어휘 equipment 장비, 자질, juvenile 청소년의, adaptation 적응, preexisting 이미 존재하는, 기존의, plasticity 가소성, dexterity 능수능란함, foraging 채집의, flint knapping 부싯돌을 쳐서 불을 붙이는 것, mutation 돌연변이, unaffordable 감당할 수 없는, morphology 형태, 체형, vertically 수직적으로, reliability 신뢰

글의 흐름 주제문은 'But clearly, once information-rich traditions are established, the selective environment changes.'이고 중괄식 구조를 하고 있다.

구조 분석 ⊙ No feedback loop yet
→ loop와 yet 사이에 'has been formed'가 생략됐다고 보라.
⊙ Such mutations can adapt morphology as well as mind to the new technology.
→ adapt A to B 구문으로 'A를 B에 적응시키다'의 뜻이다.

175
정답 ②

정답 해설 이 글은 풍요로운 정보의 전통이 어떻게 유전 환경을 바꿔 세대 간 학습 전승을 용이하게 하는지를 주장하고 있다. 따라서 주제는 ② 학습의 전승을 가능하게 하는 풍요로운 정보 전통과 돌연변이가 적절하다.

① 성공적으로 복원되나 피드백 고리가 없는 부모의 능력
② 학습의 전승을 가능하게 하는 풍요로운 정보 전통과 돌연변이
③ 사회적 학습에의 적응을 통해 전승되는 부모의 능력
④ 석기시대의 도래를 촉발시켰을 수도 있는 환경 변화
⑤ 우세한 유전자 변이 획득에 따르는 혜택과 비용

176
정답 ⑤

정답 해설 풍요로운 정보의 전통이 확립되면 유전 환경이 바뀌어 세대 간 학습의 신뢰를 높이는 쪽으로 유전자 변이가 이뤄진다고 했으므로(빈칸 다음 다음 문장 참조) 빈칸에 들어갈 말은 ⑤의 '자연선택 환경이 변한다.'이다.

① 혁신 움직임이 사그라진다.
② 피드백 고리가 풀어진다.
③ 사회적 학습 추구가 지속된다.
④ 사회가 전반적으로 빠르게 안정된다.
⑤ 자연선택 환경이 변한다.

[177~178]

지문 해석 리스크 포트폴리오(위험 분산책)은 왜 사람들이 종종 다른 분야에서는 일상적이면서 그들 삶의 한 분야에서 독창적이 되는지를 설명해준다. T. S. Eliot의 기념비적인 작품 황무지는 20세기 가장 주목할 만한 시 중 하나로 칭송받아오고 있다. 그러나 그것을 1922년에 발표한 후 엘리어트는 직업적 모험을 품는다는 생각을 거부한 채 1925년까지 런던에서 은행 일을 계속했다. 소설가 Aldous Huxley가 그를 공식 방문한 뒤 말한 것처럼 엘리어트는 "어떤 은행원보다 더 은행원다웠다." 마침내 은행 직을 그만두었을 때도 그는 여전히 독립하지 않았다(전업 작가로 나서지 않았다). 생활의 안정을 위해 그는 그 후 40년 동안 출판 일을 하면서 틈틈이 시를 썼다. 폴라로이드 창업자인 Edwin Land의 말처럼, "자기가 독창적인 한 분야를 제외한 다른 분야에서의 확고한 태도에서 오는 감정적, 사회적 안정 없이는 어느 누구도 한 분야에서 독창적일 수 없다." 하지만 일상의 직업이 우리의 최상의 일(작품 활동)을 방해하지 않을까? 창조적 성취는 시간과 에너지의 커다란 영역 없이는 융성하기 어렵고, 회사는 집중적 노력 없이 발전할 수 없으리라는 것이 상식적 판단이다. 그러한 가정은 균형 잡힌 위험 분산책이라는 중요한 이점을 간과하는 것이다. 한 분야에서 안정감을 갖는 것은 다른 분야에서 독창적일 수 있는 자유를 우리에게 준다. 우리의 기본을 재정적으로 다짐으로써 우리는 설익은 책을 펴내거나 조잡한 예술 작품을 팔고, 검증되지 않은 사업을 시작하는 압박에서 벗어난다.

글의 소재 독창적이기 위한 조건으로서의 위험 분산

주요 어휘 portfolio 포트폴리오(위험을 회피하기 위해 다양한 금융상품에 분산 투자하는 것), conventional 재래적인, 일상적인, landmark 기념비, hail 칭송하다, embrace 품다, 포용하다, strike out on one's own 독립하다, distract 정신을 혼란하게 하다, 방해하다, shoddy 조잡한, untested 검증되지 않은

글의 흐름 주제문은 'Risk portfolios explain why people often become original in one part of their lives while remaining quite conventional in others.'이고 주제문의 주장을 뒷받침하기 위해 T. S. Eliot과 Edwin Land의 경우를 예로 제시하고 있다.

구조 분석 ⊙ No person could possibly be original in one area unless he were possessed of the emotional and social stability ~

➡ 가정법 과거의 형식을 취하고 있으며 unless 이하가 가정법

조건절이기 때문에 be 동사로 were를 썼다. '~하지 않다면 어느 누구도 ~하지 않을 것이다.'로 해석한다. possibly는 강조의 부사다.

177 정답 ②

정답 해설 어느 한 분야에 모든 것을 쏟아붓기보다는 안정적 생계 수단 확보 등을 통해 적절히 위험을 분산하는 전략이 독창적이 되는 데 더 효과적이라는 게 위 글의 논지이므로 제목으로는 ②의 '창조적이기 위해 리스크를 상쇄하라'가 적절하다.
① 리스크 없이 소득 없다.
② 창조적이기 위해 리스크를 상쇄하라.
③ 쇠는 뜨거울 때 때려라.
④ 필요하면 베팅을 늘려라.
⑤ 독창성은 위험을 피하지 않는 데 있다.

178 정답 ①

정답 해설 빈칸 다음 문장은 '하나의 영역에서 안정감을 갖는 게 다른 분야에서 독창적이 될 수 있는 자유를 준다'고 주장한다. 이는 곧 독창적이기 위해 리스크를 분산하라는 뜻이므로 빈칸에는 ①의 '균형 잡힌 위험 분산책'이 오는 것이 적절하다.
① 균형 잡힌 위험 분산책
② 공격적인 투자 전략
③ 보다 포괄적인 접근
④ 선택과 집중 전략
⑤ 투자 우선순위 계획

[179~180]

지문 해석 인간 통합의 과정은 하나의 분명한 형태를 취해 왔는데 그것은 이질적 집단 사이에 유대를 맺는 것이다. 유대는 계속해서 다르게 행동하는 집단들 사이에서조차 맺어질 수 있다. 사실, 유대는 숙적 사이에서조차 형성될 수 있다. 전쟁 자체가 가장 강력한 인간 유대 중 몇몇을 맺을 수 있다. 역사가들은 종종 세계화가 1913년 처음 절정에 이르렀다가 양차 대전과 냉전 시기에 장기간 쇠퇴했고 1989년 이후에야 회복했다고 주장한다. 이것은 경제적 세계화에 대해서는 맞는 말일 수 있으나 군사적 세계화라는 다른, 하지만 마찬가지로 중요한 동인을 무시한다. 전쟁은 사상과 기술, 인간을 상업보다 훨씬 빠르게 확산시킨다. 1918년 미국은 1913년보다 유럽과 더 밀접한 관계를 유지했다. 그러다가 둘은 전쟁 사이의 기간 동안 표류하다가 결국 2차 세계대전과 냉전에 의해 서로 운명을 떼려야 뗄 수 없는 밀접한 관계로 발전했다. 전쟁은 또한 사람들로 하여금 서로에게 더욱 관심을 갖게 만든다. 미국은 냉전 기간만큼 러시아와

밀접한 관계를 유지한 때가 없었는데, 그때 모스크바 복도에서 기침 소리만 나도 워싱턴 사람들을 복도에서 왔다 갔다 하게 만들었다. 사람들은 무역 파트너보다는 적에 대해 훨씬 더 관심이 많다. 대만에 대한 미국 영화 한 편당 약 50편의 베트남 영화가 있다.

글의 소재 인간 유대의 생성자로서의 전쟁

주요 어휘 distinct 뚜렷이 구별되는, 다른, sworn enemy 숙적, decline 감소, 쇠퇴, recuperate 회복하다, interwar 전쟁 사이의, inextricably 매우 복잡하게, scramble 분주하게 움직이다

글의 흐름 주제문은 'War itself can generate some of the strongest of all human bonds.'이다.

구조 분석 ⊙ the two then drifted in the interwar years, only to have their fates meshed together inextricably by the Second World War and the Cold War.

➜ to 부정사의 결과의 부사적 용법이다. 이 경우는 '결국 ~하게 된다'로 해석한다.

⊙ For every American film about Taiwan, there are probably fifty about Vietnam.

➜ 각각의 미국의 대만 영화에 대해 약 50편의 베트남 영화가 있었다는 말은 베트남을 소재로 한 영화가 약 50배 많았다는 말이다.

179
정답 ②

정답 해설 이 글은 이질적 집단 간의 유대 형성이 인간 통합의 가장 두드러진 특징이고 이런 유대는 전시 상황에서 아군 또는 적과의 밀접한 관계에서 가장 극명하게 드러난다고 주장한다. 따라서 주제는 ② 강력한 인간 유대의 창조자로서의 전쟁이 적절하다.

┌ ① 유감스러운 냉전 시대의 유산
│ ② 강력한 인간 유대의 창조자로서의 전쟁
│ ③ 경제적 세계화 대 군사적 세계화
│ ④ 적 사이의 이념적 기술적 교류
└ ⑤ 격동의 인간 경험이 초래하는 감정 변화

180
정답 ⑤

정답 해설 밑줄 친 부분은 글자대로는 미국에서 제작되는 대만 영화 한 편당 베트남 영화는 50편이라는 뜻이지만 문맥상 미국은 대만(교역 상대)보다는 적(베트남)에 관심이 크다는 것을 뜻한다. 이는 바로 앞 문장에 대한 부연 진술이다. 따라서 정답은 ⑤이다.

[181~182]

지문 해석 글쓰기는 힘들고, 좌절감을 안겨주고 심지어 무섭기

까지 하지만 동시에 놀라울 정도로 성취감을 느끼게 한다. 그래서 글을 쓸 때 정해진 일상성을 갖는 일이 중요하다. 가장 성공한 작가들의 공통적 특질을 하나 꼽는다면 그것은 그들 모두가 규칙적으로 모습을 드러낸다는 것이다. 글을 자정에 쓰건, 새벽에 쓰건, 마티니 두 잔을 곁들인 점심 후에 쓰건 그들에겐 정해진 일상성이 있다. 계획이 없는 목표는 단지 바람일 뿐이라고 생텍쥐페리는 말했다. 그리고 정해진 일상성이 계획이다. 전념을 다하는 계획인 것이다. 정해진 일상성은, 그것이 심리적 장애물이건 감질나게 하는 파티 초대장이건 당신의 글쓰기를 방해하는 모든 장애물을 없애는 데 도움이 된다.

하지만 그것은 그 이상이다. 당신이 하루 중 특정한 시간에, 오로지 사색을 위해 마련된 환경에서 글을 쓸 때 당신은 창의성에 도움이 되는 것들을 경험한다. 시간과 공간의 규칙성은 당신의 마음이 상상력의 문간을 거닐고 당신의 이야기에 완전히 집중하도록 하는 초청장 역할을 한다. 일상은 당신의 이야기와 연관된 인지적 신호를 촉발해 당신이 잠재의식 속에 소용돌이치는 사상과 이미지, 감정 그리고 문장들을 습득하도록 돕는다. 만일 당신이 특정 시간과 공간을 글쓰기용으로 지정해 그것을 성스럽고 일상적인 것으로 만든다면 삶을 방해하는 초조함을 극복하고 그 불협화음을 넘어서는 것이 어려워진다(쉬워진다). 일상성과 반복성은 상상의 영역 깊숙한 곳으로 당신을 이끄는 안내자와 같다.

글의 소재 글쓰기에서 일상성의 중요성

주요 어휘 daunting 힘든, fulfilling 성취감을 느끼게 하는, trait 특질, martini 마티니 칵테일, obliterate 없애다, 말살하다, obstacle 장애물, hinder 방해하다, tantalizing 감질나게 하는, rumination 사색, 반추, trigger 촉발하다, cognitive 인지의, cloak 망토, ~를 입히다, swirl 소용돌이치다, anoint 약을 바르다, 성스럽게 하다, 지정하다, transcend 초월하다, 극복하다, intrusive 침해하는, fretfulness 초조함, cacophony 불협화음

글의 흐름 주제문은 'That's why having a writing routine is so important'인 두괄식 문단이고 주제문에 이어 글쓰기에서 일상성이 중요한 두 가지 이유, 즉 방해 요소 차단과 창의력 증진이 제시되는 구조다.

구조 분석 ⊙ That's why having a writing routine is so important.

➜ is와 why 사이에 선행사 the reason이 생략된 관계부사 구문이다. 이럴 때 That's why를 For the reason으로 바꿔 '그런 이유로 ~하다'로 해석하면 매끄럽다.

⊙ The regularity of time and place serves as an invitation for your mind to walk through the doorways of your imagination and fully concentrate on your story.

➜ to walk는 invitation을 꾸며주는 형용사적 용법이고 for your mind는 to walk의 의미상 주어이고 fully concentrate는 to walk와 병렬구조다.

181

정답 해설 이 글은 글쓰기 할 때 routine을 유지하는 게 왜 중요한지 그 이유와 routine의 효능에 대해 설명하고 있다. 따라서 이 글의 주제는 ①의 '글쓰기에서 일상성의 중요성'이다.

① 글쓰기에서 일상성의 중요성
② 글쓰기에서 정해진 일상을 반복하는 일의 위험성
③ 직업적 성공의 결정적 요인으로서의 목표 설정
④ 일상의 변화가 가져오는 혼란과 좌절
⑤ 모든 문학적 글쓰기에 필요한 상상력과 집중력

182

정답 ⑤

정답 해설 이 글은 글을 쓸 때 왜 우리가 일상성을 유지해야 하는지 일상성의 중요성을 강조하고 있다. 글쓰기 전용의 시간과 공간, 즉 routine을 마련하면 삶의 초조함을 극복하기 어려워진다는 (e) 문장은 routine을 부정적으로 보기 때문에 전체 맥락에 어긋난다. harder를 easier로 바꿔야 한다. 따라서 정답은 ⑤다.

17. 장문의 이해 Ⅱ - 1지문 3문제

정답

		183 ②	184 ②	185 ⑤
186 ②	187 ④	188 ③	189 ②	190 ④
191 ⑤	192 ②	193 ⑤	194 ①	195 ⑤
196 ⑤	197 ③	198 ④	199 ④	200 ④

[183~185]

지문 해석 전 세계 대도시에 점점 높은 빌딩들이 끊임없이 세워지고 있다. 외부로 확장하기보다는 높이 솟는 빌딩이 건축의 보편적인 주제가 되었는데 그래야 사람들이 좀 더 가까이서 생활하고 일할 수 있기 때문이다. 이것이 이상적인 해결책으로 보이지만 거기에는 문제점도 있다. 대부분 고층 빌딩의 상층부는 대개 전망이 환상적이지만 그와 동시에 많은 주민들을 그것들의 그림자 속에 살게 만든다.

이 새로운 빌딩들은 도시의 스카이라인을 바꿀 뿐만 아니라 도시에 의도하지 않았던 영향을 미친다. 이 육중한 건축물들은 거리를 어둡게 하고 공원 같은 공공장소에 그림자를 드리운다. 이런 점점 커져만 가는 건축물들이 많은 성장 도시에서 논란을 불러일으키고 있다. 때로는 도시가 확장할 공간이 없는 경우도 있고 도심에 주거 및 사무 공간에 대한 추가 수요가 있는 경우도 있다. 어느 경우든 많은 주민들은 달가워하지 않는다. 논란의 초점은 종종 새로운 빌딩의 위치나

자연광의 부족, 혹은 그것이 도시에 미치는 부정적 영향 등이다. 이들 건물이 그 지역의 공기를 어떻게 바꾸는지, 혹은 다른 재산 가치에 어떤 영향을 미치는지 등과 같은 보다 현실적인 걱정도 있다.

고층 빌딩은 도시의 성장이 장기 거주민들에게 의도하지 않은 영향을 미칠 수 있음을 종종 상기시킨다. 새 건물이 드리우는 그림자가 일조권을 불평등의 한 징표로 탈바꿈시킬 수 있다. 일부 지역에서 자연광은 부유층만이 누리는 사치품이 되었고 그 과정에서 공공의 허락을 받지 않은 경우도 종종 있다. 이런 일은 부가적인 일자리와 사업 기회를 제공하는 성장의 결과로 생기지만 문제는 건물의 배치나 그 건물 아래 있는 거리, 주거지, 공공장소 등이 받을 영향이다. 주택이나 사무 공간에 대한 수요가 시민의 우려보다 우선하는가? 어떤 이들은 새 건물이 도시에게서 가치를 빼앗기보다는 더해준다고 주장한다. 대형 건물과 건축 스타일의 발전이 없다면 많은 세계 도시들이 오늘날 보여주는 매력을 잃는다는 것이다. 하지만 시민들이 그로부터 얼마나 혜택을 얻을 수 있는지에 대해 의문을 품는 이들도 있다.

글의 소재 도시 고층 빌딩의 빛과 그림자

주요 어휘 spark 불을 붙이다, placement 배치, skyscraper 마천루, access to sunlight 일조권, override ~에 우선하다

구조 분석 ⊙ The arguments often focus on the placement of new buildings, the necessity for natural light, or the negative effects it will have on the city.

→ it은 the necessity for natural light를 가리키며 '자연광의 부족'을 뜻한다.

⊙ The skyscrapers are often a reminder that the growth of cities can have unintended consequences for longtime residents.

→ reminder는 '~를 상기시켜 주는 것'이고 that은 동격의 that 이다. 이 문장은 The skyscrapers often remind that ~로 바꿔 쓸 수 있다.

183
정답 ②

정답 해설 이 글은 현대식 고층 빌딩이 나타나게 된 배경을 말 하면서, 그로 인한 긍정적 · 부정적인 영향들을 소개한 글이다. 그러므로 ②가 제목으로 가장 적절하다.

① 도심 고층 빌딩에 대한 끊임없는 수요
② 현대식 고층 빌딩의 빛과 그림자
③ 현대 건축 디자인의 눈부신 발전
④ 고층 빌딩이 도시 미관에 기여하는 바
⑤ 지속 가능한 도시 개발의 조건

184
정답 ②

정답 해설 (A)가 포함된 문장의 다음 문장(Some argue that new buildings add more value to a city than they take away from it.)으로 미루어 보았을 때, '고층 빌딩 건설이 초래 하는 긍정적인 효과가 부정적인 효과보다 더 중요한가?'를 묻 는 내용이 와야 한다. 즉, '주택 및 사무 공간에 대한 수요가 시 민의 우려보다 우선하는가?' 하는 내용이 와야 하므로 빈칸은 override가 타당하다.

① 용서하다
② 우선하다
③ 창조하다
④ 바꾸다
⑤ 자극하다

185
정답 ⑤

정답 해설 (e)는 세계의 도시를 가리키고, 나머지는 모두 고층 빌딩을 가리킨다. 같은 말의 반복을 피하기 위해 다양한 대체 어구가 사용되고 있음을 주목하자.

[186~188]

지문 해석 지난달 보스턴 레드삭스 경기에서 Tonya Carpenter 에게 일어난 일 때문에 야구계가 충격에 빠졌다. 그녀가 3루 쪽 두 번째 열에서 관전하고 있을 때 부러진 야구배트가 관중석으 로 날아들었다. 부러진 배트는 그녀의 머리를 때려 치명상을 입 혔다. 그녀는 병원으로 이송돼 몇 가지 수술을 받은 뒤에야 겨 우 목숨을 건졌다.

이 사건은 스포츠 경기에서의 안전과 책임에 대해 많은 문제점 을 제기했다. 각 팀은 관중의 안전 보장에 책임이 있는가? 파울 볼을 잡기 위해 대부분 구장 홈플레이트 뒤에 설치한 보호망을 구장 전체에 설치해야 하는가? 관중들에게 조심하라는 경고 문 구가 입장권에 인쇄돼 있기는 하지만 그것이 입장권 소지자에 게 책임을 떠넘기기에 충분한가? 구매할 입장권이 없고, 따라서 경고 문구를 볼 기회도 없는 경우는 어떤가? Tracey DeBriga 는 아들의 유소년 리그 게임을 보다가 야구공에 맞았다. 그녀가 깔고 앉은 담요를 정리하는데 투수가 잘못 던진 공이 담장을 넘 어 그녀의 얼굴을 때렸다. 그녀는 중상을 입었고 결국 엄청난 병원비를 지불해야 했다.

병원비 지불을 위해 그녀는 야구팀과 야구 리그 측을 상대로 손 해 배상 청구 소송을 제기했다. 주최 측은 관중들이 부상 걱정 없이 안전하게 관전할 수 있는 공간을 제공할 의무가 있다고 그 녀는 주장한다. 그녀의 이러한 주장은 입장하는 팬들의 수에 비 해 외야석이 충분하지 못하다는 사실에 의해 뒷받침됐다. 만일 안전한 자리에서 관전했더라면 부상당하지 않았을 거라고 그녀 는 주장한다. 결국 법원은 야구장을 찾은 관중 각자에게 책임이 있다며 DeBriga에게 패소 판결을 내렸다. 법원은 이러한 종류 의 이벤트에 참가할 때 관객이 주의할 것으로 기대되기 때문에 주최 측은 부상에 대해 책임이 없다고 말했다. 더군다나 주최 측 은 안전한 관전 구역을 제공할 의무도 없다고 법원은 덧붙였다.

글의 소재 야구장 안전사고의 책임

주요 어휘 bring up 제기하다, what if ~한 경우는 어떤가?, errant 길을 잘못 든, hefty 많은, 두둑한, bleacher 야구장 외 야석, rule against ~에 패소 판결을 내리다, liable for ~에 대 해 책임이 있는

구조 분석 ⊙ struck her in the face

→ 신체 접촉을 나타내는 관용 표현으로 동사 + 사람 + 전치사 + the + 신체 부위의 어순을 따른다. (e.g. She patted me on the back. He seized me by the sleeve.)

186
정답 ②

정답 해설 야구장 안전사고와 관련된 소송에서 피해자인 관중 이 패소한 내용을 소개하고 야구장 안전사고의 일차 책임은 관 중 자신에게 있음을 암시한 글이므로 제목은 ②가 적절하다.

① 준비가 안 됐으면 야구장 방문을 삼가라.
② 야구 관람은 본인 책임
③ 불행은 홀로 오지 않는다
④ 야구의 인기 요인은?

⑤ 나쁜 일은 언제 어디서든 일어나기 마련

187
정답 ④

정답 해설 '입장권이 없고, 따라서, 경고문구도 접할 수 없다'는 흐름이므로 (A)에는 '인과'의 연결사가, (B)에는 법원이 판결 내용을 추가하는 것이므로(It added) '추가'의 연결사가 각각 와야 한다.

188
정답 ③

정답 해설 'She was setting up a blanket to sit on when an errant throw went over the fence and struck her in the face.'에서 알 수 있듯이 Tracey DeBriga는 타자가 아닌 투수의 공을 맞았다. 따라서 ③은 이 글의 내용과 일치하지 않는다.

[189~191]

지문 해석 전통적으로 아빠보다는 엄마가 애들을 잘 돌보는 것으로 여겨져 왔다. 일반적으로 엄마가 배려심이 더 많고 애들의 감정과 더 잘 통한다. 아빠는 애들과 장난하는 데 관심이 많고 우스꽝스러운 짓을 잘 해낸다. 가령 한 연구에 의하면 다섯 달 젖먹이를 돌보는 엄마는 놀 때 아기들과 눈을 맞추고 그들의 동작을 그대로 담아낸다고 한다. 반면에 아빠들은 행동이나 동작으로 애기들을 자극해 웃게 하는 경향이 있다. 새 연구에 의하면 이 두 육아 스타일 모두 어린이의 정서적 안녕에 좋고 전반적인 발달에 도움이 된다고 한다.
과거에 연구원들은 육아 평가에서 아빠에게 낮은 점수를 줬다. 그러나 연구에 참여한 아이들을 인터뷰해 보니 그들은 아빠를 높게 평가하고 아빠와 관계가 좋다고 한다. 이 일로 연구원들은 이전 실험의 정당성을 의문시하게 됐다. 그들은 초기 평가가 잘못됐다는 것을 알았는데 그 평가가 엄마가 잘하는 몇몇 솜씨를 중심으로 이뤄졌기 때문이다. 다정다감하기, 위로의 느낌 전하기 등인데 이는 일반적으로 아빠들의 강점이 아니다.
아빠들은 애들을 격려하고 자신감을 심어주는 데 강점이 있다. 이런 요소를 평가 항목에 포함시키자 아빠들의 점수가 상당히 좋아졌다. 아빠의 소란스럽고 다소 무계획적인 놀이 방법이 결국은 애들의 모험심과 탐구심을 키우는 데 도움이 됐음이 드러났다. 반면 엄마들은 놀 때 애들을 부추겨 육체적으로 과감하라고 가르치는 경우가 많지 않다.
결국 연구원들은 아빠의 육아와 놀이 방법이 엄마와는 다른 방식으로 애들의 발달에 도움을 준다는 것을 깨달았다. 아빠들은 육체적인 면과 놀이를 이용해 웃음을 유도하고 감정을 고조시키지만 보다 중요한 것은 그들이 아이들로 하여금 최고조에 이른 감정을 조절할 수 있도록 도와준다는 것이다. 아빠와 놀 때 애들은 종종 흥분하거나 화내기도 하지만 자신의 감정을 조절

해 도전하는 임무를 끝낸다. 감정이 상황을 지배하지 못하게 하는 이런 능력을 통해 아빠는 애들한테 자신감을 불어넣어 주는 것이다.

글의 소재 아빠 육아법의 경쟁력

주요 어휘 typically 전형적으로, 일반적으로, interact 상호작용하다, mirror 그대로 담아내다, stimulate 자극하다, parenting 육아, overall 전반적인, development 발달, evaluation 평가, speak highly of ~을 칭찬하다, validity 정당성, 타당성, be based on ~에 근거하다, affectionate 다정다감한, strong suit 높은 패, 강점, criteria 기준, criterion의 복수, boisterous 시끌벅적한, physicality 육체적임, 육체적인 힘, heighten 고양시키다

글의 흐름 ⊙ 주제문은 'In the end, what researchers have learned is that a father's style of parenting and play helps a child develop in a different way than their mother's style does.이다. in the end같은 결론/요약의 연결사를 품는 연결사가 있는 문장이 주제문일 경우가 많다.

구조 분석 ⊙ For example, one study shows that mothers interacting with five-month-old infants are more likely to <u>look</u> into the child's eyes during playtime and <u>mirror</u> their movements.
→ mirror their movements에서 mirror는 타동사로 쓰였고 mirror their movements는 look into the child's eyes와 병렬 구조이다.

⊙ This led researchers to question the validity of their previous experiment.
→ 무생물 주어 구문이기 때문에 '이것이 ~를 ~로 이끌었다'보다는 '이로써 ~는 ~하게 되었다'로 해석하는 게 자연스럽다.

⊙ the reason the initial evaluations were wrong was because they were based on skills that mothers were typically better at.
→ the reason 다음에 관계부사 why가 생략됐다. 이 문장은 the reason is that(because) 구문으로 '~한 이유는 ~때문'의 뜻이다.

189
정답 ②

정답 해설 이 글은 최근 재발견된, 자녀 교육에서 아버지의 상대적 강점을 연구 사례를 들어 예시하고 있다. 따라서 정답은 ②이다.
① 아빠와 엄마의 자녀 교육 스타일의 유사성
② 재발견된 아빠 자녀 교육법의 강점
③ 균형 잡힌 아빠 엄마 교육의 중요성
④ 엄마 교육의 보조 수단으로의 아빠 교육
⑤ 아빠 교육이 낮게 평가돼 온 이유

190

정답 해설 앞에서 엄마의 이야기를 한 뒤에 아빠를 말하고 있기 때문에 (A)에는 '전환'의 연결사인 on the other hand가 적합하다. 또, (B)에는 마지막 단락에서 여태까지 내용을 종합하는 것이기 때문에 '결론/요약'의 연결사 In the end로 시작하는 것이 타당하다.

191

정답 ⑤

정답 해설 마지막 단락의 'but the key is that they also help the children control these emotions in their heightened state.'로 ⑤가 이 글의 내용과 일치함을 알 수 있다.

① → 아빠에 해당하는 말이다.

② → 과거에 연구원들은 육아 평가에서 아빠에게 낮은 점수를 줬다.

③ → 초기의 교육 평가는 엄마가 잘하는 솜씨를 중심으로 이루어졌다.

④ → 아빠의 시끌벅적한 교육이 모험심 키우기에는 더 효과적이다.

[192~194]

지문 해설 툼 레이더는 단지 영화일 뿐 아니라 흔치 않은 고대 풍습으로 중국 전역에서 실제 일어나고 있는 일이다. 결혼 못 하고 죽은 여인들이 무덤으로부터 파내지고 그들의 시신이 결혼 못 하고 죽은 아들을 영혼 결혼시켜 주려는 가족에게 팔려나가고 있다. 일단 영혼 결혼이 끝나면 여인의 시신은 신랑의 가족묘로 옮겨져 묻힌다.

전통적으로 중국에서 영혼 결혼은 죽은 이들을 위한 것이었다. 그러나 지금은 살아있는 '신랑'과 죽은 '신부' 사이에서도 드물지 않게 볼 수 있다. 살아있는 친척들은 그들의 식구가 죽은 후 외롭지 않게 하려고 이런 영혼 결혼을 치른다. 그것은 또한 가족이 망자의 이루지 못한 소원을 들어주는 방법이기도 하다. 살아있는 가족은 죽은 아들의 소원을 풀어주지 못하면 그가 성나고 불안에 헤매는 영혼이 될 것으로 믿는다.

영혼 결혼이라는 콘셉트가 간단해 보일지 모르나 그것은 그리 쉽게 치러지지 않는다. 산 사람에게 적용되는 똑같은 기준이 영혼에도 적용된다. 풍수 전문가가 가족을 도와 영혼 신부를 고르고 신부 가격과 지참금을 정하는데 여기에는 보석, 하인 그리고 저택이 포함될 수 있다. 하지만 이런 혼수와 돈거래는 형식적인 것으로 실제 돈을 주고받지는 않고 혼수도 단지 종이 장식일 뿐이다.

최근 폐지된 한 자녀 정책과 전통적인 남아 선호로 안타깝게도 중국에는 남자 인구가 여자보다 월등히 많고 그래서 산 신부 죽은 신부를 막론하고 신부가 충분치 않다. 이런 현실은 불법적인 묘지 도굴이나 유골 매매 같은 사태를 불렀다. 돈을 손쉽게 벌려는 자들은 심지어 살인까지도 서슴지 않는다. 이런 불편한 진실이 지난 8월 한 중국 남자가 중매쟁이로 가장하고 정신지체 여인 두 명을 살해함으로써 만천하에 드러났다. 영혼 결혼이 죽은 식구에게 바치는 가슴 뭉클한 헌사이건, 범죄율을 높이는 섬뜩한 의식이건 전통은 전통이다. 이런 풍습이 중국에서 사라질 기미가 보이지 않기 때문에 우리는 단지 그것이 한 사람을 죽여 다른 사람의 영혼을 만족시키는 식의 폭력적이고 불법적인 쪽으로 흐르지 않기만을 바랄 뿐이다.

글의 소재 중국의 영혼 결혼 풍습

주요 어휘 tomb raid 도굴, make amends for 보상하다, fengshui 풍수, dowry 신부지참금, outnumber 숫자가 더 많다, make a quick buck 돈을 손쉽게 벌다, mentally disabled 정신 장애의, grisly 섬뜩한

글의 흐름 ⊙ 주제문은 'Tomb raiding is a real thing happening throughout China as a part of an unusual, ancient custom.'으로 두괄식 구조이다.

192

정답 ②

정답 해설 이 문제는 이 글이 무엇을 말하고 있는지를 묻고 있다. 이 글은 중국에서 성행하는 영혼 결혼의 이모저모를 살피고 있다. 때문에 정답은 ②이다.

① 망자의 치유 수단인 영혼 결혼

② 중국에서 성행하고 있는 영혼 결혼

③ 망자의 못 이룬 꿈에 대한 보상의 중요성

④ 영혼 결혼에 따르는 복잡한 절차

⑤ 오랜 전통을 지켜나가는 의미

193

정답 ⑤

정답 해설 빈칸이 있는 문장에서 필자는 한 사람의 '무엇'을 만족시키기 위한 영혼 결혼이 다른 사람을 죽이는 식의 폭력적이고 불법적인 쪽으로 흐르지 않기를 바란다고 했으므로 '무엇'에 해당하는 가장 적절한 말은 ghost이다.

① 요구

② 관심

③ 자존심

④ 웰빙

⑤ 영혼

194

정답 ①

정답 해설 둘째 단락의 두 번째 문장인 'However, now it's not uncommon to have a living "husband" and a dead "wife."'

로 ①이 이 글의 내용과 일치함을 알 수 있다.

- ② → 여성의 시신은 신랑의 가족묘에 묻힌다.
- ③ → 산 사람의 결혼 절차가 그대로 적용된다.
- ④ → 형식적일 뿐이고 실제 지불되지는 않는다.
- ⑤ → 이 관습의 끝은 보이지 않는다(there is no end in sight for this custom).

[195~197]

[지문 해석] 1973년에 스티븐 킹은 빈털터리가 되었다. 그는 이 동식 가옥에 살았고 철선과 접착테이프로 얼기설기 엮은 낡은 뷰익을 몰았다. 그가 동 메인의 사립 고교인 햄프든 아카데미에서 영어를 가르치는 동안 아내인 태비는 던킨 도너츠에서 야간 근무를 했다. 생계 해결을 위해 킹은 여름이면 업소용 세탁공장에서 일했고 경비원이나 주유소 보조로 부업을 했다. 겨우 걷기 시작한 애와 갓난아기를 먹여 살리고 틈나는 대로 소설을 써야 했으므로 돈 — 그리고 소설 쓸 시간 — 벌기가 여간 어렵지 않았다. 킹은 타자기조차 마련할 여유가 없어서, 그는 태비가 대학 때부터 쓰던 구식 모델을 함께 써야 했다. 태비는 세탁실에 임시 책상을 하나 만들어 세탁기와 건조기 사이에 끼워 넣었다. 매일 저녁 태비가 기저귀를 갈고 음식을 하는 사이 킹은 가방 속에 채점 안한 시험지들을 무시하고 세탁실에 파묻혀 글쓰기에 전념했다. 초기 결과는 신통치 않았다. 킹은 그의 단편소설들을 카발리에나 펜트하우스 같은 남성 잡지사에 보냈다. 그가 운이 좋으면 이따금 소액 수표가 우편함 속에서 발견되기도 했다. 그것은 정부의 복지 혜택을 겨우 면하게 할 정도의 액수였다.
어느 날, 햄프든의 영어 과장이 킹으로선 거절하기 어려운 — 그러리라고 그가 생각한 — 한 가지 제안을 했다. 토론 클럽에 새 지도교사 한 명이 필요했는데 킹 본인만 원하면 얻을 수 있는 자리였다. 연 300달러를 여분으로 버는 거니까 많지는 않아도 그의 가족의 10주치 식료품비 정도는 충당할 수 있었다. 여분의 수입이 생긴다는 점에 마음이 끌려 그는 집에 와서 태비도 그 소식에 열광하겠거니 생각했다. 그러나 그녀는 그리 달가워하지 않았다.
"글 쓸 시간이 있겠어요?" 그녀가 물었다.
"아니 별로." 내가 대답했다.
그러자 태비가 "그럼 하지 마세요."라고 말했다.
그래서 킹은 그 직을 거절했다. 그것은 잘된 결정이었다. 일 년이 채 안 돼 그는 캐리라는 베스트셀러를 써서 트레일러 신세를 면할 수 있었다.

[글의 소재] 무명 시절의 스티븐 킹

[주요 어휘] second-shift 야간 근무 조, scrape by 근근이 살아가다, moonlight 부업하다, be one's for the taking 원하기만 하면 얻을 수 있는, a good call 잘된 결정

[구조 분석] ⊙ It was just enough money to keep the King family off of welfare.

→ 여기서 keep A off of B는 keep A off B와 같은 구문으로 'A를 B에게서 떼어놓다'는 뜻이다. 킹의 가족을 (정부의) 복지 혜택으로부터 떼어냈다, 즉 정부의 복지 혜택을 면하게 했다는 뜻이다.

⊙ he would write his way out of that trailer with a bestseller called Carrie.

→ 동사 + one's way out of 구문으로, '~함으로써 ~로부터 벗어나다'의 뜻이다. (e.g. He tried to explain his way out of the difficult situation. 그는 설명을 통해 곤경을 벗어나 보려 하였다.) (e.g. She elbowed her way out of the crowd. 그녀는 팔꿈치로 밀치며 군중으로부터 벗어났다.)

195 정답 ⑤

[정답 해설] 제시된 요약문은 '경제적 어려움 속에서도 굽히지 않는 킹의 분투적 글쓰기가 결국 _____을 가져왔다.'라는 내용이다. 따라서 이 글의 말미에 베스트셀러로 트레일러 신세를 면할 수 있었다는 내용으로 보았을 때, 빈칸에는 ⑤의 'a dramatic turnaround(극적 반전)'가 타당하다. ③의 경우, 트레일러 신세를 면한 것을 '졸부'라 표현한 것은 지나치다.

- ① 더욱 깊어가는 고통
- ② 심각한 부부간의 불화
- ③ 졸부의 탄생
- ④ 성공적인 학문적 성취
- ⑤ 극적 반전

196 정답 ⑤

[정답 해설] 글의 마지막 부분의 'So King turned down the job.'과 'Within a year, he would write his way out of that trailer with a bestseller called Carrie.'로 ⑤가 이 글의 내용과 일치함을 알 수 있다.

- ① → 가방 속에 채점 안 한 시험지들을 무시하고 세탁실에 파묻혀 글쓰기에 전념했다.
- ② → 정부의 복지 프로그램 신세를 겨우 면할 만큼의 액수였다.
- ③ → 킹 본인만 원하면 얻을 수 있는 자리였다.
- ④ → 태비도 그 소식에 열광하겠거니 생각했다. 그러나 그녀는 별로 달가워하지 않았다.

197 정답 ③

[정답 해설] 나머지의 'he'는 이 글의 중심인물인 Stephen King을 가리키지만 ⓒ의 'he'는 King에게 debate club의 a new faculty advisor를 제안한 the head of Hampden's English department를 가리킨다.

[198~200]

[지문 해석] 19세기 원소주기율표를 개발한 러시아 화학자 멘델레예프는 화학 역사에서 중요 인물을 가리는 어떤 리스트에서도 빠지지 않는다. 그런 그가 노벨상 수상 초기에 생존해 있었음에도 불구하고 노벨상을 타지 못했다. 문제는 1895년 노벨이 '바로 전 해에 인류에 큰 공헌을 할 가능성이 발견된 사람'에게 상을 주라는 유언을 했다는 점이었다. 따라서 1901년 수상을 필두로 수상 초기에는 주로 선정 당시 업적을 대상으로 했다. 그러나 1900년에 노벨상을 주관하는 노벨위원회가 노벨의 유언에 대한 유권 해석을 구체화한 규정을 발표했는데, 수상은 최근 업적을 우선 대상으로 삼되 이전 업적의 중요성이 최근에 알려졌을 경우 이전 업적도 포함한다는 내용이었다. 불활성 기체 원소가 1904년 노벨 물리학과 화학상의 주제로 떠올랐을 때 멘델레예프 지지자들은 이 두 번째 해석을 주목했다. 그들은 이 해석에 따라 멘델레예프의 19세기 주기율표가 수상 후보로 오를 수 있다고 생각했다. 그 결과 멘델레예프는 1905년 노벨상 수상자 후보에 올랐다. 그러나 상을 타지는 못했다. 그는 이듬해 또다시 후보에 올랐는데 이때 수상 후보를 추천하는 노벨상위원회는 그의 추천을 4대 1로 표결했다. 그러나 수상자를 최종 결정하는 스웨덴 왕립 과학 아카데미가 투표 결과를 인정하지 않았다. 대신 위원 수를 4명 추가해 다시 표결하게 했다. 재표결 결과는 5대 4로 앙리 므와상 쪽으로 기울었는데 일차불소를 분리하고 전기로를 개발한 그의 공로를 인정한 것이다. 왕립 아카데미는 이 표결을 받아들였다. 학자들은 왕립 아카데미의 주요 멤버인 스반테 아레니우스가 멘델레예프의 수상을 저지했을지 모른다고 믿는다. 자신의 이온 해리 이론 – 전해질이 물속에서 이온으로 해리된다는 생각 – 을 멘델레예프가 집요하게 그리고 공개적으로 비판한 데 대해 그가 못마땅해 했기 때문이다. 아레니우스는 멘델레예프의 업적이 낡은 것이라 생각했을 수도 있다. 멘델레예프는 1907년 사망해 노벨상 수상의 기회를 영영 놓치고 말았다. 수상을 위해서는 과학자가 생존해 있어야 한다는 노벨의 또 다른 유언 내용 때문이었다.

[글의 소재] 멘델레예프의 노벨상 수상 실패

[주요 어휘] periodic table 주기율표, contemporaneously 동시대에, inert gas 불활성 기체, fluorine 불소, ionic dissociation theory 이온해리 이론, electrolyte 전해질, dissociate 분리되다, 떨어지다

[구조 분석] ⊙ But in 1900, statutes that embodied an official interpretation of the will by the Nobel Foundation, which administers the prize, stated that the awards should primarily honor recent achievements but could also be granted for earlier work whose significance had recently become apparent.

→ statues가 이 문장의 주어이고 stated가 동사, that 이하가 목적절이다.

⊙ They thought those discoveries made Mendeleev's 19th-century periodic table work Nobel-eligible.

→ those 이하는 those discoveries(S) + made(V) + Mendeleev's 19th-century periodic table work(O) + Nobel-eligible(OC)로 구성되는 5형식 문장이다.

⊙ Arrhenius's ionic dissociation theory, the idea that electrolytes dissociate in water to form ions.

→ the idea that ~에서 that은 동격의 that이고 that절의 수식을 받는 the idea가 다시 theory와 동격을 이루고 있다.

198 〔정답 ④〕

[정답 해설] 이 글은 멘델레예프가 원소주기율표 완성이라는 뛰어난 공적에도 불구하고 왜 노벨상을 수상하지 못했는지 세 가지 이유를 들어 설명하고 있다. 따라서 이 글의 가장 알맞은 제목은 ④이다.

① 노벨상 선정 과정에서 발견되는 제도상 허점
② 노벨상 수상을 좌우하는 무시 못 할 요인, 운
③ 현대 화학에 대한 멘델레예프의 독보적 기여
④ 무엇이 멘델레예프의 노벨상 수상을 막았나?
⑤ 과학계에 만연하는 불화와 반목

199 〔정답 ④〕

[정답 해설] 밑줄 친 빈칸 부분 앞 내용인 'Mendeleev died in 1907 and therefore never got another chance because of another stipulation in Alfred Nobel's will'로 다음의 빈칸에 이어질 노벨의 유언 내용이 '노벨상은 살아있는 사람에게만 주어져야 함'임을 추론할 수 있다.

① 출신성분이 의심스러운 사람은 수상할 수 없다
② 과학적 업적은 모든 이념적 차이를 초월해야 한다
③ 수상을 위해서는 과학자의 업적이 독특하고 창의적이어야 한다
④ 수상을 위해서는 과학자가 생존해 있어야 한다
⑤ 노벨상위원회 투표가 모든 다른 결정에 우선한다

200 〔정답 ④〕

[정답 해설] 'However, the Royal Swedish Academy, which makes the final prize decisions, did not accept the vote.'로 노벨상에 대한 최종 결정은 노벨상위원회가 아니라 스웨덴 왕립 과학 아카데미가 함을 알 수 있다. 노벨상위원회는 후보를 추천할 뿐이다. 따라서 ④는 이 글의 내용과 일치하지 않는다.

18. 2025학년도 사관학교 1차 선발 시험

정답

01 ②	02 ④	03 ④	04 ③	05 ①
06 ⑤	07 ④	08 ③	09 ②	10 ②
11 ①	12 ④	13 ③	14 ②	15 ⑤
16 ①	17 ②	18 ①	19 ②	20 ②
21 ③	22 ④	23 ④	24 ⑤	25 ①
26 ⑤	27 ③	28 ④	29 ③	30 ⑤

01   정답 ②

지문 해석 조도照度는 아주 단순히 일정한 표면적에 도달하는 광원에서 발산되는 빛의 양을 말하며 촉광이나 미터법 체계에서는 룩스로 표시된다. 건조 환경에서 조도는 미묘한 차이를 보이는 공간 구성물에 형태와 선명성을 가져다준다. 그것은 (What→It) 복합 공간의 여러 층을 드러내기도 하고 숨기기도 하는 빛과 어둠의 크레셴도인 시각적 극단의 세기를 조절할 수 있다. 이런 원리는 건축 조명 설계에서 실제로나 현상학적으로 대단히 중요한데 이는 그것이 우리로 하여금 한 공간을 통해 나아가고 그 공간 안에서 과제를 수행하게 하기 때문이다. 더구나 조도는 공간에 대한 우리의 정서적 반응에서 매우 중요한 역할을 한다. 어둠에 대한 우리의 내재적인 공포나 빛에 이끌림은 우리 사회가 안전을 확보하고 정서적 안도감을 주는 수단으로서의 빛에 신뢰를 보내는 양식에 영향을 끼쳐 왔다. 끝으로 "조도"라는 말은, 적정 수준으로 관리하면 생명의 지속성을 보장하지만 극단으로 흐르면 그것의 수령자에게 물리적인 해를 끼칠 수 있는 빛과 에너지의 양을 나타냄을 우리는 잊지 말아야 한다.

글의 소재 인간의 삶에서의 조명의 역할

주요 어휘 footcandle 촉광, metric 미터법의, nuanced 미묘한 차이를 보이는. crescendo 크레셴도(점점 세어짐), intrinsic 내재적인, gravitation 인력, 이끌림, reassurance 안심, sustenance 지속성, recipient 수령인

구조 분석 ⊙ This principle is of great practical and phenomenological importance in architectural lighting design, as

it allows us to navigate our way through, or perform tasks within, a space.

→ a space가 전치사 through와 within의 공동목적어로 쓰인 생략구문으로 '~navigate our way through a space or perform tasks within a space'가 생략 전 문장이다.

정답 해설 ②: 여기서 what은 관계대명사로 쓰였다고 볼 수밖에 없으나 그럴 경우 what이 유도하는 명사절이 문장 끝까지 이어져 술부를 갖지 못하고 따라서 문장이 성립하지 않는다. 그러므로 what의 자리에는 일반대명사 it이 와야 한다.

① 앞에서 이미 문장이 완결됐으므로 이후 나오는 동사 measure는 반드시 분사 형태가 돼야 한다. 그중 수동의 의미로 'the quantity of light'를 꾸며줘야 하므로 과거분사 'measured'가 온 것은 타당하다.

③ 앞의 'to navigate'과 병렬구조를 이루고 있으므로 동사 원형 perform이 온 것은 타당하다. to 부정사가 병렬구조를 이룰 경우 to는 흔히 생략된다.

④ 다음 문장이 완전한 문장이므로 전치사(in)+관계대명사 (which)가 나온 것은 옳다.

⑤ 주격관계대명사 that의 동사이고 선행사는 a quantity of light or energy로 단수이므로 ensures로 수 일치시키는 것은 문법적으로 타당하다.

02   정답 ④

지문 해석 칼 포퍼는 명확하게 사실로 입증될 수 있는 이론은 없다고 주장한 것으로 종종 전해진다. 그러나 그는 이보다 훨씬 더 급진적인 견해를 지녔다. 그는, 아직 틀렸음이 적극적으로 입증되지 않은 이론들 가운데 우리가 다른 것보다 어느 하나를 믿어야 할 이유가 절대 없다고 생각했다. 최상의 이론조차 명확히 입증할 수 없다는 게 아니다. "최상의 이론" 따위는 없으며 "살아남은 이론"이 있을 뿐인데 모든 살아남은 이론들은 동등하다는 것이다. 따라서 포퍼의 견해에 따르면 한 살아남은 이론이 다른 것보다 우월함을 뒷받침하는 증거를 모으려 하는 것은 쓸데없는 짓이다. 그러므로 과학자들은 가능한 많은 아이디어를 논박함으로써 살아남은 이론의 풀의 크기를 줄이는 데 힘써야 한다. 과학적 연구조사는 본질적으로 논박의 과정이어서 과학자들은 오류를 증명하는 사람이요, 틀렸음을 드러내는 사람이요, 파괴자다. 포퍼식 연구조사의 논리는 과학 종사자들에게 살인자의 결단력을 요구한다. 이론을 대할 때 그들은 이론을 이해했으면 그것을 없애야 한다는 생각을 먼저 가져야 한다. 과학자들이 모든 추측의 도살을 위해 한마음으로 매진할 때 비로소 과학은 발전한다.

글의 소재 칼 포퍼의 급진적 이론관

주요 어휘 radical 급진적인, disprove 잘못됐음을 입증하다,

consequently 따라서, 그러므로, refute 논박하다, inquiry 연구조사, debunker 틀렸음을 드러내는 사람, liquidate 청산하다, slaughter 도살, 도축, speculation 추측

구조 분석 ⊙ he thought that of the theories that have not yet been positively disproved, we have ~

➜ 첫 번째 that는 목적절을 유도하는 접속사, 두 번째 that는 선행사 theories를 수식하는 주격관계대명사다. 'of ~ disproved'는 전치사구(부사구)로 of는 '~중에서'의 뜻이고 목적절 that절의 주어는 we이다.

정답 해설 ④의 문장은 목적어 a murderous resolve를 취하므로 ④는 수동형이 아닌 능동형 requires가 돼야 한다. 원래 require A of B(=A에게 B를 요구한다) 문형이나 목적어(a murderous resolve)를 강조하기 위해 뒤로 뺀 도치문이다. 영어에서는 중요한 어구일수록 뒤로 빼는 경향이 있다(end focus 법칙)

① reason를 수식하는 to부정사의 형용사적 용법으로 쓰임은 타당하다
② 이 문장의 목적어 themselves가 주어와 같기 때문에 재귀대명사를 쓴 것은 타당하다. 재귀대명사의 재귀적 용법이다.
③ essentially는 문장 전체를 수식하는 부사로 문장의 맨 앞으로 와도 같은 뜻이다.
⑤ 강조의 Only if~ 절 때문에 주절이 도치돼 will science progress 어순을 취했으며 동사 원형 progress가 온 것은 옳다.

03 정답 ④

지문 해석 마음챙김은 당신의 모든 생각을 쓸어내기 위해 강력한 마인드 컨트롤을 필요로 한다는 식의 사고방식은 옳지 않은데 이는 그렇게 함으로써 당신은 의식과 무의식 속에서 당신의 모든 생각을 적으로 취급하고 그것들을 제거하려 하기 때문이다. 하지만 당신의 생각들은 실제로 당신의 육체적 정신적 상태의 정확한 반영이다. 당신의 육체적 정신적 상태가 변하지 않는다면 당신 생각의 패턴 역시 변하지 않고 그대로이다. 사실 올바른 노력과 적절한 컨트롤은 효율적인 마음챙김 학습과 수련에 열쇠다. 마음챙김을 수련할 때 우리는 종종 호흡, 생각의 과정, 몸의 느낌이나 감각 등 한 가지 목표에 상당한 노력을 쏟아붓는다. 그러나 집중적이고 힘들여 하는 수련은 우리 마음을 쉽게 피로하게 하고 스트레스 호르몬(코티솔)을 감소시켜(→증가시켜) 몸과 두뇌/마음 상태를 악화시키고 손상을 입힌다. 휴가기간 중 집중적인 마음챙김 명상으로 부작용 사례가 발생할 수 있음을 몇몇 연구가 보여줬다. 따라서 마음챙김 (수련)에 마인드 컨트롤만을 사용하는 것은 마음과 마음챙김 수련을 위한 자연스러운 방법이 아니다.

글의 소재 올바른 마음챙김 수련법

주요 어휘 mindfulness 마음챙김, appropriate 적절한, efficient 효율적인, deteriorate 악화시키다, adverse 역逆의, 반대되는,

구조 분석 ⊙ However, intensive and effortful practice makes our mind fatigue easily

➜ fatigue를 목적보어로 취하는 5형식 문장이다. makes가 사역동사라 fatigue가 원형을 취했다.

정답 해설 같은 문장 전반부에서 집중적인 수련이 마음을 피로하게 한다고 했으므로 스트레스 호르몬은 증가하는 게 논리적으로 맞기 때문에 ④의 decreases는 increases로 바꿔야 한다. 정답 ④.

04 정답 ③

지문 해석 내가 사는 고장의 과학박물관에는 마인드볼이라는 신기한 게임이 있다. 두 명의 플레이어가 긴 테이블의 반대편 끝에 앉는다. 그들 각각은 전극을 장착한 머리띠를 두르는데 전극은 두뇌 표면에서 일어나는 전기 활동의 일반 패턴을 포착하도록 고안되었다. 두 플레이어 사이에는 쇠공이 놓여있다. 이 공을 마음의 힘으로 테이블의 맞은 편 끝으로 밀어내는 것이 목표이고 이를 먼저 해내는 플레이어가 승리한다. 추진력은—이것은 각 플레이어의 전극에서 측정돼 테이블 밑에 숨겨놓은 자석을 통해 공으로 전달된다.—두뇌가 이완됐을 때 발생시키는 알파파와 세타파의 합산이다. 더 많은 알파파와 세타파를 발생시킬수록 더 많은 힘을 공에 정신적으로 행사할 수 있다. 기본적으로 마인드볼은 누가 가장 활동적인지(→비활동적인지)를 겨루는 게임이다. 보는 것도 재밌다. 플레이어들은 눈을 감거나 심호흡을 하고 어설프게 요가 자세를 취하는 등 릴렉스하려고 안간힘을 쓰는 것이 역력하다. 공이 테이블의 자기 쪽으로 향할 때 그들이 느끼는 공포는 상대방의 지나친 열의와 늘 균형을 이루고 큰 쇠공이 왔다 갔다 하면 두 플레이어는 번갈아 냉정을 잃는다. 애쓰지 않으려고 애쓰는 것이 얼마나 어려운지에 대한 더 나은, 더 응축된 실례를 당신은 애써 찾을 필요가 없을 것이다.

글의 소재 애쓰지 않으려고 애쓰는 마인드볼 게임

주요 어휘 electrode 전극, convey 전달하다, essentially 본질적으로, 기본적으로, vaguely 애매하게, 어설프게, balance out 균형 잡다, overeagerness 지나친 열의, alternately 번갈아, condensed 응축된, illustration 실례, 삽화

구조 분석 ⊙ ~ both players alternately losing their cool as the big metal ball rolls back and forth.

➜ 종속절 주어 both players가 주절의 주어와 달라서 살려놓은 분사구문으로 볼 수도 있고 both 앞에 with가 생략된 부대

상황의 전치사구로 볼 수도 있다.

정답 해설 ③의 전 문장에서 추진력은 뇌가 이완됐을 때 나오는 알파파와 세타파의 합산이라 했으므로 마인드볼은 활동성이 아닌 비활동성을 겨루는 게임이다. 따라서 active는 inactive로 고쳐야 한다. 정답 ③.

05 　　　　　　　　　　　　　　　　　　　 정답 ①

지문 해석 오늘날의 테크노 세상에서 우리는 더 이상 현실과 가상 사이에 명확한 구분선을 그을 수 없다. 이것이 게임에 대해 의미하는 바는 무엇인가? 그것은 게임이 오늘날 기술을 매개로 한 어떤 경험보다 현실적임을 의미한다. 게이머는 새로운 세계에서 힘과 개성을 발휘한다. 그녀의 경험과 행동들은 현실적이다. 또한 게임은 사회적이다. 현대적인 게임은 종종 많은 플레이어를 참여시키고 상호적이며 역할 놀이를 요구한다. 게이머들은 새로운 사람을 만나고 우정과 애정 관계를 발전시킨다. 따라서 그들은 감정적 경험을 포함한 실제 사회 경험을 하게 된다. 이러한 경험들은 단순히 스크린이나 무대에서 일어나는 것에 대한 반응이 아니라 게이머가 게임 환경에서 다른 이들과 나누는 상호작용의 결과다. 게이머들의 사고나 상호작용, 참여, 감정은 허구적이지도 가상적이지도 않다. 그것들은 완전히 현실적이다. 따라서 현상학적으로 게이머들은 이 세상을 떠나 다른 세상으로 가는 것이 아니다.

글의 소재 가상 게임의 현실성

주요 어휘 distinction 구분, 특성, agency 대리인, 동인(動因), 힘, contemporary 현대적인, 동시대의, interactive 상호적인, phenomenologically 현상학적으로

구조 분석 ⊙ These experiences are not a mere response to what happens on the screen or on stage, but are the result of the interaction of the gamer with others in the game environment.

➡ not A but B 구문＝A가 아니라 B다. 전치사 to는 관계대명사 what이 유도하는 명사절 전체를 목적어로 취한다.

정답 해설 현대의 가상게임은 현실성과 사회성이 대폭 강화돼 게이머는 이의 참여를 통해 실제 현실과 다름없는 사회 생활을 경험하고 공유한다는 것이 이 글의 일관된 주장이므로 정답은 ① '가상 게임은 실제 현실과 같은 사회적 활동이다.'이다.

06 　　　　　　　　　　　　　　　　　　　 정답 ⑤

지문 해석 인문학자들이 자연 과학에서 배울 것이 많다면 그 역도 또한 사실이다. 인문학자들은 과학적 연구에 기여할 것도 많다. 생물학과 인지과학의 발견물들이 전통적인 학문적 경계

를 모호하게 만들기 시작하자 이 분야 연구자들은 그들의 작업이 그들로 하여금 전통적으로 핵심 인문학의 영역이었던 수준 높은 문제와 접촉하게 만들었음을 알게 되었고, 이 분야에 대한 정식 훈련 부족으로 그들은 종종 어둠 속을 헤매거나 이미 있는 것을 새로 만드느라 시간을 낭비했다. 여기가, 인문학자들이 과학적 탐구의 결과물들을 설명하고 해석하는 데―이는 인문학과 자연과학의 구분선 양쪽에 있는 학자들이 서로 대화할 때에만 일어날 수 있는 어떤 것이다.―중추적인 역할을 할 수 있고 또 해야 하는 바로 그 지점이다. 전통적으로 첨예했던 인문학과 자연과학의 구분은 더 이상 설 자리가 없음이 점점 분명해지고 있고 이는 이전의 구분선 양쪽의 연구자들이 철저하게 더욱 학제적이 될 것을 요구한다.

글의 소재 인문학자들의 자연 과학 분야 기여의 당위성

주요 어휘 humanist 인문학자, reverse 역(逆)의, cognitive 인지의, disciplinary 규율의, 학문의, domain 영역, grope 더듬다, reinvent the wheel 이미 있는 것을 새로 만드느라 시간을 낭비하다, expertise 전문지식, crucial 중차대한, 중추적인, divide(n) 구분, 경계선, viable 생존할 수 있는, 실행할 수 있는, interdisciplinary 학제적인, 학문 간의

구조 분석 ⊙ and often their lack of formal training in these areas leaves them groping in the dark or attempting to reinvent the wheel.

➡ 이 문장은 주어(lack), 동사(leaves), 목적어(them), 목적격 보어 2개(groping~, attempting~)로 구성된 5형식 문장이고 2개의 목적격 보어는 등위접속사 or로 연결돼 병렬구조를 이루고 있다.

정답 해설 위 글은 인문학자가 자연과학의 발전에 기여할 필요성을 강조하며 그 구체적 방법으로 학제 간 교류 협력을 제시하고 있으므로 정답은 ⑤ '과학적 발견에 대한 인문학의 기여는 학제적 교류를 통해 이뤄질 수 있다.'이다.

① 인문학의 사변적 이론들은 경험적 연구로 예증될 수 있다.

② 자연과학과 인문학은 각자 자신의 분야와 노선에 집중해야 한다.

③ 자연과학자들은 인문학 연구를 통해 철학적 내용을 보강해야 한다.

④ 자연과학과 인문학의 진정한 통합은 서로를 내포함으로써 가능하다.

07 　　　　　　　　　　　　　　　　　　　 정답 ①

지문 해석 다른 영장류와 비교해 우리 인간은 이상하리만큼 사회적, 협조적이다. 고분고분하게 비행기 좌석에 앉아있고, 집을 짓기 위해 집단 노동을 하고, 서로 다른 기술을 전공하고 집단 내의 구체적 역할이 강제하는 삶을 산다. 인류 최근의 진화 역

사를 봤을 때 이는 영장류가 해내기에는 대단히 어려운 마술이다. 벌집 생활은 (말 그대로) 개미에게는 손쉽게 할 수 있는 일이다. 그들은 같은 유전자를 가지고 있어서 공동선을 위해 희생하는 것은 사실상 희생이 아니다.―내가 개미라면 공동선은 곧 나의 선일뿐이다. 하지만 인간은, 타인에게 조종당하고, 오도당하고, 착취당하는 위험을 극도로 경계해 친척이나 동료 부족 구성원과 단지 제한적으로만 협동하도록 진화된 유인원이다. 그러나 우리는 열 지어 행진하고 고분고분히 줄지어 앉아 학과를 암송하고, 사회 규범에 순응하고 때로는 병정개미를 무안에 이르게 할 정도의 열정으로 목숨을 희생한다. 각진 영장류의 말뚝을 둥근 사회적 곤충의 구멍에 박으려 하는 것은 어려울 수밖에 없다.

[글의 소재] 이해하기 어려운 인간의 사회성과 협동성

[주요 어휘] primate 영장류의 동물, freakishly 이상하리만큼, trick 마술, 계략, 속임수, pull off 해내다, 성공하다, evolutionary 진화론의, no-brainer 쉽게 할 수 있는 일, acutely 극도로, alert 경계하는, manipulate 조종하다, exploit 착취하다, conform to ~에 순응하다, norm 규범, enthusiasm 열정, put someone to shame (너무 뛰어나) ~를 부끄럽게 하다, ~를 무안에 이르게 하다, be bound to 꼭 ~하다

[구조 분석] ⊙ not only do we sit obediently on airplanes, we labor collectively to build houses

→ not only ~ but also구문에서 but also 부분이 생략됐다. not only의 부정어 not 때문에 조동사 do가 앞으로 빠지는 도치문이 됐다.

⊙ This is quite a trick for a primate to pull off, considering our most recent evolutionary history.

→ 'quite a trick for a primate to pull off'는 '영장류가 해내기에는 (너무 어려운) 마술'의 뜻으로 'too tricky for a primate to pull off'로 바꿔 쓸 수 있는 'too ~ for ~ to ~' 용법의 변형으로 볼 수 있다. considering은 '~를 감안하면'을 뜻하는 전치사로 쓰였다.

[정답 해설] square(round) peg in a square(round) hole = 적재적소를 의미하고 a square peg in a round hole이나 a round peg in a square hole은 부적절하거나 어울리지 않는 상황을 상기하면 밑줄 친 부분은 '(제한된 협동이라는) 유인원의 처지를 무시하고 이를 사회성 뛰어난 곤충의 현실에 적용하려는 부적절한 상황'을 뜻함을 알 수 있다. 따라서 정답은 ④ '유인원의 특징을 억누르고 공동의 이익을 추구하다.'이다.
① 유인원과 개미에 대한 인간의 우월성을 격하시키다
② 유인원과 곤충의 협력을 강제하다
③ 벌집 곤충을 조종해 유인원 류의 특징을 받아들이게 하다
⑤ 공동선에 기여하는 유인원의 능력을 극대화하다

08

정답 ③

[지문 해설] 대수大數의 법칙은 확률이론과 통계학의 토대 중 하나다. ① 그것은 장기적으로 미래 사건의 결과를 꽤 정확히 예측할 수 있음을 보장한다. ② 가령 이것은, 의무적으로 지불해야 할 전망치를 알 수 있게 하기 때문에 금융회사가 보험이나 연금 상품 가격을 매길 수 있도록 자신감을 부여하고, 카지노가 결국은 항상 도박 고객들로부터 이익을 올리도록 보장한다. ③ 하지만 그것은 한 사람이 각각의 시행 결과가 서로 연관됐다고 가정하는 이른바 '도박사의 오류'다. ④ 그 법칙에 따르면, 한 사건의 발생을 더 많이 관찰할수록 그 결과의 측정된 확률(또는 승산)은 관찰이 시작되기 전에 산출한 이론적 전망치에 끊임없이 가까워진다. ⑤ 달리 말하면 다수의 시행에서 얻은 평균적 결과는 확률 이론을 사용해 산출한 기대치에 가까운 수치며 시행의 횟수를 늘리면 그 기대치에 한층 더 가까워진다.

[글의 소재] 확률 이론과 통계학에서 적용되는 대수의 법칙

[주요 어휘] foundation 기초, 초석, probability 확률, reasonable 합리적인, 적정한, fallacy 오류, assume 가정하다, 전제하다

[구조 분석] ⊙ and increasing the number of trials will result in that average becoming an even closer match.

→ 전치사 in의 목적어는 becoming(동명사임. 현재분사가 아님) 이하이고 that average는 동명사 becoming의 의미상 주어다.

[정답 해설] 이 글은 사건의 시행 횟수를 크게 늘리면 결국 그 결과치는 이론적 확률에 수렴한다는 대수의 법칙을 설명하고 있다. 각각의 시행 결과가 서로 연관됐음을 가정하는 '도박사의 오류'는 이런 흐름과 무관하다. 따라서 정답은 ③이다.

09

정답 ②

[지문 해설] 기업 윤리는 스캔들에서 태어난다. 그것은 이어지는 스캔들의 파장과 함께 소생하는 것처럼 보인다. 그런데 여기는 두 가지 문제가 있다. 첫 번째는 우리 세계가 너무 연관돼 있어 우리는 기업을 더 이상 자체 도덕 코드를 지닌 하나의 독립된 사회 내 기관으로 볼 수 없다는 점이다. 기업은 어떤 경우에도 사회 안에 존재해야 한다. 이것은, 우리가 기업가는 경제적 이익을 극대화하는 사람일 뿐 다른 사람일 수 없다는, 이제는 다분히 상투어가 돼버린 담론을 더 이상 받아들일 수 없음을 의미한다. 기업은 우리 사회 안에 세워져 전 세계적으로 연관을 맺고 있는 대단히 인간적인 기관이다. 두 번째 문제는 스캔들로 재탄생함으로써 기업 윤리가, 기업은 도덕적으로 의심스러운 상태에서 출발한다는 추론을 결코 피할 수 없다는 것이다. 기업은 그것이 세상에 가져다주는 선에 대해서는 어떤 공적도 얻지

못하면서 단지 악에 대한 문제들만 얻는 듯이 보인다. 사실 자본주의는 당연히 우리가 발명한 최고의 사회 협력 시스템이다. 그러나 그럼에도 그것은 최고의 사상가들의 비판적 시험을 견뎌야 한다. 그것을 더 나은 것으로 만들기 위한 바로 그 이유 때문이라 하더라도 말이다. 자본주의가 의심의 여지없이 도덕적으로 훌륭하다거나 의심의 여지없이 도덕적으로 문제가 있다고 쉽게 가정하는 것은 학자적 규범과 현실적 규범을 모두 위반하는 것이다.

글의 소재 기업 윤리가 앉고 있는 내재적인 문제들

주요 어휘 regenerate 재생하다, interconnected 상호연관된, subject to ~에 매어있는, thoroughly 철저하게, presumption 추정, 추론, norm 규범

구조 분석 ⊙ But, <u>if it is</u>, then <u>it</u> must stand the critical test of our best thinkers, <u>if for no other reason than to make it better.</u>

→ 두 if 구문은 모두 생략 구문으로 앞 문장은 'if it is the greatest system of social cooperation that we have ever invented'가, 뒤 문장은 'if it must stand the critical test of our best thinkers for no other reason than to make it better.'가 각각 생략 전 문장이고 두 if는 모두 even if의 뜻이다. 이 문장의 it는 모두 capitalism을 가리킨다.

정답 해설 이 글은 기업이 단순한 이윤 추구 집단이 아닌 사회적, 인간적 집합체로 발전하고 있고, 자본주의 자체가 구성원들의 끊임없는 비판을 감수해야 하는 현 상황에서 기업 윤리가 겪을 수밖에 없는 두 가지 문제점을 지적하고 있다. 따라서 정답은 ② '기업 윤리의 내재적 난제'다.

① 스캔들을 잊고 혁신하자!
③ 인권 단체의 피할 수 없는 장애물
④ 기업 윤리: 떠오르는 학자적 규범
⑤ 성공의 열쇠로서의 기업 윤리

10   정답 ②

지문 해석 The European Mediterranean Seismological Centre (EMSC)는 최근 지진의 영향에 대한 현장 목격담을 목격자들로부터 신속히 수집하기 위한 한 방식을 시행했다. 이 방식은 지진의 영향력에 대한 신속 평가의 불확실성을 감소시키는 데 확실히 도움을 주기 때문에 대단히 중요하다. 페이스북이나 트위터 같은 소셜 미디어가 지진 탐지를 위한 유용한 네트워크로 고려될 수 있다. 소셜 네트워크로부터의 데이터 채굴은 지진 발생 구역을 탐지하고 결정하기 위해 사용돼 왔고 United States Geological Service에 의해 Twitter Earthquake Detector (TED)가 개발되기에 이르렀다. 그러한 미디어를 활용한 지진 조기 탐지는 기본적인 지진 탐지 패러다임에 근본적

인 변화를 의미한다. 소셜 네트워크에 실린 정보는 지진파보다 훨씬 빠르게 이동해 지진 발생 후 수 분 내에 신속하고 신빙성 있는 탐지를 가능하게 한다. 이탈리아 지역의 경우 TwiFelt라는 소프트웨어 시스템이 2012년부터 시행되고 있다. 그 목적은 트위터 흐름을 분석해 지진 감지 지도를 실시간으로 제공하는 것이다.

글의 소재 소셜 미디어를 활용한 지진 탐지

주요 어휘 Mediterranean 지중해의, seismological 지진의, implement 시행하다, in situ 현장의, assessment 평가, detection 탐지, represent 대표하다, 상징하다, 의미하다, radical 근본적인, 급진적인

구조 분석 ⊙ Information carried by social networks travels much faster than seismic waves, <u>allowing</u> a fast and reliable detection within a few minutes of an earthquake's origin.

→ 분사구문으로 allowing은 'and it allows ~'로 바꿀 수 있다.

정답 해설 이 글은 소셜 미디어가 지진의 조기 탐지에 활용되고 있고 이에 따라 지진 탐지의 근본 패러다임이 변화하고 있음을 구체적인 실례를 들어 설명한다. 따라서 이 글의 제목은 ② '소셜 미디어: 신속 지진 탐지기'가 적절하다.

① 재난 구조에 소셜 미디어를 이용하라!
③ 지진학에서 데이터 채굴은 시기상조
④ 톱다운 정보 수단으로서의 시민
⑤ 소셜 미디어를 통해 퍼지는 지진 관련 루머

11   정답 ①

지문 해석 낮에, 따분한 활동을 하다가도 졸리면 당신은 충분한 수면을 취하지 않았다고 전문가들은 말한다. 만약 당신이 늘 자리에 누운 지 5분 이내에 잠들면 아마 당신은 심각한 수면 결핍을 가지고 있고 심지어 수면 장애를 겪고 있을 수도 있다. 늘 깨어있는 사람이 매우 짧은 시간 잠드는 것, 즉 마이크로 수면은 수면 결핍의 또 다른 징표다. 많은 경우에 사람들은 자신이 마이크로 수면을 경험한다는 것을 알지 못한다. 서구 산업사회에서 소위 '초를 양쪽에서 태우는(무리해서 일하는)' 만연된 관행은 너무도 많은 수면 결핍을 초래해 비정상적인 수면이 이제는 거의 표준이다. 수면 결핍은 위험하다는 점을 많은 연구들은 분명히 밝히고 있다. 운전 시뮬레이터를 이용하거나 손-눈 협응 과제를 수행하는 테스트를 받는 수면 결핍자들의 수행력은 술 취한 사람과 비슷하거나 그보다 더 낮다. 또한 수면 결핍은 신체에 미치는 알콜의 영향을 증대해 피곤한 사람이 술을 마시면 푹 쉰 사람보다 신체 기능이 훨씬 더 약해질 것이다.

글의 소재 수면 결핍의 부작용

주요 어휘 severe 심각한, deprivation 결핍, disorder 장애,

microsleep 마이크로 수면, widespread 널리 퍼진, 만연한, burn the candle at both ends 무리해서 일하다, intoxicated 술·마약에 취한, magnify 확대하다, impair 손상시키다, 약화시키다

[구조 분석] ⊙ The widespread practice of "burning the candle at both ends" in Western industrialized societies has created so much sleep deprivation that what is really abnormal sleepiness is now almost the norm.

➜ so ~ that 용법=너무 ~해서 ~하다. what은 선행사가 포함된 관계대명사로 명사절을 유도해 that절의 주어로 기능한다.

[정답 해설] 위 글은 수면 결핍을 겪는 사람이 실생활에서 어떤 부작용을 겪는지 다양한 사례를 들어 논증하고 있다. 따라서 글의 주제는 ① '수면 결핍의 고질적 징후들'이 적절하다.
② 심각한 수면 결핍이 통근 운전자에 미치는 영향
③ 술 취한 사람과 수면 결핍자의 유사성
④ 서구 산업 사회의 전통적인 수면 관습
⑤ 수면 결핍자의 높은 알콜 의존도

12
[정답 ④]

[지문 해석] 즐거운 Veteran's Day 되세요. 이 글을 읽는 여러분 건강이 함께하기를 빕니다. 국방도서관 관장으로서 저는 지난 책 무료 증정 이벤트가 대박이었다는 소식을 기쁜 마음으로 전해드립니다. 저는 많은 지역 문화 행사에 중추적 역할을 해온 도서관을 대표한다는 데 큰 자부심을 느끼고 있습니다. 또 우리 도서관의 최근 행사 하나를 기쁜 마음으로 알려드릴까 합니다. 우리는 이번 주말부터 연말까지 매주 토요일 오후 6시에 무료 영화 관람 행사를 계획해 왔습니다. 영화 상영은 3층 Eisenhower Community Room에서 있습니다. 일반 시민에 개방됩니다. 영화 목록은 매달 1일 저희 웹사이트에서 업로드 됩니다. 이번 토요일 상영될 첫 번째 영화는 Black Hawk Down입니다. 오셔서 무료 영화를 즐기세요.

[글의 소재] 무료 영화 상영 고지
[주요 어휘] giveaway 무료 증정, instrumental 중요한
[구조 분석] ⊙ I hope this message finds you well.
this message 이하는 동사 + 목적어 + 목적보어의 5형식이다. 목적보어 well은 형용사로 쓰였고 'healthy'의 뜻이다.
[정답 해설] 'We have planned a free movie showing every Saturday at 6 P.M.'에서 이 글의 목적이 무료 영화 상영을 알리려는 것임을 알 수 있다. 따라서 정답은 ④ '도서관의 무료 영화 상영 행사를 안내하려고'이다.

13
[정답 ③]

[지문 해석] 언어적 상호작용의 중요성을 알면 부모의 행동과 의사결정력이 생길 수 있다. 유아가 깨어있을 때 그들과 상호작용하는 것, 그리고 그들 또한 상호작용으로 응하고 있고 우리가 하는 말의 의미를 찾으려 애쓰고 있다는 것을 존중하는 것이 중요하다. 이를 실행하기 위한 한 방법은 그들이 대화에 기여하는 것(아무리 사소해도)을 인정해 주는 것이다. 부모는 또 양육자나 보모들이 이런 식의 상호작용에 전념한다는 증거를 찾아야 한다. 보모가 유아와 같이 있으면서 TV를 본다든지 유아가 깨어있을 때조차 전화 통화에 많은 시간을 보내는 경우가 흔하다. (유아에게는) 젖병과 깨끗한 기저귀 이상이 필요하다. 상호작용하는 유아라는 새로운 시각은 양육에는 보호 관리 이상이 포함된다는 것을 의미한다. 양육을 위한 새로운 직무 기술서에는 '민감하고 호응하는 태도라는 형태의 양육자 자극이 요구됨'이라는 문구를 추가해야 한다. 부모는 아기들과 이야기하는 데 열의를 보이는, 공감적이면서 격려적인 보모를 찾아야 한다. 연구에 의하면, TV에서 나오는 언어 자극은 유아의 언어 학습 준비를 돕지 못한다. 오직 사람과의 대화만이 그러하다.

[글의 소재] 이상적인 유아 양육자의 조건으로서의 공감과 격려
[주요 어휘] interaction 상호작용, alert 조심하는, 깨어있는, acknowledge 인정하다, meager 사소한, custodial 보호감호의, 양육의, description 기술서, 설명서, stimulation 자극, responsive 호응하는, empathic 공감하는, converse with ~와 대화하다

[구조 분석] ⊙ When infants are alert, it is vital to interact with them and to respect that they are interacting in return and working on finding meaning in what we say.

➜ 등위접속사 and로 연결된 병렬 구조가 두 번 연속 나오고 있다. 병렬 구조에서는 동사의 형태(원형이나 ~ing)가 일치하는지 확인하는 것이 중요하다.

[정답 해설] 이 글은 유아와의 언어 소통과 공감의 중요성을 강조하고 있고 글의 말미 'Parents should ~'에서 그런 양육자를 찾을 것을 권고하고 있다. 따라서 정답은 ③ '부모는 유아와 공감하며 언어적 상호작용에 적극적인 양육자를 찾아야 한다.'이다. 명령문이나 should, must 등 강한 표현을 포함한 문장이 주제문일 경우가 많다.

14
[정답 ②]

[지문 해석] Maurice Wilkins는 뉴질랜드에서 태어났고 아버지는 의사였다. 그가 여섯 살 때 Wilkins 가족은 잉글랜드 Birmingham으로 이사 갔다. 그는 1935년 Cambridge의 St. John's College에 들어가 물리학을 공부했고 1938년에 학사학위를 받았다. 이차세계대전 도중 그는 University of

California, Berkeley에서 2년 동안 Manhattan Project에 참여했다. 전쟁 후 원자탄의 영향에 공포를 느낀 Wilkins는 또 다른 과학 분야로 전과하기로 결심했다. 영국으로 돌아온 Wilkins는 University of St. Andrews in Scotland에서 강의했다. 1946년 그는 King's College 생물물리학과에 합류해 1970년부터 1980년까지 학과장으로 일했다. 그곳에서 그는 DNA의 엑스레이 회절 연구로 이어진 일련의 연구조사에 착수했다. James Watson과 Francis Crick과 함께 그는 DNA의 분자 구조 결정에 기여한 바를 인정받아 노벨 생리학/의학상을 공동 수상했다.

글의 소재 Maurice Wilkins의 약전

주요 어휘 biophysics 생물물리학, investigation 수사, 연구조사, diffraction 회절, physiology 생리학, determination 결정, molecular 분자의

구조 분석 ⊙ After the War, horrified by the effects of the atomic bomb, Wilkins decided to move into another branch of science.

→ Having been이 생략된 분사구문이다. 이 문장을 완전한 절로 고치면 'As he had been horrified by the effects of the atomic bomb,'이다.

정답 해설 Wilkins가 St. John's College에서 학위를 받은 것은 1938년이다. 따라서 정답은 ② '1935년에 St. John's College에서 학위를 받았다.'이다.

15 정답 ⑤

지문 해석 북서항로의 도전을 적대적 환경의 도전으로 축소하는 것은 지나치게 단순화하는 것이다. 도전적 환경은 매우 경쟁적인 시장에서 전장에 이르기까지 여러 가지 형태를 취할 수 있다. 하나의 도전 상황을 다른 것과 비교할 때 우리는 가변성, 예측 가능성, 위험의 심각성, 외부 도움이 가능한지 여부, 노출 기간 등 많은 차원에서 구분 지을 수 있다. 이 모든 변수들이 높은 리더십 환경을 찾기는 드물다. 화재 진압은 위험한 일이지만, 숙련된 소방관에게 불은 예측 가능한 방향으로 움직이고 그것의 위험에 노출되는 시간은 비교적 짧다. 핀테크 스타트업을 창업하는 데는 매우 변동성이 크고 예측불가능한 상황이 따르지만 항상 더 많은 투자를 요청할 수 있는 선택권이 있다. 북서항로를 항해하는 것은 모든 차원에서 도전이었다. 위협은 많은 형태로 나타났고 매우 예측이 불가능한 성격이었으며 모두 잠재적으로 치명적이었던 데 반해 외부 지원은 배제되었고 노출은 장기적이었다. 그러므로 이런 상황에서 탐험대들을 이끄는 것은 다차원적 도전이었다.

글의 소재 Northwest Passage의 도전적인 항해 환경

주요 어휘 reduce A to B A를 B로 축소하다, hostile 적대

적인, differentiate 차별화하다, 구분하다, variability 가변성, predictability 예측 가능성, hazard 위험, external 외부의, duration 기간, exposure 노출, variable 변수, fin-tech 첨단 기술을 이용한 첨단 금융 기술(financial technology의 준말), lethal 치명적인, intervention 개입, rule out 배제하다

구조 분석 ⊙ Leading expeditions in this environment was thus a multi-dimensional challenge.

→ 여기서 Leading은 현재분사가 아닌 동명사이기 때문에 단수was로 수 일치시켰다. Leading expeditions는 탐험대들을 이끄는 것으로 해석해야 한다.(선도적인 탐험대들로 해석하면 안 된다.)

정답 해설 글 후반부에서 알 수 있듯 북서항로는 다차원적 도전이 도사리고 있는 매우 위험한 항로다. 이런 북서항로의 도전을 적대적 환경의 도전이라고 축소하는 것은, 즉 일언이폐지 해 말하는 것은 지나치게 단순화하는 것이다. 따라서 정답은 ⑤ oversimplify이다.

16 정답 ①

지문 해석 1830년대와 40년대에 몇몇 유럽 국가들은 통계의 열정에 사로잡혔다. 그것은 이전에는 숨겨졌거나 당연시 여겨졌던 것들을 보이게 만들었다. 가난한 사람들은 세어질 때에만 사회적 실체로 보였고 그에 따른 추상 개념으로서의 '빈곤'의 출현은 도덕적 책무를 일깨우는 데 도움을 주었다. 통계학회와 학술지가 창립됐고 사회적 데이터를 수집, 평가, 저장하기 위한 정부 부서가 신설되었다. 정치는 그 어느 때보다 정확한 정보에 의존했다. 1801년 프랑스에서는 체계적이고 정기적인 데이터 수집이 도 단위에서 시행됐다. 시민 사회 깊숙이 침투하기를 꾀했던 나폴레옹 정부는 그에 대한 가능한 많은 정확한 정보가 필요했다. 영국에서도 훨씬 덜 발달된 지역 관료주의에도 불구하고 의회 정부는 노동자 구역 위생에서 군내 병사들의 의료 환경에 이르기까지 모든 종류의 것들에 대한 경험적 사실을 광범위하게 활용했다. 이들의 수집은 임시 왕립위원회에 위임됐고 그들의 결론은 당시 정부와 그 비판자들에게 공개적으로 제공됐다.

글의 소재 유럽에서의 통계학의 태동

주요 어휘 be gripped by ~에 사로잡히다, entity 실체, 존재, emergence 출현, 부상, commitment 책무, 헌신, call into being 새로 만들다, evaluate 평가하다, institute(v) 도입하다, 시행하다, prefecture 도, 현(지방행정구역), make inroads into ~에 침입하다, extensive 광범위한, entrust 위임하다, ad hoc 임시의, 특별의

구조 분석 ⊙ government offices were called into being to gather, evaluate, and store social data.

→ to gather 이하는 government offices를 꾸며주는 형용사 구이나 바로 뒤에서 수식할 경우 주어가 너무 길어져 따로 떼어 후치시켰다. 긴 부분은 가급적 뒤로 빼는 것이 영어 문장의 관행이다. (end weight법칙)

정답 해설 통계학회와 저널이 창립되고 통계 관리를 위한 정부 부서가 신설됐다는 빈칸 다음 3번째 문장으로 보아 빈칸에는 통계의 열정에 사로잡혔다는 내용이 타당하다. 정답은 ①이다. ②의 경우는 데이터 수집에 대한 규제(regulation)를 시행했다는 것이므로 본문과는 정반대의 뜻이다.

② 데이터 수집에 대한 규제를 시행했다
③ 시민에게 국가 소유의 데이터를 무료 제공했다
④ 압도적 통계로 공포에 떨었다
⑤ 경제적 불평등을 극복하는 데 전념했다

17 _{정답 ②}

지문 해석 러시아 군인들이 얼마나 준비가 안 됐는지를 보여주는 많은 증거가 있었다. 벨라루스와 러시아 내에서 '훈련 중'이라고 생각했던 러시아 군인들은 자기들 휴대전화로 집에 전화해—우크라이나 통신망으로—자기들이 속아서 갑자기 실제 전투에 투입됐다는 불안한 마음을 가족이나 여자 친구에게 털어놨다. 틱톡이나 인스타그램에 게시물을 올리는 이도 있었다. 다시 한 번 우크라이나는 그런 아마추어리즘을 이용할 위치에 있었다. 비밀 감시센터에 몸을 숨긴 신병들은 분주히 전화나 SNS 전화의 위치를 추적하고 그 정보를 군과 공유해 정밀 타격에 나섰다. 침공이 펼쳐지는 것을 보면서 미 국방성 관리들 또한 러시아 보급과 병참 작전이 절망적으로 교란되거나 지체되고 있다는 증거로 아연했다. 러시아는 며칠 이상의 전투를 지속할 충분한 식량을 가져오지 못했을 뿐 아니라 키우로 향하는 러시아군 행렬은 완전히 멈춰버렸다.

글의 소재 러-우 전쟁 초기의 엉성한 러시아군 준비 상태

주요 어휘 angst 불안, exploit 이용하다, recruit 신병, tucked away 몸을 숨긴, geolocate 위치를 추적하다, precision 정밀, unfold 전개하다, 펼쳐지다, be struck by 갑자기 어떤 생각이 들다, snarl 교란하다, backlog 지체시키다, sustain 지속하다, column 행렬, stall 멈추다

구조 분석 ⊙ ~ to call home to express their angst to family members and girlfriends that they had been deceived and were suddenly in a real battle.

→ that는 동격의 that로 angst를 부연 설명하며 '~라는 불안'으로 해석한다.

정답 해설 통신 보안이 생명인 군에서 개인 전화를 사용해 위치를 노출시키거나 보급선이 교란되고 군 행렬이 멈춘 것은 모

두 러시아군의 전쟁 준비에 문제가 있음을 보여준다. 일 처리가 프로답지 못하고 미숙한 아마추어리즘의 증거를 보여준 것이다. 따라서 증거의 내용을 묻는 빈칸에는 ② '러시아군이 얼마나 준비가 덜 됐는지'가 정답이다.

① 어떻게 신병들이 전장에서 도망쳤는지
③ 러시아가 왜 병참 작전에서 실패했는지
④ 정보전에서 우크라이나는 어떤 핸디캡이 있었는지
⑤ 러시아와 우크라이나의 긴장은 얼마나 심각한지

18 _{정답 ①}

지문 해석 여러 가지 면에서 불확실성은 만연하고 삶이라는 바로 그 스크립트에 쓰인 것으로 이해될 수 있다. 이 때문에 확실성에 대한 갈망은 아직 이해될 수 없고, 정도는 훨씬 덜 하지만 통제될 수 없는 인지된 현상의 흐름을 저지하는 수단이 됐을 뿐이다. 따라서 불확실성을 극복하고 대신 확실성을 추구하는 욕망의 상호작용은 인간과 사회에 현재와 미래에 영향을 미치는 한 방법으로 각인됐다. 이 상호작용은 매우 오래된 것으로 안전과, 생존과 안락, 웰빙에 필요하다고 여겨지는 물질적, 기술적, 사회적 보호에 대한 인간의 희망에 뿌리를 두고 있다. Mokyr는 서구 자본주의 사회가 어떻게 불확실성에 관한 불안을 줄이려는 체계적인 시도에 빚지고 있는지를 보여준다. Mokyr에 의하면 기술적 진보에 대한 강한 믿음과 다양한 측면에서 삶의 계속된 개선은, 계몽주의 철학 운동에서 태동해 발전했고, 무엇을 알고 그것을 폭넓은 활동으로 실제로 실험하려는 인간적 욕망에 '공간'을 창조한 추론에 근거를 두고 있다.

글의 소재 불확실성을 줄이고 확실성을 추구하는 인간의 욕구

주요 어휘 pervasive 만연하는, craving 갈망, stem(vt) 저지하다, inscribe 각인시키다, be indebted to ~에 빚지다, reasoning 추론, emerge 부상하다

구조 분석 ⊙ the strong belief in technical progress and the continuous improvement of various aspects of life are rooted in the reasoning that emerged and developed in the philosophical movement of the Enlightenment and which created a "space" for humans' "desire to know" and practically experiment with a wide range of activities.

→ 이 문장의 주어는 belief ~ and ~ improvement, 동사는 are rooted이고 'that ~ Enlightenment'와 'which ~ activities'는 모두 선행사 reasoning를 수식하는 이중 주격 관계대명사 절이다. 복잡해 보이지만 두 개의 명사구(주부)와 두 개의 형용사절(관계사절)로 이뤄진 1형식 문장이다.

정답 해설 빈칸 앞의 두 문장에서, 불확실성을 극복하고 확실성을 추구하는 욕망의 상호작용이 인간 사회에 각인됐고 이 상호작용은 인간의 안전 욕구에 근거한다고 밝히고 있으므로 이

를 부연 설명하는 빈칸에는 ① '불확실성에 관한 불안을 줄이다'가 적절하다.

② 과학 분야에서 선조를 능가하다

③ 확실성 해석 상 오류를 제거하다

④ 인간 추론의 잠재력을 최소화하다

⑤ 과부하 걸린 정보의 세계에서 살아남다

의해 결정된다는 말이니까 결국 민주주의를 하냐 못하냐의 의사소통에 의해 결정된다는 말이다. 따라서 빈칸에 들어갈 말은 ② '민주 국가는 그들의 의사소통 문화에 의해 정의된다.'가 적절하다.

① 민주주의에서 미디어가 곧 의사소통 문제를 해결할 것이다

③ 개인주의와 집단주의 간 갈등은 불가피하다

④ 민주주의는 끝없는 대중 강론이 아닌 질서로 꽃피운다

⑤ 민주주의는 사회경제적 역동성에 의해 지속된다

19 정답 ②

지문 해석 민주주의에 대한 너무도 많은 설명들이 입법 과정이나 정책 결과를 강조하지만 이런 것들은 종종 의사소통과 정치 문화의 깊은 연관성을 놓친다. 문화가 논의될 때 흔히 자유민주주의적 가치의 맥락에서 논의된다. 그러나 우리가 묻고자 하는 것은 그러한 가치의 결합가를 결정하는 것은 무엇이냐는 것이다. 민주주의가 그것을 지탱하는 문화의 질에 따라 지속되거나 붕괴된다면 그런 가치들이 어떤 조건 하에서 긍정되거나 거부되는지 우리는 알아야 한다. 우리는 그런 조건들이 미디어에 의해 촉진되는, 사회의 설득을 위한 의사소통 수단에 의해 결정된다고 믿는다. 실제로 민주 국가는 그들의 의사소통 문화에 의해 정의된다. 민주주의가, 꼭 해야 하는 것을 집단적으로 결정하는 시민들로 구성된다면 그들이 서로를 설득하는 방식이 뒤따르는 거의 모든 것을 결정한다. 그리고 그것이 미디어 생태계에 정치학의 우두머리라는 특권을 부여한다. Marshall McLuhan이나 Neil Postman 같은 그것의 주요 실천가 중 몇몇은 미디어 환경이 우리가 무엇에 주목하는지 뿐만 아니라 세계에서 어떻게 생각하고 적응해 나갈지도 결정한다는 것을 감지했다.

글의 소재 민주주의의 근간, 의사소통

주요 어휘 account 설명, 계정, legislative 입법의, outcome 결과, valence 결정가, prop up 지탱하다, affirm 확언하다, 긍정하다, reject 거부하다, facilitate 촉진하다, persuade 설득하다, consist of ~로 구성되다, privilege(v) 특권화하다, foremost 선구적인, practitioner 실천가, sociologist 사회학자, orient oneself 적응하다

구조 분석 ⊙ We believe those conditions are determined by a society's tools of communication, facilitated through media, to persuade.

→ 'facilitated through media'와 'to persuade'가 모두 'tools of communication'을 수식한다.

정답 해설 빈칸 바로 앞 문장에서 필자는 그런 조건들은 설득의 의사소통 수단에 의해 결정된다고 주장하는데 그런 조건들이란 다시 그 전 문장에서 보듯 자유민주주의적 가치가 긍정되거나 부정되는 조건을 말한다. 즉, 자유민주주의적 가치가 긍정되고(민주주의) 부정되는(비민주주의) 조건은 의사소통 수단에

20 정답 ②

지문 해석

2013년 1월 26일 한 무리의 알카에다 전사들이 사하라사막 남단의 고대 도시 Timbuktu로 들어왔다.

(B) 거기서 그들은 아랍어와 몇몇 아프리카어로 천문학에서 지리학, 역사, 의학에 이르는 주제에 관해 쓰인 3만장의 원고를 소장한 중세 도서관에 불을 났다. 서구에 알려지지 않은 이것은 대륙 전체의 지혜를 모은 것이었고 아프리카가 전혀 목소리를 내지 못한다고 여겨지던 시기에 아프리카의 목소리였다.

(A) 이 사건을 목격한 Bamako 시장은 원고를 태운 것을 '세계 문화유산에 대한 범죄'라 불렀다. 그는 옳았다. 아니 옳았었을 수 있다. 그가 거짓말하고 있었다는 사실만 아니면.

(C) 사실은 그 일이 있기 직전 아프리카 학자들은 고서를 임의로 끌어 모아 테러리스트들이 태우도록 내버려 뒀다. 오늘날 그 콜렉션은 말리의 수도 Bamako에 숨겨져 높은 습도 속에 썩어가고 있다. 책략으로 구출한 것이 다시 한 번 위험에 처한 것이다. 이번에는 기후 때문에.

글의 소재 테러리스트 방화에 살아남은 아프리카 원고

주요 어휘 heritage 유산, medieval 중세의, manuscript 원고, astronomy 천문학, entire 전체의, assortment 모음, 분류, ruse 책략, rescue 구출하다, be in jeopardy 위험에 처하다,

구조 분석 ⊙ And he was right—or he would have been, if it weren't for the fact that he was also lying.

→ 주절에서는 가정법 과거완료가, 조건절에서는 가정법 과거가 각각 쓰인 혼합 가정법이다. 그가 옳았을 수도 있었다는 과거의 사실을 가정하기 때문에 주절에는 가정법 과거완료가, 조건절에서는 그가 거짓말한 사실 여부를 판단하는 시점은 현재이기 때문에 현재 사실의 반대를 나타내기 위해 가정법 과거가 각각 쓰였다.

정답 해설 먼저 (A)의 첫 문장은 burning을 언급하고 있으므로 주어진 글에 이어질 수 없다. (C)의 말미는 humidity나

climate를 언급하고 있으므로 (A)는 (C) 뒤에 올 수도 없다. (A) 갈 곳은 (B) 다음뿐이다. (B) - (A) 결정. (C) 또한 첫 문장이 'for the terrorists to burn'을 언급하므로 주어진 글 다음에 올 수 없다. (B) - (A)는 이미 결정됐으므로 (C)가 갈 곳은 (A) 뒤뿐이다. 그래서 (B) - (A) - (C) 순서가 도출된다. (A) 끝 문장의 lying과 (C) 첫 문장의 In fact에서 단서를 얻을 수도 있다. '거짓말하는 것'과 '사실은'은 강한 논리적 연관성을 갖기 때문에 (C)는 (A) 다음에 오는 것이 자연스럽다(머리의 단서는 꼬리에서 찾아라.-수미상응).

21 정답 ③

【지문 해석】

> 거래적 인간관계에서 믿음의 필요성은 명백하다. 그것은 고전적으로 부모-아이 관계나 환자-보호자 관계 같은 책무와 상호의존에 의해 주도되는 다른 비거래적 관계에서도 명확하다.

(B) 덜 일반적으로 인식된 것은 표면적으로 거래적으로 보이는 상호작용조차 암묵적 신뢰를 깊이 배경으로 했을 때에만 일어나는 그 정도다. 거리 노점상에게 핫도그 하나를 사려고 4불을 지불할 때 돈-소시지 교환은 일일이 나열하기가 불가능할 정도로 많은 가정들을 전제로 한다.

(C) 핫도그는 제대로 조리됐다. 누군가 그것을 고의적으로 오염시키지 않았다. 내가 건네는 달러는 위조가 아니다. 핫도그에는 (적어도 대부분은) 소고기거나 돼지고기가 들어있지 개고기가 아니다. 이 중 어떤 것도 명시적으로 표현되지 않지만 그럼에도 그것은 확고하게 당연시된다.

(A) 그런 이유로 이따금 터져 나오는 배경 신뢰의 아이템 위반이 큰 파장을 부른다. 한 지역 노점상의 핫도그에 개고기! 공원에서 가짜 돈 건네는 한 지역 아버지! 선정적인 타블로이드 표제는 우리가 이런 기본적인 배경 전제들을 얼마나 깊이 신뢰하는지 그리고 그것들이 얼마나 드물게 위반되는지를 더욱 굳게 할 뿐이다.

【글의 소재】 인간 거래에서 신뢰의 중요성

【주요 어휘】 transactional 거래의, obvious 명백한, commitment 책무, interdependence 상호의존, classically 고전적으로, occasional 이따금 발생하는, vendor 노점상, lurid 선정적인, reinforce 강화하다, fundamental 기본적인, 근본적인, interaction 상호작용, implicit암묵적인, 내밀한, exhaustively 철저히, deliberately 고의로, contaminate 오염시키다, counterfeit 위조된, explicitly 명시적으로

【구조 분석】 ⊙ the money-for-wiener trade rests upon a set of assumptions so long it would be impossible to exhaustively list.

→ so long 이하는 'so ~ that=너무 ~해서 ~하다' 형식에서 that이 생략된 형태이며 의미상 'a set of assumptions'를 수식하는 형용사절이다.

【정답 해설】 (A)는 'these items of background faith' 때문에, (C)는 'the hot dog' 때문에 주어진 글 다음에 올 수 없다. 따라서 첫 문장은 (B)이다. (B)는 끝 문장에서 '핫도그 거래는 수많은 전제 조건들에 달려있다.'고 했고 그런 조건은 (C)에서 구체적으로 예시되므로 (B) - (C)가 자연스럽다. 구정보(the hot dog) vs 신정보(a hot dog)의 선후관계로 봐도 그렇다. 따라서 올바른 순서는 (B) - (C) - (A)다. 또, (A) 첫 문장에서 '그래서 background faith가 깨지면 큰 스캔들이 발생한다.'고 말하므로 논리상 이 말 바로 앞에는 faith가 잘 지켜진다는 내용이 와야 한다. (C)의 마지막 문장 '이것은 명시적으로 표현되지 않지만 그럼에도 확고하게 당연시된다.'는 내용이 이에 부합한다. 여기서 (C) - (A)를 미리 결정할 수도 있다.

22 정답 ①

【지문 해석】 신세계가 탄생했는데 거기에서는 단지 사용이 쉽고 복잡한 생각을 요구하지 않는다는 이유만으로 이미지가 말들을 죽였다. 편지에서 이메일로, 이메일에서 페이스북으로, 마침내 페이스북에서 인스타그램으로 의사소통 수단의 진화는 매우 계열적이다. 시간을 요하는 문자에서 그림이나, 비디오, 이모티콘 같은 어린애도 쉽게 다룰 수 있는 도구로의 이동은 놀라운 속도는 물론 전례 없음을 특징적으로 보여주는 과정이었다. 사실상 지난 천년동안 인류의 발전은 복잡한 사유에 기반을 둬 왔고 그것은 문자를 필요로 했으며 문자는 독서를 요구했다. 하지만 독서는 타고나는 것이 아닌 문화적인 산물이다. 그리고 신경과학이 보여주듯 독서는 평소에는 분리돼 있는 뇌의 부분들을 연결해 준다. 독서와 문자의 종언은 이러한 연결이 사라지고, 더 신속하고 멀티태스킹, 그러나 깊은 사고와 이해는 문자와 시간을 요하므로 운명적으로 표면에 머물 수밖에 없는 또 다른 뇌의 출현을 의미한다. 그림이나 셀피, 이모티콘이나 간단한 문장으로 시나 소설, 과학 논문을 쓰는 것은 불가능하다.

【글의 소재】 사이버 시대 문자의 종언과 그 의미

【주요 어휘】 paradigmatic 계열적인, characterise 특징지우다, rapidity 신속, precedent 전례, millennia 천년, innate 타고난, vanish 사라지다, emergence 출현, 부상

【구조 분석】 ⊙ The end of reading and of written words means the vanishing of these connections, and the emergence of a different brain, maybe speedier and multitasking, but destined to remain on the surface since deeper thought and understanding require words and time.

→ 이 문장은 vanishing과 emergence 두 개의 목적어를 취하고 있다. 'maybe ~ on the surface'는 a different brain를 꾸며주는 형용사구이고 'since deeper ~ words and time'는 'destined to remain ~'을 수식하는 부사구다.

정답 해설 ④ 다음 문장에 지시사 'these connections'가 나오지만 바로 앞 문장에는 이를 받을 말이 없다. 따라서 여기가 흐름이 끊어진 곳이고 주어진 문장이 들어갈 자리다. 'these connections'에 대한 언급은 주어진 문장에 나온다(connects). 지시사가 나오면 그 지칭 대상이 반드시 앞 문장에 들어있어야 함을 상기하면 쉽게 풀 수 있는 문제다.

23
정답 ④

지문 해석 창조적 영장류로서 인간은 측면적 사고에 결정적으로 의존한다. 우리는 끊임없이 이어지는 신기한 통찰력과 기존 지식의 지속적인 재구성을 필요로 한다. 어린이들은 전전두피질이 미발달 상태라 이 점에서는 수퍼스타다. 그러나 그들을 창조적으로 만든 바로 그것이 그들의 창조물 대부분을, 적어도 목표 지향적 어른의 실용적 관점에서 보면 쓸모없는 것으로 만든다. 바비 인형 머리를 한 레고 사람들이 운전하는 포스트 아포칼립스, 쓰레기 부품으로 조립한 차량이 나오는 기괴하게 뒤틀린 레고 세계 또는 공식적인 영국식 차 파티에 등장하는 슈퍼히어로 피규어와 봉제 인형 전시장은 인상적인 창의적 사고를 반영한다. 그러나 지금 사회가 정말로 필요로 하는 건 새 백신과 더 효율적인 리튬이온 배터리다. 당신의 목표가 실현 가능한 문화 혁신이라면 당신의 이상적인 인간형은 어른의 몸을 가졌지만 단기간이라도 어린이의 마음을 가진 사람이다. 즉, 인지 통제가 덜 되고, 경험에 대한 높은 개방성과 예측 불가능한 방향으로 헤매는 경향이 있는 마음을 지닌 그런 사람 말이다.

글의 소재 문화 혁신에 어린이의 마음이 필요한 이유

주요 어휘 primate 영장류, crucially 결정적으로, prefrontal 전전두엽의, pragmatic 실용적인, bizarrely 기괴하게, distort 왜곡시키다, scavenged 쓰레기를 뒤져 찾은, menagerie 전시장, out-of-the-box 격외의, 창조적인, implementable 실현 가능한, downregulated 규제가 작은, heightened 고양된

구조 분석 ⊙ But the very thing that makes them so creative renders most of their creations useless, at least from the pragmatic perspective of goal-oriented adults.

→ 주절과 종속절(thing을 수식하는 관계대명사절)이 모두 S+V+O+OC 형식의 두 개의 5형식 문장으로 이뤄진 문장이다.

정답 해설 주어진 문장에서 사회가 진짜 필요로 하는 건 new vaccines이나 리튬이온 배터리라고 했고 이는 실용성을 강조하기 위해 예로든 물건이다. 이 문장이 But로 시작되는 꺾이는 문장이기 때문에 바로 앞에는 실용적이지 못한 내용이 나와야 한

다. ④ 앞 문장을 보면 창조적인, (그러나 실용적이지 않은) 여러 어린이용 물건을 예로 들고 있다. 역접의 연결사와 함께 반대 예가 이어지는 주어진 문장은 이곳에 와야 한다. 주어진 문장의 실용성이 ④ 다음 문장에서 실현 가능성implementable으로 이어지기 때문에 흐름도 자연스럽다. 정답 ④.

24
정답 ⑤

지문 해석 미국 문화의 위대한 신화는 그때나 지금이나 민주주의는 언어를 통한 것이든 인쇄된 것이든 자유로운 표현 위에 세워진다는 것이다. 아이디어 시장에서 나온 상투어들로 포장돼 있지만 그런 신화에는 장점이 없지 않다. 원칙의 문제로나 권력에 대한 견제로나 자유로운 표현은 스스로를 정당화시킨다는 생각에는 지혜가 담겨 있다. 하지만 종종 그 대가가 크다. 진실이 항상 성취하지는 않고 공공 영역은 통제할 수 없다. 이것이 새로운 미디어 기술이 정보 공간에 밀려들 때마다 다시 배우는 교훈이다. 1938년 Orsen Welles와 그의 Mercury Theater 극단은 H. G. Wells의 소설 *The War of the Worlds*의 라디오 버전을 생방송했다. 이 프로그램이 실제 공포를 불러일으켰다는 증거는 많지 않지만—Welles는 방송의 서두와 말미에서 프로그램은 드라마이고 실제 사건의 뉴스 보도가 아니라는 것을 명백히 했다.—그 방송은 신문의 비중 있는 보도 대상이 됐음을 우리는 안다. 라디오는 이미 1934년 설립된 연방통신위원회의 규제 하에 있었지만 한 매체는 다른 매체와 맞섰다.

↓

사상의 자유롭고 공개적인 교류는 미국 민주주의의 초석이라 일반적으로 믿어지지만 1938년 라디오 생방송의 경우에서 보듯 그 대가는 새로운 미디어를 통한 허위사실의 의도치 않은, 그리고 통제할 수 없는 유포일 수 있다.

글의 소재 자유로운 표현의 장점과 위험성

주요 어휘 shibboleth 상투적인 어구, justification 정당화, win out 성취하다, contain 담다, 통제하다, perpetually 끊임없이, touch off 불러일으키다, garner 얻다, coverage 보도, regulation 규제, confront 맞서다

구조 분석 ⊙ There is wisdom in the notion that free expression is its own justification, as a matter of principle and as a check on power.

→ that는 동격의 that이며 명사절을 유도하고 notion을 부연 설명한다.

정답 해설 본문 전반부에서 미국 민주주의가 자유로운 표현에 기반을 둔다는 신화는 장점이 있고 또 자유로운 표현은 스스로 정당화시킨다고 했으므로 자유로운 표현이 미국 민주주의의 중요한 역할을 하는 것이 분명하다. 따라서 요약문 (A)에는 초석, 기둥, 기반 같은 말이 와야 한다. 한편 글 후반부는 당시 새로운

매체인 한 라디오가 전쟁 드라마를 생방송했는데 이 프로그램이 패닉을 불러일으킨 증거는 많지 않지만 신문이 이를 비중 있게 보도했음을 지적해 이를 실제 상황으로 오인한 적지 않은 동요가 있었음을 암시한다. 이는 라디오 매체의 진의가 왜곡 전달된, 즉 허위 사실이 유포돼 파장을 일으킨 사례로 볼수 있다. 따라서 (B)에 들어갈 말은 유포가 적절하다.

[25~26]

(지문 해석) 자연 진화는 오늘날에도 큰 관심을 받고 있는 신호 유형과 탐지 및 위치 추적 기술을 생산했다. 박쥐는 끊이지 않는 연구 대상이다. 그들은 입으로(일부는 코로) Chip이나 Click으로 불리는 짧은 초음파 신호(주파수 100 kHz 이상)를 발사하고 몇 미터 떨어진 물체의 존재로 인한 반향을 듣는다. 그들의 뇌는 각 귀에 감지되는 반향의 지연이나 주파수, 강도를 근거로 물체의 정확한 위치를 재구성한다. 박쥐의 주된 먹이인 곤충이 단지 몇 미터만 떨어져도 이를 찾아내는 데는 높은 민감도가 요구된다. 발사된 신호는 협대역, 즉 일정한 주파수(CF)와 광대역(주파수 변조, FM 또는 Chirp) 성분을 둘 다 가지고 있다. Chirp라 불리는 선형 주파수 변조 신호는(비선형 변조와 함께 발전된 신호 포함) 박쥐에 의해 발사된 신호 중 하나이며 1942-1943년 이래 독일과 연합국에 의해 레이더 응용을 위해 연구돼 왔다. 박쥐가 발사한 신호의 첫 번째 분석이 이보다 불과 4-5년 전에 이뤄졌다는 점은 주목할 만하다. 동일한 지속 시간과 에너지를 갖는 일반 직사각형 펄스와 관련해, 이러한 유형의 신호는 거리 해상도, 다시 말해 거리 측정에서의 구분 능력의 극적인 개선을 가능하게 한다. 신호 뿐 아니라 박쥐가 장애물과 먹이의 위치를 알아내는 과정이 레이더 관점에서는 대단한 관심거리이다. 전통에 의하면 Chirp이라는 이름은(새가 지저귀는 소리와 같다) 1950년대 펄스 압축을 개발한 미국 실험가 B. M. Oliver에 기인하는데 그는 레이더 발사에는 총 소리가 아닌 새가 지저귀는 소리가 나야한다고 말했다.

(글의 소재) 박쥐 생태를 응용한 레이더 발명

(주요 어휘) detection 탐지, localization 위치 측정, emit 발산하다, ultrasonic 초음파의, reconstruct 재구성하다, on the basis of~를 기반으로, ~를 근거로, locate 위치를 찾아내다 component 구성 요소, linearly 직선으로, date back to ~로 거슬러 올라가다, with respect to ~와 관련해, rectangular 직사각형의, resolution 해상도, discrimination 구별, measurement 측정, obstacle 장애물, compression 압축

(구조 분석) ⊙ Not only signals, but also the processes by which the bats locate obstacles and their prey are of great interest from the radar point of view.

→ not only A but also B 구문으로 'A 뿐만 아니라 B도'의 의미다. B=the processes에 맞춰 동사를 수 일치시켰다. of + 추상명사가 be동사와 함께 쓰이면 형용사 역할을 한다는 점

도 아울러 챙기자. ~ are of great interest ＝ ~ are greatly interesting.

25 [정답 ①]

(정답 해설) 이 글은 초음파를 발사해 먹이를 탐지하는 박쥐의 독특한 능력과 이를 레이더 개발에 응용해온 인간의 노력을 소개한 글이다. 따라서 이 글의 제목으로는 ① '박쥐가 울 때 우리는 레이더를 배운다'가 적절하다.

② 군비 경쟁: 레이더 기술의 어머니

→ 이 글은 군비 경쟁에 대한 글이 아니다.

③ 아쉽다! 박쥐가 보여준 레이더 개발 가능성을 놓치다니

→ 놓치지 않았다.

④ 박쥐의 반향 위치 측정: 먹이 탐지와 포획을 위한 적응력

→ 박쥐 얘기로는 부족하다. 레이더가 나와야 한다.

⑤ 칩, 클릭, 칩: 군사 정보 획득에 동물 이용

→ 본문에 군사 정보 획득에 대한 언급은 없다.

26 [정답 ⑤]

(정답 해설) 앞 문제 해설에서 밝혔듯 이 글은 초음파 신호를 발생시키고 이를 이용해 먹이를 탐지하는 박쥐의 생태를 레이더 개발에 응용한다는 내용이다. 그런데 빈칸 문장의 주어가 자연 진화이고 이는 곧 박쥐의 진화로 해석할 수 있으므로 술부는 신호 발생과 먹이 탐지와 관련된 내용이 올 가능성이 크다. 이에 가까운 것은 ⑤ 뿐이다. ③은 '수동적인 수용기'를 언급하나 박쥐는 능동적으로 신호를 발생시켜 대상을 탐지하므로 정 반대다.

① 항공분야에서 비행 부대의 가치를 강조했다

→ 전혀 동떨어진 내용이다

② 우리에게 깊이 탐지, 항해술, 시각 해상도를 가르쳤다

→ 깊이 탐지나 항해술은 언급되지 않았다

③ 전기 신호 탐지를 위한 수동적 수용기 이용을 밝혀냈다

→ 문제 해설 참조

④ 기술의 참된 정의와 적절한 기능을 소개했다

→ 본문 내용과 거리가 멀다

[27~28]

(지문 해석) 좁은 의미의 문화유산은 의미 있고, 보존과 후대로의 전수 가치가 있다고 인정되는 문화 요소의 저수지로 이해될 수 있다. 하지만, 넓은 의미의 문화유산은, 그 안에서 과거 문화 자원과 그 의미가 사회적 상호작용을 통해 세워지는 역동성 있는 광범위한 구역으로 이해된다. 일단 이 광범위한 구역에서 빠

져나오면 그 저수지는 단지 다양한 형태로 내장된, 공허하고 의미 없는 인공물과 사상의 컬렉션이 된다. 그러한 문화유산의 이해는 Maurice Halbwachs가 도입한 집단적 기억의 사상에 뿌리를 두고 있다. 과거에 대한 우리의 기억은 사회적으로 형성된다고 그는 주장한다. 어느 정도는 사회적 조건이 우리가 무엇을 어떻게 기억하는지를 결정한다. 사회적으로 결정되는 전통과 문화유산의 현상은 Eric Hobsbawn and Terence Ranger에 의해 강조되는데 그들은 전통은 재현되는 게 아니라 발명된다고 본다.

문화유산의 광범위한 성격에 대한 믿음은 어떤 인공물이나 행태적 패턴이 후세에 전승될 것인가를 결정하는 기준이 안정적이라는(→불안정하다는) 확신에 근거한다. 한편으로 문화유산의 저수지는 선택에서 자유롭지 못하고 세계적 흐름, 신기술, 경제, 문화 정책이나 정책 결정자의 정서에 의해 결정된다. 다른 한편으로 그런 저수지는 지속적인 재해석의 대상이어서 문화에 참여하는 개인의 사회적 지위, 배경, 개인사, 문화적 능력에 의해 영향 받는다. 사회적 상호작용은 문화유산 이전의 본질이다.

글의 소재 사회적 산물로서의 광의의 문화유산

주요 어휘 reservoir 저수지, preservation 보존, transfer 전승, dynamic 역동적인, discursive 광범위한, extract 추출하다, 빼내다, artefact 인공물, 공예품, embedded 내장된, reproduce 재생하다, 재현하다, 복제하다, conviction 확신, behavioural 행태의, posterity 후세, be subject to ~에 매어있다, continual 끊임없는, reinterpretation 재해석, competence 능력, transition 이전, 전승

구조 분석 ⊙ Once extracted from this discursive area, the reservoir becomes just an empty and meaningless collection of artefacts and ideas embedded in various forms.

→ Once와 extracted 사이에는 it is가 생략됐다. 시간과 조건의 부사절에서 주절과 종속절의 주어와 시제가 같으면 부사절(종속절)의 주어와 be동사는 흔히 생략된다.

27

정답 ③

정답 해설 이 글은 문화요소의 저수지라는 좁은 의미에서의 문화유산이 아닌 사회적 상호작용에 의해 결정되는 역동적이고 가변적이고 늘 재해석되고 불안한 넓은 의미의 문화유산에 초점 맞추고 있다. 본문 셋째 줄 역접의 연결사와 함께 통념―좁은 의미의 문화유산―이 깨지면서 필자의 주장―광의의 문화유산―이 나오는 문장이 주제문이다. 따라서 정답은 ③ '사회적 산물이라는 광의의 문화유산의 특성'이 타당하다.

① 문화유산 보존의 중요성

② 문화유산 인공물 저수지를 짓는 절차
④ 사회단체의 폭넓은 세계 유산 지정 노력
⑤ 역사적 가치에 따라 인공물을 분류하는 확립된 기준

28

정답 ④

정답 해설 본문 마지막 두 문장에서 보듯 인공물 저수지를 결정하는 요인은 매우 다양하고 저수지 자체가 끊임없이 재해석되므로 후손에 물려줄 인공물이나 행동패턴을 결정하는 기준은 안정적이 아니라 불안정하다가 맞다. 따라서 (d)는 unstable로 바꿔야 한다. 정답 ④.

[29~30]

지문 해석

(A) 사라는 의사가 되기를 꿈꿨다. 초등학교 이후 그녀는 자신이 의사가 될 거라는 데 한 점의 의심도 품지 않았다. 어느 날 어린 시절 친구인 아만다가 그녀의 집을 찾아왔다. 그녀 또한 의학 분야 진로를 꿈꿔서 그들은 같은 아이비리그 학교에 들어갈 계획을 세웠다. 사라와 아만다의 부모는 둘이 모두 대학가는 데는 찬성했지만 딸들이 선택한 진로에 대해선 전혀 다른 태도를 보였다.

(C) 사라의 부모는 딸을 지지하는 쪽이었다. 그들은 그녀에게 출세를 학교 성적이나 포상과 연관시키지 말고 자신의 가치관을 세우고 이해하라고 격려했다. 사라는 아만다에게 그녀 부모는 그들의 계획을 어떻게 생각하느냐고 물었다. 그들이 한번 이상 걱정된다는 말을 했다고 그녀가 밝혔다. 아만다는 공부에 재능이 있었기 때문에 이 말을 듣고 그녀는 놀랐다. '여자애들은 과학에 약해' 같은 고정관념 문화 속에서 딸을 키워서 아만다의 부모는 그녀가 그런 진로에 소질이 있는지 없는지에 대해 의심을 품었다.

(D) 대학 입학 후 두 친구는 첫 번째 작은 좌절을 경험했다. 그들은 중간고사 생물학 시험에서 나쁜 성적을 받았다. 아만다는 화났다. 그녀는 나쁜 성적이 부모님이 내내 얘기해 오던 것을 입증했다고 생각했다. 사라도 실망했지만 그녀는 훌훌 털어버렸다. 그녀는 친구에게 그녀가 새 장소에서 수업, 사교 모임, 여학생 클럽 의무사항을 곡예 하듯 해내고 난생 처음 가족과 떨어져 살고 있다는 점을 상기시켰다.

(B) 아만다는 아직 그녀의 추론에 설득당하지 않았다. 그런 사소한 시험에 낙제한다면 그녀가 의사될 소질이 없는 게 분명하지 않을까? 그녀는 학과를 바꿀 것을 고려하고, 심지어 아예 학교를 그만둘 생각까지 했다. 사라는 동요되지 않았다. 그녀의 개인적 가치관이, 단지 과학을 못해서 그녀의 학문적 수행이 동료보다 못하다는 위험한 문화적 메시지에 흡수되는 것으로부터 그녀를 보호했다. 이것은 길 위의 작은 턱일 뿐이고 사라는 몇

년 후 두 친구 모두 의사의 꿈을 이룰 수 있음을 알았다.

글의 소재 사라와 사만다의 대조적 가치관

주요 어휘 sliver 조각, hatch 부화하다, convince 설득하다, 확신을 주다, reasoning 추론, flunk 낙제하다, perturb 동요시키다, absorb 흡수하다, peer 동료, 또래, supportive 지지하는, identify 동일시하다, 신분을 밝히다, accolade 찬사, 포상, reveal 폭로하다, stereotype 고정관념, setback 좌절, disappoint 실망시키다, shrug it off 훌훌 털어버리다, juggle 저글하다, 둘 이상의 일을 동시에 하다, sorority 여학생 클럽, obligation 의무

구조 분석 ⊙ he reminded her friend that she was in a new place, juggling classes, social events, sorority obligations and living away from family for the first time in her life.

→ 'juggling classes ~ sorority obligations'는 분사구문으로 계속 진행을 나타내며 'and she juggled ~'로 패러프레이즈 된다. 같은 분사구문이 등위접속사 and와 함께 'living away ~ in her life'로 이어지는 병렬구조다.

29 정답 ③

정답 해설 주어진 글 (A)가 두 부모의 매우 다른 태도를 언급하며 끝맺고 있으므로 사라 부모의 태도가 나오는 (C)가 (A) 다음에 이어져야 한다. (B)는 첫 문장에서 사라의 추론을 언급하고 있고 이런 내용은 (C)에 없으므로 (C) 다음에 올 수 없다. (C) 다음에 올 수 있는 것은 (D) 뿐이다. 따라서 올바른 순서는 (C) - (D) - (B)이다. 정답은 ③이다.

30 정답 ⑤

정답 해설 (e)는 사만다를 가리키고 나머지는 모두 사라를 가리킨다. 따라서 정답은 ⑤ (e)이다.

19. 2025학년도 경찰대학교 1차 선발 시험

정답

01 ①	02 ②	03 ③	04 ③	05 ①
06 ②	07 ④	08 ①	09 ④	10 ④
11 ③	12 ②	13 ⑤	14 ②	15 ④
16 ⑤	17 ②	18 ①	19 ①	20 ③
21 ④	22 ②	23 ①	24 ①	25 ②
26 ②	27 ⑤	28 ①	29 ④	30 ④
31 ⑤	32 ③	33 ⑤	34 ④	35 ⑤
36 ③	37 ①	38 ②	39 ⑤	40 ④
41 ③	42 ④	43 ③	44 ⑤	45 ⑤

01 정답 ①

02 정답 ②

03 정답 ③

04 정답 ③

05 정답 ①

06 정답 ②

07 정답 ④

08 정답 ①

지문 해석 인도에서 성장기를 보내면서 나는 Kolkata에 있는 조부모님을 방문하며 여름방학을 보내곤 했다. 매일 오후, 할머니는 힌두교 신의 석상들이 작은 나무 좌대에 놓여있는 가족 기도실을 마주보며 거실 매트에 편안히 앉으셨다. 그녀는 눈 감고 손가락으로는 염주를 돌리고 크리슈나 이름을 속삭이듯 낭송하며 30분 동안 가만히 앉아 계셨다. 그 명상의 시간이 할머니가 신과 모종의 교감을 이루는데 도움을 줬는지를 객관적으로 알 수 없지만 그녀가 그것으로부터 여러 방식으로 도움을 받았음을 암시하는 과학적 증거가 점점 늘어갔다. 그 명상 실천은 그녀가 스트레스를 관리하는 효과적인 접근법이었을지 모른다. 그것은 어쩌면 나이와 관련된 인지 저하를 늦추는 데 도움이 됐을 지도 모른다. 또 그것은 십중팔구 그녀의 통증 다루는 능력

을 높여줬을 것이다. 주의를 현재에 집중하는 연습이라 폭넓게 정의되는 명상은 어떤 형태로든 전 세계 종교 전통에 의해—대부분 영적 깨달음 추구에 뿌리를 두고—수천 년 동안 실천돼 왔다. 오늘날 명상의 인기는 정신 건강과 스트레스 해소의 중요성에 대한 인식과 병행해 커지고 있다.

글의 소재 할머니 명상법의 효능

주요 어휘 worship 숭배, 기도, throne 왕좌. 좌대, communion 교감, cognitive 인지의, decline 저하, 하락, enhance 높이다, 고양하다, quest 추구, enlightenment 각성, 깨달음, in parallel with ~와 병행해, awareness 인식

구조 분석 ⊙ Defined most broadly as the exercise of focusing one's attention on the current moment, meditation in some form has been practiced for millennia by religious traditions around the world ~.

→ Defined 앞에 being이 생략된 분사구문으로 패러프레이즈하면 'As it is defined ~'이 된다. 또 과거분사로 시작하는 분사구문은 주절의 주어를 수동으로 꾸며주는 식으로, 즉 '~로 정의되는 명상은' 식으로 해석하면 자연스러운 경우가 많다.

정답 해설 ① 이 문장에는 동사가 없어 1문장 1동사 원칙에 위배된다. 따라서 settling의 자리에는 준동사가 아닌 동사(settled)가 와야 한다. 정답 ①.

② 의문사 whether 이하가 명사절을 유도해 know의 목적어로 쓰인 것은 문법적으로 옳다.

③ 여기서 likely는 부사로 쓰였고 probably의 뜻이다.

④ 문장 맨 앞에 Being이 생략된 분사구문으로 Defined의 쓰임은 옳다(구조 분석 참조).

⑤ 명상의 인기가 나날이 커지고 있음을 나타내기 위해 현재완료 계속의 용법이 사용된 것은 문법적으로 옳다.

09 정답 ④

지문 해석 화는 분명히 공격과 관계가 있지만 둘이 똑같지는 않다. 화내지 않고 공격적일 수 있고 마찬가지로 공격적이지 않으면서 화낼 수도 있다. 하지만 그 둘(화라는 감정과 공격이라는 행동)은 서로 연결돼 있고 생물학적 기반을 두고 있어서 명백한 존재가를 가진다. 화는 항상 대폭 증가된 에너지의 분출을 가져 오고 생물학적 기반을 두지만 몇몇 심리학자들에 의해 대체로 사회적으로 형성되는 것으로 여겨진다. 다시 말해, 어떤 사람은 다른 사람보다 기질적으로 화를 내는 쪽으로 더 기울 수 있지만 이것을 표현하는 정도는 십중팔구 사회적으로 결정된다. 가령 우리 문화에서는 남자아이가 여자아이보다 더 공개적으로 화를 내도록 장려되고 분노 조절 강의를 듣는 비율은 여자보다 남자가 훨씬 높다. 이것들은 생물학적 차이가 아니라 학습된 차이이다.

글의 소재 화냄의 사회적 성격

주요 어휘 aggression 공격, one and the same 똑같은, burst 분출, temperamentally 기질적으로, prone to ~하는 경향이 있는, proportion 비율

구조 분석 ⊙ Anger always results in a much increased burst of energy and, although biologically based, is seen by some psychologists as largely socially constructed.

→ 등위접속사 and로 연결된 병렬구조로 'although biologically based' 삽입절 다음의 is를 results와 수, 시제 일치시켰다.

정답 해설 ④ 5형식 문장을 수동태로 바꾼 문장이다. 5형식을 수동태로 바꿀 때는 반드시 목적보어로 쓰인 원형부정사 앞에 to를 붙여야 한다. 따라서 take는 to take로 바꿔야 한다. 정답 ④.

① equally가 부사로 쓰여 형용사 possible를 수식한 것은 문제가 없다.

② 'although it is biologically based'에서 it is가 생략된 형태로 문법적으로 옳다. 시간이나 조건, 양보의 부사절에서 주절과 종속절의 주어와 시제가 같으면 '주어 + be동사'는 생략될 수 있다.

③ 뒤 문장이 완전하기 때문에 ③의 자리에는 관계부사가 오거나 '전치사 + 관계대명사'가 와야 한다. 따라서 여기서 to which가 쓰인 것은 문법적으로 옳다.

⑤ '학습된'이라는 의미의 형용사로 쓰여 differences를 꾸며 준 것은 타당하다.

10 정답 ④

지문 해석 최근 수십 년간의 정치적, 사회적 변화의 결과 문화적 다원주의는 이제 대체로 이 사회의 구성 원리로 인정된다. 인종 간, 집단 간 차이를 지울 것을 약속한 멜팅팟 사상과는 대조적으로 오늘날 어린이들은 다양성이 삶의 활력소라고 배운다. 미국은 많은 다른 집단에 주거지를 제공했고 그들이 자신의 문화유산을 유지하거나, 동화하거나 아니면 흔히 그러하듯 두 가지 다 하거나를 허용했다. 선택은 그들의 몫이지 국가의 것이 아니다. 그들은 문화적 다원주의가 자유 사회의 규범 중 하나이며 집단 간 차이는 해결해야 할 문제가 아니라 국가적 자원이라고 배운다. 실제로, 미국만의 독특한 특징은 공동의 문화가 하위문화의 상호작용으로 만들어졌다는 점이다. 그것은 이민자, 아메리카 인디언, 아프리카인(노예와 자유인)과 그들의 후손들에 의해 시간을 두고 영향 받은 문화다. 미국의 음악, 미술, 문학, 언어, 음식, 옷, 스포츠, 휴일, 관습은 모두 한 나라 안의 다양한 문화가 뒤섞인 결과를 보여준다. 역설적으로 들릴지 모르나 미국은 다문화적인 공동의 문화를 가지고 있다.

글의 소재 미국의 문화 다원주의

주요 어휘 pluralism 다원주의, melting pot (사상 인종이 뒤섞여 녹는) 용광로, 멜팅팟, assimilate 동화하다, as is often the case 흔히 그러하듯이, norm 규범, subsidiary 부수적인, 하위의, descendant 후손, paradoxical 역설적인, multicultural 다문화의

구조 분석 ⊙ Paradoxical though it may seem, the United States has a common culture that is multicultural.

➔ 원래 문장 'Though it may seem paradoxical'에서 강조를 위해 paradoxical이 앞으로 나오면서 도치 구문이 됐다. 도치문에서 though는 as로 바꿔도 같은 뜻이다.

정답 해설 (A) 문장에서 아이들은 다양성이 삶의 활력소라 배운다고 했는데 이는 멜팅팟과 대조되므로 네모 안에는 contrast가 맞다. (B) 문장에는 세 개의 선택지가 or로 연결 제시되는데 나머지 두 개가 '동화되는 것'과 '둘 다'이므로 첫째 선택지는 동화되지 않고 개별성을 유지하는 내용이어야 한다. 따라서 네모 안에 올 말은 maintain이다. (C)는 미국의 문화 다원주의가 구체적으로 예시되는 문장이므로 '한 나라에 다양한 문화가 뒤섞인 결과'라는 내용이어야 한다. 따라서 (C)에는 diverse가 적절하다. 정답 ④.

11 정답 ③

지문 해석 지식과 힘의 상호 관계에 대한 일반적 이해는 자주 "아는 것이 힘이다."라는 문구로 표현된다. 계통학 연구에서 푸꼬는 이 표현의 논리를 뒤집는다. 우리에게 힘을 주는 것은 지식의 습득이 아니라고 그는 주장한다. 대신 지식은, "힘이 지식이다."라는 말을 해야 할 정도로 이미 언제나 깊이 힘을 부여받고 있다. 따라서 푸꼬의 분석에 의하면, 지식은 결코 힘과 동떨어진 것이 아니라 힘을 행사하기 위한 구체적인 수단이다. 이런 식으로 지식은 단순히 한 개인이나 사회 구조 안에서 구현되는 어떤 것이 아니라 신체적 힘에 의한 강제나 처벌로 표현된다. 힘은 "지식"의 체계 안으로 성공적으로 변환돼 자명한 진실의 베일 아래서 하는 성찰에서 벗어날 때 가장 강력한 형태로 나타난다. 푸꼬에 따르면 힘과 지식의 불가분성은 너무도 철저해서 그는 자주 둘을 힘/지식이라는 용어로 묶는다.

글의 소재 푸꼬의 지식관

주요 어휘 genealogical 계통학의, reverse 뒤집다, contend 주장하다, aquition 습득, be invested with ~를 부여받다, embody 구현하다, brute 신체적 힘에 의한, coercion 강제, potent 강한, conjoin 결합하다

구조 분석 ⊙ Instead, knowledge is already always deeply invested with power in such a way that it must be said that "power is knowledge."

➔ 앞의 that은 'such ~ that' 용법에서 부사절을 유도하는 접

속사 that이다. 뒤의 that는 가주어 it의 진주어로 명사절을 유도하는 접속사다.

정답 해설 글의 중반에서 푸꼬는 지식이 힘이 아니라 힘이 지식이라 하여 논리를 뒤집었으므로 (A)에 들어갈 말은 reverses가 합당하다. (B) 문장에서 필자는 지식이 힘과 동떨어진 것이 아니라고 했으므로 그것은 힘을 거부하는 것이 아니라 행사하는 수단이어야 논리적으로 맞다. 따라서 (B)에는 exercising이 적절하다. 이 글은 힘과 지식의 불가분성을 일관되게 주장하고 있으므로 (C) 들어갈 말은 inseparability가 타당하다. 따라서 정답은 ③이다.

12 정답 ②

지문 해석 라이벌 회사 간의 경쟁은 상품과 서비스에서 혁신을 가져올 것이라고 모든 경제학 교과서는 당신에게 말할 것이다. 그러나 혁신을 장거리 관점에서 볼 때 경쟁은 우리가 보통 생각하는 것보다 좋은 생각의 역사에 덜 중심적이다. 표준 교과서들이 그러하듯 혁신을 개인과 기관의 차원에서 분석하는 것은 우리의 시각을 (넓힌다→좁힌다). 그것은 독점적 연구와 "적자생존" 식 경쟁의 역할을 과장하는 혁신 상을 만든다. 장거리 관점 식 접근은 우리로 하여금 순전히 경쟁적인 체제보다 개방성과 연관성이 결국 혁신에 더 소중함을 알게 할 것이다. 그러한 혁신의 양상은 인정받을 만한데 그 이유는 부분적으로 왜 좋은 아이디어가 태어나는지를 역사적으로 이해하는 것이 본질적으로 중요하기 때문이고 그리고 또 그러한 양상을 수용함으로써 우리는 좋은 아이디어를 키우는 일을 더 잘 해내는 환경을—그 환경이 학교든, 정부든, 또는 사회 운동이든—조성할 수 있기 때문이다. 우리는 창조를 가능케 하는 많은 연관된 환경에 우리 마음을 열 때 보다 창조적으로 생각할 수 있다.

글의 소재 창조의 모태로서의 개방성과 연관성

주요 어휘 overstate 과장하다, proprietary 독점적인, survival of the fittest 적자생존, connectivity 연관성, intrinsically 본질적으로, embrace 껴안다, 수용하다, nurture 양육하다,

구조 분석 ⊙ Analyzing innovation on the scale of individuals and organizations—as the standard textbooks do—broadens our view.

➔Analyzing는 동명사로 쓰였고 주어가 동명사구라 동사를 단수로 수 일치시켰다.

정답 해설 ② 다음 문장에서 그것(혁신을 개인과 단체 차원에서 분석하는 것)은 독점적 연구와 적자생존 식 경쟁의 역할을 과장한다는 부정적 내용으로 보아 이러한 분석은 우리의 시각을 넓히는 것이 아니라 좁히는 것이다. 따라서 broadens는 narrows로 바꿔야 한다. 정답 ②.

13

[지문 해석] 긴 소개가 필요 없는 위대한 미국 작가 Edgar Allan Poe는 현대 단편 소설을 창시한 작가 중 한 명이다. 현대 단편 소설은 스토리를 현대의 현실주의적 배경에 설정한다는 점에서뿐 아니라 그 형식이 단일한 극적 사건에 초점 맞춘다는 점에서 이전의 이야기나 우화 형태와는 다르다. Poe의 경우 이 단일 사건은 보통 죽음과 살인이 따르는 비정상적인 행위와 매우 자주 관련이 있다. 그런 불쾌한 사건을 살인자 자신의 관점에서 서술함으로써 Poe 단편소설의 독자는 어떻게 자기가 범행을 저질렀는지를 세세하게 공들여 설명하는 공격자의 생생한 목소리를 들어야하는데 이는 Poe의 발명품이었다. 이런 양식의 스토리텔링의 단점은(→장점은) 그것이 작가로 하여금 인간의 마음이라는 신비한 물건을 매우 친밀하고 극단적인 방식으로 탐구할 수 있게 한다는 점이다.

[글의 소재] Poe의 혁신적인 소설 작법

[주요 어휘] concentrate 집중하다, abnormal 비정상적인, typically 전형적으로, 보통, disturbing 불쾌한, murderer 살인자, aggressor 공격자, intimate 친밀한

[구조 분석] ⊙ A modern short story is different from earlier forms of tales and fables not only in that it sets the story on a modern realistic background but also in the way its form concentrates on a single dramatic event.

➡ that 이하는 전치가 in의 목적어인 명사절이다. 전치사는 원칙적으로 절을 목적어로 취하지 못하나 'except that'(~라는 점을 제외하고), 'save that'(~라는 점을 제외하고), 'but that'(~이 아니라면) 등의 경우는 예외적으로 허용된다.

[정답 해설] ⑤ 문장의 서술부에서는 작가가 인간의 마음이라는 신비한 물건을 친밀하고 극단적인 방식으로 탐구한다는 긍정적인 내용이 이어지므로 논지의 일관성 상 ⑤에는 disadvantage(단점)이 아닌 advantage(장점)라야 맞다. 정답 ⑤.

14

[지문 해석] Virgil의 뛰어난 시는 그에게 라틴어 권 최고의 시인이라는 유산을 안겼다. 중세와 르네상스 내내 그의 명성은 커져만 갔다. 인쇄기가 발명되기 전, 필경사의 손을 통해 전승되던 고전 텍스트가 귀했던 때 Virgil의 시는 글을 이해하는 계층에 보급됐고 그들 사이에서 그는 고대의 가장 중요한 작가로 여겨졌다. 그는 이태리어의 단테, 영어의 밀턴 그리고 Aeneid를 중세 모험담 Le Roman d'Eneas로 개작한 무명의 프랑스 시인을 포함해 시인들에게 언어를 뛰어넘어 영감을 주었다. 후에 기독교 문화권이 된 곳에서 Virgil은 이교도 예언자로 간주됐는데 이는 그의 작품 중 몇 구절이 예수 재림을 예언한 것으로 해석됐기 때문이다. 르네상스 작가들 사이에서 Virgil은 그의 생생한 인간 감정 묘사로 높이 평가됐다. 한편 현대 비평가들은 덜 관대했다. Virgil의 시는 흔히 그의 그리스 선배들의 시, 특히 호머의 서사시로 추정되며 역시 트로이전쟁을 그린 *Iliad and the Odyssey*와 비교돼서 평가된다. 대부분의 현대 작가들은 Virgil의 시를 호머의 시에 비교하면 창백해진다(초라해진다)고 생각한다.

[글의 소재] 라틴어 권 최고의 시인으로 칭송받았던 Virgil

[주요 어휘] masterful 거장다운, 뛰어난, scribe 필경사, literate 문해의, 글을 이해하는, anonymous 무명의, 익명의, medieval 중세의, pagan 이교도의, prophet 예언자, portrayal 묘사, predecessor 전임자, 선배, pale(vi) 창백해지다, 초라해지다, in comparison to ~와 비교해

[구조 분석] ⊙ Most contemporary scholars hold that Virgil's poetry pales in comparison to Homer's.

➡ hold는 '~라 생각하다'를 뜻하고, pale은 원래 '창백한'을 뜻하는 형용사지만 여기서는 '빛을 잃다,' '초라해지다'라는 뜻의 자동사로 쓰였다.

[정답 해설] 본문에서 Vilgil의 명성은 중세와 르네상스 내내 그의 명성은 커져만 갔다고 했으므로 선택지 ② '그의 명성은 르네상스 동안 쇠퇴했다.'는 사실이 아니다. 따라서 정답은 ②다.
① 그의 능수능란한 라틴어 시가 그를 저명한 시인으로 만들었다.
③ 그는 다른 언어의 시에 영향을 미쳤다.
④ 그의 시는 분명히 인간 감정을 표현했다.
⑤ 그의 시는 현대 비평가들에 의해 호머의 시보다 낮게 평가된다.

15

[지문 해석] Alice James는 항상 어떤 유명인의 형제자매로 분류된다. 그녀의 오빠인 소설가 Henry James와 철학자 William James는 둘 다 자기 분야에서 중요 인물이다. 그녀의 가족 자체가 매사추세츠 Cambridge의 유명하고 존경받는 가문이었다. 하지만 막내딸 Alice는 열여섯 살 때 처음 신경쇠약을 앓은 후 늘 문제 거리였다. 또 그녀는 여러 가지 건강상 문제에 시달렸다. 한편 그의 오빠들은 그들의 공적 이력에서 점점 유명해지고 있었다. Alice James는 마흔 넷의 나이로 죽었지만 인생의 마지막 3년 동안 자신의 사상에 대한 매우 흥미로운 기록을 남겼다. 그러나 그녀는 너무 약해 글을 쓸 수조차 없었다. 그녀의 절친 K. P. Loring이 그녀가 하는 말을 대신 써줬다. Loring은 또 Alice의 오빠들과 그녀 자신을 위해 Alice의 일기 한 권을 출간했다. 그녀의 일기를 읽을 때 어려운 점은 분노와 자기 연민 그리고 물론 그녀가 느낀 고통을 이해하는 것이다. 당시 여성은 늘 남자 의사에 의해 연구되고 치료돼야 할 '사례' 혹은 '문제'로 여겨졌기 때문에 우리는 그녀의 경험이 여성 특유의 경험이었음을 또한 잊지 말아야 한다.

글의 소재 Alice James의 생애 약전

주요 어휘 household 가구, 가정, mental breakdown 신경쇠약, challenge 도전, 난점, journal 저널, 일기, appreciate 감상하다, 이해하다, 감사하다, feminine 여성의

구조 분석 ⊙ The challenge in reading her journal is to appreciate the mixture of anger, self-pity, and, of course, the pain the writer feels.

→ 'is'가 동사이고 'to appreciate'가 보어인 2형식 문장이다. 'to appreciate'는 to 부정사의 명사적 용법으로 '~하는 것'으로 해석한다. 예정이나 운명, 능력 등을 나타내는 'be to'용법이 아님을 주의하라.

정답 해설 절친 Loring이 Alice의 말을 받아써 책으로 냈다는 말이 본문에 나오므로 ④ '그녀는 그녀의 사상에 대한 구술된 저작물을 남겼다'는 본문의 내용과 일치한다.

① 그녀는 Cambridge의 하류층 가정 출신이다.

→ Cambridge의 유명하고 존경받는 가문이었다.

② 그녀는 집에서 맏이다.

→ 집안의 막내였다

③ 그녀의 오빠들은 명성을 얻지 못했다.

→ 둘 다 자기 분야에서 중요 인물이다.

⑤ 그녀의 일기는 다른 여성에 대한 연민으로 가득하다.

→ 자기 연민으로 가득하다

16
정답 ⑤

지문 해석 미국이 분석철학으로 넘어간 데에는 몇몇 중요한 인물과 단체, 사건들이 중간 역할을 했다. 그 한 인물이 Morris Cohen(1880 - 1947)이다. 러시아에서 태어난 그는 City College of New York에서 교육받았다. 1905년에 Harvard에서 박사학위를 받은 그는 1912년부터 1938년까지는 City대에서, 1938년부터 1941년까지는 University of Chicago에서 각각 가르쳤다. 논리학과 과학철학에 대한 관심으로 유명했던 그는 철학 분야 지식 습득에 어떤 비과학적인 방법도 인정하지 않은 헌신적인 동식물학자였다. 제자 중 한 명이 체코슬로바키아 태생 Ernest Nagel이었는데 그는 City대에서 학사학위를 받은 후 1931년 Columbia University에서 박사학위를 취득했다. 1960년대 Rockefeller University에서의 1년을 제외하고 그는 직장 생활을 Columbia University에서 과학철학을 가르치거나 쓰고, 논리학이 철학의 핵심임을 설명하면서 보냈다.

글의 소재 Morris Cohen과 그의 제자 Ernest Nagel의 간략한 캐리어 소개

주요 어휘 transition 전환, 이행, 전이, mediate 중재하다, committed 헌신적인, naturalist 동식물학자, 박물학자, capable of ~을 할 수 있는, attain 습득하다, centrality 중심성

구조 분석 ⊙ he spent his career at Columbia University teaching and writing about the philosophy of science and explaining the centrality of logic to philosophy.

→ 이 부분을 절로 패러프레이즈하면 'explaining that logic is central to philosophy.'이다.

정답 해설 본문에 Nagel은 Rockefeller University에서의 1년을 제외하고 직장 생활을 Columbia University에서 보냈다는 말이 있기 때문에 ⑤ 'Nagel은 직장 생활 대부분을 Columbia University에서 보냈다.'는 사실에 부합한다.

① Cohen은 Czechoslovakia에서 태어났다.

→ 러시아에서 태어났다.

② Cohen은 1941까지 City College of New York에서 가르쳤다.

→ 1941년까지 University of Chicago에서 가르쳤다.

③ Cohen는 논리학에만 관심 있었던 것으로 유명했다.

→ 논리학과 과학철학에 대한 관심으로 유명했다.

④ Nagel은 1931년 Harvard University에서 박사학위를 받았다.

→ 1931년 Columbia University에서 박사학위를 받았다.

17
정답 ②

지문 해석 교육 측면에서 역사학은 항상 언론의 좋은 대우를 받은 것은 아니다. 1656년 아들에게 충고하며 Francis Osborne은 그 과목에 대해 전혀 열의를 보이지 않았다. 자기 생애에 벌어진 내전들(현대사)에 대한 상충된 보도를 들은 그의 경험이 그로 하여금 덜 최근 벌어진 사건들에 대한 기록의 신뢰성에 대해 회의적이게 만들었다. 그런 역사적 기록들은 '거짓 아니면 기껏해야 부수적인 믿음'을 제공할 가능성이 크고, 그래서 심각한 연구를 보장받기 어렵다고 그는 결론 내렸다. 아들이 신뢰하기 어려운 역사를 공부하며 시간을 낭비하게 될지도 모른다는 Osborne의 걱정은 역사를 이상적으로 어떤 종류—과거에 대해 확실하고 '사실적인' 지식을 생산하는 그런 종류—의 것으로 이해했음을 의미했다. 그런 모델은 Osborne 시대에도 이미 도전 받고 있었지만 어느 정도는 우리 시대까지 지속돼 오고 있다.

글의 소재 역사학에 대해 회의적이었던 Osborne

주요 어휘 in terms of ~ 측면에서, ~에 관해, receive a good press 언론의 좋은 대우를 받다, enthusiastic 열정적인, contradictory 모순적인, 상충된, contemporary 동시대의, 현대적인, reliability 신뢰성, contingent 임시의, 부수적인, warrant 보장하다, 정당화하다, anxiety 걱정, 불안, potentially 잠재적으로, imply 의미하다, 함축하다, factual 사실적인, persist 지속하다

구조 분석 ⊙ Osborne's anxiety <u>about</u> <u>his son</u> potentially <u>wasting</u> his time by studying history that is unreliable, <u>implies an understanding of history as being ideally of a certain kind</u>—the kind that yields certain, 'factual' knowledge about the past.

→ wasting은 about의 목적어인 동명사이고 그 의미상 주어는 his son이다. implies 이하를 절로 바꾸면 'implies that he understood history as being ~'가 된다.

정답 해설 빈칸 문장에서 그가 내전에 대한 상충되는 보도를 들었다고 했고 다음 문장에서도 역사 기록이 거짓되고 기껏해야 부수적인 믿음을 줄 가능성이 크다고 말하고 있는 것으로 보다 Osborne은 기록의 신뢰성을 의심했음을 알 수 있다. 따라서 빈칸에 적절한 말은 ② reliability다.

① 연속성

③ 재발견

④ 간결성

⑤ 예측 가능성

18
정답 ①

지문 해석 모든 지능은 가르쳐져야 한다. 인간의 두뇌는 유전적으로 사물을 분류하도록 준비돼 있지만 고양이와 개를 구분하기 이전의 어린애처럼 십여 개의 예를 더 봐야 한다. 이것은 인공 지능에 대해서는 더욱 사실이다. 가장 잘 프로그램화된 컴퓨터조차 적어도 천 번의 체크 게임을 해야 좋은 성적을 낼 수 있다. AI의 비약적 발전의 일부는 세계에 대해 수집된 엄청난 양의 정보에 있는데 이것이 AI가 필요로 하는 학습을 제공한다. 대규모 데이터베이스, 자가 추적, 웹 쿠키, 온라인 발자국, 수 테러바이트의 기억 장치, 수십 년의 연구 결과, 그리고 전 디지털 영역이 모두 AI를 스마트하게 만드는 스승들이다. Andrew Ng는 그것을 이렇게 설명한다. "AI는 로켓 추진선을 건조하는 것과 유사하다. 당신에게는 거대한 엔진과 많은 연료가 필요하다. 로켓 엔진은 학습 알고리즘이지만 연료는 알고리즘에 먹이는 방대한 양의 데이터다."

글의 소재 인간 지능이나 AI에서의 학습의 필요성

주요 어휘 genetically 유전적으로, be primed to ~할 준비가 돼 있다, distinguish 구분하다, breakthrough 돌파구, 비약적 발전, lie in ~에 있다, incredible 믿기 어려운, 놀라운, self-tracking 자가 추적, storage 저장, 기억 장치, entire 전체의, akin to ~와 유사한

구조 분석 ⊙ A human brain, <u>which is genetically primed to categorize things</u>, still needs to see a dozen examples as a child before it can distinguish between cats and dogs.

→ 관계대명사의 계속적 용법으로 양보절을 유도하며 'though

---

it is genetically primed to categorize things,'로 패러프레이즈할 수 있다.

정답 해설 빈칸 문장에 이어지는 다음 두 문장에서 '인간의 두뇌는 고양이와 개를 구분하기 이전의 어린애처럼 십여 개의 예를 더 봐야 한다.'고 했고 '인공 지능은 더욱 그러하다'고 했는데 이는 모든 지능은 학습되는 것임을 말해준다. 따라서 빈칸에 들어갈 적절한 말은 '가르쳐져야'이다. 정답 ①.

② 스스로를 뛰어 넘어야

③ 혼자 힘으로 사고해야

④ 규칙에 의해 통제돼야

⑤ 모든 확률을 계산해야

19
정답 ①

지문 해석 어원학은 말의 뿌리, 즉 어원에 대한 학문이다. 그것은 '사실의'를 뜻하는 희랍어 어근 *etymos*에서 유래했다. 어원의 중요성과 의미는 크다. 일반적으로 어원과 의미의 관계에는 두 가지 상반된 프로세스가 작동한다. 첫째는 어원의 연결고리가 서서히 약화되고 있다는 것이다. 말들이 그들의 원래 의미에서 꾸준히 멀어지는 경향을 보이는 것이다. 이와 상반된 것은 연결고리를 되살리려는, 즉 말들을 그들의 과거와 '말이 되게' 만들려는 욕구다. 사람들은 말들에 대한 <u>기억하기 쉽고 논리적인 기원을 좋아해서</u>, 그것들이 없으면 만들어내기까지 한다. 어떤 말들은 실제로 매우 인상적인 어원을 가지고 있다. 우리는, *sandwich*가 Earl of Sandwich에서 유래했고 그는 광적인 도박꾼이어서 24시간 게임 도중 테이블을 떠나지 않으려고 부분적으로 토스트 빵 사이에 끼워 넣은 차가운 쇠고기를 먹고 버텼다는 것을 (한번 들으면) 잊기 어렵다. 이리하여 *sandwich*가 탄생했고 1762년에 처음 기록됐다.

주요 어휘 etymology 어원, 어원학, derive 파생하다, implication 의미, 함축, contradictory 모순되는, 상충된, gradual 서서히 진행되는, erosion 잠식, 약화, contrary 반대되는, striking 인상적인, compulsive 강박감에 사로잡힌, 광적인, bout 한 판 승부, sustain oneself 목숨을 연명하다, 버티다

구조 분석 ⊙ <u>Contrary</u> to this <u>is a desire</u> to revive the link, to get words 'to make sense' with their past.

→ 보어(Contrary) + 동사(is) + 주어(a desire ~)의 어순을 취한 도치구문이다. 영어에서는 주어가 너무 길면 문장 뒤로 빼는 경향이 있다(end weight법칙).

정답 해설 빈칸 바로 앞 문장에서 '연결고리를 되살리려는, 즉 말들을 그들의 과거와 '말이 되게' 만들려는 욕구'를 언급하고 있고 논지의 일관성 상 이러한 어원 친화적 논조는 그대로 빈칸 문장에 이어져야 한다(두 문장은 역접 관계가 아니다). 선지 중 어원 친화적인 내용은 ① 뿐이다. 정답 ①.

20

지문 해석 우리의 직관은 체스전문가에게 보드 게임 분석은 반사작용이라는 것이다. 실제로 최고 수준의 체스 선수는 한 번 슬쩍 보기만 해도 판세를 평가하고 말들의 배치를 상세히 기억할 수 있는데 이는 그가 그것을 자동적으로 의미 있는 덩어리로 나눠 분석하기 때문이라는 사실을 연구는 입증한다. 더구나 한 최근 연구는 이러한 나누는 과정이 정말 무의식적임을 보여준다. 간이 게임은, 그것을 안 보이게 하는 마스크 사이에 끼워놓은 상태로 20 밀리세컨드 동안만 보일 수 있는데도 여전히 체스 마스터의 결정에 영향을 미칠 수 있다. 실험은 전문가 급 체스 선수에게만, 그리고 그가 왕이 장군을 받는 상황인지 아닌지를 결정하는 등 의미 있는 문제를 해결할 때에만 유효하다. 그것은 시각 체계가 말들의 정체(룩인지 기사인지)와 그들의 위치를 고려해 재빨리 이 정보를 의미 있는 덩어리로(검은 왕이 장군 당하고 있음) 묶는다는 것을 의미한다. 이러한 정교한 작전이 전적으로 의식적 인식 밖에서 일어난다.

글의 소재 무의식적으로 이뤄지는 체스 판세 분석

주요 어휘 intuition 직관, parsing 분석, reflex 반사작용, configuration 배치 상태, segment 분할하다, unconscious 무의식적인, flash 비추다, 잠깐 보여주다, invisible 보이지 않는, under check (체스에서) 왕이 장군 받고 있는, sophisticated 정교한, operations 작용, 작전

구조 분석 ⊙ only if they are solving a meaningful problem, such as determining if the king is under check or not.

→ 밑줄 친 부분은 determining의 목적어인 명사절이며 이 때 if는 whether로 바꿀 수 있다.

정답 해설 체스 전문가가 순식간에 체크 판세를 읽는 것은 그것을 의미 있는 덩어리로 나누기 때문이고 그 나누는 과정은 정말로 무의식적이라 했으므로(this segmenting process is truly unconscious) 빈칸에 들어갈 말은 ③ '전적으로 의식적 인식 밖에서 일어난다.'가 적절하다.

① 마스터의 의식이 깨어있을 때만 일어난다.

② 의미 있는 인식과 더불어 의식적으로 펼쳐진다.

④ 세심한 분석과 반복을 통해 성공한다.

⑤ 다감각 정보는 서로 합칠 수 있음을 입증한다.

21

지문 해석 18-19세기에 유럽에서 일어난 산업혁명(그리고 이와 관련 있는 농업혁명)은 일의 성격을 바꿨을 뿐만 아니라 사회 구조, 성(性)과 친족 관계 그리고 지배적인 인간 거주 형태를 극적으로 변화시켰다. 잠재적 산업 노동자들이 농촌에서 신흥 제조업 중산층의 공장이 위치한 도시로 대거 이주한 결과 농촌

과 도시의 구성과 둘 사이의 관계가 완전히 역전됐다. 그 당시 일어난 인구학적 변화의 정도는 19세기 초 인구 2만 이상의 영국 도시가 15개였지만 세기 말에는 185개였다는 조사가 잘 보여준다. 실제로 1800년에는 유럽 인구의 2.2 퍼센트만이 인구 10만 이상의 도시에 산 것으로 추정된다.—오늘날 그 지정학적 공간은 압도적으로 도시화되고 고도로 산업화됐다.

글의 소재 산업 혁명이 도시-농촌 간 인구 구성에 미친 영향

주요 어휘 kinship 친족, dominant 지배적인, rural 농촌의, urban 도시의, overturn 뒤집다, 역전시키다, emerging 떠오르는, bourgeoisie 중산층, demographic 인구학적, underline 강조하다, estimate 추산하다, geopolitical 지정학적인, predominantly 압도적으로, urbanize 도시화하다

구조 분석 ⊙ In particular, the composition of, and link between, the rural and the urban was completely overturned.

→ 'the rural and the urban'이 전치사 of와 between의 공동 목적어다. 이 부분을 패러프레이즈하면 'the composition of the rural and the urban and the link between the rural and the urban'이다.

정답 해설 빈 칸 문장 뒤에는 산업 혁명으로 농촌 인구가 대거 도시로 이동해 도시 인구가 폭발적으로 증가한다는 내용이 이어지고 이는 사람들의 거주 형태에 큰 변화가 일어났음을 의미한다. 따라서 산업혁명이 무엇을 변화시켰는지를 묻는 빈칸에는 ④ '지배적인 인간의 거주 형태'가 적절하다.

① 몇몇 국가의 지리적 특성

② 제조업의 시스템

③ 사회 정의와 평등의 개념

⑤ 노동자 계급의 정의

22

지문 해석 당신은 속담에 나오는 유리컵을 반만큼 찬 쪽으로 보는 인간 유형인가, 아니면 반만큼 빈 쪽으로 보는 유형인가? 좀 더 낙관적인—유리컵이 반만큼 찬 쪽으로 보는—태도를 가진 사람들은 다른 사람들보다 육체적 장애와 관련된 스트레스를 포함한 스트레스의 영향으로부터 강한 회복력을 보이는 경향이 있다. 예를 들어, 연구자들은 낙관주의를 심장병이나 암 환자의 낮은 정서적 스트레스 수치 그리고 암 환자가 보고하는 낮은 고통 수치와 연관시킨다. 임신한 여성들의 낙관주의는 심지어 예컨대, 더 무거운 신생아의 몸무게로 측정되듯 더 나은 출산 결과를 예측하기도 한다. 또한 관상동맥 우회 수술 환자의 낙관주의는 수술 후 합병증이 더 적게 나오는 것과 관련이 있다. 그와 반면에 더 비관적인 태도를 가진 사람은 우울증과 사회적 불안의 형태로 나타나는 더 큰 정서적 스트레스를 보고하는 경향이 있다.

낙관주의와 비관주의의 긍·부정적 임상 효과

주요 어휘 proverbial 속담의, optimistic 낙관적인, resilient 회복력이 있는, disorder 장애, 병, investigator 조사자, 수사관, outcome 결과, coronary artery 관상동맥, bypass 우회, postoperative 수술 후, complication 합병증, pessimistic 비관적인, depression 우울증, anxiety 걱정, 불안

구조 분석 ⊙ investigators link optimism to lower levels of emotional distress among heart disease and cancer patients and to lower levels of reported pain among cancer patients.

→ 'link A to B and to C'의 병렬 구조다. link A to B=A와 B를 연관시키다

정답 해설 (A) 앞 문장에는 낙관적인 사람이 병에 대해 회복력을 보인다고 말하고 (A) 문장에서는 이를 심장병과 암환자 등 구체적인 예를 제시하므로 (A)에는 예시의 연결사가 적절하다. (B) 앞 문장까지 낙관주의에 대해 설명하다가 (B) 문장에서는 비관적 태도를 가진 사람에 대한 서술로 180도 바뀌었기 때문에 빈 칸에는 전환이나 대조의 연결사가 필요하다. 따라서 정답은 ②다.

23

정답 ①

지문 해석 NASA가 일찍이 기획한 가장 대담한 심우주 미션 중 하나가 가장 홍보가 덜 된 것 중 하나임이 드러나고 있다. 목표는 지구로부터 수백만 킬로 떨어져 태양 궤도를 도는 1992KD라는 이름의 큰 소행성이다. 하지만 목적지는 그 여행을 할 우주선의 수행 성과에 따라 가변적이다. 나사가 발사한 무수한 다른 무인 우주선과 크게 다르지 않아 보이지만, 그 우주선은 영화 *2001 Space Odyssey*에 나오는 독립식 작동 컴퓨터 HAL와 비교돼 온 전자두뇌로 항해하고, 오랫동안 기술적 환상의 소재였던 이온 엔진 시스템을 추진해 우주 공간을 움직일 것이다. 모든 것이 계획대로 진행된다면 이달 말 발사 예정인 Deep Space 1호는 신세대 우주선의 선두주자가 될 것이다. 비행 기획자들은 그 우주선이 성분과 표면 구조 등 목표 소행성에 대한 흥미로운 관측을 수행하기를 바라지만 DSI의 일차적 임무는 NASA가, 위험도가 너무 높아 일반의 관심도가 높은 미션에서는 시도할 수 없다고 생각해 온 다수의 신기술이 정당했음을 입증하는 것이다.

글의 소재 NASA의 소행성 탐사선 Deep Space 1호

주요 어휘 daring 대담한, publicize 공표하다, 홍보하다, asteroid 소행성, destination 목적지, incidental 부수적인, ~에 따르는, liken 비교하다, 비유하다, propulsion 추진, forerunner 선구자, composition 구성, prime(a) 일차적인, assignment 과제, 임무, high-profile 대중의 관심도가 높은, 세간의 이목을 끄는

구조 분석 ⊙ DS1's prime assignment is to validate a host of new technologies NASA had always considered too risky to try on a high-profile mission.

→ technologies와 NASA 사이에 목적격 관계대명사 that(which)가 생략됐다. 관계사절의 목적어는 선행사인 technologies, 목적격 보어는 'too risky to try on a high-profile mission'이다.

정답 해설 NASA가 발사 예정인 소행성 탐사선 Deep Space 1호의 여러 첨단 기능과 수행할 임무, 발사 의의 등이 이 글의 주된 내용이므로 이 글의 제목으로 가정 적절한 것은 ① '스마트한 신종 우주선'이다.
② 무인 로켓의 발사
③ 실패한 DSI의 고난도 기술들
④ 컴퓨터화 된 엔진 시스템의 성능
⑤ 대형 소행성을 항해할 새로운 미션

24

정답 ①

지문 해석 소는 민감한 동물이다. 그들은 먼 거리에서 포식자를 탐지하기 위한 몇 개의 감각적 적응 능력을 진화시켜 왔다. 그들은 개나 고양이에 뒤지지 않는 예민한 후각과 청각을 가지고 있다. 코끼리는 결코 잊지 않는다고 사람들은 말하지만 소도 그렇다. 그들은, 그들이 아는 사람은 물론 함께 지내는 동료의 사진을 식별할 수 있다. 찰스 다윈은 인간과 동물은 둘 다 감정 표현의 유사성을 가진다고 주장했다. 물론 우리는 쾌락이나 공포 같은 기본 감정을 분별할 수 있다. 하지만 개를 우리에게 사랑받게 하는 것은, 그들 식 애정 표현 방식이라고 우리가 보는 것—눈빛에 나타난 주인과 함께 있고 싶어 하는 동경이나 기꺼이 즐겁게 하려는 마음—을 그들이 확실히 해 낼 수 있는 능력이다. 소가 당신을 사랑하는 것을 어떻게 알 수 있나? 당신이 개에 대해 아는 것과 거의 같은 방식이다. 나의 소 Ricky Bobby는 행복하게 내 옆에 누워 뿔 달린 머리를 내 무릎에 올려놓는다. 그는 내가 쓰다듬어 주는 것을 좋아하고 심지어 배를 어루만져 달라고 돌아눕기까지 한다.

글의 소재 애완동물로서의 소

주요 어휘 cattle (집합적) 소, a suite of 한 조의, 몇 개의, sensory 감각의, 지각의, adaptation 적응, detect 탐지하다, endear 사랑받게 하다, apparent 명백한, capacity 능력, overall 전반적인, willingness 의지, lap 무릎, belly rub (애완동물의) 배 어루만지기

구조 분석 ⊙ But what endears dogs to us is their apparent capacity for what we take as their version of love.

→ 두 what는 모두 선행사를 포함한 관계대명사이고 둘 다 the thing that(which)로 바꿔 쓸 수 있다.

이 글은 개나 고양이에 버금가는 소의 탁월한 지각 능력, 식별 능력, 애정 표현 능력 등 우리가 모르는 소의 여러 가지 인간 친화적 모습을 소개하고 있다. 따라서 이 글의 제목으로는 ① '소도 애완동물이 될 수 있다.'가 적절하다.

② 애완동물은 감정 변화를 표현한다.

③ 야생 동물 길들이는 법

④ 소를 차로 안전하게 집으로 데려오는 방법

⑤ 다윈의 동물 행태 발견

25 정답 ③

생명과 재산을 보호하고 질서를 유지하는 목표 때문에 그리고 날씨와 상관없이 하루 24 시간 근무하기 때문에 경찰이 스스로를 돌보지 못하거나 그럴 의지가 없는 사람을 돌보도록 요청받는 것은 불가피하다. 거기에는 어린 아이, 어르신, 정신병자와 노숙자가 포함된다. 물론 경찰이 그런 사람들을 돕는 것은 거기까지다.—경찰은 다른 사람의 애들을 키우거나 정신병자를 치료하거나 이 나라의 노숙자를 위해 집을 지을 수 없다. 그러나 경찰은 가난한 사람을 위해 임시 숙소나 교통편을 제공하거나 주선할 수 있고 또 자주 그렇게 한다. 또 그들은 병원 이송을 돕고 사람들이 이용할 수 있는 프로그램이나 서비스를 활용할 수 있도록 정보를 제공한다. 경제가 어려울 때나 사회적 프로그램들이 자금 부족을 겪을 때 그리고 많은 시민들이 불우한 사람들에게 등을 돌릴 때 경찰의 도움은 자주 스스로를 제대로 돌보지 못하는 사람에게 유일한 선택이다.

사회적 약자를 돕는 경찰의 적극 서비스

inevitable 불가피한, properly 적절히, assistance 도움, 지원, temporary 임시의, shelter 숙소, 피난처, referral 병원 이송, take advantage of 활용하다, struggle 분투하다, underfunded 자금 부족을 겪는, turn a cold shoulder to ~에게 등 돌리다.

⊙ They also make referrals and provide information so that people can take advantage of programs and services available to them.

➡ 'so that ~ '용법으로 '~하도록'의 뜻이며 so와 that 둘 중 하나는 생략 가능하다.

이 글은 국민의 생명과 재산 보호와 질서 유지라는 기본 의무를 넘어 주거 마련이나 교통편의 제공, 환자 이송 등 사회적 약자를 위해 경찰이 할 수 있는 적극 서비스에 대해 상술하고 있다. 따라서 ③ '스스로 돌보지 못하는 사람을 위해 경찰이 여기 있다!'가 이 글의 제목으로 타당하다. 사회 통념이 깨지면서 필자의 주장이 시작되는 However 이후의 문장 흐름에 주의하라.

① 잠재적 문제를 항상 감시하는 경찰

② 경찰의 주요 목표: 중범죄 예방하기

④ 다양한 갈등 해결은 누가 맡아야 하나?

⑤ 경찰 서비스의 중추로서의 순찰

26 정답 ②

종교적 그리고 도덕적으로 계몽적인 드라마—각각 기적극, 도덕극이라는 이름이 붙음—의 긴 전통이 있었지만 영국의 첫 공공 극장은 1576년에야 지어졌다. 이것은 Gamini Salgado가 적절히 명명한 '영국 역사 상 드라마 글쓰기의 최전성기'의 촉매제가 되었다. 엘리자베스 시대의 무대 환경은 지금 완전히 정확하게 재현하기는 어려우나 전반적으로 원시적이었다. 이러한 불충분함을 보충하기 위해 완전히 새로운 언어 매체가 창조됐다. 극적 환상을 불러일으키기 위한 최소한의 소품과 효과만을 갖춘 빈 무대에서 위대한 드라마작가들은, 특히 셰익스피어는 전적으로 개성이 부여된 언어 매체, 즉 그들의 창조물이 철학을 이야기하고, 고통스러워하고, 웃고, 앓고 죽는 말들의 세계를 통해 비범한 경험의 다양성과 폭넓은 인물들을 창조했다.

엘리자베스 시대 영국 연극계에 분 언어 혁명

enlightening 계몽적인, term(v) 명명하다, playhouse 극장, catalyst 촉매, efflorescence 전성기, reconstruct 재구성하다, 재현하다, accuracy 정확성, primitive 원시적인, compensate for ~을 보상하다, inadequacy 불충분함, property 소품, individuate 개성을 부여하다, philosophize 철학적인 이야기를 하다, agonize 고통스러워하다

⊙ To compensate for these inadequacies, a whole new linguistic medium was created.

➡ 밑줄 친 'To compensate'는 목적의 부사적 용법이며 '~하기 위해'로 해석한다. 문장이 'to 부정사'로 시작하고 커마와 함께 주절로 이어질 경우 'to 부정사'는 십중팔구 목적의 부사적 용법이다. 이때 'to 부정사'의 의미상 주어는 주절의 주어다.

엘리자베스 시대의 열악한 무대 환경을 보충하기 위해 등장인물의 언어에 개성을 부여하는 등 언어 혁명을 일으켜 무대 경험과 인물의 폭을 넓히고 급기야 연극 최전성기를 이룩했다는 게 이 글의 요지이므로 이 글의 제목으로 가장 적절한 것은 ② '엘리자베스 시대 무대와 언어 혁명'이다.

① 엘리자베스 시대 극장의 기술적 진보

③ 셰익스피어의 효과적인 원시 무대 사용

④ 영국의 종교극 쇠퇴

⑤ 중세 도덕극의 부상

27

지문 해석 당신을 고착시키는 모든 무쾌감적 선택의 배후에는 당신이 규칙에 도전한다면 당신(또는 당신의 삶)이 무너질 거라는 믿음이 있다. 이것은 강력한 신화다. 그것은 당신을 완전히 마비시킬 수 있다. 당신 자신에게서 그것을 제거하는 유일한 방법은 당신의 정신력을 시험해 보는 것이다. 삶의 문제들을 참아 넘기는 것을 중단하고 변화를 향한 걸음을 내딛기 전에는 자신이 실제 얼마나 강한지 아는 사람은 많지 않다. 그것이 쉽지는 않을 것이다. 당신은 몇 번은 넘어지겠지만 무너지지는 않는다. 그 반대로 당신의 삶을 통제할 수 있는 능력을 주장하면 할수록 당신은 더 강해질 것이다. 정신력을 키우는 것은 육체적 능력을 키우는 것과 같다. 훈련을 많이 할수록 강해진다.

글의 소재 정신력을 키우는 법

주요 어휘 anhedonic 쾌락을 추구하지 않는, myth 신화(근거 없는 믿음이라는 부정적 뉘앙스일 때가 많다.), paralyze 마비시키다, rid A of B A에서 B를 제거하다, put A to the test A를 시험하다, put up with ~을 참다, assert 주장하다,

구조 분석 ⊙ Behind every anhedonic choice that keeps you stuck is the belief that you (or your life) will fall apart if you challenge the rules.
→ the belief가 주어인 1형식 도치문이다. 장소의 부사구가 문두로 나와 도치된 경우이며 여기서도 무거운 부분을 뒤로 보내는 'end weight' 법칙이 적용됐다.

정답 해설 이 글은 무너질 것이 무서워 도전을 거부하고 문제를 안고 사는 삶에서 벗어나 변화하고 도전하면서 육체의 힘을 키우듯 정신력을 키우라고 충고하는 내용이다. 따라서 이 글의 주장으로 적절한 것은 ⑤ '스스로 연약하다고 생각하지 말고 정신적으로 강해져라.'이다.
① 항상 현실적 계획을 세워야 한다고 생각하지 마라.
② 당신의 성공에 도움을 주는 조건을 확인하라.
③ 큰 꿈 하나를 선택해 그것을 현실로 만들라.
④ 도달 가능한 목표를 세우고 작은 진보의 발걸음을 즐겨라.

28
정답 ①

지문 해석 어떤 명확한 범주도 모든 재즈를 아우르지는 못한다. 각 연주자의 표현법이 그 자체의 스타일이다. 모든 다른 음악과 마찬가지로 재즈는 세 가지 예술 활동 즉, 창작, 연주, 듣기로 구성된다. 전통적인 서구 유럽 음악에서 이 세 가지 활동은, 항상 동일한 한 사람에 의해 이뤄지는—그런 경우가 꽤 자주 있기는 하지만—않는다. 하지만 재즈에서는 연주자가 세 가지를 동시에 결합하는 것이 필수적이다. 음악 창작은 모든 재즈 연주의 적극적인 일부이며 전개되는 창작품에 대한 연주자의

이해에 의존하며 이 이해는 그들의 잘 듣는 능력에 의해서만 얻어지는 이해다. 그들은 동료 연주자들에게서 듣는 것에 즉각적으로 반응해야 하고 그들의 기여(조언)는 펼쳐지는 주제나 분위기와 맞아떨어져야 한다. 따라서 재즈에서 모든 음악 창작 행위는 그것을 창작하는 연주자만큼 개성이 강해야 한다.

글의 소재 연주자의 개성을 중시하는 재즈 음악의 특징

주요 어휘 clear-cut 명확한, encompass 포함하다, 아우르다, comprise 포함하다, instantaneously 즉각적으로, consistent 일관성 있는, 맞아떨어지는, unfold 펼쳐지는, 전개되다

구조 분석 ⊙ Musical creation is an active part of any jazz performance and depends on the performers' understanding of the developing creation, an understanding gained only by their ability to listen well.
→ 'an understanding ~'은 동격의 명사구이며 앞의 'performers' understanding ~' 부분을 부연 설명한다.

정답 해설 창작, 듣기, 연주가 반드시 한 사람에 의해 이뤄지고 무엇보다 연주자의 개성이 중시되는 재즈 음악의 특징을 설명한 글이므로 주제로 적합한 선지는 ① '연주자의 개성을 반영하는 재즈의 특질'이다. 이 글은 미괄식 구성으로 맨 끝 문장이 주제문이다. 이에 주의하면 어렵지 않게 정답을 찾아낼 수 있다.
② 멋진 연주를 위한 재즈 작곡법
③ 재즈와 서구 음악의 유사성
④ 현대 재즈계의 유명 인사들
⑤ 전통음악이 재즈에 미친 영향

29
정답 ④

지문 해석 컴퓨터를 이용한 교육이 대학 교육 과정의 성격 자체를 바꾸고 있다. 점점 더 많은 수의 학생들이 대학 교육을 원하지만 그들은 낮 시간 동안 일을 해야 하는데 주변에 저녁에 강의를 제공하는 대학이 없을 수 있다. 이 문제에 대한 해결책은 원격 학습이라 불리는데 이는 학생은 대학 강의에 등록하지만 대학에 직접 출석할 필요는 없다는 것을 의미한다. ① 대학에서 제공되는 학과 강의들은 녹화돼 언제라도 학생들이 가능한 시간에 PC로 시청할 수 있도록 준비된다. ② 따라서 컴퓨터 기술이 강의를 학생에게 전달하기 때문에 강의는 시간이나 공간과 무관하게 제공된다. ③ 어떤 대학들은 현재 이런 기술을 통해 전체 학위 과정 프로그램을 학생들에게 제공하고 있다. ④ 그래서 원격 학습은 계속 일을 미루거나 마감일을 맞추지 못하는 학생들에게 좋은 선택이 될 수 없다. ⑤ 학생은 물리적으로 전혀 대학에 출석하지 않고도 대학에서 학위를 받을 수 있다.

글의 소재 대학 교육의 성격을 바꾸는 컴퓨터 원격 학습

주요 어휘 instruction 교육, 지시, enroll 등록하다

구조 분석 ⊙ A student can earn a degree from a univer-

sity without ever having physically attended the university.
→ 학위 받는 것보다 학교에 출석하는 것이 한 시제 앞서기 때문에 완료 동명사를 썼다. ever는 부정의 강조를 나타낸다.

정답 해설 이 글은 컴퓨터를 이용한 원격 학습이 대학 교육의 양상을 바꾸는 최근의 추세를 설명하고 있는데 ④는 원격 학습이 학생의 선택이 될 수 없다고 주장하므로 전체 흐름에 어긋난다. 따라서 정답은 ④다.

30
정답 ④

지문 해석 데카르트가 데카르트식 이원론자였다는 것은 상식이다(단지 상식에 불과할 것이다!). (①) 누구나 아는 것처럼, 데카르트는, 두 개의 세계가 있는데 하나는 정신적 대상의 세계이고 다른 하나는 동물이나 인간의 몸 같은 물질적 대상의 세계라고 생각했다. (②) 정신적 대상은 의식 상태이며(예를 들어 고통, 시각적 경험, 신념, 욕망, 공포, 즐거움), 물질적 대상은 거의 시계태엽 장치의 복잡한 조각들이다. (③) '내부 세계'의 아이템들은 '자기 성찰'이라 불리는 특별한 능력을 행사함으로써 이해되고 '외부 세계'의 대상들은 오감에 의해 감지된다. (④) 대부분의 '상식' 아이템처럼 독서의 중요성은 비판적 조사 없이 자주 당연시된다. (⑤) 정신적 상태와 신체의 상태는 논리적으로 독립적이지만 인과적으로 상호 연관돼 있어서 인과적 상호작용은 그야말로 각자 개인에게서 마음을 몸에 붙이는 접착제다.

글의 소재 데카르트 이원론

주요 어휘 Cartesian 데카르트의, dualist 이원론, conscious-ness 의식, complex 복잡한, clockwork 시계태엽장치, faculty 능력, 교수진, introspection 자기 성찰, perceive 감지하다, critical 비판적인, 중요한, causally 인과적으로, interrelated 상호 연관된, interaction 상호작용

구조 분석 ⊙ As everyone knows, he held that there are two worlds, one of mental objects and one of material things, including animals and human bodies.
→ 'held'는 'thought'의 뜻이고 앞뒤의 one은 모두 'a world'를 가리키는 부정대명사다.

정답 해설 우리 세계는 정신세계와 물질세계로 이뤄졌고 이 두 세계는 인과적으로 연관돼 있다는 데카르트 이원론을 설명하는 글이다. 독서의 중요성이 무비판적으로 받아들여진다는 내용의 ④는 전체 흐름과 관계가 없다. 따라서 정답은 ④다.

31
정답 ⑤

지문 해석 인류는 역사를 통틀어 기술 변화를 경험해 왔다. 하지만 기술이 우리 사회의 사회적 정치적 구조를 근본적으로 뒤

바꾼 경우는 좀처럼 없었다. (①) 더 흔하게, 우리가 사회적 세계의 질서를 잡아가는 기존의 틀은 신기술을 맞추고 흡수한 다음 식별 가능한 범주 내에서 진화하고 개혁한다. (②) 사회 구조의 완전한 변화를 강요하지 않으면서 자동차는 말을 대신했다. (③) 소총이 머스킷총을 대신했지만 재래적인 군사 활동의 일반적 패러다임은 큰 변화가 없었다. (④) 우리가, 세계를 설명하고 질서를 잡아가는 지배적인 양식에 도전하는 기술을 맞닥뜨린 경우는 좀처럼 없었다. (⑤) 하지만 AI는 인간 경험의 모든 영역을 변화시킬 전망이다. 그리고 변화의 핵심은 결국 철학적 차원에서 일어나 인간이 현실과 그 안에서 우리의 역할을 이해하는 방식을 뒤바꿀 것이다.

글의 소재 AI가 가져올 근본적인 사회 변화

주요 어휘 fundamentally 근본적으로, preexisting 기존의, adapt 적응시키다, 맞추다, absorb 흡수하다, recognizable 알아볼 수 있는, 식별할 수 있는, replace 대신하다, shift 변동, 변화, musket 머스킷총, conventional 전통적인, 재래적인, unaltered 변하지 않는, encounter 조우하다, 맞닥뜨리다, prevailing 지배적인, 우세한, ultimately 결국, 궁극적으로,

구조 분석 ⊙ Only rarely, however, has technology funda-mentally transformed the social and political structure of our societies.
→ 부정어 rarely가 문장 앞에 오는 바람에 조동사(has)+주어(technology)+본동사(transformed) 형식의 도치구문이 됐다.

정답 해설 주어진 글에 역접의 연결사가 있으므로 글의 흐름에 반전이 이뤄지는 곳에 유의하면서 읽어 나간다. ⑤ 전까지는 여러 변화가 일어났으나 부분적 변화에 그쳤을 뿐 사회 질서나 지배적 양식을 뒤바꾼 근본적인 변화는 일어나지 않다가 ⑤ 다음 문장에 그런 변화가 철학에도 일어나 현실 인식에 근본적인 변화가 일어날 것이라고 말해 이 부분에서 논리적 단절이 있음을 알 수 있다. 따라서 주어진 글이 들어갈 자리는 ⑤다, 정답 ⑤.

32
정답 ③

지문 해석 물고기자리 하면 흔히 밧줄로 서로를 묶은 한 쌍의 물고기를 상상한다. 이런 이미지는 기원전 2천년 고대 이집트와 이후 바빌로니아 문헌에 기록돼 있다. 이 두 물고기가 왜 묶여 있는지는 이 고대 자료에는 기록되지 않고 있지만 이후 그리스 로마 신화는 약간의 설명을 해 준다. 신들이 끔찍한 괴물 타이폰과 대항하고 있었을 때 아프로디테와 에로스는 전장에서 멀리 떨어져 있었던 것으로 전해진다. 사랑과 욕정의 신으로서 그 둘은 세상을 부수는 큰 위협 앞에 할 수 있는 것이 별로 없었다. 도피할 곳을 찾다가 그 둘은 물고기로 변신해 안전을 위해 서로를 묶고 유프라테스 강으로 뛰어들었다. 이것이 당시 모습이 별자리의 행태로 포착된 순간이었다. 대체 버전에는 Pisces의 물

고기 두 마리가 신들을 등에 태우고 도망가서 구출하는 것으로 나온다. 도움에 대한 보상으로 물고기들은 밤하늘에 자리 잡게 됐다.

(글의 소재) 물고기자리 탄생 설화

(주요 어휘) constellation 별자리, ancient 고대의, millennium 천년, BCE(Before Common Era) 기원전, lust 욕정, in the face of ~의 면전에서, capture 포획하다, 포착하다, refuge 피난, alternative 대체의, 대안의, rescue 구출하다, reward 보상

(구조 분석) ⊙ An alternative version has the two fish of Pisces rescuing the gods who rode away on their backs.

→ 동사(has) + 목적어(the two fish of Pisces) + 목적보어 (rescuing ~)의 5형식 문장이다. 진행이나 계속의 의미가 있을 경우 사역동사 have는 동사의 진행형을 목적보어로 취할 수 있다.

(정답 해설) ③ 다음 문장 '이때가 바로 그것이 이 별자리의 형태로 포착되는 순간'은 앞에 동적인 장면이 있을 때 가능한 표현이다. 그런데 앞에는 '이 둘이 할 수 있는 것이 별로 없었다.'는 상태를 서술한 문장이라 흐름이 어색하다. 따라서 주어진 글의 '물고기로 변신해 강으로 뛰어드는' 동적인 장면은 ③에 삽입돼야 흐름이 자연스럽다. 정답은 ③.

33   정답 ⑤

(지문 해석) 일차세계대전 직후에 쓴 글에서 프랑스 철학계의 한 예리한 관찰자는 "철학적 연구가 우리 사이에서 지난 30년 보다 더 풍성하고 더 진지하고 더 강렬했던 적이 없었다."고 평가했다. 이런 전성기는 새로운 교육 시스템에서 차지하는 철학의 위치 때문이었는데 이것은 사기를 떨어뜨린 보불전쟁에서의 패배 이후 제3공화국이 수립했다. 프랑스인들은 나폴레옹 3세가 Sedan에서 포로로 잡힌 데 굴욕감을 느꼈고 오랜 파리의 포위로 황폐해졌다. 또한 그들은, 대부분의 중산층이 코뮌의 급진적 사회주의가 벌인 73일 간의 무정부상태라고 여겼던 것을 무서워했다. 새 공화국이 벌인 정신적 회복 노력의 많은 부분은 제도적 종교의 전통적인 가치를 거부하는 것에 의해 주도됐고, 공화국은 그것을 계몽적인 세계관으로 대체하려 했다. 이 야심찬 사업의 주요 수단은 교육 개혁, 구체적으로 학문과 이성, 휴머니즘에 헌신하는 대학 시스템의 수립이었다. Albert Thibaudet가 3공화국을 "교수 공화국"으로 부르자 이 개혁의 중요성이 한층 돋보였다.

(글의 소재) 프랑스 3공화국의 야심찬 교육 개혁

(주요 어휘) acute 예리한, scene 장면, ~계(界), abundant 풍성한, intense 강력한, flowering 개화, 전성기, in the wake of ~이후의, demoralizing 사기를 저하시키는, defeat 패배, humiliate 굴욕감을 느끼게 하다, capture 포획, anarchy 무정부상태, radical 급진적인, restoration 회복, rejection 거부,

institutional 제도적인, replace A with B A를 B로 대신하다, enterprise 큰 사업, specifically 구체적으로, dedicated to ~에 헌신하는, highlight 강조하다, 돋보이게 하다

(구조 분석) ⊙ They had also been terrified by what most of the bourgeoisie saw as seventy-three days of anarchy under the radical socialism of the Commune.

→ what은 선행사를 포함한 관계대명사이고 관계사절 안에서 목적어로 쓰였다. see A as B=A를 B라 여기다.

(정답 해설) 맨 끝 문장에 나오는 지시사가 들어간 표현 'this reform'을 주목하자. 지시사는 독립적으로 쓰일 수 없고 지칭 대상이 반드시 앞 문장에 들어있어야 한다. 그런데 여기서는 앞 문장에 this reform을 받을 말이 없다. 그것은 주어진 문장에 나온다(educational reform). 따라서 주어진 문장이 들어갈 곳은 ⑤다. 정답 ⑤.

34   정답 ④

(지문 해석)

"농부가 더 많은 가뭄을 필요로 하는 것처럼 국유림은 더 많은 도로를 필요로 한다." 우리는 어떤 사람이 더 많은 도로는 국유림에 나쁘다는 것을 청중에게 설득하려고 이 말을 하는 것을 들었다.

(C) 하지만 이 말은 논증이 아니다. 그것은 숲에 도로를 건설하는 것을 부정적으로 표현하는 진술일 뿐이다. 어떤 작가들은 논증을 누군가에게 무엇을 설득하려는 시도로 정의한다. 이것은 옳지 않다.

(A) 논증은 결론을 입증하거나 뒷받침하려는 시도다. 당신이 누군가를 설득하려 할 때 당신은 그/그녀를 당신의 관점으로 끌어오려고 시도한다. 설득하려 하는 것과 논증하려는 것은 논리적으로 차이가 분명한 일이다. 실제로 당신이 누군가에게 무엇을 설득할 때 당신은 논증의 방법을 쓰기도 한다.

(B) 그러나 모든 논증이 설득을 시도하는 것도 아니고 설득하려는 시도에 논증이 따르지 않는 경우도 많다. 사실 논거를 들이대는 것은 흔히 사람을 설득하는 가장 비효율적인 방법 중 하나다.—이것이 물론 논증에 신경 쓰는 광고주들이 드문 이유다. 사람들이 가장 약한 논증으로 설득당하면서 종종 가장 훌륭한 논증으로도 마음이 움직이지 않는 것은 유명하다.

(글의 소재) 논증과 설득의 상관관계

(주요 어휘) drought 가뭄, persuade 설득하다, distinct 다른, 각별한, argument 논증, 논거, 주장, effective 효율적인, notoriously 악명 높게, undisturbed 마음이 움직이지 않는, 방해받지 않는, remark 발언, statement 진술

구조 분석 ⊙ People notoriously are persuaded by the weakest of arguments and sometimes are undisturbed by even quite good arguments.

→ notoriously는 문장 전체 수식부사로 'It is notorious that ~'으로 패러프레이즈할 수 있다.

정답 해설 먼저 (C)의 the remark가 눈에 들어온다. 여기서 the는 대표단수의 the가 아니기 때문에 지칭 대상, 즉 '누가 한 발언'이 있어야 한다. 이것은 주어진 글 안의 인용부호 문장에서 쉽게 찾을 수 있다. 따라서 주어진 문장에 이어질 단락은 (C)다. (C)는 일부 작가는 argument를 누군가에게 무엇을 설득하는 것으로 정의하는데 이것은 옳지 않다고 끝맺는다. 그렇다면 이어지는 문장에는 'argument의 쓰임이 설득이 아닌 다른 것'이라는 내용이 들어있어야 한다. 이 말은 'argument는 결론을 증명하거나 뒷받침하기를 시도한다.'는 (A)의 첫 문장에 제시되고 있다. 따라서 글의 순서는 (C) - (A) - (B)이다. 정답 ④.

35

정답 ⑤

지문 해석

좋은 비판적 사고는 인지적 기술이다. 일반적으로 기술을 개발하는 데는 세 가지 조건—이론의 학습, 신중한 연습, 그리고 올바른 태도 갖기—이 필요하다.

(C) 이론이라 함은 기술을 습득하기 위해 알아야 하는 규칙과 사실을 말한다. 예를 들어 우리는 농구의 규칙—가령 공을 발로 차서는 안 된다는 것—을 알지 않고서는 훌륭한 농구 선수가 될 수 없다. 마찬가지로 비판적으로 생각하는 데는 어느 정도 논리학을 알 필요가 있다.

(B) 하지만 이론을 아는 것과 그것을 적용할 수 있다는 것은 다르다. 자전거를 탈 때 자전거의 균형을 잡아야 한다는 것을 이론상으로는 알지 모르지만 그것(아는 것)이 그것(균형 잡기)를 실제 할 수 있다는 것을 의미하지는 않는다. 그래서 연습이 등장하는데 그것은 연습이 이론적 지식을 실제 능력으로 바꿔주기 때문이다.

(A) 그러나, 당신의 연습이 효율적이고 지속가능한지에 대해서는 당신의 태도가 큰 차이를 가져온다. 만약 당신이 피아노 치기가 싫다면 당신에게 피아노 치라고 강요하는 것은 장기적으로 효율적이지 못하다.

글의 소재 기술 개발의 삼 요소: 이론, 연습, 태도

주요 어휘 critical 비판적인, cognitive 인지의, deliberate(a) 신중한, 사려 깊은, sustainable 지속가능한, in the long run 장기적으로, actually 실제로, translate A into B A를 B로 번역하다, A를 B로 변환하다

구조 분석 ⊙ By theory we mean the rules and facts we have to know in order to possess the skill.

→ 원래 'mean A by B＝B는 A를 의미하다' 구문이지만 목적어 부분(the rules and facts ~)이 길어 후치시키고 'by B'를 문장 앞으로 뺀 도치구문이 됐다. end weight 법칙이 적용된 또 하나의 예다.

정답 해설 (A)는 '그러나 연습이 효과적인 데는 태도가 중요하다'고 말하고 이는 연습에 대한 설명을 전제하는 말이므로 주어진 문장 뒤에 올 수 없다. (B) 역시 '이론은 아는 것과 적용하는 것은 별개다.'라는 취지의 말은 이론에 대한 언급이 있은 후에 할 수 있는 말이다. 이론에 대해서는 (C)에 설명돼 있다. 따라서 주어진 글 뒤에 올 수 있는 것은 (C) 뿐이고 올바른 순서는 (C) - (B) -(A)이다. 정답 ⑤.

36

정답 ③

지문 해석

문제 해결과 관련해 우리가 언어적 추론을 사용해서 쉽게 풀지 못하는 문제를 푸는 데 이미지를 쓰면 도움이 될 수 있다.

(B) 예를 들어 뉴욕에 사는 영업사원이 워싱턴 DC, 버펄로, 시카고 세 도시를 운전해서 가야한다고 하자. 만약 그녀가 위의 순서로 여행해 뉴욕으로 되돌아온다면 그녀는 최단거리를 여행하지 않을지 모른다.

(C) 그래서 그녀는 마음의 눈으로 미국 지도를 그리고 몇 차례 가상 여행을 해 볼 수 있다. 워싱턴을 방문하고 나서 버펄로를 간다면, 그리고 버펄로 다음에 시카고를 여행하고 뉴욕으로 돌아온다면 일부 왔던 길을 되짚어 가게 된다는 것을 깨닫는다.

(A) 그때 그녀는 워싱턴으로 차를 몬 다음 시카고를 여행하고 그리고 나서 버펄로를 방문하고 뉴욕으로 돌아보면 운전 시간을 여러 시간 절약할 수 있다는 것을 알게 된다.

주요 어휘 in regard to ~와 관련해, imagery 이미지(집합적), verbal 말씀의, reasoning 추론, hence 따라서, 그래서, virtual 가상의, partially 부분적으로, retrace (왔던 길을) 되짚어가다

구조 분석 ⊙ In regard to problem solving, imagery can be used to help solve problems that one could not easily solve using verbal reasoning.

→ using 앞에 전치사 by가 생략됐다고 보라.

정답 해설 (A)와 (C)의 첫 문장에 나오는 she를 받을 말이 주어진 글에 없기 때문에 둘 다 주어진 글 다음에 올 수 없다. 따라서 주어진 말에 이어지는 단락은 (B)다. (A)는 she가 이미 가상 지도를 이미 보고 알게 된 바를 설명하고 있고 (C)에는 가상 지도가 처음 언급되므로 (C)가 (A)보다 앞서야 한다. 따라서 올바른 글의 순서는 (B) - (C) - (A)다. 정답 ③.

37

지문 해석 정말로 스마트해지려면 온라인 집단은 한 가지 최종 규칙—직관에 반하는 규칙인데—을 지켜야 한다. 구성원들은 아무리 서로 접촉을 많이 해도 지나칠 게 없다. 가장 일을 잘하기 위해서는 집단적 그룹의 구성원들은 독립적으로 생각하고 일할 수 있어야 한다. 이 규칙은 1958년 사회 과학자들이 브레인스토밍의 여러 기술을 시험하면서 탄생했다. 그들은 생각을 자극하는 질문을 하나 제시했다. 만일 사람이 양 손에 엄지손가락을 하나씩 더 가진다면 어떤 이익과 문제가 생기겠는가? 그들은 두 가지 다른 유형의 집단 브레인스토밍 해답을 얻었다. 한 그룹의 구성원들은 얼굴을 마주보며 작업했고 다른 그룹은 구성원들이 각자 독립적으로 작업하고 최종적으로 답을 모았다. 얼굴을 마주 보며 작업한 구성원들이 더 생산적이라고 당신은 기대할지 모르지만 그것은 사실이 아니다. 독립적으로 작업한 구성원의 팀이 거의 두 배 많은 아이디어를 냈다. 전통적인 브레인스토밍은 혼자 생각하고 결과를 모으는 것만큼 잘 작동하지 않는다.

⬇

브레인스토밍에서 직접적으로 접촉한 그룹 구성원들은 물리적으로 서로 떨어져서 작업한 이들보다 적은 아이디어를 냈는데 이는 우리의 직관에 반한다.

글의 소재 보다 효율적인 독립적인 작업과 결과 취합법

주요 어휘 counterintuitive 직감에 반하는, pose 제시하다, 제기하다, thought-provoking 생각을 자극하는, emerge 떠오르다, 부상하다, face-to-face 직접 대면의, productive 생산적인

구조 분석 ⊙ The members can't have too much contact with one another.

➜ 'can't ~ too' 구문으로 '아무리 ~해도 지나치지 않는다.'를 의미한다.

정답 해설 브레인스토밍 결과 독립적으로 작업한 팀이 얼굴을 마주 보고 작업한 팀보다 거의 두 배 많은 아이디어를 냈다고 했으므로 (A)에는 fewer가, 그리고 이런 결과는 얼굴을 마주하면서 일하는 쪽이 더 효율적일 거라는 일반의 생각과는 상반된 것이므로 (B)에는 intuition이 각각 적절하다. 정답 ①.

38

지문 해석 첫 번째 컴퓨터가 출현한지 얼마 안 돼서 그들의 큰 실수는 농담의 소재가 됐다. 프로그래밍의 작은 실수가 고객의 은행 계좌를 없애버리거나 이상한 액수의 청구서를 발송하거나 컴퓨터를 계속 똑 같은 실수를 되풀이하는 순환 고리에 빠지게 했다. 이런, 사람을 화나게 하는 상식 부족이 그들의 사용자 대부분으로 하여금 기계는 결코 지능적이 될 수 없다는 결론을 내리게 했다. 물론 오늘날 컴퓨터는 더 잘 한다. 어떤 프로그램은 체스 게임에서 사람을 이길 수 있다. 심장마비를 진단하는 프로그램도 있다. 하지만 아직 침대를 만들거나 책을 읽거나 아기를 돌보는 기계는 없다. 대부분의 사람이 할 수 있는 종류의 일을 컴퓨터는 할 수 없게 만드는 것은 무엇인가? 그들은 더 많은 메모리 용량, 속도 또는 복잡한 특성을 필요로 하나? 그들은 엉뚱한 명령어 세트를 사용하나? 그도 아니면 인간의 두뇌만이 가질 수 있는 마술적 속성이 그들에게 결여돼 있나? 이들 중 어떤 것도 오늘날 기계들의 결점에 대해 책임이 없다고 나는 주장한다. 그게 아니고 그 모든 (능력의) 한계들은 프로그래머들이 그들을 프로그래밍하기를 택하는 뒤떨어진 방식에서 온다.

⬇

초기 컴퓨터들이 큰 실수를 저질렀지만 현대의 기계들은 체스나 의료 진단 같은 임무에서 뛰어나나 내재적인 기술적 한계 때문이라기보다 구식 프로그래밍으로 인해 기본적인 인간의 활동에서는 고전한다.

글의 소재 오늘날 컴퓨터의 특장과 한계

주요 어휘 blunder 큰 실수, tiny 매우 작은, wipe out 없애버리다, outlandish 이상한, 이국풍의, madden 화나게 하다, beat ~에게 이기다, 물리치다, diagnose 진단하다, heart attack 심장마비, complexity 복잡성, instruction 지시, 교육, attribute(n) 속성, argue 주장하다, 논증하다, 다투다, out-of-date 구식의

구조 분석 ⊙ This maddening lack of common sense led most of their users to conclude that machines could never become intelligent.

➜ 동사＋목적어＋목적보어의 5형식 문장이다. 'lead to'에는 두 가지 중요한 쓰임이 있는데, 하나는 여기서처럼 'lead somebody to 동사원형＝사람으로 하여금 어떤 행동, 생각을) 하게하다'이고 다른 하나는 'lead to＋명사 또는 ~ing＝~을 초래하다'이다.

정답 해설 지문 중간쯤에 오늘날 컴퓨터는 성능이 좋아져 체스에서 사람을 이기거나 의료 진단을 내린다는 말이 있으므로 (A)에는 excel이 적절하다. 글 후반부에서 필자는 메모리 용량이나 속도 등 컴퓨터의 여러 기술적 한계들을 열거한 후 그것들이 결함의 원인은 아니라고 주장하기 때문에 (B)에 들어갈 말은 limitations가 타당하다.

[39~40]

지문 해석 폼페이는 기원후 79년 Vesuvius산의 파멸적인 분출로 파괴돼 주민들을 켜켜이 쌓인 화산재 아래 묻어버렸다. 그러나 이 고대 로마도시의 비극적 운명 이야기에는 그 이상이 있다. 전문지 *Frontiers in Earth Science*에 발표된 한 연구는 폼페이는 그와 동시에 대규모 지진으로 파괴됐다는 증거를 제공

한다. 이 발견은 그 도시의 붕괴에 대한 새로운 연대표를 설정하고 연구에 대한 새로운 접근법이 충분히 연구된 고고학 현장에서 추가적인 비밀을 드러낼 수 있음을 보여준다. 연구자들은 지진 활동이 그 도시의 파괴에 일조했다는 생각을 항상 가져 왔다. Pliny the Younger는 Vesuvius산의 분출에 격렬한 흔들림이 뒤따랐다고 보고했다. 그러나 지금까지 이러한 역사 기록을 뒷받침하는 어떤 증거도 발견되지 않았다. 이태리 출신 Domenico Sparice가 이끄는 한 연구팀이 이런 기록상의 갭을 조사하기로 결정했다. Sparice 박사는 당시까지만 해도 폼페이 발굴이 지진이 고대 건물에 미치는 영향을 다루는 고고지진학 분야의 전문가를 포함하지 않았다고 말했다. 이 지역 전문가들의 공헌이 그 발견에 열쇠였다고 그는 말했다. Sparice 박사는 "지진활동도의 영향이 과거 학자들에 의해 추측됐지만 우리의 연구 전에는 어떤 사실적 증거도 보고되지 않았다."면서 그 발견이 "매우 고무적"이었다고 덧붙였다. 연구팀은 Insula of the Chaste Lovers 지역에 집중했다. 이 지역은 빵집과 집 등 몇 채의 건물을 에워싸는데 그 집에서는 화가들이 용암 분출로 방해받아 그림에 칠한(→그림에 칠하지 못한) 채로 남겨둔 것이 분명했다. 발굴과 세심한 분석 후 연구자들은 Insula의 벽들이 지진 때문에 무너졌다고 결론 내렸다.

[글의 소재] 지진: 폼페이 붕괴의 추가적인 이유

[주요 어휘] catastrophic 대재앙의, eruption 분출, entomb 묻다, 매장하다, simultaneously 동시에, wreck 파괴하다, timeline 연대표, reveal 폭로하다, 밝히다, archaeological 고고학적, seismic 지진의, be accompanied by ~이 뒤따르다, violent 격렬한, account 설명, 기록, 계정, excavation 발굴, archaeoseismology 고고지진학, speculate 추측하다, 투기하다, encompass 포함하다, 에워싸다, interrupt 방해하다,

[구조 분석] ⊙ Dr. Sparice said that excavations of Pompeii to date had not included experts in the field of archaeoseismology, which deals with the effects of earthquakes on ancient buildings.

➔ 'to date'는 '지금까지'의 뜻이지만 과거 상황에서 쓰였기 때문에 '당시까지'로 해석해야 한다. 또 과거 완료(had not included)가 쓰여 당시까지만 해도 ~전문가를 포함하지 않았다는 뜻이므로 주의하라.

39 정답 ⑤

[정답 해설] 이 글은 폼페이 파괴와 관련해 Sparice 박사 연구팀이 고고지진학적 접근을 통해 학계의 추측으로만 나돌았던 지진 촉발설이 사실이었음을 입증했고 이는 기존의 용암 분출설이 폼페이 파괴의 유일한 원인이 아니었음을 의미한다. 따라서 이 글의 제목으로 적절한 것은 ⑤ 'Vesuvius산의 분출이 폼페이의 유일한 킬러가 아니었다.'이다. 정답 ⑤.

40 정답 ⑤

[정답 해설] (e) 바로 앞에 화가들이 용암 분출로 방해받은 것이 분명했다고 했으므로 그림을 완성하지 못한, 즉 칠하지 못한 상태로 남겨둬야 논리적으로 맞다. 따라서 (e)는 uncolored 등으로 바꿔야 한다.

[41~42]
성격은 일상생활에서 확실한(확실히 나타나는) 인간 조건의 여러 부분 중 하나다. 우리들 모두는 독특하며 이러한 독특함을 강조하는 것이 성격에 대한 연구인 반면 심리학의 다른 대부분은 사람들 간 유사성을 강조한다. 성격의 어떤 부분들은 타고나는 것처럼 보이며 또 학습되는 것처럼 보이기도 한다. 확실히 성격은 환경적 필요를 통해서든 믿음이나 가치관, 견해, 판단을 통해서든 또한 문화의 영향을 받는다.

그 성격을 어떤 쪽에서 들여다보든 혹은 이론화하든 그것이 진공 속에 존재하지 않는다는 점은 확실하다. 한 사람을 구성하는 것은 이드, 에고, 수퍼 에고, 실현적 자아일 수도 있고, 일련의 학습된 사회적 행태나 한 묶음의 특질일 수도 있다. 그것(성격)이 이 중 어떤 것이냐는 맥락, 즉 어느 둘도 똑 같지 않은 일련의 상황이나 경험에 의해 결정된다. 일반적인 성격이나 어떤 이의 개별적인 성격을 보는 가장 좋은 방법은 상호작용이라는 눈을 통해서다. 사람들은 서로 다른 이에게 영향을 끼치기 때문에 환경 없이 존재할 수 없다. 따라서 성격은 개별적 환경에서 존재하는 대로 이해하는 것이 제일 좋다. 성격은 외따로 존재할 수 없다.

[글의 소재] 성격 형성의 사회성

[주요 어휘] obvious 분명한, 확실한, unique 독특한, whereas ~인 반면, remainder 나머지, built in 내장된, 태생의, be made up of ~로 구성되다, actualise 실현하다, trait 특질, context 맥락, in particular 개별적인, make sense of ~을 이해하다

[구조 분석] ⊙ Whichever of these it might be occurs within a context or a series of situations or experiences, no two of which are the same.

➔ 이 문장은 주어는 'Whichever of these it might be'이고 동사는 occurs인 1형식 문장이다. 여기서 it는 personality를 가리킨다.

41 정답 ③

[문제 해설] 성격을 보는 데는 개성/유사성, 생래적 결정론/학습 결정론 등 여러 시각이 있으나 분명한 것은 인간은 홀로 살 수 없고, 따라서 성격은 필연적으로 환경의 지배를 받을 수밖에 없음을 역설한 글이므로 제목으로는 적절한 것은 ③ '성격의 이해: 독특함, 문화, 맥락'이다. 정답 ③.

42

문제 해설 빈칸 문장에 이어지는 글에서 인간은 환경 없이 존재할 수 없고 서로 영향을 미친다고 했으므로 성격을 이해하는 최상의 방법은 사람들이 서로 교류하고 영향을 주고받는 환경, 즉 상호작용을 이해하는 것이다. 따라서 빈칸에 가장 적절한 말은 ④ 상호작용이다. 정답 ④.

[43~45]

지문 해석

소피아는 North High 고등학교의 벽돌담에 기대며 손가락으로 낙서를 따라가고 있었다. 이미 마지막 종이 울렸고 학생들이 빠르게 빠져나가고 있었다. 언니 사라를 찾아 주변을 둘러보았으나 그녀를 찾을 수 없었다. 한 숨을 내쉬며 그녀는 집을 향해 걷기 시작했다. 다음 주면 학교 장기 자랑이 있고 그녀는 노래 부르기를 신청했다. 그녀는 노래하기를 좋아하지만 단 한 번도 많은 청중 앞에서 노래해 본 적은 없다.

(C) 소피아는 걸으며 생각에 빠져 졸업반 반장인 자넷이 바로 앞에 다가설 때까지 그녀를 알아보지 못했다. 자넷과 사라는 서로 아는 사이였지만 소피아는 그녀에게 말을 건넨 적이 없다. "안녕, 소피아" 자넷이 활짝 웃으며 말했다. "자넷 안녕. 무슨 일이야?" 그녀가 놀라며 대답했다. "너 장기자랑 신청했다며?" "뭐 부를 건데?" 자넷이 말했다. 소피아는 긴장했다. "잘 모르겠어." "아직 생각 중이야." 그녀가 말했다. "커피 한잔 하면서 그 얘기 좀 할까?" 자넷이 또 다시 웃었다.

(D) 그들은 그 동네 카페에 들어가 학교와 음악에 대해 얘기했다. 자넷은 말하기 편한 성격이고 소피아는 그녀와 함께 있어 마음이 편했다. "너 어떤 음악 좋아해?" 자넷이 물었다. "클래식 록을 좋아해." "그래서 클래식 록의 어쿠스틱 버전을 해 볼까 생각 중이야."라고 소피아가 답했다. 자넷의 눈이 번쩍했다. "그럼 딱이다 얘. 내가 기타를 조금 치거든. 너하고 같이 연주할 수 있을지 몰라."

(B) 소피아의 눈이 휘둥그레졌다. "정말? 환상적이겠네!" 그들은 다음 한 시간을 계획을 짜고 연습하며 보냈다. 그들이 헤어졌을 때 소피아는 자넷이 그녀를 많이 도와줘서 자신감이 커졌다. 집으로 걸어오는데 저녁의 태양이 도시를 황금빛으로 물들였다. 그녀는 예상치 못한 순간들과 새 친구들이 모든 것을 더 좋게 만들 수 있다는 것을 깨달았다. 장기자랑은 더 이상 두려워할 어떤 것이 아니라 그녀가 빛을 낼 수 있는 기회였다.

글의 소재 학교 장기자랑과 소피아의 되찾은 자신감

주요 어휘 graffiti 낙서, sign up to 동사 또는 sign up for 명사 ~를 신청하다, confident 자신감 있는, grab a coffee 커피를 마시다

구조 분석 ⊙ The talent show was no longer something to be scared of but a chance for her to shine.

→ 여기서 of를 반드시 써야 하는 데 그 이유는 이렇다. 밑줄 친 부분을 절로 바꾸면 'something that should be scared of (by her)'이고 이를 다시 능동으로 바꾸면 'something that she should be scared of'가 된다. 이것을 관계사절 이전의 문장으로 환원하면 'She should be scared of something.'이 되는데 여기서 of는 생략할 수 없다.

43

정답 해설 (B)는 시작이 누구와의 대화 상황이어서, (D)는 첫 문장의 They를 받을 말이 주어진 글에 없어서 각각 주어진 글 다음에 이어질 수 없다. 주어진 글 뒤에 이어질 수 있는 것은 (C) 뿐이다. (C)는 자넷이 소피아에게 커피 한 잔 하자고 초청하는 말로 끝나므로 카페로 들어가는 말로 시작하는 (D)로 이어지는 것이 자연스럽다. 따라서 올바른 글의 순서는 (C) - (D) -(B)이다. 정답 ③.

44

정답 해설 (e)는 Janet를 나머지는 모두 Sophia를 가리킨다. 따라서 정답은 ⑤다.

45

정답 해설 소피아는 원래 기타를 칠 줄 안다고 했으므로 소피아가 가르쳤다는 ⑤는 지문 내용과 다르다. 정답 ⑤.

Chapter Ⅰ 글의 핵심 이해

1. 글의 주제

001 ④	002 ①	003 ②	004 ③	005 ⑤
006 ④	007 ④	008 ②	009 ④	010 ⑤
011 ⑤				

2. 요지 · 주장

	012 ④	013 ③	014 ③	015 ③
016 ②	017 ③	018 ②	019 ②	020 ①

3. 글의 제목

021 ②	022 ③	023 ②	024 ①	025 ④
026 ③	027 ①	028 ⑤	029 ⑤	

Chapter Ⅱ 어휘·어법·세부 내용 파악

4. 어법

				030 ④
031 ⑤	032 ⑤	033 ①	034 ②	035 ③
036 ④	037 ⑤	038 ②	039 ②	

5. 어휘

				040 ⑤
041 ③	042 ⑤	043 ④	044 ②	045 ①
046 ①	047 ⑤	048 ④		

6. 세부 내용 파악

			049 ③	050 ⑤
051 ③	052 ③	053 ⑤	054 ②	055 ③
056 ②	057 ④	058 ⑤	059 ④	060 ①
061 ③	062 ③			

Chapter Ⅲ 추론적 이해

7. 지칭 추론

		063 ⑤	064 ①	065 ②
066 ④	067 ②			

8. 빈칸 추론

		068 ②	069 ②	070 ⑤
071 ③	072 ②	073 ④	074 ②	075 ②
076 ①	077 ①	078 ①	079 ⑤	080 ③
081 ④	082 ⑤	083 ①	084 ①	085 ①
086 ④	087 ②	088 ④	089 ②	090 ②
091 ④	092 ②	093 ②	094 ⑤	095 ①

9. 함축적 의미 추론

096 ④	097 ④	098 ③	099 ③	100 ①

Chapter Ⅳ 글의 흐름 이해

10. 무관한 문장 파악

101 ④	102 ④	103 ④	104 ②	105 ④
106 ④				

11. 문장 삽입

	107 ③	108 ⑤	109 ④	110 ④
111 ③	112 ②	113 ⑤	114 ③	

12. 글의 순서

				115 ⑤
116 ⑤	117 ⑤	118 ④	119 ⑤	120 ③
121 ③	122 ①	123 ②	124 ②	125 ⑤

13. 요약문 완성

126 ④	127 ④	128 ③	129 ③	130 ④
131 ②	132 ②	133 ③	134 ①	135 ③
136 ③	137 ②	138 ②	139 ④	140 ③
141 ②				

Chapter Ⅴ **종합적 이해**

14. 글의 목적

	142 ②	143 ③	144 ⑤	145 ③
146 ③				

15. 심경 · 태도 · 분위기

	147 ⑤	148 ③	148 ①	150 ①
151 ④	152 ④			

16. 장문의 이해 Ⅰ - 1지문 2문제

		153 ⑤	154 ④	155 ④
156 ③	157 ③	158 ④	158 ②	160 ⑤
161 ⑤	162 ①	163 ②	164 ②	165 ③
166 ⑤	167 ④	168 ②	169 ①	170 ⑤
171 ②	172 ③	173 ②	174 ⑤	175 ②
176 ⑤	177 ②	178 ①	179 ②	180 ⑤
181 ①	182 ⑤			

17. 장문의 이해 Ⅱ - 1지문 3문제

		183 ②	184 ②	185 ⑤
186 ②	187 ④	188 ③	189 ②	190 ④
191 ⑤	192 ②	193 ⑤	194 ①	195 ⑤
196 ⑤	197 ③	198 ④	199 ④	200 ④

Chapter Ⅵ **사관학교 & 경찰대학교 기출문제**

18. 2025학년도 사관학교 1차 선발 시험

01 ②	02 ④	03 ④	04 ③	05 ①
06 ⑤	07 ④	08 ③	09 ②	10 ②
11 ①	12 ④	13 ③	14 ②	15 ⑤
16 ①	17 ②	18 ①	19 ②	20 ②
21 ③	22 ④	23 ④	24 ⑤	25 ①
26 ⑤	27 ③	28 ④	29 ③	30 ⑤

19. 2025학년도 경찰대학교 1차 선발 시험

01 ①	02 ②	03 ③	04 ③	05 ①
06 ②	07 ④	08 ①	09 ④	10 ④
11 ③	12 ②	13 ⑤	14 ②	15 ④
16 ⑤	17 ②	18 ①	19 ①	20 ③
21 ④	22 ②	23 ①	24 ①	25 ③
26 ②	27 ⑤	28 ①	29 ④	30 ④
31 ⑤	32 ③	33 ⑤	34 ④	35 ⑤
36 ③	37 ①	38 ②	39 ⑤	40 ⑤
41 ③	42 ④	43 ③	44 ⑤	45 ⑤